Cases in Public Relations Management

The Rise of Social Media and Activism

Second Edition

Patricia Swann

NEW YORK AND LONDON

Second edition published 2014
by Routledge
711 Third Avenue, New York, NY 10017

and by Routledge
2 Park Square, Milton Park, Abingdon, Oxon OX14 4RN

Routledge is an imprint of the Taylor & Francis Group, an informa business

First edition published 2010 by Routledge

Library of Congress Cataloging-in-Publication Data
A catalog record has been requested for this book.

ISBN: 978-0-415-51770-6 (hbk)
ISBN: 978-0-415-51771-3 (pbk)
ISBN: 978-0-203-52339-1 (ebk)

Typeset in StoneSerif
by Apex CoVantage, LLC

Printed and bound by CPI Group (UK) Ltd, Croydon, CR0 4YY

With love and appreciation to my husband, John, for reading and editing each case study.

For my daughters Martha, Sarah, and Olivia, whose youthful outlook provided inspiration for the selection of the cases.

And, for my friend and mentor, Raymond Simon, a pioneer in public relations case studies.

CONTENTS

PREFACE

This edition of *Cases in Public Relations Management* presents an insider perspective of organizations from a public relations and management perspective. While it was tempting to feature successful, prize-winning campaigns recognized by the public relations industry, this book took a different approach. It sought cases that provided interesting scenarios that any practitioner might encounter on the job—including a number of difficult situations. All the cases have a problem or opportunity. They are designed to challenge you to think analytically, strategically, and practically.

You may disagree with the strategies and tactics used. The idea was not to deconstruct exemplary cases, although some are, but to challenge you to assess the situations based on what you know about communication theory, ethics, the public relations process (research, planning, communication tactics, and evaluation), and management practices. You'll discover a lot of different opinions from your peers and there will be plenty of topics for great discussions.

All the cases in this textbook actually happened, and many were widely reported in the news media. Whenever possible, practitioners involved were interviewed to provide the fullest picture. In a few instances, the organization chose not to participate, mostly due to ongoing legal issues surrounding the case. In those instances, I consulted the public record and talked to industry insiders with knowledge about the case.

The idea behind this book is that we learn best from experience. Many practitioners shared their experiences in order to help the next generation of public relations professionals learn from their experiences. I hope you will share your experiences with your classmates and listen to what they have to say. Hopefully, this book is the next best thing to being there. I think you will agree that public relations is interesting and challenging—and definitely never dull.

WHAT'S NEW IN THIS BOOK?

This edition has twenty-seven new case studies and a few favorites from the first edition. So, it is pretty much a new book. I did retain some of the organizations from the first edition but rewrote the case based on new campaigns and different situations. There is one new chapter, entitled "Activism," to emphasize the growing power of activists, particularly in democracies. The rest of the chapters have been revised and retitled to better reflect the profession. The appendices provide information on how to analyze the cases.

WEB RESOURCES

Nearly every case has supplemental materials for the student (and teacher) that will enrich your understanding of the case, including videos, brochures, reports and other communication tactics from the case scenario. Information on related research is also provided. You can access this book's web resources at: www.routledge.com/cw/swann

AUTHOR'S BLOG

A blog called "Cases in Public Relations Management" was created since many of these cases will be playing out in the news media or new material will be available in the future. This blog highlights other cases in the news media that relate to the topics in the textbook or to the cases themselves. This blog is also a platform for showcasing what public relations classes are doing for learning activities. So, please share what you are doing with the cases. The blog can be found at: www.casesinprmanagement.com

LET ME KNOW WHAT YOU THINK

I am interested in your comments—good or bad—about the cases and if you have an idea for a new case for the next edition. Please e-mail me at pswann@utica.edu and let me know what you think. Or, join me on the book's blog and add your comments there. Thanks!

Patricia Swann
Utica College
pswann@utica.edu

CHAPTER 1

A Brief Introduction to Public Relations

HAVE AN ORGANIZATIONAL PURPOSE

What is "public relations"? If you asked a hundred people, you would probably get a hundred different replies—and several confused looks!

Whether you're a student getting ready to enter the public relations field or a practitioner already on the job, the answer to this question will provide focus, direction, and purpose for your career. A clear understanding of what public relations is, and how it contributes to organizational effectiveness, is necessary to making a difference in your organization.

Often, practitioners fall into the trap of being defined by the most visible and technical aspects of their job. "I write news releases." "I write and edit the company newsletter and other publications." "I get the media to cover our events." "I handle our company's communication." These are examples of practitioner products or "outputs."

What these responses do not convey is the strategy: *why* practitioners do all these communication-related activities. For example, a news release published or broadcast in the mass media about an organization's open house can help meet some obvious needs, such as increasing awareness of the event and the organization, and possibly getting people to attend the event. But why does the organization want people to attend an open house in the first place? How does the event, and publicizing it, tie in with the mission and goals of the organization? Who does the organization want to attract to the event? What specific groups? Men, women, kids, senior citizens, parents, singles, working professionals, job seekers—what the news release says, and how and when it says it, could make a big difference in its published/broadcast appeal to members of different groups. The result could be a well-attended open house or a public relations problem.

Defining What We Do

A good definition of public relations helps define the practitioner's organizational role. One early definition of public relations was created at the World Assembly of Public Relations in Mexico City in 1978:

> Public relations practice is the art and social science of analyzing trends, predicting their consequences, counseling organizational leaders, and implementing planned programs of action which serve both the organization's and the public's interest.

Scott M. Cutlip, Allen H. Center, and Glen M. Broom, authors of *Effective Public Relations*, wrote one of the best-known definitions:

> Public relations is the management function that establishes and maintains mutually beneficial relationships between an organization and the publics on whom its success and failure depends.

Robert Health and Timothy Coombs's more detailed definition captures the complexity of its five characteristics:

> Public relations is the management function that entails planning, research, publicity, promotion, and collaborative decision making to help any organization's ability to listen to, appreciate, and respond appropriately to those persons and groups whose mutually beneficial relationships the organization needs to foster as it strives to achieve its mission and vision.

Interestingly, these definitions do not contain the word *communication*. What they emphasize instead is building relationships with specific groups of people, because organizations and entities do not exist on their own; they are created to meet a need—almost always to provide goods and/or services for consumption. They rely on outside people or other organizations to buy those products and services or to support their mission.

Inherent in the concept of building relationships is trust. Solid relationships require trust, which is often achieved over time by both words and deeds. The concept of transparency is an important factor in building and sustaining trust, since stakeholders want to know how decisions are made at the top levels. Public relations practitioners are experts in managing the relationship-building programs that promote understanding of an organization by its important constituents. Practitioners also counsel management to consider the consequences of organizational actions on its publics.

The Value of Public Relations

Public relations should have a purpose, and this purpose should provide value for an organization. What would happen if the public relations function was eliminated from your organization? Would anyone notice?

When public relations programs are not linked to the mission of an organization, public relations practitioners are often caught up in the production of meaningless work. In an effective public relations office, practitioners know their organization's mission and support it. For example, businesses that produce a product in a competitive environment may focus on product quality as a way to distinguish themselves from competitors. Public relations can help develop employee relations programs that promote a healthy and friendly working environment, resulting in high morale, pride in workmanship, and—ultimately—a better product.

While many public relations practitioners are doing good work, sometimes their efforts are ignored because they fail to demonstrate the value of public relations in ways that management can appreciate.

Public relations legend Patrick Jackson once summed up the contributions of public relations for organizations. These nine contributions were featured in *Public Relations Strategies and Tactics:*

- *Awareness and information*—Public relations provides publicity and promotion to raise awareness and aid sales and fundraising efforts.
- *Organizational motivation*—Public relations builds internal relationships to foster positive morale, teamwork, productivity, and corporate culture.
- *Issue anticipation*—Public relations through environmental monitoring, research, and connections with its publics can provide an early warning system of potential problems.
- *Opportunity identification*—Public relations through environmental monitoring, research, and connections with its publics can identify new markets, products, methods, allies, and positive issues.
- *Crisis management*—Public relations can manage an appropriate response to crisis situations that will minimize the harm to an organization's reputation and allow it to continue functioning.
- *Overcoming executive isolation*—Public relations through research and counseling keeps management in touch with what is happening so that appropriate decisions are made.
- *Change agentry*—Public relations can assist with organizational changes through communication and other activities to ease resistance to change and promote a smooth transition for those affected by the changes.
- *Social responsibility*—Public relations can take the lead in helping organizations act responsibly in such areas as the environment, workplace issues, and philanthropy. These actions can lead to greater public trust and positive feelings for the organization, which can increase mutual understanding and translate into increased sales and use of services.
- *Influencing public policy*—Public relations can use its connections to government officials and other influential individuals or groups to gain acceptance for the organization's activities, products, or services and also remove political barriers.

Management Support

If a CEO understands the value of public relations to the company, all is well. If, on the other hand, a public relations department is known in the company for producing "fluff" and "bells and whistles," watch out! In bad times, companies find they can do without the bells, whistles, and fluff because they have no real value. Strategic public relations can build this internal understanding by demonstrating its value to an organization, especially the positive outcomes generated by the building of relationships with the organization's key stakeholders.

The commitment to establishing lasting and mutually beneficial relationships with key publics has to come from the organization's leadership ranks, where organizational policies and management strategies are determined. To be effective, public relations must have a seat at the management table to guide the organization's public relations and communication strategy. Organizations that "talk the talk" but aren't committed to "walk the talk" have often strayed from their missions. They may have made a series of decisions based on short-term gain, without considering their publics—and the effects on long-term relationships. Public relations plays an important organizational role in helping management understand the consequences of its actions and its responsibility to do the right thing.

Management will support things that make a positive and measurable difference for an organization, especially communication and relationship building activities that build stakeholder awareness and understanding of organizational initiatives. But simply "getting the word out" has been complicated by the explosive growth of communication outlets and the fragmentation of audiences. Managing the communication function today involves many strategic decisions such as selecting the most appropriate and effective delivery vehicles, creating and producing effective messages for those delivery vehicles, and evaluating the effectiveness of the communication.

The complexity of communication strategy is underscored in democratic societies that encourage open and liberal debate of virtually any topic. In the U.S., the First Amendment protects the right of organizations and individuals to freely express themselves in most situations. Citizens are free to criticize organizations, their products or services, and their leaders. Public relations helps organizations participate strategically in the "marketplace of ideas," so that viewpoints important to the organization are present in public debates that could affect an organization—including debates that aid the promotion of products and services.

Some of these public debates take place at the legislative level. Newly proposed legislation that could have positive or negative consequences for an organization may involve public relations practitioners who influence the debate and the legislative outcome by providing information; this strategy is often accomplished through government affairs and lobbying activities.

While organizations cannot participate in every conversation and debate taking place, public relations can identify and prioritize the communication needs most important to an organization and then create an effective communication plan.

Management understands and wants communication with a defined purpose that protects and enhances the organization.

Business Sense

One factor preventing some public relations practitioners from entering the ranks of management is a lack of understanding of basic business principles, management strategies, and number-crunching. Most executives have business management backgrounds and are driven by business goals and strategies that help organizations achieve their missions.

Public relations practitioners pride themselves on their communication skills, but some are unprepared or unable to read a balance sheet or explain a campaign's return on investment. Executives are not enthusiastic about departments that spend large sums of money; they want to see how such spending changes customer attitudes, boosts the consumption of the company's products or services, and increases profits. Public relations should not merely make a difference to an organization's bottom line; it should communicate that difference to top executives.

To be a part of management, a public relations practitioner should understand the language of business, how the organization operates, how it makes money, and how its strategic plan meets current and future challenges.

This textbook will introduce basic business terms, concepts, and management skills to begin building a business management foundation. Students and professionals can also read the business sections of their daily newspaper, watch cable and broadcast TV business shows, or take introductory college business courses to learn more about the business world. Case study, which this text employs, has its roots in business education. It started at the Harvard Business School (HBS) when Arch Wilkinson Shaw began teaching a course using real examples of business problems. In 1921, HBS's first case study, "The General Shoe Company," was created to prepare business majors for the realities of the business world. The 1999 report of the Commission on Public Relations Education, "Public Relations Education for the 21st Century: A Port of Entry," recommended a minor or double major in either business or the behavioral sciences.

Public Relations as Activism

Most of the discussion so far has been about public relations functioning within the traditional organizational sphere. Some scholars, however, are calling for the need to expand our thinking of public relations especially as change agents for social change. Kristin Demetrious, Derina Holtzhausen, Timothy Coombs, and others have questioned organizational public relations' role in society. Some argue that unethical public relations practices enacted at the organizational level oppress social movements and that activists need to assert asymmetrical and persuasive methods to force organizations to act socially responsibly.

THE PUBLIC RELATIONS PROCESS

Public relations helps build strategic relationships with stakeholders to solve problems and take advantage of opportunities, whether the client is an individual, a small organization, or a large entity. How an organization goes about solving its public relations problem or turning an opportunity into a windfall is determined by its public relations strategy—its overall game plan.

Public relations success rarely results from such one-shot activities as issuing a news release or brochure. Many practitioners, especially those just entering the field, find themselves tackling many writing tasks, planning special events, and working with the news media. Important as they are, these tasks are just part of what effective public relations practitioners do; they are, in effect, all examples of steps in a process. Most introductory public relations textbooks mention such public relations process models as research, action planning, communication, and evaluation (RACE), or research, objectives, programming, and evaluation (ROPE). The models RACE and ROPE are helpful because both easy-to-remember acronyms contain the four major aspects of the public relations process.

An organization begins the process by first recognizing that it has an opportunity or a problem important enough to the mission (or, in drastic cases, the survival) of the organization for some kind of action. This opportunity or problem starts the public relations process. Public relations practitioners at the management level follow these basic steps:

- Research the issue that prompts the organization's concern (i.e., the opportunity or problem).
- Develop goals and objectives that address the opportunity or problem.
- Develop a public relations strategy that addresses goals and objectives.
- Select and implement the communication tactics that would best achieve the strategy's goals and objectives.
- Evaluate the effectiveness of the public relations program in reaching its goals and objectives. Practitioners must complete the public relations process and evaluate the results of their efforts so that management can clearly see a return on its investment in money, staffing, and time. That requires research and evidence.

For example, a practitioner issues 300 news releases in a year and tracks the number of impressions (printed appearances or hits) generated in the media. The chief executive is unimpressed; he or she wants to know how the news releases helped increase demand for the company's products and services. Were the stories counted in the media positive about the organization, and did customer or other key publics' attitudes positively change after the public relations effort? If the practitioner can demonstrate those results, the CEO will see the value of public relations.

Although the words *management level* are used to describe the practitioner who carries out the public relations process, any practitioner with knowledge of this four-step process can use it—whether the practitioner's title carries the manager designation or not. Student interns and practitioners who are just beginning their careers may be assigned to "technical" communication roles within a public relations department or firm.

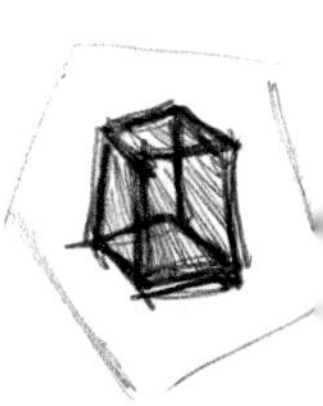

These entry-level positions are mostly concerned with message creation—the third step of the public relations process. While communication technician positions are excellent gateways into the professional world of public relations and important to the overall effectiveness of public relations work, practitioners assigned to such positions must keep in mind their work is just one step of the process. Writing news releases, features, and speeches, producing publications, creating audiovisuals, taking photographs, and coordinating press conferences or arranging media coverage are important activities; but if they are not connected with research, planning, and evaluation, they can easily miss their objectives.

To be effective, public relations needs all four steps; usually, only upper-level management can make sure all four steps happen. Scholar David M. Dozier said that practitioners at the management level have strategic and operational management knowledge that includes developing goals, objectives, and strategies to solve problems or take advantage of opportunities, managing communication programs, and managing people and budgets. He also said managers have the ability to carry out research, including environmental scanning, counsel management (negotiation knowledge) on its options when dealing with its publics, and understand the use of persuasion to achieve organizational goals.

Stakeholders and Publics

People who are affected in some way by the decisions of an organization are called stakeholders. They can include employees, neighbors, shareholders, consumer advocates, the media or governmental officials; they can be people with no formal tie to the organization other than an interest in it and/or its products or services.

Stakeholders who become more aware and active when they recognize a problem caused by an organization's actions can be described as publics.

Building Strategic Relationships

Relationships don't simply happen. In our daily lives we seek relationships with people because they fulfill some personal need: They are fun to be around, they share our interests in music or sports, or maybe they come from a similar background.

Organizations also seek relationships with certain groups of people because they are important to achieving the organization's mission, enhancing its reputation, or protecting its long-term survival. But not all publics are supportive of the organization. Ronald D. Smith said in *Strategic Planning for Public Relations,* "A public is like your family. You don't pick them; they just are . . . Publics may be helpful or annoying, friendly or not, but an organization must deal with them regardless."

According to situational theory, organizations create publics when their actions positively or negatively impact others. Researchers James Grunig and Todd Hunt segmented publics as *nonpublics,* those who are not affected by the organization's actions and do not interact with the organization; *latent publics,* those who are affected by the organization's actions but are not yet aware of it; *aware publics,* those who are aware that the organization is affecting them but have not taken any action; and *active publics,* those who do something about the organization's impact on them. Active publics can emerge at any time; often their appearance is anticipated but sometimes it is not. Public relations can facilitate the process of creating positive relationships.

Strategic relationships are often built over time through actions and words. Consider that good relationships, such as those between roommates in college or spouses in marriage, do not just happen. Strong relationships are developed as each participant observes and learns about others through experience—what they do, as well as what they say. Dialogue, in which both parties exchange information, is an effective means for two parties to work out problems. Trust, the ability to rely on the other party, builds as evidence accumulates that the person or organization is sincere, that it can deliver on its promises, and that it can and does follow through.

Good relationships should offer something of value to each participant. When a person or organization creates a relationship solely for its own gains, the relationship won't last long. Not many people are interested in being taken advantage of or being used without receiving something in return, even if it is just a sincere thank-you. Mutually beneficial relationships have a great advantage over the one-way kind too. They are much stronger over time, and can stand up to occasional mishaps and larger difficulties—both of which are bound to happen in any long-term relationship.

An Effective Early Warning System

Public relations can help organizations anticipate problems or see opportunities by identifying issues and trends. This function is called *environmental scanning* and, in fact, is an early warning system for organizations. Practitioners who scan the environment pay attention to what's happening to similar organizations or industries and apply the knowledge and lessons occurring to their own particular environment.

While organizations may have good environmental monitoring systems in place to gauge trends and anticipate issues, problems will still emerge. Human error and natural disasters are a part of life and are, therefore, inevitable. Since organizations cannot anticipate every problem, some day a crisis will come. It is then—in a time of crisis—when public relations can be especially valuable. Answering the "what if" with a strategic plan involves *issues management.*

The goal of the public relations practitioner should be to anticipate, identify, and plan for problems, but when a crisis strikes, public relations should be ready to respond with appropriate strategies. One goal of this book is to help you develop strategic thinking skills so you can anticipate and solve problems as they emerge.

In a 24/7 news environment, a rapid and expert response with the news media is required to prevent nearly instant and significant damage to an organization's carefully constructed reputation. Case studies, in particular, have provided new insights for practitioners managing crisis situations. Public relations practitioners play an important role not only in managing chaotic communication in a crisis environment but—more importantly—in counseling senior management to do the right thing, be truthful, accept responsibility if the organization made a mistake, and take immediate action to repair any damage.

Counseling Senior Management

If an organization is out of sync with public expectations and norms, or its survivability is threatened, public relations can counsel management on communication strategies or policy changes, which might help remedy or lessen the problem. This works best when the counsel is given directly to the chief executive officer. Many times senior management loses touch with how the rest of the world operates due to executive isolation or too much focus on short-term goals. To be effective in an advisory role, public relations practitioners need to maintain their management independence, not simply report up the chain of command. Direct access to senior management and involvement in management decision making are ultimately where practitioners can be most effective.

Leaders who think only they can see the problem clearly and only they have the solution to their problems tend to surround themselves with "yes people," subordinates who do not dare question the wisdom of their boss. Practitioners are seldom effective in such situations and are unlikely to be part of the organization's decision making. Public relations practitioners must choose their battles wisely. When problems are serious, involving long-term negative consequences or legal and public safety issues, public relations practitioners must take a stand for what is right—despite potential personal consequences.

In severe situations, such as the Enron business scandal, any employee may become the moral compass of an organization. These whistle-blowers have insider knowledge that may be unknown to others in the organization, including the public relations practitioner. Once a whistle-blower goes public with accusations of illegal activity or safety violations, the organization will face increasing pressure to mend its ways. Unfortunately, whistle-blowing can also mean damage to the organization's reputation: hardly the most strategic way to solve problems and move forward.

Do the Right Thing

What prevents people from doing the right thing? Most of us know people who have done bad things—often because they do not think they will be caught or because the right thing may not be that obvious. Sometimes the dynamics of a situation—peer pressure, fear, rapidly unfolding events—makes people act in a way that they would not normally do if they had more time to think carefully and consider the consequences.

In the management of communication programs for organizations, many public relations problems can occur in what an organization communicates or doesn't communicate, and whether those words match the organization's deeds. Just about every veteran public relations person will say that the best practice is simply to always tell the truth. But this is not as easy as it sounds. During a crisis, for example, a practitioner may be prevented from communicating certain information due to legal issues involved. Sometimes practitioners are not fully informed of the details of a situation. Inexperience and not thinking through the consequences of one's actions often lead to mistakes.

Codes of conduct can be helpful, and the college classroom is one of the best times to study these guidelines; there is no pressure from the work world to distract you. You do not want to be digging through your desk files looking for a copy of your code of conduct during a crisis! Just as a student learns the skills of research, writing, and planning in public relations, the study of ethics is a valuable tool for achieving personal excellence in effective public relations.

Ethical behavior comes from the shared values held by a group or community. These core values are what individuals in the group or community decide are important. One core value in the Public Relations Society of America's code of conduct is honesty. This value relates to communicating accurate and truthful information. Core values help establish the ground rules for what is considered right and wrong within that group.

The Public Relations Society of America Member Code of Ethics

This book will use the Public Relations Society of America Member Code of Ethics (see Appendix G) to examine the ethical dimensions of the cases. Many organizations also have their own codes of conduct that reveal not only their rules for conduct but also something about their culture, the way they do things, and what they value.

The Public Relations Society of America (PRSA) code covers six core values: advocacy, honesty, expertise, independence, loyalty, and fairness. *Advocacy* recognizes that public relations practitioners play an essential role in bringing another voice to the marketplace of ideas within a democratic society. *Honesty* (truthfulness) is necessary to maintain credibility and trust with publics. Objective counsel to others *(independence)* keeps organizations in touch with their environment.

Practitioners with *expertise* can build mutual understanding between organizations and their publics. Practitioners are not only *loyal* to their organizations or clients; they are also obligated to protect the public interest. *Fairness* means that organizations do not take unfair advantage of people and groups that they deal with, even when the organizations have more resources and power. People's opinions and their right to express them are also respected.

Public relations plays an important role in organizations and, by extension, in our society. Future practitioners who understand their ethical role will contribute positively to their employer and society by increasing understanding between organizations and their publics.

The PRSA Code of Ethics and its core provisions are provided in Appendix G.

HOW PUBLIC RELATIONS RELATES TO OTHER DISCIPLINES

Public relations, as a communication and business discipline, shares many common characteristics with advertising, marketing, marketing communication, and journalism. Practitioners should be aware of these commonalities and how public relations practice may differ in its approach.

Advertising

Advertising is space or time purchased within the mass media for the purpose of persuading people to do something, such as buy a product, attend an event, or support a cause. Advertising is considered a controlled medium because the organization pays to control the appearance, content, and timing of the advertisement's placement in a mass medium, such as newspapers, radio, television, or the Internet. A newspaper, for example, cannot change the wording of a print ad or its size. It must be printed exactly as it is provided by the organization.

Marketing professionals mostly use advertising, but sometimes public relations practitioners will use ads to promote a public relations activity or support an image campaign to enhance an organization's reputation. This is true especially in the nonprofit world, where marketing is frequently incorporated into the public relations role. A college may create newspaper ads to announce new graduate programs or announce upcoming admission days. In corporate or agency settings, the role of advertising is often relegated to marketing.

When the message contains sensitive wording and any slight change could affect its intended meaning, especially during a crisis or other momentous situation, paid advertising is often used. For example, when a company must recall a product, it will want a carefully crafted message for its publics that explains what the organization has done and is doing to protect its product's users. When oil companies are trying to explain why corporate profits are at all-time highs, they will want to develop carefully worded messages to explain the situation. Often these advertisements or commercials are created when an organization thinks its messages are not getting through or are inaccurately portrayed in the news media.

Marketing

Marketing focuses on increasing customers and sales for an organization's product or service. Marketing is also concerned with ensuring the product or service is designed to meet customer needs, is attractively packaged, is distributed efficiently, and satisfies customers. Marketing professionals conduct research to find out what type of products consumers want and at what cost.

The public relations profession has learned a great deal from marketing's strong reliance on research and planning to make decisions tied to the bottom line—making money by selling products or services. Public relations has steadily incorporated research and planning with goals, objectives, and strategies as part of its work.

Public relations has also taught marketing a few things—most notably that relationships matter and that catering to consumer behaviors exclusively can create many problems down the road. Paid advertising, a major tool of marketing, isn't as effective as it once was as consumers rely more and more on other sources of information.

Marketing's use of communication to raise awareness and create effective messages is another area that overlaps with public relations. Marketing's messages can be informative and persuasive—to build excitement and desire for a product or service. Advertising created for a public relations campaign may also have specific tasks, such as introducing new college degree programs or inviting people to an open house.

Marketing also values understanding its key publics. Market research helps segment the organization's publics so that messages are created in the form of advertisements or commercials and delivered with precision to the right people through the right communication channels such as newspapers, radio, television, the Internet, special events, and clothing. Besides advertising communication, marketing also uses celebrity endorsers and sponsorships, just as public relations does to communicate with its publics.

However, public relations messages often try to reach several key publics, beyond customers or potential customers. Employees, for example, are a key public that public relations traditionally seeks to build a strong relationship with, while marketing is more outwardly focused. Non-customers, such as activists and legislators proposing regulations, can potentially have great impact on an organization, and therefore demand the attention of public relations.

Public relations seeks to enhance the organization's reputation—not just its bottom line. It is typically a long process to build the necessary positive relationships that result in good reputations. Sometimes it requires organizations to change and adapt to new ways.

Integrated Marketing Communication

The fact that marketing and public relations use many of the same communication tactics has led many organizations to blend the two functions into what is commonly called *integrated marketing communication* (IMC). This approach coordinates the communication activities of the marketing and public relations departments that, in the past, often operated independently. For some organizations, a lack of coordination between these departments has sometimes led to embarrassing mixed messages to key publics.

The concept of coordinating all organizational communication is a good idea. However, some researchers and educators are uncertain if complete merging of marketing and public relations is always in the best long-term interests of an organization. The driving need to produce profit and the potential for executive isolation can create an environment in which clear, unbiased thinking about long-term consequences of organizational actions is not always present. As a result, the hard sell might come first, and relationship-building activities second—or not at all.

Public relations should maintain its independence within the organization, allowing practitioners to counsel management about the long-term consequences of proposed actions—before decisions are made. For example, although a product campaign might be wildly successful in the short term, a questionable ad campaign or product can produce serious long-term consequences for an organization if all key publics are not considered.

Journalism

Journalists such as Ivy Lee were at the forefront of the development of modern-day public relations. Lee is credited with developing the corporate news release and using media relations techniques. Early on, corporations realized the need to recruit journalists to develop their media relations programs so that they could capture their share of the public discussion in newspapers, magazines, and radio. After all, who could better understand the needs of journalists and package information the way they wanted it than a former journalist?

To this day, many public relations professionals have previous journalism experience. The common background and the traditional emphasis on media relations have created strong ties to the journalism profession.

Journalists and public relations practitioners package information for public consumption, and the two can often develop a close, dependent relationship. Journalists often rely on public relations professionals to provide ideas and information for their stories; public relations relies on journalists for access to a credible mass media vehicle that can distribute organizational messages to a wide audience at little expense.

Journalists are in the business of gathering and synthesizing information and converting that information into products that people want to read, hear, or view. The product—news content—can be informative, entertaining, or useful in some way to consumers' daily lives. Journalists judge whether or not information is newsworthy based on any of the following characteristics: timeliness, prominence, proximity, significance, unusualness, human interest, conflict, and newness. Journalists gather and package news content that is truthful and represents, to the best of the journalist's ability, a balanced account of what happened. If information supplied by the organization is considered newsworthy, the journalist will start his or her work. A journalist might speak to representatives of the organization that issued a news release but will probably also interview someone independent of the organization, such as competitors, consumers, or industry experts.

Public relations practitioners have no control over the final version of a journalist's story. However, sometimes they can help shape the content by providing information from the organization or by suggesting "third-party endorsers," independent experts who have in-depth knowledge of specific issues. Journalists like using such sources because they can lend credibility to a news story; public relations practitioners may benefit because the experts may support or be sympathetic to the organization's perspective.

Public Relations' Advocacy Role

Public relations practitioners, unlike journalists, are hired by organizations to advocate their interests and to promote their views in public discourse. Notions of balance and objectivity, very important to journalists, do not apply to public relations in the same way. Still, truthfulness in all communication is the foundation that establishes the integrity of organizational public relations. But providing balance—both sides of the story—is not a common tactic in public relations. For example, when a new product is launched by an organization, a public relations practitioner probably won't focus on information in its news release or other promotional material about other products that compete for the customer's pocketbook. The practitioner likely will focus exclusively on its product's attributes, gathering accurate and positive information from product engineers, users, and outside experts.

Public relations practitioners' advocacy role takes them beyond writing for the mass news media. They produce many other types of communication products, including newsletters, direct mailers, and web content. Their function within an organization is also much broader than writing. Public relations practitioners develop opportunities for interpersonal communication including special events and information exchanges such as product demonstrations. Public relations skills should also include counseling management, research, and planning.

Journalists, in comparison, have a more focused function; they gather and synthesize information for publication in a growing variety of multimedia formats.

Journalists representing mass media are writing for a broad, general audience. Public relations practitioners segment the general public into key publics with messages created to address their interests and concerns in communication styles appropriate to each particular public. The key is to make sure that each message, no matter the target audience, is both easily understood and engaging.

PUBLIC RELATIONS, COMMUNICATION, AND RELATED THEORIES

How do organizations create effective public relations and communication programs? Successful practitioners know that program goals and communication strategies must be grounded in public relations and communication theories. Every case in this textbook can be analyzed through the lens of one or more relationship, behavior and mass communication theories. A short summary of some of these theories is provided in the book's Appendix C.

CHAPTER 2

Ethics and the Law

Public relations has been front-page news, and the news has not always been flattering. Negative incidents brought to light by the national media have dealt largely with the ethics of organizations covertly influencing public opinion through public relations programs. And, in some cases, the focus of news coverage was simply shady business dealings.

Ethics provides the framework for deciding what behavior is right and what is wrong. On the surface, it seems so simple. After all, who doesn't know to tell the truth, play fairly, and avoid injuring others? In the business world, however, the black-and-white differences often turn gray when decisions are made in a hurry or management directs others to carry out questionable practices. For young and inexperienced practitioners, relying on superiors to do the right thing—a common assumption—may be naive. Textbook authors Lattimore et al. noted some of the troubling questions a practitioner may confront. Will he or she:

- Lie for a client or employer?
- Engage in deception to collect information about another practitioner's clients?
- Help conceal a hazardous condition or illegal act?
- Present information that presents only part of the truth?
- Offer something (gift, travel, or information) to reporters or legislators that may compromise their reporting or decision making?
- Present true but misleading information in an interview or news conference that corrupts the channels of government?

Ethical decision making is best learned before one enters the workforce, away from the pressures of the job. Preventing ethical problems requires a system for determining what's right and wrong. Most professions provide a code of conduct to guide people in their decision making. The Public Relations Society of America (PRSA) has a code of ethics that embodies "professional values . . . vital to the integrity of the profession as a whole." A thorough understanding of this code of ethics will help a young practitioner make the right decisions even when that might mean confronting a client or boss who possesses more power, authority, and experience. The International Association of Business Communicators (IABC) also has an excellent code of ethics that is available at its website, www.iabc.com.

A common theme that runs through many of PRSA's core values is protecting the public interest. This includes providing honest and accurate information so that customers can make the correct purchasing decisions. At its extreme, it includes protecting the public health if a product or service is found to be harmful.

The PRSA code has six core values: advocacy, honesty, expertise, independence, loyalty, and fairness. It also has six code provisions: free flow of information, competition, disclosure of information, safeguarding confidences, conflicts of interest, and enhancing the profession.

PRSA's "Ethical Decision-Making Guide Helps Resolve Ethical Dilemmas," by Kathy R. Fitzpatrick, offers the following process:

- Define the specific ethical issue/conflict.
- Identify internal/external factors (e.g., legal, political, social, economic) that may influence the decision.
- Identify key values.
- Identify the parties who will be affected by the decision and define the public relations professional's obligation to each.
- Select ethical principles to guide the decision-making process.
- Make a decision and justify it.

LEGAL ISSUES IN PUBLIC RELATIONS

Beyond ethical issues, some actions can ensnare an organization legally. Legal issues encountered by public relations practitioners include:

- *Defamation*—Defamation refers to the negative and harmful use of language that is directed at a person, particularly an individual who is considered a private person. Libel refers to published defamation and slander refers to spoken defamation. The best defense against an accusation of libel defamation is the truth. "Stated as opinions" is also a good defense. Actual malice must be proved for public figures.
- *Privacy*—Invading someone's privacy can bring trouble. Revealing private facts without legitimate public concern and secretly gathering information on individuals, such as taping a conversation, or misappropriation of a person's name or image is not allowed unless permission is granted by the individual. It is harder to invade someone's privacy if he or she is a public figure, e.g., elected officials and celebrities.

- *Financial information*—Publicly traded companies are regulated by the U.S. Securities and Exchange Commission. Withholding "material" information that could have a financial impact on stockholders is not allowed. "Full and prompt disclosure" of material information is required.
- *False or deceptive advertising*—False or deceptive advertising and publicity such as deceptive testimonials or claims about the product are not allowed by the Federal Trade Commission.
- *Copyright*—Use of copyrighted information created by an individual or organization is not allowed without the permission of the copyright holder. Fair use of copyrighted materials is generally allowed with limits for nonprofit or noncommercial educational purposes, or for comment for reviews, or for transformation into a new creative work. Use of copyrighted work must be limited to excerpts and the use of this material must not affect the potential market for or value of the copyrighted work.
- *Trademark*—Trademarks prevent the use of names, logos, slogans, mascots, and other products without permission of the owner.
- *Service mark*—Service marks are similar to trademarks and protect symbols and words associated with services and programs rather than products.

1

What Would You Do?

Dr Deborah Silverman, APR, Fellow PRSA

INTERNS POSTING FALSE REVIEWS

You are an intern for a large marketing and public relations firm. Its clients include a company that manufactures computer games. Your internship supervisor at the firm asks you to write glowing reviews of one of the client's new computer games and to post the reviews in the Apple iTunes Store under several different account names. She urges you to give the game four or five stars and to include comments such as "Terrific new game—can't wait to tell my friends about it!"

You have tried the game and know that it's not a five-star game, but you want to please your internship supervisor because you hope to land a public relations job at a PR firm after graduation and you would like to use your supervisor as a reference. Besides, you have read lots of fake reviews for other products on the Internet, so maybe this isn't such a big deal.

What is the ethical situation or conflict? What should you do?

PAYING FOR POSITIVE ONLINE NEWS STORIES

You have just been hired as the media relations manager for a large municipal utility company. You learned that your predecessor spent $80,000 in taxpayer funds on a consultant who wrote positive promotional stories about the utility, which were then placed on a news website. The website is affiliated with the consultant's public relations firm.

The website is indexed by Google News and is labeled as a news channel by Google News, so whenever Internet users type the name of the utility company into Google News, they get a series of positive articles about the utility company.

Your utility company serves nearly three million residents of a large metropolitan area. It has been fighting what company leaders call "inaccurate stories in the news media" about its finances, including an investigation by the county's prosecutors of travel expenses for the company's board members and their spouses.

The utility company's leaders are pleased with the online coverage that has resulted from the promotional stories on the news website. In fact, there has been a large spike in traffic to the utility company's own website, and your new boss—the vice president for communication—believes that this tactic is more effective than traditional news releases.

You, however, are not so sure. The contract with the consultant is up for renewal for another six months, and you need to make a decision on renewal by the end of the week.

What is the ethical situation or conflict? What should you do?

THE THREATENING TWEET

You are the marketing manager of a company that manufactures video games. You hired a public relations firm to promote your newest game, "Rock On Forever." The PR firm sent copies of the game to many game reviewers, but the best of the reviews were half-hearted and lukewarm. In fact, most reviewers recommended not purchasing the game until the problems were ironed out.

These reviews angered the president of the public relations firm, who took to Twitter to proclaim: "Game reviewers went too far . . . we are reconsidering who will get games next time." Almost immediately, he regretted that tweet, and he apologized several times on Twitter, but you've heard from many angry game reviewers today, furious because of the threat that they might not receive review copies of video games in the future. Your company has dealt with these reviewers for years, and they have given balanced, fair reviews on past video games.

What is the ethical situation or conflict? What should you do?

FOOD FOR THOUGHT

You are an assistant account executive at a large public relations firm, which is working on a major special event for a public relations client: a series of elaborate dinners at an "underground restaurant" in the city to promote the client's line of frozen foods. Food bloggers will be invited to the dinners, which will be prepared by a famous chef, and a food industry analyst will offer his thoughts on the latest food trends. Food bloggers will receive an extra pair of dinner tickets as a prize for their readers and the dinner promises to include "an unexpected surprise."

You've been carefully reading the blogs posted by the food bloggers who have been invited to the dinners; you know they prefer to eat organic, fresh food rather than highly processed frozen foods. You are also troubled by the fact that your boss plans to use hidden cameras at the dinners to record the reactions of the food bloggers when they learn that the main course is actually a frozen dinner entrée from the PR client's product line.

What is the ethical situation or conflict? What should you do?

GETTING HAMMERED

You are the vice president of public relations for a nonprofit organization whose mission includes blood donations; you supervise a staff of twenty-five public relations professionals, including ten in the social media department. You make a habit of spot-checking social media daily for mentions of your organization.

One morning while you are monitoring Twitter, you discover a curious tweet from one of your social media employees that mentions a specific brand of beer. It reads, "John found five more six-packs of [name of] beer . . . we do it right when we drink. #gettinghammered." The message was tweeted to all 200,000 followers of your organization on Twitter.

What is the ethical situation or conflict? What should you do?

Dig Deeper

One area of ethical concern for public relations professionals is the proper use of testimonials and endorsements, especially in blogs. Read the document "FTC Publishes Final Guidelines Concerning the Use of Endorsements and Testimonials" available on the textbook's companion website. Explain the concept of "material connections" and how public relations professionals can prevent ethical situations from arising.

Another FTC settlement involved Reebok's proof for the claims for advertising products. The FTC's response is available on the textbook's companion website. What PRSA code principles are involved with this case?

2

City Utility or Cash Cow?

Top Agency Accused of Overbilling City

THE LOS ANGELES DEPARTMENT OF WATER AND POWER

The Los Angeles Department of Water and Power (LADWP), established in 1902, served 3.9 million residents with an annual budget of $4 billion in 2011. LADWP was financed by sales of water and electrical services. No tax support was received and Los Angeles customers purchased 168 billion gallons of water during 2011. It was the largest power and water utility in the United States with 7,221 miles of pipe and 60,115 fire hydrants. It supplied about 22 million megawatt hours of electricity a year for Los Angeles customers. About 9,200 employees were employed in 2011.

The Public Affairs division of LADWP is responsible for media and community relations (media response, informational field trips, Speaker's Bureau, and special events, such as the annual Light Festival), advertising and publications (*Contact* and *Intake* newsletters, customer bill inserts, and brochures), environmental communications and educational programs (Science Bowl and Adopt-a-School). It produces news releases, media advisories, fact sheets, and news conferences. It also keeps the news media informed during emergencies, such as power outages and watermain breaks. In addition to the media team, there are photographers, graphic artists, and web content editors.

Beyond media relations, the public affairs staff supports many educational projects for water and power conservation efforts, power safety, water quality issues, water supply and infrastructure issues, power supply, power content, power loads, historical information, employee relations materials, and business and consumer materials.

While the case study happened in 2004 it still offers important lessons involving ethics and the workplace.

NOT BUSINESS AS USUAL

When the LADWP board requested an 18 percent water rate increase over two years for infrastructure repairs, federally mandated quality improvements, and security measures, it raised questions. Still, more than a decade had passed since the last rate increase; most water users understood both the need for system repairs and increased post-9/11 protection of public drinking water.

LADWP, the largest municipal utility in the nation, provided its nearly four million residential and commercial users electricity and safe drinking water at rates lower than most California communities. Apart from its low rates, LADWP was a success story because it provided the LA city government with much-needed revenue: 7 percent of LADWP's annual estimated electric revenues and 5 percent of its water revenues went to the city's general fund. Also, LADWP required no tax support since its operations were financed by the sale of water and electric services.

With all those facts and figures on its side, no doubt LADWP officials hoped for easy city council approval of the proposed rate hike. But neighborhood council members and some city council members questioned the increase and requested more information.

PAYMENT DENIED; AN AUDIT BEGINS

Three months after LADWP requested an 18 percent rate increase, LA City Comptroller Laura Chick's review of invoices from an outside public relations firm for LADWP-related work sparked concern; payment was denied until more information and clarification of the bills were provided by FleishmanHillard.

Two weeks later, April 1, 2004, Chick announced an audit of the city's multimillion dollar contract with FleishmanHillard for questionable expenses and LADWP's oversight of the contract.

According to Chick's office, FleishmanHillard had been paid more than $24 million by LADWP from 1999 to 2004.

The *Los Angeles Times* and the *Daily News of Los Angeles* reported that FleishmanHillard officials "could not be reached for comment." The *Los Angeles Times* reporter's 7 p.m. call did not include further attempts to reach FleishmanHillard executives by cell phone or other means. FleishmanHillard, with an international reputation for crisis management and high ethical standards, was suddenly putting its reputation to the test.

As readers of the *Los Angeles Times* and other local news sources began to learn about the inner workings of LADWP, it became clear that the rate proposal and FleishmanHillard contract were in trouble. In a series of news articles, editorials, and columns, the *Los Angeles Times* and other local news media questioned LADWP's dealings with the nationally respected public relations firm FleishmanHillard:

- Why was a $3 million annual contract necessary for public relations services provided by FleishmanHillard when LADWP was a monopoly? As LA councilman Jack Weiss put it, "I've always wondered why a public utility needs an outside public relations firm to convince people to flick on their light switch and turn on their water faucet."

- Why did LADWP's corporate communications budget increase by $1 million, to $13.3 million in 2003 2004, when it also had its $3 million Fleishman Hillard contract? According to news accounts, twenty-three LADWP communication employees were paid from $41,154 to $108,242 a year.

- Wasn't the $425-an-hour fee charged by FleishmanHillard's LA office top executive excessive? A January 3, 2003, bill for 2½ hours of "strategic counsel" cost customers $1,062 and never stated who got the strategic counseling; that month alone, nearly $20,000 was charged by that one executive for strategic counsel. Why was there a $1,275 bill for three hours so that a FleishmanHillard executive could attend "a lunch and a traveling exhibit on the DWP"?

- Why, questioned LA City Comptroller Chick, was the LADWP paying $50 to $100 for quarter-hour periods in which FleishmanHillard employees were just leaving telephone messages or sending e-mails?

- Why was $175,000 paid for a LADWP parade float in the shape of a boombox or $1.2 million spent on a sponsorship pact with the Los Angeles Dodgers?

A week after the city comptroller announced her audit, investigations were launched by the Los Angeles County District Attorney's office and the U.S. Attorney's Office in the Central District of California to determine if Mayor James K. Hahn sought contributions in return for city contracts. (No allegations were raised by investigators that FleishmanHillard received any direct benefit as a result of its contributions or other support.)

Expanded scrutiny of LADWP's professional relationship with FleishmanHillard revealed that $137,000 in political contributions were made to Mayor Hahn and other city politicians by the firm and its executives. The firm also provided pro bono services to Hahn and held fundraising events for him. The contributions and pro bono work had been reported the previous May by local news organizations.

The *Los Angeles Times* reported July 15, 2004, that FleishmanHillard routinely inflated billing to LADWP, according to two former firm employees. Two days later seven former FleishmanHillard employees told the *Los Angeles Times* that they "were encouraged or directed to inflate bills" to DWP. One of those former employees was Diana Greenwood, daughter of *Los Angeles Times* editor Noel Greenwood, who worked on the DWP account in 1999. She told the *Los Angeles Times* that practices like submitting false time sheets were "wrong, unethical and done on a regular basis" at FleishmanHillard.

The day the initial allegations by former employees appeared in the *Los Angeles Times,* John Graham, chairman and chief executive officer of FleishmanHillard, sent an e-mail to employees, stating:

> *Today, the* Los Angeles Times *ran a major article alleging that, over a period of years, some employees in our Los Angeles office intentionally billed a client, the* Los Angeles

Department of Water and Power, for work that was never performed. The article included allegations of other billing irregularities, as well as claims of preferential treatment given to individuals connected to this client.

After 38 years at our firm, I cannot tell you how much this situation personally hurts me. In the nearly 60 years that FleishmanHillard has been serving thousands of clients, never before have such allegations been leveled against the people at our firm.

There are two things I want you to know. First, we are conducting a detailed review of the process and procedures related to our work on Los Angeles municipal projects. If we confirm any wrongdoing—including anything related to the allegations in the Times*—we will take appropriate steps. Second, we are proud of the work our people have done and the results they have produced for the Los Angeles Department of Water and Power.*

You have my full assurance that FleishmanHillard remains committed to its fundamental values of the exceptional work, quality client service, and the highest standards of ethics and integrity.

Los Angeles City Attorney Rocky Delgadillo filed a lawsuit July 16, 2004, against FleishmanHillard for alleged overbilling based on his office's investigation and the *Los Angeles Times* report. In a news release announcing the lawsuit, Delgadillo said, "This is a case of outright fraud. The ratepayers of this city were ripped off—intentionally and maliciously." The lawsuit claimed "FleishmanHillard knowingly and consistently falsified invoices for inflated hours and claimed to provide work that was not performed."

FleishmanHillard's own investigation was conducted by independent attorneys and its results were turned over to public investigating authorities. The agency also fully cooperated with the public investigation.

Graham sent another internal e-mail July 16, 2004, to FleishmanHillard employees:

Recent allegations about past events in our Los Angeles office are very disturbing because, if they are true, then a small group of people has violated what we stand for as an agency and put our most valuable asset—our reputation—at risk.

We are investigating and we will discover what happened. If we confirm any wrongdoing, we will share that information with the appropriate authorities and take the necessary corrective actions, up to and including termination.

We have expanded the scope of our internal review to ensure it includes all aspects of the recent allegations in the Los Angeles Times *and we have added dedicated and independent legal experts to conduct that review. The legal investigators will share their findings promptly with appropriate authorities.*

Also, today we are placing Doug Dowie on administrative leave of absence. We believe that is best for Doug and the firm.

I deeply regret any pain this has caused you and the uncertainty it has raised for our clients. I promise you that we will take every necessary step to resolve these issues as soon as possible. Please distribute this to your staff as appropriate, and contact me if you have questions or concerns.

Meanwhile, Richard Kline, a Los Angeles FleishmanHillard executive, told the *Los Angeles Times* July 17, 2004, that "the firm has not concluded on the basis of published reports that Dowie did anything wrong. We are intensifying our investigation. We absolutely have not reached any conclusion."

The same news article quoted portions of the July 16, 2004, internal memo to senior managers from Graham.

FleishmanHillard announced publicly on July 20, 2004, it would not renew its contracts with LADWP or harbor department and would terminate its contract with the airport department. The firm also named Kline as the office's new general manager.

A public statement issued by FleishmanHillard's Kline explained the company's actions:

We are in the business of client service. Unfortunately, our representation of the Department of Water and Power has become part of a larger public debate that has diverted attention from the department's important work to the provider of its communication services. That does not serve our client's best interests. Ideally, public attention would be on the department's work, rather than on the provider of its communications services. As a result, we believe the best course for DWP and our firm is to end the relationship.

Although our representation of the Port and the Airport is not being debated today, we want to take this voluntary step so it does not become an issue for our clients.

We believe we have accomplished much and performed properly in our work for these agencies.

Our work for the LADWP began by helping it prepare for energy deregulation. Today, the challenges are more numerous, including encouraging the wise use of scarce water supplies, environmental threats, state and federal legislation that could have detrimental impacts on the LADWP and the city, as well as the issues of diversity and economic development.

For the Port, our work has included helping promote initiatives to clean the air, including the AMP program to allow ships to use cleaner shore-side power. Although we have a contract with the airport, we have not done any work there for some time. We value the opportunities we had with these agencies to help them achieve their communications goals. We will work with each of them, as needed, to ensure an orderly transition.

Los Angeles Times writer David Stratified noted that FleishmanHillard had made an amateur's mistake of "becoming the story." He raised the question of how a top public relations firm could not see the signs of trouble when, nearly a year before the alleged overbilling scandal broke, the media had begun to explore the relationship between FleishmanHillard and Mayor Hahn, focusing on political contributions.

An internal memo from Graham to FleishmanHillard employees July 29, 2004, outlined new steps the firm would implement to prevent future ethical problems. Graham said:

> *For nearly six decades, one of the cornerstones of our corporate philosophy has been our commitment to the highest ethical standards. That is why the recent allegations of billing irregularities in our Los Angeles office are so disturbing; they run counter to everything that this agency has stood for in 58 years . . . Once all the facts are known, we will move swiftly to address any shortcomings. In addition, if the results of our investigation uncover any improper billings, we will reimburse clients.*

The actions outlined in the memo included:

> ***Office Meetings****—I have directed each of our regional presidents to work with their general managers to conduct staff meetings over the next two weeks, to reinforce the firm's commitment to operating with the highest standards of client service, integrity, and business conduct and to reinforce that we would never accept or condone any misrepresentation of client billing. In addition, I will schedule conference calls with each of our U.S. offices and our partner companies, and I will meet with our California staff in person.*
>
> ***Ongoing Time Certification****—As you know, we recently began a new time entry and billing certification process. With each time entry on a client account, every staff member now must certify that they have reviewed and understand the firm's time entry policy, and that the time being entered is an accurate account of time worked. Further, each manager who is responsible for approving invoices will sign a statement certifying that they understand the firm's billing policy, and that all time being charged to a client is accurate.*
>
> ***Public Service Sector Training****—To address the increasingly sophisticated compliance requirements of our public service accounts, all employees working on local or state government contracts will complete the same training process the firm uses for employees working on federal contracts. This enhanced training, conducted by our experienced contract managers working in Washington, D.C., and by outside experts as needed, will ensure that every team member working on a public service client is fully aware of the key operating provisions and expectations of relevant client contracts.*
>
> ***Client Reassurance****—Our nearly 100 Client Relationship Managers (CRMs), along with our regional presidents and general managers, are in ongoing communication with our clients around the globe. In discussing this matter, our CRMs and regional leaders have the authority to take any necessary steps to ensure that our clients have absolute confidence in our billing practices. In addition, going forward, we will conduct regular audits of our work performed on behalf of any regulated or public service sector clients.*

> ***Enhanced Ethics Program***—*I understand and appreciate that we are an organization of highly ethical individuals. However, when our ethics are called into question, even in just one isolated area, it is appropriate to take steps to ensure we have the benefit of the best and freshest thinking. Therefore, we have engaged a respected, independent ethics expert to assess the ethical commitment of the firm. This individual, who is on the faculty of a major U.S. university and is an active ethics leader in the United States and Europe, has finished the first phase of his review and will work with a subcommittee of the firm to put in place a curriculum of "case-based" ethics training for all staff. This approach will complement our operating policies and allow everyone to even further engage in living this core value. By year's end, every FH employee will be introduced to this approach to ethics training.*
>
> ***Hotline***—*Within the next 10 days, we will announce a hotline giving every employee and anyone associated with our firm, from clients to suppliers, the ability to anonymously report any questionable or unethical behavior 24-hours a day, seven days a week. Every call to the hotline will result in a notification to me; Agnes Gioconda, our Chief Talent Officer; and the appropriate regional president.*
>
> ***New Approach to Political Contributions***—*We have revised our policies on political contributions to eliminate all contributions of corporate funds to candidates or ballot issues. In addition, we now require a three-part approval process at the local, regional, and corporate levels for any solicitation of political contributions from employees on FH premises, or on FH time, or using our name.*
>
> 
>
> ***Exit Interviews***—*We are revamping our existing process. Going forward, talent development liaisons in St Louis will conduct all exit interviews, which will be reviewed by our Chief Talent Officer and the appropriate regional president.*
>
> ***Client Satisfaction Survey***—*As always, we will thoroughly examine the results of this fall's annual client satisfaction survey and conduct follow-through one-on-one discussions with our clients on all matters such as account billing, administration of their business, and the results we generate.*

Graham sent an e-mail to all FleishmanHillard employees worldwide on August 9, 2004, explaining the new ethics hotline. He noted:

> *Let me emphasize that incidents of questionable or unethical behavior reported on the hotline—anything you feel runs contradictory to our core values or is a potential violation of the law or our operating policies—will be taken very seriously.*

Graham assured employees the hotline would protect the identity of the caller, that senior management would be engaged, and that there would be an investigation "to address any shortcomings we identify."

Throughout the controversy, Richard Kline, FleishmanHillard's regional president and LA general manager, participated in hundreds of interviews with the news and trade media, including a Q&A with *PR Week* and an opinion piece for the *Los Angeles Daily News*.

The Public Relations Society of America responded to the controversy by e-mailing a professional standards advisory to its membership. The advisory reminded its nearly 20,000 members that it is wrong to claim "compensation or credit for work that was never performed." Such practice is "unethical and weakens the public's trust in the public relations profession" and may be illegal.

In announcing the city comptroller's audit results in November 2004, Chick said, "What my audit finds are millions of dollars of bills that boggle the mind and defy common sense. FleishmanHillard treated the ratepayers of Los Angeles like a cash cow, milking them for millions."

The following year, FleishmanHillard agreed to a $5.7 million settlement of a civil suit with Los Angeles on April 19, 2005. The settlement included a $4.5 million cash payment and the forgiveness of approximately $1.2 million in outstanding bills.

The announcement was accompanied by a FleishmanHillard news release that carried statements from Kline, FleishmanHillard's Los Angeles general manager and regional president:

> *We sincerely apologize to the citizens of Los Angeles and to City officials. Other than these recent problems in our Los Angeles office, we have never had an issue of this type in the almost 60-year history of our firm. We take full responsibility for any billing issues, and we have taken steps to ensure the integrity of our billing process.*
>
> *We have a strong and entirely new management team in Los Angeles, and we have moved forward with numerous new policies and procedures to highlight the importance of adhering to the highest ethical standards. With the proposed payment under this civil settlement, we believe we have taken a significant step in setting this matter right.*
>
> *We have offered this substantial payment for several reasons: first, out of basic respect for the citizens of Los Angeles, because we failed to meet our standards or those of the City with regard to this billing; second, because we know the ongoing costs of litigation in this matter would be significant; and finally, because resolving this dispute will help us focus on restoring our reputation in Los Angeles and serving our clients.*

According to City Attorney Delgadillo's news release announcing the nearly $6 million settlement: "A review of the evidence by a forensic accounting team in support of the City Attorney's litigation efforts found the city stood a high likelihood of recovering $850,000 if the case went to trial." Delgadillo said in the release, "Those who attempt to defraud the city will find that my office will continue to be a watchdog, unafraid to take on those who seek to cheat our residents—no matter how well-connected."

POSTSCRIPT

The 18 percent water rate request was reduced to 11 percent and passed. The acting head of LADWP, Frank Salas, was demoted to his former post as LADWP's chief administrative officer. Los Angeles Mayor James Hahn banned all city agencies from contracting with public relations firms. The *Los Angeles Times* reported that the nine-campus Los Angeles Community College District decided to review its invoices from a $395,000 annual contract with FleishmanHillard. The college's review turned up no irregularities; FleishmanHillard did not submit a proposal to renew its contract with the college.

The *Los Angeles Times* reported August 31, 2004, that Los Angeles city comptroller Chick denied payment to Lee Andrews Group, a consulting firm, for June and July invoices totaling $74,000 for LADWP because the invoices did not provide enough information. Chick requested that Lee Andrews Group resubmit its bills "in a format that specifies the services, products or deliverables that were provided." The article went on to explain the problem:

> *The rejected invoices include 23 hours of work billed by company President Donna Andrews at $218 per hour in May for "strategic planning" and "administration." Other workers at the firm billed for the same services at rates ranging from $56 to $200 per hour. And the invoices included $45,000 for "planning and coordination of business breakfasts."*

Two former Los Angeles FleishmanHillard executives, which included Fleishman-Hillard's former Los Angeles general manager Doug Dowie, were convicted May 16, 2006, by a federal court jury on conspiracy and wire fraud charges for their involvement in overbilling the LADWP; the two executives were also terminated by FleishmanHillard. A third former executive pleaded guilty to three counts of wire fraud.

Mayor Hahn lost reelection in May 2005 to Antonio Villaraigosa, the city's first elected Latino mayor. The new mayor a few months later appointed a new five-member Board of Commissioners for LADWP.

QUESTIONS FOR DISCUSSION

1. Why does a public utility and monopoly need private public relations services—or even internal public relations staff?
2. What could LADWP have done to prevent this overbilling situation? What policies or procedures would you recommend for the utility's public affairs office?
3. Do you think that FleishmanHillard responded appropriately to this crisis? What were its response options?

4. Examine the ethical guidelines implemented by FleishmanHillard during the crisis. Do you think the response was adequate, or would other actions or guidelines have been helpful?
5. What are the implications of this case for the public relations field?

Dig Deeper

Read "Public Relations Agency Compensation: Enhancing Value through Best Practices" provided by the Council of Public Relations Firms available on the textbook's companion website. What practices are recommended to improve the agency relationship with its clients? Would these suggestions have helped prevent the overbilling situation in the case study "City Utility or Cash Cow"? What are the current public relations billing models?

WEB RESOURCES: DIG DEEPER

Examine the bills submitted by FleishmanHillard to LADWP. What is your impression of the tasks and amounts in the billing? Do they seem reasonable? Why or why not? Describe other billing options beyond hourly billing.

3

"In Washington, I'm Karen Ryan Reporting"

When Is a "Reporter" Not a Reporter?

Can one word make a difference?

When combined with election year politics and journalistic ethics, the answer is yes!

The ethical debate, some of it over the word *reporting,* began with a front-page story in *The New York Times*. This article detailed a federal investigation by the U.S. Government Accountability Office into new Medicare materials issued by the Health and Human Services Department (HHS).

Some of the informational materials were packaged as a video news release (VNR), the video equivalent of a print news release, and explained the benefits of a new Medicare drug benefit. Some versions of the VNRs, according to *The New York Times,* showed video clips of President George Bush receiving a standing ovation at a December 2003 bill-signing ceremony. The Medicare legislation had been hotly debated in Congress; opponents of the administration plan said the $400 billion program (which later was revised to $534 billion) was too costly and didn't provide better benefits for recipients.

Produced by Home Front Communications, a Washington, D.C., video production company, two of the Medicare VNRs ended with a woman's voice saying, "I'm Karen Ryan reporting." A Spanish-language version of the VNR featured a man who identified himself as a reporter named Alberto Garcia interviewing a Bush administration official. VNRs are broadcast-quality story packages that can be used in their entirety or partially in local television broadcasts. In addition to the complete "story," most VNRs include additional video ("B-roll" video) and suggested scripts, so that local TV news staff can construct their own video report.

One VNR script suggested this introduction: "In December, President Bush signed into law the first-ever prescription drug benefit for people with Medicare. Since then, there have been a lot of questions about how the law will help older Americans and people with disabilities."

REPORTER KAREN RYAN HELPS SORT THROUGH THE DETAILS

The ninety-second prepackaged VNR script follows:

Voice-over:	When President Bush signed the Medicare Prescription Drug Improvement and Modernization Act into law last month, millions of people who are covered by Medicare began asking how it will help them.
Tommy Thompson (Secretary HHS):	This is going to be the same Medicare system only with new benefits, more choices, more opportunities for enhanced benefits.
Voice-over:	Most of the attention has focused on the new prescription drug benefit that takes effect in 2006. In the meantime, Medicare will offer some immediate help through a discount card. There will be more than one to choose from.
Leslie Norwalk (HHS Acting Deputy Administrator):	In June of this year, seniors will have access to a drug discount card that Medicare endorses, giving them discounts on their prescription drugs.
Voice-over:	And some lower-income seniors get additional help: a $600 credit. Starting in 2005, the law provides new preventive services, such as a physical exam for all beneficiaries within the first six months of enrollment in Medicare.
Leslie Norwalk:	This preventative benefit, along with others, including cholesterol screening, diabetes screening, and heart disease screening, should help seniors stay healthy and have a better quality of life.
Voice-over:	Medicare officials emphasize that no one will be forced to sign up for any of the new benefits.
Tommy Thompson:	It's completely voluntary. Seniors will be able to partake in the new Medicare system or the old Medicare system.
Voice-over:	Officials urged people to call 1–800-MEDICARE for more information about the new law.
Voice-over:	In Washington, I'm Karen Ryan reporting.

Ryan was not a news reporter, although she had been a television journalist at one point in her career. She was a public relations consultant and the operator of Karen Ryan Group Communications. For the Medicare VNRs, she had been hired to read the Medicare script provided by Home Front Communications, a company subcontracted for the project by the public relations firm Ketchum. Production cost for the VNRs was $43,000. Critics said that the use of the word *reporting* or *reporter* in the VNRs was misleading because viewers had no way of knowing that the report they were seeing was paid for by its subject—the federal government—and was not the work of an objective journalist.

Three days after the *New York Times* article, the American Society of Newspaper Editors, the largest organization of supervising newspaper editors, joined several other journalism groups in protesting the use of people posing as journalists by sending a letter to Tommy Thompson, secretary of HHS. The society's president, Peter Bhatia, wrote,

> *It is fair, of course, for the government to communicate with citizens via press releases on video as well as print. It is not ethical or appropriate, however, to employ people to pose as journalists, either on or off camera.*

In addition to ethical considerations, critics pointed to legal concerns. Use of federal money for "publicity or propaganda purposes" without congressional authorization, *The New York Times* pointed out, is illegal according to the U.S. Government Accountability Office. The article detailed the scope of the publicity campaign:

> *$12.6 million for advertising this winter; $18.5 million to publicize drug discount cards this spring, about $18.5 million this summer, $30 million for a year of beneficiary education starting this fall, and $44 million starting in the fall of 2005.*

The Medicare VNRs were part of HHS's $12.6 million educational campaign funds to promote the drug benefit program. Bill Pierce, a spokesperson for HHS, said forty stations in thirty-three markets had aired all or part of the video news release. Defending the distribution to the media, he said, "That's their choice. They know who sent it to them. They know this came from somebody with a viewpoint."

Ryan, stung by critics who called her an "actor," "hooker," and "phony," agreed with Pierce. The VNRs were clearly labeled as coming from HHS. Ryan responded:

> *It's not about playing a reporter; I never pretended to do that. In just about every VNR a voice-over will say, "I'm so-and-so reporting." You're not telling a newsroom this is the way the story goes. You're telling them this is what a cut spot looks and sounds like with your information. Some of the coverage made it sound like HHS had a casting call and I was the best actor for the job.*

HHS and Ryan said the ultimate responsibility for the use of the video belonged to the local television stations. The VNRs "were clearly marked as originating from the government."

Ryan noted that deceiving the news media runs contrary to good media relations; it's a cooperative and respectful relationship built on trust. "PR people and news people have worked together for quite a while," she said. "It's not a deceitful, terrible relationship. A TV producer would never know to cover certain things if a PR person never called."

Kevin Foley, president of KEF Media Associates in Atlanta, said, "The media are the filter here and they have to pass judgment on what airs. They are not unwitting victims. If we can provide quality news content, why wouldn't they consider airing it?"

The symbiotic relationship that exists between journalists and public relations professionals is often viewed as a necessary evil by journalists, who may need assistance with background information, interviews with employees, or access to facilities. Journalists may not have the resources of expertise, time, or personnel to cover stories without the help of public relations. Because public relations practitioners are advocates for their organization, their efforts are often viewed with a healthy dose of caution.

Public relations practitioners have always provided journalists with "information subsidies," usually in the form of print news releases, but also increasingly in VNR formats. As long as the information coming from the organization is clearly labeled for the journalists, it should be treated equally. Public Relations Society of America president Judith Turner Phair testified at a Senate Committee hearing on prepackaged news stories:

> *Just as "print" news releases follow the style of print journalism, VNRs utilize a format that is most adaptable to electronic media. Both print and video news releases present information in a way that is preferred by these respective media and that meets public information needs and interests.*
>
> *But we also believe that VNRs should be produced and disseminated with the highest levels of transparency, candor, and honesty. To provide open communication that fosters informed decision, we must do more than simply funnel information through the media to the public. We must reveal the sponsors for causes and interests represented and disclose all financial interests related to the VNR.*

Another criticism of the Medicare VNRs concerned their dissemination. The VNRs were distributed through CNN Newsource, a service that allows television stations to download news footage produced by CNN or other affiliates as well as video news releases. Some news managers misread the label or thought the package was an actual news report. A month after the controversy began, CNN Newsource changed the way it transmitted video news releases. The producer of the VNR is identified, the footage is labeled as a VNR, and it is transmitted separately from real journalist-produced news footage under its own heading. News stations can also bar news releases from being sent or just receive B-roll footage of VNRs.

POSTSCRIPT

What the U.S. Government Accountability Office Said

A sixteen-page decision issued May 19, 2004, by federal investigators of the U.S. Government Accountability Office found the Health and Human Services Medicare VNRs crossed the legal line and violated the government's publicity and propaganda prohibition because the packages were not attributed to the Center for Medicare Services (CMS). Even though the stations received VNRs clearly labeled as such, viewers did not know they were watching material packaged by the federal government—not journalists:

> *Nothing in the story packages permits the viewer to know that Karen Ryan and Alberto Garcia were paid with federal funds through a contractor to report the message in the story package. The entire story package was developed with appropriated funds but appears to be an independent news story. The failure to identify HHS or CMS as the source within the story package is not remedied by the fact that the other materials in the VNR package identify HHS and CMS as the source of the materials or that the content of the story package did not attempt to attribute the agency's position to an individual outside the agency.*

A second GAO opinion issued in January 2005 found similar problems with video news releases disseminated by the Office of National Drug Control Policy as part of its National Youth Anti-drug Media Campaign.

In congressional testimony, a GAO representative noted that federal agencies "have a right to inform the public about their activities and to defend the administration's point of view on policy matters," but there are statutory limitations on an agency's information dissemination. In particular, the publicity and propaganda prohibition enacted in 1951 states: "No part of any appropriation contained in this or any other Act shall be used for publicity or propaganda purposes within the United States not heretofore authorized by Congress."

Under this regulation, GAO has identified several specific activities as illegal: "One of the main targets of this prohibition is agency-produced material that is covert as to source. Our opinions have emphasized that the critical element of covert propaganda is concealment of the government's role in producing the materials."

A subsequent investigation of seven federal departments by the GAO in 2005 found that during 2003, 2004, and the first two quarters of 2005, $1.6 billion in contracts was spent with public relations firms, advertising agencies, media organizations, and individual members of the media.

What the U.S. Department of Justice Said

The U.S. Department of Justice disagreed with the GAO's opinion. A separate July 30, 2004, opinion issued by the General Counsel Office of Health and Human Services stated:

> *But we believe a line must be drawn to distinguish legitimate governmental information from improper governmental advocacy. The VNRs at issue here did not advocate a particular policy or position of HHS and CMS, but rather provided accurate (even if not comprehensive) information about the benefits provided under a recent Act of Congress: the MMA. Informing the public of the facts about a federal program is not the type of evil with which Congress was concerned in enacting the "publicity or propaganda" riders.*

What the Federal Communication Commission Said

The Federal Communication Commission issued a public notice April 13, 2005, reminding all broadcast stations and cable systems of their legal obligations to "clearly disclose" to listeners and viewers "the nature, source, and sponsorship of the material they are viewing," especially when dealing with political material or controversial issues. The sponsorship identification rules are part of the Communications Act of 1934. Violations could result in fines up to $10,000, license revocation, or imprisonment of up to a year.

What Other Investigations Said

A 2005 report by minority leaders in Congress entitled "Federal Public Relations Spending" noted:

> *In 2004, the Bush administration spent over $88 million on contracts with public relations agencies. The value of federal contracts with public relations agencies has increased significantly over the last four years. In 2000, the last year of the Clinton administration, the federal government spent $39 million on contracts with major public relations agencies. By 2004, the value of these public relations contracts had grown by almost $50 million, an increase of 128 percent.*
>
> *The center for Medicare and Medicaid Services spent over $94 million on contracts with public relations agencies over the last four years, the most of any federal agency.*

QUESTIONS FOR DISCUSSION

1. Using the PRSA Code of Ethics as your guide, what values and code provisions could you point to that apply to this case?
2. What does the publicity and propaganda prohibition related to the federal agency's information dissemination activities mean?

3. What was the difference between legitimate governmental information and improper governmental advocacy?
4. What steps could HHS have taken to prevent this controversy?
5. If printed news releases are accepted by the journalism world, why are video news releases different? How could a reader tell if a newspaper published a news release without changing its contents or identifying the source?
6. Is it acceptable for the federal government to spend millions of dollars informing taxpayers of a new program?
7. What are the elements of a video news release? What is "B-roll"? Do video news releases present both sides of a story?

Dig Deeper

Video news releases and multimedia news releases are effective ways to tell an organization's story. Read the report entitled "Fake TV News—Widespread and Undisclosed" by PR Watch that is available on the textbook's companion website. What ethical issues were identified with the news media's use of video news releases? How can public relations practitioners help protect the integrity of the news media when they prepare video material for the news media? What principle or principles from the PRSA Code of Ethics are involved?

In the specific case of Station KMSP-TV what did the FCC penalize the station for doing? The FCC notice of penalty for KMSP is provided on the textbook's companion website.

CHAPTER 3

Corporate Social Responsibility

What is the corporation's responsibility to social issues facing the world? According to the European Union, corporate social responsibility (CSR) goes beyond voluntary efforts such as corporate philanthropy and foundation grants. CSR is:

> *A concept whereby companies integrate social and environmental concerns in their business operations and in their interaction with their stakeholders on a voluntary basis as they are increasingly aware that responsible behavior leads to sustainable business practices.*

For many business people, the concept of CSR runs contrary to a fundamental truth—that businesses exist to meet the needs of their private interests and to maximize their profits. As the economist and Nobel laureate Milton Friedman put it in 1962, the "business of business is business."

But if businesses are seen more as a part of the "basic structure of society" rather than as independent private concerns that should be left alone to do their work, then a shift in the corporate obligation to societal issues changes dramatically.

As the scholars Kenneth Amaeshi, Paul Nnodim, and Onyeka Osuji noted in *Corporate Social Responsibility, Entrepreneurship, and Innovation*, the major philosophical differences between capitalism and CSR are stark (Table 3.1).

Traditional business advocates worry that reducing the corporation's single-mindedness on its business operations (private interests) and maximizing profits will ultimately weaken its ability to compete. Those in the CSR movement propose that maximizing profit can be done while taking into account the "social and moral obligations firms have toward the larger society," according to Amaeshi et al.

What are these social and moral obligations? Social responsibility can include sustainability, sustainable development, environmental management, business ethics, philanthropy and community investment, worker rights and welfare, human rights, corruption, corporate governance, legal compliance, and animal rights, as described in *Corporate Social Responsibility: A Research Handbook*.

In the sustainability movement, leading economic powers, such as the U.S., are consuming more resources compared with developing countries. Consider

TABLE 3.1 The differences between capitalism and CSR

	CAPITALISM	CSR AGENDA
Motivation/drive	Self-interest	Collective/communal interests
Goal orientation	Profit	Social welfare
Process	Efficiency	Equity/fairness
Guide	Rationality (logic)	Empathic rationality
Performance criterion	Shareholder value	Externalities (impacts)
Nature of firms	Private institutions	Social institutions
Governance of firms	Contractual (legal entity concepts)	Networked governance
Dominant strategy	Competing with strife	Competing responsibly
Dominant operational time horizon	Short-term	Long-term

some of these findings from Worldwatch Institute, a nonprofit research and policy organization:

- The U.S., with less than 5 percent of the global population, uses about a quarter of the world's fossil fuel resources—burning up nearly 25 percent of the coal, 26 percent of the oil, and 27 percent of the world's natural gas.
- 12 percent of the world's population lives in North America and Western Europe and accounts for 60 percent of private consumption spending, but a third of humanity who live in South Asia and sub-Saharan Africa account for only 3.2 percent.
- New houses in the U.S. were 38 percent bigger in 2002 than in 1975, despite having fewer people per household on average.

The Living Planet Report, published by the World Wide Fund for Nature (WWF), links excessive consumption to environmental degradation. Among its findings:

- 51 percent of the freshwater animal species of the world are declining in number.
- A recent survey found one in four vertebrate species to be in sharp decline or facing serious pressure from human activities.
- One of every eight known plant species is threatened with extinction or is nearly extinct.

- One in ten tree species—some 8,750 of the 80,000 to 100,000 tree species known to science—are threatened with extinction.
- The overall rate of extinction is estimated to be 1,000 to 10,000 times higher than it would be naturally, and appears to be increasing. The last time such a mass extinction is believed to have occurred was sixty-five million years ago, when a dramatic shift in global climate patterns ended the age of the dinosaurs.
- The average American consumes about fifty-three times more goods and services than someone from China.

Just because a country can afford and is capable of consuming vast quantities of resources does not make it morally right, according to sustainability advocates. Over-consumption may lead to unintended consequences. Climate change, for example, is seen as a sustainability issue because of its connection to greenhouse gases produced by human activities.

These types of threats have led the U.S. to develop national policies and programs for sustainable development. The government created the first national policy for environmental sustainability—the National Environmental Policy Act—in 1969 and established the Environmental Protection Agency in 1970. The U.S. has also developed laws and policies to address social issues including fair labor practices, human and animal rights, and business ethics and corruption. Still, advocates say much more needs to be done.

In the past decade public support for CSR has grown. The American public is supportive of businesses expanding their missions to include more active engagement in social issues. According to the 2010 *Cause Evaluation Study* by the well-known cause marketing and public relations firm Cone Communications:

- 88 percent of Americans say it is acceptable for companies to involve a cause or issue in their marketing. This record number represents a 33 percent increase since Cone began measuring in 1993 (66 percent).
- 85 percent of consumers have a more positive image of a product or company when it supports a cause they care about.
- 90 percent of consumers want companies to tell them the ways they are supporting causes. Put another way: More than 278 million people in the U.S. want to know what a company is doing to benefit a cause.

PHILANTHROPY AND CAUSE-RELATED MARKETING

Businesses can donate money or in-kind services to a cause in support of CSR activities by nonprofit organizations. This charitable giving is called philanthropy and it generally results in a tax write-off for the business.

Another way businesses can support CSR initiatives is to work with a nonprofit organization involved in social or environmental projects. The nonprofit enters into a marketing relationship with a business to sell products that benefit both parties in some way. The nonprofit benefits by extending its cause to the people serviced by the business, and it may also benefit in a share of the revenue generated by the sales of products or services. The business benefits reputationally by supporting a popular cause and by selling more products or services. Some examples of successful cause-related marketing campaigns include Yoplait's "Save Lids to Save Lives" in support of Susan G. Komen for the Cure and General Mills' Box Tops for Education which benefited schools. Businesses should consider the match between the product/service and the nonprofit organization to ensure consumers can make the right connections.

PUBLIC RELATIONS AND CORPORATE SOCIAL RESPONSIBILITY

With growing consumer interest in CSR, public relations is strategically positioned within organizations to help leaders develop and implement CSR goals as part of business strategy. In the article "Corporate Social Responsibility," Robert Heath and Lan Ni provided examples of how the public relations practice can contribute directly or indirectly to establishing a CSR culture in an organization. Public relations can:

- support top-down commitment of organizational leadership to create a CSR program and culture;
- assist with the creation of a CSR framework;
- assist with the creation of a CSR position statement;
- develop a CSR ombudsman program;
- develop CSR audits and reports;
- encourage stakeholder involvement;
- encourage corporate governance involvement;
- create awareness;
- manage key messages;
- manage stakeholder relationships.

If an organization commits to CSR, it should encourage transparency to ensure that its actions are ethical and that it receives the goodwill from its stakeholders. Organizations that don't carry out their promises or over-promise results risk boycotts and "shaming" campaigns organized via social media. The term "greenwashing" refers to organizations promoting their environmental activities for reputational gain and failing to live up to their promises. The term "pinkwashing" similarly calls out organizations that use breast cancer campaigns to cover up actions, especially their products or services, that could cause cancer.

4

Food for Thought

Pig Stalls Become Focal Point of Animal Rights Debate

From Wilbur in *Charlotte's Web* to Porky Pig and Babe, fictional pigs are cute, cuddly, and smart, but real pigs are a commodity—and a multibillion dollar industry. Driven by consumer demand for affordable meat, pork production in the United States has evolved from family farms to what critics call "factory farming." These large-scale farms raise large numbers of animals in confined spaces, which are now common in the production of meat, milk and eggs.

For large-scale pork producers, a successful operation begins with an efficient breeding system. Unlike adult females on small farms, a sow in a factory farm setting is confined during her 114-day gestation period in a "sow gestation stall," about two feet wide by seven feet long. Pork producers say the system provides a safer and more efficient way to produce healthy piglets, with between 2 and 2.1 healthy litters each year. Animal welfare groups, such as the Humane Society of the United States (HSUS), maintain the use of what they call "gestation crates" is inhumane and unhealthy for pigs.

FIGURE 3.1 *Sows in gestation crates.*
http://video.pork.org/
The National Pork Board

ANIMAL WELFARE AND ANIMAL RIGHTS

Most Americans know little about where their food comes from and how it's produced. For some, the hard-working family farmer raising pigs to take to market conjures up a pleasant image: a small farm with a few animals in an open field. With few exceptions, that idea is long gone. "Factory" farms, on the other hand, present a very different picture; they are large facilities built for efficiency.

In recent years, a wave of news reports, books, documentaries, and research have explored factory farming and depicted some of the industry's operations in unflattering detail. Consumers began to take note.

Critics of large-scale farming, such as the HSUS, say that animals that live indoors can live in such close confinement that their natural social behaviors are often curtailed or prevented. Instead of the large number of small family farms that helped feed Americans in the 20th century, large-scale farms are relatively few in number. According to the National Pork Board, the top twenty-five pork producers account for about half of the breeding herd in the United States. Still, there are about 67,000 hog farmers in the United States.

According to a 2012 Gallup poll, 5 percent of Americans considered themselves vegetarians and 2 percent said they were vegans.

While most Americans don't have a problem with a meat-based diet, some people believe animals deserve more protections and even rights. The term "animal welfare" refers to the physical and psychological well-being of animals. Researchers and activists have developed indicators including behavior, physiology, longevity, and reproduction to measure how well an animal is doing.

Animal welfare proponents believe that animals are sentient creatures; they can feel, perceive, be conscious and have subjective experiences. While there are many points of view, adherents to animal welfare want to minimize what they describe as adverse effects of animal treatment, particularly for those animals that benefit humans.

Animal rights adherents go even further. They believe that animals should not be treated as property and that their use by humans is not acceptable. Animal rights activists oppose the use of leather clothing and the consumption of animals. Animal rights groups, such as People for the Ethical Treatment of Animals (PETA), advocate for vegan or meatless diets. Eating animals, they contend, is cruel.

The pork industry say it is bad business to mistreat pigs and that pig farmers take great care to feed and shelter their animals properly. In fact, the pork industry argues gestation stalls are a safer and more nutritional way to raise sows indoors.

Pig farmers say to meet the growing demand for meat products nationally and globally and stay in business, farmers must be efficient and use factory farming methods.

So, what's right? Since one cannot ask pigs what they think, and no one knows for certain if animals are aware or can perceive their situation as humans would, the issue poses a problem with ethical and emotional dimensions.

This case study examines the HSUS's campaign to eliminate sow gestation crates and the pork industry's response to its pressure tactics between 2010 and 2012.

THE HUMANE SOCIETY OF THE UNITED STATES

The HSUS, established in 1954, has sought to improve the welfare of animals, acknowledging that such changes often occur incrementally. According to its website, the HSUS seeks to protect animals by advocating for better laws and conducting campaigns to change industries; it also conducts investigations into animal cruelty and cares for animals through a network of five sanctuaries and rehabilitation facilities.

Over the years the HSUS gathered support for a number of state and federal legislative initiatives such as the Humane Slaughter Act of 1958 and the Animal Welfare Act of 1966. Some of its recent campaigns have included farm animal protection, animal fighting, puppy mills, animals in laboratories and the fur trade.

Charity Navigator, an independent nonprofit organization that evaluates American charities' financial health and accountability/transparency, gave the HSUS a four-star rating in 2012, the highest possible. Charity Navigator noted that the HSUS's fundraising efficiency was 18 cents for every dollar raised. Most of its budget was devoted to program expenses (77 percent), and administrative expenses were low at 3.7 percent. In 2011, the charity had total revenues of more than $167.7 million, a sizeable amount to fund many activities on behalf of animals.

However, another organization, Charity Watch (American Institute of Philanthropy), in 2012 gave the organization a "D" for high fundraising costs—spending up to 48 cents per dollar raised.

Since 2001, the HSUS has campaigned to reduce what it deems "the suffering of animals," which has included many initiatives such as ending "cruel confinement of farm animals," "cruel slaughter practices" and "force-fed animals." The HSUS publicized the severe confinement of calves, pigs and hens in factory farm settings and pressured producers, legislators, and others through a variety of tactics. In particular, it estimated that sow gestation crates were used by 70 percent of U.S. pork producers.

THE U.S. PORK INDUSTRY

The U.S. pork industry has undergone major changes since 1985. According to the National Pork Board, "output per breeding animal has more than doubled in the past 30 years, while the U.S. breeding herd has been reduced by more than 50 percent" due to advances in technology and economies of scale. Pork is much healthier too. Pork tenderloin is as lean as skinless chicken breast, according to the National Pork Board. Six of the most common pork cuts have, on average, 16 percent less fat and 27 percent less saturated fat than pork sold before 2004, according to the U.S. Department of Agriculture (USDA). Worldwide, pork is the most widely eaten meat, beating out chicken by nearly 10 percent, according to the USDA Foreign Agricultural Service. One study found that each market hog represents 371 servings of pork, based on a 265-pound market weight hog and 70 percent yield and 8-ounce servings. Ninety-four percent of U.S. households consumed pork, according to a National Pork Board consumer segmentation study in 2010.

There are a host of co-products beyond food that are derived from hogs today, including insulin used in the treatment of diabetes, hog heart valves used to replace diseased human heart valves, and hog skin used to treat severe burn victims. Many consumer products are derived from hogs, including quality leather for clothes, shoes, and handbags, and many other products from hog bones, hair, and fatty acids and glycerin.

PORK INDUSTRY ADVOCACY ORGANIZATIONS

The country's pork industry is represented by two major organizations: the National Pork Board and the National Pork Producers Council, along with other state and national groups. These organizations have worked on behalf of pork producers to tell the hitherto untold story of what the industry has accomplished in the last twenty years.

The National Pork Board and its funding apparatus were established in 1986 by Congress to help about 67,000 hog farmers increase demand for pork products. The Board's Pork Checkoff Program is the industry's funding source for consumer advertising and research to improve production and marketing. The program collects a small fee for every hog sold in the U.S. and on imported hogs or pork products, generating about $78 million in 2012. About 20 percent of the collected funds are returned to the pork state associations for their own projects.

The National Pork Board's mission is to "harness the resources of all producers to capture opportunity, address challenges and satisfy customers."

The other leading pork organization is the National Pork Producers Council, which is the public-policy/lobbying arm of the industry and represents forty-three affiliated state pork associations. Its mission is:

> *to fight for reasonable legislation and regulations, develop revenue and market opportunities and protect the livelihoods of America's 67,000 pork producers. Public-policy issues on which it focuses are in the areas of agriculture and industry, animal health and food safety, environment and energy and international trade.*

The National Pork Board and the National Pork Producers Council work together on many projects that improve the industry and its reputation. In 2012, the National Pork Board allocated $69.2 million, spending $52.7 million in three areas: domestic marketing, science and technology research, and communication and producer outreach. Funding for the National Pork Producers Council is voluntary and not published.

Beyond the sow confinement issue, the pork industry faced other concerns. According to the National Pork Board's five-year 2010 strategic plan, the industry

FIGURE 3.2 *Erin Ehinger from Dykhuis farms talks about sow care including the use of sow gestation stalls.*
http://video.pork.org/
National Pork Board

was grappling with high feed and energy costs, soft demand for pork due to food consumption patterns that emphasized less meat in diets, and activist groups that attacked the pork industry's handling of public safety issues including environmental stewardship (air, water, and land quality), and animal welfare issues. The pork industry was also dealing with an American public that erroneously connected the H1N1 ("swine flu") virus with pigs, had little connection to modern farms and did not understand how hard it was to produce high-quality meat at affordable prices. This was especially true during conditions of drought or too much rain due to climate change.

A National Pork Board survey of pork producers determined that activist groups were the most significant force facing the industry in 2009. Producers and other stakeholders wanted the National Pork Board to improve the industry's image and address animal care issues (the top third and fourth priorities respectively) with its Checkoff Program resources.

THE HSUS CAMPAIGN

In 2001 voters in Florida amended their constitution to ban the use of gestation stalls. This event ignited efforts by the HSUS, which used a variety of pressure tactics to increase public awareness and action about sow gestation crates, claiming these were used by 60–70 percent of U.S. pork producers. The tactics included publicizing scientific research, undercover investigative reports, legal actions, lobbying for policy and legislative changes, and shareholder activism, that supported the HSUS' belief that sow gestation crates equated to animal mistreatment.

SCIENTIFIC RESEARCH

One of the tactics the HSUS has employed is the use of third-party expert sources to support its goals. One important study that was promoted by the HSUS and undertaken by the Pew Commission on Industrial Farm Animal Production was called "Putting Meat on the Table: Industrial Farm Animal Production in America."

This 2008 study was funded by the Pew Charitable Trusts and the Johns Hopkins School of Public Health. This report recommended abolishing gestation stalls. In its executive summary it said:

> *Gestation crates, the most restrictive farrowing crates, battery cages, and other intensive confinement systems fail to allow for even these minimal natural behaviors . . .*
>
> *. . . The Commission believes that ethical treatment of animals raised for food is essential to, and consistent with, achieving a safe and sustainable system for producing food animals. Practices that restrict natural motion, such as sow gestation crates, induce high levels of stress in the animals and threaten their health, which in turn may threaten human health. There is growing public concern for ethical treatment of farm animals that will lead to new laws and regulations governing farm animal treatment unless the industry voluntarily adopts third-party, consensus-based standards for animal well-being.*

FIGURE 3.3 *A report funded by The Pew Charitable Trusts and Johns Hopkins Bloomberg School of Public Health was critical of farm factory practices.*
http://www.ncifap.org/
Pew Commission on Industrial Farm Animal Production (PCIFAP)

The Commission recommended phasing out gestation crates:

Phase out the most intensive and inhumane production practices within a decade to reduce the risk of IFAP to public health and improve animal well-being (i.e., gestation crates and battery cages).

GESTATION CRATES:

Problems & Solutions

Most mother pigs in the U.S. pork industry are confined in "gestation crates" for virtually their entire lives. These crates are about the same width and length of a pig's body, preventing the animals from even turning around.

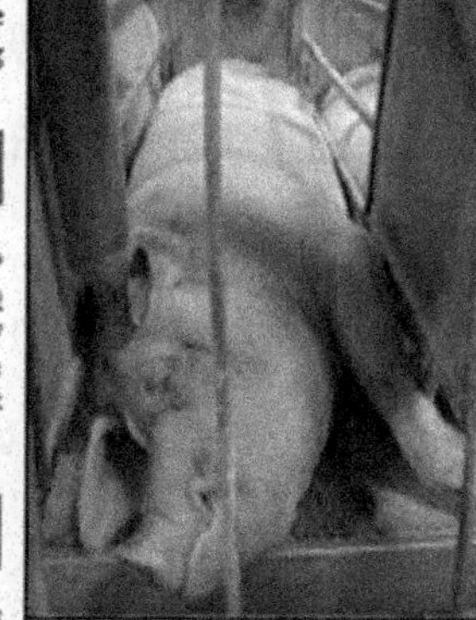

THE SCIENCE IS CLEAR

Renowned animal welfare scientist Dr. Temple Grandin says, "We've got to treat animals right, and gestation stalls have got to go." The Pew Commission on Industrial Farm Animal Production—which was funded by the Pew Charitable Trusts and Johns Hopkins School of Public Health, and included the former U.S. Secretary of Agriculture—recommended that "all systems that restrict natural movement," including gestation crates, be phased-out.

THE ECONOMICS STACK UP

The alternative is "group housing," which affords animals greater freedom of movement. Iowa State University conducted a two-and-a-half year long economic analysis of the issue and found that that "group housing...resulted in a weaned pig cost that was 11 percent less than the cost of a weaned pig from the individual stall confinement system."

LEGISLATION AND FOOD RETAILERS FAVOR GROUP HOUSING

Nine states (Florida, Maine, Colorado, California, Ohio, Rhode Island, Michigan, Oregon and Arizona), as well as the E.U., have passed laws to ban the use of gestation crates. Over 30 of the world's largest food companies—Costco, McDonald's, Burger King, ARAMARK, Sodexo, Wendy's, Oscar Mayer/Kraft, Kroger, Safeway, Target, Supervalu, Subway, Sysco, Denny's, ConAgra Foods, Hillshire Brands (Jimmy Dean, Ballpark, and Hillshire Farm), Cracker Barrel, Sonic, Dunkin Brands, CKE Restaurants (Carl's Jr. and Hardee's), Baja Fresh, Kmart, Heinz, Wienerschnitzel, Jack in the Box, Qdoba, Harris Teeter, Brinker International (Chili's), Royal Caribbean Cruise Lines, Carnival Cruise Lines, Bruegger's Bagels, Einstein Noah Restaurant Group, The Cheesecake Factory, Campbell's Soup, Wolfgang Puck Restaurants, Compass Group, TrustHouse and Bon Appétit Management Company—have announced that they will eliminate gestation crates from their supply chains. **Chipotle, Whole Foods** and others *only* use gestation crate-free pork.

"McDonald's believes gestation stalls are not a sustainable production system for the future...[and] wants to see the end of sow confinement in gestation stalls in our supply chain."

"Wendy's is working with its U.S. and Canadian Pork Suppliers to eliminate the use of sow gestation stalls over time. We believe that confining pigs in gestation stalls is not sustainable over the long-term, and moving away from this practice is the right thing to do."

"[Burger King] pledges to eliminate gestation crates for breeding pigs...[and will] only purchase pork from suppliers that can demonstrate documented plans to end their use of gestation crates."

FIGURE 3.4 *A fact sheet from the Humane Society of the United States that summarized its position on the sow gestation crate issue.*
http://www.fmi.org/docs/animal-welfare/hsus-gestation-crate-factsheet.pdf?sfvrsn=3
Courtesy of The Humane Society of the United States

The Union of Concerned Scientists also issued a report in 2008 entitled "CAFOs: The Untold Story of Confined Animal Feeding Operations," which focused on the negative safety and environmental effects of factory farming.

These reports generated numerous news media stories. *The New York Times* wrote in an editorial based on the reports: "In short, animal husbandry has been turned into animal abuse" and called for changes.

The HSUS invested in reporting the research of others to support HSUS views. These reports were heavily annotated examinations of animal welfare issues in factory farming.

For example, its January 2012 report, "Welfare Issues with Gestation Crates for Pregnant Sows," was fourteen pages in length, with half of these devoted to footnotes. According to this report, "Crated sows suffer a number of significant welfare problems, including elevated risk of urinary tract infections, weakened bones, overgrown hooves, lameness, behavioral restriction and stereotypies." The report notes that sows are unable to participate in normal behaviors such as grazing, rooting, walking, and lying down. As a consequence of confinement, abnormal behaviors such as "repetitive bar-biting, head-weaving" and "chewing motions with an empty mouth" occur. Many of the sources are scientific research articles published in journals such as the *Journal of the American Veterinary Medical Association* and *Animal Science*.

These types of reports attempted to counteract other third-party voices such as that of the American Veterinary Medical Association (AVMA). The AVMA said in a statement that gestation crates "may minimize aggression and injury, reduce competition, and allow individual feeding and nutritional management, assistant in control of body condition," but that crates "restrict normal behavioral expression." The AVMA endorsed more research into housing systems that would increase sow welfare.

The HSUS report recommended alternative feeding methods, such as an electronic sow feeder system that eliminates sow aggression and provides for individual feeding care. Another report that the HSUS promoted, "The Economics of Adopting Alternatives to Gestation Crate Confinement of Sows," tackled the economics of using different feeding systems, showing that there were viable alternatives.

THIRD-PARTY ENDORSEMENTS

In addition to the scientific reports that functioned as third-party endorsements, the news media and others supported the HSUS viewpoints in editorials and columns or provided credibility to the cause by including the HSUS information. One major endorsement was quoted in HSUS literature and on its website from the famed animal welfare scientist Dr. Temple Grandin, although pork industry advocates noted that she was not a welfare expert on sow gestation housing options. She said: "We've got to treat animals right, and gestation stalls have got to go. Confining an animal for most of its life in a box in which it is not able to turn around does not provide a decent life."

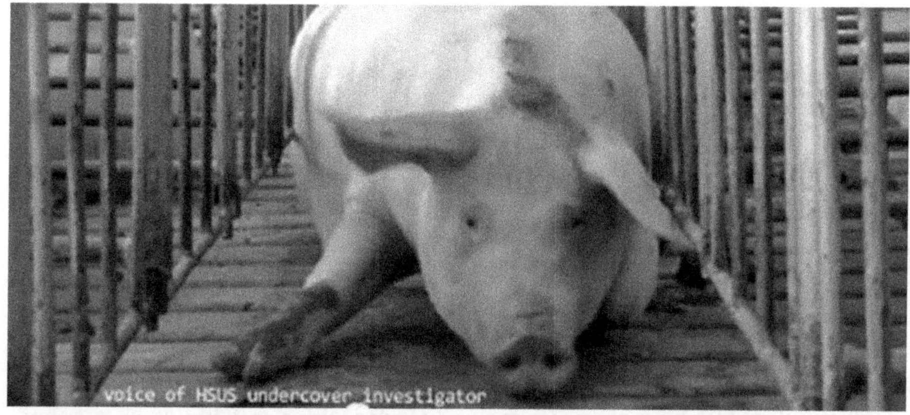

FIGURE 3.5 *A still from the undercover video investigation by the Humane Society of the United States into farm factory practices at Seaboard. http://www.humanesociety.org/news/press_releases/2012/01/pig_gestation_investigation_013112.html*
Courtesy of The Human Society of the United States

UNDERCOVER INVESTIGATIONS

Three major undercover investigations were conducted by the HSUS regarding the use of sow gestation crates. The first targeted Smithfield Foods, a company that pledged in 2007 to phase out the use of gestation crates over the next ten years, but in 2009 delayed its plans. In 2010, an HSUS undercover investigator witnessed cramped gestation crates, sows with open pressure sores and wounds that sometimes became infected, the use of gate rods to make a sow move, mishandled piglets, and premature piglets that fell through floor slats into manure pits. The video recorded alleged mistreatment issues, further strengthening the purported evidence of animal abuse. Shortly after the HSUS released the video and report, Smithfield recommitted to phasing out gestation crates by 2017, according to a company statement.

Another undercover investigation at two other major pig-breeding producers' facilities (Seaboard and Prestage Farms) released in 2012 found the following alleged problems: physical mistreatment, untreated pressure sores/wounds, unsanitary conditions in gestation crates, and dead pigs in gestation crates and pens. National news media such as Reuters and The Associated Press wrote stories based on the report and graphic video.

The HSUS also performed an undercover investigation of Wyoming Premium Farms, exposing workers punching and kicking mother pigs, kicking piglets like balls, whipping them around by their hind legs, smashing them into concrete floors, and throwing them high into the air. These videos and first-person accounts provided evidence for legal claims against the companies and nine charges of animal cruelty were brought against workers at the farm.

LEGAL TACTICS

The HSUS filed complaints to challenge the pork industry's position that sow gestation confinement was humane and ethical, a description the HSUS called "deception by omission," according to a HSUS statement. In 2012, the HSUS filed a complaint with the Federal Trade Commission alleging that the National Pork Producers Council's public descriptions of its animal welfare commitment (specifically its "We Care" and "Pork Quality Assurance Plus" training and certification programs) were misleading, due to the industry's prevalent use of sow gestation crates. The HSUS said in a statement: "The pork industry spends millions misleading the public about its animal welfare record while allowing pigs to be crammed into tiny gestation crates where they can't even turn around for months on end."

The National Pork Producers Council responded with a criticism of what it characterized as Big Brother-type tactics, and stated:

> *The FTC complaint is the latest attack by animal-rights activists on America's hog farmers, an assault that seems obviously in response to the U.S. pork industry's strident opposition to congressional legislation that would allow federal bureaucrats to tell farmers how to raise and care for their animals.*

The HSUS also lodged a complaint with the Federal Trade Commission (FTC) against Seaboard Foods, one of the largest pork producers in the country. The HSUS claimed that the company's "Sustainability & Stewardship Report" contained falsehoods:

> *Seaboard is issuing unlawfully false or misleading representations about the animal welfare practices of its wholly owned subsidiary Seaboard Foods, one of the largest pork producers in the country. Seaboard Foods' "Sustainability & Stewardship Report," accessible through both the Seaboard Corporation and Seaboard Foods websites, and videos and other statements available on the Seaboard Foods website are replete with false and/or misleading representations about Seaboard's animal welfare practices, claims that animals raised to produce Seaboard products are raised "free from cruelty" and only in accordance with the "most humane practices."*

A similar legal complaint filed with the U.S. Securities and Exchange Commission (SEC) against Smithfield Foods, a supplier of McDonald's, said that a Smithfield video misrepresented to viewers its animal welfare and environmental standards.

> *On March 7, 2011, Smithfield posted on its investor relations website a press release announcing the launch of a series of informational videos—New Smithfield Foods Educational Video Series Helps Take the Mystery Out of Pork Production. The release directed investors to visit websites hosting seven videos purporting to show how we raise our pigs and how our environmental and animal handling sustainability practices work every day.*
>
> *As detailed more fully below, these videos are replete with false and/or misleading representations—both express and implied—about Smithfield's animal welfare and*

environmental practices. These claims are material and misleading to stakeholders concerned about corporate social responsibility (CSR).

The video noted that Smithfield "provides animals with 'ideal' living conditions and that their animals' 'every need is met' despite the fact that the vast majority of its breeding sows are confined in gestation crates."

When Seaboard Foods challenged the allegations in the videos, the HSUS filed more complaints with the SEC and FTC for Seaboard's alleged false and misleading statements.

LEGISLATIVE EFFORTS

There are no federal animal welfare laws regulating the treatment of "food animals" while they're on the farm. While all fifty states had cruelty statutes in 2012, most exempted common farming practices, such as close confinement housing systems.

Each year, the HSUS ranks each state on its animal protection laws, including laws protecting farm animal welfare. It gives annual Humane Legislator of the Year awards to those legislators who have pressed for effective laws to protect animals. Citizens are encouraged to participate in its Humane Lobby Day events. These sponsored events give animal welfare activists information about effective lobbying and bills under consideration in their state legislature. The HSUS offers to make appointments for these citizen lobbyists to meet face-to-face with their legislators or staff to seek support for particular animal welfare bills.

By 2012, eight states had passed legislation banning the use of sow gestation stalls/crates. Bills introduced in state legislatures often sought to ban the use of such confinement units and require enough room for sows to turn around or more. Generally, the legislation developed a gradual phase-out process over several years to mitigate the economic impact on pork producers. On this issue, the U.S. lagged behind Sweden and the United Kingdom, both of which had already banned the sow gestation crates by 2012; a limited European Union ban took effect in 2013.

SHAREHOLDER MEETING TACTICS

Shareholders of publicly traded companies have voting rights on issues that affect their corporations. Shareholders also have the right to speak at annual meetings, although the corporation's bylaws dictate the scope of such speeches. Usually, they are short, under five minutes, and speakers are limited to two presentations during a single meeting. To raise awareness and pressure companies to change their practices, the HSUS purchased shares in various companies that either produce or purchase pork in order to present resolutions or proposals asking for the phasing out of sow gestation crates. Companies targeted include Seaboard Foods, Bob Evans Farms restaurant chain and food producer, Tim Horton's Restaurants, CKE Restaurants (which owns Hardee's and Carl's Jr restaurant chains), Domino's Pizza, Bravo Brio Restaurant Group, Steak 'n Shake, and Jack in the Box.

Shareholders also have the right to inspect their corporation's records. In one instance, the HSUS asked Hormel Foods to "disclose to shareholders how many breeding pigs are confined in gestation crates for its products, and any progress the company has made moving toward more humane housing methods."

THE PORK INDUSTRY'S RESPONSE

The pork industry used its marketing, communication and lobbying resources to advocate for industry priorities. In 2010, the pork industry identified "operating freedom" as its top critical issue, followed by "enhanced demand and competitive global advantage." Operating freedom was defined in its strategic plan as: "the rights and ability of U.S. farmers to produce pork in a socially responsible and cost competitive manner."

This included the following strategies:

1. Evaluate consumer perception, provide timely research, and lead discussions throughout the food chain that result in the adoption of socially responsible best management practices that reflect pork producers' ethical principles.

2. Work with the National Pork Producers Council and state pork organizations to increase awareness and understanding, among key target audiences, of the pork industry's stewardship activities and the value of modern production practices. A benchmark survey will measure progress annually.

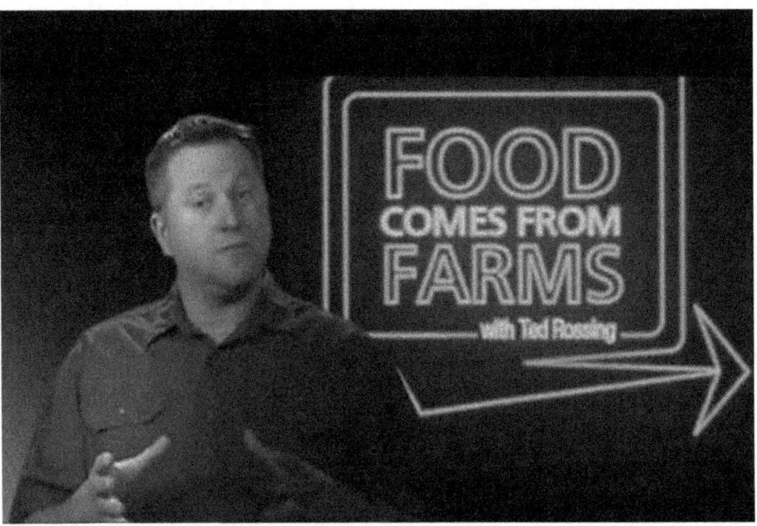

FIGURE 3.6 *Ted Rossing from the National Pork Board talks about sow care including the use of sow gestation stalls.*
http://video.pork.org/
National Pork Board

3. Work with the National Pork Producers Council and state pork organizations to provide pork producers with the tools to assist them in the development of a favorable business climate within their local communities.
4. Manage issues to minimize current and emerging threats that endanger consumer demand and/or producer productivity.

In 2012, the National Pork Board spent $12.7 million to support operational freedom strategies, $34.8 million to support pork's image and increase market demand for pork, and $5.1 million to increase market demand for U.S. pork globally.

LOBBYING

The pork industry's lobbying effort focused on preventing any new regulations or laws that would mandate how farmers should take care of their animals. Its lobbying efforts were guided by the National Pork Producers Council. This organization is involved in the political process through PorkPAC, its political action committee. According to the website OpenSecrets.org, PorkPAC gave $356,993 to federal candidates (32 percent Democrats and 68 percent Republicans). These contributions support candidates that agree with the pork industry on regulatory issues and provide access and credibility when dealing with Members of Congress. PorkPAC educates and supports candidates at the state and federal levels who support the U.S. pork industry. The National Pork Producers Council also interacts with federal agencies

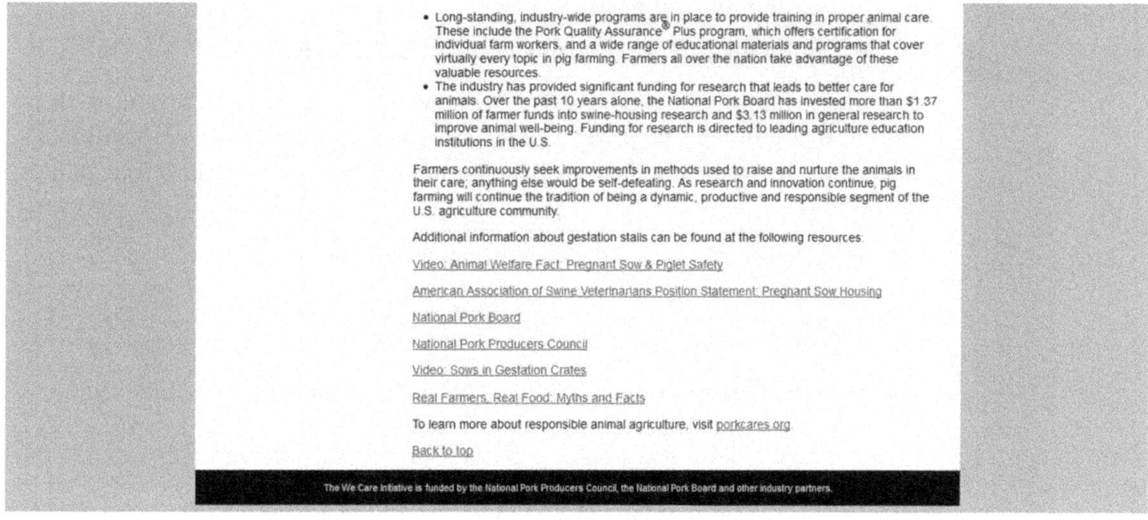

FIGURE 3.7 *Answers on the Gestation Stalls website, which was developed by the National Pork Board's We Care program to combat criticism of gestation stalls.*
http://www.porkcares.org/
National Pork Board

such as the Agriculture Department to provide information and work on mutually beneficial activities.

The National Pork Producers Council trains pork industry business people and farmers to engage with their own elected public officials and become grassroots activists. It also supports the Swine Veterinarian Public Policy Advocate Program that trains veterinarians to advocate for the pork industry.

"WE CARE" INITIATIVE

Another way of helping producers maintain operational freedom involved doing a better job of projecting a more socially responsible image and actively telling its story to its key stakeholders. The industry's social responsibility program, We Care, was a good start to delivering key messages to its public and building understanding.

The cornerstone of the industry's safe and humane production practices and environmentally sound farming methods was its six ethical principles. Developed in 2008, these principles would guide producers, suppliers and sellers. Included was a principle for animal "well-being":

- Produce safe food.
- Protect and promote animal well-being.
- Ensure practices to protect public health.
- Safeguard natural resources.
- Provide a safe work environment.
- Contribute to a better quality of life in our communities.

"Producers realize that pigs are living beings and, as such, they must receive a level of care that promotes their well-being," according to a National Pork Board publication. Under "animal well-being," the National Pork Board described four guiding principles:

- Provide feed, water and an environment that promotes the well-being of our animals.
- Provide proper care, handling and transportation for pigs at each stage of life.
- Protect pig health and provide appropriate treatment, including veterinary care when needed.
- Use approved practices to euthanize, in a timely manner, those sick or injured pigs that fail to respond to care and treatment.

The We Care program included training programs (Pork Quality Assurance Plus and Transport Quality Assurance) to support animal well-being, safety and quality. These training programs provided the current best practice for handling animals and ensuring their safety. By the end of 2012, 57,000 individuals had received certification and 16,487 sites (75 percent of the U.S. pig inventory) had been assessed.

THIRD-PARTY ENDORSEMENTS

The National Pork Board uses respected supporters of its stand. The AVMA and the American Association of Swine Veterinarians (AASV) have reviewed the existing scientific literature on gestational sow housing and have published position statements that concluded that both types of housing (open and confined) have advantages and disadvantages. These organizations said that the housing system should:

- minimize aggression and competition among sows;
- protect sows from detrimental effects associated with environmental extremes, particularly temperature extremes;
- reduce exposure to hazards that result in injuries, pain or disease;
- provide every animal with daily access to appropriate food and water;
- facilitate observation of individual sow appetite, respiratory rate, urination and defecation, and reproductive status by caregivers;
- allow sows to express most normal behavior patterns.

The pork industry noted that support for both open and confined housing systems from these veterinarian organizations was further evidence that the industry was operating within socially responsible parameters.

ACTIVISM

Authentic voices for the pork industry were available for no cost. Open house kits were available for farmers to host their own open house and interact with community members. The kit included newspaper advertisements, a sample agenda, sample press release, and other tools to promote the open house. Farmers could tell their own story about raising healthy and well-cared-for animals. Another outreach program designed for producers and other industry volunteers was Operation Main Street. This educational program provided materials and talking points for small and large group presentations about where their food comes from and how modern agriculture is meeting consumer demand responsibly. So far, more than 5,000 presentations have been made to consumers with a total audience reach of twenty-four million.

RESEARCH

Which housing system is best for sows is still a matter of evolving science. The pork industry's review of the available science has determined "that both individual and group housing systems are acceptable for providing for the well-being of the sow.

Regardless of the system used, the caretaker's husbandry skills and ability to provide good care most influences the well-being of the sow."

The AVMA's Task Force on the Housing of Pregnant Sows conducted a thorough and objective review of the scientific evidence, including peer-reviewed science, relating to the impact on the health and welfare of keeping breeding sows. Entitled "A Comprehensive Review of Housing for Pregnant Sows," the 2005 report concluded:

> *Considering all factors, all sow housing systems in current use have advantages and disadvantages for animal welfare. Current group systems allow freedom of movement and social interaction. However, these same systems, when they fail to work well, lead to problems, especially in the areas of aggression, injury and uneven body condition. When they lack manipulable material, sows in group systems are also unable to forage. Current stall systems minimize aggression and injury, reduce competition, allow individual feeding, and assist in control of body condition. Stalls, however, also restrict movement, exercise, foraging behavior, and social interaction. Because the advantages and disadvantages of housing systems are qualitatively different, there is no simple or objective way to rank systems for overall welfare. There is no scientific way, for example, to say how much freedom of movement is equal to how much freedom from aggression or how many scratches are equal to how much frustration. In such cases, science can identify problems and find solutions but cannot calculate and compare overall welfare in very different systems. Ideally, sow housing systems should do the following:*
>
> - *Minimize aggression and competition among sows.*
> - *Protect sows from detrimental effects associated with environmental extremes, particularly temperature extremes.*
> - *Reduce exposure to hazards that result in injuries, pain, or disease.*
> - *Provide every animal with daily access to appropriate amounts and types of food and water.*
> - *Facilitate observation of individual sow appetite, respirator rate, urination and defecation, and reproductive status by caretakers.*
> - *Allow sows to express most normal patterns of behavior.*

A 2004 study conducted meta-analyses of existing scientific data on housing systems for gestating sows (McGlone et al.) and found that sows' stress levels measured by blood cortisol, productivity and behaviors were similar for stalls and group pens.

The pork industry cautioned in one of its publications, "Swine Facts on Animal Welfare": "Because animal welfare can easily become an emotional issue, it's important to base decisions around sound science. Otherwise, changing the dynamics of the farm may impair rather than enhance welfare."

The pork industry created the Animal Welfare Committee more than twenty years ago to review the science of animal welfare to inform production practices on the farm. It approved this resolution in 2002:

Animal welfare guidelines developed without a sound scientific basis put the welfare of the animal and the sustainability of the producer's operation at risk. Therefore, the National Pork Board continues to support sound science as the only basis for animal welfare guideline decision-making.

The Swine Welfare Assurance Program (SWAP) was created by the National Pork Board. It maintained and promoted scientifically sound animal care practices; the "Swine Care Handbook" was published in 2003 based on current scientific research. Elements of SWAP were later incorporated into the Pork Quality Assurance Plus program.

Investment in sow housing research became the industry's top research priority, with $367,794 funding research projects in 2012. Between 2002 and 2012, $1.8 million had been invested in sow housing research. The National Pork Board's website provides written summaries and other publications.

PUBLIC RELATIONS AND MARKETING

The National Pork Board monitored and evaluated traditional as well as social media sites for issues management activity. Its communication staff worked with the news media requests and reached out to specific reporters influential to the national debate. The board relied on current science and experts in the industry to tell its story.

The pork industry's main consumer site is PorkBeInspired.com, which contains thousands of recipes and information about the nutritional benefits of pork.

A site called PorkCares.org is the industry's social responsibility site and features its We Care initiatives. It features an industry progress report, entitled "Responsible Farming: Our Heritage, Our Future," created in 2012 as a response to growing public interest in modern-day farming. It tracks the We Care initiatives in areas such as food safety, animal well-being, environmental stewardship, and worker safety. The site hosts many videos focusing on farmers and We Care principles: "Doing What's Right: A Long-Term Commitment," "Food Safety: The Highest Priority," "Today's Hog Farmers Provide Better Animal Care and Food Safety," and "Benefits of Modern Farming: A Largely Untold Story."

Dr. Paul Sundberg, vice president of science and technology, said on framing the discussion about sow gestation crates:

We rely on the best measurements of animal welfare that we have—an evaluation of the sow's production, physiology and behavior. Any attempt to evaluate welfare status without considering all three together can be misleading because the scientific consensus is that all three considerations must be taken into account. Trying to put forth one as a credible assessment of welfare is misleading.

FIGURE 3.8 *The National Pork Board's We Care program created a corporate social responsibility report in 2012 to show the industry's progress on social and animal welfare issues.*
http://www.porkcares.org/
National Pork Board

Some key talking points that the Pork Board used to build understanding included:

- *Today's pigs are raised by farmers who have dedicated their life to providing for the best in health, well-being and safety of their animals and about the safety of the food they produce.*
- *Pork producers also recognize that today's consumers are asking more questions about where their food comes from and how it is raised. That's why we welcome every chance we get to talk to people about modern pork production.*
- *Modern pork production facilities of all sizes provide animals with an environment designed especially for them to keep them safe, healthy and comfortable. This means they don't get chilled in harsh winter weather or swelter during hot summers, which can predispose them to disease.*
- *Pork producers believe in continuous improvement. If we can improve their product, or the way we raise our pigs or the things we do to keep the environment safe for our families and our neighbors, we do it.*

DOING WHAT'S RIGHT. A LONG-TERM COMMITMENT.

America's pork producers supply the highest quality and safest pork in the world. We've earned the trust of generations of consumers by delivering on our promise to produce pork responsibly.

Our goal is to demonstrate that we are doing the right things every day in important areas such as food safety, animal well-being, safeguarding natural resources and improving the quality of life in our communities. We're proud to demonstrate that our commitment to responsible, ethical farming is stronger today than ever before.

FOOD SAFETY: THE HIGHEST PRIORITY

Providing safe, wholesome food is the pork industry's most important responsibility. On the farm, many factors can have an impact on food safety, which is why today's farmers use a wide variety of technology, techniques and expertise to minimize food safety threats as much as possible. The typical hog farm today does look different from farms many decades ago. Family farmer Brad Greenway opens his doors to show you why he has made

FIGURE 3.9 *The National Pork Board's We Care social reponsibility website includes reports, family farm testimonials, and other resources for consumers and farmers. On its home page it frequently addresses issues about farm safety and animal welfare.*
http://www.porkcares.org/
National Pork Board

- *Pork producers are like the vast majority of all Americans. When it comes to managing our farms, we do the right thing for the right reasons. When mistakes are made, we fix them immediately.*
- *As a pork producer, I am committed to producing safe, wholesome pork in a socially responsible way. No one cares more than I do, as a U.S. pork producer, about producing high-quality products, taking care of their animals and natural resources, and contributing to their communities.*
- *Pork producers have adopted a Statement of Ethical Principles that guides their everyday actions. So consumers know we share their values when it comes to food safety, animal well-being, participating in the life of our communities, and protecting both the environment and public health.*

Another website developed by the National Pork Board (http://video.pork.org/default.aspxNational Pork Board) included videos of various industry representatives, with many farmers describing their farming practices in detail. The videos sought to build understanding about modern farming and demonstrate the industry's commitment to animal welfare, the environment, health and safety, and the community. One video featured Neil Dierks, CEO of the National Pork Producers Council:

> *Pork producers take their role very seriously. In fact, nobody cares more and nobody has more on the line when it comes to food safety, health, animal care, the environment, and being responsible citizens. After all, pork producers' very existence depends on these things.*

Social media efforts include farm bloggers such as the moms and pork producers Heather Hill (ThreeKidsandlotsofPigs.com and @ProudPorkMom) and Jo Windmann (TheBaconBlogger.blogspot.com and @JoWindmann) who live by the We Care principles, a Twitter account (#porkcares) that discusses socially responsible farming practices, and a Facebook page that features farmers and pork industry news and supports its We Care efforts.

The National Pork Board and the National Pork Producers Council's websites were geared toward producers' needs.

MCDONALD'S WORKS WITH SUPPLIERS TO PHASE OUT STALLS

While pork producers and suppliers were pressured to change their ways, the news media attention was minimal. That wasn't the case with companies farther along the food chain: those that dealt directly with consumers. With millions of dollars spent annually to promote their companies' socially responsible actions and in the glare of the media spotlight, restaurants and other food service companies were monitoring the sow gestation stall issue.

Without a doubt, reputational risks were evaluated with an eye toward a greater commitment to animal welfare. In 2011, Hormel Foods, the maker of Spam, and

Sonic Corporation, owner of the largest chain of drive-in restaurants in the U.S., announced policies to move away from extreme confinement of farm animals. McDonald's, the nation's largest restaurant chain, issued a joint announcement with the HSUS on February 13, 2012, that it would require its U.S. pork suppliers to phase out the use of sow gestation stalls.

"We are beginning an assessment with our U.S. suppliers to determine how to build on the work already underway to reach that goal," said Dan Grosky, senior vice president of McDonald's North America Supply Chain Management. "In May, after receiving our suppliers' plans, we'll share results from the assessment and our next steps." The McDonald's–HSUS announcement included an endorsement from renowned scientist Dr. Temple Grandin: "Moving away from gestation stalls to better alternatives will improve the welfare of sows and I'm pleased to see McDonald's working with suppliers toward that end."

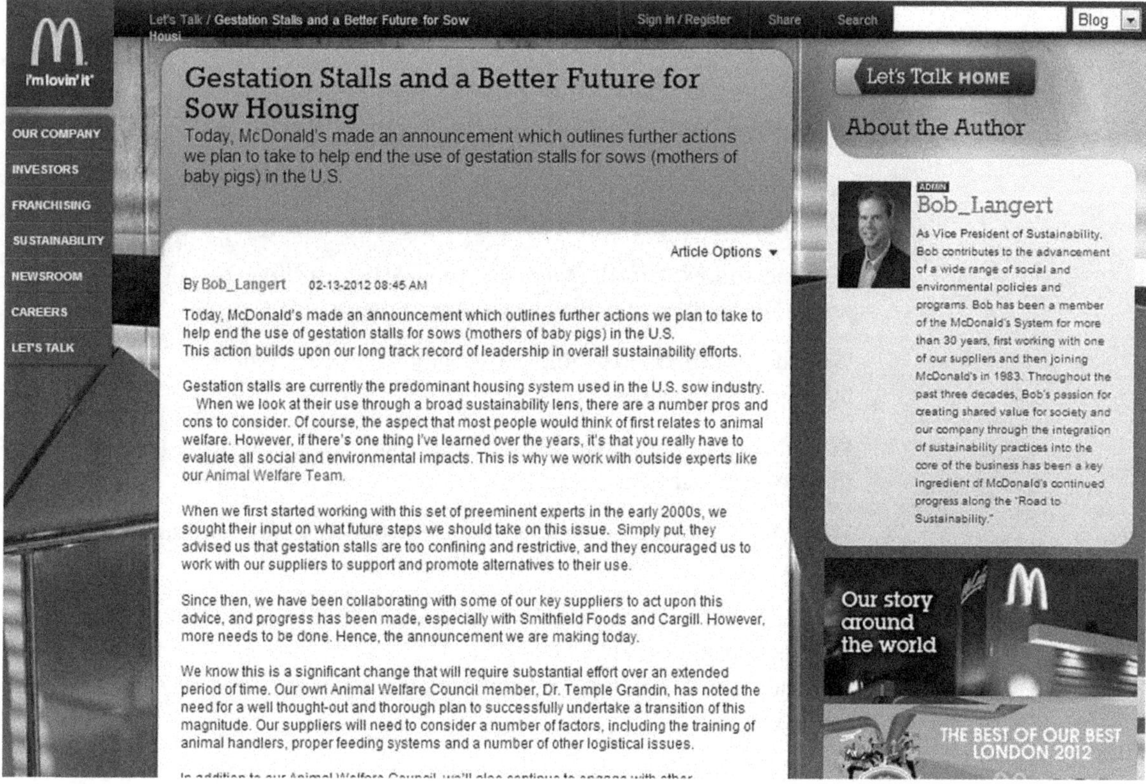

FIGURE 3.10 *McDonald's sustainability blog announced its intention to discontinue buying from suppliers who used sow gestation crates.*
http://community.aboutmcdonalds.com/
McDonald's

Within hours, the National Pork Board responded, noting that

> *there are numerous ways, including sow gestation stalls, to provide proper care for sows. Each housing system, including gestation stalls, open pens, free-access stalls and pastures, has welfare advantages and disadvantages that must be considered by an individual famer.*

Its position, the National Pork Board said, was supported by the available science. The AVMA and the AASV also based their positions on the available scientific evidence, which concluded that both systems were acceptable.

Less than a month later, Bon Appétit Management Company and Wendy's made an announcement similar to McDonald's, followed by Burger King and others. Compass Group, the largest food service company in the world, also announced a new policy that would phase out the use of gestation crates.

QUESTIONS FOR DISCUSSION

1. What is factory farming? What do critics say about this type of farming?
2. What is the difference between animal welfare and animal rights advocates?
3. What was the goal of the HSUS regarding the issue with pig stalls?
4. Describe and explain the tactics of the pork industry regarding the pig stall issue. In your opinion, how effective were these strategies and tactics?
5. Describe and explain the tactics of the HSUS regarding the pig stall issue. In your opinion, how effective were these strategies and tactics?
6. What do you think is the role of the National Pork Producers Council in establishing ethical business practices?
7. What led to the response of some restaurant companies to move away from the use of sow gestation stalls?
8. What do you think are the effective elements of the pork industry's We Care campaign?
9. After seeing the HSUS undercover investigation video at Smithfield Foods (see the video *Undercover at Smithfield Foods* on the HSUS website and the textbook's companion website), how do you think it supported the case against sow gestation crates?
10. How did the HSUS use the Pew Commission on Industrial Farm Animal Production report and other scientific reports as a pressure tactic?

Dig Deeper

Read the pork industry's social responsibility report "Responsible Farming," available on the textbook's companion website. Explain how the industry is responsible, professional and caring. Review the pork industry's video entitled *Life in Confinement*, available on the textbook's companion website. What arguments does the pig farmer make for raising pigs in confined spaces? The HSUS produced two graphic undercover videos on the mistreatment of pigs in large-scale farms. Review the video *Shocking Animal Cruelty at Tyson Foods Supplier* or *Undercover Video Documents Abuse of Pigs at Okla. Factory Farms*, available on the textbook's companion website, and explain how these videos can harm the pork industry's reputation. How should the pork industry respond to these types of videos?

5

Apple iProblem

Subcontractor Worker Issues Bring Negative Attention

What is the true cost of an Apple iPhone or an iPad? That was the question Americans began to ask when it was learned that one of Apple's major suppliers might be mistreating its factory workers. There is the cost of the product but there are other costs as well—human costs, environmental costs, and reputational costs.

Many Americans learned about working conditions in Chinese factories that Apple contracted with to manufacture iPhones and iPads after *The New York Times'* January 26, 2012, devastating front-page story, which included interviews with former Apple executives and other industry insiders detailing unsafe working conditions, excessive overtime, crowded dorms, and underage workers. Follow-up reports by the news media described the results of "squeezed [profit] margins" that led suppliers to cut costs. Some of the problems included:

- The use of poisonous chemicals to clean iPhone screens injured 137 workers at an Apple supplier factory; the chemical, n-hexane, can cause nerve damage and paralysis. It was used because the chemical evaporated much quicker than rubbing alcohol, thus allowing more screens to be cleaned per minute.
- An explosion occurred at one factory that polished iPod cases, caused by a build-up of aluminum dust; four died and eighteen were injured. Seven months later, another factory explosion from aluminum dust injured fifty-nine workers. Proper ventilation would have prevented the dust build-up.
- Worker stress levels and other conditions contributed to many employee suicides and more suicide attempts; hotlines to report abusive conditions, seek mental counseling or discuss workplace problems were not available. The average factory workers were young, between the ages of 18 and 25, and from rural villages, hundreds of miles from home. During a two-day protest about 150 workers threatened mass suicide atop a Foxconn factory that assembled

FIGURE 3.11 *Local and mainland Chinese university students, dressed as the Foxconn workers, hold a mock iPad with a skeleton print outside an Apple Premium Reseller shop in Hong Kong Saturday, May 7, 2011. They denounced Apple Inc. and its Chinese supplier Foxconn Technology Group for the alleged dire working conditions of their workers.*
© Kin Cheung/AP Photo/Corbis

Microsoft's Xbox, protesting working conditions that were described as "military" fashion.

- Minimum wages required overtime work in order to live in an urban center and still be able to save.

FOXCONN

Apple does not own factories. Instead, it contracts out its massive manufacturing business to suppliers. The biggest contract supplier for Apple is Hon Hai, better known as Foxconn, headquartered in Taiwan. It is the world's largest contract electronics manufacturer, was founded in 1974 and ranked No. 60 in *Fortune*'s Global 500 in 2011. The original equipment manufacturer of Apple Computer's iPod, Foxconn operates thirteen factories in nine Chinese cities. Foxconn has nearly a million employees who work at various mega-sized factories, manufacturing a whopping 40 percent of the world's consumer electronics for companies like Amazon, Dell, Hewlett-Packard, Nintendo, Nokia, and Samsung. At the Chengu Foxconn factory there are 120,000 employees and at Shenzhen there are, by some estimates, 250,000–420,000 employees. Foxconn factories are like self-contained cities with shopping, banks, Internet

FIGURE 3.12 *Relatives of Foxconn suicide worker urge further investigation: Parents and elder sister of Foxconn employee Ma Xiangqian, who committed suicide by jumping off a building, show the photo of Ma Xiangqian and signs saying "We Appeal to the Investigation Team from the Central Government to Thoroughly Investigate the Case of Ma Xiangqian," outside the Foxconn plant in Longhua town, Shenzhen city, south China's Guangdong province, May 29 2010. Foxconn insisted, that the spate of suicides among its workers (thirteen attempted suicides and eleven deaths alone in 2010) was a result of social problems and not alienating work conditions and refused to compensate victims' relatives. But the victims' families insisted that responsibilities be investigated. Public opinion has began to question the Chinese model of development. The Taiwan company, a world leader in the manufacture of electronic and computer parts, insisted that the working conditions were good.*
© Imaginechina/Corbis

cafes, restaurants, recreational facilities including swimming pools, basketball courts and soccer fields, and dormitories. While these amenities may sound good to the average American worker, long working hours at Foxconn factories—sometimes as many as seventy hours a week—and huge numbers of workers with no family members nearby make these services essential to the factories' efficiency.

APPLE

In early 2012, Apple was the most valuable company in the world in terms of market capitalization, according to Forbes.com. Apple reported a market cap of more than

$620 billion in shares trading at over $662 per share on August 20, 2012. It also had a huge reserve of cash—$97.6 billion in February 2012. Apple, the innovative technology leader, was breaking profit and sales records during this time of media scrutiny; revenue for the full fiscal year (ending in September) was $156.5 billion. *Fortune* magazine gave Apple the top ranking as the world's most admired company in 2012, ahead of Google and Amazon.com.

Apple's rapid product innovation kept consumers coming back for new product models and the latest technology developments, including new updates of iPods, iPads, iPhones, and new Macs. While this fast-paced innovation leads to demand for more product it also leads to stresses on the supplier, which is pressured to have workers willing to work continuous shifts and extended overtime, while living in crowded conditions, as factories rush to fill orders and still maintain a profit.

IHS iSuppli, a technology marketing company, estimated that an iPhone 4S with 16GB cost $188 in materials and $8 for manufacturing costs for a total of $196 in 2011. It retailed for $199–$399. In 2012, the average Foxconn employee was 23 years old and made $403 a month, which often included long working days, according to the Fair Labor Association audit. Most employees traveled great distances from their homes to land a job at Foxconn and save enough money in order to support their families or get a head start in life. While Foxconn minimum wages are some of the highest offered, the company did not fully understand workers' stress and ability to adapt to strange new environments.

CULTURE OF SECRECY

A veil of secrecy has surrounded Apple's product development and production. Keeping new products under tight wraps created industry buzz and endless speculation by industry watchers and reporters. The secrecy also helped build product anticipation from its legions of fans. Steve Jobs, Apple's leader and supreme innovator who died in 2011, perfected the product launch to attract as much media attention as possible by unveiling the newest product to a great fanfare at a major computer conference. The secrecy also had another important function: it protected Apple's intellectual property from corporate spies intent on industrial espionage. Even contract supplier names were never revealed, nor did suppliers admit what products they produced. This lack of transparency increased the difficulty of labor organizations to monitor what was going on in the factories. Reporters were in the same situation.

APPLE'S RESPONSE TO THE *NEW YORK TIMES* ARTICLE

On January 13, 2012, almost two weeks before the *New York Times* article appeared, Apple issued a news release entitled "Apple's Supplier Code of Conduct and 2012 Progress Report." The release brought readers to a web page that provided details of Apple's efforts in labor and human rights, worker health and safety, and environmental impact. It included its code of conduct, auditing reports, and education and development initiatives.

After the *New York Times* article, Apple's CEO Tim Cook responded with an e-mail to Apple employees. The letter was reprinted in 9to5Mac.com, a web news site that covers Apple. In it he stated that Apple cares about every worker in its supply chain and that accidents were "deeply troubling" and problems with working conditions were "cause for concern."

> *Any suggestion that we don't care is patently false and offensive to us. As you know better than anyone, accusations like these are contrary to our values. It's not who we are.*
>
> *For the many hundreds of you who are based at our suppliers' manufacturing sites around the world, or spend long stretches working there away from your families, I know you are as outraged by this as I am.*

Cook then detailed the many actions that Apple had taken to improve worker conditions, including Apple factory inspections, FLA (Fair Labor Association) audits, and employee education on their rights. Cook said, "We know of no one in our industry who is doing as much as we are, in as many places, touching as many people."

APPLE'S MONITORING EFFORTS

Sweatshops have always existed. In the United States, many American immigrants in the late 19th and early 20th centuries endured harsh and unsafe working conditions in order to make a new life. In the 1990s, when American companies began relocating their manufacturing facilities overseas in order to use cheaper labor in foreign countries to produce their goods, reports of worker abuse made media headlines. For example, throughout the 1990s Nike, the world's leading manufacturer of athletic shoes and apparel, was derided by human rights activists and labor unions, who called news media attention to the many harsh working conditions; these included its use of child labor in Cambodia and other countries involving worker abuse incidents in its factories. Kathy Lee Gifford, the famous co-host of the nationally broadcast *Live with Regis and Kathy Lee*, was engulfed in scandal in 1996 when activists and the news media revealed that her WalMart clothing line was manufactured in foreign sweatshops. Gifford had federal authorities investigate her subcontractor and later supported legislative and White House administrative efforts to eliminate sweatshop abuses. Eventually, her clothing line was dropped by WalMart in 2003 in favor of a more trendy line.

During the 1990s, the Fair Labor Association (FLA) and other human rights groups were formed to focus attention on factory sweatshops and environmental problems caused by these companies. To combat these negative issues American companies began to implement codes of conduct for their suppliers. However, Apple did not join FLA's membership at the time.

In 2005 Apple did establish its own suppliers' code of conduct, based on the standards set by the Electronics Industry Citizenship Coalition, which encourages technology companies to operate with "social, environmental and economic responsibility." Critics said it was an organization with few teeth.

Rumors of harsh working environments at Foxconn began to surface in 2006. One of the earliest media reports was from the *Daily Mail*, a British daily newspaper that secretly visited a Foxconn factory in Shenzhen, China, where Apple iPods were made. The news report, "The Stark Reality of iPod's Chinese Factories," said employees were poorly paid, forced to work overtime—some working fifteen-hour days—and unable to sit down during twelve-hour shifts. The article also claimed that as many as a hundred workers lived in one dormitory room. Reports from other news organizations followed, detailing similar working conditions.

In Apple's 2007 four-page "Supplier Responsibility Progress Report," it noted the 2006 negative press coverage of one of its suppliers:

> *In the summer of 2006, we were concerned by reports in the press alleging poor working and living conditions at one of our iPod final assembly suppliers in China. In response, we conducted a thorough audit of the facility and worked closely with the supplier to correct any practices or incidents that did not conform to our Supplier Code of Conduct.*

Apple also expanded its audit to all its Mac and iPod final assembly manufacturers. It published its first report in February 2007.

FIGURE 3.13 *Apple's 2012 "Supplier Responsibility Progress Report."*
http://images.apple.com/
Apple

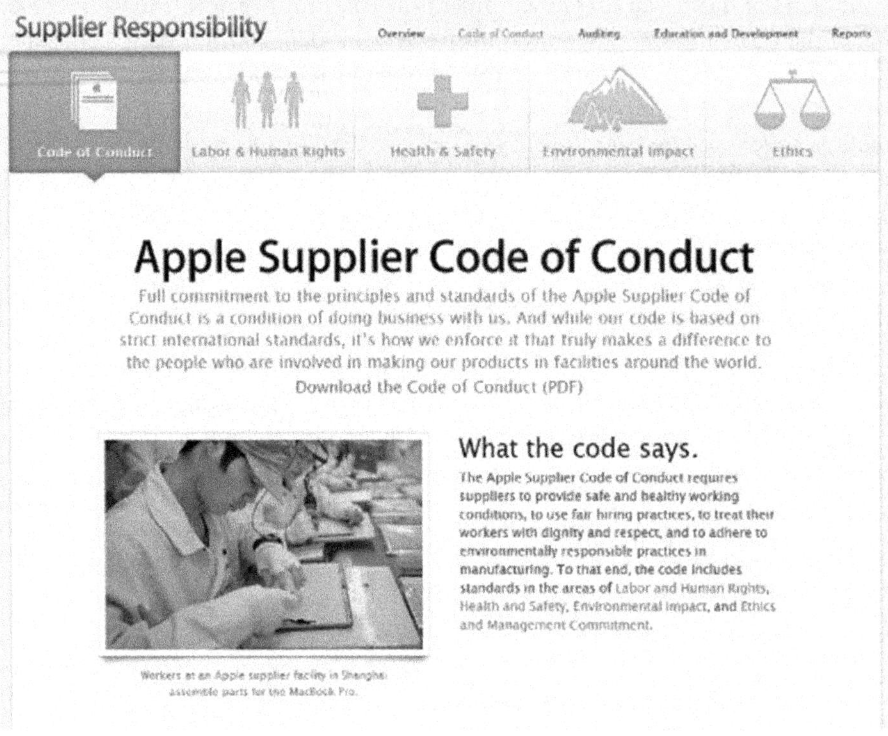

FIGURE 3.14 *Apple Supplier Responsibility Accountability website. http://www.apple.com/*
Apple

It was based on third-party experts who reviewed company records, interviewed more than 500 employees, and conducted inspections of eleven factories, including dining halls and dormitories. It found that some employees witnessed workers "required to stand in a corner or do pushups" as a method of discipline; three suppliers used wage deductions as a disciplinary measure; 38 percent of employees worked more than sixty-hour weeks and 29 percent of employees interviewed worked more than six consecutive days. The audit also discovered that 15-year-olds were hired and that records had been falsified.

While problems were identified, the brief audit report did not offer many details and often seemed to minimize any problems. Here's an example from Apple's audit report stemming from the employee interviews:

> *The overwhelming majority of employees interviewed were pleased with the work environment and how they were treated. We also heard a lot of positive comments about amenities offered by these suppliers, including educational opportunities, the quality of food in dining halls, Internet access, recreational options such as gymnasiums and sports leagues, talent shows, TV rooms and movies. The most common complaint we heard was about long lines—specifically the lines for bus*

> *transportation to get to work, the lines to badge in and out of work areas and the lines at the cafeterias.*

After the 2006 audit, Apple's senior managers and its auditors met with managers at the factories to develop corrective plans, and Apple's executives met with executives from each supplier to finalize the plans. Follow-up audits were conducted to verify the corrective actions. These audits continued every year and uncovered numerous violations, which were followed up with meetings and corrective plans.

Criticism by human rights and workers' rights organizations continued and the news media filed reports on alleged abuses whenever information could be found by enterprising journalists or activists. Critics charged that moving the entire manufacturing operation out of the United States and into China had economic as well as reputational value as real third-party information was difficult to come by behind gated factories. Apple critics said it used its distant location, labor policies, and audits as a shield.

In Apple's 2011 "Apple Supplier Responsibility Report" thirty-six core violations were reported from audits of 127 facilities:

> *eighteen facilities where workers had paid excessive recruitment fees, which we consider to be involuntary labor; ten facilities where underage workers had been hired; two instances of worker endangerment; four facilities where records were falsified; one case of bribery; and one case of coaching workers on how to answer auditors' questions.*

The report also addressed the suicides at the Shenzhen facility and the 137 workers at the Suzhou facility of Wintek, an Apple supplier, who became ill after using the toxic chemical n-hexane used in cleaning agents.

The first reports and worker protests over the chemical poisoning began in 2009, according to one activist group that also detailed other worker abuses such as use of student workers and excessive work hours without appropriate time off.

Apple's corrective actions regarding the use of n-hexane called for the elimination of the chemical's use and free medical care and monitoring of those workers affected.

While difficult to confirm, it appears that at least ten Foxconn employees committed suicide in 2010 alone. Apple hired top suicide prevention specialists who accompanied Apple's COO Tim Cook and other Apple executives to meet with Foxconn CEO Terry Gou and members of his staff to review suicide prevention measures. Another team of suicide prevention experts conducted a deeper investigation into the suicides to recommend future prevention strategies.

Foxconn hired more psychological counselors, established a twenty-four-hour care center and attached large nets to factory buildings to prevent suicides. The suicide prevention team recommended better training of its hotline staff and care center counselors, the establishment of an employee assistance program that provided mental health care, expansion of social support networks, and the building of factories in rural areas of China so workers did not travel long distances from their families.

While Apple focused on these efforts, including training employees on their rights, eliminating underage workers and onerous recruiting fees imposed on immigrant workers, the minimum wage was also an issue. Young employees left their rural homes and traveled hundreds of miles to obtain factory work and save money in order to start a new life back home.

The basic salary for an assembly-line worker in Shenzhen in 2010 was about $132 a month (83 cents an hour), according to *The New York Times*.

By 2012, some factories were offering $285 per month ($1.78 an hour), still considered by Chinese standards a low living wage, according to Business Insider, SAI, a business news website. A growing number of employee protests sought to raise it. Most workers could not live and save on that amount so they frequently worked sixty or more hours a week. Worker protests sometimes led to promises of higher wages but these were not always kept. Workers were hesitant to protest because they did not want to lose their jobs; they could see hundreds of youthful job seekers lined up each morning waiting for an opportunity to work. The average work day is 8 a.m. to 8 p.m. with an hour off for lunch and dinner breaks, for assembly-line jobs that are often mind-numbingly boring and repetitive.

In addition to the rash of suicides and other problems, a large explosion in 2011 killed four Foxconn employees and injured eighteen. The explosion was due to a build-up of aluminum dust from polishing Apple products without adequate ventilation.

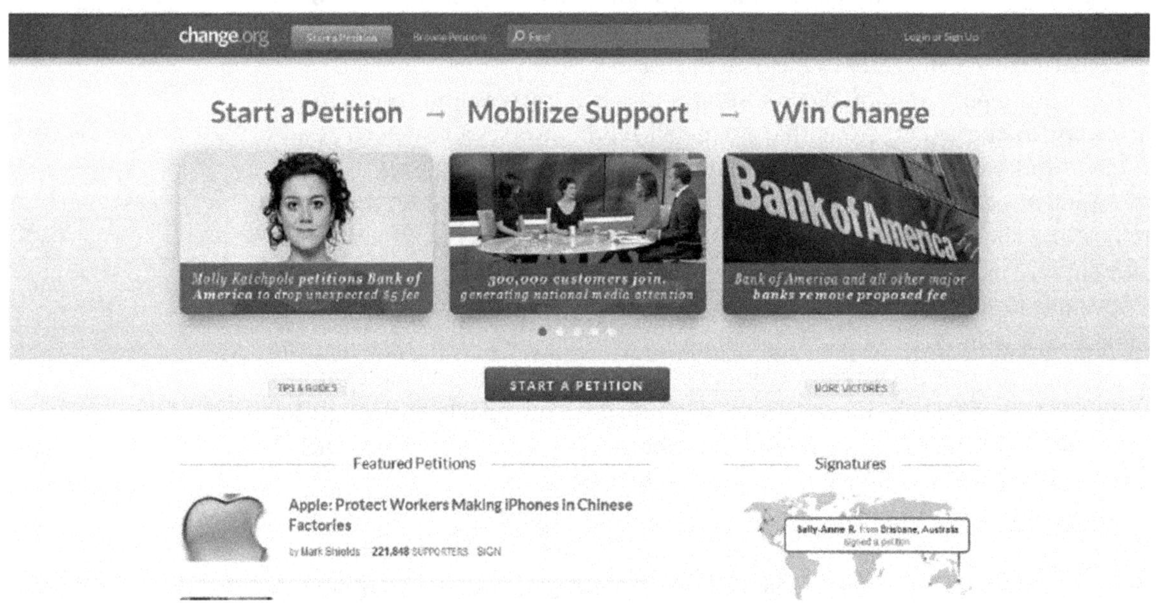

FIGURE 3.15 *Change.org petition to protect Chinese workers making iPhones.*
http://www.change.org/
Change.org

Americans began to wonder what price they were really paying for their Apple products.

TRANSPARENCY CONCERNS

While Apple's efforts to mitigate and eliminate supplier problems were steps in the right direction, critics questioned Apple's true commitment to workers' rights and safety issues. In particular, the rash of suicides, large worker wage protests, and workplace explosions caught people's attention as nonprofit organizations and the news media reported on these sensational problems. However, no reporters had ever been allowed into a Foxconn factory and Apple refused to release a complete list of Apple's suppliers. Apple was also criticized for its auditing process because, while it was publicized as conducted by third-party auditors, critics wondered how truly independent the process really was, especially since problems continued and rumors were rampant.

Eight days before the *New York Times* exposé was published in January 2012, Apple released a list of its suppliers for the first time and announced that it had joined the Fair Labor Association as a participating company, which cost $250,000. FLA had been in discussions with Apple for five years regarding its membership. It also announced that FLA would independently audit its supplier companies and report detailed findings on FLA's website. Apple would align its compliance program with FLA's within two years. A month later, FLA launched an independent investigation into labor rights allegations at Foxconn.

FLA'S AUDIT

FLA is a coalition of universities, nonprofit organizations and businesses committed to improving the health, safety, fair treatment, and respect of workers worldwide. Its process is more than a compliance audit; it examines how well the entire worker life cycle works, from hiring to termination. It uses a nine-step sustainable compliance methodology to identify "root causes of noncompliance so that sustainable solutions can be developed and implemented," according to its website. Those steps include: desktop research, policy and procedures review, task and risk mapping, opening meeting, workflow mapping, management and worker interviews, observation and documentation review, cross checking and triangulation, closing meeting and root cause analysis and reporting. In addition to its sustainable compliance assessment, a worker perception and satisfaction survey was administered to 35,000 randomly selected Foxconn workers.

The month-long investigation of three Foxconn factories confirmed many of the news media's reports. The biggest problems included:

- **Working hours**—During peak production times, Foxconn workers "exceeded both the FLA code standard and the Chinese legal limits." For example, this occurred in November and December of 2011 when one-third to a half of employees said they worked more than seventy hours a week. The Chinese legal limit is forty hours a week with up to thirty-six hours of overtime each month. The FLA standard is sixty hours a week, including overtime. Some employees "worked more than seven days in a row without a required minimum twenty-four-hour break." Nearly half of the workers surveyed said that they had worked eleven or more consecutive days without a break.

- **Health and safety**—The report revealed that "workers felt generally insecure regarding their health and safety. The issue of aluminum dust of particular concern . . ." Inconsistent policies, procedures, and practices were also cited. FLA recommended that workers be more involved in the health and safety committees. It also noted that high turnover of workers required frequent health and safety training.
- **Industrial relations and worker integration**—Many workers were "largely alienated, in fact or in perception, from the factories' safety and health committees and had little confidence in the management of health

FIGURE 3.16 *Fair Labor Association's independent investigative report on Foxconn.*
http://www.fairlabor.org/
Fair Labor Association

and safety issues." The investigation also noted that the committees were mostly reactive to health and safety issues instead of preventive.

- **Compensation and social security insurance**—14 percent of workers who had unscheduled overtime may not have received fair compensation. However, while employees were concerned about the impact of long working hours on themselves, they wanted the opportunity to "boost their pay." A majority of workers said "their salary was not sufficient to cover their basic needs." FLA recommended a study to examine the spending patterns to develop a "basic needs wage." The investigation also noted problems with workers' access to social security, unemployment, and maternity coverage.

On March 29, 2012, FLA announced in a news release that it was able to secure from Foxconn: "commitments that will reduce working hours to legal limits while protecting pay, improve health and safety conditions, establish a genuine voice for workers, and will monitor on an ongoing basis to verify compliance."

Auret van Heerden, president and CEO of FLA, said in the same news release: "If implemented, these commitments will significantly improve the lives of more than 1.2 million Foxconn employees and set a new standard for Chinese factories."

TARNISHED APPLE

Public awareness of Apple's supplier problems through media accounts grew as more news media followed FLA's investigation. National Public Radio's *This American Life* carried a monologist's theatric description of the dire working conditions at Foxconn in January 2012. Written by Mike Daisey, "The Agony and the Ecstasy of Steve Jobs" was a blisteringly funny yet serious look at the price paid for high-tech toys. One listener launched a petition on Change.com. Within weeks over 250,000 Apple users called on the company to build the first "ethical" iPhone. Protests were planned at Apple stores around the world. Another social activist website, the Sum of Us, also launched a petition drive calling for improved worker conditions.

Apple and Foxconn made the decision to allow certain media outlets the rare opportunity to report inside its Chinese factories. It invited ABC's *Nightline* anchor Bill Weir to report from its Shenzhen and Chengdu factories during the time that FLA was conducting its audit. Why ABC? Critics noted (as did ABC) that the CEO of ABC's parent company Disney sits on Apple's board.

Still, *Nightline* had access to any employee or manager in the factories, although the visits were expected. In one startling admission, Weir interviewed Louis Woo, a former Apple executive who advises Foxconn CEO Terry Gou. He said:

> *You being here is part of the openness, part of the learning, part of the change that Foxconn is undergoing. Of course you can argue that we should have opened up five years ago. Well five years ago, we are under the radar screen, nobody really knows us, we are doing well. Why should I open it up?*

The most common complaints that ABC heard were employees suffering from "soul-crushing boredom," "deep fatigue" and "not enough overtime." Some employees complained of cramped living conditions in the dormitories.

Foxconn did issue a statement, published by ABC News, to clarify some points about the *Nightline* report, including the issue of salaries:

> *We have over 75 percent of the employees in the category of earning at least 2,200 RMB ($349/month) basic compensation standard. That means they are earning 13.75 RMB ($2.18) per hour. If they work overtime on the weekend, they will earn 27 RMB ($4.28) per hour.*

The second news outlet granted access to Foxconn factories was reporter Rob Schmitz of the nationally syndicated show American Public Media's *Marketplace*. This invitation was the result of Schmitz fact-checking anti-Apple monologist Daisey's claim to have met victims of the n-hexane poisonings at an Apple iPhone assembly line. Schmitz confronted Daisey on a subsequent episode of *This American Life*, during which Daisey admitted he had not met with poisoned workers but had talked to people who knew of people poisoned. *Marketplace* had critically reported on Foxconn working conditions since 2010. Its series of reports cited many of the concerns raised by other news coverage.

While no news media accounts discuss the public relations activities of Foxconn, a *Marketplace* interview with one of Foxconn's CEO advisers and main spokesman, Louis Woo, provided some insight into the public relations strategy to a reporter:

> *Terry Gou was always confident that Foxconn was doing the right thing, so he never thought he needed the help. "Until the spate of suicides in 2010 when Terry asked me to come in to help on this issue, we never hired a PR company," he tells me. "Even two years ago, we were doing, what? Eighty billion U.S. dollars a year? I don't think you can imagine any company anywhere in the world with the size of $80 billion of revenue a year without a PR company."*

APPLE'S ACTIONS

Apple's 2013 "Supplier Responsibility Progress Report" began with an "Our Commitment to Transparency" section that discussed Apple's seven-year-long commitment to sharing its audit findings "the good and the bad . . ." The section concluded this way: "At Apple, we care just as much about how our products are made as we do about how they're designed. We know people have very high expectations of us. We have even higher expectations of ourselves."

The report provided Apple's highlights for the 2012 year:

- *We conducted 393 audits at all levels of our supply chain—a 72 percent increase over 2011—covering facilities where more than 1.5 million workers make Apple products. This total includes 55 focused environmental audits and*

40 specialized process safety assessments to evaluate suppliers' operations and business practices. In addition, we conducted 27 targeted bonded labor audits to protect workers from excessive recruitment fees.

- *Taking on the industrywide problem of excessive work hours, we achieved an average of 92 percent compliance with a maximum 60-hour work week. We are now tracking more than 1 million workers weekly and publishing the results monthly on our website.*
- *In 2012, Apple became the first technology company to join the Fair Labor Association (FLA). At our request, the FLA conducted the largest-scale independent audit in its history, covering an estimated 178,000 workers at our largest final assembly supplier, Foxconn. The FLA's independent findings and progress reports have been published on its website.*
- *We extended our worker empowerment training programs to more workers and more managers. In 2012, 1.3 million workers and managers received Apple-designed training about local laws, their rights as workers, occupational health and safety, and Apple's Supplier Code of Conduct. That's nearly double the number of workers trained by this program since 2008.*
- *We increased our investment in our Supplier Employee Education and Development program—which offers workers the opportunity to study business, computer skills, languages, and other subjects at no charge—expanding from four facilities to nine. More than 200,000 workers have now participated in the program.*
- *Continuing our efforts to protect the rights of workers who move from their home country to work in our suppliers' factories, we required suppliers to reimburse US$6.4 million in excess foreign contract worker fees in 2012. That brings the total repaid to workers to US$13.1 million since 2008.*

QUESTIONS FOR DISCUSSION

1. What did the *New York Times* story on January 26, 2012, uncover about the Apple subcontractor Foxconn?
2. How did Apple respond to the *New York Times* January 26, 2012, article?
3. Why was Apple reluctant to make public its list of suppliers and subcontractors?
4. Why did critics criticize Apple's auditing system for its subcontractors?
5. Why was FLA the right move for Apple?
6. What were the cultural issues involved with Foxconn and media relations?

7. What role did culture play in this case?
8. Was the Foxconn factory tour for ABC's *Nightline* anchor Bill Weir the best solution for building trust and understanding?
9. American Public Media's *Marketplace* was allowed access to Foxconn staff and facilities. What did its reporter find out about its public relations efforts?

Dig Deeper

Audits are an effective research tool to examine what organizations are offering to address an opportunity or problem, such as labor practices or communication. Public relations professionals use audits as a first-level examination of its communication efforts. Read the article "How to Conduct a Social Media Audit" available on the textbook's companion website. What kind of information does this provide a practitioner and what other types of information would you need to make improvements to an organization's social media program?

6

Developing Wines with a Conscience

South African Wine Industry Confronts Societal Issues

More consumers are increasingly aware that their inexpensive products come at a cost to those who produce them. For years, many developing countries have produced cheap goods for customers in developed nations, but now more end users are demanding proof of better working conditions for those who make such products. The UK, Sweden, Netherlands, and Germany are the biggest importers of South African wine. Canada, the United States, and other European nations are also important markets for South African wine.

A fair labor accreditation program for South African wine producers and farmers began in 2002 as an outgrowth of an ethical trading initiative spearheaded by several large grocery chains in Britain. Brits and others wanted to be sure the wine they were enjoying was produced under decent working conditions.

South Africa has about 3,500 primary wine producers and nearly 600 wine cellars where grapes are crushed.

The country produces about 10 percent of the imported wine consumed in the United Kingdom, which accounts for nearly half of South Africa's wine exports. According to some research, sales would increase if consumers knew both producers and workers in South Africa were treated fairly; many older consumers still associate South Africa with apartheid, the brutal policy of racial separation that officially ended in 1994.

SOUTH AFRICA'S WINE INDUSTRY

The major wine region in South Africa is located in the fertile region of Western Cape near the coast, although other regions produce wine as well. Winemaking in South Africa dates back to 1659 under the egis of the Dutch East India Company.

FIGURE 3.17 *Woman working in the vineyards at Paul Gluver Estate. http://gallery.wosa.co.za/*
WOSA (Wines of South Africa)/Charmaine Greiger

South Africa ranks ninth in volume production of wine globally, producing 3.8 percent of the world's wine. Some 275,000 people are employed both directly and indirectly in the South African wine industry, including the production and promotion of its wines. About half of the jobs include 160,000 workers from historically disadvantaged groups such as farm laborers. There are 3,500 primary producers, but 43 percent of these are small mixed farms, and about 570 wine cellars where grapes are crushed. A sizeable portion of the wine industry is connected to its wine tourism which currently boasts nineteen official wine routes.

Many of the wine brands produced in South Africa are Caucasian owned due to the country's colonial history and apartheid. The industry is dominated by a small handful of corporations that account for the branded wholesale wine business, including the huge Distell and Treasury Wines, the Company of Wine People, DGB, and KWV. During the 1980s there were international trade sanctions that prevented South African wine from being exported to many countries, including the United States. This changed when apartheid ended in 1994 and the global market opened up.

Civil rights and economic opportunity for black Africans has been slowly progressing. Black agriculture business ownership, for example, was fairly uncommon. In 2012, the South African government issued a historic charter agreement (AgriBEE, Black Economic Empowerment Act) between the industry and the government to ensure that a more racially representative ownership structure developed in agriculture. By 2013, there were more than thirty black-owned wine brands in South Africa. Educational programs to develop the business skills and knowledge to manage businesses are another effort by the wine industry and its charitable partners.

Another issue facing the wine industry is the protection of its amazing biodiversity; the Cape winelands are home to 9,600 plant species. According to UNESCO, 70 percent of the plants are unique to the region and about 1,435 species are identified as threatened. The Cape region's "Cape Floral Kingdom" is a world heritage site and has been identified as one of the world's eighteen biodiversity "hot spots." The wine industry has developed some set-aside programs to protect the natural fauna and manage its cultivated vineyards efficiently.

Wines of South Africa (WOSA), established in its current form in 1999, is the wine industry's trade association representing all South African producers of wine who export their products. Its mandate is to promote the export of all South African wines in key international markets including the United Kingdom, Germany, Sweden, and the Netherlands. More recently, WOSA has also been developing markets for South African wines in the United States, Canada, Russia, and Asia, according to the WOSA website. WOSA is funded by a levy per liter, raised on all bottled natural and sparkling wines exported

WOSA's additional activities support the Cape's growing wine tourism and marketing training seminars for members. WOSA brings wine and lifestyle journalists to the Cape on an ongoing basis.

Its website also notes WOSA's business scope:

- Enhance the image and reputation of the South African wines in key international markets.
- Assist with the development of new export markets.

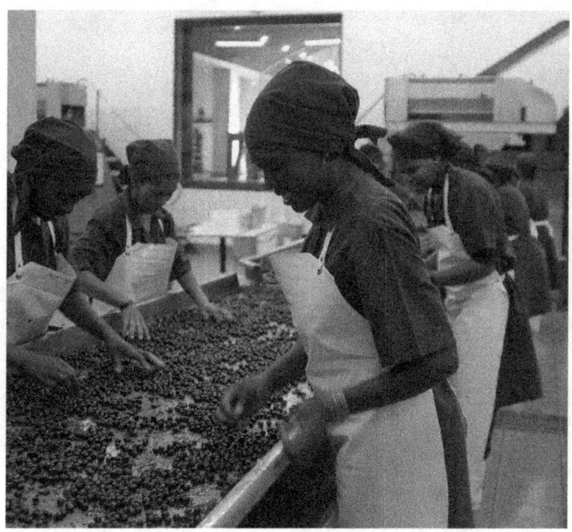

FIGURE 3.18 *Workers sorting grapes at Lourensford.*
http://gallery.wosa.co.za/
WOSA (Wines of South Africa)/Charmaine Greiger

- Assist with capacity building among exporters.
- Facilitate the development of SA wine tourism.

While it is not explicitly stated, WOSA has endorsed and spearheaded programs that address socially responsible business practices, which are key to its global image and reputation. These include support of sustainability and biodiversity protection initiatives, training and educational programs for future business leaders, and monitoring programs for the ethical production of wine. WOSA endorses the Fairtrade Label South Africa and the Wine Industry Ethical Trade Association. To combat alcoholism, virtually all of South Africa's wine producers contribute voluntarily to the Industry Association for Responsible Alcohol Use (ARA) fund.

WINE INDUSTRY ETHICAL TRADE ASSOCIATION

The Wine Industry Ethical Trade Association (WIETA) partners with WOSA to promote voluntary compliance to an ethical fair labor program. It receives funding from WOSA, which launched the organization in 2002. South Africa is the only wine industry in the world that has an independent organization focusing exclusively on promoting ethical standards.

WIETA members include vineyards and other businesses related to growing grapes for winemaking purposes. While there are about 4,000 wine producers and cellars, just 135 businesses are members of WIETA. Its mission is to improve working conditions for employees in the wine industry by encouraging fair prices for grapes, decent living wages, the right to bargain, safe working conditions, and the elimination of child labor, discrimination, and excessive work hours.

FIGURE 3.19 *Farm children at an afterschool centre on Dennegeur, Franschhoek.*
http://gallery.wosa.co.za/
WOSA (Wines of South Africa)/Anna Lusty

WIETA explained some of its guiding principles and goals in 2012:

The WIETA code of good practice is premised on the base code of the International Labor Conventions' Ethical Trading Initiative and also incorporates South African labor legislation. It precludes the use of child labor, asserts that employment should be freely chosen, and that all employees should have the right to a healthy and safe working environment. Among the conditions it sets are that workers should have the right to freedom of association, a living wage and to be protected from unfair discrimination. Worker housing and tenure security rights should also be respected.

Currently, seventy-nine cellars and farms are WIETA accredited. In the future, the whole supply chain, i.e., not just the cellars but all the producers and suppliers, will be audited. The South African wine industry's campaign for ethical best practice is unique in the world, and brand owners, farmers, trade unions and NGOs are standing together behind this drive to ensure that everyone in the production chain follows good labor practices. There are just over 3,500 primary producers, and 43 percent of these are small, mixed farms which supply less than 100 tons of wine grapes annually. A total of 573 cellars crush grapes. This translates into a huge challenge. Some of the big producers, however, have been working with their producers for a while to ensure that they can be accredited, and have indicated that they will be writing into their 2013 or 2014 contracts that all farms supplying them must be WIETA accredited. WIETA is gearing up with trainers and auditors to meet this challenge, and it is envisaged that by the end of 2014, 60 percent of South Africa's winegrowers will be accredited.

According to WIETA's code of conduct its specific principles include:

- Child labor shall not be utilized.
- Employment shall be freely chosen.
- All shall have the right to a healthy and safe working environment.
- All shall have the right to freedom of association.
- All shall have the right to a living wage.
- Working hours shall not be excessive.
- Harsh or inhumane treatment is prohibited.
- Unfair discrimination is prohibited.
- Regular employment shall be provided.
- Workers' housing and tenure security rights will be respected.

One of the most widespread problems has been the paternalist labor relations that exist between vineyard owners and their workers and that are often exacerbated by the fact that most winery owners speak English or Afrikaans while many workers tend to speak Xhosa—meaning communication and relations can be difficult.

WIETA has a long-term aim of empowering workers, to allow them to have a say in their working conditions. It has created informational materials, including a photocomic book, that educate workers of limited reading skills about WIETA's audits and its code.

Membership in WIETA is voluntary and includes cellars, cooperatives, and corporate businesses involved in South African winemaking. Its members must permit regular auditing of their businesses as outlined in the code. Companies audited by WIETA are assessed on their compliance with more than one hundred individual items by means of visual inspection, interviews of a representative sample of workers, interviews with key management staff, and inspection of documents held by the company.

In the past, WIETA's social audit has examined "young workers" issues that, for example, have included these items:

- The TES employer [temporary employment supplier] has a photocopy of all its employees' ID books, including seasonal and contract workers.
- There are no children under the age of 15 working on the farm.
- Where work is given to young workers (between the ages of 15 and 18), the employer has:
    - Obtained the consent of the parents concerned;
    - Made inquiries at the young person's school (if any) in order to ensure that the work does not interfere with his/her schooling activities.
- Work given to young workers does not involve
    - Work with pesticides or any agro chemicals;
    - Work with dangerous cutting or other machinery.
- Young workers work no more than thirty-five hours per week.

FIGURE 3.20 *WIETA auditor talking to a farm worker.*
http://www.wieta.org.za/
Wine Industry Ethical Trade Association

- Young workers are paid at least the current hourly minimum wage prescribed by law (Sectoral Determination for Agriculture under the BCEA) (current amount R4.87 per hour).

WIETA monitors code compliance with independent social auditors trained by WIETA. Those who meet the code's criteria are accredited, and WIETA accreditation can be used as part of the business's marketing strategy.

The first round of audits held in 2004 at thirty wine-related businesses resulted in four accreditations. While not a large number, this represented significant progress considering that only a decade had passed since the initial introduction of labor legislation for South African farms. The following year, another twelve audits were conducted. By the end of the 2006 accreditation cycle, twenty wine-producing operations had achieved the rigorous accreditation. In 2012, seventy-nine cellars and farms were accredited.

Early audits, according to WIETA, revealed that many workplaces have been found not to comply with health and safety regulations, often through a lack of understanding of the risks of certain winery practices. In this respect WIETA has served to educate the wineries and limit the dangers that workers may face.

As in most wine-producing regions, many workers in South African vineyards are temporary, and labor brokers who contract this seasonal labor force have been found to commit the most rights infringements by not always paying a decent wage or formally contracting their workers. WIETA is working to ensure that labor rights are respected throughout the supply chain.

Many winery owners did not know that using certain filtration media can cause silicosis and were inadvertently putting their cellar workers at risk. Now that WIETA has educated them on the problem, preventative measures can be taken. Housing for temporary cellar workers has also been improved, and since the WIETA inspections members have taken steps to rectify problems experienced by seasonal workers engaged through employment services, as many of the latter were not complying with

FIGURE 3.21 *WIETA auditor conducts a focus group with workers.*
http://www.wieta.org.za/
Wine Industry Ethical Trade Association

their legal obligations. WIETA has considered carrying out further inspections during season time to ensure that standards are being maintained throughout the year.

HUMAN RIGHTS WATCH ISSUES CRITICAL REPORT

Human Rights Watch (HRW), a nonprofit independent investigative human rights organization, issued a critical report and news release August 23, 2011, entitled "Ripe with Abuse: Human Rights Conditions in South Africa's Fruit and Wine Industries," that was based on more than 260 interviews with farm and production workers. HRW found examples of many labor abuses including: forced evictions, and poor labor, health and housing conditions. Pay for farm workers was one of the lowest in South Africa's formal employment sector, and women were paid even lower rates than men. Unsafe exposure to pesticides and lack of safe drinking water and toilets near fields were also cited. The illegal "dop" payment system, in which farm workers are compensated for their labor in wine, is still practiced and creates unsafe work environments and alcoholism. Workers reported many obstacles to creating unions.

The HRW report also criticized the effectiveness of WIETA's efforts. Some excerpts from the report stated:

- *[T]he WIETA code simply requires compliance with South African law, including compliance with the Extension of Security of Tenure Act, with the notable addition of a provision calling for payment of a "living wage."*
- *WIETA did not audit "down the supply chain" (although this is envisioned for the future), but only audits the workplace of the member. Since many WIETA members are wine producers who do not grow crops themselves but source them*

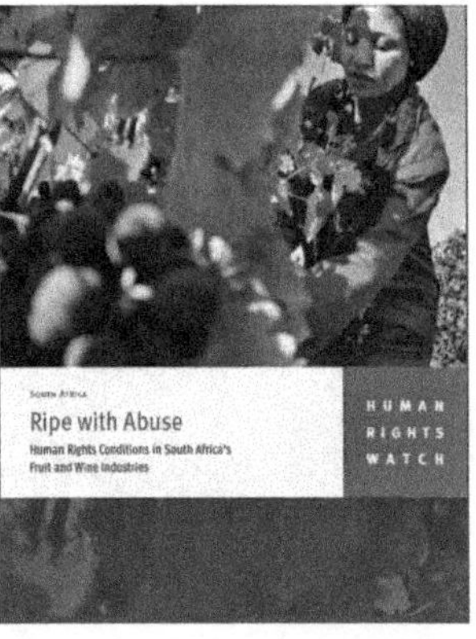

FIGURE 3.22 *Cover of Human Rights Watch report* Ripe With Abuse: Human Rights Conditions in South Africa's Fruit and Wine Industries.
http://www.hrw.org/
Courtesy of Human Rights Watch

from a variety of suppliers, many audits have not been of farms or primary input suppliers. WIETA is thus unable to guarantee that farm workers who work on farms that supply to accredited members work under decent conditions.

- *WIETA did not conduct annual audits.*

Su Birch, CEO of WOSA, the wine industry trade group, challenged the HRW report. In a news release entitled "WOSA Questions Bias of Human Rights Watch on Wine Farming" issued by WOSA on August 23, 2011, Birch questioned the HRW report findings, noted the significant progress made by the industry in worker rights and complimented the work of WIETA:

> *Su Birch, CEO of Wines of South Africa (WOSA), has challenged the Human Rights Watch report entitled "Ripe with Abuse: Human Rights Conditions in South Africa's Fruit and Wine Industries." She said the 96-page report, purporting to accurately document conditions on farms, had used a questionable basis for the selection of many of the respondents interviewed in the study, while interviews with workers had not been independently verified and nor had employer reaction to allegations been sought. As a result, it was extremely difficult to respond to specific allegations highlighted by the study.*
>
> *According to its authors, the report was based on interviews in 2010 and 2011 with "over 260 people, including 117 current or former farmworkers and an additional 16 farm dwellers."*
>
> *Birch said: "Readers of the report have no basis for understanding how representative the sample of respondents is. The study relies on anecdotal evidence that uses the cover of respondent protection to avoid substantiating the claims it makes. Moreover, the media release, provocatively entitled 'South Africa: Farmworkers' Dismal, Dangerous Lives' and distributed internationally to announce the report, does not present a sufficiently comprehensive picture of conditions across the wine industry and as a result, is potentially misleading.*
>
> *"Like the report itself, the release disingenuously plays down the significance of the wine industry's substantial direct and indirect contribution to improving working conditions through organisations such as the Wine Industry Ethical Trade Association (WIETA), and Fairtrade. It also makes scant mention of empowerment initiatives. With positive examples of the progress made in redressing past wrongs rendered virtually inaccessible to all but the most serious readers, the report negates the work of those who should be allowed to stand out as role models to their peers."*
>
> *In contrast with the report's virtual dismissal of the role of WIETA, she said the organisation had continued to expand its involvement with producers. WIETA CEO Linda Lipparoni had confirmed that membership of the organisation this year, was up 29 per cent on 2010 and had continued to strengthen since its inception in 2002.*
>
> *"Many WIETA members are now writing WIETA compliance requirements into their supplier contracts," said Lipparoni. "There are over 80 farms being audited under the Wine Supply Chain Support Programme in 2011."*
>
> *She added that WIETA's approach to auditing was a developmental one. "WIETA has implemented a capacity building programme for small producers and suppliers. It involves*

comprehensive training and awareness workshops for both managers of small wineries and farms, and workers' rights awareness sessions for farm workers."

She confirmed that auditing for accreditation took place every three years which was in line with international best practice.

"In partnership with the Ethical Trade Initiative (ETI) in the UK, WIETA is also implementing a three-year training programme focusing on understanding and addressing discrimination and sexual harassment," added Lipparoni. "The project involves the participation of over 150 farms in the Western Cape in training managers, supervisors (including team leaders) and workers."

Birch said that as far as Fairtrade was concerned, South Africa had the highest number of Fairtrade-accredited wine producers worldwide.

Birch added that another example of the report's questionable approach was the accusation levelled at farmers for not affording their workers protection when spraying for pests, without including any mention of the far-reaching Integrated Production of Wine (IPW) eco-sustainable principles that set very clear guidelines regarding the use of pesticides and the need for worker protection. Monitoring for IPW compliance included blood testing amongst workers to check for pesticide residues. "Compliance is regularly and independently monitored. Producers who flout the regulations not only run the risk of losing their IPW accreditation but also their ability to export."

Referring to the housing conditions highlighted in the report, she said: "While we are not disputing that there are transgressions and that these are taken very seriously by the wine industry, at no stage does the report contextualise the provision of housing for workers. Wine farmers are currently providing housing for over 200,000 workers which represents an investment of billions of rands. As one of South Africa's most progressive wine producers, Charles Back recently commented on his blog: 'I seriously doubt whether there is any other industry that provides this magnitude of housing relative to the value of the industry itself. Just imagine what the effect on the bottom line would be if some of our listed companies had to start to provide housing for their workers!'"

She said the industry's support for measures to address alcohol abuse amongst workers, as well as Foetal Alcohol Syndrome (FAS) had been given glancing attention and was almost buried within the report. The Industry Association for Responsible Alcohol Use (ARA) imposed levies on members, who were producers of wine as well as other beverages, to initiate widespread anti-alcohol abuse programmes, including in the Winelands, and research into FAS. Amongst the particularly active producers in this regard were Distell and Wine Cellars SA (WCSA), with the latter representing over 60 large producers.

ARA director Adrian Botha said: "Success is partly dependent on breaking the cycle of poverty and providing value-based education."

Leading South African wine producer, Distell, whose portfolio accounts for a third of the country's total still and sparkling wine production confirmed that Distell-owned and LUSAN-owned farms, (in which Distell has a 50 per cent stake), were unionised. Heidi Bartis, the company's communication manager said: "Annual negotiations take place between union members and the relevant unions and a substantive agreement is reached for a 12-month period. Where applicable, housing is made available but is linked to employment. In some instances housing is made available rent-free, with water and electricity also provided at no cost. Free transport on some farms is offered to labourers to do their week-end shopping and to attend sports, school, religious and cultural events. Workers can join subsidised medical funds, while a mobile clinic service provides additional health support to labourers and their families. Functional literacy programmes, specialised agricultural training and crèche facilities are also available to workers across some of the farms."

Birch stressed that the report had the potential to do great harm to the industry that was already battling in the face of a strong rand and a protracted global economic downturn, without the benefit of the government support that its global competitors enjoyed. "Ironically, it could also jeopardise the jobs of the very people it claims to be championing.

"In the interests of the continuity of the industry and its capacity to create employment and sustainably improved working conditions, the wine sector deserves to be monitored with fairness and not to be undermined by assertions based on what appears to be random anecdotal evidence.

"Let me make it very clear: we condemn out of hand any and all human rights abuses on wine farms. Our disappointment in the bias of the report is in no way an indication of our support for inhumane practices. It expresses our concern that trade and consumers all over the world could become alienated from South African wines. We call on Government to partner the wine industry in accelerating reform and in rooting out problems."

FIGURE 3.23 *Patrick Ngamane, winemaker, at Hartenberg Estate.*
http://gallery.wosa.co.za/
WOSA (Wines of South Africa)/Anna Lusty

WIETA IMPLEMENTS ETHICAL SEAL PROGRAM

In the wake of the HRW report, WIETA took further action to help wine producers and farmers comply with growing consumer expectations for socially responsible business practices. CEO Linda Lipparoni announced in May 2012 plans to develop an ethical seal for wine producers and farmers. WIETA said it is believed to be a world first among wine-producing countries; its seal is a parallel effort to Fairtrade or Fair for Life. Lipparoni explained the goal of its seal, which would be placed on wine bottles for producers meeting criteria, in a WOSA news release entitled "SA Wine Industry's Planned Ethical Seal, Arguably a World First":

> *"By introducing the seal, we want to acknowledge and accredit wineries and farms that follow ethical practices and to protect them from any potential negative publicity resulting from those who flout the law.*
>
> *"After almost twenty years of democracy and exposure of the country's wine producers to international best-practice, we have reached a level of maturity where no abuses of human rights should be countenanced. The industry has no place for the few who, by perpetuating unfair, inhumane labor practices, are tarnishing the majority who recognize that the ethical treatment of workers is both a moral and a legal obligation . . ."*
>
> *Lipparoni said the fully traceable seal was being modeled on South Africa's sustainability seal developed to promote awareness of the production integrity followed at every stage of the supply chain from vineyard to bottle.*
>
> *She confirmed the fast-tracking ethical program would be implemented in three phases, starting with the simultaneous training of workers, owners and management in labor law and the WIETA code of fair trading principles. All training manuals would be supplied free of charge by WIETA.*
>
> *After the initial training phase, all producers would be required to complete assessment forms to determine their level of compliance and would be given further support from WIETA in taking the necessary steps to address gaps.*
>
> *In the final stage of the process, producers would be required to pass a full WIETA audit, involving on-site inspections.*
>
> *To be entitled to carry the ethical seal, brand owners would have to enter an annually renewable, legally binding agreement with WIETA. To ensure total traceability brand owners would have to identify all their suppliers. At least 60 percent of these suppliers would also have to be WIETA-accredited, with the other 40 percent having to demonstrate that they were preparing themselves for accreditation.*
>
> *Lipparoni confirmed that WIETA was also considering the recognition of ethical, health and safety audits undertaken by other recognized bodies to facilitate the accreditation process.*
>
> *[CEO of VinPro, Rico] Basson added that the longer-term goal was to ultimately have a single seal, issued by the Wine & Spirit Board, that would confirm both production integrity and fair working conditions, as well as certified wine of origin information, such as vintage date and varietal.*

AFTERMATH

Worker protests and strikes ensued in fall 2012 in the Western Cape wineland region over worker pay for fruit workers (mostly table grapes, not wine grapes). According to news reports, strikes continued until workers were promised by the government a wage increase to $12 a day, up from $8. One industry group, VinPro, temporarily withdrew its support of WIETA after alleging that some members of WIETA's board had been involved "in incidents of violence and intimidation that accompanied farm worker strikes," according to a WIETA news release entitled "VinPro Resumes WIETA Support." The news release stated that VinPro reversed its decision because WIETA was enforcing its own code of conduct for its members and adhering to "stricter corporate governance."

The HRW report increased interest in the WIETA accreditation process including the supplier farms. South African wine companies in cooperation with WIETA decided to have 60 percent of all winegrowers accredited by the end of 2014. By the end of September 2012, WIETA had announced the first twenty-six wines to carry the new ethical seal for complying with fair labor practices.

QUESTIONS FOR DISCUSSION

1. What are the ethical issues that motivated the creation of WIETA?
2. What are the elements of a social audit? What aspects of the audit would resonate most with American and European consumers?
3. How is this type of accreditation good for business?
4. What are some of the social and environmental issues that Americans are interested in?
5. What were the concerns of HRW regarding WIETA?
6. What does auditing down the supply chain refer to? Why is it important for producers?
7. Assess the response of the wine industry's trade association WOSA to HRW's report. Was it effective? Why?
8. WIETA proposed an ethical seal for producers and farmers who successfully completed the fair labor practices audit. What was a potential weakness of the program?

Dig Deeper

Read HRW's "South Africa Ripe with Abuse" report, available on the textbook's companion website. What are some of the report's recommendations to resolve some of the problems in manufacturing wine in South Africa? What are the limitations of Fairtrade and WIETA programs according to HRW?

CHAPTER 4

Media Relations

Journalism has been undergoing profound change in recent years, as the production, delivery, and consumption of news evolve. Traditional media are competing with a slew of new news and infotainment organizations along with the increasing availability of news content for free. With every technology innovation, such as mobile devices, there are changes in how news is consumed. It is a tough environment for the working journalist—one that presents an opportunity for public relations professionals.

For public relations professionals, monitoring journalism's continuing evolution is a must; practitioners who stay up to date will be able to more effectively provide information to journalists. There are many organizations that track trends in journalism. Some include: *Columbia Journalism Review*, *Editor & Publisher*, Pew Internet for Civic Journalism, Poynter Institute of Media Studies, National Press Club, the Association for Journalism Education and Mass Communication (AEJMC), and National Public Radio's *On the Media*.

Beyond the traditional news media, there are thousands of other publications and websites that carry news and feature content about virtually every conceivable industry and topic. These industry publications and Internet sites generally do not have large writing staffs and rely on freelance writers; opportunities abound. But among this overabundance lies a problem. With so many places to develop news content placement today, careful research must be conducted to create a strategy that maximizes the result of the time invested. Which media to target for news pitches should be based on the reading and viewing behaviors of key publics.

Media relations is often one of the first tasks a new public relations practitioner is assigned, and it is a high-visibility activity for any public relations professional. The results are viewed by the masses, and that can both raise awareness and help shape public opinion about the organization and its mission.

Media relations is described as the practitioner's *relationship* with the editors and reporters of the mass media that function as communication channels directly to the organization's stakeholders. These placements in the news media are prized for two reasons.

First, these types of news media placements (news stories, features, editorials, etc.) are viewed as more trusted information sources by readers, viewers, and listeners. The audience assumes a trusted and credible journalist has done independent research. The resulting story, which may include an organization's name and positive information about the organization, sounds more credible because it has been filtered and deemed newsworthy by a journalist and editor. This outside recognition is called *third-party endorsement*.

Second, unlike advertising, the information placement is free when included in a news story. Depending on the publication's circulation or audience reach, this could produce significant return on investment.

The emphasis on relationship building with journalists is important because the practitioner often works hard to create a positive rapport with the key beat reporters and editors likely to make decisions on editorial content. Editors function as gatekeepers, sifting through hundreds of news releases and calls weekly from organizations eager for media coverage.

Public relations practitioners who understand the challenges faced by journalists today can package newsworthy material in the accepted news format, are accessible to journalists on deadline, and are professional in their interactions will likely experience more success in their news media efforts.

To break through the clutter of competing news items, practitioners and news editors have shared many dos and don'ts that will go a long way toward building solid relationships with the media. Here are some key factors to keep in mind.

HELP A REPORTER OUT

In 2008, Peter Shankman created Help a Reporter Out (HARO), now owned by Vocus, Inc., to connect expert sources with journalists working on relevant stories. Journalists can submit their queries for information sources without cost and gain access to many potential sources. Other similar services include SourceWire, Expert Central, and Expert Click. These and other useful journalism sources that public relations practitioners should know about are found at JournalismToolbox.org.

DO THE RESEARCH—KNOW THE NEWS OUTLET

Editors often ignore story requests, or "pitches," because the practitioner is obviously not familiar with the type of editorial content sought by a particular news outlet. Read, watch, or listen to the news outlet to determine if a particular story fits the organization's editorial focus. Often the news organization's website provides past issues or articles that will serve as a guide for editorial content. Practitioners also use electronic media directories, such as Cision/Bacon's and Gebbie Press directories, to get editorial information as well as contact and deadline information and circulation figures. News release distribution services, such as PR Newswire and Marketwire, offer some of the same services. Magazines often have editorial calendars in which they seek specific types of editorial material months in advance. Organizational news can be shaped for potential publication in the styles, health, viewpoints, and other special sections and segments featured in newspapers, television, radio, and online news outlets. A practitioner can also research specific reporters and their specialized areas of interest. If a reporter has written on a particular topic before, he or she may be interested in story pitches that present a new development or unique twist.

THINK AND WRITE LIKE A REPORTER

The news release is the standard document that makes the case for news coverage. Like journalism itself, the news release has seen some new trends including the multimedia news release that provides a number of elements often found in a press kit. Those include video and audio clips, photo galleries, graphics, background material, hyperlinks to other information, and more.

Editors often tell reporters "don't bury the lead," and the same advice applies to practitioners preparing news releases. Many news releases end up in the trash because they do not meet the basic requirements of news or the writer "buried" the most important story element too far down in the text to effectively capture an editor's attention. Editors suggest getting to the point fast, in the title/headline and within the first paragraph of the news release. Busy editors and reporters do not have the time to read two pages of background information to find out if your news release has anything important. News organizations are looking for news. While news can be defined in many ways, the following elements are often cited as meeting news criteria: timeliness, prominence, proximity, significance, unusualness, human interest, conflict, and newness.

- *Timeliness* refers to when the event occurred; old news usually does not appeal to news operations. A news item can also be timely if it is relevant to holidays, observances, or other national or international events in the news.
- *Prominence* refers to the type of people involved in the news item. Well-known people, such as celebrities, professional athletes, or elected officials, are often of interest to news audiences.
- *Proximity* refers to where the news is happening. A train wreck, murder, or a new factory opening may be big news in a community but not if it happened in a far-off city. People generally have a natural curiosity about what's happening in their community. The "news hole," the space not occupied by advertising, is only so big each day, so some newsworthy stories don't make the cut if they occur too far outside the media's audience reach.
- *Significance* can be defined by its impact on people and things, such as the environment or an industry. A story can be judged newsworthy if it affects a significant number of people. Significance also refers to who the affected people are and where they live.
- *Unusualness* is something that turns your head when you see it. Everyday occurrences do not normally make news. It is the unusual, out-of-the-ordinary event that attracts the audience's attention. A new twist on a

common occurrence, such as a giant birthday cake in celebration of an organization's 100th anniversary, might attract media interest. Often, these unusual stories are quick "fillers" that show up increasingly on traditional and non-traditional news websites—including those of the major news networks. If something is out of the ordinary and in keeping with an organization's strategic communication goals, a little effort could make it a story, or even an Internet sensation.

- *Human interest* relates to a good story told well about a person or people; it has interesting story elements that hold the audience's attention. The story can be about anything, including the first female firefighter in a community or the postal worker who climbed Mount Everest. Usually every organization has interesting human interest stories to tell. Colleges often use a graduate who has overcome overwhelming obstacles to help illustrate a media pitch for commencement ceremony coverage.

- *Conflict* occurs when people or organizations disagree. When these disagreements are made public, they often make news in the form of boycotts, strikes, rallies, and other public demonstrations.
- *Newness* is a common news peg for pitches. Organizations always have new products or services to introduce or a new version of an existing product that is somehow different.

Beyond what makes news, reporters and editors appreciate information that is written in journalistic style—using the Associated Press style and the inverted pyramid of information organization. Releases written concisely with no jargon or technical terms stand a better chance of being read. State the newsworthy aspect of the news release early with all the necessary information to cover the event including the who, what, where, when, and why of the story. Suggest organizational leaders or experts who are available to talk to a reporter.

Offer *exclusives*. Sometimes, human interest and other feature stories that are not major announcements can be offered to a single news organization. Or, sometimes, a major story may have many different angles that you can offer exclusively to different news outlets.

In addition to these elements of news, there is another way to get your story into the news by helping reporters with their analysis of the bigger story. Digging deeper into the root causes and history of an issue can provide opportunities for the organization to provide the bigger perspectives, such as healthcare issues that result from new legislation.

RESPECT DEADLINES

Many news operations are working under stressful deadlines, often compounded by small staffs. One of the best ways to earn a good reputation with editors and reporters is to respect their deadlines. When a reporter calls, return that call immediately—not in two hours or the next day.

Practitioners should be accessible. Many news operations collect news past regular business hours, especially for morning newspapers or evening or late news shows, so provide an e-mail address as well as office, home, and cell phone numbers to reporters.

If a reporter asks a question and you don't know the answer, tell the reporter that you don't know but will find out and call back. Always ask how much time you have before a reporter's deadline.

Because news organizations often have companion websites, speed is essential in an increasingly competitive news environment. No longer are local television stations putting together a few daily newscasts. They are posting their stories throughout the day online and reporting updated versions on newscasts and podcasts, which feature downloadable digital content. The same is true for newspapers and radio news organizations.

A practitioner's respect for deadlines will be appreciated by reporters. After all, most professionals today have access to their e-mails and phone messages 24/7. There really are few excuses for not getting back to a reporter today or asking an associate to do so if the practitioner is unavailable. Over time, journalists remember who is a reliable source of information and will turn to that practitioner for future stories.

BUILD A LASTING RELATIONSHIP

Reporters are busy people, often overworked and underpaid. Traditional newsrooms across the country are shrinking, and reporters are asked to do more than report. Some take photos and video; many blog and tweet about their reporting experiences. There is a lot of pressure to do more with less. Public relations professionals who can provide useful information in the format needed are valuable to the reporter.

Take the time to know the reporter as a person. Over time, find out something about him or her. Read the reporter's stories and mention the ones you enjoyed reading. If a reporter does a good job on a story involving your organization, take the time to thank that reporter with a note or e-mail.

If a reporter makes an error, remain calm and ask the reporter how the erroneous information got into the story. If the error is big, ask for a correction. Always think long term. Establishing trust is crucial to building a relationship. Always tell the truth and provide accurate information.

Never ask for favors, such as a request for story placement. Offering gifts to reporters, even those of nominal value, can be unethical because journalists must remain neutral and independent in their reporting. Gifts can be interpreted as bribes to garner positive coverage or to minimize negative stories. If the public thought that journalists could be bought, their credibility as an independent news source would be damaged.

In the end, a good relationship will be mutually beneficial. Even when a reporter is writing a negative story about an organization, it is often the best strategy to be a part of the story and respond when called by a reporter. The reporter will respect the public relations professional's efforts to make the story present the relevant voices of the situation.

As you develop a strong relationship to a reporter, ask him or her to be part of your LinkedIn or some other professional social network group so that you can maintain your connection to that journalist as he or she moves on to different jobs.

UNFILTERED ORGANIZATIONAL INFORMATION

Once, the news media was a gatekeeper; editors decided which news items were worthy of publishing or broadcasting to the masses. But those days are gone. Thanks to the Internet, editorial and publishing functions are in the hands of the many, as bloggers and other content creators decide what is news—and aggregators distill offerings from hundreds of news organizations for countless audiences. The result: endless opportunities for organizations to produce relevant content that informs and maybe even entertains its target constituents.

More people are bypassing news organizations or looking for even more information by going directly to the source for news about a particular organization or entity. Many organizations post their news updates on their websites, especially on "newsroom" or media centers' pages. Press release archives, executive speeches, annual reports, photos, videos, and other news information are available to anyone.

Multimedia news releases can contain photos, video stories and "B-roll" video, podcasts, audio, and hyperlinks to micro-websites, quotes, and more bulleted information. A study conducted by PR Newswire found that multimedia news releases were significantly more attention-getting than text-only news releases.

The online newsroom continues to be a smart investment for organizations since news reporters go online to familiarize themselves with the organization or news items. Once a story is published or aired, consumers can go to the organization's website to find out more.

More information on enhancing an organization's website content is available in Appendix D.

SOCIAL MEDIA

Social media, such as Facebook, Twitter, YouTube, Flickr, Pinterest, and countless other programs, have revolutionized how organizations and individuals share information and develop relationships. These technologies provide significant opportunities for public relations professionals to reach stakeholders in interactive ways. They provide excellent sounding boards for soliciting feedback on an organization's services and product quality, for example.

What's important to understand about social media is that organizations cannot control the conversation as they might have done with their corporate blogs or news releases. In the social media world, the openness of communication is integral to its functioning. Users who suspect that an organization is, for example, deleting posts or somehow manipulating the conversation will get "outed" or alternate sharing sites will be developed by the users. Organizations should participate in these conversations and use these platforms as a way to educate users on why the organization is doing what it's doing and to promote its activities, products, and services. It should also analyze the conversations to understand how the organization is being perceived by its stakeholders.

Journalists are using social media to connect their readers as well and to seek information for stories being written.

Public relations professionals should be knowledgeable about the application of social media to the overall public relations strategy for the organization. If done right, social media can put a human face on an organization's actions, educate and persuade its stakeholders, and provide true two-way conversations that can benefit both parties.

7

Are You Pouring on the Pounds?

Debating the Link between Sugary Drinks and Obesity

HEALTH AND THE CITY

Every New York City mayor leaves a legacy. Rudolph Giuliani, a two-term mayor, was the "master of disaster" for his leadership during the 9/11 terrorist attacks. Giuliani was also "America's Mayor" for making the Big Apple's public spaces much safer.

Michael Bloomberg, the billionaire businessman, was nicknamed the "Nanny Mayor" for his efforts to prod or force New Yorkers to lead healthier lifestyles. Several of his initiatives were initially controversial but later adopted by other cities, states, and the federal government, and supported by the public. During his three terms, New York City Mayor Bloomberg:

- Made all workplaces including bars and restaurants smoke-free; by 2012, thirty states had legislation prohibiting smoking in enclosed public spaces.
- Eliminated the use of artificial trans-fats in restaurants and other food service establishments; Philadelphia, Boston, and the entire state of California, among many other jurisdictions, followed suit.
- Required chain restaurants with more than fifteen outlets to post calorie counts on menus; today, any restaurant in the country with more than twenty locations is required to post the calorie counts of its menu items.
- Banned smoking in public parks, plazas and beaches.

Bloomberg launched the National Salt Reduction Initiative to reduce salt in food by encouraging manufacturers and restaurants to reduce sodium in food by 25 percent. He advocated a voluntary breastfeeding initiative called Latch on NYC, a program which encourages participating hospitals to support breastfeeding by not automatically providing infant formula unless medically required or specifically requested by the mother. Before receiving formula, moms are offered breastfeeding support and counseled on its benefits.

FIGURE 4.1 *This full page advertisment was run in* The New York Times *by ConsumerFreedom.com.*
http://www.consumerfreedom.com/
Courtesy of The Center for Consumer Freedom

Some of Bloomberg's more controversial public health initiatives are related to his efforts to wean New Yorkers off sugary drinks. He supported New York State proposals for a penny-per-ounce tax on sugary drinks in 2009 and 2010, although these taxes were not ultimately included in the final state budgets; *The New York Times* reported that the soda industry spent $13 million in 2010 to lobby New York State elected officials against the tax. In 2010 Bloomberg proposed a two-year pilot project to eliminate sugary drinks from the list of allowable products food stamps can be used to purchase, a proposal which was rejected by the U.S. Department of Agriculture. In 2012, Bloomberg used his authority to request that the New York City Board of Health amend the city's health code to limit the size of sugary drinks offered or sold in restaurants and by other food vendors to 16 ounces.

THE LINK BETWEEN OBESITY, DIABETES, AND SUGARY DRINKS

Obesity in the United States reached epidemic proportions by 2004 when nearly 25 percent of adult Americans were obese, according to the Centers for Disease Control (CDC). By 2010, 36 percent of adults and nearly 17 percent of youth were considered obese. Research has linked several chronic diseases to obesity including heart disease, stroke, some types of cancer, and type 2 diabetes. Obesity is expensive too. According to one investigation, "In 2008, medical costs associated with obesity were estimated at $147 billion; the medical costs paid by third-party payers for people who are obese were $1,429 higher than those of normal weight," according to *Health Affairs*, a health policy journal, and cited by the CDC.

Changing patterns of food consumption and physical activity led researchers to isolate the major factors within these two areas. One line of research focused on sugary drinks. Americans consumed 13.8 billion gallons of calorically sweetened beverages in 2009; the number of calories from sugary drinks consumed by the average person was 70,000, according to *Health Affairs*. Some researchers found that sugary drinks were a major source of added sugar in the American diet. One of the first significant longitudinal studies in 2004 collected data from 51,603 women. It found "weight gain over a four-year period was highest among women who increased their sugar-sweetened soft drink consumption from one or fewer drinks per week to one or more drinks per day," according to the *Journal of the American Medical Association*. It also found "women consuming one or more sugar-sweetened soft drinks per day had a relative risk of type 2 diabetes."

Many more studies followed, and in 2010 a meta-analysis study reported:

> *that higher consumption of SSBs [sugar-sweetened beverages] is significantly associated with development of metabolic syndrome and type 2 diabetes. It provides further support to limit consumption of these beverages in place of healthy alternatives such as water to reduce obesity-related chronic disease risk.*

Studies were pointing to sugary drinks as a major driver in the rising obesity and diabetes trends.

According to the CDC, in 2011 there were 25.8 million Americans with diabetes and the cost of their care was $174 billion annually. The CDC issued an alarming news release in 2010 that predicted that a third of Americans could have diabetes by 2050, based on a study in the journal *Population Health Metrics*. These figures were widely quoted in news articles. Medical experts were especially concerned about the increasing numbers of children with diabetes.

Another study conducted by researchers at the University of California, San Francisco, found that a one-cent-per-ounce tax on sugary drinks would "prevent nearly 100,000 cases of heart disease, 8,000 strokes, and 26,000 deaths over the next decade," according to a UCSF news release. The researchers estimated that $13 billion would be raised in revenue and would save the public about $17 billion over the next decade in healthcare costs.

Based on the growing evidence about sugary drinks, health experts suggested sweetened beverage consumers to "rethink your drink" and simply substitute sugary drinks with water or other healthier, low-calorie alternatives.

In May 2012, the Institute for Medicine issued a report, entitled "Accelerating Progress in Obesity Prevention: Solving the Weight of the Nation," that recommended far-reaching strategies, including the possibility of a sugary soda tax, to curb the "obesogenic" environment that could lead to 42 percent of the population labeled as obese by 2030. This report coincided with HBO's four-part film series entitled "Weight of a Nation," which was produced in collaboration with the Institute of

Medicine, Centers for Disease Control, the National Institutes of Health, and others and aired in May 2012. It was a powerful production that generated buzz for discussion, including in Congress.

NEW YORK CITY RESPONDS

In New York City, the health effects of obesity are great. By 2012, more than half of New York City adults were overweight or obese (58 percent), according to the New York City Health Department Community Health Survey, and 21 percent of its children were obese, according to the CDC. According to the city's health department, more than 5,000 deaths and $4 billion in direct medical costs could be linked to obesity annually in New York City.

New Yorkers like their sugary drinks. According to a city health survey:

> *More than 30 percent of adult New Yorkers report drinking one or more sugary drinks per day. These rates are much higher in minority and low-income communities. Many residents in low-income neighborhoods report drinking four or more sugary drinks daily.*

New York City children were also big sugary beverage drinkers. Forty-four percent of children aged 6–12 years consumed more than one sugary drink per day, according to the city's Child Health Survey. For every sugary drink added to a child's daily diet "his/her odds of becoming obese increased by 60 percent," according to a study published in *The Lancet*. "These drinks are now the primary source of added sugars . . . in children's diets," according to the city's health department.

The New York City Department of Health and Mental Hygiene collaborated with healthcare organizations and experts to devise solutions to the problem of obesity and its related healthcare issues. To educate residents about obesity issues, the Department of Health created multiple informational campaigns that ran between 2010 and 2013.

ARE YOU POURING ON THE POUNDS?

An informational campaign called "Are You Pouring on the Pounds?" was created to raise awareness about the link between weight gain and sugary drinks. Starting in 2009, the New York City Department of Health and Mental Hygiene developed posters, subway ads, internet videos, and television commercials to show New Yorkers what they were really drinking. The ads used humor and, in some cases, alarming images to make their point, and over several waves of the campaign, "Pouring on the Pounds" has become a recognizable brand and part of the parlance of the mainstream media coverage of obesity.

In the first video, *Man Drinking Fat*, a can of liquefied fat is being poured into a tall glass and a young man in profile chugs it down. "Drinking one can of soda a day . . . can make you 10 pounds fatter a year." The next scene shows a table place setting with 10 pounds of liquefied fat raining down on a plate. Next, examples of sugary drinks are displayed, with the text: "Don't drink yourself fat.

ARE YOU POURING ON THE POUNDS?
DON'T DRINK YOURSELF FAT.
Cut back on soda and other sugary beverages.
Go with water, seltzer or low-fat milk instead.
NYC

FIGURE 4.2 *The Department of Health's "Are You Pouring on the Pounds?" health campaign poster.*
http://www.nyc.gov/
Courtesy of The New York City Department of Health

Cut out soda and other sugary beverages." Another scene displays alternatives with this text: "Go with water, seltzer, or low-fat milk instead." This video went viral, with over half a million views in its first two weeks on YouTube.

The next video, entitled *Man Eating Sugar*, shows the same young male actor sitting at a diner counter consuming packets of sugar one after the other while two people sitting next to him stare in disbelief. The superimposed text says,

> *You'd never eat sixteen packs of sugar. Why would you drink sixteen packs of sugar? There are sixteen packs of sugar in one 20 oz bottle of soda. All those extra calories can bring on obesity, diabetes and heart disease. Go with water, fat-free milk, seltzer, or unsweetened tea instead.*

The final scenes show examples of the problem drinks with suitable drink substitutes.

Man Walking Off Soda shows the man from the previous videos happily walking in New York City in numerous and rapidly edited shots. As the actor's pace begins to slow down, superimposed text says: "You have to walk the three miles from Union Square to Brooklyn to burn off the calories from one 20 oz. soda." In the next scene, healthier drink alternatives are shown with the text: "Go with water, seltzer, fat-free milk, or unsweetened teas."

Each video was released with complementary subway ads. For instance, subway posters showing maps of NYC routes to burn off different sugary drinks were released in coordination with the *Man Walking Off Soda* video. Two television commercials, both released in 2011, took a more hard-hitting tack, graphically illustrating the health consequences associated with obesity.

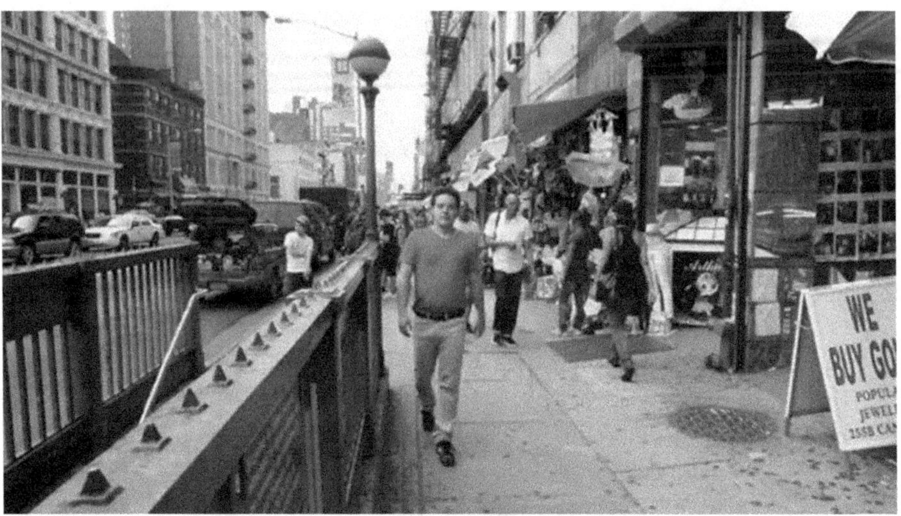

FIGURE 4.3 *This New York City Department of Health commercial "Man Walks off Soda" was an entertaining companion to the print advertising. http://www.youtube.com/*
Courtesy of The New York City Department of Health

You have to walk the **3 MILES** from Union Square to Brooklyn
to burn off the calories from **ONE 20oz. SODA**
ARE YOU POURING ON THE POUNDS?
Sugary drinks can bring on obesity, type 2 diabetes and heart disease.
FOR HEALTHY ALTERNATIVES: go to nyc.gov and search for Eating Healthy or call 311.
NYC Health

FIGURE 4.4 *This subway poster by New York City's Department of Health showed how far one had to walk in order to make up for the sugary drink calories.*
New York City Department of Health
Courtesy of The New York City Department of Health

Street intercept and online surveys after two waves of the campaign showed strong recall of both the ads—especially the subway ads—and the slogan "Are You Pouring on the Pounds?" The city continues to build on this campaign with new creative development and through social media channels such as Facebook, Twitter, and Tumblr.

CUT YOUR PORTIONS, CUT YOUR RISK

In 2012, the city launched a new information campaign aimed at educating consumers about portion sizes and the link to obesity and other health-related risks.

In a news release announcing the campaign, the city's Health Commissioner Dr. Thomas Farley said:

> *The portion sizes that are marketed are often much more than humans need. We are warning people about the risks of super-size portions so they can make more informed choices about what they eat. Consuming too many calories can lead to weight gain, which greatly increases the risk of type 2 diabetes. If New Yorkers cut their portions, they can cut their risk of these health problems.*

The city's news release also said:

> *Most adults only need to eat 2,000 calories per day, and children need even fewer. But with Americans eating out more often than they did forty years ago, staying within these recommendations has become more difficult. A beverage at a fast food chain has increased fourfold since 1955, from 7 ounces to 32 ounces. During the same time, french fry portions have more than doubled, from 2.4 ounces to 5.4 ounces. As a result, recent studies show that one-third of New Yorkers eating at chain restaurants consume more than 1,000 calories at lunchtime alone.*

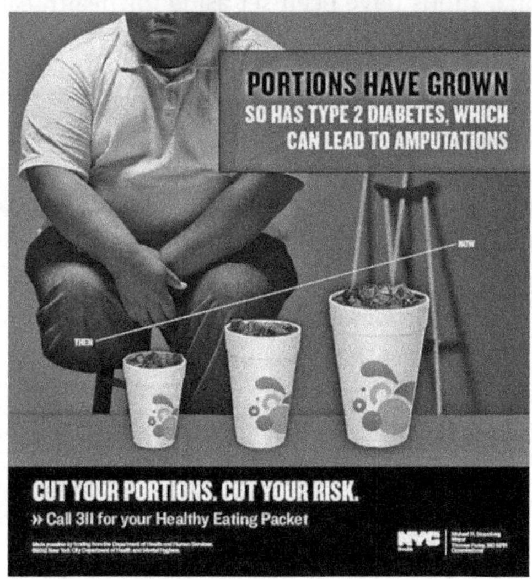

FIGURE 4.5 *The Department of Health's "Cut Your Portions" health campaign poster.*
http://www.nyc.gov/html/doh/downloads/pdf/cdp/portion-campaign-ads.pdf
Courtesy of The New York City Department of Health

Experts noted that the original Coca-Cola bottle size was 6.5 fluid ounces, nearly half the size of today's soda can (12 fluid ounces) and dwarfed by the popular 20-ounce size plastic bottles. Part of this campaign focused on the increasing beverage sizes offered at food retailers. One poster showed an amputee with different sized drinks. The text said "Portions have grown. So has type 2 diabetes, which can lead to amputations. Cut your portions, cut your risk." Other posters used hamburgers and french fries in different portions. Viewers were directed to call for further information. This campaign provided consumers with a free Healthy Eating Packet that contained:

- **"Counting Calories? Read 'Em Before You Eat 'Em" brochure**—provides information on daily calorie needs and tips for making healthy choices.
- **"Are You Pouring on the Pounds?" health bulletin**—provides tips on how to cut back on soda, juice, and other sugary drinks.
- **"Make New York City Your Gym" health bulletin**—provides information on the importance of being physically active and gives tips on how to incorporate free or low-cost exercise into daily routines.
- **"Eating Out, Eating Well" health bulletin**—provides information on making smart choices when eating out.
- **"My Plate Planner" placemat and magnets**—provides guidance on creating a healthy and balanced meal for both adults and children.

Between 2009 and 2012, the educational campaigns to help reduce sugary drinks in New Yorkers' diets cost $2.8 million, of which 87 percent was financed by the federal government. Additional funds have been set aside for health campaigns related to sugary drink consumption in 2013.

BEYOND INFORMATION

Coordinated with the city's education campaigns were many activities and services to aid New Yorkers in making healthy lifestyle changes. These included support for farmers' markets, mobile green cart vendors who brought fresh produce to underserved areas of the city, fitness programs, nutrition education in schools and daycare centers, and several publications that provided useful advice on shopping choices, exercise, and nutrition.

The "Make NYC Your Gym" initiative encouraged cycling on the 200 miles of bike lanes in the city and walking tours of hundreds of landmarks. For example, walking the Brooklyn Bridge provides 1.1 miles of exercise, walking the circumference of Yankee Stadium provides 1 mile of exercise, and the Coney Island Boardwalk provides 2.5 miles of exercise. New Yorkers were advised to get off the subway one stop early and take the stairs instead of the elevator to get more exercise.

Even workplaces were targeted for healthier choices. Employers were encouraged to offer healthy snack alternatives at meetings, such as low-calorie beverages or water, diet sodas, and unsweetened tea, and offering fresh fruit and/or vegetables.

Employer cafeterias were also encouraged to take simple steps to provide healthier choices by simply moving candy, cookies, chips, and other unhealthy foods away from the cash register to discourage impulse purchases of "junk" foods, according to one of the city's brochures.

AMENDING THE CITY'S HEALTH CODE

The most controversial aspect of the city's efforts to slim New Yorkers' waistlines was Bloomberg's proposal to limit the size of sugary drinks offered or sold to 16 ounces in food service establishments such as restaurants, movie theaters, and delis. It did not cover convenience stores such as 7–11s or grocery stores, which are regulated by the State Department of Agriculture and Markets. That meant the Big Gulp was not covered by the proposal but mega 64-ounce movie drinks were. Alcoholic beverages were also not covered, since the service of alcohol is regulated by the state. Beverages with fewer than 25 calories, like some unsweetened teas, lightly flavored waters, or diet drinks were also acceptable. The health code proposal was part of a number of recommendations announced by the Mayor's Task Force on Obesity on May 31, 2012.

Bloomberg provided his first interviews and photo op to *The New York Times* and *New York Post* on May 30, 2012. In the photo, Bloomberg posed behind five increasingly large drinks with the corresponding sugar amounts represented by sugar cubes placed in front of the drinks. The KFC 64-ounce drink had fifty-four teaspoons of sugar and 780 calories. Bloomberg's website and Twitter account also had information about the proposed amendment.

Critics immediately called the restrictions infringements on personal freedom and bad for businesses, especially small businesses, that rely on drink sales for much of their revenues; single-drink soda sales are considered high profit margin items and can easily return an 80 percent profit. The New York Beverage Association said, for example, that one deli operator claimed 85 percent of his summer profits came from drink sales.

Bloomberg's strategy to change the city's health code was seen by some as an end-run around his detractors, since the city's health board members, who voted on the proposal, are appointed by the mayor (with the consent of the city council) and were deemed friendly to the amendment. Bloomberg said he was willing to consider all available legal means to confront the city's obesity epidemic. He told *The New York Times* in an article published May 30, 2012, a day before the task force's announcement: "Obesity is a nationwide problem, and all over the United States, public health officials are wringing their hands saying, 'Oh, this is terrible.' New York City is not about wringing your hands; it's about doing something."

The New York Times also quoted Stefan Friedman, spokesman for the New York City Beverage Association, part of the soda industry's national trade group:

> *The New York City health department's unhealthy obsession with attacking soft drinks is again pushing them over the top. It's time for serious health professionals to move*

on and seek solutions that are going to actually curb obesity. These zealous proposals just distract from the hard work that needs to be done on this front.

The obesity task force included representatives from eleven city agencies. One of its goals was to cut the city's adult and childhood obesity rates by 10 and 15 percent respectively by 2016. One way to achieve this goal was to reduce the consumption of sugary drinks by limiting drink sizes. It was noted in the proposal that customers who wanted more than 16 ounces could purchase more than one beverage. The taskforce likened the proposed cap on sugary drink portion sizes to the government's restrictions on lead in paint and trans-fats in foods.

BLOOMBERG'S ACTIONS

Bloomberg used his bully pulpit to convince New Yorkers that the portion cap on sugary drink sizes was the right thing to do. He actively participated in national and local news interviews and took part in events that put a spotlight on the problem. For example, he conducted a news conference at Montefiore Medical Center on June 5, 2012, with healthcare professionals. Montefiore is located in the Bronx, which is considered ground zero for the obesity epidemic in New York City. The news conference included several statements from various healthcare professionals in support of the proposed ban and the need for bold action to avert a healthcare disaster. Here are a few of the statements made at this event:

"We see the often grave health impacts of the obesity epidemic every day across our public hospital system with ever increasing numbers of overweight patients presenting with diabetes, hypertension and congestive heart failure," said HHC [NYC Health and Hospitals Corporation] President Alan D. Aviles. "While there is no single action that will help all patients avoid or reduce excess weight gain, a sensible restriction on the available portion size of sugary beverages can increase the odds."

"Mayor Bloomberg's proposed ban on the sale of large sugary drinks is an important step in the fight against obesity," said Montefiore Medical Center President and CEO Dr. Safyer. "I've watched for years as sugary beverages and unhealthy foods have been marketed to our children, while the obesity epidemic exploded. What we need now are far-reaching measures to protect our children from the risks of diabetes, heart disease, and cancers associated with obesity."

"The importance of Mayor Bloomberg's initiative cannot be overstated," said Montefiore Executive Vice President and Chief Operating Officer Dr Ozuah. "As Physician in Chief of the Children's Hospital at Montefiore, it's been incredibly challenging to watch more and more children coming in each year with complications from obesity-related illnesses. With this ban, my hope is that children, as well as adults, can begin establishing healthier habits and working towards a healthier future."

Bloomberg enlisted the support of dozens of healthcare researchers, professionals, elected officials, pop star icons, and many other influential people to go on record with their support of the initiative.

THE BEVERAGE INDUSTRY RESPONDS

Two national industry groups opposed the health code amendment: the American Beverage Association (ABA), with the local New York City Beverage Association; and the National Restaurant Association, and its associated New York City Restaurant Association.

No industry likes regulations, especially if it affects profit. Kelly Brownell, a professor at Yale University and director of the Rudd Center for Food Policy and Obesity, said the profit margin of selling sugary drinks is "enormous—90 percent," according to theatlantic.com. He also said that profits increase with the size of the drink sold.

One of the core strategies of the ABA was to refute the research on the link of sugar-sweetened beverages to obesity and other health problems. While many studies pointed to sugar-sweetened beverages as a major driver for obesity, the ABA used its chief scientist Maureen Storey to reexamine the available government data on obesity and sugar-sweetened beverages. Storey published "The Shifting Beverage Landscape" in 2010 in the peer-reviewed journal *Physiology & Behavior*; it found that the beverage industry was evolving:

- Between 1970 and 2006, Americans had added 600 additional kilocalories per day (although another study found the increase to be between 200 and 300 kilocalories per day). While added fats increased 35 percent during this period, added sugars declined 11 percent.
- In 2005–2006, calories from sodas, sports drinks, sweetened bottled water, and energy drinks comprised 5.5 percent of the total American diet. "Grain-based desserts" were the number one source of calories, 6.5 percent. All desserts (grain-based, dairy-based and candy) added 11 percent of calories in the American diet.
- The production of full-calorie sodas' calories per ounce decreased 24.4 percent between 1988 and 2008.
- By 2008, bottled water was 29 percent of the market share, while carbonated soft drinks decreased 70 percent to less than 50 percent, according to the Beverage Marketing Corporation.

Two researchers from Cornell, Brian Wansink and David Just, writing for theatlantic.com, said the proposed soda size limit would not work because people "buy the size they want." While their research showed that when people were given larger portions in social settings they drank and ate "substantially more," it was because they weren't paying attention. But in situations where portions were forced on research participants, it didn't work. The researchers favored incentives to beverage makers and consumers to promote or purchase low- or no-calorie drinks.

A more grassroots group, funded by the ABA, was organized, called New Yorkers for Beverage Choices. It had about 1,500 individuals, businesses, and community organization members opposed to restricting drink sizes by the summer of 2012.

According to *The New York Times*, workers paid by New Yorkers for Beverage Choice collected petition signatures against the new regulation and created Facebook and Twitter pages to "say no to a #sodaban." The group's supporters wore t-shirts that said: "I Picked My Beverage All by Myself."

Another nonprofit group, called the Center for Consumer Freedom, supported by the food industry and individuals, also responded. Coca-Cola likewise took an active role in the debate.

Statements and news releases quickly followed the May 30, 2012, proposed cap on large soda sizes.

DAY ONE—MAY 31, 2012

New York City Beverage Association's spokesman Stefan Friedman said in an e-mail statement to news media:

> *The city is not going to address the obesity issue by attacking soda because soda is not driving the obesity rates. In fact, as obesity continues to rise, [Centers for Disease Control and Prevention] data shows that calories from sugar-sweetened beverages are a small and declining part of the American diet. It's time for serious health professionals to move on and seek solutions that are going to actually curb obesity. These zealous proposals just distract from the hard work that needs to be done on this front.*

While PepsiCo deferred to the ABA, Coca-Cola took an active role in the debate and issued a website media statement May 31, 2012:

FIGURE 4.6 *The New Yorkers for Beverage Choices group developed a television commercial called "Take a Stand" that asked viewers if they were going to let someone else tell them what they could drink. It ended in a texting request.*
http://nycbeveragechoices.com/
New Yorkers for Beverage Choice

> *The people of New York City are much smarter than the New York City Health Department believes. We are transparent with our consumers. They can see exactly how many calories are in every beverage we serve. We have prominently placed calorie counts on the front of our bottles and cans and in New York City, restaurants already post the calorie content of all their offerings and portion sizes—including soft drinks.*
>
> *New Yorkers expect and deserve better than this. They can make their own choices about the beverages they purchase. We hope New Yorkers loudly voice their disapproval about this arbitrary mandate.*

The ABA's blog also responded to the announcement in an entry May 31, 2012, titled "Here They Go Again: Nanny Bloomberg's Obsession with Soda":

> *New York City Mayor Michael Bloomberg is taking his unhealthy obsession with soft drinks to a new level, this time proposing to ban sugar-sweetened beverages larger than 16 ounces from city restaurants, movie theaters, stadiums and food trucks. This is not the first time the New York City Health Department, under the direction of Mayor Bloomberg, has rallied against the consumption of our industry's products as an alleged means to reduce obesity.*

The blog entry, one of many to follow, criticized the Department of Health's previous information campaigns as misleading. The writer said the industry had "taken and continues to take bold action to help address the complex issue of obesity." These actions included providing more drink choices, more portion sizes, and easier-to-read calorie labels on every bottle, can, and pack.

> *However, New York City is not going to address the obesity issue by attacking soda because soda is not driving the obesity rates. According to government data, sugar-sweetened beverages account for only 7 percent of calories in the average American's diet. So while obesity rates continue to climb, beverage calories continue to decline.*

Readers were directed to Let'sClearItUp.org and DeliveringChoices.org, both ABA websites that provided more information on the beverage debate from the drink industry perspective. The blog entry ended with "These zealous proposals just distract from the hard work that needs to be done on this front."

The ABA ran a full-page advertisement May 31, 2012, in *The New York Times*. It refuted the Department of Health's facts with a different use of CDC data. The ad featured cartoon talking balloons that said: "Are soda and sugar-sweetened beverages driving obesity? Not according to the facts." The ad then listed:

- **FACT**: According to CDC data, sugar-sweetened beverages make up just 7 percent of the average diet.
- **FACT**: According to CDC data, added sugar from soda has declined 39 percent since 2000. And sugar-sweetened beverages are not the No. 1 source of added sugars in our diets—food is.
- **FACT**: According to the Beverage Marketing Corporation, there has been a 23 percent reduction in the average calories per serving from beverages sold between 1998 and 2010.

The facts make it clear—beverage calories and added sugars have decreased for more than a decade, while the CDC reports obesity rates continue to climb. America's beverage companies have been doing our part to help curb obesity by offering more products in smaller portion sizes and lower or no calories. And while New York City had its own school program, our industry's efforts in New York State and across the country have led to 88 percent fewer beverage calories in schools overall. For more information, visit letsclearitup.org.

The Academy for Nutrition and Dietetics issued its statement May 31, 2012, that urged more research before the beverage proposal was approved. The academy said it would study the proposal and others. Registered dietitian and Academy president Sylvia Escott-Stump said in a statement on its website May 31, 2012:

To date, most bans and taxations like the New York proposal are based on theoretical models. There is conflicting research on whether these programs actually result in behavior change that leads to positive health outcomes.

As a science-based organization, the Academy of Nutrition and Dietetics believes there must be an evaluation component to these programs. We need to measure behavior changes across the population as a result of the program. Then, we can determine if the changes are long-term and whether they contribute to a reduction of chronic diseases like obesity and diabetes.

The New York State Restaurant Association issued this statement from Andrew Moesel, spokesperson for the NYC Chapter of the organization:

We appreciate the Mayor's concern for public health but the current proposal goes much too far. No one understands private enterprise and business better than the mayor. People want choices. Restaurants are serving the public what it wants and we all hope that will continue. If we want New York City to remain the restaurant capital of the world, we must stop placing these burdensome restrictions on what can and can't be served here.

DAY TWO—JUNE 1, 2012

In an interview published June 1, 2012, in theatlantic.com, the New York City Health Commissioner, Thomas Farley, said that while the mayor cares about what New Yorkers think, it's not the only consideration:

"Sure, we care what people think, and we have reason to think a lot of people are supporting of this," he said. "The other thing, though, is that we have a board of health in New York City for a reason, and that is to take the issue of protecting the health of citizens out of the political process and put it in the hands of health experts."

Farley said unusual action was needed because "obesity is a crisis" and lives were at stake. He reminded readers that many people opposed the indoor smoking ban proposed by the Bloomberg administration years earlier:

"It's common for any policy that's a big change for people to have an initial reaction that's a little skeptical," Farley said. "But our experience has been, with some of these other policy changes, that after that initial skepticism was overcome and the policy was put into place, not only are they popular, but people say, 'Why didn't we do this earlier?'"

Michael Jacobson, co-founder and executive director of the Center for Science in the Public Interest, a nonprofit health advocacy organization, supported Bloomberg's efforts in an opinion column on usnews.com:

Don't underestimate New York City Mayor Michael A. Bloomberg. And don't be surprised if, five years from now, 32- and 64-ounce Cokes are hard-to-find relics. We won't miss them nor should we: If there are a hundred things we should do to make a dent in rates of obesity in children and in adults, the first ten of those things should be strategies to reduce consumption of soda and other sugary drinks.

Dawn Sweeney, president and CEO of the National Restaurant Association, offered a counterview along with Jacobson's column on usnews.com. She said it had taken a "proactive role in helping the country deal with issues related to food and healthy living." She went on to say: "Mayor Bloomberg's proposal is another example of consistent targeting of restaurants for excessive regulation and placing bureaucratic mandates on the industry that even some City Council members have called unfair and inconsistent."

The *New York Post* wrote an editorial entitled "Mike: Downsize It" that supported Bloomberg's efforts to curb sugary drink consumption. After citing research, its editorial ended this way:

We've never been fans of coercive government measures. But this one seems less onerous than most.

It's certainly worth a try.

On CNN's *EarlyStart* morning news program, Coca-Cola's Chief Scientific and Regulatory Officer Dr. Rhona Applebaum said that the real solution was not soda but physical activity. Applebaum agreed that the rising rates of obesity were a national tragedy but:

what's even a bigger tragedy . . . is that we've taken physical education and physical activity out of our schools . . . We're not saying that diet should not be addressed; absolutely; we want our public and consumers to have a sensible balanced diet but they also have to have regular physical activity. So if they want to put their money where their mouth is let's look at our environment, let's look at our schools; let's increase school activity.

Applebaum said in another interview on foxbusiness.com that Coke began calorie labeling in 2009 to help consumers make informed decisions, and Coca-Cola had recently introduced the 90-calorie 7.5-ounce mini-can "designed to help people manage their portions."

DAY THREE—JUNE 2, 2012

The Center for Consumer Freedom, supported by the food industry and individuals, developed a full-page color ad that ran in *The New York Times* June 6, 2012. Its headline was "The Nanny: You only *thought* you lived in the land of the free." It featured an image of Bloomberg wearing a frumpy pale blue dress suit and matching pastel scarf, with his arms outstretched in a protective embrace. The ad's copy said:

> *Bye Bye Venti—Nanny Bloomberg has taken his strange obsession with what you eat one step further. He now wants to make it illegal to serve "sugary drinks" bigger than 16 oz. What's next? Limits on the width of a pizza slice, size of a hamburger or amount of cream cheese on your bagel? New Yorkers need a mayor not a nanny. Find out more at ConsumerFreedom.com.*

The *New York Times* op-ed columnist Frank Bruni wrote "Trimming a Fat City," which endorsed Bloomberg's anti-obesity efforts; his column began this way:

> *While Michelle Obama focused on carrots, Mayor Michael R. Bloomberg brandished a stick. It's what we deserve.*
>
> *Cry all you want about a nanny state, but as a city and a nation we've gorged and guzzled past the point where a gentle nudge toward roughage suffices. We need a weight watcher willing to mete out some stricter discipline.*

COCA-COLA'S MEDIA RELATIONS

Coca-Cola increased its efforts to tell the industry's story in the news media by offering Katie Bayne, Coca-Cola's president of sparkling beverages in North America, as a spokesperson on the debate.

In an interview with *USA Today*, June 7, 2012, she used similar facts quoted in the June 1, 2012, ABA *New York Times* ad. She said sugars from soda consumption had decreased 39 percent from 1999 through 2010 while obesity rates increased, including a 13 percent increase for children and 7 percent increase for adults.

Bayne also said Coca-Cola beverage line introduced twenty new low-calorie or no-calorie drinks in 2011 and offered 150 low-calorie or no-calorie beverages in the United States; that was about one-third of its U.S. beverage portfolio.

In another *USA Today* story with a Q&A with Bayne, she said:

> **Q:** *Is anyone at Coca-Cola trying to figure out a way to get sugar out of all drinks?*
>
> **A:** *There is a large portion of the population that relies on the carbohydrates and energy in our regular beverages. When my son gets home from school, he needs a pick-up with calories and great taste.*
>
> **Q:** *But critics call soft drinks "empty" calories.*

A: *A calorie is a calorie. What our drinks offer is hydration. That's essential to the human body. We offer great taste and benefits whether it's an uplift or carbohydrates or energy. We don't believe in empty calories. We believe in hydration.*

Bayne told *USA Today* that she personally drank diet Coca-Cola products in her typical day but sometimes had an 8-ounce regular Coke in midafternoon as a "pick-me-up" instead of a candy bar or cookie. Bayne did not prohibit her own children from drinking sugary drinks but encouraged them to make good choices. She said that a 12-ounce regular Coke had 140 calories, similar to what's in a lunch-size bag of pretzels.

Coca-Cola issued a statement on its website June 20, 2012, titled "Statement on NYC Health Department new initiatives to 'solve' the obesity problem over the next 18 months":

Our concerns with Mayor Bloomberg's proposal are well known. We know the Mayor has the best intentions for his city. However, we believe the best way to tackle obesity is by working together. As a team, we can make a lot more progress. People can consume calories from many different foods and beverages, so it makes no sense to single out sugar-sweetened beverages.

We have a record of working together to create solutions:

The School Beverage Guidelines, developed in partnership with President Clinton, have decreased calories from our beverages in schools by 88 percent between 2004 and 2010.

Our work with First Lady Michelle Obama's "Let's Move!" initiative placed clear calorie information on the front of nearly every bottle and can our industry produces.

We have a program in the Bronx that is educating people by promoting no and low calorie beverages.

KEY POINTS: RESTRICTIONS TARGETING THE SALE OF ANY FOOD OR BEVERAGE LIMIT CHOICE AND WON'T SOLVE OBESITY

- *Since people consume calories from many foods and drinks, restrictions on sugar-sweetened beverages are unlikely to impact obesity.*
- *If NYC's Department of Health can restrict the sale of a safe, legal product like a soda, then what's next? Will coffee trucks be banned from selling Danishes and street vendors from selling pretzels, slices of pizza or hot dogs?*
- *Coca-Cola believes New Yorkers don't need the Mayor to make beverage decisions for them.*

- *There is no data backing the City's proposal to target beverages in containers larger than 16 oz. We believe health policy should be driven by facts, not agenda.*

OBESITY IS A COMPLEX PROBLEM THAT CAN'T BE BLAMED ON A SINGLE FOOD OR BEVERAGE

- *When it comes to losing and maintaining weight, all calories count. It's wrong to single out anything for causing people to be overweight or obese. People consume calories from many different sources.*
- *Calories from sugar-sweetened beverages are a small fraction of the American diet—on average, approximately 7 percent. Between 1999 and 2008, obesity rates continued to rise while Americans' added-sugar consumption from soda decreased by 39 percent.*
- *A sensible diet isn't about eliminating specific foods or beverages. It's about creating balance by staying active, making choices that are right for you and enjoying what you eat and drink.*

COCA-COLA IS COMMITTED TO WORKING WITH ALL SECTORS OF SOCIETY TO FIND SOLUTIONS TO OBESITY

- *To help change the way people think about nutrition and exercise we need to work together.*
- *Coca-Cola was the first beverage company to voluntarily put calorie information on the front of nearly all of our bottles and cans. We give people the information they need to make choices right for them.*
- *We support choice by providing a variety of beverage options and sizes, including many no-/ and low-calorie options and 7.5 oz. mini cans.*
- *We offer more than 700 beverage choices in the U.S. including sodas, water, juices, teas and energy drinks. This includes 150 low- and no-calorie beverages to help people manage their calorie intake.*
- *Where full-calorie beverages are sold, we offer people no- and low-calorie alternatives.*

LOBBYING EFFORTS

According to news reports, Coca-Cola and other soda companies met with New York City mayoral candidates and City Council members in a session that included discussion of the new sugary drink regulation. According to *The New York Times*, the ABA had several political consultants "including the strategists responsible for the 'Harry and Louise' television commercials" that helped defeat President Bill Clinton's 1990s healthcare plan. Large soda companies also have their strategists and consultants.

THE ABA

While Coca-Cola representatives were frequently quoted in the news media, the ABA, a Washington-based marketing and lobbying group, was the main industry voice. In addition to its media interviews, advertising and social media (primarily its blog), the ABA responded to another attack on sugar-sweetened beverages (SSBs) from the American Medical Association's report condoning taxes on SSBs to fund anti-obesity educational campaigns. The ABA's June 19, 2012, statement also addressed the link between obesity and sugar-sweetened beverages. Below is a portion of the ABA's statement from its website:

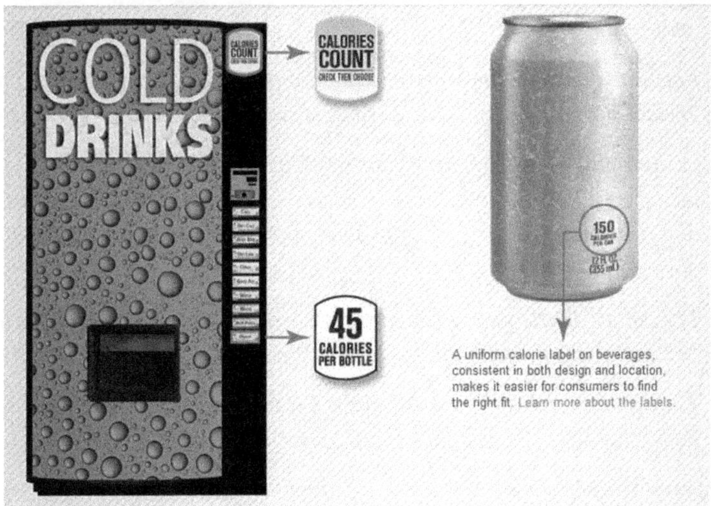

FIGURE 4.7 *The American Beverage Association developed a "We Deliver" corporate social responsibility website. Calories were one of several issues discussed.*
http://www.deliveringchoices.org/
American Beverage Association, We Deliver

On Sugar-Sweetened Beverages and Obesity:

- *Singling out sugar-sweetened beverages as the "single best thing to do for weight loss" is misleading and ignores government data. Calories from sugar-sweetened beverages—including soft drinks, juice drinks, flavored waters and other beverages—make up only 7 percent of calories, on average, in the American diet, according to a National Cancer Institute analysis of government data submitted to the U.S. Dietary Guidelines Advisory Committee. That means that 93 percent of calories come from other sources.*
- *Since 1998, the average calories per serving from beverages decreased 23 percent due in part to the innovation of more low- and zero-calorie beverages.*
- *Added sugars consumed from soda decreased 39 percent since 2000, per CDC data.*
- *From 1999 to 2010, full-calorie soda sales have declined 12.5 percent.*
- *Yet, obesity rates continued to rise over the same time period.*

On Industry's Efforts to be Part of Meaningful Solutions:

- *America's beverage companies are delivering more choices, smaller portions, fewer calories and clearer labels across the country. By doing so, our companies are making a meaningful difference for families and individuals in our communities—making it easier to choose the drink that's right for them.*

Clear Calorie Labels:

- *America's beverage companies are delivering on their Clear on Calories commitment to place clear calorie labels on the front of every bottle, can and pack they produce.*
- *We are placing total calories on the front of all bottles and cans up to and including 20 ounces to help consumers choose the beverage that's right for them and their families. For packaging larger than 20 ounces, the labels provide calories per serving.*
- *The calorie labels put this information right at the fingertips of consumers so they can make a choice that's right for them.*
- *The beverage industry announced the Clear on Calories initiative in support of First Lady Michelle Obama's "Let's Move!" campaign.*

Beverages in Schools:

- *We recognize that schools are unique places where parents want greater control over what their children eat and drink when they're not around. That's why we successfully implemented national School Beverage Guidelines.*
- *The guidelines removed full-calorie soft drinks from all schools and replaced them with more lower-calorie, smaller-portion options. Under the voluntary Guidelines, only juice, low-fat milk and water are allowed in elementary and*

middle schools, with the addition of lower-calorie and portion-controlled beverages in high schools.

- *Through the guidelines, the signatory companies drove an 88 percent reduction in beverage calories shipped to schools since 2004.*

More Choices:

- *Through innovation, our companies have broadened their product portfolio, offering beverages in a wide variety of type, portion size and calories. These innovations are evident on store shelves and in vending machines throughout our communities.*
- *The broad choices in beverage type include soft drinks, ready-to-drink teas, water, sports drinks, flavored and enhanced waters, juices, energy drinks and more.*
- *The new choices include an ever-increasing selection of low- and no-calorie beverage choices, as well as mid-calorie beverages. The innovation pipeline continues as our companies remain engaged in developing even more beverage options to fit the ways people live.*

Smaller Portions:

- *Delivering a range of portion sizes is another way to help individuals and parents choose beverages that are right for them and their families. Soft drinks and other beverages packaged for individuals are now available in portion sizes ranging from 20-ounce bottles to 7.5-ounce cans, with several options in between.*
- *Through its School Beverage Guidelines, the beverage industry voluntarily reduced juice portion sizes in K-12 schools and capped portion sizes on sports drinks, which are only offered in high schools, to 12 ounces. The range of portion sizes for beverages—including more smaller-portion options—provide for even more choice.*

Fewer Calories:

- *Through innovation and initiative, America's beverage companies are cutting calories in stores and in schools across the country.*
- *In the marketplace, the development of more low- and no-calorie beverages has helped drive a 23 percent reduction in the average calories per serving since 1998, according to Beverage Marketing Corporation, a leading analyst of industry sales data.*

OTHER EFFORTS BY THE ABA

By August 2012 the ABA had launched a website, Let's Clear it Up, which focused on various negative soda/beverage rumors, news accounts, and studies. The consumer-friendly, easy-to-read site responded in simple language and graphics. For example, on its home page in 2012, it said:

Myth: *The obesity epidemic can be reversed if people stop drinking soda.*
Fact: *Sugar-sweetened beverages account for only 7 percent of calories in the average American's diet, according to government data.*

Myth: *Mayor Bloomberg will reduce obesity by banning soda and other beverages in containers larger than 16 ounces sold in select locations throughout New York City.*
Fact: *Not likely, especially when soda is not driving obesity according to the facts:*

- *By nearly every measure, the contribution of calories from beverages to the diet is declining, yet obesity is still rising.*
- *Since 1998, the average calories per serving from beverages is down 23 percent due to more low- and zero-calorie beverages.*
- *Added sugars consumed from soda are down 39 percent since 2000, according to the CDC.*
- *Food is the no. 1 source of added sugars in the diets of Americans, according to a recent data brief from the Centers for Disease Control and Prevention.*
- *Sugar-sweetened beverages—like soda, ready-to-drink teas, sport drinks, juice drinks and flavored waters—account for only 7 percent of calories in the average American's diet, according to government data. With 93 percent of our calories coming from other foods and beverages, meaningful steps to reduce obesity need to look at the bigger picture.*
- *From 1999 to 2010, full-calorie soda sales have declined 12.5 percent.*

The ABA, with the support of the Coca-Cola Company, Dr. Pepper Snapple, PepsiCo, SunnyD, and others, developed the Delivering Choices social responsibility website that showcases how the beverage industry is voluntarily making decisions that benefit people and communities.

RALLIES FOR AND AGAINST

In addition to the city's health department and health community's support for the limitations on sugary drinks, other advocacy groups and citizens rallied support, including one rally on the steps of City Hall on June 11, 2012, that attracted community leaders from the Greater New York Hospital Association, Children's Museum of Manhattan, United Way of New York City, and others.

On July 9, 2012, the Million Big Gulp March attracted a small group including a City Council member to protest the new regulation.

AFTERMATH

On September 13, 2012, the New York City Board of Health approved the Portion Cap Rule eight to zero with one abstention on the sale of large sugary drinks at restaurants, street carts, and movie theaters. A month later, the ABA, the National

Restaurant Association and other businesses filed a lawsuit to overturn the new regulation. The day the regulation was slated to take effect, a court struck down the regulation for being too arbitrary in its application.

The City responded:

> *Without a portion cap on sugary drinks, it would be harder to tackle an obesity epidemic that kills more New Yorkers than anything other than smoking and causes misery for many thousands more who suffer from heart disease, diabetes and other debilitating illnesses. Sugary drinks are a leading cause of this epidemic. Today's decision threatens the health of New Yorkers, but we are confident that we will win on appeal.*

QUESTIONS FOR DISCUSSION

1. Explain Mayor Michael Bloomberg's strategy for reducing consumption of sugary drinks in the health code.
2. What type of appeals did the Department of Health use in its information campaigns ("Are You Pouring on the Pounds?" "Cut Your Portions, Cut Your Risk")? What were the most effective in your opinion? Why?
3. What evidence did the Department of Health use to support its campaign to reduce sugary drink consumption? How did the beverage industry refute these claims?
4. What third-party endorsements did the mayor and the Department of Health use for their campaigns?
5. What were the strategies of the beverage industry to defeat the health code proposal to limit sugary drink consumption in New York City?
6. What is the purpose of the Delivering Choices website, developed by the ABA?
7. New Yorkers for Beverage Choice is called a grassroots organization but some have called it a front group for the beverage industry. What is the difference between the two?
8. What is the purpose of the Let's Clear It Up website developed by the ABA? What other issues are confronting the beverage industry?

Dig Deeper

Read the transcript of New York City's Department of Health and Mental Hygiene's public hearing on the proposed amendment to the public health code limiting sugary drink sizes, available on the textbook's companion website. What were some of the arguments for and against the amendment? What arguments were most effective? Why?

New York City initiated another controversial educational campaign on teen pregnancy. Review the campaign materials available on the textbook's companion website. What were the appeal strategies used in the messages? Were they effective? Explain.

8

Face Value

Face Transplant Surgery Balances Privacy, Ethics and Publicity

Author's note: This case study was written with assistance from Dr. Marjorie Kruvand, assistant professor, Loyola University Chicago.

For organizations and institutions, news media attention is a double-edged sword; publicity can have favorable or unfavorable consequences. The cost of successful media relations, such as a positive front-page article touting an organization's newest product, is negligible when compared to paid advertising. News media placements, especially in credible news operations, can be effective in generating positive consumer awareness, attitudes, and behaviors.

However, news media outlets are independent operations with a mission—providing balanced, reliable information that readers want to read. Reporters don't rely only on what an institution says; they dig deeper and seek other authoritative—and sometimes critical—sources. More broadly, the "news media" also includes infotainment outlets that may operate under less stringent journalistic and ethical guidelines; these "tabloid-style" media usually emphasize the more shocking aspects of a story.

Since organizations can spend enormous amounts of money developing a positive brand or public image, careful dealings with the news media are not only sensible but essential for business today. When the Cleveland Clinic was ready to perform the first near-total face transplant in the United States, it knew that it had an exceptional opportunity to promote its world-class medical research and services. The clinic also needed to put ethical issues and the privacy of the patient and donor first.

BACKGROUND

The Cleveland Clinic, located in Cleveland, Ohio, is world renowned for its medical research and healthcare services. Since its founding in 1921, it has produced many important medical innovations including the development of coronary artery bypass surgery techniques, discoveries about the physiological electrical systems in the brain and the nervous system, and the development of an artificial kidney for hemodialysis, according to its website. In 2004, the clinic took the first steps to another major medical first: the nation's first face transplant. This long process began with seeking approval from the clinic's Institutional Review Board (IRB), which protects the rights and welfare of research subjects, and carefully considering the ethical issues surrounding this new procedure and the potential negative consequences for the patient.

Of greatest concern was whether this experimental procedure provided enough benefit to the patient to outweigh the serious health and psychological risks. Some said the procedure was cosmetic, not life-saving, and therefore not necessary since it did not sustain life functions, as do heart, liver, and kidney transplants. It was also a risky procedure. A human face transplant had never been done at the time of the IRB approval. There was a significant chance that the complex operation would not be successful and, if it did work, the patient would have to take a complex daily regimen of anti-rejection drugs for life.

Because the surgery would create intense media interest, the patient's mental stability and resilience were a concern. It was assumed that despite strict privacy laws protecting hospital patients, it was likely that the news media would find out the transplant recipient's identity while the individual was in the hospital or when he or she was released from the hospital. The patient would need to be able to deal with the media spotlight. After ten months of discussion and review, the IRB gave its approval for face transplant surgery.

People severely disfigured by accidents, fires and other mishaps think the procedure is worth the risk. While transplant surgery is necessary to restore basic biological functions, it also restores a sense of humanity. As one of the physicians concerned in the following case later noted:

> *We are such social creatures; our whole world revolves around our interaction with society. When you strip that away from somebody, they will try anything to be able to get that back. Connie never said, "I want to look like a certain person or look like me again"; she said, "I want to look human again."*

Dr. Maria Siemionow, who would become the surgical team leader for the first U.S. face transplant, put it simply: "You need a face to face the world."

Even though the operation was years away, the IRB announcement in and of itself was big news, generating 3,000 media calls. The clinic's communication office, which had rarely used outside public relations agencies before, found the media interest challenging. The primary strategy was to direct media inquiries to an exclusive given to the Cleveland *Plain Dealer*, which provided good background information about the ethical considerations and the amount of work that was being done to prepare for this medical milestone. The staff had also provided materials such as a news release and background information to explain the clinic's methodical, responsible approach.

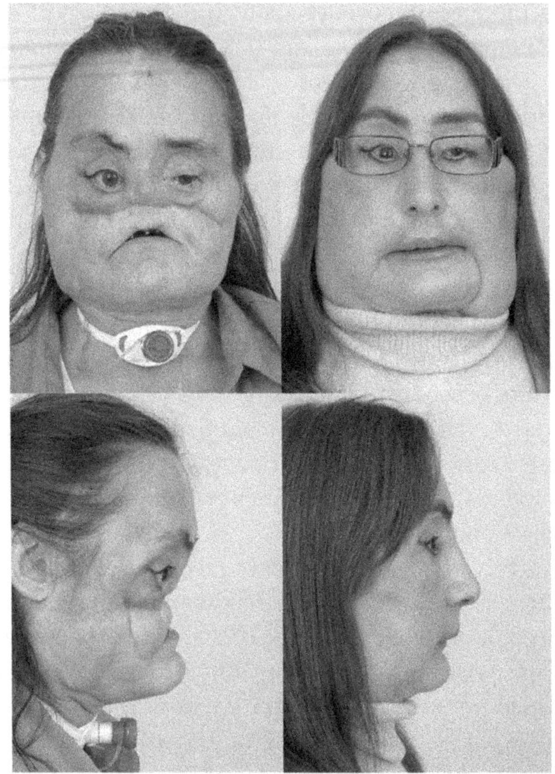

FIGURE 4.8 *Before and after photos of the patient.*
Cleveland Clinic: http://www.clevelandclinic.org/
Courtesy of Cleveland Clinic

It took four years after the IRB approval for the Cleveland Clinic to prepare its surgical team and select the right candidate for the near-total face transplant.

Connie Culp was 40 years old and a mother of two when her husband shot her in the face. The shotgun blast took away her nose, an eye, upper jaw and upper lip, palate, and lower eyelids. She couldn't eat solid food, drink from a cup, smell, or taste. Since she no longer had a nose, she breathed through a hole cut into her throat. Thirty reconstructive face surgeries failed to resolve lingering medical issues; skin grafts from her body did not begin to restore her beautiful face. Her physical appearance was so alarming it caused adults to cringe and children to call her a monster.

Meanwhile, in 2005 a French hospital performed the world's first face transplant. Cleveland Clinic's Executive Director of Corporate Communications Eileen Sheil used the opportunity to study the French hospital's media relations efforts. It was most instructive. The international coverage focused more on ethical issues than the medical milestone. Other problems included the media's early publication of the identities of the transplant donor and recipient, with their photos. And there were sensational aspects of the coverage: the recipient's alleged suicide attempt that occurred well before the transplant procedure and reports that the patient and surgical team had made a movie deal three months before the surgery.

THE MEDIA RELATIONS PLAN

The negative coverage in the French case led the Cleveland Clinic to consider a different approach. To protect the privacy of patient and donor, tight control of their personal information would be maintained; initially only the hospital's executive leadership and the surgical team would know who the patient and donor were and when the operation would take place. This privacy protection would extend throughout the patient's hospital stay. The goal was to focus the media's energies on the medical aspects of the procedure and the significance of this transplant milestone as the nation's first near-total face transplant. Ethical arguments supporting the surgery were also developed.

According to Siemionow's book *The Know-How of Face Transplantation*, Sheil said that the clinic's media alert, news release, and fact sheet contained information to protect the privacy of the patient. For example, the news release said: "For the privacy and protection of those involved, no information will be released on the patient, the donor or their families. (A written statement from the patient's sibling is available at www.clevelandclinic.org/face.)"

News of the operation was not disclosed until eight days after the surgery. Sheil said:

> *Before going public, we wanted to see how the patient would respond to the surgery; mainly, would the transplant show signs of rejection? We knew that we could not wait long, though. News of the face transplant was sure to leak eventually, as employees secretly tell their families, who tell their friends, who call the media.*

Sheil also said the delay provided time to "prepare the announcement in the way that would be most effective."

Several steps were taken by the clinic's corporate communication office to accomplish these goals, according to the clinic and research by Marjorie Kruvand, assistant professor at Loyola University Chicago:

- Information about the transplant surgery was not released until eight days after the surgery. The first public announcement was an e-mail message to all Cleveland Clinic employees closely followed by the media advisory to news reporters for a news conference the next day.
- The communication team worked with the surgical team to coordinate key messages focusing on the significance of the medical procedure and the ethical guidelines followed.
- Statements were prepared ahead of time for both a successful and unsuccessful outcome.
- A mock news conference was provided to help coach medical personnel on how to answer questions effectively.

- The news conference, held eight days after the surgery, emphasized the transplant's medical significance, the careful preparation by the surgical team, and the ethical basis and guidelines for the procedure. A logistics team helped make the conference a professional event. Reporters unable to attend the conference could hear it using a conference phone line.
- To stress the ethical reasoning behind the surgical procedure, the chairman of the Department of Bioethics at the Cleveland Clinic was the third speaker, following the president and chief executive officer's and the surgical team leader's remarks.
- Reporters' questions were anticipated and responses developed.

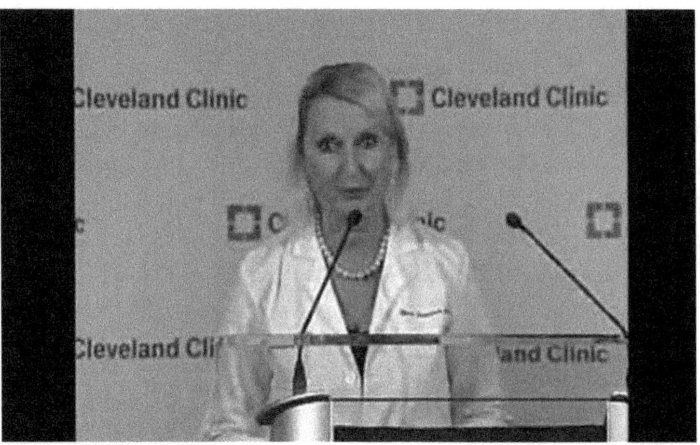

FIGURE 4.9 *Cleveland Clinic news conference with Dr Siemionow.*
http://www.clevelandclinic.org/
Courtesy of Cleveland Clinic

FIGURE 4.10 *Cleveland Clinic news conference with Dr Eric Kodish, chair of the Department of Bioethics.*
http://www.clevelandclinic.org/
Courtesy of Cleveland Clinic

- The media kit comprised an agenda, news release, fact sheet, bios and photos of the transplant team, a statement from the patient's sibling, background information on the clinic, and a list of media relations contacts. There was also a CD with B-roll of the surgery, photos, and animation of the procedure.
- An Internet microsite was developed to make communication material available after the news conference.

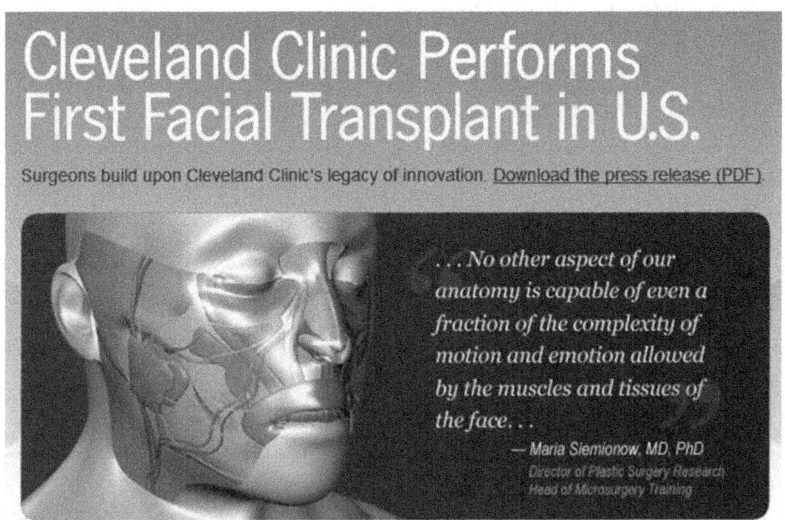

FIGURE 4.11 *A micro website was developed for the news media to help educate and answer questions.*
http://www.clevelandclinic.org/lp/face_transplant/
Courtesy of Cleveland Clinic

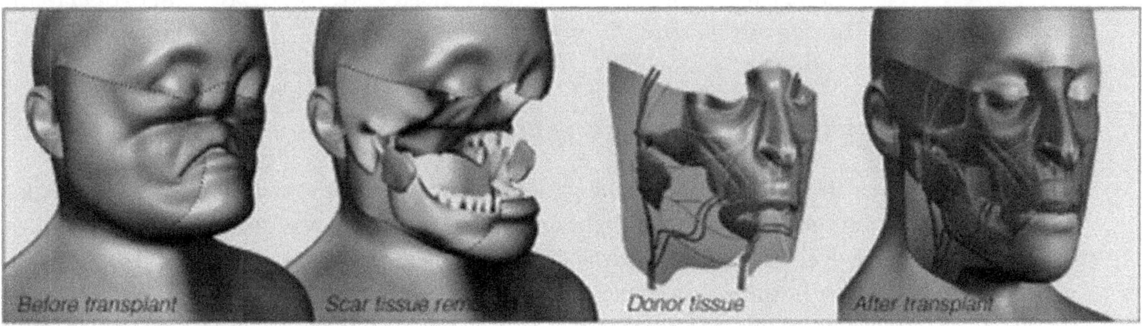

Much More Than a New Look

A team of eight surgeons at the Cleveland Clinic have performed the world's most complex face transplant to date. The 23-hour procedure involved removing scar tissue from the unnamed patient, who had lost her nose and palate because of trauma, and grafting on facial skin, muscle, bone and blood vessels from a dead donor.

SCHEMATIC ILLUSTRATIONS BY THE CLEVELAND CLINIC

FIGURE 4.12 *Much More than a New Look.*
http://www.clevelandclinic.org/graphic
Courtesy of Cleveland Clinic

The news conference attracted international interest and news coverage. Nearly all of it was positive; the focus was on the medical achievement and how the patient had benefited from the transplant.

The New York Times headlined its front-page article, "In an Extensive and Intricate Operation, a Face is Remade":

> *Only the forehead, upper eyelids, lower lip, lower teeth and jaw are hers.*
>
> *The rest of her face comes from a cadaver.*
>
> *In a 23-hour operation, transplant surgeons have given nearly an entire new face to a woman with facial damage so severe that she could not eat on her own or breathe without a hole in her windpipe, doctors at the Cleveland Clinic said here on Wednesday.*
>
> *The highly experimental procedure, performed within the last two weeks, was the world's fourth partial face transplant, the country's first, and the most extensive and complicated such operation to date.*

The Washington Post began its front-page in-depth story, "Surgeons Say Recipient of Face Transplant 'Is Doing Well,'" this way:

> *Surgeons yesterday provided details of the first face transplant done in the United States, a painstaking 22-hour operation to stitch most of a dead woman's face onto a recipient so horribly disfigured that she was willing to undergo the risky surgery in the hopes of being able to smile, smell, eat and breathe normally again—and go out in public without frightening children.*
>
> *In a procedure done sometime in the last two weeks, the thirty-member Cleveland Clinic team replaced about 80 percent of the woman's face—essentially re-creating the entire middle portion, including her lower eyelids, nose, cheeks and upper jaw, along with the supporting bones, muscles, nerves and arteries.*
>
> *The operation, transferring everything except the upper eyelids, forehead, lower lip and chin, marks the first time the controversial procedure has been performed in North America and the most extensive face transplant yet.*

MEETING THE NEWS MEDIA

After the surgery, neither the patient's nor the donor's identity was revealed. Anonymity prevailed for fifty-eight days after the patient was discharged from the hospital, even as she stayed in the Cleveland area for follow-up care.

The hospital was concerned about Culp's transition into public life when she returned home. The news media were keenly interested in who she was and what she looked like, but the idea of Culp being pursued and overwhelmed by reporters eager for her story was not a pleasant prospect. The hospital communication director discussed helping Culp face the news media for her first public appearance. Culp agreed to the hospital's plan: a small news briefing with trusted reporters who would, hopefully, focus on the medical issues and benefits rather than her appearance.

Nearly five months after her surgery, on May 5, 2009, the media were invited to the Cleveland Clinic without the knowledge that they would meet Culp. Sheil and her staff planned the event carefully:

- The briefing began with Culp's surgical team leader, Dr. Siemionow, discussing the significance of the near-total face transplant and how the surgery had restored important bodily functions for Culp, such as breathing through her nose, regaining her sense of smell, and being able to eat solid food.
- Medical team members described the patient's medical trauma; before and after photos of Culp were displayed. While her appearance was not perfect, it had greatly improved. Future surgeries would give her a more natural appearance.
- After the medical team finished its presentation, Culp was escorted into the room and gave a brief statement. She thanked the surgical team and discussed some of her experiences living with severe facial disfigurement. Mostly, she was upbeat and positive—and thankful. Culp said she wanted to help build understanding: "When somebody has a disfigurement and don't look as pretty as you do, don't judge them, because you never know what happened to them. Don't judge people who don't look the same as you do. Because you never know. One day it might be all taken away."
- She did not take questions and was escorted out of the room.
- At that time, the medical team who cared for Culp was available for interviews.
- A media kit included information about Culp's physical progress and restored functions, before- and after-surgery photos, and a five-year photo progression of Culp to show what she would look like after minor cosmetic surgeries were performed.

Shortly after the news briefing, Culp conducted one national broadcast news interview with Diane Sawyer of ABC News for ABC's *Good Morning America* and *Nightline*. Finally, ten months after the transplant surgery, Culp and the lead physician of her transplant team, Dr. Siemionow, appeared together on *The Oprah Winfrey Show*.

RESULTS

From the initial IRB announcement in 2004 through 2009, there were at least 1,190 stories written, according to a Lexis search. The communications staff had received more than 5,000 media inquiries. The news coverage was positive for the Cleveland Clinic, adding to its reputation for cutting-edge medical science. It also built support and acceptance for a new controversial procedure. The clinic was portrayed as sensitive to the needs of patients and protective of their privacy. Culp was portrayed as positive, thankful, and caring: she wanted to build understanding for others in similar situations. Her cheerful and positive outlook garnered sympathy and admiration for her, and it helped underscore the need for her face transplant procedure.

According to Siemionow's book *The Know-How of Face Transplantation*, Sheil noted the media relations success was due to careful preplanning:

> *We were . . . providing reporters with what they needed before they had even asked for it—detailed technical information, graphics, photos, video, and easy access to all of it. In making their jobs easier for them, we helped to ensure that our message was understandable, meaningful, and translatable to the general public. To do that, we provided—among other information—a timeline and background sheet on Ms. Culp's injuries, surgery, complications, medications, and future.*

QUESTIONS FOR DISCUSSION

1. How would you apply the theory of agenda building to this case?
2. How would you apply the concept of "information subsidies" to this case?
3. What were some of the less traditional "information subsidies" provided to the media? How effective were they in communicating the clinic's key messages?
4. How did the French face transplant inform the Cleveland Clinic communications department?
5. What are the ethical issues presented by this case study that had to be considered by the public relations staff at the Cleveland Clinic? Why was the Cleveland Clinic so concerned about these ethical issues?
6. There were three major communication activities in this case study: the IRB announcement; the post-surgical news conference, and the news briefing to introduce Connie Culp, the patient, to the news media. While no social media was used in this case study, what, if any, social media could be used and how?
7. The Cleveland Clinic exercised strict control of information with the news media. Why was this necessary?
8. Cleveland Clinic has a sophisticated corporate communications department. What are the benefits of an in-house public relations and media relations team?

Dig Deeper

Read the research article entitled "Facing the Future: Media Ethics, Bioethics, and the World's First Face Transplant" by Marjorie Kruvand and Bastiaan Vanacker available on the textbook's companion website. What lessons regarding media relations and ethics did this provide to the Cleveland Clinic communications staff? What media ethics issues emerged from this situation?

9

Only in Texas

School District's $60 Million Stadium Attracts Media

It's not every day that a public relations manager is given a giant-sized publicity opportunity. In this case, Allen Independent School District (ISD), just twenty-two miles northeast of Dallas, had a unique chance to showcase itself through a new facility—a huge football stadium. Even with such seemingly great news, this announcement needed to be handled with a smart strategy.

MORE THAN A GAME

Every fall across Texas, the Friday night high school football game is *the* social event of the week. It is estimated that more than 40,000 Texas students—100,000 if you count the non-varsity players—are involved in 600 weekly varsity football games. The intensely charged football environment has united families and communities for generations. Football in Texas starts with Pee Wee leagues and continues with high school, college, and the professional competition. However, most Texans would agree that it's high school football that garners the most hometown enthusiasm.

Some say football inspires a nearly religious fervor in Texas, with legions of fanatical fans and a high level of community support for local high school teams. *Friday Night Lights*, a 2004 film classic about the Odessa, Texas, Permian High School Panthers' pursuit of the 1988 state championship illustrated the intensity of small-town football.

"It's all everybody talks about all the time," said Jordan Shipley, in an ABC report about high school football's importance to Burnet, Texas. "Friday nights the whole town just shuts down and everybody just goes to the football game."

ALLEN—A RAPID GROWTH CITY

Allen, Texas, home to Allen ISD, was once a small farming community; its population ballooned from 2,000 in 1970 to 84,000 in 2010, according to the U.S. Census.

FIGURE 4.13 *The Allen Independent School District's Eagle Stadium during the opening game 2012.*
Allen Independent School District
Courtesy of Allen Independent School District

Officials estimate Allen's population will expand to about 95,000 before the city runs out of room.

Well-to-do commuters took advantage of Allen's relatively close proximity to Dallas, and the growing community has become an upper-middle-class suburb with high-end retail and entertainment businesses. Allen's **median** household income was $100,843 in 2009, compared to the national **median** of $49,000.

To promote and develop Allen's identity as an upscale bedroom community, the city's economic development corporation has cultivated a strong base of business and industrial companies, including data centers attracted by access to large electrical substations and transmission lines. One million square feet of retail space and 500,000 square feet of office space have been created through a public–private partnership with developers.

Beyond business, Allen has worked hard to develop amenities that a wealthier population expects. It has a $52.6 million event center with a 7,500-seat arena that hosts minor league hockey, arena football, indoor soccer, and concerts; plus a wakeboarding park, municipal golf course, a skate park with BMX tracks, and indoor swimming pools. There are plenty of retail stores for shopping, including a factory outlet mall. And there's culture—the Allen Philharmonic and the Civic Ballet.

ALLEN ISD—A HIGH-PERFORMANCE SCHOOL DISTRICT

One of the essential ingredients of successful economic development is a community's school district. High-income parents want the best for their children, and businesses need a stable employee pool to draw from. In this regard, Allen has a good story to tell: one school district with sixteen elementary schools, three middle schools, a freshman center, and a single high school—which looks more like a college campus.

The district prides itself on achievement for every student. *U.S. News and World Report* ranked the 5,700-student high school 99th out of 1,842 schools in the state of Texas, and 1,219th out of 21,776 schools nationwide. Eighty-five percent of Allen students go on to college. At least 70 percent of Allen graduates take either the SAT or ACT, and 40 percent or more scored at or above the criterion recommended by the Texas Education Agency (SAT 1110; ACT Composite 24). The Allen ISD's 2010 average SAT score of 1,080 beat the state average by 95 points. Fifteen percent of eleventh and twelfth graders took at least one advanced placement (AP) or international baccalaureate (IB) examination, and 50 percent of eleventh and twelfth grade students scored at or above the criterion on at least one examination (three and above for AP; four and above for IB). In 2011, eleven Allen High School seniors were named 2011 National Merit Scholarship Competition finalists. Four Allen seniors were National Merit Scholarship Award winners, while two others won corporate-sponsored National Merit Scholarship Awards. An Allen middle-school robotics team won second place overall in 2011 at the Texas BEST Competition hosted at the University of North Texas in Denton.

FIGURE 4.14 *The Allen Independent School District's Eagle Stadium during the state championship 2012; the Eagles won.*
Allen Independent School District
Courtesy of Allen Independent School District

STATE BUDGET EDUCATION FUNDING

In 2011 the Texas legislature cut $5.4 billion from 2012 public school funding statewide to help close a $4.3 billion budget gap and to offset future federal funding cuts to the military and Medicaid. School officials argued that rising state testing requirements and continued enrollment growth required more funding, not less; Texas was averaging roughly 80,000 new students annually. The 2012 budget year was the first time state funding had not increased in more than sixty years.

In 2012, nearly 600 of the state's 1,024 school districts sued the state in multiple lawsuits, claiming that the school finance system failed to adequately and equitably pay for public education in Texas. Governor Rick Perry refused to reinstate educational funding in 2011, saying that schools needed to better manage their resources.

Thanks to soaring oil and gas production, by August 2012 Texas ended its budget year with a $3.7 billion surplus; tax revenue estimates for the 2012–2013 budget year were also looking favorable. The fiscally conservative governor, however, called it a "rainy day" fund and asked local governments and schools to live within their means.

ALLEN ISD—BUDGET

With less state aid, Allen's school board approved a 2011–2012 budget of $132.7 million, $4.5 million less than the previous year.

The legislature's education aid cuts meant Allen ISD was projected to lose $18–23 million in state and federal aid over the two-year 2011–2013 budget cycle.

For most school districts, the annual operating budget is labor intensive with approximately 80 percent going toward salary and benefits. Managing the large reduction in state and federal funds for 2011–2012, Allen ISD's Board of Trustees froze all salaries and benefits for the year. In the past, raises and benefit adjustments had ranged from $2 million to $4 million, according to the district's budget publication. While student enrollment grew 13.6 percent from 2007 to 2011, the total staff grew by 7.6 percent; teaching staff grew by 8.1 percent.

To cut costs, the district reduced eighty-four positions through attrition in 2011–2012, saving $3 million, and made an additional $1.5 million in cuts to non-instructional areas such as administration, maintenance, and energy expenses. State law required classroom staffing for kindergarten through grade four with a 22:1 ratio of students to teacher. The district staffed the 2011–2012 year at 24:1 for K-4 with a waiver from the Texas Education Agency. At the secondary level, and grades five through six at the elementary level, the district attempted to maintain a ratio of 28:1, but some classes exceeded that goal. The reduction in teaching positions increased class sizes in all grades in the district.

Cuts to the Allen ISD were $9 million for 2011–2012. An additional $3 million was cut in 2012–2013, according to officials.

The board asked voters to raise the maintenance and operations tax rate to $1.17 per $100 of property value from $1.04, according to *The Bond Buyer*; the increase would raise $10 million, which would help balance the budget and hire additional teachers to meet student growth over the next two years. The debt service tax rate remained at 50 cents per $100 of assessed value, the same rate since 2009, according to *The Bond Buyer.*

School districts have two separate budgets—one for operational expenses and day-to-day functions: salaries, benefits, and supplies, and another for capital expenses to fund new buildings, renovate existing buildings, perform technology upgrades, and purchase new buses. In Texas and many other states, communities vote annually on school district operating budgets while capital project budgets are brought before voters in a separate vote when needed. Most capital projects involve long-term borrowing through the issuance of bonds. By law, districts cannot use money in capital budgets for operating expenses, such as teacher salaries.

In just two years, Allen residents approved $338 million in capital projects. In 2008, residents approved a $219 million bond project to construct two new elementary schools, renovate and expand existing school facilities, upgrade security and technology, and purchase more buses. The construction of one of the approved new elementary schools was delayed a year because the district did not have the operational funds to run and maintain it.

In 2009, the district also approved $119 million for a new performing arts center ($23.3 million), a combined district transportation and student nutrition service center ($36.5 million), and a multipurpose stadium ($59.6 million). The $119 million bond project passed with a solid 63 percent positive vote.

When the school board opened the floor for public comment in 2012 on the proposed budget adoption that included teacher and staff cuts, there were no

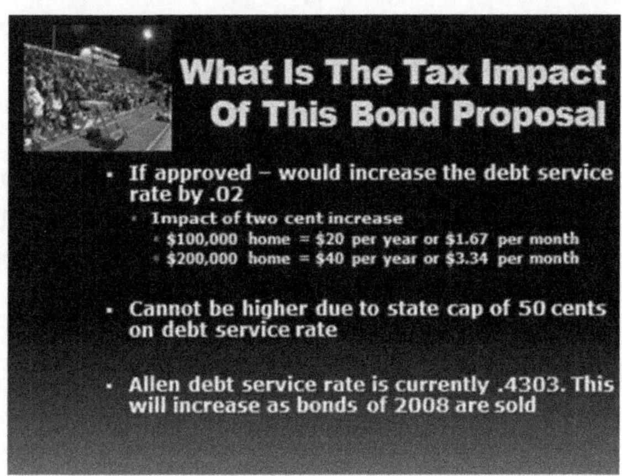

FIGURE 4.15 *The Allen Independent School District used community presentations with PowerPoints as well as printed materials such as newsletters to explain the ramifications the stadium and arts center capital project would have on residents.*
Allen Independent School District
Courtesy of Allen Independent School Distric

comments. The only negative community response came from some residents upset with the proposed district transportation and student nutrition service center location. They were afraid the congestion, pollution, and noise from hundreds of school buses might lower their property values. A small group created a website called StopTheBarn.org to protest the "bus barn" and what members described as a waste of public funds used to build it. There were no complaints from families with children, according to the district.

ALLEN'S HIGH SCHOOL FOOTBALL STADIUM

Planning for a new stadium began in 1995, but new school construction was a higher priority for the fast-growing district. By 2012, the district's double-digit enrollment growth over the past decade had begun to decline to a more manageable level of 7 or 8 percent per year. The 2008 and 2009 bond issues would be the last major construction projects needed by the district.

The old stadium, built in 1976, was by 2009 considered substandard in every way. The need for a new facility was highlighted when the Allen Eagles won their first state championship in 2008. Even visiting team coaches supported the construction of a new facility, since their players had to dress in the school gymnasium and play on faded turf. The press box was compared to a "gutted-out mobile home."

But the real outcry came from Allen's own citizens, who were tired of being shuttled to the home game from distant parking areas, sitting on rented temporary bleachers, and using portable toilets for the overflow crowds; the old stadium had only 7,000 permanent seats and one set of bathrooms. Of course, attendees who found substandard conditions were lucky; many families were shut out of games completely due to lack of seats. The year before the new stadium opened, 400 families competed in a lottery for seventy tickets. Rented bleachers cost the district $250,000 annually. Allen residents expected better for their community and for their students.

Many out-of-staters and even some Texans questioned the $60 million price tag for a sports facility at a time when education budgets were being slashed. "What do I say to that?" Allen's district athletic director Steve Williams responded to a *Fox Sports Southwest* reporter's question. "I say we're in a community that overwhelmingly voted to build this stadium."

The stadium was considered a student-centered project since thousands of students are involved each year, either directly in football, marching band, cheerleading, color guard and drill team, or as spectators. The varsity football team has around one hundred players, with another one hundred on two junior varsity teams, and 256 intending to play freshman football. The marching band is the largest such high school ensemble in the nation, with about 800 members. The stadium could also be used for concerts and Allen High graduation, weather permitting.

While the stadium is grand in every way, it's affordable entertainment for everyone for the season's six home varsity games. Adult tickets are $6, students' are $4.

FIGURE 4.16 *The Allen Independent School District made good use of its district Facebook page by providing updates on the construction.*
http://www.facebook.com/allenisd
Courtesy of Allen Independent School District

FIGURE 4.17 *The district used its Facebook page to continue the good vibes from its inaugural game August 31, 2012. It posted more than forty photos from the game.*
http://www.facebook.com/allenisd
Courtesy of Allen Independent School District

FIGURE 4.18 *The school district provided frequent updates on the stadium construction. Here's one from September 2, 2011.*
https://www.facebook.com/allenisd
Courtesy of Allen Independent School District

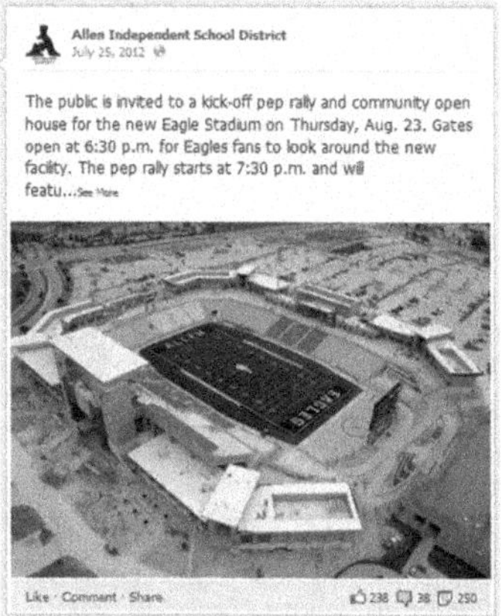

FIGURE 4.19 *The District's Facebook page began promoting its Pep Rally July 25, 2012, for its new stadium a month prior to its opening.*
https://www.facebook.com/allenisd
Courtesy of Allen Independent School District

Tickets at the gate are $8 for general admission and $10 for visitor reserved. During its first game, 22,000 people brought in $126,000 in ticket sales and $76,000 in concession sales, said Allen's public relations manager Tim Carroll.

Carroll said the stadium generates its own revenue to cover operating expenses, although it will never be able to recoup the building expenses. The stadium had sold eight of its ten founding sponsors when it opened. The main sponsors will generate $105,000 annually. Another four minor sponsors will generate $15,000 annually.

Anthony Gibson, Allen's fine arts director, summed up the feelings of many when he told *The New York Times*, "There's an energy you can't describe. When they say football is like religion in Texas, it's true. From little kids all the way to the Super Bowl, we do football right."

The nearly $60 million stadium included the following features:

- A seat capacity of 18,000 with concrete seats; 5,000 reserved seats with seatbacks
- Artificial turf, the same as carpets the Dallas Cowboys Stadium
- A sunken bowl collegiate design
- A scoreboard video display in HD and LEDs
- A two-tiered press box
- 1,500 parking spots
- Full-service concession stands at all four corners
- Restrooms throughout the complex
- A Wall of Honor plaza
- Concrete seating instead of all-aluminum benches
- A customized weight room
- A workout room and coaches' offices for the wrestling team
- Indoor hitting areas for golf teams.

NOT THE BIGGEST

With the stadium's substantial (and much-publicized) price tag during an era of cutbacks and austerity in most parts of the nation, Allen ISD's officials needed to put things into perspective for those unfamiliar with Texas football culture.

Allen's new facility was not the biggest high school football stadium in Texas. In fact, it was only the fourth-largest, tying with Buccaneer Stadium in Corpus Christi. The bragging rights for the largest Texas stadium went to Alamo Stadium in San Antonio with a seating capacity of 23,000. There are ten stadiums in Texas with seating capacities of 16,500 or more, according to TexasBob.com, a website dedicated to keeping track of about 1,200 high school sports stadiums in Texas. The website estimates that 40 percent of all football stadiums in Texas have artificial turf.

Other stadium amenities, such as electronic scoreboards, have become much sought-after items for bigger and better bragging rights. For its season opener in 2012, Carthage High School, in Carthage, Texas, unveiled a new 1,200-square-foot video scoreboard with instant replay, color and animated graphics, player photos with stats—and a $750,000 price tag. The giant display screen was approved by 70 percent of local voters who were proud of their three-time state champions.

MEDIA COVERAGE

Allen ISD's Director of Public Information and Community Services Tim Carroll received inquiries from many national and international news outlets, including the *Dallas Morning News, The New York Times,* The Associated Press, *NBC Nightly News, CBS News, ABC World News* and ABC's *Good Morning America,* Britain's Sky News network, and London's Mail Online. Carroll told *USA Today*: "We still get a lot of that Texas stereotype stuff: Everything is bigger in Texas, and people in Texas will do anything to outdo each other," Carroll said. "[Dallas Cowboys owner] Jerry Jones didn't do us any favors by building the mother of all football stadiums."

Carroll, who was also president of the Texas School Public Relations Association when the stadium opened, had thirty-two years in school public relations including nearly eighteen years at Allen. He was accredited by the Public Relations Society of America and handled all internal and external public relations for the school district.

PARENT AND STUDENT COMMUNICATION

Allen ISD continually updated parents and students on the progress of the stadium construction through a variety of channels including its parent newsletters, student newspaper, the district's Facebook page, and its district athletic department website.

STATE CHAMPS

Allen had more to celebrate than just a new stadium. Its football team brought home the Class 5A Division I state title after beating Lamar from Houston, Texas, 35–21 in front of over 48,000 fans at the Cowboys Stadium.

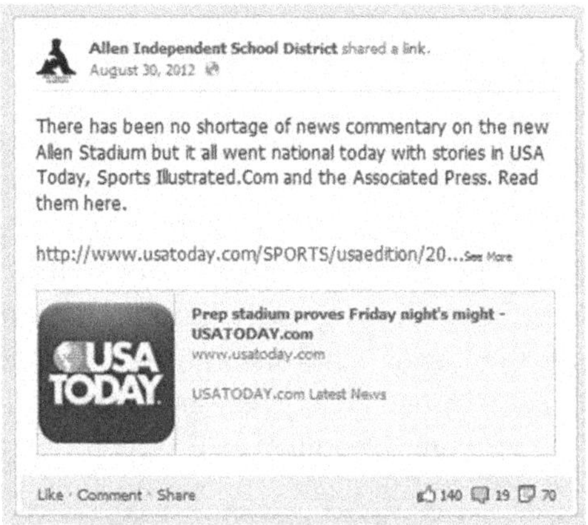

FIGURE 4.20 *The national news coverage included The New York Times, USA Today, Sports Illustrated, and many others. The district alerted residents to the national growing interest in their stadium on its district Facebook page.*
https://www.facebook.com/allenisd
Courtesy of Allen Independent School District

QUESTIONS FOR DISCUSSION

1. Review the Allen ISD's 2009 bond proposal presentation (on the textbook's companion website) and describe the strong and the weak aspects of the presentation.
2. What were the positive aspects of this stadium project for the school district?
3. What were the potential negative aspects of the stadium project?
4. What were the key messages developed for this publicity campaign?
5. How would you prepare for the initial announcement of this stadium project? What tactics would be involved?
6. In this publicity campaign, the district superintendent did not play a major role as spokesperson. Most media requests were answered by the district's athletic director and the public information officer. How would you prepare the athletic director for the media coverage?
7. Social media did not play a major role in this publicity campaign; however, the district did have a significant Facebook presence. Examine the district's Facebook page during the time the stadium opened. What would you recommend regarding its Facebook page and other social media tactics?

Dig Deeper

For background information, review Allen ISD's 2011–2012 budget book. Review Allen ISD's public information materials for its stadium (and other projects) bond issue available on the textbook's companion website. What limitations do taxpayer-supported school districts have when communicating information for public votes? What persuasive arguments did the district make to engineer consent for the stadium bond vote?

10

Two Employees with a Video Camera

Social Media and a Damaged Global Domino's Brand

One of the steps of crisis planning is to imagine "worst-case scenarios" that could occur, and develop appropriate responses ahead of time. It's not a perfect strategy, but practitioners can have basic responses ready to modify at a moment's notice to contain or minimize a difficult situation as quickly as possible.

Sometimes, however, a response tactic or strategy can occur on the spot.

This case study on Domino's Pizza has taken on historical significance in the public relations world. It examines one of the first social media-only responses by an American-owned international corporation during a crisis. It occurred in 2009 when YouTube was four years old and many corporations had not developed social media platforms. In this case, Domino's Pizza was just weeks from launching its own Facebook and Twitter platforms when two rogue employees decided to pull a prank with a YouTube video that went viral.

DOMINO'S PIZZA

Domino's Pizza originated in 1960 when two brothers borrowed $900 and purchased a pizza store in Ypsilanti, Michigan, according to Domino's history. In 2004 Domino's went from a private to a publicly traded company on the New York Stock Exchange, with the ticker symbol "DPZ." Its mission is: "Exceptional franchisees and team members on a mission to be the best pizza delivery company in the world."

The U.S. pizza market is a $32.4 billion business with chain and mom-and-pop operations. Domino's domestically has focused its efforts on the delivery market. In 2011, it had a 94 percent on time delivery performance.

Domino's uses a master franchise model in which individuals can purchase the right to operate a Domino's Pizza store. The corporation provides the food and supplies, equipment, marketing, technology, legal and other administrative services to maintain quality consistency and efficiencies between stores. Domino's has sixteen regional dough manufacturing and supply chain centers, one thin-crust manufacturing center, a vegetable processing center, and an equipment center in the United States to ensure food consistency.

According to its financial profile, in 2011 it was serving more than one million customers a day as a global corporation with more than 10,000 stores. More than 400 million pizzas were consumed with global retail sales of over $6.9 billion in 2011, $3.4 billion of it in the U.S.

TWO EMPLOYEES' PRANK GOES VIRAL

For a pizza company like Domino's, there are a number of negative scenarios to prepare for, including "total product failure"—a disaster category that includes serving tainted or harmful food.

On Easter Sunday, April 12, 2009, two Domino's employees, Kristy Hammonds and Michael Setzer, videotaped a series of gross-out antics at work, such as topping food orders with cheese one of them had shoved up his nose. Hammonds narrated:

> *In about five minutes these will be sent out and somebody will be eating these—yes, eating these. And little do they know that the cheese was in his nose and that there was some lethal gas that ended up on their salami. Now that's how we roll at Domino's.*

Another video contained even viler footage. Setzer was shown wiping his backside with a sponge, which he then used to wash a dish. Yuck.

The videos were posted the next day, Monday, April 13, 2009. It took just a few days for this worst-case scenario to go from a few online videos to a national media sensation. On Monday, five short videos were uploaded to the popular video-sharing site YouTube; people began to view them and pass them along. Within hours, The Consumerist, an online resource for consumer-driven advice and a subsidiary of *Consumer Reports* magazine, and an activist website called Good as You, displayed them on their sites as well, accompanied by outraged comments. According to one report, the founder of Good as You e-mailed Domino's Pizza vice president of corporate communications Tim McIntyre about the video thirty minutes before Domino's social media team knew about it.

By 10 p.m., Monday, April 13, 2009, the whole thing was playing out on the Consumerist website, with a growing discussion thread displaying the posts of those who had simply seen the videos and wanted to comment on them, along with posts by more active Internet users—who wanted to get to the bottom of the situation:

- A reader of the Consumerist e-mailed McIntyre. Domino's then attempted to remove the videos from YouTube but first needed the written permission

FIGURE 4.21 *Readers of* The Consumerist, *a publication of Consumer Reports, helped Domino's track down the two employees with digital sleuthing techniques.*
http://consumerist.com/
Consumerist.com

of the person who had uploaded them, the copyright owner—Hammonds. (They would not be removed until Wednesday night.)

- Three especially capable cyber-sleuths, Amy Wilson, her boyfriend Jonathan Drake, and Paris Miller, managed to figure out in about two hours which Domino's location had become the setting for a viral video (it was Conover, North Carolina). They used the YouTube videos' user name, a glimpse through a window of a Jack in the Box in the video, and some cyber-tracking using Google maps. Then they alerted the *Hickory Daily Record* and WBTV television near Conover.
- Another alert Internet user tracked down McIntyre's e-mail address to let him know about the videos and the Domino's store location by 11 p.m. Fortunately, McIntyre was in the habit of checking his e-mail after work hours and immediately went into action.
- And in his post, another visitor to the site wrote that he had telephoned the Domino's store manager and asked if she knew "christi and michael [the two employees] . . . and what they'd done?"

The Consumerist's discussion thread also displayed McIntyre's grateful e-mail responses to those who had helped.

DOMINO'S RESPONSE

The morning after the discovery, Tuesday, April 14, McIntyre focused his initial efforts on verifying the details of the video with the franchise owner, according to an interview in the *Public Relations Strategist*. This included finding out if the contaminated food had been served to customers (it had not) and contacting the police and the health departments.

Still images from the videos of the two employees were sent to all franchise owners looking for the two employees.

Domino's quickly determined that the food had not been delivered or eaten by customers because no sandwich orders had been made at the time. All orders are networked on Domino's PULSE point-of-sale system, a national computerized management information system that streams all store data into a central processing center for real-time management analysis, planning, and communication. McIntyre said the store manager checked the customer orders with the food that Hammonds and Setzer prepared on the video at the approximate time and determined that they were not real customer orders. This data system also allowed the communication department to share updates in real time to store managers.

Throughout the day, the Domino's communication team provided briefings to its leadership team and posted updates to the Consumerist discussion thread. McIntyre shared an apologetic e-mail from Hammonds; the videos weren't "real," and the whole thing was intended to be a joke:

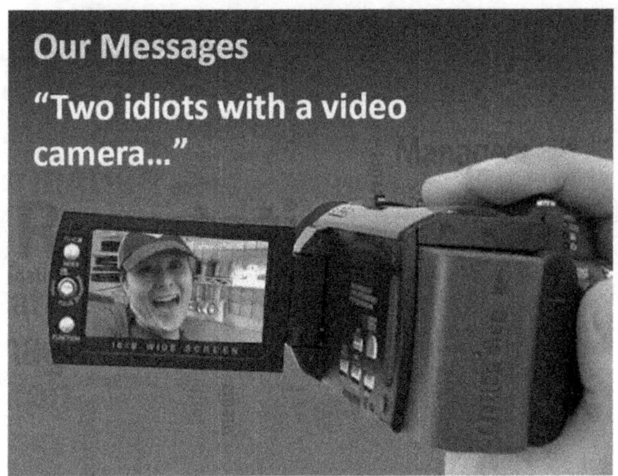

FIGURE 4.22 *Domino's Pizza developed three key messages during the crisis including that the rogue employees were "Two idiots with a video camera," "They don't represent the rest of us," and "Nothing is more sacred than your trust."*
Domino's Pizza
Courtsey of Domino's Pizza

> *I am sorry about all of this! It was all a prank and me nor Michael expected to have this much attention from the videos that were uploaded! No food was ever sent out to any customer. We would never put something like that on you tube if it were real!! It was fake and I wish that everyone knew that!!!! Michael never would do that to any customer, EVER!! I AM SOO SORRY! You see all the time of the pranks that people upload and the pranks need to seem real in order to get a laugh out of people but this prank was very very immature and I am sorry for the embarrassment that I have caused your company!*

By the end of Tuesday, more than 250,000 people had viewed the videos on the Consumerist, Good As You, and other sites. Many of those who posted comments wrote that they would never eat at a Domino's again. While Hammonds denied that the food had been served to customers, one of the videos seemed to indicate otherwise: it showed a store monitor with customer orders on it, and Hammonds said the food was going to customers. There were no indications in the videos that the food had been destroyed or that the food had been eaten by customers.

Posts on Twitter were being monitored by Domino's social media team. According to *Public Relations Strategist*, McIntyre said:

> *The initial chatter was, "Oh, my gosh. Look at this horrible thing." We started communicating on Twitter, saying, "Yeah, we know. Domino's has found them. It's a hoax." But most of the chatter on Twitter was less about the actual video and more about "Does Domino's know this?" "What is Domino's doing about it?" "How come they're not talking to anybody?" Well, we were talking to the people who were in the core audience from the beginning.*

Domino's activated a temporary Twitter account, @dpzinfo, on April 15, 2009, to respond to customers about the incident. An example of a tweet by Domino's corporate social media person said: "To all that have messaged, RT'd or given a vote of confidence: THANK YOU! It's been a heck of a day, but we're glad to be out here with you."

On Wednesday, April 15, the offending videos were gone from YouTube, but were still available on other websites—and they began to spread. A spark had lit a fire that would soon become a firestorm. Another McIntyre e-mail was posted on the Consumerist website saying that Domino's chief of security had spoken to the franchise owner "who was dumfounded . . . The challenge that comes with the freedom of the internet," McIntyre wrote, "is that any idiot with a camera and an internet link can do stuff like this."

This crisis unfolded the week after Easter when many of Domino's top executives were on vacations with their families. Domino's president, Patrick Doyle, was vacationing in Florida with his family when the videos went viral. He had been in contact regularly with McIntyre and others as the situation developed and decided to return Wednesday, April 15, two days after the videos' YouTube appearance. McIntyre said that at the time there were 350,000 views on YouTube. The question was

FIGURE 4.23 *Patrick Doyle, CEO of Domino's Pizza, developed a YouTube video statement to respond to the viral videos from the rogue employees. No news release was issued.*
Domino's Pizza
Courtesy of Domino's Pizza

whether to respond with a traditional news conference, news release, or statement, or a combination of all three.

McIntyre was against a large-scale response since the videos had not reached a large national audience. "I could have reached every news editor with a press of the button for about $1,000 with PR Newswire—and everyone would know," McIntyre said. But, "did we need to put out a candle with a hose?" Someone then suggested, "Let's address this with people who have already seen the videos," said McIntyre. Domino's would develop its own YouTube video response using the same search terms and tags. The idea seemed appropriate to the situation and Doyle, who had just gotten off the plane, agreed to do it.

Doyle sat down with McIntyre and developed about five talking points for a statement. Less than an hour after Doyle had arrived, McIntyre's staff was setting up an office video camera with no special lighting at Domino's headquarters and created some cue cards for the taping. After just one take, the video was reviewed and uploaded to YouTube by that evening, April 15, 2009. "We were nervous because no one had ever done this before," McIntyre said. Doyle's statement said:

> *Hello, I'm Patrick Doyle, President of Domino's USA. Recently we discovered a video of two Domino's team members who thought their acts would be a funny YouTube*

> *hoax. We sincerely apologize for this incident. We thank members of the online community who quickly alerted us and allowed us to take immediate action. Although the individuals in question claim it's a hoax, we are taking this incredibly seriously. This was an isolated incident in Conover, N.C. The two team members have been dismissed and there are felony warrants out for their arrest. The store has been shut down and sanitized from top to bottom. There is nothing more important or sacred to us than our customers' trust. We are re-examining all of our hiring practices to make sure that people like this don't make it into our stores. We have across the country auditors in our stores every day of the week making sure that our stores are as clean as they can possibly be and that we are delivering high quality food to our customers—day in and day out. The independent owner of that store is reeling from the damage that this has caused and it's not a surprise that this has caused a lot of damage to our brand. It sickens me that the actions of two individuals could impact our great system where 125,000 men and women work for local business owners around the U.S. and more than sixty countries around the world. We take tremendous pride in crafting delicious food that they deliver to you every day. There are so many people who have come forward with messages of support for us and we want to thank you for hanging in there with us as we work to regain your trust. Thank you.*

McIntyre said the point of the video statement was that "We are the victims and we still apologized"—in other words, Domino's was victimized but it was taking charge of the problem and fixing it. A short time later, Domino's posted a statement on its corporate website that said how the two employees had dishonored "the hard work performed by 125,000 men and women working for Domino's."

> *In the last 24 hours, videos of two of Domino's Pizza employees appearing inappropriately within one of our franchise restaurants have been circulating online.*
>
> *Since the videos first surfaced yesterday, the two workers have been identified, fired and the affected franchisee has filed a criminal complaint against them, and there are warrants for their arrest.*
>
> *The opportunities and freedom of the internet is wonderful. But it also comes with the risk of anyone with a camera and an internet link to cause a lot of damage, as in this case, where a couple of individuals suddenly overshadow the hard work performed by the 125,000 men and women working for Domino's across the nation and in sixty countries around the world.*
>
> *We apologize for the actions of these individuals, and thank you for your continued support of Domino's Pizza.*

No news release was sent or news conference was held. McIntyre told *AdAge* that Domino's decided on a strategy of direct response to the YouTube platform because it wanted to talk directly to the YouTube audience. He stressed that Domino's did not communicate aggressively on multiple platforms, saying, "the company can deal with tens of thousands of impressions [on YouTube], but a strong response from Domino's would alert more consumers to the embarrassment."

McIntyre said that many employees at Domino's headquarters asked to help answer a flood of incoming phone calls and e-mails from concerned customers. McIntyre's team put together some talking points and provided customer training. The talking points were also shared by the company's computerized management information system so that managers and delivery people could answer questions about the situation. The talking points included:

- It's an isolated event that happened in North Carolina.
- The two employees don't represent who we are.
- We don't tolerate this sort of behavior.

McIntyre said that drivers and managers were given permission to say in their own words how they felt personally about the situation. "We basically gave them permission to be angry."

THE FALLOUT

But by late Wednesday, April 15, 2009, the two employees' video had been viewed by nearly one million people. Domino's corporate video had 66,000 views. This strategy of containment was quickly dashed. "Domino's" as a search term had exceeded the wildly popular celebrity Paris Hilton.

That night, The Associated Press carried its first story, saying the two employees had been fired, criminal charges had been filed, and the franchise had been closed for sanitation. This alerted all traditional media outlets and many newspapers printed the wire story.

The next day, Thursday, April 16, the major television networks and news media, such as *The New York Times*, BBC News, and NBC's *Today Show* had stories. The *Times* reported that a research firm that conducts daily consumer surveys on various brands had seen Domino's quality perception among consumers go from "positive to negative" in just a couple of days. References to the video dominated the first page of Google search for the term "Domino's."

While it's estimated that millions saw the videos in broadcast news stories and online, the crisis was of short duration—basically four days. Once the apology was made, the miscreants arrested and the restaurant sanitized, there really wasn't much more to talk about.

Much of the media coverage focused on how companies needed to react in order to protect their brands on the Internet, especially with the emerging social media tools.

Fortunately, Domino's wasn't the only YouTube video sensation attracting attention; the amateur singing sensation Susan Boyle's performance video was taking the Internet by storm, and other "real" news was on its way, including a threatened swine flu outbreak.

Still, plenty of bloggers shared their opinions on Domino's situation, both as it was unfolding and later. Most liked the fact that Domino's top executive had responded to the crisis within forty-eight hours, although sooner would have been better. At the time, no CEO had ever before delivered a crisis response statement on YouTube. Some pundits complained that Doyle should have responded sooner, and some had suggestions for his video. He did not look directly into the camera, they said, which gave the impression that he was reading a script, and he should have used his own words to show he was upset and determined to make things right for his customers.

Others noted that Domino's strategy of targeted response on YouTube and its e-mails to the Consumerist's discussion thread did not go far enough. Domino's, they argued, should have had a Twitter account actively responding to people's concerns from the start. They noted that the company's Facebook and MySpace web pages were not part of a coordinated response. Domino's did not have a strong search profile on the Internet, and search engine optimization (SEO) and online reputation management (ORM) strategies were lacking.

In keeping with a more traditional crisis response strategy, Domino's spokesperson McIntyre was available for media interviews to provide a continuous source of information from Domino's about its response to the situation.

OTHER CASES

At the time, social media were still relatively new to businesses in 2009. Most companies were trying to figure out how to incorporate social media platforms such as Twitter and Facebook into their business and marketing plans. Still, there were examples of similar crises to show practitioners the way. In 2004, for example, the famous bike lock maker Kryptonite had a similar situation—total product failure, first demonstrated by a viral Internet video and eventually reported by the mainstream media, causing brand damage. The year before the Domino's debacle, Burger King learned about the power of YouTube when one of its employees decided to take a bath in the kitchen sink and posted the video. And JetBlue took a major reputational hit in 2007 when passengers were stranded on the tarmac for nearly eleven hours. Angry passengers used social media to make sure that everyone knew about the terrible conditions endured—no water, overflowing toilets, no information, and no option to deplane.

In just a few years, companies found their crisis response strategies outdated and in need of rebooting for the Internet age. Now, when an embarrassment can become a crisis in a matter of minutes, public relations practitioners have to be ready to respond in the social media universe.

AFTERMATH

Both Hammonds and Setzer were charged and arrested with adulterating food, according to the *Hickory Daily Record*. Hammonds pleaded guilty to a lesser charge and received a suspended sentence, probation, and community service. Setzer took an Alford plea in which he admitted no wrongdoing but received a suspended sentence and supervised probation.

Domino's Pizza celebrated its fiftieth anniversary in 2010—the year it reinvented its pizza recipe—and now offers a variety of Italian dishes including artisan-style pizzas. It removed the word "Pizza" from its name to better represent its full menu including non-pizza products.

QUESTIONS FOR DISCUSSION

1. What are the reputational issues posed by this type of crisis?
2. How could Domino's have prepared for this incident? Would media monitoring have helped? Why or why not?
3. Tim McIntyre, Domino's vice president of corporate communications, later told *The New York Times:* "What we missed was the perpetual mushroom effect of viral sensations." How could this situation be mitigated?
4. Why are openness and dialogue important for a business website and social media platforms?
5. Domino's mentioned its auditing system in which auditors visit stores to check for cleanliness. How does this relate to the incident?
6. Domino's used the term "hoax" to describe the incident by the two employees. Did Domino's communicate strongly enough that the tainted food was not served?
7. Many companies have taken control of their online reputation and have created their own "online search profile." If Domino's had optimized ten of its own positive videos on YouTube, what would have been the effect on searches?
8. One critic said that Domino's should have asked employees to create and post their own videos and optimized them to occupy the top spots for video searches under "dominos." What effect would this have had on employees' morale?

Dig Deeper

The response video by Domino's Pizza CEO Patrick Doyle is available on the textbook's companion website. Domino's Pizza is a publicly traded company that must answer to its shareholders. Examine the Domino's Pizza 2012 Investor Presentation available on the textbook's companion website. What is its "investment thesis"? How does this company provide shareholder value?

Using Domino's Pizza's annual report, available on the textbook's companion website, what are its competitive strengths, particularly with its brand image? Summarize its business strategy. What was its marketing operations brand message? What else does the annual report provide that is useful for a public relations professional?

CHAPTER 5

Conflict Management

Conflict represents a recognizable and significant disagreement of ideas or interests between two or more parties. The severity of a conflict can range from minor problems to full-scale wars. Much has been said about crisis communications over the years, but less has been said about the other phases of conflict management. Dennis Wilcox, author of *Public Relations: Strategies and Tactics*, described the conflict management life cycle that starts with the proactive phase, and continues with the strategic, the reactive, and the recovery phases:

- The proactive phase includes environmental scanning, issues tracking, issues management, and the crisis plan.
- The strategic phase includes risk communication and conflict positioning while adapting the crisis plan.
- The reactive phase includes crisis communication, conflict resolution, and litigation public relations.
- The recovery phase includes reputation management and image restoration strategies.

PROACTIVE PHASE: LOOKING FOR RISKS AND MANAGING ISSUES

Most crises are not unforeseen "acts of God," such as tsunamis, earthquakes, or tornadoes. If fact, hindsight shows that most crises simmered for months—even years—before boiling over onto the front page.

Crises such as WalMart and bribes in Mexico, the BBC's child sex-abuse failures, CIA Director David Petraeus' affair with his biographer, and J.P. Morgan's $7 billion trading mishap involved either improper business dealings, lapses in personal integrity, or outright illegal activity. While much of Hurricane Katrina's devastation of New Orleans and the Gulf Coast could not have been prevented, better planning and coordination of emergency services would have minimized the disaster.

Public relations research has focused on more than what to do in a crisis. Minimizing an organization's risks, managing issues to prevent a crisis from happening, and image repair strategies have received much-needed attention. There is a great deal of information available on issue management and crisis communication, online and in print. Here is a quick review of some key points to consider.

The first step in preventing a crisis situation is to conduct risk assessment, an internal activity that identifies potential problem areas for an organization. Public relations personnel should be familiar with internal reports and customer relations activity. By learning from others' mistakes, organizations can potentially reduce their own risks. After Katrina struck, for example, other hurricane-prone communities reviewed their risks and vulnerabilities. The public relations office can address identified risks with appropriate risk communication efforts such as safety guidelines, and user warnings for products.

Environmental scanning, an external activity, requires careful, objective scrutiny of an organization's outside environment. This monitoring activity looks for problems faced by the organization, by similar organizations, and even by organizations in other industries. Monitoring can be as simple as reviewing feedback from customers via toll-free telephone call lines, letters, e-mails, or web postings. Practitioners should also read industry reports, trade publications, and other information sources to keep current with industry trends that might reveal potential threats to the organization.

Because organizations can face a variety of problems, public relations has a role in identifying, prioritizing, and managing problems that can become serious issues. Practitioners, along with management, need to decide which problems have the potential for becoming major issues that could escalate into crises if not managed properly.

By asking "what if" questions and thinking "worst-case scenario," organizations can begin to develop a crisis plan that anticipates possible scenarios—from severe crises, such as a product failure, facility destruction, or employee strike, to moderate or minimal crises with appropriate response options for each situation. Each crisis plan should include a crisis management team that taps key individuals responsible for carrying out portions of the plan. Public relations' role is to coordinate and manage the communication activity during the crisis. Other typical team members include the organization's heads of facilities, human resources, technology services, and security.

Plans are worthless if they are shelved and forgotten. A crisis plan should be revisited by an organization on a regular basis and tested and updated through simulations. The crisis team must know its role and be able to react quickly. Hospitals and other emergency response agencies have been leading the way in crisis response simulations. Thorough testing reveals gaps and identifies areas in need of further development.

STRATEGIC PHASE: RISK COMMUNICATION, CONFLICT POSITIONING

When there is time before the crisis hits, practitioners can create messages known as risk communication to alleviate the effects of the impending crisis. For example, when a hurricane is on track to hit a community, messages should be developed to provide information on whether or not to evacuate, where shelters are located, etc. Health messages can be created when a public health threat is found. For example, the government has developed a website called Flu.gov to provide citizens with useful information on prevention, symptoms, and treatment.

Conflict positioning can include a number of strategies including the development of key messages specific to the crisis issue, collecting evidence to bolster the organization's viewpoint regarding the crisis issue, securing credible third-party organizations and experts who can speak out knowledgably on behalf of the organization, preparing the organization's leadership to handle media attention, and, if the crisis is expected to attract large numbers of journalists, preparing a media center.

REACTIVE PHASE: CRISIS RESPONSE STRATEGIES

When proactive strategies such as risk and issues management cannot prevent a crisis from occurring, practitioners can still manage the crisis based on research and best practices. Researchers such as Timothy Coombs have developed helpful typologies to describe organizational responses. They have identified at least seven basic ways an organization can react in times of crisis. The response typology represents a range of strategies, from preemptive action strategies to strategic inaction.

Some researchers view organizational responses as a continuum from defensive to accommodative strategies. Reactive defensive responses include: "prebuttal," attacking the accuser, embarrassment, threat, denial, excuse, justification, and strategic silence. Accommodative responses include: concession, ingratiation, concern, condolence, regret, apology, investigation, corrective action, restitution, and repentance.

Depending on each situation, an organization can try one strategy or move to another. When the public holds an organization responsible for a crisis, defensive strategies often do not improve the organization's image, and accommodative strategies are recommended.

The textbook *Strategic Planning for Public Relations* discusses the variety of reactive responses used by organizations:

- **Preemptive action strategy**
  - **Prebuttal:** An organization tries to be the first one to tell the story and set the tone before other versions of the story are published.
- **Offensive response strategies**
  - **Attack the accuser:** An organization may decide to attack its accuser when its logic or facts are faulty or if the accuser is negligent or malicious.
  - **Embarrassment:** This strategy uses shame or humiliation to lessen the accuser's influence.
  - **Threat:** An organization threatens its accusers with harm from such things as lawsuits or exposure.

- **Defensive response strategies**
  - **Denial:** An organization can deny that a problem exists or that the organization had any role in the crisis.
  - **Excuse:** An organization can minimize its responsibility for the crisis. Any intention to do harm is denied, and the organization says that it had no control over the events that led to the crisis. This strategy is often used when there is a natural disaster or product tampering.
  - **Justification:** Crisis can be minimized with a statement that no serious damage or injuries resulted. Sometimes, the blame is shifted to the victims. This is often done when a consumer misuses a product or when there is an industrial accident.

- **Diversionary response strategies**
  - **Concession:** An organization gives the public something it wants, which is valued by both groups, as a step toward repairing its relationships with its publics.
  - **Ingratiation:** Actions are taken to appease the publics involved. Consumers who complain are given coupons, or the organization makes a donation to a charitable organization.
  - **Disassociation:** This strategy distances the organization from the wrongdoer who has ignored or exploited the company's policies.
  - **Relabeling:** Sometimes, devising a new name for a product, service, or organization is used if the old one has negative connotations.

- **Vocal commiseration strategies**
  - **Concern:** The organization does not admit guilt but does show concern for the situation.
  - **Condolence:** This is a more formal vocal response than the concern response. Condolence recognizes the sorrow of personal loss or misfortune experienced by others, but the organization does not admit guilt.
  - **Regret:** This strategy, according to Ronald Smith, "involves admitting sorrow and remorse for a situation." An organization may or may not accept fault for the situation.
  - **Apology:** The organization takes responsibility and asks forgiveness. Some compensation of money or aid is often included.

- **Rectifying behavior strategies**
  - **Investigation:** This is a short-term strategy to examine the facts that led to the situation. Depending on what is found, an organization can take further action.

- **Corrective action:** Steps are taken to repair the damage from the crisis and to prevent it from happening again.
- **Restitution:** The organization offers to provide publics with ways to compensate victims or restore the situation to its former state.
- **Repentance:** An organization fully accepts responsibility for the situation and offers to change its practices that led to the situation.

- **Strategic inaction**

  - **Silence:** Every so often, an organization may choose to remain silent when it is under siege. This strategy has been used to protect victims' privacy or some other higher cause. Sometimes a short statement explaining why the organization will not respond is helpful. This strategy is not the same as "no comment," which usually implies some wrongdoing by the organization.

ACTIONS TO TAKE DURING A CRISIS

Researchers and experts in crisis communication have many suggestions for what to do in a crisis. *Public Relations Strategies and Tactics* and other books have created basic communication tactics in times of crisis. Following are some of the most important actions related to the communication function.

Put the Public First

An organization should act to immediately minimize or stop any negative effects on the public stemming from the organizational crisis. Sometimes an organization may need to take a drastic step, such as recalling a product from store shelves. While this action may cause immediate economic hardship for the organization, in the long run customers will remember this act and respond favorably.

Take Responsibility

Whether or not the crisis is caused directly by the organization, the organization involved should take a leadership role in resolving it. Fix the problem first—determine the blame later. Such action demonstrates that the organization is more concerned about stopping any negative impact on consumers, the community, or the environment than its own bottom line.

Be Honest but Don't Speculate

Stick to the facts as the situation unfolds. Often, in times of crisis, facts may be few at the onset, but an organization needs to be up front about what it knows. Public relations practitioners frequently work with legal counsel to determine what can be said in times of crisis without incrimination. A simple statement, such as "The cause of the accident is not known but an investigation is underway," is better than "no comment." People tend to view "no comment" statements as an organization's attempt to hide information. Resist the temptation to speculate on a cause or other unknown aspects of the crisis. Constant changing or rephrasing the "facts" makes an organization look disorganized or possibly incompetent.

Be Accessible and Accommodate the Media: Communicate Frequently

In today's competitive 24/7 news environment the news media and their companion websites seek constant updates or new perspectives for their audiences. If an organization does not make itself available to the news media, reporters will go elsewhere for the story—sometimes to the detriment of the organization. If an organization's leadership is not available, for example, the news media may seek out employees as they leave work. If they have not been briefed on the situation, employees may speculate or discuss rumors that can lead to misinformation—or worse. The news media can also go to outside experts who may speculate on the situation. It is far better to participate in the news coverage than ignore it, even when the organization's motives are good and the leadership would rather work full time on resolving the crisis.

From the onset, an organization should come forward with its version of the facts as they are known. Legal counsel often guides the process to ensure that information released to the public is appropriate. Depending on the intensity of the crisis, including situations with ongoing threats to human safety, the organization's top leadership should meet frequently with reporters through news conferences. Its website should include video or transcripts of its news conferences, as well as news releases, and other available background material. Log all media requests and respond immediately to top-tier media, such as national newspapers, television news shows, and the Associated Press, along with the local news media. When possible, respect the news media's deadlines, although companion websites are now making such deadlines largely irrelevant since news can be instantly posted.

Designate a Single Spokesperson/Create Message Points

A crisis requires the active participation of the organization's leadership in solving the problem. To ensure that the perspective of the organization is reflected accurately during a crisis, a single spokesperson can be designated, or specific message points that are used by senior leaders. During major crisis situations, the spokesperson should be the CEO or other high-ranking official. A single spokesperson, trained in media relations, can focus on the organization's positive steps and key messages. Having more than one spokesperson can result in conflicting messages or faulty information unless everyone follows the key messages.

Monitor News Coverage

Since a crisis can make it difficult to find the time to monitor news coverage, this is a task that can be delegated to a news and Internet monitoring service or to a crisis communication firm. Analysis of news coverage can uncover how well an organization's key messages are penetrating the news media so that adjustments can be made during the peak interest period of the crisis. If erroneous information circulates, it is necessary to create a rapid response strategy to correct the errors. This involves directly responding to the information and explaining the inaccuracies with factual, confirmable information.

Communicate with Key Publics

During a crisis, public relations staff are so involved in meeting media requests that key publics are sometimes lost in the shuffle. Direct communication should be considered for investors, employees, retailers, and customers since they are stakeholders and actively seek information. Employees particularly need accurate information during a crisis since this information may play a part in effectively combating the crisis situation. Investors, as part owners of publicly held organizations, will want information about what the organization is doing to address the crisis and protect their investment. For product-related crises, retailers and customers will want specific information on affected products: is the product being recalled, is it safe to use under certain conditions, and so forth. The organization's website can be especially helpful in creating distinct messages for these publics and can be used to interact with individuals through e-mail. Organizations should also consider a toll-free telephone number and a call center to respond to individual inquiries.

Consult Crisis Communication Experts

Crises are often overwhelming situations that require sustained around-the-clock effort to respond to countless media inquiries and key publics within a relatively short period of time. This effort can quickly exhaust staff, and their objectivity can be lost due to stress and internal pressures. Before a crisis strikes, organizations can develop partnerships with public relations firms that have crisis communication experience. This partnership can provide additional staffing, resources, and objective counsel during a crisis. Some businesses offer crisis communication Internet modules that can be remotely created and updated if a public relations practitioner is unable to reach his or her office or the organization's Internet service is disrupted.

RECOVERY PHASE: IMAGE REPAIR AND REPUTATION MANAGEMENT

Once the crisis has died down and the organization is able to devote time to normal business activities, the recovery phase can begin. Image repair strategies actually start during the crisis with reactive strategies such as launching investigations or offering apologies.

After the crisis is the period where actions speak louder than words, and stakeholders will be watching to see if the organization does more than talk. It is important for the organization to keep open communication between its stakeholders regarding the follow-up actions after the crisis. If an investigation is launched, the results of that investigation should be communicated. If a policy is changed or new organizational services are developed, those should be communicated. Some organizations involved in large crises develop webpages devoted to the recovery phase activities. This can also include educational efforts to explain how the organization is responding. It can include testimonials from employees, third-party endorsements, and messages from its key leadership.

The organization may fund activities that contribute new knowledge to the situation that caused the crisis through research grants and scholarships. Sometimes, this includes preserving and displaying artifacts from the event itself.

Depending on the circumstance of the crisis, the organization must still maintain relationships with its stakeholders and manage its brand reputation.

11

"Lean Finely Textured Beef" or "Pink Slime"?

Consumers Ask: "What is this Stuff?"

What's in your hamburger? Consumers found out some unappetizing facts when the news media, a popular cooking chef, and a mommy blogger with a Harvard law degree turned a little-known meat processing method into a consumer controversy that spelled disaster for one company.

QUESTIONS ABOUT FOOD SAFETY

Safety concerns about the U.S. meat supply had been growing for years. In 1993, four children died after eating under-cooked Jack in the Box restaurant hamburgers contaminated with *E. coli*, bacterial contamination that can occur when fecal matter comes into contact with food. "Mad cow disease" (bovine spongiform encephalopathy) made its first U.S. appearance in 2003, leading to new regulations for the beef industry.

Frozen hamburger maker Topps Meat Co. went out of business after recalling 21.7 million pounds of beef contaminated with *E. coli* in 2007—the second largest beef recall in U.S. history. The wave of consumer lawsuits forced it into bankruptcy a few months later. Meat wasn't the only problem. There were major *E. coli* and salmonella outbreaks during the 1990s and 2000s, as onions, fresh spinach, tainted peanut butter, jalapeño and Serrano peppers, and eggs sickened thousands of Americans.

Local and national media offered extensive coverage of the outbreaks, focusing on the often large numbers of people affected by illness and the long period of testing needed to isolate the source of the contamination. The government issued warnings, telling consumers to avoid certain foods, and recalled affected items. Critics called for more government regulations to test food; industry associations generally resisted more regulation, arguing it would hurt the food industry and raise prices.

Riding the wave of growing national consumer concern, the national news media, independent film makers, and authors began to dig deeper into how the food industry worked. *Food Inc.*, a documentary film released in 2008, decried the corporatization of the rural farm; *Fast Food Nation*, a 2001 best-selling book, along with others painted similarly negative portraits of the modern food industry. On October 4, 2009, *The New York Times* published a front-page article entitled "The Burger that Shattered Her Life." The 5,000-word feature, which won a Pulitzer Prize, probed questionable meatpacking industry safety practices, focusing on Stephanie Smith, a 22-year-old woman who ate an undercooked hamburger and nearly died from the *E. coli* contamination. The otherwise healthy dance instructor ended up with severely damaged kidneys and permanent paralysis from the waist down.

The reporter discovered an industry with many safety lapses and secretive practices. For example, some meat grinding/packing companies were not allowed to test shipments of "trimmings" for *E. coli* before they were ground into hamburger derived from multiple sources of varying quality.

Trimmings are low-grade fatty cuts of meat that are either closest to the fat layer under the hide, which can have fecal smears on it, or near the intestinal track, where fecal matter resides naturally. Varying qualities of meat trimmings are used to produce ground beef: hamburger. *The New York Times* article traced the ingredients used to produce Smith's hamburger; 10 percent came from "fine lean textured meat" produced by a company called Beef Products, Inc. (BPI) through a treatment process:

> *it bought meat that averages between 50 percent and 70 percent fat, including "any small pieces of fat derived from the normal breakdown of the beef carcass." It warms the trimmings, removes the fat in a centrifuge and treats the remaining product with ammonia to kill* E. coli.

The *New York Times* article also noted that BPI's "lean finely textured beef" (LFTB) was approved for use in federal school lunch programs. Government inspectors had found and stopped the use of BPI's tainted LFTB in 2006, 2008, and 2009.

In addition to the article on Smith's frightening *E. coli* experience, the *Times* did a follow-up front-page story on BPI entitled "Company's Record on Treatment of Beef is Called into Question" on December 31, 2009. Pointing out that "The federal school lunch program used an estimated 5.5 million pounds of the processed beef" in 2008, the article questioned the safety of BPI's process: "Since 2005, *E. coli* has been found three times and salmonella forty-eight times, including back-to-back incidents in August in which two 27,000-pound batches were found to be contaminated. The meat was caught before reaching lunch-room trays."

BPI's "exemption from routine testing" was revoked by USDA as a result of the *Times* investigation. The *Times* report included USDA's own school lunch division testing results—results that were news to USDA officials.

"Although no food outbreak has been tied to BPI," its officials said they were continually improving their processes "to ensure that they are scientifically sound and protect public health," according to the *Times* article. BPI's founder and owner declined to be interviewed for the article or to allow access to company production facilities. In a response to a written question by the *Times* reporter, an official said, "BPI's track record demonstrates the progress BPI has made compared to the industry norm . . . Like any responsible member of the meat industry, we are not perfect."

The article used the term "pink slime" to describe LFTB. The term was coined by USDA microbiologist Gerald Zirnstein, who said in an e-mail to colleagues: "I do not consider the stuff to be ground beef, and I consider allowing it in ground beef to be a form of fraudulent labeling."

LEAN FINELY TEXTURED BEEF

The manufacturing of LFTB in the United States was largely handled by two businesses—BPI and Cargill. According to a Congressional research report, "a substantial portion—about 25 percent—of a beef carcass is lean beef trimmings." The report also explained the business side of LFTB:

> *Total production of LFTB and FTB [finely textured beef] in the United States has been reported to be about 850 million pounds per year. Another analyst estimates that BPI and Cargill produced about 600 million pounds in 2011, and at the peak of production, around 2009 or 2010, produced 725 million pounds annually. It takes about two to three pounds of 50 percent lean trimmings to make one pound of LFTB, thus adding substantial value to more than 1 to 2 billion pounds of low-valued 50 percent beef trimmings. Some cattle and beef analysts have argued that it would take an additional 1.5 million head of cattle to produce the beef necessary to replace the use of LFTB and FTB.*

BEEF PRODUCTS, INC.

BPI was the brainchild of Eldon Roth, who discovered a new way to process some of the lowest grade meat trimmings safely.

As the *Times* described, fatty trimmings, previously used in the production of dog food and cooking oil, were heated and then centrifuged to separate the meat from the fat. The meat was then treated with a small amount of ammonium hydroxide gas to eliminate bacterial contaminants, and then flash-frozen.

In 2001, BPI's process was approved by the Food and Drug Administration and the U.S. Department of Agriculture; the processed material was added to about 80 percent of the country's hamburger supply. This included most of the major fast-food restaurants including MacDonald's, Burger King and Taco Bell—and school cafeterias.

BPI, headquartered in Dakota Dunes, South Dakota, operated plants in Iowa, Kansas, Texas, and Nebraska. At its peak production, BPI manufactured 500 million pounds of LFTB, according to *Bloomberg BusinessWeek*.

BPI also had a known record for food safety. The International Association for Food Protection presented BPI with its Black Pearl award for advancing food safety and quality in 2007. It was one of the first meat processers to test for the major strain of *E. coli* and for five other strains of *E. coli*. The Agriculture Department's school lunch program had private labs test nearly 7,000 samples of LFTB since January 2010 and found no evidence of *E. coli* or salmonella, according to *The New York Times*.

AMMONIUM HYDROXIDE IS NOT AN INGREDIENT

Critics of LFTB focused on two things: the meat trimmings were low quality and they were treated by a chemical called ammonium hydroxide which was used to kill any harmful bacteria. A Congressional research report said:

> *Ammonium hydroxide is used directly in baked goods, cheese, chocolates, and puddings. In addition, ammonium hydroxide is a processing aid in dairy products, confections, baked goods, breakfast cereals, eggs, fish, sports drinks, beer, and meat. It is used as a leavening agent and pH control agent in food production. The use of ammonium hydroxide is based on its status as an FDA "generally recognized as safe" (GRAS) substance that is used according to current good manufacturing practices.*

Regarding the safety of ammonium hydroxide and why the chemical was not included in labeling of meat products that used LFTB, the same Congressional research report stated:

> *There is no evidence in the available information on . . . ammonium hydroxide . . . that demonstrates, or suggests reasonable grounds to suspect, a hazard to the public when it is used at levels that are now current or might reasonably be expected in the future.*
>
> *Federal regulations require that ingredients used in foods be included on food labels. When USDA approved BPI's use of ammonium hydroxide as an antimicrobial intervention; USDA determined that it was a processing aid and not an ingredient.*

JAMIE OLIVER'S FOOD REVOLUTION

After the 2009 *New York Times* articles, there was little news on BPI until ABC aired a report on "Jamie Oliver's Food Revolution," April 12, 2011. During the show, Oliver brought onto the stage a brown cow covered in white broken lines indicating where various meat portions were located. The leftover trimmings, "the bits that no one wants," and "not fit for human consumption," were then discussed.

In the report, Oliver provided a crude simulation of how LFTB is created. He placed meat trimmings into a consumer dryer to heat the meat fat and separate the meat from the fat and then pulled out a jug of ammonia labeled with a skull and cross bones. He doused the meat trimmings with a water and ammonia solution, admitting he didn't know how much ammonia BPI used, and explained that the water and

FIGURE 5.1 *In ABC television show Jamie Oliver's Food Revolution, the chef took aim at lean finely textured beef claiming it was pink slime. He used household ammonia mixed in with the beef to demonstrate how the beef was sanitized.*
http://www.youtube.com/watch?v=wshlnRWnf30

ammonia solution killed the harmful *E. coli* and salmonella bacteria. He drained the meat and ground it. The result looked like ground hamburger found in a store.

Oliver told an appalled audience of parents and young children:

> *If you have a pile of regular ground meat and you want to stretch it further you're allowed to add up to 15 percent of this product in any patty in any mincemeat. So basically what I'm telling you is that this is a thinner. Can you imagine how happy an accountant is? You just turned dog food into potentially your kid's food. The other thing is the USDA who are employed to protect you people have made it legal to not have to register on any form or labeling the ammonia. They say that it's processed not an ingredient and they publicly say that pink slime is safe to eat.*

There was no formal response from BPI immediately after the show.

THE DAILY IGNITES THE FIRE

While Jamie Oliver's colorful video report got the attention of some consumers and bloggers, not much else happened. Then, on March 5, 2012, The Daily, an independent digital news organization, wrote a piece on the BPI process that featured the perspectives of Zirnstein, the USDA microbiologist who coined the term "pink slime," and former USDA scientist Carl Custer. Both expressed safety concerns about LFTB. The Daily report said that USDA planned to purchase seven million pounds of LFTB for school lunch programs, while fast-food restaurants McDonald's, Burger King and Taco Bell had quietly stopped their use of LFTB by January 2012.

The Daily article caught the attention and ire of Bettina Elias Siegel, a Harvard law graduate with two kids and an interest in school food. She had started a blog called *The Lunch Tray* in 2010 as an outgrowth of her involvement with a Huston school food program and was dismayed to discover that LFTB was still in school food. She had read the *New York Times* articles and was familiar with the "Jamie Oliver's Food Revolution" report. On March 6, 2012, Siegel launched a petition drive on Change.org, asking Agriculture Secretary Tom Vilsack to get rid of LFTB in the federal school lunch program. Within two weeks, her petition had more than 250,000 signatures.

Siegel's petition made her another voice in the debate. Her advocacy for nutrition in schools and her status as a mother made her a source for news reports. Her blog also tracked the growing news attention and voices that were critics of LFTB.

On March 7, 2012, ABC investigative reporter Jim Avila's report on *World News with Diane Sawyer* put the issue squarely on the national agenda:

> *And now, a startling ABC News investigation, a whistle-blower has come forward to tell consumers about the ground beef a lot of us buy at the supermarket. Is it what we think it is? Or is it padded with a filler the whistle-blower calls pink slime?*

The report, titled "70 Percent of Ground Beef at Supermarkets Contains 'Pink Slime,'" told viewers that Zirnstein grinds his own hamburger because he doesn't trust store-bought or restaurant hamburger anymore. "It's economic fraud. It's not fresh ground beef. It's a substitute. It's a cheap substitute being added in," Zirnstein said. Custer, another USDA microbiologist, called LFTB a "salvage product." The report described LFTB as "beef trimmings that were once used only in dog food and cooking oil, but now [are] sprayed with ammonia to make them safe to eat."

The report linked former Under Secretary of Agriculture Joanne Smith, who had ties to the beef industry, as the person responsible for approving LFTB.

More national news outlets started covering the story, including *The Washington Post*, MSNBC, CBS, and The Associated Press. Despite the industry's insistence that LFTB was safe, the term "pink slime" entered the public vocabulary.

Some of ABC's nearly 7.1 million viewers and other news readers reacted by passing on the story link in tweets and Facebook postings. The following night, ABC's *World News* responded to viewer questions on what grocery stores had LFTB-free hamburger. Publix, Costco, HEB, and Whole Foods responded that their hamburger never had LFTB.

FAST-FOOD RESTAURANTS

Prior to the March 7, 2012, ABC report and the flurry of other national news and Internet reports about LFTB, three fast-food restaurants had stopped using LFTB—McDonald's, Burger King, and Taco Bell. Spokespeople for the restaurants did not tie their decision to the news coverage but one newspaper, the *Argus Leader*, reported that Taco Bell had

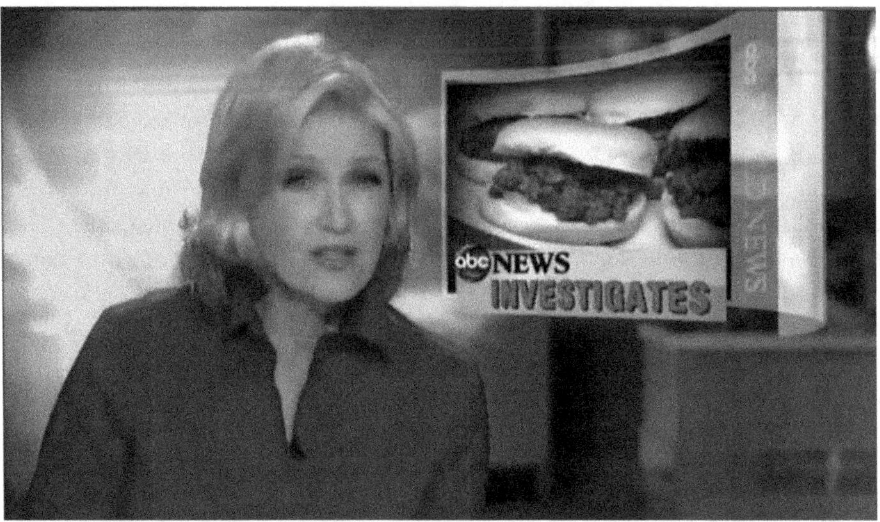

FIGURE 5.2 ABC News *anchor Diane Sawyer introduced the nation to the phrase "pink slime" to describe lean finely textured beef, March 7, 2012. http://abcnews.go.com/blogs/*
ABC

discontinued the use of LFTB sometime after the Jamie Oliver show. Here's McDonald's statement on the issue released during the controversy:

> *Burgers are at the heart of the Golden Arches, and the fact is, McDonald's USA serves 100 percent USDA-inspected beef—no preservatives, no fillers, no extenders—period.*
>
> *For a number of years prior to 2011, to assist with supply, McDonald's USA used some lean beef trimmings treated with ammonia in our burgers. We were among other food retailers who used this safe product.*
>
> *At the beginning of last year, we made a decision to stop using this ingredient. It has been out of the McDonald's USA supply chain since last August. We wanted to be consistent with our global beef supply chain and we're always evolving our practices.*

PRESSURE BUILDS

Animals and children are topics that can elicit strong emotions from people, especially if there is the potential for harm or mistreatment. In this case, parents did not want to think that their children might be eating "pink slime."

On March 15, 2012, citing consumer demand, USDA announced it would allow school districts to choose meat with LFTB or without it. This was a blow to the meat industry, particularly BPI, since many school districts across the country bought meat through USDA programs. The USDA's news release stated:

In response to requests from school districts across the country, the USDA announced today that it will offer more choices to schools in the National School Lunch Program when it comes to purchases of ground beef products.

USDA only purchases products for the school lunch program that are safe, nutritious and affordable—including all products containing Lean Finely Textured Beef. However, due to customer demand, the department will be adjusting procurement specifications for the next school year so schools can have additional options in procuring ground beef products. USDA will provide schools with a choice to order product either with or without Lean Finely Textured Beef.

USDA continues to affirm the safety of Lean Finely Textured Beef product for all consumers and urges customers to consult science based information on the safety and quality of this product. Lean Finely Textured Beef is a meat product derived from a process which separates fatty pieces from beef trimmings to reduce the overall fat content.

The next day, Jamie Oliver launched the bright pink StopPinkSlime.org website, providing links to ABC news coverage, a petition, and a link to tweet consumer concerns about LFTB to the USDA. A Facebook page by the same title was launched a month later to provide more information and discussion on the topic.

The uproar continued to grow. On March 18, 2012, Congresswoman Chellie Pingree (D-ME) wrote Agriculture Secretary Tom Vilsack urging him "to immediately ban the use of [LFTB] in school lunches." A few weeks later, she introduced a bill called the REAL Beef Act, calling for labeling LFTB on packages of meat. Pingree's supporters were pitted against the elected officials who represented the states where BPI operated and those with significant cattle production.

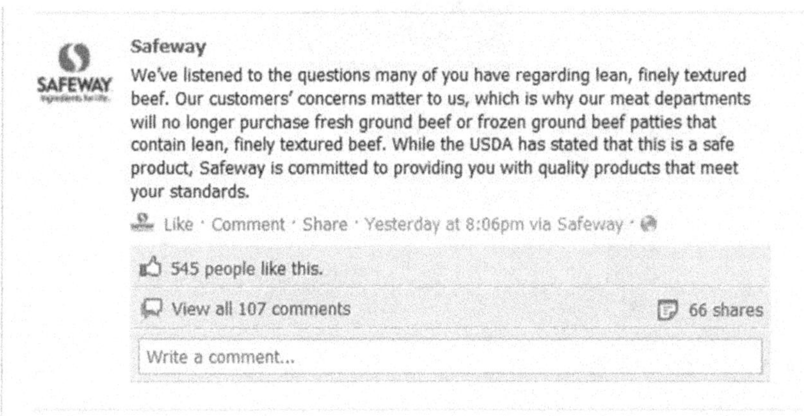

FIGURE 5.3 *Safeway posted its announcement to discontinue carrying meats with lean finely textured beef on its social media and website accounts March 21, 2012.*
http://www.facebook.com/Safeway?ref=ts&fref=ts
www.facebook.com/safeway

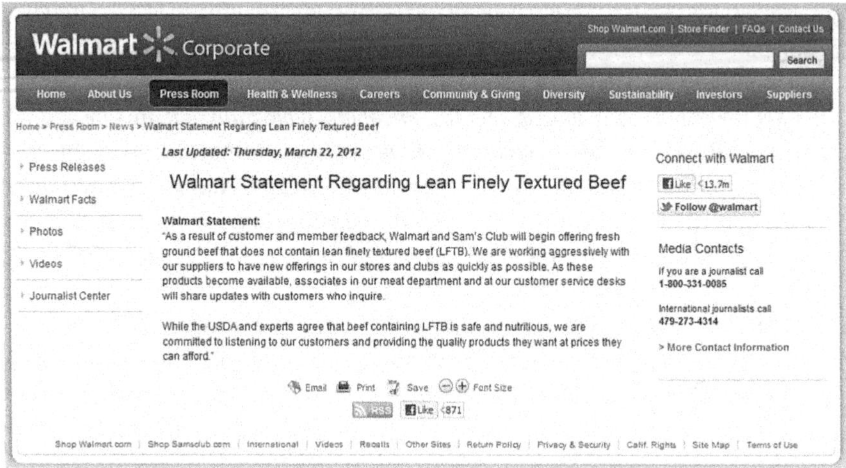

FIGURE 5.4 *Walmart announced it would provide ground beef without lean finely textured beef on March 21, 2012.*
http://news.walmart.com/
Walmart

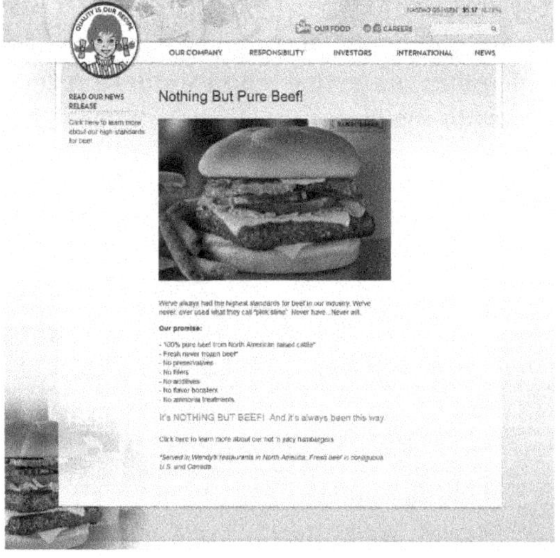

FIGURE 5.5 *Wendy's took advantage of the national discussion about lean finely textured beef to proclaim on its website that it did not use the product.*
http://wendys-prod.serverside.net/Our-Company/Nothing-but-Beef!/
The Wendy's Company

Meanwhile, by March 23, 2012, many supermarkets had bowed to consumer pressure to ban LFTB from meat products, including Kroger, BJs, Giant Food Stores, Wegmans Food Markets, Supervalu, Food Line, and Safeway, Inc. WalMart announced it

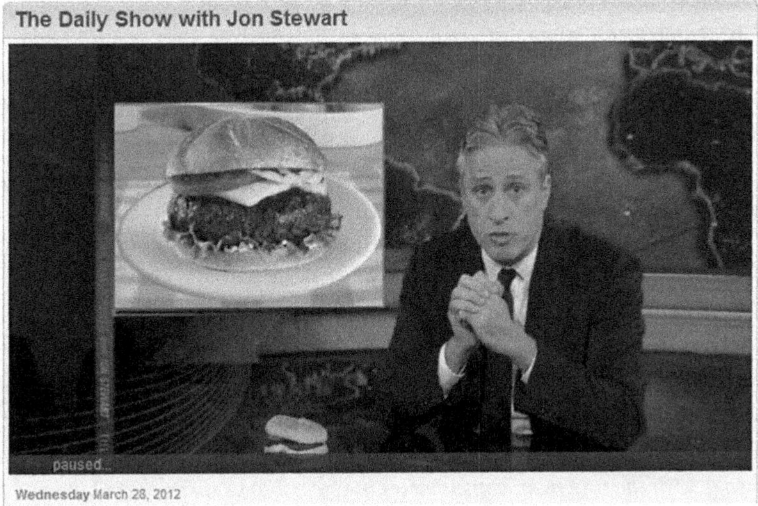

FIGURE 5.6 *Three weeks after the first* ABC News *report, the comedian Jon Stewart performs "The Hunger Shame-Pink Slime" on* The Daily Show. *http://www.thedailyshow.com/*
ABC The Daily Show with Jon Stewart

would begin offering meat without LFTB. Whole Foods, A&P, and Costco stressed that they had never sold meat with LFTB. The Wendy's company ran a full-page ad in eight major newspapers reassuring its customers that it had never used LFTB in its food.

Just three weeks after ABC's initial reports about LFTB, three of the four BPI plants closed and the Nebraska plant reduced its operations.

Comedians were using the LFTB saga for material. Jon Stewart called LFTB "ammonia-soaked centrifuge-separated byproduct paste." In a segment he mused how to solve the crisis: remove the filler from hamburger. But simple solutions are never easy because:

> *then a news report followed about the operating plants closing and people losing their jobs. We're a pink slime-based economy. So by not putting pink slime in my kids' mouths, I'm taking slime out of the mouths of kids of hard-working slime packers just trying to put slime on their families' dinner table. I feel guilty and nauseous. Well played Meat Industry! Well played!!*

A Harris Interactive poll commissioned by Red Robin Gourmet Burgers found that 88 percent of Americans were aware of the "pink slime" issue and 76 percent said they were "at least somewhat concerned."

USDA'S RESPONSE

USDA's top official did not respond to the controversy until March 22, 2012, after much of the damage had already occurred to BPI's reputation.

Dr. Elisabeth Hagen, Under Secretary for Food Safety, posted on her blog this statement under the headline "Setting the Record Straight on Beef":

As the head of USDA's public health agency, I am responsible for ensuring that the nation's commercial supply of meat, poultry, and egg products is safe for American families. I approach this role not only as a food safety expert and a physician, but also as a mother. And I want to address the national conversation over the last few weeks about the safety of Lean Finely Textured Beef (LFTB).

I believe it is important to distinguish people's concerns about how their food is made from their concerns about food safety. The process used to produce LFTB is safe and has been used for a very long time. And adding LFTB to ground beef does not make that ground beef any less safe to consume.

We are lucky to live in a country with strong food safety standards. I certainly understand that there are processes and methods in food production that may be troublesome to some, regardless of their impacts on food safety. Choosing what food to serve at your kitchen table is a very personal decision, and thankfully we have many choices at the grocery store that fit a variety of budgets. We hope that we can continue to engage with the American consumer on the steps USDA takes every day to make sure the meat they buy is safe to eat.

BPI'S AND THE MEAT INDUSTRY'S RESPONSE

BPI worked with Ketchum, an international public relations agency, during the crisis starting March 4, 2012, although Ketchum later withdrew because of a client conflict. The American Meat Institute, an industry association representing meat producers and processors, issued a statement and a fact sheet on the LFTB process on March 8, 2012, the day after the ABC News story aired:

Boneless Lean Beef Trimmings (BLBT) Is A Safe and Wholesome Beef Product Made By Separating Lean Beef From Fat

Thursday, March 8, 2012

(Attribute Statement to American Meat President J. Patrick Boyle)

Washington, DC, March 8, 2012—Boneless lean beef trimmings (BLBT) is a safe, wholesome and nutritious form of beef that is made by separating lean beef from fat. To make the product, beef companies use beef trimmings, the small cuts of beef that remain when larger cuts are trimmed down. These trimmings are USDA inspected, wholesome cuts of beef that contain both fat and lean and are nearly impossible to separate using a knife. When these trimmings are processed, the process separates the fat away and the end result is nutritious, lean beef. It's a process similar to separating cream from milk.

One process uses food grade ammonium hydroxide gas, something commonly used in the production of many foods, to destroy bacteria. Whatever process is used, it is all done under the watchful eye of USDA inspectors and according to strict federal rules. Lean finely textured beef is blended into foods like ground beef. Producing BLBT ensures that lean, nutritious, safe beef is not wasted in a world where red meat protein supplies are decreasing while global demand is increasing as population and income increases.

Some recent media reports created a troubling and inaccurate picture, particularly in their use of the colloquial term 'pink slime.' The fact is, BLBT is beef. The beef trimmings that are used to make BLBT are absolutely edible. In fact, no process can somehow make an inedible meat edible; it's impossible. In reality, the BLBT production process simply removes fat and makes the remaining beef more lean and suited to a variety of beef products that satisfy consumers' desire for leaner foods.

In fact, BLBT is a sustainable product because it recovers lean meat that would otherwise be wasted. The beef industry is proud to efficiently produce as much lean meat as possible from the cattle we raise. It's the right thing to do and it ensures that our products remain as affordable as we can make them while helping to feed America and the world.

Consumers with questions are encouraged to visit http://www.meatmythcrushers.com/. For information on the use of ammonium hydroxide in other foods, visit http://www.foodinsight.org/Resources/Detail.aspx?topic=Questions_and_Answers_about_Ammonium_Hydroxide_Use_in_Food_Production.

Note to media: A photograph that is being used in many stories is NOT boneless lean beef trimmings and should not be used in connection with stories about BLBT.

BPI issued a statement March 8, 2012, to the news media:

At Beef Products, Inc., we produce lean beef from trim. Trim is the meat and fat that is trimmed away when beef is cut into steaks and roasts. This lean beef is used in hamburger, sausage, ground beef, and as a valuable ingredient in many other foods. We use a natural compound—called ammonium hydroxide, which is widely used in the processing of numerous foods, such as baked goods, cheeses, gelatins, chocolate, caramels, and puddings—to slightly increase the pH level in beef and improve its safety.

A diverse group of experts who follow food quality and safety, including:

- *John Block, former United States Secretary of Agriculture in Illinois from 1981 to 1986 and currently Senior Policy Advisor at Olsson Frank Weeda Terman Matz PC;*
- *Chuck Jolley, journalist and president of the Meat Industry Hall of Fame;*
- *Keith Nunes, executive editor of* Food Business News*;*
- *Gary Acuff, Ph.D., Professor & AgriLife Research Faculty Fellow, Director, Center for Food Safety, Texas A&M University;*
- *Nancy Donley, founder of STOP Foodborne Illness and member of the United States Department of Agriculture's National Advisory Committee on Meat and Poultry Inspection;*
- *Linda Golodner, former president, National Consumer League;*
- *Carol Tucker-Foreman, Distinguished Fellow, the Food Policy Institute, Consumer Federation of America and former Assistant Secretary of Agriculture;*
- *and Bill Marler, the nation's leading foodborne illness attorney;*

say these things about BPI and its lean beef:

"The boneless lean beef is made from the same high quality USDA-inspected trimmings as other ground beef" John Block.

"BPI produces a boneless lean beef product from trim that is usually lost. Its primary uses are for hamburger patties, taco meat, chili and sausages. It has two primary benefits: It's a very low-cost [ingredient] and it is as close to an absolutely safe product as humanly possible to produce" Chuck Jolley.

"Negative publicity about the company's process and the use of the compound ammonium hydroxide, a critical component of the process, is at the heart of Beef Products' recent challenges. This is distressing, because ammonium hydroxide was designated as "generally recognized as safe" for use in food by the Food and Drug Administration in 1974 and it has been used as a leavening agent in baked foods as well as a way to manage the pH in many types of food products since then. In 2001, the Food Safety and Inspection Service, the regulatory arm of the U.S. Department of Agriculture that regulates the U.S. meat and poultry industry, approved the use of ammonium hydroxide as a food safety tool" Keith Nunes.

"[The video depicting the use of household ammonia with ground beef] is a terrible misrepresentation" . . . "I'm glad they use it [ammonium hydroxide] because anything that can help improve the safety of the product is certainly a product that will be on my table" Gary Acuff.

"We are encouraged to see a company like BPI taking the bull by the horns and independently testing for these killer pathogens before being required by government, but we need the entire industry involved and that will only happen when government mandates it" Nancy Donley.

"I have been to many factories, many plants, in my career at the National Consumers League. BPI is an outstanding plant: when you go in you go through a room where the air is actually cleaned, it's an amazing plant" Linda Golodner.

"Eldon Roth of Beef Products, Inc., who just won the Beef Industry Vision Award, has been extraordinarily creative in developing ways to protect consumers from pathogens in meat" Carole Tucker-Foreman.

"BPI has demonstrated a commitment to food safety. I see it as a big step in the right direction" Bill Marler.

Beef Products, Inc., is the world's leading producer of lean beef processed from fresh beef trimmings. BPI® Boneless Lean Beef, is approximately 94 percent lean beef, and made with great attention to food safety and quality.

In response to the heightened media coverage and petition, the Beef is Beef website was launched March 9, 2012 by BPI, based on an earlier version called "Pink Slime is a Myth." The company used the product name "Boneless Lean Beef Trimmings" instead of LFTB.

BPI spokesman Rich Jochum defended LFTB for schools March 12, 2012, saying that it "(1) improves the nutritional profile, (2) increases the safety of the products and (3) meets the budget parameters that allow the school lunch program to feed kids nationwide every day."

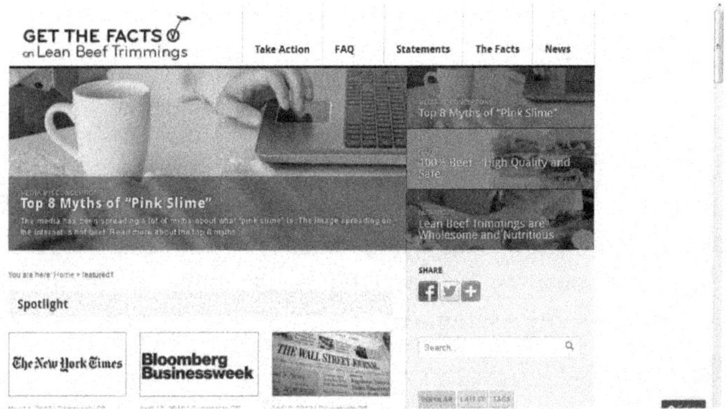

FIGURE 5.7 *BPI's educational website about its product, lean finely textured beef, was modified at least three times during the crisis. It started as "Pink Slime is a Myth" and morphed into "Beef is Beef" during the crisis, and a subsequent version was "Get the Facts on Lean Beef Trimmings."*
www.beefisbeef.com/
www.BeefisBeef.com

FIGURE 5.8 *Janet Riley, senior vice president, public affairs and member services, for the American Meat Institute provided logical and reassuring facts about the process of making lean finely textured beef in a video hosted on BPI's Beef is Beef website.*
http://www.beefisbeef.com/
American Meat Institute

Critics responded that (1) better quality of meat to start with was always more nutritious and desirable, (2) *The New York Times* investigation found no evidence that LFTB actually improved meat safety when it was mixed in with meat from other sources, and (3) BPI was a for-profit company and, therefore, driven by profit.

Two days later its Beef is Beef website expanded its news release with statements supporting LFTB from prominent government leaders, academics, food safety experts, and consumer groups entitled "100% Beef—High Quality and Safe." Other items included an electronic letter-writing campaign to request that grocery stores provide the choice to purchase beef with LFTB.

Eldon Roth, the owner of BPI, did not interact often with the news media, relying more on his spokesman to handle media interviews. Instead, Roth's name was penned to a letter in a full-page advertisement in *The Wall Street Journal* March 23, 2012, that characterized the criticism against LFTB as a "campaign of lies and deceit" to drive "BPI out of business." He noted that BPI's commitment to safety was "unsurpassed." Here is the entire statement:

> *"Pink Slime" Libel to Cost This Country Jobs*
>
> *Before last summer, we could not have imagined the personal, professional, financial and spiritual impact of the campaign of lies and deceit that have been waged against our company and the lean beef we produce. But over the last several weeks, that campaign has been joined by entertainment media, tabloid journalists, so-called national news—and all to what end? The clear goal expressed by the campaign organizer—put BPI out of business.*
>
> *It is simply amazing how this mis-information campaign can take a company and product that has long been recognized for its quality and safety and turn the public perception so negative that it now may result in the loss of over 3,000 jobs (direct employment and companies that rely upon our business) and affected their families and communities.*
>
> *Our record is unsurpassed. NEVER has a foodborne illness been associated with our lean beef over thirty years. In nearly 300,000,000,000 meals, we have been a recognized leader in food safety by groups such as the International Association for Food Protection. Look at the overwhelming support from food scientists, USDA officials, Consumer Advocate organizations, academia and customers we have received reaffirming the wholesomeness, nutrition and safety of our lean beef.*
>
> *As the founder of the company, I can personally guarantee that in our thirty year history,* ***we have never produced "pink slime."***
>
> *Eldon Roth*
> *President & CEO*

The Wall Street Journal advertisement also contained an endorsement opinion piece from Nancy Donley, founder and president of STOP Foodborne Illness, whose child died after eating *E. coli* contaminated meat. Donley wrote that she was

> *impressed by [BPI's] complete commitment to the safety and wholesomeness of the meat products they produced. I was also impressed by the food safety culture they instilled throughout their company . . . I have personally visited their plant and the categorization of calling their product "pink slime" is completely false and incendiary.*

The full ad was available on the Beef is Beef website.

In addition to the websites and statements, two petition sites were developed to support BPI. One was on Change.org, called "Sustainable Food Petition: Beef is Beef" and another was "Address Libel, Slander and Social Media Influencing Government Agency Decisions," posted at whitehouse.gov.

BPI suspended operations in Texas, Kansas, and Iowa on March 26, 2012. Its Nebraska plant was left partially operational. In a statement issued on the Beef is Beef website, Roth said because of "recent unfounded and misguided attacks on our Boneless Lean Beef Trimmings, we have had to make some unfortunate and very difficult business decisions."

NEWS CONFERENCE WITH POLITICAL MUSCLE

Three days later, on March 26, 2012, reporters (including ABC investigative reporter Jim Avila), five governors and lieutenant governors, other government officials along with Dr. Hagen, U.S. Under Secretary of Food Safety, toured the Nebraska plant. Guests were served juicy burgers with BPI's LFTB after the news conference. T-shirts with "Dude, It's Beef" were distributed.

The Food Safety News website reported that during the press briefing those reporters questioned whether two large anonymous donations influenced Nancy Donley's STOP organization favorably toward BPI. She denied any influence by BPI. Similarly, Iowa Governor Branstad, who was at the news conference, denied any influence by BPI's $152,000 contribution to his 2010 campaign and his decision to speak out in support of the company.

According to Food Safety News: " 'None whatsoever!' shouted Branstad. 'Let me tell you this, I will always fight for my constituents and I will always fight for what's right, and I will never be intimidated by anybody in the press who tries to make those accusations.' "

Several other elected officials denounced the "smear campaign" against BPI by issuing statements and airing their views in the news media. The Associated Press reported that BPI had "donated more than $800,000 to state and federal candidates over the past decade." Later, Congressman Bruce Braley (R-IA) called for a Congressional hearing about "false" news media claims regarding LFTB.

BPI created an illustrated "Get the Facts on Lean Beef Trimmings" handout that explained how its product was produced safely and nutritiously. Its Beef is Beef website also had FAQs, and a page to lobby elected officials and grocery stores and tweet "the truth" about LFTB. The site linked to supportive news articles and BPI statements. One interesting link described independent studies that showed people preferred the taste and texture of ground beef mixed with LFTB.

Throughout the crisis, BPI had support from the American Meat Institute (AMI) and the National Meat Association (NMA), industry associations. Both issued news releases after the first ABC report aired March 7; NMA's release was titled "BPI's Beef is Beef." The AMI issued three news releases, including "Boneless Lean Beef Trimmings is a Safe and Wholesome Beef Product Made by Separating Lean Beef from Fat," "Statement of the American Meat Institute About Impact of 'Pink Slime' Scare Campaign," and "AMI Issues Newsroom Advisory Urging Media to Stop Using Term 'Pink Slime.' "

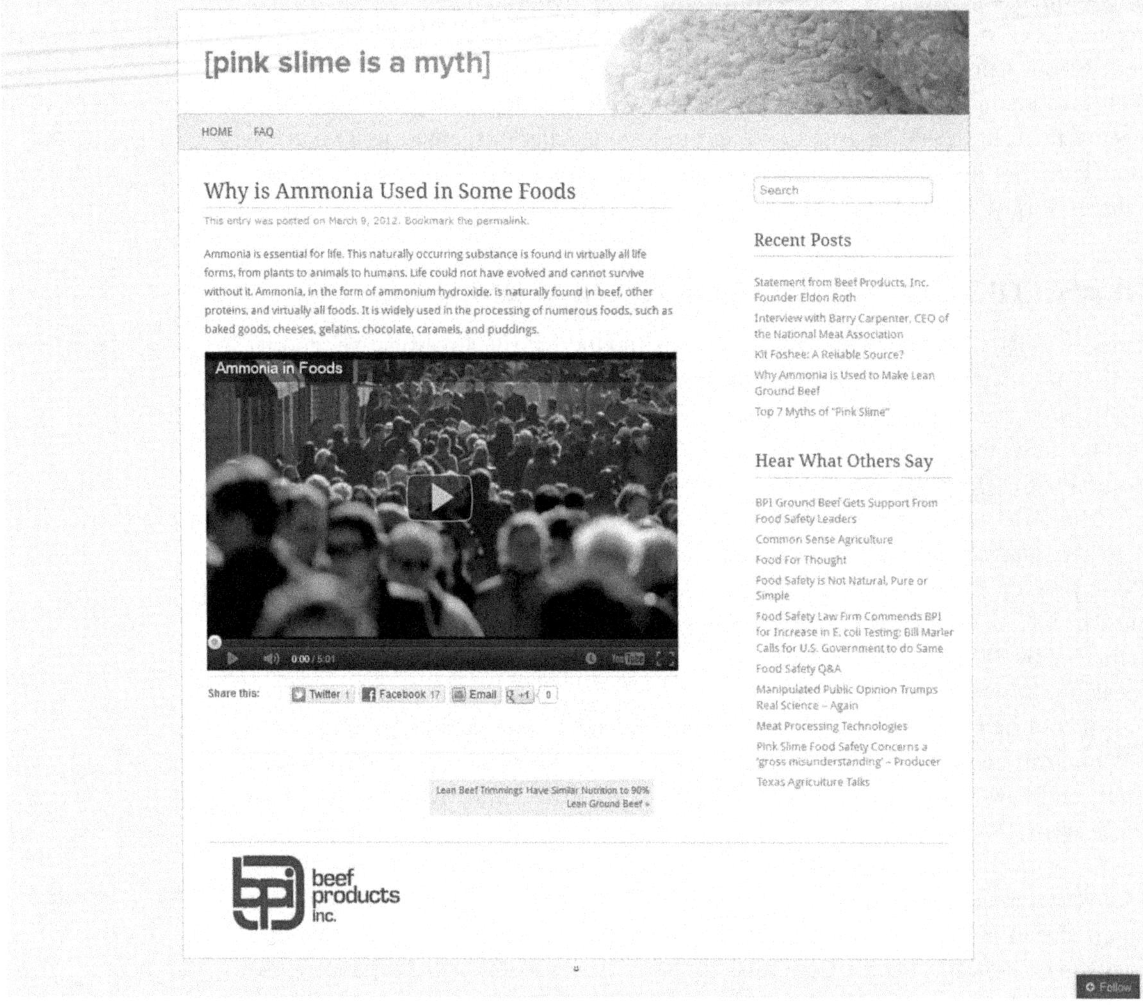

FIGURE 5.9 *The Beef is Beef website is optimized for "pink slime" Google searches and tackles the use of ammonia in its beef production.*
http://www.beefisbeef.com/myths/
www.BeefisBeef.com

WENDY'S PROMOTION

During the controversy, the Wendy's restaurant company promoted its no-LFTB burgers on its website and in advertising that appeared across the country. Under the title "Nothing but Pure Beef!" and a photograph of a huge burger with all the fixings, the Wendy's website said: "We've always had the highest standards for beef in our industry. We've never, ever used what they call "pink slime." Never have . . . Never will." The site then recited its promise to customers: 100 percent pure beef

GET THE **FACTS**

What You Need to Know about **Lean Beef Trimmings**

Lean Beef Trimmings are **100% BEEF** Wholesome and Nutritious

- It's 100% beef and processed from beef trimmed from steaks and roasts
- The process removes the fat from the meat, resulting in a 94-97% lean beef
- Ammonium hydroxide is only one part of the robust food safety system
- Ammonium hydroxide is found naturally in all proteins we eat — plant or animal — and one of its roles is to prohibit bacteria from forming
- Ammonium hydroxide is widely used in everyday cooking from baking powder to cheese to chocolate

Lean Beef Trimmings are Nutritious, Substantially Identical to **90% Lean Ground Beef**

They are a good or excellent source of protein, iron, zinc and many B-vitamins

Bun — 2 oz = 50 mg (440 ppm*)

Bacon — 1 oz = 16 mg (160 ppm)

Condiments — 2 oz = 50 mg (400 ppm)

Cheese — .8 oz = 38 mg (813 ppm)

Beef — 1.6 oz = 20 mg (200 ppm)

To provide perspective, ammonium hydroxide-based compounds can be found in every component of a bacon cheeseburger (bun, bacon, cheese, condiments, and beef) between the naturally occurring levels and small amounts used to make food safer.

*ppm = parts per million of ammonium hydroxide

GET THE **FACTS**

Visit **www.beefisbeef.com** for more information

FIGURE 5.10 *This BeefisBeef poster explains the benefits of lean finely textured beef, especially that it is "100% beef."*
http://www.beefisbeef.com/
Courtesy of BPI

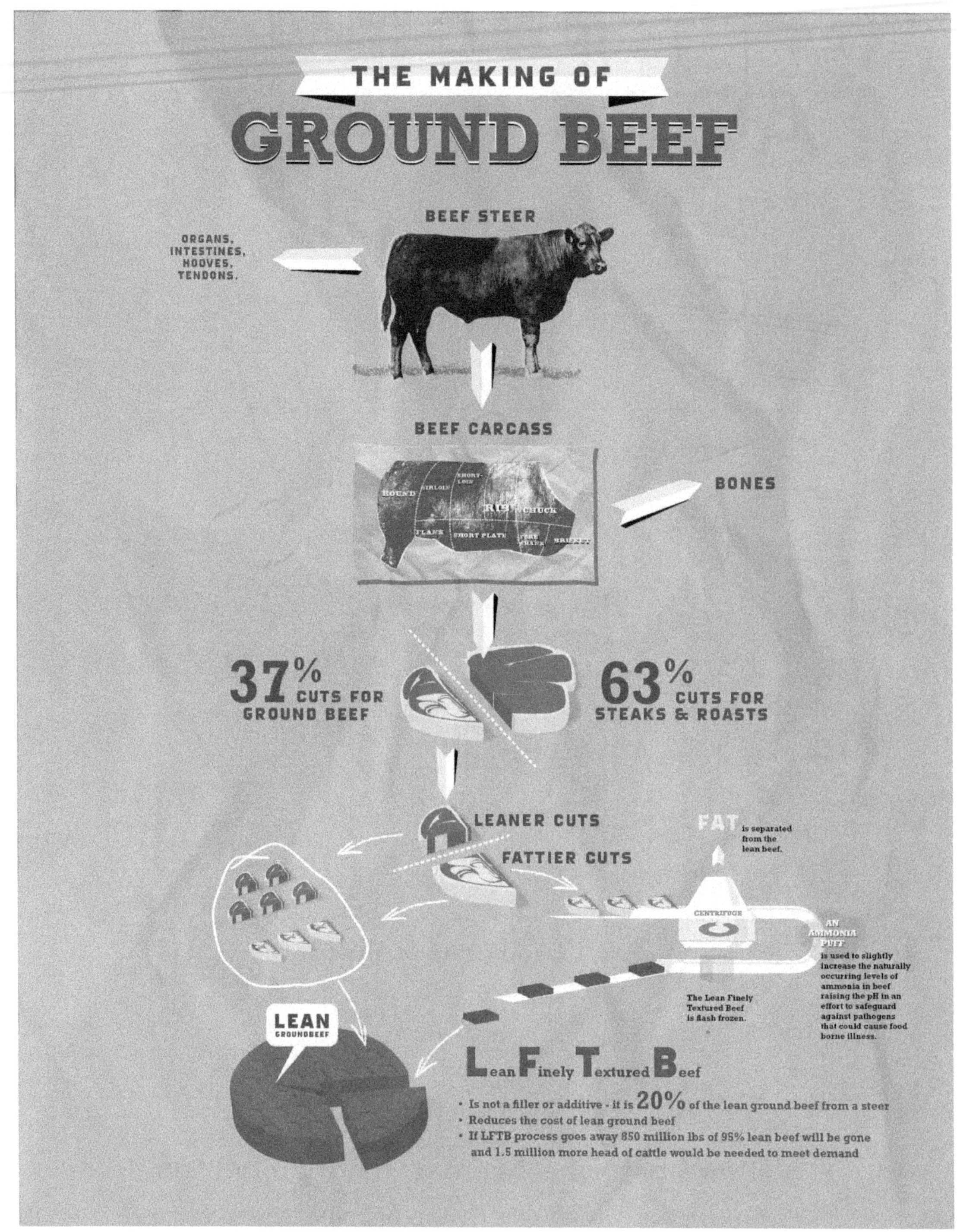

FIGURE 5.11 *This Beef is Beef poster explains the process of making lean finely textured beef. http://www.beefisbeef.com/*
Courtesy of BPI

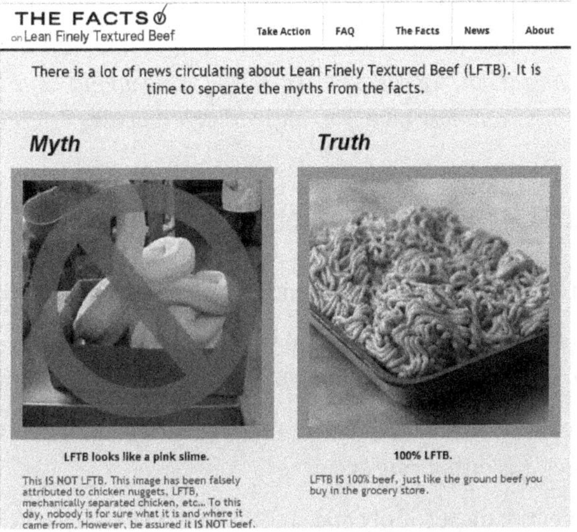

FIGURE 5.12 *The Beef is Beef website tackled several myths about pink slime. This page clarified what lean finely textured beef really looks like, according to BPI.*
http://www.beefisbeef.com/
Courtesy of BPI

from North American-raised cattle; fresh, never frozen, beef; no preservatives, fillers, additives, flavor boosters, or ammonia treatments.

In full-page ads it asked "Where's the Pure Beef?—At Wendy's, that's where!" It then mentioned its promise to its customers about the pureness of its beef.

The advertising caught BPI's public relations agency Ketchum in the controversy since the Omnicom PR firm had developed the Wendy's ad. Ketchum resigned from the account to avert conflicts of interest between its clients.

AFTERMATH

After suspending operations in March, BPI announced that it was closing three plants May 8, 2012, which eliminated 650 jobs in Texas, Kansas, and Iowa. Its Nebraska plant continued operations at a reduced level.

By mid-May 2012, just three states had ordered school lunch beef with LFTB, according to MarketingandTechnology.com.

On September 13, 2012, BPI filed a lawsuit against ABC News and others for "knowingly and intentionally publishing false and disparaging statements regarding BPI and its product, lean finely textured beef (LFTB)," according to a BPI news release. The news release went on to state:

> *"Through nearly 200 false, misleading and defamatory statements, repeated continuously during a month-long disinformation campaign, ABC and other individuals knowingly misled consumers into believing that LFTB was not beef and not safe for*

public consumption, which is completely false," said Dan Webb, Chairman, Winston & Strawn LLP. "BPI has filed suit because their business has been severely damaged by this conduct. As a result, we will be asking a jury to award BPI more than $1 billion in compensatory and statutory damages, plus punitive damages."

QUESTIONS FOR DISCUSSION

1. If LFTB is 100 percent beef, as BPI said, then why were critics concerned?
2. "Pink slime" was coined by a former USDA meat inspector/microbiologist. How did this term emerge? Did this person's credentials add credence to the term?
3. Why is the term "pink slime" more effective and memorable that "lean finely textured beef"? Is either one accurate?
4. Concern over the meat supply and the "filler" had existed for three years before the ABC reports began. How could BPI have prepared for this issue?
5. Did Jamie Oliver's report present the issue in an unbiased manner?
6. How did ABC News' coverage influence the controversy?
7. Why did some critics say LFTB was a public health issue?
8. What was BPI's response to the criticism? What tactics did BPI employ to combat the news media coverage?
9. Did a news conference featuring elected officials who had received campaign contributions from the meat industry do anything to advance BPI's cause?
10. What were some of the tactics used on the Beef is Beef website? What were effective persuasive elements of the website?
11. The LFTB controversy demonstrates that consumers' perceptions and understanding of modern food production can quickly affect meat-related business. How should the meat industry use the lessons of this case study?

Dig Deeper

BPI created a full-page newspaper advertisement to respond to the growing criticism of lean finely textured ground beef in the news media; this is available on the textbook's companion website. It uses a third-party endorser and a message from BPI's founder Eldon Roth. Analyze the strategy behind this ad as well as its effectiveness. What other strategies could have been used?

Review BPI's legal complaint against ABC News for its coverage of BPI's lean finely textured beef, available on the textbook's companion website. What is the basis for the lawsuit? What is ABC's defense?

12

The Politics of Pink

Susan G. Komen for the Cure Steps into Partisan Minefield

Each year about 230,000 women discover they have invasive breast cancer, and about 40,000 succumb to the disease. While death rates have decreased in recent years due to treatment advances, and earlier detection through screening and awareness, the human toll is immense. Everyone would agree the goal is to find a cure. But not everyone agrees with the means to that end.

SUSAN G. KOMEN FOR THE CURE

Before Susan G. Komen died at age 36 from breast cancer, she asked her sister, Nancy Brinker, to promise to help find a cure for the terrible disease. In 1982, Brinker created "Susan G. Komen for the Cure," a nonprofit foundation that has raised more than $2.2 billion to fund breast cancer research, health services, and advocacy, making it the largest breast cancer charity in the world. Its ubiquitous pink ribbons, symbolizing breast cancer advocacy, and its Race for the Cure fundraising events have global cachet. Each year it provides tens of millions of dollars in grants to thousands of organizations to fund research, health services, and advocacy projects.

Before the controversy, it was one of the top nonprofit brands in the country, according to a Harris poll.

Brinker has served as Komen's chief executive officer since 2009. While she is no stranger to politics, having served as ambassador to Hungary and U.S. Chief of Protocol during President George W. Bush's administration, Komen has always maintained a nonpartisan stance. Komen for the Cure was considered a "safe" charity—a rallying point for all women united in fighting a common menace.

Its leadership has maintained that its purpose is to help women and to find a cure for breast cancer. In 2011, Komen spent 83 percent of its money on its mission. Thirty-seven percent went to education, 23 percent to research, 16 percent to screening and 7 percent to treatment. Administrative costs included 7 percent and fundraising 10 percent, according to The Associated Press.

FIGURE 5.13 *Part of Susan G. Komen's image repair included the "We Are Susan G. Komen" campaign with women who were personally affected by breast cancer telling their stories about SGK.*
http://ww5.komen.org/
Courtesy of Susan G. Komen for the Cure

For nearly twenty years, the beloved foundation had encountered relatively few flaps during its existence. Usually, any criticisms were connected with its sponsors. These marketing problems have gotten a name—"pinkwashing." The term was used to characterize marketing campaigns that were questionable fits for Komen or somehow misled customers.

For example, KFC, the fast-food fried chicken restaurant, was criticized along with Komen for allowing KFC to conduct a six-week fundraising and awareness campaign in 2010 using Komen's seal of approval. KFC changed the color of its packaging, including its famous food buckets, to pink. The campaign also had the iconic KFC colonel donning a pink suit instead of his usual white outfit. The campaign raised a record $4.2 million but was criticized for the food's high fat content which was most popular in lower socioeconomic neighborhoods.

PLANNED PARENTHOOD

The Planned Parenthood Federation of America was established in 1916 by Margaret Sanger to provide birth control services. Since then it has expanded its mission to provide health and family planning services, including birth control, testing for sexually transmitted diseases, and cancer screening.

Planned Parenthood health clinics provide 640,000 breast exams, 585,000 pap tests, and nearly 4.5 million tests and treatments for sexually transmitted diseases annually. It is also a major provider of contraceptive services. According to the national organization, its clinics perform approximately 330,000 abortions each year, about 3 percent of its overall services. Twenty percent of all women in the U.S. have visited a Planned Parenthood health center. Forty-five percent of Planned Parenthood's budget is funded by government grants and reimbursements, although no government money can be used to fund abortions.

For many years, Komen for the Cure provided grants to Planned Parenthood clinics in local communities through Komen's affiliate network. These grants were awarded according to a review by the affiliate of gaps in local breast health services, to provide women in rural and underserved communities with free or low-cost clinical breast exams, breast health education, and referrals for mammograms. The Komen funding over five years provided nearly 170,000 clinical breast exams that resulted in 6,400 referrals for mammograms. In 2011, Komen gave Planned Parenthood $680,000 to fund clinical breast exams to nineteen affiliate programs throughout the U.S. Over a period of nearly twenty years, Komen had given $9 million to Planned Parenthood, according to Brinker in an interview with Andrea Mitchell on MSNBC.

PRESSURE

Planned Parenthood is no stranger to hardball high-pressure tactics; it is the target of regular protests from legions of dedicated volunteers opposed to abortions. It has been investigated for numerous alleged illegal activities. Many activist groups have tried to disrupt and abolish Planned Parenthood.

For example, Americans United for Life, a national anti-abortion group, suggested in a report that Planned Parenthood may be using public money to fund abortions in violation of federal prohibitions. The report also identified other potential misconduct, and the group urged Rep. Cliff Stearns (R-Fl.), a staunch anti-abortion Congressman, to open a congressional investigation into Planned Parenthood's finances and practices, which he did in September 2011.

For the nation's largest abortion provider, this type of investigation was nothing new and was considered a cost of doing business; Planned Parenthood inevitably drew lots of unwanted attention to any organization that did business with it. And that's exactly what happened when anti-abortion groups eventually discovered the link between Komen and Planned Parenthood.

Life Decisions International, the publishing division of the Southern Baptist Convention, pulled its pink Bibles in December 2011 to prevent money generated by the Bibles' sales for the Komen charity ending up in Planned Parenthood's budget. Komen was added to LDI's boycott list.

Some Roman Catholic bishops criticized Komen for its ties with Planned Parenthood as well.

KOMEN ADOPTS A NEW POLICY

In 2011, Komen for the Cure granted more than $60 million to breast cancer research and another $103 million in grants to about 2,000 community health organizations for breast cancer and breast health services, primarily for low-income and uninsured women. These included screenings, help with living expenses, transportation to treatment, patient navigation and support programs, education, and advocacy. In an effort to strengthen the impact of its grants to organizations, Komen adopted new performance criteria to measure the effectiveness of participating organizations' work with Komen's grant money. The board also "implemented more stringent eligibility standards to safeguard donor dollars." This new policy, adopted on November 29, 2011, prohibited grants to organizations under investigation. This meant the Congressional investigation of Planned Parenthood made it ineligible for future funds. While Komen did not publicly announce its new policy, it did communicate the change to its U.S. affiliates with a December 16, 2011, memo that explained the new policy and included talking points on the updated granting criteria and a Q&A. And on December 16, Komen's president called Planned Parenthood's president to break the news. Planned Parenthood had learned of the new policy weeks earlier from an anti-choice blog that had published the story. While the new policy criteria were applied to all its funding applicants, Planned Parenthood was the only organization affected by the policy change.

Planned Parenthood requested a meeting with Komen's board. Komen ignored the request to meet and defended its new grant policy in a response letter.

Planned Parenthood notified its Congressional supporters about the policy change.

The Associated Press broke the story nationally late on January 31, 2012. The focus of the story was speculation that the policy was actually a ploy by Komen to eliminate its ties with Planned Parenthood. Cecile Richards, president of Planned Parenthood, put it this way: "It's hard to understand how an organization with whom we share a mission of saving women's lives could have bowed to this kind of bullying."

The Associated Press story immediately ignited a firestorm on both sides of the abortion debate. Meanwhile, Planned Parenthood took to social media and e-mail to distribute its message of disappointment about Komen's decision to its supporters, requesting an "emergency donation."

Planned Parenthood issued the following statement January 31, 2012:

> *"Alarmed and Saddened" by Komen Foundation Succumbing to Political Pressure, Planned Parenthood Launches Fund for Breast Cancer Services*
>
> *NEW YORK—Planned Parenthood Federation of America today expressed deep disappointment in response to the Susan G. Komen for the Cure Foundation's decision to stop funding breast cancer prevention, screenings and education at Planned Parenthood health centers. Anti-choice groups in America have repeatedly threatened the Susan G. Komen for the Cure Foundation for partnering with Planned Parenthood to provide these lifesaving cancer screenings and news articles suggest that the Komen Foundation ultimately succumbed to these pressures.*
>
> *"We are alarmed and saddened that the Susan G. Komen for the Cure Foundation appears to have succumbed to political pressure. Our greatest desire is for Komen*

to reconsider this policy and recommit to the partnership on which so many women count," said Cecile Richards, president of Planned Parenthood Federation of America.

In the last few weeks, the Komen Foundation has begun notifying local Planned Parenthood programs that their breast cancer initiatives will not be eligible for new grants (beyond existing agreements or plans). The Komen Foundation's leadership did not respond to Planned Parenthood requests to meet with the Komen Board of Directors about the decision.

To ensure that the Komen Foundation's decision doesn't jeopardize any woman's access to lifesaving screenings and services, Planned Parenthood has launched a Breast Health Emergency Fund. The fund will offset the support that nineteen local Planned Parenthood programs stand to lose from Komen. The Komen-funded Planned Parenthood programs have helped thousands of women in rural and underserved communities get breast health education, screenings, and referrals for mammograms.

"While this is deeply disturbing and disappointing, we want to assure women who rely on Planned Parenthood for breast care that we're still here for them, and we always will be. The new fund we're launching to support these services will ensure that the Komen Foundation's decision doesn't jeopardize women's health," added Richards.

Over the past five years, Planned Parenthood health centers with Komen program funding have provided nearly 170,000 clinical breast exams out of the more than four million clinical breast exams performed nationwide at Planned Parenthood health centers, as well as more than 6,400 mammogram referrals out of 70,000 mammogram referrals. Anti-choice groups in America have repeatedly threatened the Susan G. Komen for the Cure Foundation for partnering with Planned Parenthood to provide these lifesaving cancer screenings.

Planned Parenthood's quality, accessibility and affordability make it a leader in identifying breast cancer early when there is the best chance of successful treatment. Nationwide, Planned Parenthood doctors and nurses provide nearly 750,000 breast cancer screenings annually, offering risk assessments, breast exams, breast health information and education, and diagnostic and surgical referrals.

Led by a generous $250,000 gift from Amy and Lee Fikes' foundation, Planned Parenthood has established a Breast Health Emergency Fund to provide immediate funding to ensure that Planned Parenthood health centers can continue to provide breast cancer screenings and care that had previously been supported by Komen.

Amy and Lee Fikes said: "Our family is saddened that the far right has relentlessly and successfully pressured the Susan G. Komen for the Cure Foundation to cut funding for breast screening, referral, and education support to low-income women who, until now, have been able to depend on the partnership between Komen and Planned Parenthood for their health. In response to this disappointing news, our family foundation has granted $250,000 to establish a Breast Health Fund at Planned Parenthood, so that their health centers across the country can continue to put the real needs of women ahead of right wing ideology. We encourage others to join us in replacing the funds lost, so that no woman's health is imperiled by Komen's unfortunate decision" . . .

Abigail Sanocki, in Denver, Colorado, is one of the thousands of women who have received critical treatment at Planned Parenthood thanks to funding from the Komen

Foundation. She said: "In January of 2010 I found a lump in my left breast. At the time I was unemployed (like many others in the nation), and considering having to ignore it. However, at my annual exam, I did have one of Planned Parenthood's doctors look at it, and was encouraged to get an ultrasound, which then led to me having to have the lump biopsied. The total estimated costs for the ultrasound and needle biopsy, which had to be done through an outside health institution, would have been over $7,000. I was nearly pennyless, without insurance, and terrified about the possibilities of where the results of this biopsy could have led . . . Without Planned Parenthood, I would still be walking around years later unsure of what was going on inside my body and the immediate future of my health."

One in five women in America has come to Planned Parenthood at some point in her life. More than 90 percent of Planned Parenthood health care is preventive, including lifesaving cancer screenings, birth control, prevention and treatment of STDs, breast health services, Pap tests, and sexual health education and information.

Planned Parenthood president Cecile Richards readily participated in media interviews. Along with the news release, Planned Parenthood also launched a breast health landing page on its website. The ensuing publicity would lead many supporters to act on both sides. Planned Parenthood announced it had received $400,000 from 6,000 donors in twenty-four hours.

U.S. Senator Patricia "Patty" Murray (D-Washington) and U.S. Representative Mike Honda (D-Calif.) issued news releases on January 31, 2012, condemning Komen's new policy and characterizing it as politically motivated. Murray directly

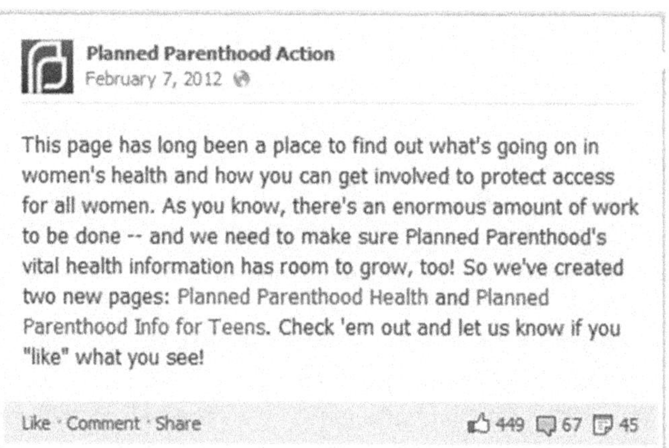

FIGURE 5.14 *With all the attention on breast cancer screenings, Planned Parenthood used its Facebook page to direct people to its Breast Health website.*
http://www.plannedparenthood.org/

connected Komen's policy decision to the "shameful 'investigation'" by House Republicans, and Honda characterized Stearn's investigation as "the latest casualty in a misguided and harmful campaign . . . to demonize the life-saving health services delivered by Planned Parenthood health centers."

The following provides a three-day analysis of Komen's response to the controversy:

DAY ONE—FEBRUARY 1, 2012

On February 1, 2012, within hours, politicians and organizations in both camps issued statements defending or attacking Komen's actions. While the news media were reporting the story, activists and individuals began to flood Komen's Facebook page with comments; Planned Parenthood also saw a steep uptick in its Facebook traffic. According to various social media tracking organizations analyzing the sites, the comments were 75–90 percent against Komen's decision. Polipulse, a social media analysis firm, said a quarter of people critical of Komen's decision would pull their donations.

Komen issued a statement later in the day that was posted on its Facebook page on February 1, 2012:

> *At Susan G. Komen for the Cure, the women we serve are our highest priority in everything we do. Last year, we invested $93 million in community health programs, which included 700,000 mammograms. Additionally, we began an initiative to further strengthen our grants program to be even more outcomes-driven and to allow for even greater investments in programs that directly serve women. We also implemented more stringent eligibility and performance criteria to support these strategies.*
>
> *While it is regrettable when changes in priorities and policies affect any of our grantees, such as a longstanding partner like Planned Parenthood, we must continue to evolve to best meet the needs of the women we serve and most fully advance our mission.*
>
> *It is critical to underscore that the women we serve in communities remain our priority. We are working directly with Komen Affiliates to ensure there is no interruption or gaps in services for women who need breast health screening and services.*
>
> *Grant making decisions are not about politics—our priority is and always will be the women we serve. Making this issue political or leveraging it for fundraising purposes would be a disservice to women.*

A similar statement by Komen was released through Business Wire February 1, 2012, around 10 p.m. GMT:

> *We are dismayed and extremely disappointed that actions we have taken to strengthen our granting process have been widely mischaracterized. It is necessary to set the record straight.*
>
> *Starting in 2010, Komen began an initiative to help us do a better job of measuring the impact of community grants. This is important because we invest significant dollars in our local community programs—$93 million in 2011, which provided for 700,000 breast health screenings and diagnostic procedures.*

> *Following this review, we made the decision to implement stronger performance criteria for our grantees to minimize duplication and free up dollars for direct services to help vulnerable women. To support this new granting strategy, Komen has also implemented more stringent eligibility standards to safeguard donor dollars. Consequently, some organizations are no longer eligible to receive Komen grants.*
>
> *Some might argue that our standards are too exacting, but over the past three decades people have given us more than just their money. They have given us their trust and we take that responsibility very seriously.*
>
> *We regret that these new policies have impacted some longstanding grantees, such as Planned Parenthood, but want to be absolutely clear that our grant-making decisions are not about politics. Throughout our thirty-year history, our priority has always been and will continue to be the women we serve. As we move forward, we are working to ensure that there is no interruption or gaps in services for the women who need our support most in the fight against breast cancer.*

Some Congressmen withdrew their support for Komen, including U.S. Senator Barbara Boxer (D-Calif.) and Representative Jackie Speier (D-Calif.).

U.S. Representative Louie Gohmert (R-Texas) said in a statement:

> *This courageous decision . . . is truly a beautiful victory for those who stand in support of the unborn. Life is sacred—it's a wonderful gift from God. It is exciting and encouraging to see this top charity, working to prevent and cure breast cancer, display such a public stance to honor the sanctity of life.*

Not only was the debate raging in the public arena but also within the Komen organization. The Connecticut affiliate of Susan G. Komen for the Cure said in a Facebook statement: "We understand, and share in, the frustration around this situation." The affiliate said it would continue to fund Planned Parenthood of New England.

Komen sought to clarify its new policy with a YouTube video posted on February 1, 2012 (and later removed), reported by Politico.com and many other news outlets. In addition to explaining the new eligibility criteria Komen president Brinker mentioned that the organization was also trying to focus on "higher impact programs."

> *These changes mean that we will be able to do more to help women and advance the fight against breast cancer. We are working to eliminate duplicative grants, freeing up more dollars for higher impact programs, and wherever possible we want to grant to the provider that is actually providing the lifesaving mammogram.*

The new policy would favor organizations that went beyond clinical breast examinations and provided mammogram services, which Planned Parenthood clinics did not do, although they did referrals based on exam results. This was a new reason to potentially disqualify Planned Parenthood from future grants. Brinker's video message further explained:

We have the highest responsibility to ensure that these donor dollars make the biggest impact possible. Regrettably, this strategic shift will affect any number of long-standing partners, but we have always done what is right for our organization, for our donors and volunteers.

Brinker concluded her video message by denying the new policy was political in nature and saying that the organization would hold firm to its new direction:

We will never bow down to political pressure. The scurrilous accusations being hurled at this organization are profoundly hurtful to so many of us who put our heart, soul and lives into this organization. But more importantly, they are a dangerous distraction from the work that still remains to be done in ridding the world of breast cancer.

The Komen news release issued the same day as Brinker's video did not mention that organizations under investigation were affected by the new disqualifying criteria or Komen's shift in funding for health services that provided direct mammogram services instead of just clinical breast examinations. The news release did not refer to the accusations of political pressure but the video certainly did—and was widely reported in the news media.

DAY TWO—FEBRUARY 2, 2012

Social media were intensely active for and against Komen and Planned Parenthood, although most of the attention was negative—and directed toward Komen.

One poster said:

Thanks SGK. You inspired me to triple my usual donation to Planned Parenthood. You have galvanized a sleeping giant: those of us who support Planned Parenthood's work and previously stood silent in the face of multifaceted attacks by the right wing. NO MORE! Adios SGKF. Big miscalculation on your part.

Robbie Schwartz Thanks SGK. You inspired me to triple my usual donation to Planned Parenthood. You have galvanized a sleeping giant: those of us who support Planned Parenthood's work and previously stood silent in the face of multifaceted attacks by the right wing. NO MORE! Adios SGKF. Big miscalculation on your part.

February 2 at 10:34pm · Like · 9

FIGURE 5.15 *Komen's facebook page had many supporters' and critics' comments. One said she would triple her donation to Planned Parenthood based on Komen's new policy.*
http://www.facebook.com/susangkomenforthecure/
Courtesy of Susan G. Komen for the Cure

Planned Parenthood supporters weren't the only ones displeased. Apparently, hackers gained accessed to Komen's website early February 2 and changed the text of one of its home page banner graphics. The particular banner was a photo showing the shoes of runners in motion. According to AtlanticWire.com, the text had been changed from: "Help us get 26.2 or 13.1 miles closer to a world without breast cancer" to "Help us run over poor women on our way to the bank."

Others encouraged boycotts of Komen's major corporate sponsors, and some focused on how Komen spent contributors' donations. For example, some questioned why Brinker earned $417,000 from the charity while only 15 percent of the organization's distributed funds went to cancer research—or finding the "cure."

New York mayor Michael Bloomberg announced he would donate $250,000 to Planned Parenthood, saying:

> *Politics have no place in health care. Breast cancer screening saves lives and hundreds of thousands of women rely on Planned Parenthood for access to care. We should be helping women access that care, not placing barriers in their way.*

LiveStrong, a charitable cancer organization founded by cancer survivor and cyclist Lance Armstrong, also announced a $100,000 donation to Planned Parenthood. Armstrong, chairman of the organization, issued a statement:

> *For fifteen years, the Lance Armstrong Foundation has served people and families affected by cancer, especially those in underserved communities. We join Mayor Bloomberg and our partners in the philanthropic community today in their efforts to preserve access to cancer screening for women throughout the U.S. The Lance Armstrong*

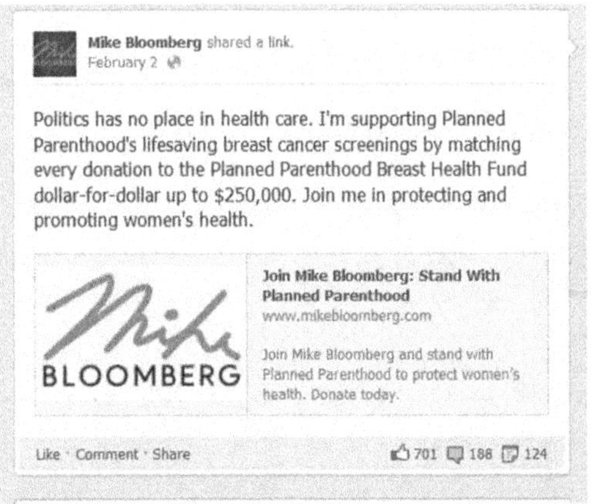

FIGURE 5.16 *New York City Mayor Mike Bloomberg pledged $250,000 for Planned Parenthood breast screenings on his Facebook page after komen's funding guidelines were changed.*
http://www.facebook.com/mikebloomberg
Michael Bloomberg

Foundation will add an additional $100,000 to Mayor Bloomberg's matching challenge to Planned Parenthood's cancer services fund.

Komen reported that its donations were up 100 percent in forty-eight hours, although no specific amount was noted.

In a conference call to reporters, Brinker said the decision had been "grossly mischaracterized" and that the Congressional investigation into Planned Parenthood was not a major factor in Komen's granting decision. The deciding factor, she said, was the fact that Planned Parenthood did not have mammography machines to provide direct diagnostic services. Some Planned Parenthood clinics in Colorado, California, and Texas, Brinker said, would likely be funded because they provided the only breast cancer screening services in the area.

Komen's Facebook page had three short separate posts focusing on the $93 million in grants it had distributed, stressing the fact that Komen was not withdrawing money from Planned Parenthood, and providing a link to a portion of Brinker's interview with Andrea Mitchell on MSNBC. Specifically, the first Facebook post included this statement:

Our Board of Directors approved new grants standards to improve direct services to women, says Komen Founder and CEO Amb. Nancy G. Brinker. Money is not being "withdrawn" from Planned Parenthood—will be invested in programs to serve low-income, uninsured and underinsured women.

Finally, after Planned Parenthood's president had already made the rounds on television and other news outlets, Brinker went on the offensive, making her first televised appearance on MSNBC.

FIGURE 5.17 *Clarifying its actions Komen explained that the change was a policy issue, not an attack on Planned Parenthood.*
http://www.facebook.com/susangkomenforthecure
Courtesy of Susan G. Komen for the Cure

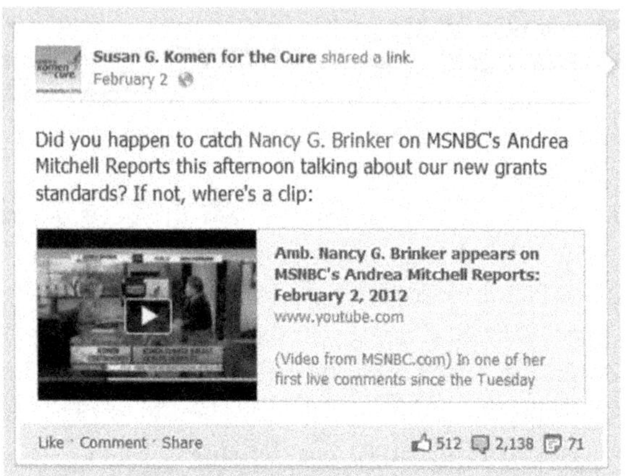

FIGURE 5.18 *Komen used Facebook to alert its supporters to favorable media coverage, although some critics felt this media interview did more harm to Komen.*
http://www.facebook.com/susangkomenforthecure
Courtesy of Susan G. Komen for the Cure

She stated that Komen was not "defunding" Planned Parenthood, that three clinics had been approved for funding in 2012, and that they might be eligible in the future. She also denied that Komen vice president Karen Handel, a Republican and previous candidate for governor in Georgia who had publicly described herself as staunchly pro-life and not a supporter of Planned Parenthood, had anything to do with the new policy; this was untrue. Brinker said Komen was concerned with improving its grant process and funding direct providers. In an eight-minute interview with Mitchell, Brinker said:

> *Karen [Handel] did not have anything to do with this decision This was decided at the board level and also by our mission . . . And let me just take a step back for a minute. We are not defunding Planned Parenthood. We have three grants that will go on this year, and they will probably be eligible for the next grant cycle.*

Later in the day, another Facebook post was uploaded to the Komen page:

> *Our supporters know that no other breast cancer organization serves women at the size and scope that Susan G. Komen for the Cure does. Screening, help through treatment, social and financial support provided $93 million in Komen community funding to 2,000 organizations last year alone.*

In the meantime, U.S. Senators Frank Lautenberg and Patty Murray and two dozen other senators signed a toughly worded letter urging Komen to reverse its decision:

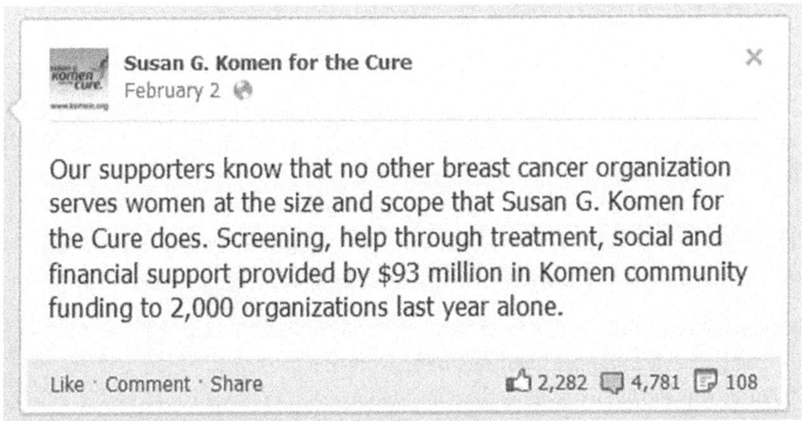
Susan G. Komen for the Cure
February 2
Our supporters know that no other breast cancer organization serves women at the size and scope that Susan G. Komen for the Cure does. Screening, help through treatment, social and financial support provided by $93 million in Komen community funding to 2,000 organizations last year alone.
Like · Comment · Share
2,282 4,781 108

FIGURE 5.19 *Komen's Facebook page reminded supporters that Komen had provided $93 million in support of community funding the previous year. http://www.facebook.com/susangkomenforthecure*
Courtesy of Susan G. Komen for the Cure

> *It would be tragic if any woman—let alone thousands of women—lost access to these potentially life-saving screenings because of a politically motivated attack.*
>
> *We earnestly hope that you will put women's health before partisan politics and reconsider this decision for the sake of the women who depend on both your organizations for access to the health care they need.*

There was support for Komen as well. *The Washington Times,* a politically conservative newspaper, reported that the Family Research Council had asked its supporters to send a thank-you e-mail to Komen, which thousands did. A website, www.thankskomen.com, was created to thank Komen. The Catholic Family and Human Rights Institute encouraged its supporters to e-mail thanks to Komen for defunding Planned Parenthood.

News reports mentioned that Komen affiliates in Arkansas, California, Colorado, Connecticut, and New York were concerned with the new policy regarding Planned Parenthood. Some affiliates in California sent a letter to its state's Congressional delegation, calling the decision a "misstep."

According to one report, a top Komen official who directed the community health programs, Mollie Williams, had resigned after the board approved its new policy in October 2011. *The New York Times* quoted her as saying "I believe it would be a mistake for any organization to bow to political pressure and compromise its mission." Kathy Plesser, a Manhattan radiologist on the medical advisory board of Komen's New York Chapter, announced plans to resign unless Komen reversed its decision.

After a board conference call later in the day, Brinker switched course.

DAY THREE—FEBRUARY 3, 2012

Mid-morning, around 11 a.m. on February 3, 2012, Komen issued a news release apologizing to the American public; in a Facebook posting that connected to the news release, the organization announced it would change its funding criteria regarding organizations under investigation:

The news release statement was slightly different than the briefer Facebook post. The news release started with an apology, followed by an explanation of its actions, and ended with a notice that it would be reaching out to key supporters:

> *We want to apologize to the American public for recent decisions that cast doubt upon our commitment to our mission of saving women's lives.*
>
> *The events of this week have been deeply unsettling for our supporters, partners and friends and all of us at Susan G. Komen. We have been distressed at the presumption that the changes made to our funding criteria were done for political reasons or to specifically penalize Planned Parenthood. They were not.*
>
> *Our original desire was to fulfill our fiduciary duty to our donors by not funding grant applications made by organizations under investigation. We will amend the criteria to make clear that disqualifying investigations must be criminal and conclusive in nature and not political. That is what is right and fair.*
>
> *Our only goal for our granting process is to support women and families in the fight against breast cancer. Amending our criteria will ensure that politics has no place in our grant process. We will continue to fund existing grants, including those of Planned Parenthood, and preserve their eligibility to apply for future grants, while maintaining the ability of our affiliates to make funding decisions that meet the needs of their communities.*
>
> *It is our hope and we believe it is time for everyone involved to pause, slow down and reflect on how grants can most effectively and directly be administered without controversies that hurt the cause of women. We urge everyone who has participated in this conversation across the country over the last few days to help us move past this issue. We do not want our mission marred or affected by politics—anyone's politics.*
>
> *Starting this afternoon, we will have calls with our network and key supporters to refocus our attention on our mission and get back to doing our work. We ask for the public's understanding and patience as we gather our Komen affiliates from around the country to determine how to move forward in the best interests of the women and people we serve.*
>
> *We extend our deepest thanks for the outpouring of support we have received from so many in the past few days and we sincerely hope that these changes will be welcomed by those who have expressed their concern.*

Komen's Facebook post was short and to the point:

> *The events of this week have been deeply unsettling for our supporters, partners and friends and all of us at Susan G. Komen. We have been distressed at the presumption that the changes made to our funding criteria were done for political reasons or to specifically penalize Planned Parenthood. They were not.*

Our original desire was to fulfill our fiduciary duty to our donors by not funding grant applications made by organizations under investigation. We will amend the criteria to make clear that disqualifying investigations must be criminal and conclusive in nature and not political. That is what is right and fair.

Planned Parenthood CEO Richards issued the following statement:

Statement by Cecile Richards, Planned Parenthood Federation of America, Regarding Today's Komen Announcement

The outpouring of support for women in need of lifesaving breast cancer screening this week has been astonishing and is a testament to our nation's compassion and sincerity.

During the last week, millions spontaneously joined a national conversation about lifesaving breast cancer prevention care and reinforced shared values about access to health care for all. This compassionate outcry in support of those most in need rose above political, ideological, and cultural divides, and will surely be recognized as one of our nation's better moments during a contentious political time. Planned Parenthood thanks each and every person who has contributed to elevating the importance of breast cancer prevention for so many women in need.

In recent weeks, the treasured relationship between the Susan G. Komen for the Cure Foundation and Planned Parenthood has been challenged, and we are now heartened that we can continue to work in partnership toward our shared commitment to breast

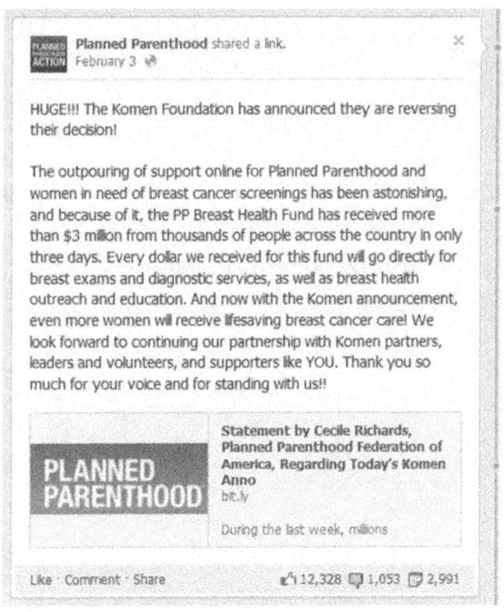

FIGURE 5.20 *Planned Parenthood announced Komen's reversal on its funding decision "HUGE!!!" on its Facebook page.*
http://www.facebook.com/PlannedParenthood

health for the most underserved women. We are enormously grateful that the Komen Foundation has clarified its grantmaking criteria, and we look forward to continuing our partnership with Komen partners, leaders and volunteers. What these past few days have demonstrated is the deep resolve all Americans share in the fight against cancer, and we honor those who are at the helm of this battle.

Planned Parenthood has been a trusted partner with the Komen Foundation in early cancer detection and prevention services. In particular, Planned Parenthood helps the Komen Foundation reach vulnerable populations—low-income women, African-American women, and Latinas—especially in rural areas and underserved communities where Planned Parenthood health centers are their only source of health care. With Komen Foundation grants, over the past five years, Planned Parenthood health centers provided nearly 170,000 clinical breast exams and more than 6,400 mammogram referrals. With the outpouring of support over the past week, even more women in need will receive lifesaving breast cancer care.

SOCIAL MEDIA'S ROLE

Throughout the controversy social media were a powerful factor in keeping the issue alive on the Internet as well as a topic of discussion in homes and public gatherings. Facebook, in particular, provided the space for individuals to share their experiences and opinions. Cecile Richards, president of Planned Parenthood, and others said social media kept mainstream media interest in the controversy alive.

FIGURE 5.21 *On Komen's Facebook page a commenter noticed Komen was apparently deleting some posts.*
http://www.facebook.com/susangkomenforthecure
Courtesy of Susan G. Komen for the Cure

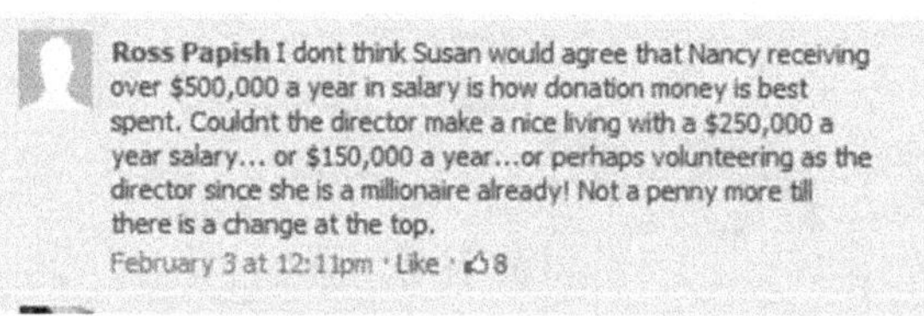

FIGURE 5.22 *Controversies can expand scrutiny into other areas of an organization. One poster on Komen's Facebook page said that Komen's CEO made $500,000 annually.*
http://www.facebook.com/susangkomenforthecure
Courtesy of Susan G. Komen for the Cure

Richards in a media conference call with reporters the day Komen reversed its decision said that Facebook had allowed Planned Parenthood to develop relationships with its supporters. It was, she said, "the authenticity of the response that carried the day." Social media activity also brought in contributions. According to Planned Parenthood, it received more than $3 million in contributions and attracted 38,000 new donors in three days. The New York *Daily News* reported Planned Parenthood did not have to do much: "All of these things were self-generated," said Planned Parenthood president Cecile Richards. "I've never seen anything catch fire like [this] . . . I do think it's a watershed moment."

According to WashingtonPost.com, Planned Parenthood's Facebook page "gets the second-most comments among nonprofits."

Planned Parenthood's Facebook page picked up more than 30,000 "likes" during the controversy. Still, Komen's Facebook page had 545,365 "likes" compared to 235,796 "likes" for Planned Parenthood. Planned Parenthood at the time had more Twitter followers, 41,295 compared to Komen's 39,086 followers.

Critics said Komen was not quick enough with Twitter and Facebook to counter the speed of the growing controversy. It did not help Komen's credibility that it was not out in front of the story; when Komen did respond it was in a defensive manner.

AFTERMATH

On February 7, 2012, Komen's Facebook page noted that it had "made mistakes" and took "full accountability" for the results. Later, another Facebook post and news release announced the resignation of Karen Handel, senior vice president for policy since April 2011.

Handel's high-profile resignation was followed by other resignations and retirements, but according to Komen they were not related to the controversy: Katrina McGhee, executive vice president and chief marketing officer, resigned but stayed with the organization for another six months as a consultant; Nancy Macgregor, vice president of global networks, retired after twenty-one years at Komen; and Joanna Newcomb, director of affiliate strategy and planning, resigned.

On August 9, 2012, Komen announced that its president, Liz Thompson, was resigning and Nancy Brinker announced that she would step down as CEO to focus on new duties in fundraising and strategic planning. According to The Associated Press, fundraising from its affiliates' fundraising race/walk events had sunk and participation had declined as much as 30 percent for some affiliate races soon after the controversy.

The Susan G. Komen annual Race for the Cure, held at various times throughout the country, saw steep declines in participation and donations. The Houston, Texas, race, for example, fell 50 percent short of its $3 million goal and significantly fewer people participated in the race activities, according to the *Houston Chronicle*. In San Francisco, registration for the race was down 50 percent, and donations were down 65 percent, compared to the previous year, according to the Los Angeles *Daily News*.

FIGURE 5.23 *Nancy Brinker used Susan G. Komen's annual leadership conference to reconnect with supporters, discuss the mistakes made in the past, and pledge to move forward.*
http://www.youtube.com/
Courtesy of Susan G. Komen for the Cure

Beyond the short-term problems of fundraising, the national office for Komen needed to repair its relationship with many of the 122 affiliate organizations who wanted more say in the future direction of Komen. With just one affiliate member serving on the national board, some said it was time to increase their voices.

Komen had a lot of work ahead as some people began to "re-think the pink" and scrutiny of the organization grew. De-Fund the Komen Foundation Facebook page and KomenWatch.org were just some examples of individuals or groups that began monitoring this charitable organization.

QUESTIONS FOR DISCUSSION

1. Who exerted pressure on Komen when it announced its grant policy changes?
2. How could issues management principles have been applied by Komen in this case?
3. Examine Komen's stated reasons for disqualifying Planned Parenthood for grant money. How did the message change and did that affect its persuasive communication strategy?
4. How did Komen's critics frame the issue? Was it successful? Why?

5. What were the internal issues with Komen's affiliates, board, and staff members that it had to deal with during this controversy? Could any of the conflict have been avoided?
6. Why do you think Komen accepted Karen Handel's resignation? What might be the strategy?
7. How can Komen rebuild relationships with its supporters?
8. How can groups on both sides of the abortion debate leverage this event to build support for their causes?

Dig Deeper

After the Susan G. Komen for the Cure crisis had subsided somewhat, its CEO Nancy Brinker took advantage of an opportunity to speak directly to its leadership about the controversy during the March 2012 Affiliate Leadership Conference. Review the video of her speech available on the textbook's companion website. What key points did Brinker make? How effective was her presentation? Does this activity help with image repair? If so, how?

13

Deepwater Horizon *Blowout*

Rehabilitating a Reputation after a Catastrophic Spill

BP, formerly known as British Petroleum, is an oil and gas company based in the United Kingdom, with global operations and 84,000 employees in 2012. It finds, extracts, transports, refines, and sells oil and gas products and has been a highly profitable company with pre-spill profits of $14 billion in 2009. Headquartered in London, BP is the second largest company in the U.K. and its brand was ranked 83rd in the world according to industry firm Interbrand. It owns oil and gas exploration rights, oil and gas fields, refineries, pipelines, large crude carrier ships, and gas stations and other oil-based products all over the world. Its chief executive officer, Tony Hayward, a geologist, was appointed from within BP's administrative ranks in 2007.

BP'S SAFETY RECORD

Before the *Deepwater Horizon* oil spill there were a number of U.S. safety and environmental incidents involving BP operations that caused some to question whether BP put profit ahead of other considerations.

BP was held responsible for a 2005 Texas City, Texas, oil refinery explosion that killed fifteen workers and injured 170; the company agreed to pay $21 million in federal fines for more than 300 safety violations. The Occupational Safety and Health Administration found more than 700 violations in a follow-up inspection in 2009, and BP agreed to pay $50.6 million for safety violations it had failed to correct following the 2005 refinery explosion. BP paid $13 million for 409 new safety violations discovered in 2009. As a result, the company invested $1 billion on safety and infrastructure improvements. One investigative report said that the Texas City disaster "was caused by organizational and safety deficiencies at all levels of the BP Corporation." Just weeks before the *Deepwater Horizon* disaster, the news media reported the same Texas City refinery plant accidentally released 500,000 pounds of toxic chemicals into the skies over a forty-day period before the mistake was discovered by workers.

A number of negative environmental incidents involving BP-owned oil wells and pipelines had occurred in Alaska. In 2006 the biggest Alaskan oil spill ever happened after a section of the 800-mile Trans-Alaska pipeline corroded and leaked more than 5,078 barrels (267,000 gallons) of crude oil into Prudhoe Bay, Alaska; another smaller leak was discovered a few months later. As a result of the leaks, BP paid $25 million in fines and was ordered to correct the problems. A smaller oil–water mixture leak occurred in 2009 during a pressure test of a pipeline at BP's Lisburne Processing Center. A 2010 investigation by ProPublica revealed various parts of the Alaskan North Slope pipelines were in such bad shape that 148 sections were labeled as in "imminent danger" of rupturing.

DEEPWATER HORIZON EXPLOSION

Technological advances in oil drilling and climbing oil prices made the Gulf of Mexico an attractive source for oil. According to the U.S. Energy Information Administration, the Gulf accounted for about 28 percent of America's domestic crude oil production and 15 percent of its natural gas in 2011.

In the Gulf of Mexico, BP operated eight so-called "deepwater" projects. It is the largest leaseholder with more than 650 "lease blocks" in waters greater than 1,250 feet, according to BP's website. Each of these sites pump out about 250,000 barrels of oil daily. Some deepwater oil projects operate in depths up to 6,000 feet. Floating oil rigs can have hundreds of workers and are like self-contained cities.

FIGURE 5.24 *Fire boat response crews battle the blazing remnants of the offshore oil rig* Deepwater Horizon, *April 21, 2010.*
https://cgvi.uscg.mil
U.S. Coast Guard

Deepwater Horizon, located forty-one miles off the coast of Louisiana, was an exploratory well operating at a water depth of about 5,000 feet. The well itself was 18,000 feet deep.

On April 20, 2010, at 10 p.m., an explosion occurred on the *Deepwater Horizon*, killing eleven workers and injuring seventeen others; 115 were rescued. The explosion was attributed to a number of factors but involved the failure of cement barriers, the "blowout preventer," a large valve designed to seal off the oil well at the wellhead, and the undetected release of hydrocarbons. Oil and gas leaking from the massive rig burned out of control for three days; *Deepwater Horizon* then sank.

The oil leak was located at the bottom of the sea floor where the wellhead joined the well. According to government investigations, *Deepwater Horizon* gushed for eighty-four days releasing nearly five million barrels of oil (200 million gallons), with about 62,000 barrels per day released, according to the Unified Command, making it the biggest oil spill in history. The blame was placed on BP, which had contracted with other companies to build the well that it operated. Eventually, the gigantic oil spill reached the Gulf shoreline and affected wildlife, the environment, and the economies of several states, especially Louisiana, Mississippi, Alabama, and Florida. The spill caused massive damage to the shrimping and fishing industries, tourism, and businesses connected to tourism as oil washed ashore in tar balls and thick sticky slicks. Massive oil plumes beneath the water's surface were also detected in the Gulf.

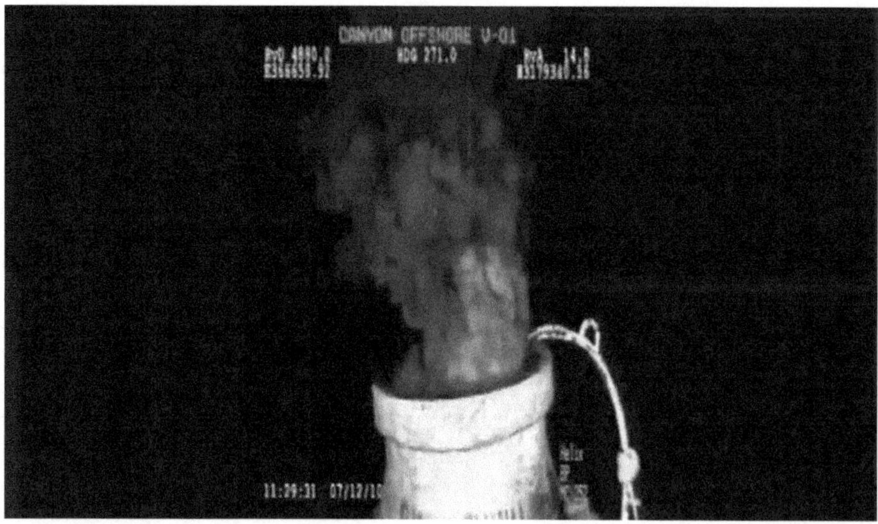

FIGURE 5.25 *The underwater camera captured images of tens of thousands of gallons of oil leaking from the oil rig.*
http://www.oilspillcommission.gov/
AP/Charlie Riedel

DEEP WATERS

As a result of the explosion and subsequent spill, BP was coping with an unprecedented disaster: trying to cap a well that had defied all sophisticated technological safeguards to prevent such an environmental catastrophe. Something like this had never happened before, and BP, as well as the entire offshore oil industry, struggled to find solutions to complex problems. Unlike ground wells that could be capped relatively easily, a deepwater well was an entirely different matter. Work had to be conducted with remotely operated robotic submersibles. Several attempts failed to stop the oil flow, including pumping first mud, then concrete into the well shaft to plug the well. BP tried lowering a large container over the well to siphon off the oil, but this failed when the container filled with ice crystals in the frigid subsea. In early June 2010 a loose cap was placed atop the blowout preventer; finally, in mid-July a tighter cap was affixed and closed off the leak. Eventually, five months after the explosion, the well was declared "dead" when a new relief well pumped in enough drilling mud and concrete to seal off the gusher.

In addition to the problem of sealing the well, numerous other issues caused concern and media scrutiny.

FIGURE 5.26 *Venice, La.—Cmdr. Virginia Kammer of the Coast Guard Gulf Strike Team conducted an interview at a pollution control staging area in Venice, La., April 30, 2010. Pollution control equipment was being deployed from staging areas along the Gulf Coast as the* Deepwater Horizon *oil spill continued to spread. U.S. Coast Guard photo by Petty Officer 3rd Class Patrick Kelley.*
https://cgvi.uscg.mil/media
U.S. Coast Guard

FIGURE 5.27 *A pelican coated in oil from the* Deepwater Horizon *oil spill.* AP Photo/Charlie Riedel

Chemical dispersants were used to break up the oil so that it could be oxidized much more easily by microbes that could consume the oil. About 1.84 million gallons of chemical dispersants were used in the Gulf of Mexico; nearly half were applied at the site of the wellhead on the ocean floor, which had never been done before. Scientists did not know for sure what detrimental effects, if any, would be caused by the use of dispersants in deep waters or on coastal shorelines.

BP's oil spill response and cleanup efforts were coordinated with the federal government's national response team comprising sixteen federal departments and agencies, including the Department of Homeland Security, Environmental Protection Agency, and Federal Emergency Management Agency. The Coast Guard directed the response, which included more than 47,000 workers and more than 6,400 vessels at its peak.

BP'S MISSTEPS

BP made a number of missteps during this crisis, some minor and others major. But taken together, they made it easy for environmentalists, politicians, media pundits, and others to cast BP as a fumbling, uncaring, and greedy multinational company that put profits ahead of everything. Here are some of the most memorable examples:

Shifting the Blame

Soon after the rig explosion, BP repeatedly placed the blame on Transocean, the rig owner, for the accident. A news release issued by BP the day after the explosion, headlined "BP Offers Full Support to Transocean after Drilling Rig Fire," said BP

FIGURE 5.28 Deepwater Horizon *oil spill.*
© Julie Dermansky/Corbis

"operates the license on which Transocean's rig was drilling an exploration well," to make clear the rig was owned by Transocean. In another news release issued April 29, nine days after the explosion, the company said "BP, as operator of the MC252 lease, continues to work around-the-clock on Transocean's subsea equipment"—again directing attention to Transocean. BP spokesman Andrew Gowers said: "This accident took place on a rig owned, managed and operated by Transocean. It involves the failure of a piece of equipment on that rig. So the unfolding events do not arise from a failure of BP's safety systems."

However, Hayward's media interviews were what people were really paying attention to. Even after President Barack Obama said May 1, "BP is responsible for this leak and will be paying the bill," Hayward was intent on shifting the blame away from BP. In a widely repeated exchange with ABC's *Good Morning America* host George Stephanopoulos on May 3, 2010, Hayward said:

> *This wasn't our accident. This was a drilling rig operated by another company. It was their people, their systems, their processes. We are responsible not for the accident, but we are responsible for the oil and for dealing with it and cleaning the situation up.*

Similar quotes provided by Hayward also appeared in many other news stories. To many Americans, this was splitting hairs and seemed like an attempt to escape responsibility for the disaster. When Stephanopoulos asked for clarification as to whether or not BP was responsible, Hayward said:

> *The drilling rig was a Transocean drilling rig. It was their equipment that's failed. It's their systems and processes that were running it.*

Well, we are clearly focused on minimizing the overall impact. We're a big company and we intend to deal with this. We take this responsibility incredibly seriously. We absolutely will prevail and we will deal with it.

Concern for Victims

BP didn't win any friends with its corporate business-as-usual attitude toward victims. A week after the explosion, reports surfaced that BP was requiring cleanup workers and people affected by the spill to sign waivers that would limit BP's liability, as well as confidentiality agreements in order to get financial relief. In the May 3 ABC interview, Hayward said: "Yeah, we've done that. That was an, an early misstep . . . frankly. We were using a standard contract. We've eliminated that."

The interview occurred on the same day that BP announced its 135 percent first quarter profit of $5.6 billion. To many, BP looked like it was trying to escape its stakeholder responsibilities by distancing itself from the crisis. This gave the appearance that it was trying to protect its financial assets while many Americans were suffering greatly from the disaster. This did not play well with the public, especially when news stories had already revealed BP's healthy 2009's pre-spill $14 billion profit. While other companies connected with the *Deepwater Horizon* did later contribute financially to the overall settlement, it was BP who shouldered the lion's share of the settlement costs.

Two days later, in an interview with *The Times* of London, Hayward said that victims would try to scam the system for profit:

Mr. Hayward reiterated a promise that BP "will honour all legitimate claims for business interruption." Asked for examples of illegitimate claims, he said: "I could give you lots of examples. This is America—come on. We're going to have lots of illegitimate claims. We all know that."

Quotes like these undermined Hayward's credibility and diminished the thoughtful gestures of concern that were expressed in one of BP's early news releases:

"We are determined to do everything in our power to contain this oil spill and resolve the situation as rapidly, safely and effectively as possible," said Group Chief Executive Tony Hayward. "We have assembled and are now deploying world-class facilities, resources and expertise, and can call on more if needed. There should be no doubt of our resolve to limit the escape of oil and protect the marine and coastal environments from its effects."

Scrambling for Solutions

BP's response indicated that the industry's impressive drilling technology in deep waters did not extend to the technology for dealing with a blowout like *Deepwater Horizon*. BP scrambled to figure out a way to stop the oil from gushing into the Gulf. It took multiple and what appeared to be somewhat clumsy efforts to finally plug the well after eighty-seven days of leaking.

There were also questions about the safety of using dispersants underwater, which had not been done before, and on such a mammoth scale. The number of unknowns and the lack of a response plan to deal appropriately with the crisis left people wondering about BP and the oil industry's priorities.

Changing Information

Originally, BP officials speculated that 1,000 barrels of oil were leaking daily. This estimate was increased nine days later to 5,000 barrels per day after mounting pressure from the Coast Guard and experts to change the flow rate. By May 14, 2010, a BP director told MSNBC that 5,000 barrels was a "good estimate" and that estimates by others of 70,000 barrels per day were "scaremongering." A month later a government panel said the flow rate was 60,000 barrels per day. By June the government was reporting that the spill "was spewing the equivalent of the *Exxon Valdez* disaster into the Gulf every two weeks or less."

A Reuters article said that documents submitted by BP to Congress showed that the well could flow as much as 100,000 barrels per day. While it is not unusual for information to change as better evidence becomes available during a crisis, the ever-shifting estimates of oil flow did not build confidence in BP's ability to handle the situation or trust in its sources.

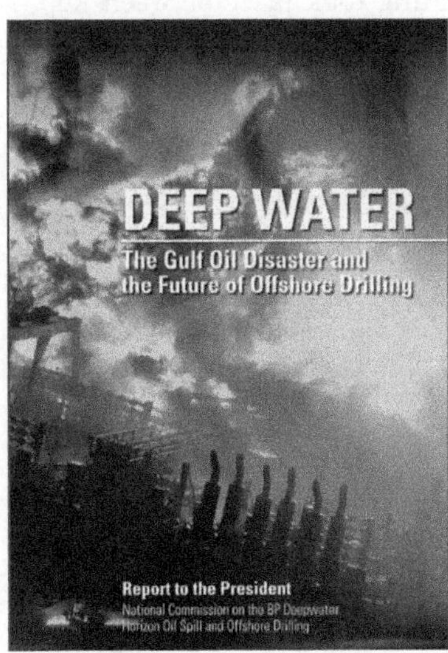

FIGURE 5.29 Deep Water: The Gulf Oil Disaster and the Future of Offshore Drilling *final report of the National Commission on the BP* Deepwater Horizon *Oil Spill and Offshore Drilling found plenty of industry issues and said the oil spill could have been prevented. http://www.oilspillcommission.gov/*

Transparency

In addition to its changing information, which didn't inspire confidence, BP was in defensive mode with mounting cleanup costs and legal suits. A day before Hayward testified to a Congressional hearing BP created a $20 billion set-aside fund for victim compensation, a figure that would later grow substantially. At a June 17, 2010, Congressional hearing fifty-nine days after the rig explosion, Hayward refused to answer many questions, infuriating lawmakers looking for answers on behalf of frustrated and upset constituents. Hayward, however, having been coached by legal and media advisers, responded cautiously or not at all.

When asked about the decisions that ultimately led to the rig explosion, Hayward responded: "I was not part of the decision-making process on this well. I had no prior knowledge." He also refused to speculate on the causes of the blowout until investigations had been completed. He did discuss BP's lines of inquiry that included the cement casing of the well, the well control procedures, and the blowout preventer.

The investigation's leader, Congressman Bart Stupak, told Hayward: "The committee is extremely frustrated with your lack of candor. You are the CEO. You have a PhD. We hope you have more candor in your responses." Even Republican members were unhappy. "You are copping out," said John "Phil" Gingrey (R-Ga.) "It seems like your testimony has been way too evasive."

An example of the level of frustration expressed by members of Congress during this highly publicized hearing took place between Rep. Peter Welch (D-Vermont) and Hayward.

FIGURE 5.30 *Tony Hayward, CEO of BP, testified to a Congressional hearing about BP's response.*

Mr. Welch: Mr Hayward, can you point to any single bad decision that was made in connection with *Deepwater Horizon*?

Mr. Hayward: As I have said often today, I am not prepared to point today, with a half-complete investigation, as to what was and was not a bad decision. There are many components to this accident, to do with, as I have said, the casing, how it was run; the cement job, how it was conducted; integrity tests that may or may not have been well-interpreted. At all stages, everyone on the rig decided that the right thing to do was to continue. We need to understand how that came about.

Mr. Welch: I understand that. But, with the benefit of hindsight and whatever investigatory work has been done, both by you and by others, at this moment, fifty-seven days after this event, is there anything you can identify that was done wrong?

Mr. Hayward: I am not able to draw that conclusion at this time.

Mr. Welch: Okay. Well, yesterday, Mr Hayward, I think BP took a very constructive step in agreeing to deposit $20 billion in an independently administered fund to compensate victims and to pay for the cleanup. It was a first step in establishing confidence in BP, confidence that BP's words would be matched by their deeds. But today, regrettably, your appearance here has done a good deal, at least for me, to erode that confidence. We know you are not an engineer, and we know that you were not on the *Deepwater Horizon*. But your answer sixty-five times that you don't know to questions that were reasonably posed to you on both sides of the aisle erodes confidence; it doesn't inspire confidence. You know, the question that any company has to ask itself is whether it has strict procedures in place to make disciplined decisions that give it confidence that, at a critical moment, where the lives of its workers and the investment of its shareholders is at stake, critical judgment will be exercised. And that is the obligation of the CEO. However it is for you to accomplish that ability to hold your workers accountable and support them; that is the job of the CEO, whether it is a small company or a large company. And at that very critical moment when that well was going to be capped and decisions had to be made about the sealing of the well, whether to use a cheaper and quicker casing design, whether to use more or fewer casing centralizers, whether to run a critical cementing test, whether or not to circulate drilling mud, it does not appear that anybody was in charge. And that is the erosion of confidence, because the lack of procedures, the lack of people being in charge, and resorting to the least-cost alternative clearly played a major role in this catastrophe.

CEO's Words and Actions

What captured the most negative attention, however, was BP's CEO Tony Hayward's words and actions. The British geologist-turned-executive did not have the ability to muster or sustain the necessary concern and compassion required by a slow-motion and lengthy crisis such as *Deepwater Horizon*.

In addition to trying to shift the blame to others, as previously described, BP tried to minimize the extent of the damage. Hayward said to *The Guardian* on May 14, 2010: "the Gulf of Mexico is a very big ocean. The amount of volume of oil and dispersant we are putting into it is tiny in relation to the total water volume." In an interview with *Sky News* on May 18, 2010, Hayward said: "It is impossible to say and we will mount, as part of the aftermath, a very detailed environmental assessment but everything we can see at the moment suggests that the overall environmental impact will be very, very modest."

However, the biggest foot-in-mouth moment came on May 30, 2010, in front of many reporters: "The first thing to say is I'm sorry. We're sorry for the massive disruption it's caused their lives. There's no one who wants this over more than I do. I would like my life back."

Two days after testifying before Congress and refusing to answer many questions related to the *Deepwater Horizon* incident, Hayward was seen on a yacht off the Isle of Wight.

MEDIA COVERAGE

Media coverage was intense. According to a study by the Pew Research Center's Project for Excellence in Journalism, the spill was one of the top three stories in the mainstream press during a fourteen-week period; it took the top spot for nine weeks. However, the news coverage never exceeded 22 percent of the "news hole."

The most intense news coverage by the mainstream media occurred from April 20 through July 28, when the story "accounted for 22 percent of the news hole, almost twice as much coverage as the No. 2 story, the economy, at 12 percent."

The report said "on Twitter, it was among the top five most tweeted topics twice during those fourteen weeks. And videos about the spill made the list of most viewed news videos on YouTube three times."

While the news media was playing a major role in reporting the crisis, the public interest was even greater. The Pew research found that between April 26 and May 23, respondents who said they were "very closely following events in the Gulf" ranged between 44 percent and 58 percent. Even as news media coverage began to subside,

FIGURE 5.31 *Venice, La.—President Barack Obama addresses the media at Coast Guard Station Venice, May 2, 2010.*
https://cgvi.uscg.mil
U.S. Coast Guard

during the June 28 to July 25 time period, "the percentage of those paying very close attention remained at near peak levels—between 43 percent and 59 percent."

Media relations became a problem as BP officials became too busy or were shielded from providing necessary access to reporters.

An Associated Press story June 11, 2010, noted that BP officials had drifted away from daily news media briefings that allowed questions. Due to time constraints, fewer briefings and more teleconferences were offered that "limited the ability to ask questions and the number of questions that could be asked." The article also said

> *In Houston, where BP has set up a U.S. command center, company PR officials have grown weary of reporters going directly to engineers and other higher-ups for information, at times trying to insist media go through them first.*
>
> *Spokesman Robert Wine said in an e-mail to The Associated Press that media visits to the Houston center are "very carefully controlled and sparingly arranged" by design.*
>
> *"The rooms that are shown are full of the teams who WILL make a difference on the result of this crisis," Wine wrote. "Every second they are not helping with media visits is time they are not doing the 'day job.'"*

It was inevitable that news media and experts compared the BP *Deepwater Horizon* blowout to another infamous industry disaster, the 1989 *Exxon Valdez* oil spill

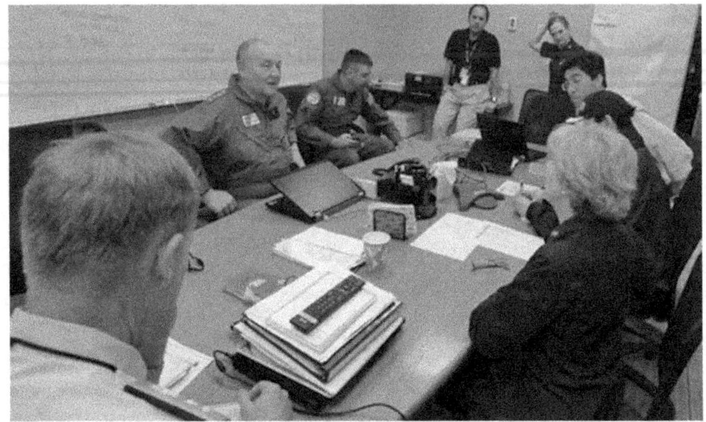

FIGURE 5.32 *Visit with Unified Command Robert, La.—U.S. Coast Guard Commandant Adm. Thad Allen met with Rear Adm. Mary Landry, the federal on-scene coordinator for the* Deepwater Horizon *incident, and other local, state and federal members participating in the unified command to discuss leveraging every available resource to respond to the BP oil spill and minimize the associated environmental risks, May 1, 2010.*
https://cgvi.uscg.mil
U.S. Coast Guard

in Prince William Sound, Alaska. The oil tanker spilled at least 260,000 barrels (11 million gallons) of crude oil on a remote and sensitive ecosystem that is still recovering. That spill covered 11,000 square miles of ocean and 1,200 miles of coastline. It was the worst manmade environmental disaster in U.S. history at the time; more than 100,000 seabirds died and the pink salmon population was severely impacted. Exxon's cleanup and litigation costs ran to about $3.5 billion, or $6.3 billion when adjusted for inflation, according to CNN.

This comparison was not helpful for BP's image as BP would go down as the biggest U.S. oil disaster of all time—and by a lot. The *Deepwater Horizon* spilled five million barrels of oil compared to just 260,000 barrels for the *Exxon Valdez* incident.

The *Deepwater Horizon* mishap, like other oil spills, was a visual story, creating an exciting event for television at each phase of the crisis response. There were the expected oil-soaked bird photos, controlled oil burns at sea, gigantic "oil plumes" beneath the sea, as well as workers, cloaked in protective clothing, combing shorelines for tar balls and other oily items.

Unlike the *Exxon Valdez* spill, the after-effects of the spill were easy for people to see personally since they affected several states' shorelines; the *Exxon Valdez* was in a remote part of Alaska. The *Deepwater Horizon* disaster was long-lasting;

FIGURE 5.33 *Gulf of Mexico.—Oil was collected in skimming booms attached to the U.S. Coast Guard cutter* Elm *approximately 21 miles off the coast of Perdido Key, Fla., June 6, 2010. The cutter, a buoy tender homeported in Atlantic Beach, N.C., was diverted from its routine duties to help with the ongoing Administration-wide response to the* Deepwater Horizon/*BP oil spill.*
https://cgvi.uscg.mil
U.S. Coast Guard

FIGURE 5.34 *Lafourche Parish, La.—Workers, contracted by BP, cleaned up oil on the beaches in Port Fourchon, La., during night operations, June 25, 2010. Night operations allowed workers to clean up while the tide was out.*
https://cgvi.uscg.mil
U.S. Coast Guard

the well gushed for eighty-four days and the cleanup continued years afterwards. When the first oil hit the Louisiana shoreline on April 30, 2010, there were dozens of news crews dipping their hands into the oily mess to show viewers the devastation up close.

Spillcam

While many BP critics praised the company for providing a live video feed of the gushing well leak, posted May 19 on a Congressional website, the images did not come voluntarily. According to Congressman Ed Markey (D-Ma.), BP waited thirty-eight days after the spill to provide the feed to Congress. The live video stream, from BP's remotely operated vehicle submarines, allowed people the chance to see for themselves what was happening and determine the spill's flow rate. The eerily silent video from 5,000 feet below the sea was disconcerting to watch without explanatory documentation and served as an unsettling and constant reminder of the work ahead. PBS developed an oil leak meter widget on its website that allowed viewers to adjust the leak rate or use suggested flow rates estimated by the Department of Energy, BP, and other experts to determine estimated total gallons leaked.

BETTER BP MOVES

Apologies

While there has been a lot of attention devoted to Hayward's gaffes, he often spoke sincerely about the tragedy. Hayward repeated BP's commitment to clean up the oil and help the people of the Gulf Coast. He made a convincing apology on behalf of

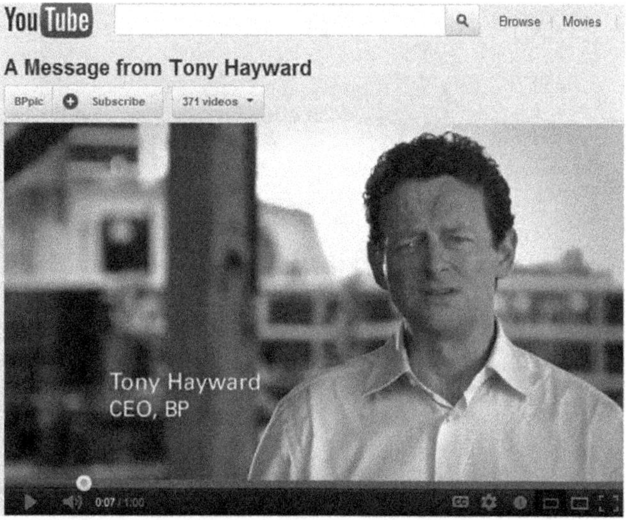

FIGURE 5.35 *A message from Tony Hayward offered a videotaped apology for the American public.*
YouTube BP Channel
BP

BP in a video statement that began airing on U.S. television June 2, 2010. Hayward was shown saying:

> *The Gulf spill is a tragedy that never should have happened. I'm Tony Hayward.*
>
> *BP has taken full responsibility for cleaning up the spill in the Gulf. We've helped organize the largest environmental response in this country's history. More than two million feet of boom, thirty planes and over 1,300 boats are working to protect the shoreline. Where oil reaches the shore, thousands of people are ready to clean it up. We will honor all legitimate claims. And our cleanup efforts will not come at any cost to taxpayers.*
>
> *To those affected and your families, I am deeply sorry. The Gulf is home for thousands of BP's employees and we all feel the impact. To all the volunteers and for the strong support of the government, thank you. We know it is our responsibility to keep you informed. And do everything we can so this never happens again. We will get this done. We will make this right.*

The commercial/video ended with a text graphic: "For information or assistance: bp.com, 866–448–5816."

Of course, not everyone was happy with this slick commercial. President Obama and others said BP should spend its money on cleanup and compensating devastated fishermen and small business owners.

Not as visible but widely reported was Hayward's other apology for his off-hand remark, reported May 30, 2010, that he wanted his life back. The unfortunate comment stirred up the blogosphere and was widely reported in traditional news outlets. Hayward's statement was posted on the BP America Facebook page June 2, 2010:

> *I made a hurtful and thoughtless comment on Sunday when I said that "I wanted my life back." When I read that recently, I was appalled. I apologize, especially to the families of the eleven men who lost their lives in this tragic accident. Those words don't represent how I feel about this tragedy, and certainly don't represent the hearts of the people of BP—many of whom live and work in the Gulf—who are doing everything they can to make things right. My first priority is doing all we can to restore the lives of the people of the Gulf region and their families—to restore their lives, not mine.*

Information Campaign

BP's information campaign to inform stakeholders and redeem its reputation began early in the crisis. BP used its own website, Facebook, Twitter, YouTube, and Flickr accounts to push out unified messages summarizing BP's latest updates about the leak, oil containment, cleanup efforts, and health, environmental, and claims issues. British-based Ogilvy & Mather worked with BP and the *Deepwater Horizon* Response center, according to Media Bistro. By June 21, 2010, *AdWeek* reported that the company's Facebook page, BP America, had only 25,000 fans and its Twitter account had just 14,800 followers two months after the explosion.

AdWeek said BP bought key search terms ("BP," "oil leak," "oil spill") to use in targeted online ads guiding people using search terms about the spill to BP's online information sites.

BP bought full-page ads in *The Washington Post* and *The New York Times* May 25, 2010. Entitled "Gulf of Mexico Oil Spill Response. What We're Doing. How to Get More Information," the text-only ad's only graphic element was a small BP sun logo in the upper-right corner to identify its owner. It began:

> *Since the tragic accident on the Transocean* Deepwater Horizon *rig first occurred, we have been committed to doing everything possible to stop the flow of oil at the seabed, collect the oil on the surface and keep it away from the shore.*
>
> *BP has taken full responsibility for dealing with the spill. We are determined to do everything we can to minimize any impact. We will honor all legitimate claims.*
>
> *This is an enormous team effort.*

The advertisement included an update on the oil spill response and thanked the efforts of "nearly 24,000 people working with BP full-time or as volunteers" to solve the problem. It provided phone numbers for shoreline oil issues, impacted wildlife, claims information, and website addresses for BP and the government/BP information sites.

The Congressional committee overseeing the BP investigation announced that BP spent $93 million on public relations in the first three months of the spill, double its normal advertising budget. Its regular corporate image advertising was pulled after the spill.

While Twitter was still relatively new to the corporate world, it was embraced by BP for communicating with stakeholders, albeit after a slow start.

BP had started using Twitter four months before the *Deepwater Horizon* spill, @BP_America. Nine days after the rig explosion, BP created a separate Twitter account called @Oil_Spill_2010. Researchers Walton et al. (2012) examined BP and the Unified Command's 1,142 tweets transmitted via Twitter between April 29 and September 19, 2010. Using the Timothy Coombs SCCT framework, their research found that 55 percent of the tweets used ingratiation, concern, and compassion message strategies while 35 percent used justification, minimization, and excuse message strategies. Walton et al. found many tweets included a link to another web page, an online video, news article, press release, or government report. About one month after the explosion, BP created a blog that encouraged followers to use the blog to file complaints, which reduced traffic on its Twitter account. In July, the U.S. government took control of the Twitter account and the name changed to @Restore_TheGulf.

BP's Facebook site, BP America, created in June 2009, began posting information May 2, 2010. It was merged for a time with the Unified Command Joint information Center's "*Deepwater Horizon* Response" Facebook page where all of the federal government agencies were working together with BP to meet crisis information needs. By October 2010, it had returned to its own Facebook presence: a BP messaging platform. Facebook was the most visible of the social media channels; however, BP did not use it as a two-way communication tool to engage its stakeholders in a conversation. Rather, BP posted many messages, links, photos, and updates.

Advertising Campaign

By June 2010, BP had selected a Washington public affairs firm, Purple Strategies, owned by two Republican and Democratic strategists, for its U.S. campaign, instead of its longtime agency WPP's Ogilvy & Mather, according to *The Wall Street Journal*. BP also hired American Anne Womack Kolton for its U.S. media relations. Kolton, also a political insider, was a former U.S. Energy Department official and aide to former Vice President Dick Cheney, according to *The Wall Street Journal*.

The news media and blogosphere were full of criticism in early June 2010 about the new series of image ads that were just rolling out. One crisis communication expert, Timothy Sellnow, a communication professor at the University of Kentucky, seemed to sum up BP's situation best in a Greenwire report:

> *"The primary story throughout the process became the solution of the week," Sellnow said. "As each of these solutions failed to work, the urgency [to stop the leak] went up."*
>
> *"From a public relations standpoint the story got away from them and became one of science and became one of consistent and persistent failures," Sellnow added. In the process, he said, the company failed to show compassion for people early on.*
>
> *"A scientific explanation to someone whose livelihood is threatened is of very little merit," Sellnow said. "They want to know, what are you going to do to compensate me.*
>
> *"You can't win the hearts and minds of people by solely emphasizing science," Sellnow added. "You need to show a concern for the people and their needs."*

The new American strategists seemed to have a better handle on the American psyche. The television, radio, and print campaign that emerged focused on what BP was doing for those affected by the crisis. Most of the early commercials featured BP workers and Gulf Coast natives (or at least employees with convincing southern accents).

BP's video commercials and messages were high-quality productions that featured BP officials, BP workers, volunteers, and citizens of the Gulf. The campaign's commercials aired frequently on national television and were available on BP's YouTube channel, created May 18, 2010. BP early on discovered Iris Cross, a community outreach director in Louisiana, who was born in New Orleans; her family still lived there. The television commercial "BP Gulf Coast Update: Our Ongoing Commitment" received more than a million hits on YouTube. Another commercial called "Gulf of Mexico Response: Communities" earned nearly 377,000 views. It was easy to see why people identified with Cross; she was a youngish American from the region and her concern for people seemed genuine.

Another BP star was Daryl Willis, born and raised in Louisiana, who volunteered for the BP claims assignment effort. He, like Cross, came across as genuine in his

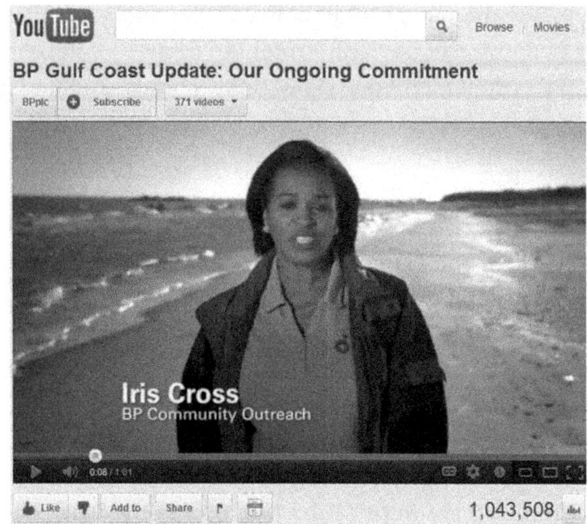

FIGURE 5.36 *BP Gulf Coast update:* Our Ongoing Commitment.
http://www.youtube.com/
BP

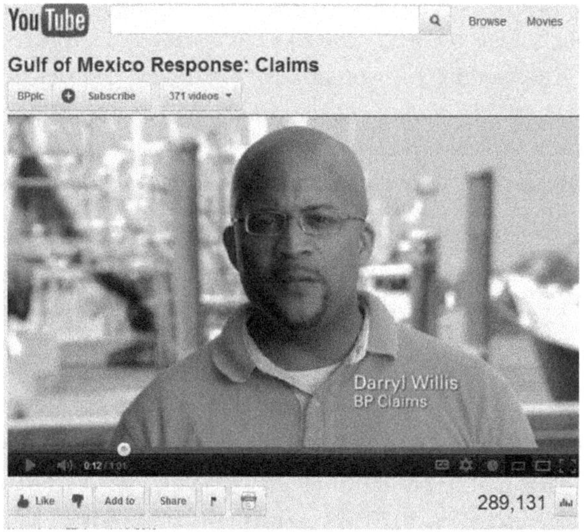

FIGURE 5.37 *BP Gulf of Mexico response: Claims.*
http://www.bp.com/
BP

concern, and he had credibility since he was native to the region. His commercial received 289,131 YouTube views.

After BP plugged the leak in September 2010, it turned its energy to expanding its image-building ads, portraying how BP was helping Gulf Coast residents get back to business as usual. BP created two major commercial campaigns, called "Voices from the Gulf" and "My Gulf," which were designed to show how BP was responding to those affected by the crisis through the voices of Gulf Coast residents. The high-quality spots were visually interesting and the stories captivating and charming.

BP found a telegenic young married couple, Bryan and Brooke Zar, whose nearly six-minute YouTube interview discussed the struggles of operating a Cajun-style restaurant alongside a leafy bayou during the crisis when seafood was unavailable. BP did another shorter version for its "Voices from the Gulf" series that showed the Zars' restaurant contracted by BP to help feed BP workers and volunteers in the region when shrimp and oysters were not available during the crisis. This video received 142,478 hits. A third video featured the Zars' Restaurant des Familles in Crown Point, Louisiana, and the Gulf's delicious seafood. "The Gulf's back," says Brooke in the video. "Our shrimpers and fishermen are back on the water; our beaches are clean—just in time for spring break." The other not-so-subtle message conveyed by the Zars was that BP cares and was taking care of those affected by the oil spill.

Other commercials featured quaint characters such as a proud old shrimper ("My Gulf Isle," "Louisiana–Shrimping by Moonlight"), gumbo cooks ("My Gulf: Making Perfect Gumbo"), and a local pottery artist who used the Mississippi clay for his creations ("My Gulf: Pass Christian, MS: Crafting Mississippi Clay").

BP's YouTube channel had many technical features related to the oil leak mission including a three-minute feature on drilling the relief well for the "final kill," which drew more than 50,000 viewers. No technology was too mundane to go

FIGURE 5.38 *"Voices of the Gulf" featured restaurant owners husband and wife Bryan and Brooke Zar.*
http://www.youtube.com/
BP

FIGURE 5.39 *"My Gulf: New Orleans, Louisiana—Cooking the perfect gumbo."*
http://www.youtube.com/
BP

unnoticed by BP's video crews. BP produced a feature on boom technology. It drew a respectable 5,587 views. Other more popular draws were videos explaining the various strategies to cap the gushing oil at the bottom of the sea. One video that provided a technical overview by a BP engineer on installing the new cap drew 165,370 views in July 2010.

BP's Website

The critiques on BP's website were mixed. While it contained a lot of information and was updated regularly, researchers Hall, Kice, and Choi (2012) said the BP crisis part of its website was too technical and not visual enough for its main audience—the Gulf Coast residents and business owners affected by the oil spill. Their research concluded:

> *BP's target audience does not appear to be the general U.S. public. Rather, BP's target audience appears to be a mirror of itself. This means that BP has tailored its message as a form of internal self-justification instead of an argument to de-vilify itself in the eyes of the general public. Similarly, BP's press releases even weeks after the spill avoided a strategy of accepting blame (Harlow et al., 2011). This fact goes a long way toward explaining dynamic narrative. As a science-driven and technology organization, BP uses the message strategy of drab technoscience with which it feels most comfortable.*

RECOVERY

By fall of 2010, with the oil well capped and the majority of the beach cleanup finished, BP was faced with the daunting task of restoring Gulf Coast businesses and BP's reputation in America. The Gulf Coast restoration would take years and a true sustained commitment from BP in words and actions were needed. The following are some BP actions that can be analyzed from the recovery phase of the crisis:

- Sponsored scientific Gulf Coast and oil spill research
- Image advertising
- Olympic sponsorships
- Tourism support and promotion
- Community support initiatives
- Risk management changes
- Communication (social media, website, etc.).

FINANCIAL IMPLICATIONS

While the acute crisis phase lasted eighty-seven days—the time between the rig explosion and final closure of the well—the negative consequences continued for years as investigations and lawsuits were filed and settled. To meet anticipated costs related to the oil spill, BP sold $35 billion in assets in 2012, and by March 2013 the company had spent $24 billion in cleanup/response costs and claims payments to individuals, businesses, and governments.

The financial impact on BP for litigation and fines was estimated between $41.9 billion and $59.4 billion by Bernstein Research, according to *The New York Times*. Here are additional details of the spill's financial consequences:

- In November 2012, BP pleaded guilty to the U.S. Department of Justice to fourteen crimes including manslaughter and environmental misconduct/neglect, which resulted in $4.5 billion in penalties. Part of the settlement required BP to appoint two monitors for safety and ethics issues and go on five years' probation. Two BP employees aboard the drilling rig were charged with manslaughter related to the rig explosion deaths.
- As part of BP's settlement with the U.S. Department of Justice in November 2012, BP admitted to providing inaccurate information to the public regarding the rate of oil released from the well, which resulted in a $525 million civil fine to the Securities and Exchange Commission for misleading investors.

- A federal civil claim for environmental fines under the Clean Water Act and the Natural Resources Damage Assessment, representing the U.S. Justice Department, Gulf states and private individuals, sought to prove that BP acted with "gross negligence and willful misconduct" instead of simple negligence. If proven true, it would quadruple the fines from $5.1 billion to $21 billion, depending on the final determination on how much oil was spilled.
- A class action lawsuit (Plaintiffs' Steering Committee) by 100,000 individuals and businesses claiming economic and medical damages from the spill could cost BP much more than its estimated $7.8 billion.

Two other companies involved with the oil spill, Transocean and Halliburton, which operated the *Deepwater Horizon* oil rig, pleaded guilty to violating the Clean Water Act and paid $1.4 billion in civil and criminal fines. Halliburton, which provided the cement that failed in the well, was also under investigation. These companies were also involved in the federal civil claim under the Clean Water Act and Natural Resources Damage Assessment which could result in billions more in fines and penalties.

BP had agreed to create a $20 billion compensation fund shortly after the disaster occurred. The resulting claims settlement, representing about 100,000 claims, did not have a cap. BP had estimated that it would pay out $7.8 billion in claims. However, that figure could go higher.

BP was back in the news in 2013 when its lawyers sought to change the terms of the court-supervised settlement claiming that some claimants' losses were not spill related despite the fact that BP set the guidelines for the affected economic loss zones and the percent of decline and incline in revenue needed to prove the claim.

BP placed full-page ads in *The New York Times* and *The Wall Street Journal* to further their case. Critics of BP noted that it was delaying and denying claim payments based on minor technicalities in order to frustrate legitimate claims.

U.S. District Judge Carl Barbier, the settlement judge, refused to temporarily shut down the settlement program to accommodate an internal investigation into alleged settlement fraud. Barbier was quoted in a July 2013 Associated Press article criticizing BP's continued tactics to evade its responsibilities after one lawyer who worked for the claims administrator Patrick Juneau was accused of misconduct:

> *"I find the recent attacks on Mr [Patrick] Juneau's [the lawyer administering the claims] character are highly offensive, inappropriate," Barbier said.*
>
> *Barbier said he found it "especially offensive" that BP CEO Robert Dudley claimed during an interview televised by CNBC on Thursday that the settlement process has been "hijacked."*
>
> *"Personal attacks, hyperbole and use of such language in my opinion crosses the line," he said.*

In a Huffington Post article, BP spokesman Geoff Morrell said the company disagreed with Barbier's ruling to continue settlement payments during the internal investigation of alleged fraud by the lawyers administering the claims.

Morrell said the company would review its legal options. "There is a material risk that payments going out the door have been and continue to be tainted by possibly fraudulent or corrupt activity, and BP should not be forced to bear the risks of improper payments pending the outcome of Judge Freeh's investigation," Morrell said in a statement.

QUESTIONS FOR DISCUSSION

1. What were some of BP's other controversies before the *Deepwater Horizon* blowout?
2. How did BP shift the blame for the *Deepwater Horizon* oil leak initially?
3. What were some of BP's missteps in handling the crisis?
4. What were the trust issues involved in this case from the public's perspective?
5. What were the visual aspects of the story that were used by the news media?
6. What were some of the most effective elements of BP's information campaign?
7. BP developed an advertising campaign that included many vignettes of people from the Gulf region. How effective were those videos?
8. How well did BP do with the media relations during the crisis?
9. Tony Hayward, BP's CEO, made some missteps during the crisis. What were they?
10. Describe BP's recovery efforts after the oil leak was sealed. What tactics were effective? Why?

Dig Deeper

A full-page advertisement during the BP oil crisis is available to review on the textbook's companion website. Bob Dudley, BP's CEO after Tony Hayward resigned, provided a different tone to BP's oil spill response. Watch the video *BP—A Year of Change* and read its accompanying transcript, available on the textbook's companion website. What message points does Dudley make for repairing BP's image? Assess the effectiveness of this tactic. View BP's sustainability report "Building a Stronger, Safer BP" available on the textbook's companion website. What are the key messages and strategies for building trust with its stakeholders?

Some of the transcripts of the BP trial are also available for background.

CHAPTER 6

Activism

As discussed in Chapter 5, conflict makes news. When organizational performance fails to live up to stakeholder expectations, pressure groups can form; these groups demand change from organizations, even governments. Their pressure tactics and the resulting conflict—often fueled by sophisticated tactics, including social media use—make activism a force to reckon with in today's 24/7 news cycle. Public relations has always recognized the role of pressure groups in the practice, but lately more attention from public relations researchers has emerged to grapple with the deeper issues involved. Public relations scholar Larissa Grunig defined activist organizations as "a group of two or more individuals who organize in order to influence another public or publics through action that may include education, compromise, persuasion, pressure tactics or force."

Activists don't just happen, although their awakening can be rapid depending on the situation. There are three stages in the evolution of publics, according to scholars James Grunig and Todd Hunt. In the first—latent—stage, a public does not recognize a situation as a problem. Second, a group recognizes a problem and moves into the aware stage. In the third stage, a public becomes active and organizes to discuss and to do something about the situation.

Activists often use many public relations strategies and tactics, including information tactics, to build influence and power. The growing availability and affordability of sophisticated communication technology over the past two decades has allowed activists to match or even surpass what their multibillion dollar organizational target can do. As researchers Timothy Coombs and Sherry Holladay noted, activists build power to persuade organizations to alter their behaviors and policies.

Patrick Jackson identified five distinct tactical areas used by activists to achieve their goals: informational activities including media interviews; symbolic activities including boycotts; organizing activities such as passing out information pieces and holding meetings; legal and legislative activities and pressuring regulatory and administrative agencies; and civil disobedience including sit-ins, blocking traffic, and trespassing.

Activists use persuasion to win over converts to their side of the issue. To be successful, activist organizations need to increase their power by: attracting new followers and political allies, and by forming coalitions; attaining media coverage that favors their point of view; and attracting monetary support. By increasing its power, an activist organization will gain the attention of the target organization and the opportunity to engage it.

Ronald Mitchell, Bradley Agle, and Donna Wood used the interesting analogy of "annoying mosquitoes" to describe activists. After all, organizations are powerful and face many issues. Still, they are restricted to some degree by their resources. Organizations prioritize what issues they must address through assessment. Mitchell et al. found three factors—power, legitimacy, and urgency—determined how organizations prioritize issues or threats. Power, in this context, refers to the ability of the public to influence the behavior of the organization; legitimacy refers to whether or not others will view the group's tactics as socially acceptable; and urgency refers to how likely the group is to take action.

It's useful to note that there are different types of crisis threats. Coombs identified what he calls "paracrisis" as "a publicly visible crisis threat that charges an organization with irresponsible or unethical behavior." This type of threat is essentially a reputational threat since there is an expectation gap between the stakeholder and the organization. Organizations dealing with paracrises may be constrained by cost of the change requested and consistency with organizational strategy. Organizations have three primary communication responses to these public challenges: refute, reform, and refuse.

Researcher Timothy Rowley has shown how activists gain power from coalition building within the organization's stakeholder networks. Activist websites and social media can play an important role in developing the activist group's legitimacy within the organization's stakeholder network. The activist website can link to other organizational stakeholders and the news media, and it can become the main source of credible information for all stakeholders. The activist can strengthen his or her influence by talking directly to other stakeholders in the organization's network and eventually gain more adherents for the cause.

Activists, like organizations, use social media to build relationships and followers. According to Tamar Ginossar, social media can obtain information, provide unsolicited information about the issue, answer questions from information seekers, provide emotional support, offer calls for action, and build conflict through complaints or criticism. Persuasion is an important activist tactic. As the term implies, activists seek action-oriented messages that are also inspirational.

activist

There are three message frames used by activists: problem identification (diagnostic frame); steps to eliminating the problem (prescriptive frame); and the call to action (motivational frame).

Frequently problem identification can be presented in many ways, from emotional to logical appeals or a mixture of both. Animal activists often use visual communication tactics, such as undercover investigative videos or photos of animal abuse, to hammer home their points. Less emotional visual tactics can still be quite powerful in cases where an organization's product or service can be shown to be faulty by demonstrating the problem with video or photos. Many other forms of evidence can be used by activists to build their case, such as financial statements, research, and third-party experts.

Strong communication skills, especially when interacting with the news media through interviews, are important factors in successful problem identification, prescriptive and motivational message frames.

Many factors affect how successful activism is in achieving its goal. Conviction is important. Activists need to be committed to the cause and feel deeply that organizations must change. A favorite organizational response is simply to ignore the complaint in hopes that the activist will give up. Resources such as time, energy, and some money are needed to keep the cause alive while building power and influence, and activists must be creative; they have to develop new ways to share the problem they are trying to solve.

ACTIVISM AND PUBLIC RELATIONS THEORY

As the Arab Spring demonstrated in 2011, the ability to communicate and bring together diverse groups for a common cause via new technologies such as Twitter, Facebook and blogs created an impressive new power for coalition building and information creation, hitherto normally controlled by the ruling government. The issue of power or the negotiation of power is at the center of a debate among public relations theorists who are grappling with how to fit today's activism into public relations theory.

For more than two decades, the excellence theory of public relations, considered the dominant public relations theory, called for symmetrical two-way communication between organizations and publics (dialogue), compromise, and shared power. Information, rather than persuasion, was considered the most ethical approach to achieving mutual understanding between the organization and its publics. Persuasion was seen by excellence theory adherents as manipulative and indicative of an organization's self-interests rather than mutual gain. Critics said the theory was not practical since organizations are unlikely to give up power and influence. Contingency theory suggested that there are many variables that lead to greater or lesser degrees of accommodation. Likewise, situational theory identifies publics (active, aware, or latent) and describes their communication behavior. The mixed-motive theory of public relations recognized each group's self-interests as a starting point for building a relationship.

On the issue of power, central to the critical public relations theorists, excellence theorists said power was not an issue. Active publics could organize into activist groups to create their own power to prevent organizations from abusing their power by ignoring or eliminating the debate.

However, postmodern public relations scholars such as Derina Holtzhausen (2007) said that excellence theory did not take into account the power imbalance that exists between organizations and their publics. Organizations often have unlimited resources, or at least more than activist groups, and sophisticated power systems that extend into the halls of government.

Holtzhausen said the individual is not powerless and called for public relations as activism. She said practitioners needed to be "change agents, serve as the conscience of the organization, and give voice to those without power in their relationship with the organization." She also noted that practitioners should resist the "dominant power structures, particularly when these structures are not inclusive."

Critical theorists in public relations accept that persuasion, rather than information, is the primary tool of public relations practitioners and that the goal is for the organization to gain control or power over its publics so that it is not constrained from achieving its goals.

While activist groups may not have as much power as organizations, there are some areas that activists can exploit to their advantage. According to researchers Coombs and Holladay, organizations today need to do more than make a profit. They are more vulnerable to rising public expectations in areas of corporate social responsibility such as environmental stewardship, human rights, workers' rights, animal rights, and many others that demand the attention of public relations managers. Missteps by organizations can have significant reputational and financial costs.

Public relations education today is mostly taught from the organizational-centric perspective that focuses on the corporation and public relations agencies rather than the activist viewpoint. That focus originated when early theorists referred to activists as "obstacles" or as organizational constraints or problems to be dealt with. Today, activist groups are considered legitimate publics.

RAISING AWARENESS

As noted above, raising awareness about an issue is necessary for activists to gain enough power to take on, and request change from, an organization. Activists seek out the news media for interviews; create events such as protests, boycotts, marches, and stunts; and offer information directly on websites through social media. The tactics can range from very basic to sophisticated media relations (see Chapter 4).

The Internet provides important ways for activists to get their positions out to the world and attract support. To be effective, activist websites should be content-rich and cater to both supporters and the news media. For example, to ensure local voices are heard on the organization's issues, many activist organizations have developed do-it-yourself media relations toolkits that include:

- Key messages
- Talking points
- Q&As
- Tips on how to reach local influencers
- Sample press releases
- Sample letters to the editor

- Tips for contributing to a blog
- Sample PowerPoint on the key issues and solutions.

With the flood of content available online today, organizations struggle with how to be seen and heard in a sea of websites. As many experts say, the world does not need another blog: it just needs one place where all the relevant information on a topic appears. One concept, "content curation," finds, organizes, and links to all relevant information on a specific topic or issue. The idea is to build a website that is the "go-to" site for news and information on a particular topic.

Enriching content on websites, also referred to as content marketing, is getting more attention these days to provide a better-quality experience for users. These quality content add-ons are also reformatted and conveyed through various social media sites managed by the organization. Beyond the basic content needs, organizations are also including:

- White papers
- E-books
- E-magazines or newsletters
- Infographics
- Case studies
- How-to's
- Q&As
- Photo galleries
- Videos
- Testimonials
- Research reports.

Much has been said about the importance of search engine optimization (SEO) so that people can find your website when they type in a key term or the name of the organization to a search engine. This continues to be crucial for developing awareness for an organization. Google Analytics provides a free service to measure a site's SEO success.

14

"Beyond Disgusting"

Bacteria-Fighting Mom Takes on Restaurant Play Areas

Erin Carr-Jordan, a mother of four, from Southeast Valley near Phoenix, Arizona, had no intention of becoming an international crusader for clean fast-food play areas. Her battle against bacteria was born of utter frustration and her determination to warn other mothers about a disturbing discovery.

It all began one morning when her young son had to make an emergency bathroom break on the way to school. Mother and son stopped at a McDonald's restaurant in Tempe, Arizona, and on the way out, he asked if he could go down the slide in the play area. Following her youngest son through the plastic tubing she was amazed and disgusted by what she saw, as she recalled the incident to CNN:

> *immediately when we entered, we noticed it was beyond disgusting. It was covered in black goo. There was so much stuff on the Plexiglas that you couldn't see out the window.*
>
> *There were large gashes in the slide. It was covered from head to toe in gang tagging and profanity. Ketchup was squirted on the wall and children's hair got stuck in it and it smelled like urine and feces.*

Carr-Jordan, a professor with a Ph.D. in educational psychology, complained on six occasions to four managers at the restaurant and its corporate headquarters for a month, but no changes were made.

Carr-Jordan wanted to know if the filthy conditions she observed were also dangerous. She shared her concerns with her long-time friend Dr. Annissa Furr, a Phoenix microbiologist and college professor, who suggested that she return to the restaurant and swab the play equipment areas for bacterial analysis. Carr-Jordan paid about $700 for the first lab analysis, although she later learned to streamline the process to a more affordable $150.

The results were startling. Thirteen different types of "opportunistic pathogens" were found, mostly consisting of fecal matter. Furr said that young children were at risk of getting sick—and for children with compromised immune systems, the pathogens were potentially deadly.

FIGURE 6.1 *The indoor play area equipment that Erin Carr-Jordan found was "beyond disgusting" for the amount of dirt and grime she found. http://www.kidsplaysafe.net/*
Courtesy of Erin Carr-Jordan

Carr-Jordan discovered that the county health department's food inspection authority did not extend to restaurant play areas. They were essentially unmonitored areas in which health and safety conditions were controlled by the restaurant management.

Furr, with a child of her own, offered to help Carr-Jordan draft state legislation to require health agencies to regulate the cleanliness of restaurant play areas.

Carr-Jordan returned to the Gilbert, Arizona, McDonald's May 10, 2011, to document the filth and inappropriate gang slang and swear words scrawled inside the tubes. She created a video that she uploaded to her newly created Kids Play Safe Facebook page on May 13, 2011, and YouTube on May 14, 2011. Carr-Jordan's first Facebook page post had the video link and said: "Hi everyone. Please watch the video and share your experiences. Together we can make a difference!"

The video, entitled *McSwarth.flv*, was a strictly amateur work—with shaky shots, some out-of-focus images, shot in available light with dizzying pans and rudimentary edits. It had the look and feel of a mother crawling through a dirty environment commenting on what she saw—with motherly dismay and some outrage in her narration. Despite its lack of high professional standards, its authenticity rang true. Here was a concerned mother who just wanted to share with other mothers what she had seen and warn them of the potentially dangerous conditions at a McDonald's restaurant.

In the eleven-minute video, she discussed and visually displayed close-up shots of the lab report's findings and concluded the video with a call to action to other parents and legislators:

> *As you can see from the video it's absolutely disgusting, but more importantly it's preventable. As parents we just need to say to McDonald's and other PlayLands that*

FIGURE 6.2 *Erin Carr-Jordan introduced her first video in her home dining room with video surveillance and lab reports.*
http://www.youtube.com/
Courtesy of Erin Carr-Jordan

FIGURE 6.3 *Erin Carr-Jordan introduced her second video with more information and lab reports.*
http://www.kidsplaysafe.net/
Courtesy of Erin Carr-Jordan

> *aren't establishing protocols for cleaning their child's PlayLand areas that we aren't going to accept it and we're not going to take our children there until they do something about it. Make no mistake about it, there are aggressive bacteria; they can and will put your child in danger. And for those children who are immunocompromised it can be potentially deadly. So I encourage you to reach out to all the people you know; share this video with them; share it with your legislature; share it with the people you know that go to McDonald's or who operate McDonald's or anyone you can think of so that we can take a stand and say that protocols need to be in place so that we can protect our children.*

Within two weeks of its posting, her video had been viewed by 5,000 people on YouTube.

Later, on June 6, 2011, Carr-Jordan uploaded a similar but shorter video to YouTube entitled *Kids Play Safe—go to kidsplaysafe.net for more info!* It included more information on the second set of lab results, the lack of regulation, and the fact that it was not an isolated incident.

NEWS MEDIA EXPOSURE

When multiple requests to McDonald's managers to sanitize the play area were ignored and calls to McDonald's national headquarters confirmed that there were no mandatory requirements for indoor play area cleanings, Carr-Jordan contacted the local Phoenix news media in mid-May 2011—and they were interested; two television stations did stories within days. Both featured interviews with Carr-Jordan and included her own video of the McDonald's in question.

The owner of this McDonald's provided a written statement to television affiliate ABC 15 KNXV-TV's May 18, 2011, story:

> *As the owner of the restaurant and a father of three kids, I am absolutely appalled by the condition of this PlayPlace. I'm disappointed we let this customer and others down. I sincerely apologize.*
>
> *Families have a high-level of trust in McDonald's. Rest assured. I have taken immediate action to address these concerns. This includes having an independent third-party thoroughly sanitize my PlayPlace.*

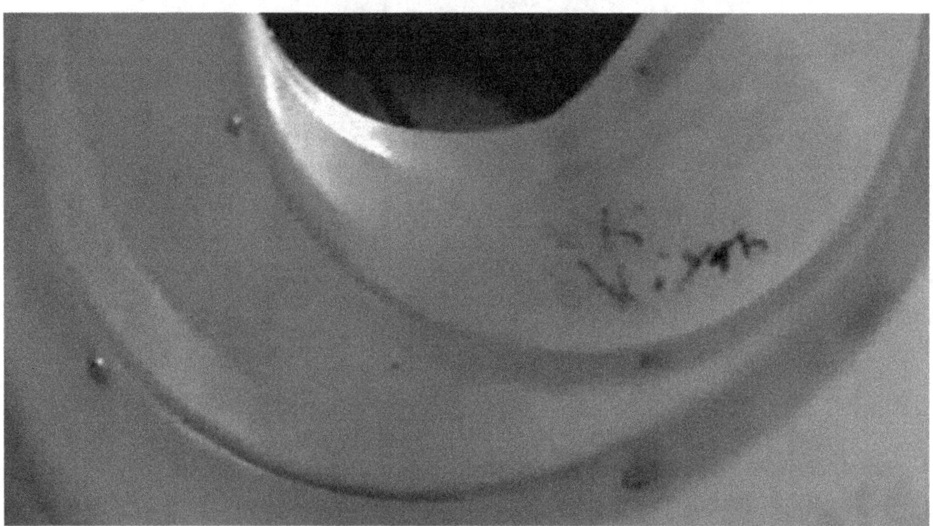

FIGURE 6.4 *The first video of an indoor play area showed excessive amounts of dirt, grime, and some unidentified substances.*
http://www.kidsplaysafe.net/
Courtesy of Erin Carr-Jordan

> *Please know we have strict requirements for daily cleaning of PlayPlaces that my management staff are required to adhere to. In this case the process was not properly followed. I will be personally monitoring the cleaning of the PlayPlace myself to ensure this doesn't happen again in the future.*

The reporter for ABC 15, Phoenix, said that a McDonald's spokesperson couldn't answer "how they were cleaned, how often they were cleaned, if at all." Carr-Jordan said that she had heard from mothers all over the country with similar stories of unclean or poorly maintained PlayLands at McDonald's. The story did show that the PlayLand in question had been cleaned. However, the next day on her Facebook page Carr-Jordan pointed out an error in the story: "One major flaw: pressure washing does NOT kill bacteria or pathogens. It just moves them around and as it dries it could make things worse. This place and countless others like it are far from clean or safe."

The CBS Phoenix affiliate also did a story featuring Carr-Jordan and the McDonald's owner's statement May 19, 2011. Carr-Jordan alerted her Facebook readers that while she appreciated the coverage, she was disappointed that the story called it an isolated case, "which it is not."

Carr-Jordan contacted the Centers for Disease Control and the state department of public health to see if these organizations could follow up on this owner's pledge and examine other restaurant play areas. Representatives from both organizations said that the issue was a state one and there were no regulations enforcing inspections of non-food areas in restaurants.

By May 25, 2011, Carr-Jordan reported on her Facebook page that consideration of her proposed Arizona legislation to regulate restaurant play areas would be postponed to the fall due to summer session. The earliest any legislative action could happen would be January 2012. That didn't bother her because she had other options for her time: "From now until then it is a grassroots effort to raise awareness."

When Carr-Jordan spoke with McDonald's national headquarters, her request to see the cleaning policy for its restaurant play areas was ignored. Transparency was an issue, she said.

These barriers did not deter Carr-Jordan. Bolstered by her convictions, the support of others, and the news media's growing interest, Carr-Jordan began drafting legislation. She also decided to mix business with pleasure with her family's summer vacation. She started visiting McDonald's PlayLands and other restaurant play areas and documenting her findings with video and microbiological analyses of surface samples. She managed to fit in more than fifty visits to restaurant indoor play areas during the summer.

As she spread awareness through her media interviews, her credibility had grown so strong that she was contacted by a California assembly office whose staffers were researching statutes and the potential health risks described in her research.

Chicago Tribune reporters followed Carr-Jordan through the twisty tubes at a Chicago McDonald's PlayLand and found similarly unsanitary conditions reported in a July 12, 2011, article. Other national news outlets began to pick up the story: *CNN Newsroom*, July 15; ABC's *Good Morning America* on August 15, 2011; The Associated Press, August 23, 2011; *The New York Times* on September 17, 2011, and even a nearly six-minute interview on Fox News' *Happening Now* on September 20, 2011.

Carr-Jordan, age 36, was articulate, poised and educated—a college professor with a Ph.D. She was also attractive and looked like a young, hip, and affluent mom. When discussing her findings, she was calm and sported a bright, friendly smile. She also carried hard-to-refute evidence within her homemade videos and microbiological lab reports that reporters were happy to share. Her message was simple and straightforward: many children's play areas need to be cleaner because some of the bacteria found could pose serious health issues.

She was also fast at thinking on her feet. When the conservative Fox News program invited her onto the show after a week of anti-regulation features, the news anchors were friendlier to Carr-Jordan's regulatory campaign. When anchor Jenna Lee introduced Carr-Jordan with a video clip of a nasty-looking indoor play area on September 20, 2011, Lee used the word "gross" to describe what Carr-Jordan had found. Lee asked Carr-Jordan to share her findings. Carr-Jordan took the opportunity to move the discussion up a notch and started by saying: "Sure. I think a better word might be 'dangerous.'" She then launched into her findings in easy-to-understand language.

Lee's Fox News co-anchor Jon Scott later posed a question he and other people were asking: Shouldn't kids get dirty and be exposed to germs to toughen them up and strengthen their immune systems? Once again, Carr-Jordan had a strong reply:

> *That's why I'm consulting with people who are microbiologists and immunologists, and who hold Ph.D. in their respective fields, and why people who are considered experts in their respective industries have commented and affirmed that these places pose a significant risk. And yes, while kids should get dirty and be exposed to dirt and have fun—that's what kids are supposed to do—they shouldn't be exposed to things that their immune system can't fight off yet. You can't fight off MRSA, you can't fight off multi-drug resistant bacteria. These are opportunistic pathogens that cause serious infections and illnesses.*

While Carr-Jordan's lab results were hard to refute, reporters sought out independent confirmation of her work. One expert was Charles Gerba, a University of Arizona professor with a Ph.D. in microbiology. He had co-authored a study of bacteria on public surfaces, entitled "Occurrence of Bacteria and Biochemical Markers on Public Surfaces," for the *International Journal of Environmental Health Research*. In the *Chicago Tribune* story July 12, 2011, Gerba was referred to as "one of the nation's foremost authorities on germ transmission." He was quoted as saying that "viruses which cause diarrhea can survive up to a month on surfaces" such as playgrounds, and that bacteria such as the deadly MRSA could be transferred in such places.

In an *Arizona Republic* newspaper story, that The Associated Press distributed August 23, 2011, Gerba agreed with Jordan's conclusions, noting that indoor playgrounds with their warm and moist environments promoted bacterial growth. "If I had a small child," Gerba said, "I'd be hesitant to let them play in there."

Reaction in the news media wasn't all positive. While the local and national news media generally provided a supportive platform for Carr-Jordan's crusade by carrying her messages and often not including negative counter viewpoints or questioning her lab research results, reader comments for online versions of articles included people who did not agree with her efforts. For example, an early news article in the *Arizona Republic*, entitled "Chandler Mom Disgusted by Fast-Food Play Areas Starts Crusade," published June 9, 2011, carried comments suggesting that if Carr-Jordan was so concerned about the health of her children she shouldn't be in a fast-food restaurant to begin with. Others said early exposure to a germy environment was healthy, and yet others derided the campaign as more useless governmental interference.

KIDS PLAY SAFE

The Kids Play Safe website was created in June 2011 to provide information about the potential dangers of indoor restaurant play areas and to share videos, photos, and other information about test sites.

FIGURE 6.5 *To promote her awareness activities, Erin Carr-Jordan developed the Kids Play Safe website that housed videos of various indoor play areas and photos of her investigations.*
http://www.kidsplaysafe.net/
Courtesy of Erin Carr-Jordan

Less than a month after she had uploaded the video of the Phoenix area McDonald's indoor play area, Carr-Jordan's thinking on the problem was evolving. She changed the name of her Facebook page to "Kids Play Safe," June 5, 2012, which quickly received 902 "likes." She then uploaded a new video that talked about a second set of lab reports, including parts of the original PlayLand video tour, and emphasized the lack of state or federal requirements for regulating restaurant play area cleanliness. Once again, she called for action and asked concerned viewers to share the video with others and support legislation to protect children. She also developed an online petition at ThePetitionSite.com.

Kids Play Safe's mission, according to the website, is:

> *Children deserve safe places to play. The current lack of regulation related to indoor playlands represents an imminent health and safety risk to children. Kids Play Safe was founded to raise awareness, conduct microbiological testing, and reach out to the media in hopes of influencing public policy and instituting change. We care deeply about what kids are exposed to, how it impacts their health and development, and are intent on making changes for the better.*

The site solicits donations to help fund the organization's efforts but little money has been donated. Visitors are asked to contact their elected officials to support legislative action to improve the safety of play areas for children, and the site allows visitors to share their own stories of what they have found at various play areas. Kids Play Safe hosts numerous videos from various restaurant play areas in eight states. The site provided links to national news stories about Carr-Jordan and her organization.

The need for legislative oversight was quickly apparent from the start of her campaign. For example, Carr-Jordan's New Mexico and Colorado lab results reported on her Facebook page found "Staph, Fungi, Mold, Bacillus, Gramm–rods, and coliforms [fecal contamination among others] at ridiculously high levels." More videos were posted about similarly "filthy" conditions at other fast-food indoor play areas. All told, lab results from the samples Carr-Jordan collected at indoor play areas in multiple restaurants in several states indicated disturbing conditions and a pattern of neglect that fed the argument for governmental regulations.

Starting in the summer of 2011, she began meeting with state legislators about the bill she was writing; she encouraged businesses to be "pro-children's health" and share her video link on their websites; and she developed a list of businesses that supported her efforts.

RESTAURANT CHAINS' RESPONSES

No restaurant chain created a news release or other statement that was available on its website regarding Carr-Jordan's efforts. She did single out Chick-fil-A as open and willing to share information on its cleaning policies. Carr-Jordan was invited to inspect any Chick-fil-A store.

Other restaurant chains did provide media statements to reporters for their stories. Here are examples that ran in some publications and television stories:

The *Chicago Tribune* carried responses from restaurant chains with indoor play areas in its article published July 12, 2011:

> *"It was unacceptable, completely unacceptable," said McDonald's spokeswoman Danya Proud, who said the video caught the attention of the restaurants' corporate offices in Oak Brook. "But it is not reflective of our business and our restaurants. As far as I'm concerned, it was an isolated matter. And we took immediate corrective action to thoroughly sanitize the PlayPlace."*
>
> *McDonald's says it requires the facilities to be thoroughly cleaned each day and the area kept free of debris and soiled surfaces. Burger King said its standards require "daily, weekly and monthly cleaning of playground equipment, pads and foams," as well as professional cleaning on quarterly basis.*
>
> *Chick-fil-A corporate spokesman Don Perry said there are regular cleaning schedules for the establishments that offer play areas. And Chuck E. Cheese's said it has eliminated ball pits, requires that "all existing play equipment is cleaned with sanitizer" and removes graffiti. Both of these companies noted that hand sanitizer is available at the playlands.*

In a July 28, 2011, news story a regional McDonald's spokesperson provided a statement for KOLD TV, Tucson, Arizona, saying that once the restaurant owner was informed of the situation, the area was cleaned. Regarding cleaning expectations the spokesperson said:

- PlayPlace components should be cleaned daily to ensure that the PlayPlace is free from debris or spills that could pose a hazard.
- Spot clean soiled surfaces with an all-purpose super concentrate solution.
- Use dedicated towels for cleaning trash receptacles.
- Pay special attention to handrails, stair treads, the slide entrance and exit, the inside of domes, entry portholes, and other areas that are touched frequently and become soiled quickly.
- Keep the PlayPlace area free of any debris.
- Spot clean the entrance and exit doors, and the windows.
- All equipment and surfaces should be spot cleaned throughout the day and cleaned thoroughly each day.
- Surfaces should be inspected frequently during each shift to check for food spills, trash, and overall cleanliness.

In *Good Morning America*'s piece on August 23, 2011, the following statements were carried by ABC's website (and other news sources):

MCDONALD'S

We put our customers first, and are taking these concerns very seriously. We've spoken with Dr. Carr-Jordan and assigned a team to review the report findings and our own existing procedures. While we have stringent sanitizing procedures for weekly, daily and even spot cleaning, we're always looking for ways to improve our standards and how they are followed at each restaurant.

Cathy Choffin, Manager of Safety and Security, McDonald's USA

BURGER KING

BURGER KING® restaurant playgrounds must be cleaned and maintained in accordance with the cleaning standards in the BURGER KING® Operations Manual. These standards include procedures for daily, weekly and monthly cleaning of playground equipment. In accordance with our policy, restaurant playgrounds are also required to be cleaned by a professional cleaning service on a quarterly basis. Burger King Corp. has contacted the franchise restaurant where the sample was taken and the franchisee has confirmed they conducted a deep cleaning of the playground this month. Additionally, the franchisee is reinforcing BURGER KING®'s standards on proper cleaning and maintenance procedures with all of its staff and management team at the restaurant.

Jonathan Fitzpatrick, Chief Brand and Operations
Officer for Burger King Corp.

CHUCK E. CHEESE'S

Our goal at Chuck E. Cheese's is to provide families with a wholesome, safe, entertaining experience. Cleanliness is a critical element toward meeting this goal. We have detailed step by step cleaning instruction manuals with video training in each of our entertainment centers. All existing play equipment is cleaned at least daily with Oasis 146 Multi-Quat sanitizer. Touch ups are completed throughout the day as needed. Additionally, we have Purell stations installed for our guests and employees to use.

Lois Perry VP, Advertising Chuck E. Cheese's

THE ROLE OF FACEBOOK

In addition to media attention, Carr-Jordan relied on social media, particularly Facebook, to build her grassroots effort while legislative efforts were slowly developing.

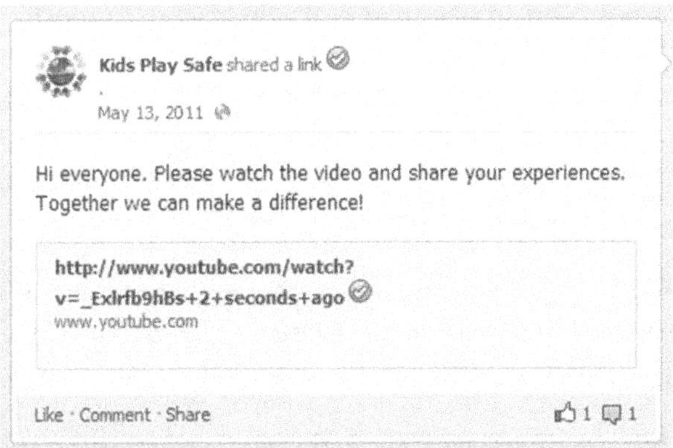

FIGURE 6.6 *Erin Carr-Jordan used a Facebook account to share her video investigation to the public.*
http://www.facebook.com/pages/Kids-Play-Safe
Courtesy of Erin Carr-Jordan

FIGURE 6.7 *Facebook became the place for updates on her campaign struggles to get indoor play areas regulated for health and safety issues. This post noted that the local daily newspaper had interviewed her.*
http://www.facebook.com/pages/Kids-Play-Safe
Courtesy of Erin Carr-Jordan

Facebook helped her to correct errors in news stories and update her supporters on any new developments with upcoming news stories or legislation. She willingly shared her victories and her disappointments with her supporters.

Supporters shared their stories about similar restaurant play areas. While she did not have massive numbers of Facebook "fans," many used the site to send her e-mails. The developing sense of community kept Carr-Jordan motivated. Others sought her help in conducting their own play area investigations. School children also contacted her for science projects—and won. Students in one San Diego nursing program did their own testing of indoor play areas.

Besides Facebook, Carr-Jordan used LinkedIn to keep in touch with journalists and other professionals with whom she had developed relationships. Her Twitter account is under her own name and is used to share updates on Kids Play Safe and a number of other topics.

Below is an example of posts from her Facebook page that demonstrate her ability to communicate frequently with her supporters:

> *May 26, 2011: More bad news today:(Since the legislature is out of session the bill I am drafting will not be reviewed until October or sponsored until January. From now until then it is a grassroots effort to raise awareness.*
>
> *May 26, 2011: Today was a good day for the cause. The story was picked up by the AZ republic and azcentral.com! I interviewed with a reporter today and the story will run within the next week. YAY!*
>
> *May 27, 2011: Also, contact NBC universal at 212–664–3720 then press 0 when it says the mailbox is unavailable (takes you to a direct operator). Email for them is story@nbcuni.com.*
>
> *May 27, 2011: Had an amazing Microbiologist comment of the lab results today. She went on the record in support of required protocols.*
>
> *May 28, 2011: Made some progress on the bill last night. Who knew drafting a bill was so complicated? The videos hit 5000 views today. I hope that means people are paying attention. I spend 2hrs per night sending it to moms grps, schools, media outlets etc and I made cards to pass out to parents during the day. Thanks to all of you for helping to spread the word.*
>
> *June 1, 2011: 2 local businesses for children agreed to put up fliers on their bulletin boards and another business owner agreed to send out the video to her entire database of parents.*
>
> *June 3, 2011: Great news today! One of the leading researchers in the area of pathogens and germs went on the record with the AZ Republic in support of our assertions and the need for regulations. In addition to the amazing Microbiologist we already have on board this is a HUGE step forward. Yay, woot woot, yippee!*

LEGAL ACTION

Carr-Jordan was not shy about expressing her concerns to restaurant managers that their play areas needed to be sanitized. In one Facebook post on October 15, 2011, she described an encounter with a McDonald's manager regarding a play area where she had discovered MRSA:

Found out that the MRSA playland was not shut down like I thought! Was told that it was disinfected and it was not. There was still sand etc all over and the swab I took was black. When I went back I was actually told to leave as I was writing my name, contact info, and lab results down for the manager on duty. Since I thought it was going to be clean I had 3 of my kiddos with me (obviously did not let them touch anything). The person who told me to leave threatened to have me arrested while my children were standing next to me. I learned today that the owner of the establishment gave that order. I also learned from him that telling the managers is a useless thing to do and that if you complain you should have a "business card" to prove you have credibility??? Why is one persons complaint more valid than another because they have credentials?

For that McDonald's owner, enough was enough. At the end of October, five months after Carr-Jordan posted her first YouTube video, she received a letter from an attorney banning her from eight McDonald's restaurants in the Tempe, Arizona, area near Phoenix. The eight included one restaurant play area in which she had found the likely presence of MRSA, the deadly antibiotic-resistant strain of bacteria. According to the *Arizona Republic*, Carr-Jordan said that she had:

approached customers with children and urged them to wash and sanitize their hands before they ate. When she observed a youngster licking the equipment, Carr Jordan said she told the manager he should close the play area. "At that point it was dangerous . . . I was very assertive; I put on my big-girl voice, but I did not yell. I can't imagine knowing there was MRSA and not doing anything. I make no apologies for what I did."

Carr-Jordan also publicized the event on her Facebook page on October 24, 2011:

Had a visitor at my home this morning at 7a. I was hand delivered a notice from the attorneys representing the owner of the MRSA location informing me that I am prohibited from entering any of his 11 McDonald's (I had only previously been to the 1). What does that tell you about him and his establishments? Im thinking it means he doesn't want me to find out what's in there! I will give you a list of the exact addresses. FYI the Chick fil A's all said I was welcome and could swab whenever I want.

In a statement provided to news outlets, McDonald's USA spokesperson Danya Proud said:

We take feedback about our restaurants extremely seriously. Over the past several months we have engaged in open and honest dialogue with Dr. Carr-Jordan in an effort to address her concerns and review her findings.

We are still committed to doing this. It appears that recent actions by Dr. Carr-Jordan have become disruptive to the employees and customers within our franchisee's restaurants, which prompted the letter from his attorney.

We remain committed to working with an internal team on ensuring that our PlayPlaces are clean and safe for all customers.

Jordan's retort came directly from her supporters: "Hey, I'm not banned, give me swabs!" said one fan posting on her Facebook page. And, with legislation already introduced in California and Illinois, it looked as though her crusade was just beginning.

LEGISLATIVE ACTION

Carr-Jordan testified at legislative hearings and spoke individually with elected officials. She obtained her first clear governmental result in her own county on September 2012 when Arizona's Maricopa County officials approved a new section in the Environmental Health Code, entitled "Indoor Play Area," that required, among other things:

Indoor Play Area surfaces that have come in contact with users shall be cleaned of visible soil as often as necessary, but not less than once per day, unless the Indoor Play Area has not been in use. The food establishment shall maintain equipment in a clean condition free of visible soil.

In 2012, a bill was introduced by California Assemblyman Michael Allen to amend the state's Health and Safety Code to include: "All premises of a food facility, including indoor and outdoor playgrounds, shall be kept clean, fully operative, and in good repair." It was approved by the house and senate but was vetoed by the state governor. The California Restaurant Association played a relatively low-key public opposition to the amendment but the association's lobbying staff were tracking it. A representative of the association said in a newspaper report that the legislation essentially singled out restaurants while other public play areas in gyms, malls, airports, and other places were not included.

Other legislative activity was percolating in Illinois and Texas.

A CITIZEN ACTIVIST

Carr-Jordan's transformation into a citizen activist was born out of frustration—when requests were ignored for correcting what she thought was an easy problem. The public health risk posed by dirty restaurant play areas made her determined to do something. "My first goal was to share information so people could make an informed decision," said Carr-Jordan. "A Law across the Fifty" came after she discovered that similar conditions existed in rich and poor, urban and rural areas.

Carr-Jordan had some personal traits that made her activism effective. First, she was highly educated. Her undergraduate degree was in broadcast journalism so she understood how journalism worked and she respected what they did. She had naturally good communication skills and knew how to tailor her responses for the news media. She had been on every major national news show, except *The Today Show*, by 2013. She had been featured on the front page of the Sunday *New York Times* and the *Chicago Tribune* among others. Her interaction with reputable journalists and broadcasters further added to her credibility.

Carr-Jordan was proactive in soliciting news coverage. When she traveled she called the news media in advance and asked if they would be interested in a story. Once reporters Googled her and learned about her crusade, many did their own investigation of indoor restaurant play areas. A second story often followed when she was in town collecting her own samples and commenting on the situation.

Her master's and doctoral degrees were in psychology, so she understood how to investigate issues and conduct research whose results could be generalized to the public. In fact, Carr-Jordan quickly decided to turn her activism into a research study with randomized data collection of indoor play areas throughout the country. This research project would be presented at an academic conference and later submitted for publication in a health journal.

While Carr-Jordan was not a microbiologist or an immunologist, nor did she pretend to be anything other than herself, she did have a close friend who was a microbiologist and educator. This friend's expertise in surface sampling for microbes quickly helped Carr-Jordan collect credible evidence for her cause. To maintain the integrity of her research findings she collected all of her data herself. Her microbiologist friend helped her understand the science behind the microbe swabbing. "I became a subject matter expert," she said. "I wanted to know everything so I could speak ethically and honestly about this situation." She also knew to defer to the experts in microbiology and immunology to further the cause.

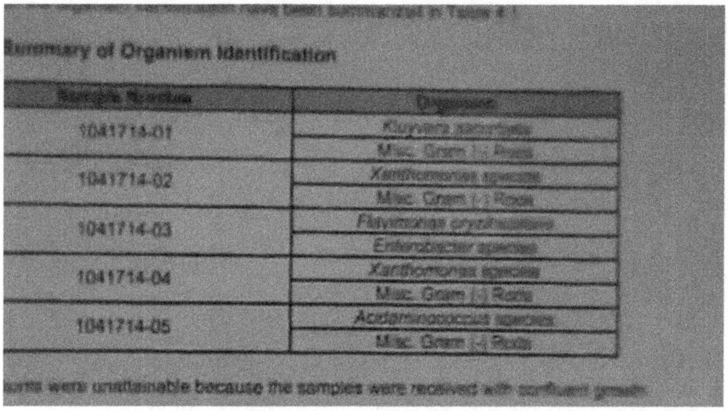

FIGURE 6.8 *The first video of an indoor play area included the lab results that were displayed by Erin Carr-Jordan on her computer.*
http://www.kidsplaysafe.net/
Courtesy of Erin Carr-Jordan

Carr-Jordan was able to finance her expenses for data collection and analysis by teaching additional courses. Between 2011 and 2012 she spent about $10,000 to analyze seventy play areas' swab findings and generate reports for her research project.

Finally, as a mother, she had a sustained interest in children's issues, especially those that could harm her kids. She found that many journalists had experienced similar situations at indoor restaurant play areas and shared her concern.

THE FUTURE

By the end of 2012, Carr-Jordan had visited twenty states and seventy locations to conduct tests on restaurant play areas. National media coverage also continued with appearances on *Anderson Cooper Live Investigates* and with Dr. Sanjay Gupta, the nationally known physician. She continued with visits to legislators regarding regulatory efforts. While restaurant play area cleanliness was her primary concern, she broadened her efforts to include the safety of play equipment. In early 2013, her website said:

> *As if the bacterial numbers aren't problematic enough, an alarming trend has emerged, broken and damaged equipment. Among the problems I have found are climbing ropes held together by string, broken second story windows, missing screws in planks, shredded climbing bumps, large cracks in slides, and unsecured platforms.*
>
> *Parents need to be aware of this information so they can take necessary precautions. Also, it is imperative that regulations be put into place so that no more children are unnecessarily endangered.*

And so, the campaign continued!

QUESTIONS FOR DISCUSSION

1. What factors mobilized Erin Carr-Jordan to become an activist?
2. What skills and knowledge did Carr-Jordan have to make her successful in raising awareness?
3. What were Carr-Jordan's tactics as she started her information campaign?
4. What made her campaign credible?
5. Beyond raising awareness about an issue what was her legislative goal?
6. How have restaurants with indoor play areas responded?
7. How could the restaurants with indoor play areas respond to minimize this issue?

Dig Deeper

View Erin Carr-Jordan's homemade video of the conditions at an indoor play area at a McDonald's restaurant, available on the textbook's companion website (*Kids Play Safe—go to kidsplaysafe.net for more info*). It does not meet professional broadcast standards but it still was effective evidence to back up her claims. What elements made this communication effective and allowed her to develop relationships with the news media?

15

Guitar Hero Strikes a Chord

Social Media Teaches Customer Service Lesson

No one likes bad service in restaurants or stores. While a few people are gutsy enough to complain and demand compensation, many choose to suffer in silence. It somehow seems easier to give up than fight for what's right. After all, dealing with an organization, especially a big one, might lead to even more frustration with nothing to show for the effort.

Dave Carroll, a 41-year-old musician from Halifax, Canada, was not easily deterred when his $3,500 Taylor six-string acoustic guitar was severely damaged by United Airlines baggage handlers at Chicago's O'Hare airport.

According to Carroll's detailed account from his blog, the incident was witnessed by a fellow passenger seated behind Carroll on the plane. The woman shouted, "Oh my God, they're throwing guitars outside," referring to the baggage handlers on the tarmac loading luggage for a quick turnaround departure. Carroll's bass player, also looking through the plane's windows, saw his bass guitar being thrown as well.

Carroll immediately alerted the plane's flight attendants who basically shooed him away, saying it wasn't their responsibility. He was directed to the gate agent, who said, "Hon, that's why we make you sign the waiver." Carroll had not signed any waiver. Throwing around expensive musical instruments was unacceptable anyhow. Carroll was told to talk to the Omaha, Nebraska, United ground crew when he landed at the next destination. When he and his bandmates arrived, it was after midnight and Carroll didn't see any United employees. He decided to leave the airport after seeing no exterior damage to his guitar's hard case. Everyone was tired and wanted to get to the hotel to sleep before their early morning departure for a week-long tour. It wasn't until later that day he discovered that his guitar's neck had been badly damaged—and he was miles away from the airport.

Thus began Carroll's extremely frustrating nine-month nightmare dealing with numerous United Airlines' customer service representatives to get $1,200 in compensation for his guitar repairs. Part of United's policy required customers to report damaged luggage claims within twenty-four hours of the flight, which Carroll was unable to do since he was miles away on tour before he discovered the damage. Finally, after many attempts to resolve the issue, Carroll was given a final, definitive answer from a Chicago customer service representative: she refused Carroll's offer to accept $1,200 in flight vouchers. The matter was closed. No vouchers, no money, no apology, no anything.

Carroll, according to his blog, realized he:

> *had been fighting a losing battle at this time and that fighting over this at all was a waste of time. The system is designed to frustrate affected customers into giving up their claims and United is very good at it. However I realized then that as a songwriter and traveling musician I wasn't without options.*

Angry but not beaten, Carroll decided on a course of action, which he shared in his last e-mail to the United customer service representative. He would write three songs about his experience with his band, Sons of Maxwell; make three music videos; and make these videos available online. His goal was to attract one million hits with all three videos.

AIRLINES IN TROUBLE

Since the terrorist attacks of September 11, 2001, followed by the recession of 2008, airlines were financially stressed and troubled for years. There had been dramatic declines in air travel and gas prices were rising. The airline industry was in a serious financial tailspin. Dramatic stories about planes filled with fliers stranded on tarmacs, in some cases, for nine hours without food, water or working toilets, were widely publicized. Lost luggage and missed connections were continual problems.

At the time Carroll was in the "ninth circle" of customer service hell, United had already entered and emerged from Chapter 11 bankruptcy protection. To stave off financial ruin with the 2008 recession, United and other airlines slashed jobs and salaries; United ended its pension plan, which was the largest corporate pension default in United States history. While United reorganized and emerged from Chapter 11, it still needed to find operational savings and shave expenses. Every United employee was affected by United's serious financial situation that lasted years. Not unexpectedly, United's service slipped and employee morale sank. Its on-time arrivals, according to the Transportation Department's Bureau of Transportation Statistics, were nearly the worst in the industry. Its surviving employees, who had lost wages and benefits, were cranky and many just didn't care.

UNITED BREAKS GUITARS: SONG ONE

Right after the July Fourth weekend, Carroll uploaded his first song video describing United's baggage handlers' outlandish handling of Carroll's guitar. That first day it received about forty hits. Carroll and his band asked their friends to pass it along to others.

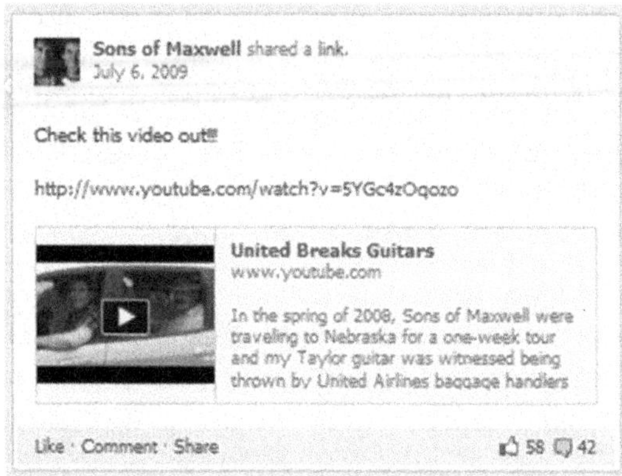

FIGURE 6.9 *Dave Carroll posted the YouTube music video of his first song and alerted friends and fans on Facebook.*
http://sonsofmaxwell.com/
Courtesy of Dave Carroll

The country–western song and music video were professionally produced. Carroll used a professional video production business in Halifax, Curve Productions, Inc., to produce the video, which featured friends dressed as baggage handlers tossing a guitar on the tarmac with Carroll and other plane passengers watching. It also featured uninterested flight crew attendants who displayed the "not my job" attitudes when Carroll tried to alert them to what was happening on the tarmac. The song was a toe-tapper and the chorus was catchy. It incorporated Carroll's dry sense of humor. It was a fun video to watch. The chorus, like the rest of the lyrics, was gentle but direct in its criticism of what had happened to him and his guitar:

I've heard all your excuses
and I've chased your wild gooses
and this attitude of yours I say must go.
United, United you broke my Taylor guitar.
United, United some big help you are.
You broke it, you should fix it.
You're liable just admit it.
I should have flown with someone else.
Or just have gone by car.
Because United breaks guitars.

Carroll's experience immediately struck a chord with the general public, who had suffered for years with poor airline service. It also had a David and Goliath appeal—the Everyman Carroll pitted against the big, bad, faceless corporation. It was a smash hit on the Internet. People happily passed it on to others, and within 24 hours it had been viewed by more than 150,000 people. People, in a cathartic mood, were sharing their own unpleasant experiences about United and other airlines using

YouTube's comment area. The video's rapid spread was helped along with viewers' Facebook postings. It surpassed Carroll's original goal of one million hits by July 10—it was an Internet viral sensation.

With an uncanny instinct for publicity, Carroll decided to quickly issue a video statement on the success of the music video. He did this July 10, four days after the video debuted, and updated his new fans on what had happened thanks to the support of viewers, which he noted: "I would like express my deep gratitude to everyone

FIGURE 6.10 *Dave Carroll made frequent use of Facebook to alert fans to what was happening with his work and the songs, including media interviews.*
http://www.facebook.com/
Courtesy of Sons of Maxwell

FIGURE 6.11 *Dave Carroll posted a YouTube video statement four days after Song One hit the Internet updating viewers on United's compensation offer and asking people to treat the United employee featured in the video with kindness.*
http://www.youtube.com/
Courtesy of Dave Carroll/Curve Productions

in the world who have supported United song One the way you have, which is more than I could ever hope, especially after two days."

He told viewers that United had contacted him to offer him compensation for his guitar. He said he was no longer seeking compensation but suggested that United provide a donation to a charity instead. He also asked viewers to be kind to the customer service representative, mentioned by last name in the video, who had ultimately refused the claim: "In my experience she was a great employee, unflappable and acting in the interests of the United's policies she represented . . . and deserves a bit of a break."

He also told viewers to stay tuned for the next song video in the planned trilogy. This statement was posted to YouTube along with *Song One*. Carroll came across as a pleasant sort of fellow who was not mean-spirited or angry. He just wanted his chance to tell his story.

The national news media picked up the story on day three of the video's debut. It was featured on several media outlets including CBS News, CNN's Wolfe Blitzer's *The Situation Room*, and *The Oprah Winfrey Show*, reaching millions of viewers who went to YouTube to view the complete video. Many more media interviews and video clip postings would follow.

In addition to Dave Carroll's Sons of Maxwell blog, he also frequently posted updates on Sons of Maxwell's Facebook page. Updates on the popularity of the video, upcoming performances, news media interviews, and Carroll's invitation to Washington, D.C., to tell his airline experience at a Congressional hearing were just some of the early and numerous posts that kept fans in the know.

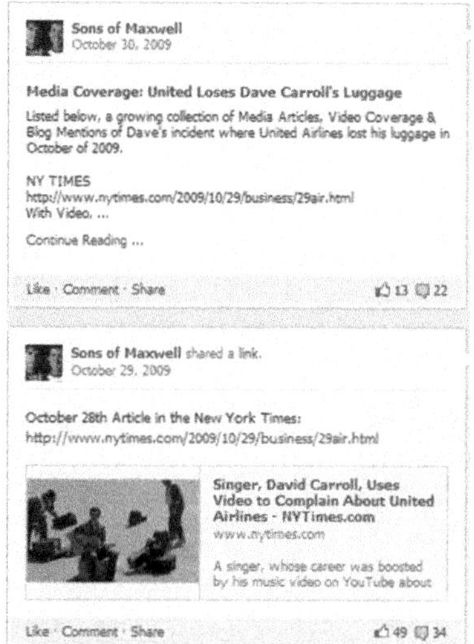

FIGURE 6.12 *Dave Carroll used Facebook to alert fans to his latest media coverage in fall 2009. By this time he was campaigning for passenger rights for air travel.*
http://www.facebook.com/
Courtesy of Sons of Maxwell

UNITED'S RESPONSE

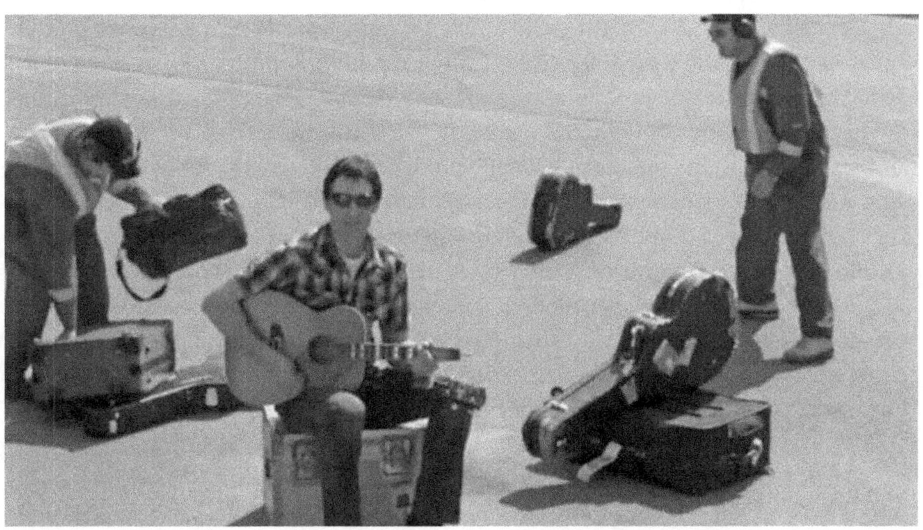

FIGURE 6.13 *A scene from "United Breaks Guitars," Song 1*
http://www.youtube.com/
Courtesy of Sons of Maxwell

The day after *Song One* was released, a United spokeswoman tweeted that "This has struck a chord with us. We're going to contact him directly and make what happened right."

In media interviews, a United representative said the video was a unique learning opportunity and asked Carroll if they might use it internally for customer service training.

After Carroll's video statement on July 10, the news media reported that United made a $3,000 donation to the Thelonious Monk Institute of Jazz.

There was no official apology, no news release, no written statement or other communication regarding the incident or its donation other than its limited media interviews from United's spokesperson. Those featured its spokeswoman's early tweet that United would contact Carroll to make amends and United's plan to use the video for customer training. United's CEO Glenn Tilton did not participate in news interviews on the subject.

SURPASSING THE GOAL

In the meantime, the video was crisscrossing the globe as people shared it on their own personal social media networks. Within a couple of days, it had surpassed Carroll's original one million hit goal. By the end of its first full week, it had been viewed by more than 2.5 million people with 13,000 YouTube comments, which expressed overwhelmingly negative sentiment toward United. It climbed to 5 million views by six weeks and 10 million views after seven months.

The second video, titled *United Breaks Guitars—Song Two,* was posted to YouTube, August 19. It detailed the endless runarounds with United's customer service department. While not as popular as the first video, it received favorable reviews and mentions online and in the news media. It also drove traffic to Carroll's first video and his blog. *Song Two* was professionally produced and featured about one hundred volunteers and friends. His musical career, which had been fairly modest before *Song One,* had received a boost which brought offers for tours and singing engagements.

By this point, Carroll also discovered that he was a hot commodity for the speaker circuit. He was being called for customer service training events. Many organizations wanted the Everyman champion to come talk to them about the power of social media and customer service expectations. Ironically, in October 2009 while Carroll was traveling to a speaking engagement, his luggage was lost. The airline? United. The luggage was found but not before he gave his presentation.

The third and final video in the *United Breaks Guitars* trilogy—*Song Three*—was released about eight months after the first video on March 1, 2010. It was another volunteer effort that included the services of a professional music producer and video production company. This time the music had a bluegrass theme and featured Canadian bluegrass legend Ray Legere on fiddle and mandolin and Jerry Douglas, who plays in Alison Krauss' band from Nashville, on dobro.

Shot in one day, *Song Three* examined Carroll's relationship with a customer service representative and how United's policies did not always work as intended. While this video didn't receive as much attention either, it fulfilled Carroll's original promise and was another professional and fun video to watch. In his blog, Carroll noted that all three videos relied on volunteers for help and cost about $2,500 to create. He clarified that normal commercial rates would have pushed the price to well over $100,000 and he thanked everyone for their support.

AFTERMATH

Carroll cofounded a company called Grapevine to help consumers and companies better use social media to resolve customer relations issues. Carroll continues to speak on customer relations and social media. In 2012 he published a book, titled *United Breaks Guitars: The Power of One Voice in the Age of Social Media,* on his experiences with United. He still writes and performs his music for audiences throughout the world.

QUESTIONS FOR DISCUSSION

1. How could the situation have been mitigated or resolved by customer relations?
2. What characteristics exhibited by Dave Carroll would suggest that he would not let his complaint go away?

3. Suggest a communication plan for United Airlines after the first video was posted to YouTube. What would be some key messages for United Airlines spokespeople?
4. Evaluate the decision to not use United Airlines' CEO Glenn Tilton in media interviews or in other communication on this subject. What are the risks of using a CEO as spokesperson?
5. Evaluate Sons of Maxwell's July and August 2009 Facebook postings. How effective were they in raising awareness and developing relationships with their readers?
6. What other ways did Dave Carroll gain support for his issue with United Airlines?
7. Humor was part of Dave Carroll's videos. Would a sense of humor from United in its communication with Carroll, have been appropriate? Explain.
8. How can public relations work with customer service departments to ensure appropriate responses to customers?
9. Describe a time you have been treated unfairly or received poor service from a business or organization. How could the situation have been resolved and what kind of communication from the organization would have been appropriate?

Dig Deeper

View Dave Carroll's first music video, entitled *United Breaks Guitars: Song One*, available on the textbook's companion website. Why do you think this video went viral? View the video statement released by Carroll entitled "United Breaks Guitars—A Statement from Dave Carroll" available on the textbook's companion website. What was its purpose?

16

Break the Silence. Make the Call.

Reaching Out to Victims and Families of Domestic Violence

The first time Kimberly's high school sweetheart hit her was two weeks before their wedding. She convinced herself that the punch in the arm was due to "wedding stress." Married at 18, she didn't know it marked the beginning of a life of violence that would hurt her for years to come.

For the next nine years, Kimberly's husband convinced her: His violent behavior was her fault. She never told anyone—family, friends, coworkers—when he hit her and threw things. Kimberly never filed a police report or showed her injuries to a doctor. Despite the beatings and death threats, she had a public image to maintain. Kimberly and her husband were active in their church; her husband was an ordained deacon. People looked up to them, Kimberly said, and often told her, "I wish we were like y'all."

At first, her husband's violent behavior happened only when they were alone. But when he began to show increasing signs of irritation with their two children, she made plans to escape. Breaking away wasn't easy; for years he had told her she was useless, stupid, and couldn't do anything on her own. With no significant work experience and no education beyond a high school diploma, Kimberly knew it would be hard. But to protect her children, she packed a few possessions and made the hardest decision of her life: a move to a family violence shelter where she and the children began a new life together.

Despite its troubled start, Kimberly's story had a happy ending. For many women trapped in abusive relationships, the outcome can be grim. In 2010, 1,095 women were killed by their male partners nationally.

The federal government's Office of Justice Programs estimates that women experience 4.8 million intimate partner physical assaults and rapes each year. Approximately 18 percent of women in the United States have experienced rape, according to the National Intimate Partner and Sexual Violence Survey (NISVS).

A 2011 study estimated that "approximately one in four women, compared to one in seven men, have been victims of severe physical violence by an intimate partner."

According to the U.S. Department of Justice in 2009:

Intimate partner violence includes violence between spouses, ex-spouses, common-law spouses and current or former boyfriends or girlfriends. Forty-six percent of intimate partner violence cases involved a defendant with a prior history of abuse toward the same victim, and the victim had reported prior violence to police in 24 percent of all cases. A direct witness to the violence was present in more than 40 percent of intimate partner violence cases.

Government statistics also noted that 22 percent of intimate violence cases were witnessed by a child. Nearly 90 percent of defendants sustained an injury, with 9 percent classified as "severe," including gunshot and stab wounds, rape, severe lacerations, and broken bones.

Domestic violence can take many forms including physical, sexual, emotional, economic, and psychological abuse.

At the time of this case study, 2003, intimate partner violence in Texas had reached nearly epidemic proportions, according to the Texas Department of Human Services. The Texas Department of Public Safety reported that in 2003 there were 185,299 incidents of "family violence" and 153 Texas women were killed by their intimate partners, representing more than 10 percent (two women per week) of the national rate at the time. The reported incidents of family violence were estimated by social agencies to be much higher than the public statistics. Just 5 percent of the victims received assistance from Texas domestic violence programs.

Through a $2.75 million grant from the State Attorney General's Office, the Texas Council on Family Violence (TCFV) developed two public awareness campaigns, "There is Help, There is Hope" and "Family and Friends," to publicize domestic violence programs and services and to provide information to the general public on ways they could assist friends and family living with domestic violence.

RESEARCH

"Domestic violence is often swept under the rug," said Kathy Miller, a former TCFV communications director. Because of its hidden nature, the scope of the problem is often difficult to grasp. Detailed information on domestic violence is often anecdotal, when it exists at all; basic statistics often underreport the problem. For example, police departments in Texas track the number of women killed as a result of domestic violence—but the data do not include women killed by ex-boyfriends. To understand the issues of domestic violence required to build an effective campaign, TCFV conducted extensive research.

Early research efforts included a statewide community audit, to determine critical needs, and thirty-four survivor focus groups. Both efforts pointed to a need for public awareness. In 2002, Saurage Research, of Houston, Texas, conducted telephone interviews with 1,200 Texans. To ensure understanding of the Hispanic population, the survey oversampled this minority population and used bilingual callers to investigate unique barriers Latino Texans face when they seek to escape domestic violence.

Six minority-only focus groups also were conducted from the total of thirty-four focus groups. Two focus groups consisted of African American, Anglo, and Hispanic Texans. Members of the six groups were drawn from both rural and urban areas of the state.

The research's key findings were:

- 74 percent said they or someone they know had experienced domestic violence.
- 31 percent had suffered "severe abuse."
- Victims first turned to friends, family, or coworkers.
- 84 percent believed they could personally make a difference on the issue.
- Many never seek help; often friends and family didn't know where to seek help. This was particularly true of Latinas.

Other important findings were:

- Victims rarely knew how to leave safely or that abuse was not normal, and never deserved.
- Victims were often unaware of the impact that abuse had on their children's behavior.
- Victims needed answers before they acted.
- Leaving an abusive relationship required tremendous courage.
- There were crucial cultural differences.

The research indicated that 31 percent of all Texans reported that they had been severely abused at some point in their lifetime. Severe abuse is defined as physical abuse, sexual abuse, or being threatened by a spouse or dating partner. The study also revealed that more than one in four Texans (26 percent) had been physically abused—hit, pushed, or choked—by their spouse or partner.

The research found several misperceptions contributing to the "barriers that domestic violence survivors face in finding pathways to safety," said Sheryl Cates, TCFV chief executive officer, in a news release announcing the survey's results. Seventy-one percent of survey respondents incorrectly blamed domestic violence survivors for their plight in response to the statement: "Victims who do not leave an abusive relationship share some of the blame for their abuse." The survey found Texans

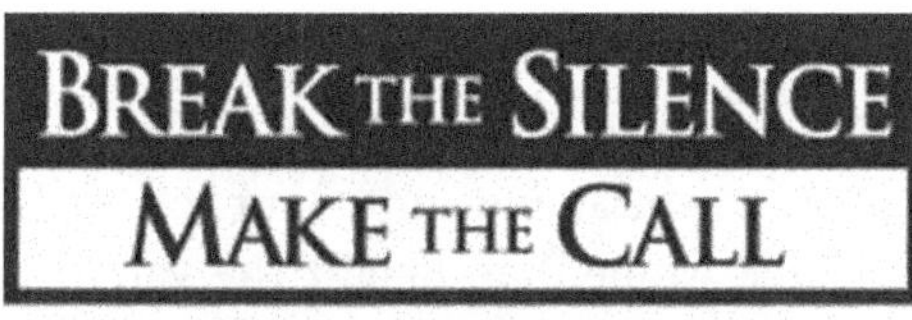

FIGURE 6.14 *The Texas awareness campaign was bilingual to support the large Hispanic population.*
Texas Council on Domestic Violence
Courtesy of Texas Council on Domestic Violence

demonstrated "a willingness to blame domestic violence on circumstances beyond an abuser's control, rather than acknowledging the abuser's culpability." More than 86 percent of Texans were willing to blame sudden financial problems or job loss for the abuse; and more than 98 percent were willing to blame alcohol or other forms of substance abuse as the cause of the domestic abuse. "While these problems can exacerbate an already abusive relationship, or increase the severity of abuse, they are not the factors responsible for that behavior," according to a TCFV news release.

The news release also said:

> *More than 96 percent of Texans failed to identify forcing your partner to have sex against their will as an act of domestic violence, and even fewer identified threatening one's partner or family, stalking or intentionally isolating one's partner from friends and family as forms of domestic violence.*

Focus groups with Hispanic victims of domestic violence, whose experiences were similar to the experiences of all victims of domestic violence, revealed four barriers that inhibited them from seeking the help they needed:

- *Isolation:* It is a common tactic used by batterers, but for Hispanic victims the feeling of isolation was often intensified by a language barrier, lack of support network, and/or the lack of legal immigration status.
- *Fear and threats:* Most often cited were threats that the abuser would report the victim to immigration services (INS) and that she would then be separated from her children or even lose them. In addition, Hispanic victims

cited threats such as being told that no matter where they went, the abuser would find them.

- *Shame:* Family plays a central and important role in Hispanic culture and, traditionally, Hispanic women are taught the value of keeping the family together at all costs. Participants cited intense shame associated with breaking up the family unit as a significant barrier to action. The shame felt by victims was often enhanced by harsh criticism from friends and families for taking such action. The intense fear of rejection from those people whose opinions they valued most often contributed to the decision not to seek assistance and to remain in an abusive relationship.
- *Lack of awareness:* Often cited by victims was the lack of awareness about available domestic violence services. Other barriers such as fear of being discovered by legal authorities and language or cultural isolation often kept Hispanic victims in the dark about the confidential support services available to them in their communities.

CAMPAIGN STRATEGY

Based on the research, TCFV targeted survivors, their family members, friends and coworkers, community and civic leaders, the business community, and the media for its awareness campaign, said Helen Vollmer, president of Vollmer Public Relations. Campaign goals included:

FIGURE 6.15 *The campaign commercials and printed materials used images of attractive middle-class women to show that abuse could happen to anyone, not just the poor.*
Texas Council on Domestic Violence
Courtesy of Texas Council on Domestic Violence

- Achieve 20 percent increase in Texas-based calls to the national family violence hotline during paid media flights.
- Mix paid and public service announcements to ensure a two-to-one minimum of free versus paid spots.
- Identify at least ten grassroots partners.
- Distribute one million educational campaign materials.

An integrated, multilingual, and culturally relevant campaign was created, said Vollmer, using existing materials, polling and research results, advertising and public service announcements, community events, media relations, business partnerships, and grassroots outreach. Communication materials emphasized the following messages:

- Legitimize victims' situation.
- Recognize they are not alone.
- Recognize abuse is not normal.
- Ensure confidentiality.
- Enable them to call for assistance.
- Reinforce public awareness with "private" awareness.

Print materials featured print ads, outdoor ads, posters and flyers, a four-page brochure, "discreet" hotline cards and envelope inserts, and media kits. A website maintained by TCFV also hosted much of the campaign's information.

Break the Silence spokespersons included survivors of family violence, friends and family touched by family violence, and local female television anchors from Belo television and cable and Univision radio and television stations. Other high-profile spokespersons included Texas First Lady Anita Perry, a former intensive care nurse who had seen firsthand the devastation of domestic violence. Texas-based musical artists Shawn Colvin and Sisters Morales were part of the campaign's launch event that reached a younger audience. Doctora Isabel, a well-respected radio psychologist with a large Hispanic following, also joined the campaign by discussing family violence issues on her show.

REACHING THE ISOLATED

Jealous batterers often isolate wives and girlfriends, limiting or preventing contact with family members or friends, TCFV's communication director Kathy Miller said. "Isolation is their number one way to control women." Since victims then often become estranged from the very family and friends most likely to help them, campaign planning included unique private communication strategies to reach women who seldom venture from the watchful gaze of jealous partners. Such strategies would have to overcome monitoring of phone and Internet communication.

FIGURE 6.16 *The "Shattered Portrait" commercial dealt with helping people understand how they could get involved and helped abused women.*
Texas Council on Domestic Violence
Courtesy of Texas Council on Domestic Violence

One technique TCFV created to meet this challenge was a "discreet" hotline card the size of a normal business card. The small size allowed women to hide it easily. In one instance, a woman kept the card in her shoe for two years before she finally called, Miller said. More than four million of the little cards were distributed to Texans in the first two years of the campaign.

TCFV considered carefully how to distribute the hotline cards and flyers advertising the hotline number so that women would see them while husbands and boyfriends would not. "We thought of any place that a woman might go that her batterer might not," said Miller. Cards and flyers were put in public women's restrooms, and at hairdressers, grocery stores, break rooms, and pediatricians' offices. To reach victims via the Internet, TCFV's website alerted users that computers could be monitored; a message on the website encouraged them to use a safer computer, such as one located at a library or community center.

Beyond isolation, the shame and the pressure to keep a family together at all costs, especially in Hispanic families, was another obstacle. Vollmer said focus groups with Latinas cited the church as a "determining factor in the decision to break the silence." Focus group participants revealed that "because the Catholic Church is such a strong proponent of the family, when women consulted priests they were often encouraged to stay and try to work things out," said Vollmer.

A second phase of the campaign that ran in 2004 addressed the need for family and friends to speak out and support women in abusive relationships. The campaign's broadcast materials included bilingual radio and television public service announcements spearheaded by BRSG Advertising and CINCO Media Communications. A partnership with the Texas Association of Broadcasters boosted the campaign's statewide airtime through the use of noncommercial sustaining announcements for television spots worth at least three times the normal paid distribution fee.

A thirty-second television spot entitled *Awakenings* featured a professionally dressed, attractive Hispanic woman:

Woman (facing camera):	*My husband used to hurt me. A lot. But I was silent because I thought I was keeping my family together. Until I saw how it was hurting my son.*
	The opening shot is followed by video of a young boy crouching in a darkened closet with angry voices in the background. The woman's narration continues:
Woman:	*He was learning to be afraid . . . just like me.*
	The final scene shows the woman holding her child, both smiling. A female announcer closes the spot:
Announcer:	*Break the silence. Make the call. 1-800-799-SAFE. Your call is anonymous.*

Vollmer said the decision to depict an upscale Hispanic woman was intentional, to show that domestic violence can happen to anyone regardless of educational level or social status.

Another campaign goal was to overcome the common belief that victims share the blame for the abuse if they don't leave a relationship. Since emotional dependency on the batterer and lack of financial resources and information often deter victims from seeking help, Vollmer said family members, friends, and coworkers may need to get involved. A television spot called *Phone Call* encouraged friends to intervene.

The thirty-second spot begins with a young white man, pacing in his apartment, looking at a photograph of an attractive young white female.

Female announcer:	*Afraid of getting involved? Imagine how she feels.*
	The spot continues with the man nervously practicing with his phone as he repeats "Hi. Hi." Finally, he makes the call.
Man:	*Hi. I've got a friend . . . I think she's being abused.*
Announcer:	*Break the silence. Make the call. 1–800–799-SAFE. Your call is anonymous.*

The TCFV campaign also posted a "Guide for Family and Friends" on its Make the Call website in English and Spanish versions. The guide explains how to recognize the signs of domestic abuse and how to get help.

The official launch of the campaign coincided with Domestic Violence Awareness Month in October. Special events included a candlelight vigil with spokespersons in English and Spanish on the steps of the state capitol building in Austin. Shawn Colvin, a Grammy-winning recording artist, and Sisters Morales, one of whom was a victim of domestic violence, were also on hand to add music and star power for the occasion. The event also featured a powerful visual element to draw attention to the women killed by an intimate partner the prior year. Lining the steps of the state capitol building were 113 life-size wooden figures painted red, each bearing the name and story of a victim. The "Silent Witnesses" exhibit was a visual reminder that two women were killed each week in Texas as a result of domestic violence.

RESULTS

In the first phase of the sixteen-month bilingual "Break the Silence" campaign, responses to the national domestic violence hotline increased dramatically: 69 percent for English-language calls, 93 percent for Spanish calls.

In a post-campaign survey, half of the respondents remembered the advertising tag line "Break the silence. Make the call." Seventy percent of respondents could recall three definitions of domestic violence, compared to 50 percent prior to the campaign.

Seventy-two percent of those who recalled the campaign considered domestic violence a serious problem in the state.

More than forty "grassroots advocates of understanding," including Texas colleges and universities and many Hispanic organizations, joined with eighty domestic violence shelters in spreading the word about the campaign and distributing materials.

Business partnerships, including corporations such as Verizon Wireless and media outlets, were formed to help distribute campaign materials through payroll stuffers, billing envelopes, and point-of-sale locations.

The campaign resulted in the formation of the Texas Business Alliance to End Domestic Violence. "With a network of partners that have multiple avenues to reach millions of employees," said TCFV Chief Executive Officer Cates, "the Alliance will have an unprecedented impact on domestic violence prevention efforts statewide by helping employees become aware of the assistance and services available to help them become safe."

Media partnerships, particularly with the Texas Broadcasting Association, extended the campaign's messages. From an investment of $160,000 the noncommercial-sustained advertising agreement yielded a $1.5 million value. The nonpaid on-air advertising netted an additional $3.9 million value.

Nationally, the overall rate of intimate partner violence declined from 1994 to 2010 by 64 percent, from 9.8 victimizations per 1,000 persons age 12 or older to 3.6 per 1,000, according to the U.S. Department of Justice.

Reported incidents of family violence in Texas have not declined, except in the year following the 2003 TCFV educational campaign: family violence declined from 185,299 to 182,087 incidents in 2004; the number of women killed also declined from 154 to 116 in 2004. (Another slight decrease in violent incidents occurred in 2005–2006.)

According to the Texas District and County Attorneys Association in 2010, 142 women were killed and there were 193,505 incidents of family violence in Texas.

QUESTIONS FOR DISCUSSION

1. How did pre-campaign research guide this campaign?
2. If you had to develop a domestic violence campaign in your state, whom would you choose as campaign spokespeople? Why?
3. What makes the campaign's slogan "Break the silence. Make the call" an effective message? What other slogans might work?
4. What were the strengths of the campaign's private (discreet) communication strategies? What other private communication strategies might be used?
5. Do you know of someone who has experienced domestic violence? What were the barriers he or she experienced in getting the help needed?
6. What new strategies for grassroots partners could be developed in this campaign? For example, what could your college or university do as a partner?
7. Beyond disseminating campaign materials, what other activities could a business partner be involved in?
8. This campaign used media partners to carry the campaign's messages to a mass public. It also used female anchors. What strategies could you develop for the news anchors?
9. How do non-commercial-sustained advertising campaigns work in this case study?

Dig Deeper

View the keynote address by journalist Paula Zahn for the National Institute of Justice Conference, available on the textbook's companion website. She discusses various issues surrounding domestic violence, including teen dating violence. How can the news media be a source for building awareness on domestic violence? What story ideas could be suggested to the news media? Read the National Institute of Justice's report "Teen Dating Violence: A Closer Look at Adolescent Romantic Relationships," available on the textbook's companion website. What are your ideas to develop an awareness program about this topic?

17

Undercover Video Captures Chicken Abuse

Animal Activist Group Targets Company

The New York Times broke the story—and buried it. The tale of chicken abuse at a processing plant only made it to page 2 of the business section, but graphic video images made it a top story for television news that evening.

A hidden video camera, installed by an undercover investigator for the animal rights group People for the Ethical Treatment of Animals (PETA), recorded in grainy black-and-white detail numerous incidents of animal abuse by employees at a Pilgrim's Pride chicken processing plant in West Virginia.

The video was so shocking that all three network television anchors cautioned viewers before airing their respective reports on July 20, 2004. CBS *Evening News* reporter Mika Brezinski's story began:

> *Some call it one of the worst cases of animal cruelty captured on videotape; shocking scenes of slaughterhouse workers kicking, stomping and throwing live chickens at a plant owned by Pilgrim's Pride, the country's second-largest poultry processor, a supplier to fast-food chain Kentucky Fried Chicken (KFC).*

ABC's Ned Potter, reporting for World News Tonight with Peter Jennings:

> *The pictures, shot with a small, hidden camera, purport to show plant employees hurling chickens against a wall, stomping on them to kill them. Kicking them like footballs, and committing other acts of cruelty. It's a far cry from the way the industry says things are supposed to be done. Workers are supposed to stun the birds before slaughter.*

CNN's Anderson Cooper, host of *Anderson Cooper 360 Degrees*, began his story this way:

> *It's enough to make a carnivore turn vegetarian, enough even to make Ozzy Osbourne from his bat-eating days gag. Caught on videotape, workers at a chicken-slaughtering plant in West Virginia torturing live birds for sport. It's the Pilgrim's Pride slaughterhouse,*

FIGURE 6.17 *A grainy undercover video shot in a chicken processing plant captured workers abusing chickens.*
http://www.kentuckyfriedcruelty.com/u-pilgrimspride.asp
Courtesy of PETA

and right now the company is anything but proud. Both Pilgrim's Pride and the company it supplies, Kentucky Fried Chicken, say they are appalled. You'll quickly see why.

The PETA investigator who took the video images also provided eyewitness testimony to other acts of cruelty. According to *The New York Times*, the investigator saw "hundreds" of acts of cruelty, including workers tearing beaks off, ripping a bird's head off to write graffiti in blood, spitting tobacco juice into birds' mouths, plucking feathers to "make it snow," suffocating a chicken by tying a latex glove over its head, and squeezing birds like water balloons to spray feces over other birds.

Similar stories about the chicken abuse at Pilgrim's Pride ran in hundreds of local and national television programs and newspapers in the week after the *New York Times* story.

The gruesome video was quickly offered to PETA website visitors, appearing in a section titled "Expose: Cruelty in the KFC Slaughter-house." The stark black-and-red webpages included video stills from the hidden camera video.

But that was just the tip of the iceberg for the curious. Visitors to the site were provided an array of information about the Pilgrim's Pride situation, including:

- A link to PETA's ongoing boycott campaign against KFC called "Kentucky Fried Cruelty."
- A two-page description of what the undercover investigator claimed to have seen.

FIGURE 6.18 *Undercover video shot in a chicken processing plant captured workers slamming live chickens against the wall.*
http://www.kentuckyfriedcruelty.com/u-pilgrimspride.asp
Courtesy of PETA

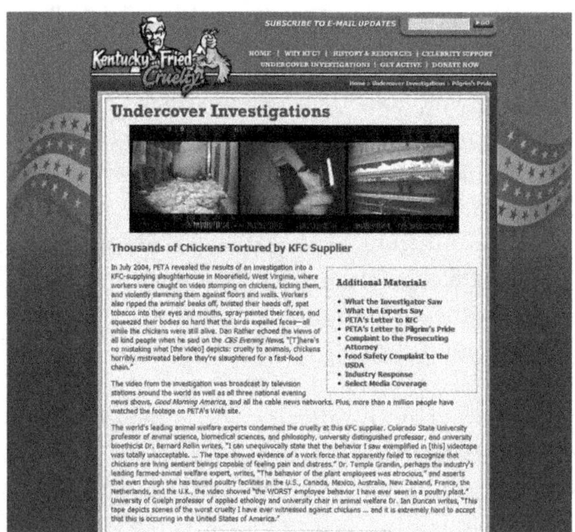

FIGURE 6.19 *PETA targeted KFC to pressure for changes in the chicken processing industry. A web page called Kentucky Fried Cruelty contained a link to the undercover video of chicken abuse at Pilgrim's Pride.*
http://www.kentuckyfriedcruelty.com/
Courtesy of PETA

- Three pages of quotes from leading and highly respected animal welfare experts and government and meat-industry advisors about their reactions to the chicken abuse, including Dr. Ian J.H. Duncan, Dr. Temple Grandin, and Dr. Bernard E. Rollin.
- PETA's letters to the Pilgrim's Pride chairman and KFC's chief executive officer detailing, among other things, the results of the undercover investigation and a plea for the use of more humane slaughter technology called "controlled-atmosphere killing."
- PETA's seventeen-page letter to the prosecuting attorney for Moorefield, West Virginia, containing thirty-five specific incidents of animal cruelty, excerpts from leading animal welfare experts commenting on the videotaped abuse, a review of slaughterhouse policies that allegedly created an environment of abuse (the letter claimed that the undercover employee did not receive training in killing methods until five months into the job, and there was no mention of animal welfare policies in the employee handbook), and a request for an official investigation of the alleged violation of the state's cruelty to animals statute.
- PETA's two-page letter to the U.S. Department of Agriculture requesting an investigation of alleged violations of poultry products inspection regulations.
- Links to free videos or downloads for *Meet Your Meat*, narrated by actor Alec Baldwin, and *Chew on This*, which alleged health risks and inhumane practices in how twenty-seven billion animals (including fish) are raised and killed for food in the United States. *The Hidden Lives of Chickens* discussed the science of chicken cognition (chickens do better than dogs or cats on scientific tests, according to PETA) and equated chicken consumption with eating dogs or cats.
- For those repulsed by the videos and information provided, PETA offered links to a free vegetarian starter kit, with reasons for eliminating animals from a healthy diet, an explanation of veganism, and a link for donations to animal rights causes.

PETA's home button on "Exposé: Cruelty in the KFC Slaughterhouse" was linked to numerous other animal rights projects, including how to organize a demonstration against KFC, and downloadable print ads and billboards supporting a KFC boycott.

PILGRIM'S PRIDE RESPONSE

Pilgrim's Pride issued a four-paragraph statement from O.B. Goolsby, president and chief operating officer the day before *The New York Times* broke the story; the message was intended, in part, to alert Pilgrim's Pride employees that media coverage of the situation was about to occur:

> *You may see coverage in the media in the coming days about a video reportedly taken in one of our chicken processing plants showing inhumane treatment of our birds. We are appalled at the treatment of the animals that was depicted in the video.*
>
> *Let me make this very clear: Pilgrim's Pride will not tolerate any mistreatment of our animals by any of our employees. Any employee who is found to have mistreated animals in violation of company policy will be immediately terminated.*
>
> *Pilgrim's Pride strictly follows the animal welfare program recommended by the National Chicken Council (NCC). This program covers all aspects of broiler chicken welfare and was developed by industry experts in consultation with academic experts from leading universities.*
>
> *Pilgrim's Pride will continue to adhere to a program of animal welfare that is designed to eliminate unnecessary harm and suffering for animals in the day-to-day operation of our production processes, and we remain committed to the highest levels of humane treatment of the animals we raise for food.*

In *The New York Times*' July 20, 2004, account, an unidentified Pilgrim's Pride spokesperson said that

> *the company had an anonymous report about poultry mistreatment at the plant in April 2004 and had made it clear to its workers that "any such behavior would result in immediate termination." In light of the tape, the company said, it will reopen its investigation.*

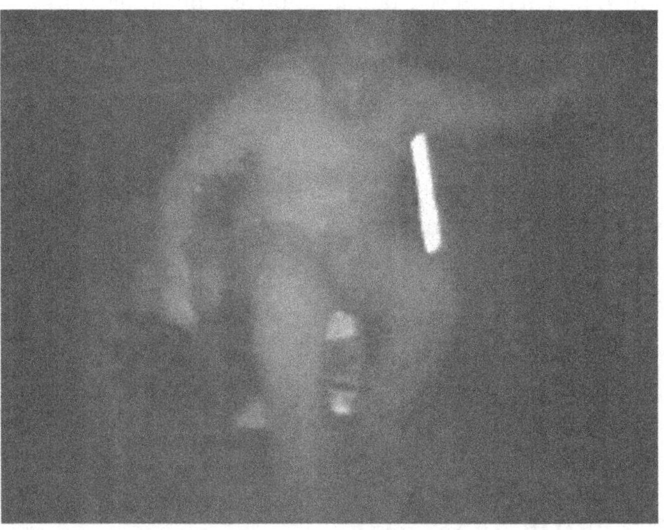

FIGURE 6.20 *This grainy undercover video of a chicken processing plant captured a worker kicking and stomping chickens.*
http://www.kentuckyfriedcruelty.com/
Courtesy of PETA

The same day, Pilgrim's Pride issued another statement by Goolsby entitled "Response to Allegations regarding Animal Welfare Practices in Moorefield, West Virginia." The statement said:

> *Pilgrim's Pride (NYSE: PPC) is appalled and outraged by the animal welfare allegations concerning our company's Moorefield, West Virginia, plant. The actions described are in complete and direct contradiction to Pilgrim's Pride animal welfare practices and policies regarding the humane treatment of poultry. KFC is a valued customer, and it's important to understand that these allegations are totally unrelated to KFC, and we regret they've been unfairly identified with this incident.*
>
> *Pilgrim's Pride does not tolerate mistreatment of animals by any employee. To make certain that this is the case, Pilgrim's is taking several steps:*
>
> - *First, an aggressive and thorough investigation was launched late yesterday when Pilgrim's Pride first became aware of the videotaped allegations. To date, one employee has been suspended without pay and three others are being investigated. Any employees who are found to have violated our policies on animal welfare will be terminated.*
> - *While we believe this is an isolated incident, earlier today Pilgrim's Pride issued a directive to management to every production facility that handles live animals to review our previously established animal welfare policies and practices in meeting with every employee and supervisor that handle live animals. Complex and plant managers at all twenty-five plants have been instructed to stop production on the current shift and hold meetings at the beginning of subsequent shifts and review animal welfare policies and Pilgrim's Pride's zero tolerance for deviation from these policies. We are also requiring signatures from every employee who works with live animals indicating that he or she reaffirms their understanding of the policies.*
> - *Pilgrim's Pride is forming an independent task force to assure the adequacy of monitoring and safeguards of animal welfare and to provide independent oversight of the Moorefield investigation.*
> - *We have also engaged Dr. Temple Grandin, one of the world's foremost experts in the field of animal welfare, to evaluate our Moorefield, West Virginia, plant in order to review our animal welfare practices.*
>
> *Pilgrim's Pride will assure that all of its locations adhere to a program of animal welfare that is designed to eliminate unnecessary harm and suffering for animals in the day-to-day operation, and we remain committed to the highest levels of humane treatment of the animals we raise for food. Pilgrim's Pride strictly adheres to the animal welfare program recommended by the National Chicken Council (NCC). This program covers all aspects of broiler chicken welfare and was developed by industry experts in consultation with academic experts from leading universities.*
>
> *Pilgrim's Pride places a high priority on humane treatment of poultry not only because it's the right thing to do, but because it also helps assure high quality, healthful products for consumers.*

This statement laid out Pilgrim's full response to the crisis, which included an internal investigation, punishment of employees implicated in the investigation, an immediate review of animal welfare policies and practices with employees throughout its facilities that handled live animals, the creation of an independent taskforce to review its animal monitoring system, and the hiring of a top expert to review the Moorefield facility and its company-wide animal welfare program. The statement also attempted to shield Pilgrim's major customer, KFC, from association with the negative incident, since KFC's only connection was as a buyer of Pilgrim's chickens. However, the scandal only added to KFC's troubles with PETA, which had earlier called for a boycott of KFC restaurants because of its commercial connection to animal housing and slaughter practices.

The next day, July 21, 2004, Pilgrim's Pride issued a third statement entitled "Pilgrim's Pride Terminates 11 Employees Based on Moorefield, West Virginia, Investigation." Among those terminated were three management-level employees and eight hourly workers. In addition to updating the public about its actions, Pilgrim's Pride took the opportunity to question why the undercover employee failed to report the incidents sooner to plant management or to an employee hotline:

> *"While we are making considerable progress with our investigation, we will continue with this investigation until we're confident that every employee—regardless of rank—who had knowledge of these incidents has been held accountable for their actions," said O.B. Goolsby, President and Chief Operation Officer of Pilgrim's Pride. He also reported that Pilgrim's Pride had placed quality assurance monitors on both shifts at the Moorefield facility to continuously audit handling practices and processing in connection with its ongoing investigation.*
>
> *"We're disappointed that the individual who surreptitiously videotaped the abuses did not report them to us when they occurred so we could have taken immediate action at that time," Goolsby said. "Had he reported the incidents to plant management and to the employee hotline, as he had been instructed during the company's animal welfare training he received on September 3, 2003, corrective and disciplinary actions would have been taken many months ago, and chickens would have been spared from suffering the types of abuses shown in the video.*
>
> *"Based on media reports of the existence of additional video footage, Pilgrim's Pride has initiated a request that all available videotape be immediately provided to the company for use in its investigation to determine whether any additional employees may have participated in or failed to report any improper practices, in direct violation of the company's animal welfare policies."*

In addition, the company announced that Dr. Grandin, one of the world's foremost experts in the field of animal welfare, would review its animal welfare practices at its Moorefield plant later in the month.

The statement also said:

> *Pilgrim's Pride places a high priority on humane treatment of poultry not only because it's the right thing to do, but because it also helps assure high-quality, healthful products*

for consumers. Pilgrim's Pride animal welfare policies are designed to eliminate unnecessary harm and suffering to animals in its day-to-day operations.

Pilgrim's Pride follows the animal welfare guidelines recommended by the National Children Council (NCC). The program covers all aspects of broiler chicken welfare and was developed by industry experts in consultation with academic experts from leading universities. Further, under the terms of Pilgrim's Pride employment, any employee who observes violations of the company's animal welfare policies is obligated to report them immediately to a supervisor.

PETA claimed its investigator twice reported the abuse and said that the plant supervisor came by regularly and witnessed the abuse.

A Pilgrim's Pride statement sent to Associated Press reporter Vicki Smith August 3, 2004, further questioned PETA's undercover tactics. It confirmed that Pilgrim's Pride had received an anonymous report April 29, 2004, of alleged mistreatment of poultry at the Moorefield facility. It also reiterated:

At that time, we promptly stopped production, addressed the allegations, and communicated the severity of these allegations to our employees, making it clear to them that any such behavior would result in immediate termination . . .

It is important to note that the "investigator" worked at the Pilgrim's Pride Moorefield plant for more than eight months, from mid-September to May 2004, and claims to have taken several hours of videotape. However, he chose to withhold this videotaped evidence from Pilgrim's Pride management until last month.

Additionally, the anonymous hotline report was not made until April 29, one day before the "investigator" showed up for work for the last time on April 30 . . . Had he presented the additional videotaped evidence earlier, corrective and disciplinary actions would have been taken many months ago, and chickens would have been spared from suffering the types of abuses shown in the video.

KFC'S RESPONSE

KFC's response was also immediate. A statement entitled "KFC Response Statement to Pilgrim's Pride Incident" released July 20, 2004, the day the story broke, also used the term "appalling" when describing KFC's reaction to the chicken abuse video.

(Louisville, KY—July 20, 2004) KFC finds the actions in the videotape appalling, wherever they have occurred. We do not tolerate animal abuse by any of our suppliers, under any circumstance.

We have notified Pilgrim's Pride that unless they can definitively assure us there are absolutely no abuses taking place, we will not purchase from this Moorefield, West Virginia facility. This facility is one of many suppliers to our Company and additionally supplies others in the fast-food industry.

We have placed an inspector on-site at this facility, who has been trained by Dr. Temple Grandin, a world-renowned animal welfare expert, to monitor activity and ensure absolutely no animal abuse. We have been in contact with Pilgrim's Pride senior management and have been assured that an immediate and thorough investigation is currently underway. We have further been assured that Pilgrim's Pride will fire any individuals involved in this alleged activity.

Pilgrim's Pride subscribes to our strict Animal Welfare guidelines and has recommitted to us they are taking the necessary actions to ensure the humane treatment of animals at all of their facilities.

The next day, at a news conference, KFC president Gregg Dedrick read a longer statement. In addition to the actions outlined in KFC's first statement, Dedrick called for the installation of security cameras at the Moorefield plant, and he noted KFC had sent a letter to all its suppliers to remind them to "strictly enforce" industry animal welfare guidelines.

Dedrick took aim at PETA for what he characterized as unfair pressure tactics. For example, KFC purchases only 15 percent of the Moorefield facility's product, yet PETA called it a "KFC facility," instead of a Pilgrim's Pride facility. He said that KFC sells "about 5 percent of all the chicken in America today" yet is singled out by PETA because its name "is synonymous with chicken":

We think it's outrageous that PETA is unfairly singling out KFC. They've done this because we're the most recognized brand selling chicken today, and our name, Kentucky Fried Chicken, is synonymous with chicken. So we have become their target. The truth is we sell about 5 percent of all the chicken in America today—that's less than the leading burger chain. But because our brand stands for chicken, they've targeted their campaign on us. Not on any other supermarket or QSR chain. Yet these companies buy their chicken from the same suppliers you do—like Pilgrim's Pride. You didn't see them hold today's press conference in Texas, where Pilgrim's Pride is located. They held it here to try to exert pressure on us . . .

Our responsibility, and we take it seriously, is to be sure we have the proper standards in place for our suppliers. While we have set standards for our suppliers, it's ultimately up to them to enforce them every day. We audit them regularly, but they have to enforce them.

I want you to know that we have the same animal welfare guidelines that our competitors do. The same standards for our suppliers as our fast-food competitors. They are on our website, KFC.com, and we have a copy available today.

We ask you today to stop being a pawn used by PETA. For example, some of the TV press coverage today said this is a "KFC videotape investigation." The Courier-Journal *today failed to mention that we're just one of the many fast-food customers of this facility—the entire article made it look like it was a KFC facility. In fact, almost all the press coverage made it look that way. And the media is not publishing all the facts. This ongoing PETA campaign of distortion, deceit and duplicity is outrageous. Their publicity ploys, like today's call for our CEO to step down, are ludicrous.*

Dedrick also mentioned examples of PETA's ongoing campaign of "distortion, deceit and duplicity" along with PETA's harassment of senior executives (including those of its parent company, Yum! Brands), their families, and neighbors. "This is not your warm and fuzzy animal rights group. This pressure through intimidation, harassment and invasion of privacy should not be tolerated. It is nothing short of corporate terrorism."

The statement ended with a recapping of the actions KFC had taken to resolve the animal abuse situation at the Pilgrim's Pride plant, including its pledge to increase audits with all its suppliers to ensure standards were met.

Both KFC statements were posted on its website. The KFC home page contained a link "KFC Sets Record Straight on Pilgrim's Pride Incident" that sent viewers to the July 21 news conference statement. The KFC website had a description of its parent company's (Yum! Brands) animal welfare program that contains guiding principles, advisory council, progress and goals, and experts' quotes. The site also contained a Yum! Brands supplier code of conduct.

THE GOVERNMENT'S RESPONSE

The U.S. Department of Agriculture (USDA) conducted a thorough investigation. According to an Associated Press article, the plant had a veterinarian and ten USDA inspectors present. A USDA spokesperson said the investigation concluded the inspectors were not aware of the abuse because their work was inside the plant and the abuse supposedly occurred in the unloading area. As of August 11, 2004, the USDA had not concluded if any federal laws had been violated since the federal Humane Methods of Slaughter Act does not cover poultry. However, in 2005 the USDA did issue a notice to poultry slaughterhouses that pursuant to the Poultry Product Inspection Act, "live poultry must be handled in a manner that is consistent with good commercial practices, meaning they should be treated humanely."

State statutes in West Virginia make animal cruelty either a felony (if the acts involve mostly torture) punishable by up to three years in prison or a misdemeanor punishable by up to $1,000 in fines and six months in jail.

LIFE GOES ON

Media interest in Moorefield (population 2,400) began to peter out a week after the story broke. However, on July 27, 2004, an Associated Press article noted that Moorefield's annual West Virginia Poultry Festival, complete with a wing sauce cook-off, beauty pageant, golf tournament, carnival, and a chicken barbecue, had taken place as scheduled. In a week's time, the story had gone from outrage to irony.

Criminal charges were never filed against the eleven employees who allegedly abused the chickens and were terminated by Pilgrim's Pride. After hearing a two-hour presentation by a special prosecutor and the undercover PETA investigator, a grand jury refused to indict four former workers PETA hoped would be convicted of felony animal cruelty.

QUESTIONS FOR DISCUSSION

1. What crisis communication concepts and practices were used in this situation?
2. Analyze the communication responses of Pilgrim's Pride and KFC during the initial phase of the crisis. Which one was more effective? Why?
3. What role does risk communication play in this situation? What might have prevented this crisis from developing in the first place?
4. The Internet played a major role in this incident. Explain how Pilgrim's Pride, KFC, and PETA used their websites to communicate. Would you do anything differently? Why?
5. PETA has been criticized as being too sensational and distorting the truth at times. What is your impression of its web communication tactics?
6. Was it right for an undercover PETA investigator to stand by while animal abuses were taking place? How do you think PETA justified this action?
7. Should organizations and activists attempt to resolve their differences in ways other than those illustrated by the Pilgrim's Pride case? What role should public relations play in this effort?
8. Many activist and protest groups use visual communication to get their point across. Provide some examples of effective visual communication used in protest events.

Dig Deeper

View PETA's undercover video on animal abuse at the Pilgrim's Pride factory (*Pilgrim's Pride Corporation Chicken Slaughterhouse Moorefield, West Virginia*) available on the textbook's companion website. While extremely poor quality, the video was still aired by the news media. What conclusions should be made by public relations professionals regarding undercover investigations within the work environment? What sort of actions can an organization take to ensure that employees treat animals humanely?

CHAPTER 7

Consumer Relations

Consumer relations embodies two areas of concern: (1) supporting marketing communication efforts to build consumer demand for products and services, and (2) maintaining mutually beneficial and lasting relationships between the organization and consumer. Inherent in the concept of consumer relations is safeguarding against questionable promotional efforts and looking out for the long-term interests of the consumer. Essentially, public relations should always take a longer view of the organization's activities to ensure consumers are not taken advantage of by shortsighted, deceptive practices or misguided policies that offend customers and noncustomers alike.

The power of the Internet has had a major impact on the ability of individuals to quickly raise an issue and organize disparate individuals around the world into formidable activist groups. A disgruntled customer or other stakeholder today can use an activist website to wage a one-person battle that will appear to be a full-fledged organizational effort. The result can be unwanted negative publicity and turned-off customers.

By paying attention to consumer needs and concerns, organizations can develop long-term relationships resulting in repeat patronage and valuable word-of-mouth endorsements from the consumer sphere of influence. Public relations practitioners can work with activists and other stakeholders who are unhappy with the organization to build understanding and minimize hostile attitudes.

MARKETING COMMUNICATION SUPPORT

Marketing has traditionally relied on paid advertising to reach the consumer market to build a customer base for products or services. While effective advertising does attract attention, its expensive production and placement costs are multiplied and complicated by an increasingly fragmented audience that gets information and entertainment from myriad sources. Clutter, the enormous number of advertisements that confront consumers daily, is also a concern. With so many advertisements assaulting the senses today, many consumers have become expert in tuning them out or using technology that removes them. Also, younger consumers are spending less time with traditional entertainment advertising sources, such as television, and more online, instant messaging friends or playing video games.

To combat these concerns, marketing has increasingly valued its partnership with public relations. Public relations expertise in media relations and special event planning is a valued part of the marketing mix for product launches and lengthy campaigns. The basic informational tactics of brochures, newsletters, direct mailers, and website material, such as backgrounders and technical specifications, are also the shared responsibility of the marketing and public relations staff.

Media relations efforts involve product mentions in the news media to raise awareness. Public relations practitioners pitch the product to reporters or editors with a news release/media kit and/or through personal contact. The goal is to gain the attention of the media gatekeepers and persuade them that the product or service is newsworthy and interesting enough for their audiences. A product that is favorably mentioned in the news portion of a publication or broadcast is usually perceived by consumers as a credible, independent evaluation (third-party endorsement) deemed worthy of extra attention. The fact that the product is mentioned by a credible outside source, when other competitors' products are not, helps establish its superiority. This is a relatively inexpensive publicity tactic to draw attention to the product and heighten consumer awareness.

Associated with media relations is speaker and media training. Public relations can help CEOs and other managers become effective spokespersons for their organizations. CEOs who participate in various high-profile industry gatherings as convention keynote speakers and panelists are often covered by the media. In addition, CEOs can be invited as talk show guests or interviewed for news and feature stories. All these efforts, if focused on the organization's mission, can help build its reputation as an industry leader.

Special events also focus or refocus consumers' attention on the product, especially when the product or service is not that much different from other competitors' products. Gala store openings, stunts, and celebrity guest appearances are some of the tactics used to attract attention. The goal of designing the right special event is to connect it logically with the product's attributes. A hybrid electric auto, for example, could travel across the country to draw attention to advances in the company's electric car line. A cake mix company might make a large White House-replica cake for a birthday gift to the President. To promote chess playing, a top-ranked chess player might play twenty young competitors simultaneously in a timed competition.

Celebrities are used frequently in special events or as product endorsers because they attract attention; companies want those star qualities transferred to the product or service. It's a tactic not without risk. For example, the U.S. Postal Service's sponsorship of Lance Armstrong, a seven-time Tour de France winner, helped connect speed, quality, and a winning image of U.S. mail service with the world's top cycling athlete. Of course, this didn't work once Armstrong admitted to doping.

When a consumer's attention is captured and he or she seeks more information about the product or service, appropriate tactics can connect with those active information seekers. A stand-alone product website or a part of the organization's website can provide a multimedia source for video, audio, and text information. Some of the most effective examples of product websites today are those promoting Hollywood's latest offerings. These can include weekly production videos and updates on the making of the big-budget film, a blog carrying the latest news, including tidbits from key movie executives, and various companion social media sites, such as Facebook fan pages. Websites frequently contain electronic versions of media kits with news releases, fact sheets, questions and answers, backgrounders, features, photos, and logos that further inform information seekers.

While emotional appeals to consumer self-interest are all important, informational tactics should also support comparison shopping. When it comes to consumer electronics, for example, specification sheets can offer more detailed technical information than advertisements have room for. Often these sheets use unfamiliar technical language, particularly for technology products. While it is acceptable to use technical terminology, it is a good idea to have a glossary of terminology to help beginners.

Once a product or service is purchased, communication efforts should continue. Many companies include short satisfaction surveys in registration materials or mail them to the customer soon after his or her purchase. Other helpful consumer relations efforts include toll-free telephone numbers or web-based customer representative chat rooms to guide customers with any product-related problems or concerns. Letters written to an organization regarding product problems should be answered and monitored for potential patterns of problems.

BEYOND THE CONSUMER

Public relations seeks to build relationships with many stakeholders to ensure the long-term viability of the organization. While the customer is a primary stakeholder for any organization, shareholders, employees, government officials, and others concerned with policies and actions of an organization are important to public relations.

In addition, public relations is concerned with identifying and managing issues from all stakeholders, including consumer complaints, that could have a negative impact on the organization. This is done by monitoring its environment and public opinion. Public relations ultimately should help organizations grow while maintaining good relationships with their stakeholders. This delicate balancing act is not always an easy task; it often requires organizations to look beyond their monthly earnings reports and see their connections to others.

18

The Five Seasons of Salem

A City Hunts for Something More than Witches

Salem, Massachusetts, residents call October their fifth season. That's because Salem is *the* Halloween destination in America. The city celebrates its witchy history with a month-long series of events culminating in a giant street party, featuring witches, goblins and zombies, and fireworks, on All Hallows' Eve.

Salem's macabre reputation dates to 1692 when Puritan villagers caught in the grip of witchcraft hysteria accused nearly 200 townspeople of witchcraft. The peculiarly bloody year-long chapter in our nation's history—when nineteen accused witches were hanged and one was crushed to death—has captivated America's imagination ever since. More than three centuries later, the city has turned a grim historical fact into a tourism bonanza.

The mystique of the Salem witch trials has grown ever stronger, reinforced by its depictions in popular culture: playwright Arthur Miller's *The Crucible* in the 1950s and several best sellers, such as *Witch-Hunt*. All have served to reintroduce the story of Salem's mass hysteria to new generations.

More than three centuries after the events depicted on stage and in film, Salem now attracts about a million visitors annually. Nearly one-third visit in October, when a full slate of Halloween activities is offered: lantern-guided walking tours, a costume parade, and haunted storytelling. Witch-related attractions—the historic Witch House (home to one of the witch trial judges), Witch History Museum, Salem Witch Museum, Witch Dungeon Museum, Spellbound Museum, and the Salem Wax Museum—all offer extended hours to accommodate enthusiastic tourists.

Police officers wear badges embroidered with a witch on a broomstick, as also is the high school athletic logo and mascot, and the school newspaper is called *The Witch's Brew*. A local microbrewery has offered a variety of Halloween-themed drinks such as Pumpkinhead ale, a Witch City Red amber, and a Black Bat stout.

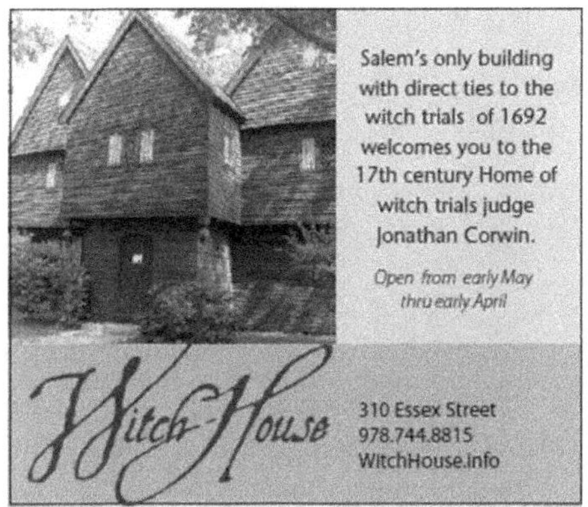

Salem's only building
with direct ties to the
witch trials of 1692
welcomes you to the
17th century Home of
witch trials judge
Jonathan Corwin.
Open from early May
thru early April
Witch-House
310 Essex Street
978.744.8815
WitchHouse.info

FIGURE 7.1 *The Witch House is owned and operated by the City of Salem. Its visitor fees provide a source of revenue to the city.*
http://www.salem.org/
Courtesy of Destination Salem

TOURISM AS ECONOMIC ENGINE

Tourism is a major economic engine for the entire state of Massachusetts, bringing in $11 billion annually and employing 124,800 people in the state, according to the state's tourism office. Salem, population 42,000, relies heavily on tourism as an economic engine; restaurants, hotels, and shops all benefit from visitors. Unlike many summer tourism destinations, Salem has its fifth season—the October celebration of the macabre brings in 300,000 with over 100,000 visiting on Halloween.

The city of Salem, chamber of commerce, and area businesses provide four weeks of Halloween activities, starting with a Grand Parade led by Salem's mayor. The month has many theatrical and musical performances inspired by the witch trials and the supernatural, a haunted movie series, magic shows, historical walking and haunted house tours, costumed parties and balls, psychic readings, and, on one occasion, a flash-mob styled Lady Gaga gathering of "little monsters" dancing to "Born this Way." It all ends with a fireworks display over the North River. Clearly, Salem knows how to handle Halloween in a big way. Locals are fond of describing Salem as "dead" after October 31. Residents who good-naturedly endure the onslaught of rowdy visitors each year call it "fall foolishness" and look forward to the peace that November brings.

Despite the snarled traffic and other temporary inconveniences thousands of ghouls and zombies bring to the city each year, October is critical to Salem's financial well-being. In recent years, it has turned a profit for the city. In 2011, the city made a net profit of $250,000 off revenues of $419,388. The city's expenses were $168,726 including extra security, staffing, supplies and event expenses. In addition, the city nets a profit of nearly $392,295 in hotel/motel tax receipts from visitors; nearly half of that amount ($163,000) is made during September, October, and November.

FIGURE 7.2 *Halloween is the main event in Salem each year. While the entire month of October is dedicated to special events and activities related to Halloween, the night itself and its preceding weekend can bring in 100,000 or more people dressed in every imaginable costume.*
https://www.salem.org/
Courtesy of Jared Charney

DEVELOPING A STABLE TOURISM EFFORT

For years, Salem's business and civic leaders have worked to extend their Halloween success beyond October. In 2007, Mayor Kimberley Driscoll led an effort to revitalize the city's "Destination Salem" tourism effort. Based on feedback from Salem businesses and a tourism research report, Driscoll redirected 25 percent of revenue from a 1 percent hotel/motel tax and other sources to Destination Salem. A new executive director for Destination Salem was hired and its office was relocated with the Office of Tourism and Cultural Affairs to City Hall to encourage collaboration. The city's contribution to the effort in 2011 climbed to half, $187,000 in hotel/motel tax revenue and a meal tax increase. While most of the city's October profits come from parking fees and meters, it also owns and operates the historic Witch House. This is the only structure still standing with a direct connection to the witch trials; its original occupant, Jonathan Corwin, was one of the judges involved in the witch trials.

Destination Salem is a public–private partnership that works closely with the city, chamber of commerce, the North of Boston Convention and Visitor Bureau, and Massachusetts Office of Travel and Tourism to publicize businesses, events, and resources in Salem. Destination Salem receives advertising revenue generated by the annual Salem guidebook, grants, and other sources. The organization publishes and distributes an annual *Visitor & Travel Guide*, and maintains the Salem.org website. Destination Salem's resources are further bolstered by the state's office of tourism services, especially its research and marketing. The state helps distribute the Salem

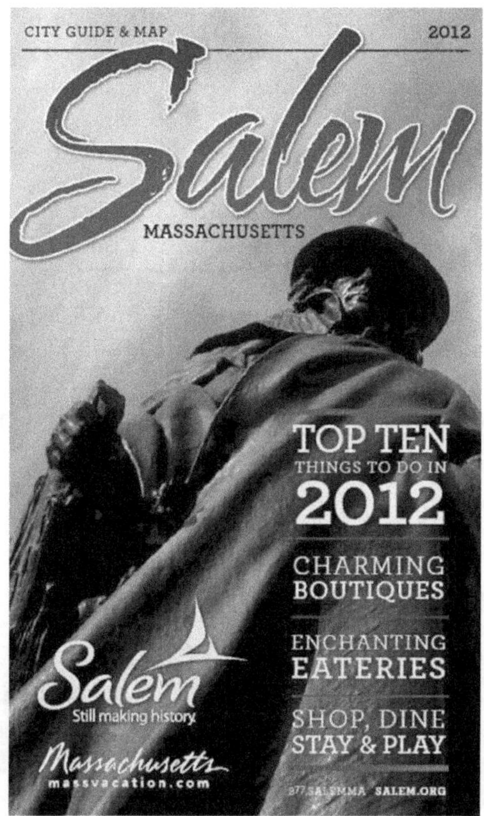

FIGURE 7.3 *Destination Salem's City Guide is the primary tourism publication available in print and digital versions.*
http://www.salem.org/
Courtesy of Destination Salem

FIGURE 7.4 *Destination Salem's tourism logo.*
https://maia.utica.edu/
Courtesy of Destination Salem

city guide to nearly 325,000 around the world; copies are distributed via direct mail request through travel agents, tour operators, AAA offices, hotels, attractions, visitors centers, and trade and consumer shows locally and around the world.

BROADENING SALEM'S BRAND

In 2010, the city hired an advertising and marketing firm to "create a brand that would work for all of Salem's industries—from tourism to Salem Hospital, from downtown shops and restaurants to Salem State University," according to a Salem news release. Rattle, an advertising and marketing firm located in Beverly, Massachusetts, was hired for $25,000 to create a new brand and positioning strategy. The mayor said the new branding effort would "appeal to a broad spectrum of stakeholders, from tourism businesses to Salem residents." Over the years, many brand statements—"taglines"—have been developed for Salem including:

- America's Bewitching Seaport
- There's No Place Like Salem
- Experience the Unexpected
- Discover the Magic of Salem.

The 2011 tagline was "Salem—Still Making History," and its campaign logo provided the viewer with two visual interpretations—a sailboat or a witch's hat. The visual illusion provided a perceptual switch between two shapes that represent Salem's major historical legacies, the Salem witch trials and its historic seaport. The clever slogan and logo were used for all events including promotion of the city's Heritage Days and Restaurant Week. The tourism campaign was integrated into all aspects of advertising including radio, print, social media, e-mail, and web marketing.

FIGURE 7.5 *Salem's logo for 2012 was "Salem Still Making History." The graphic had two views: a witch's hat and a sailboat, which combined both tourism themes.*
http://www.salem.org/
Courtesy of Destination Salem

The campaign's marketing included new communication tools such as a free Salem Guide app for devices like the iPhone and iPad. A Haunted Happenings App was also developed to help people plan their visits with business listings, photos and information.

SALEM'S HISTORIC SEAPORT

Beyond Salem's well-known witch trial history, the city has a lesser-known but also important tourism draw. One of America's oldest seaport settlements established four years before Boston, Salem is a port community of historic significance and the city's 18.5 miles of tidal shoreline have many stories to tell. Salem residents were involved in privateering during the Revolutionary War and were instrumental in opening the New World to global trade. Salem was the first to bulk import black pepper—then a rare spice in America—from the East Indies. In 1654, daring sea captains sailed from Salem to Sumatra to establish a bulk pepper trade that lasted nearly a century. By the early eighteenth century, Salem was a bustling seaport that created some of the continent's first millionaires; their fortunes were based on trade with the East and West Indies, Africa, China, Russia, Japan, and Australia.

The city is fortunate to have the federally funded Salem Maritime National Historic Site with its historic wharves, functioning iron works operation, and several carefully preserved buildings, including: the 1761 Derby house, 1780 Hawkes house, 1819 Custom House, the 1800 West India Goods Store, and the 1672 Narbonne house. Salem was the first national historic site in the National Park System,

FIGURE 7.6 *The* Friendship, *a reconstruction of a 171-foot three-masted Salem East Indiaman built in 1797, and other maritime offerings are a major attraction for Salem visitors.*
Rowlandw from http://commons.wikimedia.org/wiki/File:2006.04.20_Salem_Friendship_Schooner.jpg

established to preserve and interpret the maritime history of New England and the United States. In 1996, the site introduced a seaworthy full-sized replica of a 1797 Salem-built three-masted cargo vessel, *Friendship of Salem*, which serves as a floating museum.

According to the National Park Service, the visitor center had nearly 378,000 visitors in 2010. The Salem Maritime Historic Site partners with the city of Salem to coordinate an Independence Day celebration, a Maritime Festival, and October's Haunted Happenings.

While Salem's rich maritime glory days were long past, city officials and tourism boosters knew there were plenty of people interested in historic maritime artifacts, historic architecture, and quaint historic cities with other attractions such as dining and shopping. Salem has attracted state funding for redeveloping its historic seaport to increase tourism. With Boston's huge tourist crowds only a few miles away, Salem and other North Shore communities were eager to cash in. One of the city's key strategies was to promote Salem as a perfect day trip for those visiting Boston.

The Salem Ferry, which began operation in 2006, connects Salem with Boston's Long Wharf in less than an hour. The cost is affordable; Boston tourists can ride the ferry and visit Salem for the day (or longer) between May and October 31. In 2010, the ferry service had 87,000 riders. Salem also is connected by rail to Boston and other Boston-area locales.

In 2010 the city received $2.5 million in federal funding for the Salem Wharf improvement project to enhance the infrastructure of its ferry landing and expand its ferry service. In 2012, another $1.75 million was allocated to begin dredging the harbor so that bigger sea vessels could visit Salem's port. The money also funded construction of a harbor walk and other improvements. Little by little, Salem has worked to provide a new source of tourism revenue based on its historic maritime history.

BEYOND THE WITCH TRIALS

Still, plenty of attractions seem to be lost among Salem's witch industry. Salem's treasure trove of historic homes, many of which were built on the fortunes of early maritime magnates, goes unnoticed by many visitors. In 2005, the city was named one of America's dozen distinctive destinations by the National Trust for Historic Preservation. How could Salem leverage its total history to build a year-round tourism trade?

Below are some of Salem's other noteworthy tourism attractions, from the city's official guidebook:

- McIntire Historic District: Home to hundreds of architecturally significant houses and buildings, this area includes historic Chestnut Street, called "the most beautiful street in America," with homes built by sea captains and merchants between 1800 and 1840. There are many examples of the Federal architecture style. Some homes, such as the Witch House, date back to 1642.

FIGURE 7.7 *Salem also has a literary side as home to Nathaniel Hawthorne, author of* The House of the Seven Gables.
Destination Salem
Courtesy of Destination Salem

- The House of the Seven Gables: The Turner-Ingersoll Mansion was made famous by author Nathaniel Hawthorne in his 1851 classic tale, *The House of the Seven Gables;* the house in which Hawthorne was born, circa 1750, is next door.
- Peabody Essex Museum: A museum that chronicles New England's storied past as well as other cultural wonders, the Peabody Essex houses the finest maritime art collection in the country. Its $125 million renovation, completed in 2003, has made it a major cultural institution in Salem. More than 100,000 people came through PEM's doors in 2012.
- Salem Maritime: *Friendship of Salem*: A full-scale replica of a 171-foot, three-masted 1797 Salem East Indiaman. *Fame:* A full-scale replica of an 1812 privateer.
- Salem Harbor: Derby Wharf and the picturesque Derby Lighthouse. Pickering Wharf: a waterfront shopping and dining village.
- Ye Olde Pepper Candy Companie: The site of the nation's oldest candy company, established in 1806.
- New England Pirate Museum: Salem docks saw their fair share of pirates in the seventeenth and eighteenth centuries, including the nefarious Captains Blackbeard, Kidd, and others who prowled the Atlantic coast looking for plunder.

MARKETING FOCUS

Destination Salem develops a marketing plan with strategies and tactics each year. The following information came from Salem's annual Marketing Plan. The full report is available on the textbook's companion website.

Tapping into the Boston Market

For several years, Salem has eyed the Boston market as a natural partner in its developing tourism efforts, especially when the North Shore, which included Salem, was promoted. Here is some statistical information about the Boston market:

According to American Express Business Insights, 81 percent of visitors to Greater Boston have graduate degrees and are college educated; 86 percent are white-collar professionals; 40 percent have a household income between $100,000 and $150,000; and 23 percent have a household income greater than $150,000. Travel by car is the dominant mode of transportation to Massachusetts, with 70 percent of visitors arriving this way, 53.4 percent originating from New England and 23.5 percent arriving from the Mid-Atlantic states. Greater Boston's overnight leisure visitors tend to be older, as the majority of visitors continue to be within the 35–54 age group. This segment has had the largest growth rate and spends the most trip dollars. Following this group, one-third of Greater Boston's overnight leisure visitors are 18–34 years of age. And the remaining 32 percent of visitors are 55 years of age or older, significantly greater than all of Greater Boston's competitors, excluding Philadelphia. Sixty-eight percent of visitors to Greater Boston are historical/cultural travelers. The historic/cultural traveler spends more money compared to the average U.S. traveler, making this a lucrative market segment for destinations and attractions. U.S. Travel Association reports that more than 30 percent of historic/cultural travelers make their destination choice by specific historic or cultural event or activity.

Boston's Cruise Tourism

In 2010, cruise travel in Massachusetts created more than 7,000 new jobs and generated nearly $460 million in direct spending. The majority of Massachusetts' 1.29

FIGURE 7.8 *The Hawkes House is a fine example of the large Federal-style homes built throughout Salem in the late 18th and early 19th centuries. Salem has a concentration of historical architecture that also draws visitors. http://www.salem.org/*
Courtsey of the National Park Service

FIGURE 7.9 *In addition to Salem's witch past, it played a significant role in maritime history. The National Park Service has developed the Salem Maritime Historic Site that includes the U.S. Customs House.* *http://www.nps.gov/sama/index.htm*
Courtesy of National Park Service

million international overseas visitors come from the United Kingdom, Germany, France, and Japan. City break travel remains strong, particularly from the United Kingdom, where consumers can choose during peak season from seven non-stop flights daily from London. Family travel also remains strong, as does shopping-break travel. With the exchange rate favorable for international travelers, it continues to be inexpensive for them to travel to Massachusetts for a shopping trip or a quick getaway as Boston is the closest U.S. port of entry to Europe. In fact, European capacity at Logan International Airport increased 19.8 percent in the second quarter of 2011, and 17.1 percent in the third quarter. The majority of international passengers are from Europe as the majority of non-stop service comes from European markets; however, this is anticipated to change starting in 2012 with the advent of the new non-stop Boston–Tokyo service on JAL.

Salem's Marketing Goals

Salem's tourism goals were to increase overnight visitation and to increase the economic impact of the visitor industry. Its specific strategies included:

1. Continuing to incorporate data realized through marketing research into communications strategies;
2. Continuing to generate leads and provide information to prospective visitors in all target market segments;
3. Developing increased focus on niche markets;
4. Actively pursuing media coverage through an integrated media relations campaign, including regularly scheduled e-blasts, pursuing placement of stories, and continuing to target a list of online publications for events/activities;

5. Continuing to develop and promote themed months that are tied into the festivals and other activities in Salem, such as November and April Restaurant Weeks, May Poetry Month, or February Salem so Sweet month, among others. These themed months will be supported by media relations efforts, as well as by developing suggested itineraries and packaging by partners;
6. Increasing the number of marketing and promotional partners working with Destination Salem;
7. Continuing to enhance website;
8. Promoting pre- and post-tours for Boston-based meetings;
9. Increasing the amount of group business during need periods;
10. Increasing participation in international marketing programs;
11. Providing leadership and guidance for the development of promotional events;
12. Providing input and advocacy to affect local and regional tourism policies.

Marketing Tactics

Salem used a variety of marketing communication and public relations tactics to achieve its goals. The following information provides a summary of the marketing tactics from Salem's annual marketing plan:

- **Advertising**—Advertising focused on promoting Salem as a destination of unique experiences, a perfect blend of the historical and the contemporary, underscored with value-added offers. Salem was positioned as a place where visitors could understand the making of history and make history themselves. Destination Salem targeted affluent consumers in New York, New Jersey, Pennsylvania, and Connecticut, as well as Massachusetts and New England households.
- **Media relations**—Salem hosted educational trips for travel writers and interviews with key partners to develop an online media library and a calendar of pitch ideas/press releases to generate exposure for Salem among target media. Destination Salem continued its social media efforts to increase awareness of Salem for visitors, planners, and the media. Destination Salem also pursued media coverage for the destination by developing and pitching story ideas, targeting niche media, and promoting new itineraries to the media.
- **Social Media**—Salem continued to build its Facebook presence and considered ways to use YouTube and Flickr. Destination Salem would create a monthly calendar of posts that highlighted positive news about Salem.

Kim Driscoll @MayorDriscoll
31 Oct
So in other places it might be newsworthy when a banana, a cowboy and a zombie walk down the street together..but not here. Gotta luv Salem!
Retweeted by Haunted Happenings
Expand

FIGURE 7.10 *Salem Mayor Kim Driscoll supported the city's Halloween festivities on the city's Halloween Twitter site. She also provided media interviews and led the costume parade.*
https://twitter.com/DestSalem
Courtesy of Destination Salem

- **E-newsletters**—Two types of e-newsletters were produced: one for locals and one for visitors/media produced on a regular basis. The one produced for local residents would promote events and specials with a shorter lead-time, helping to address short-term business needs.
- **Content Development**—Topics for niche itineraries to be listed on the website and promoted to the media would include: buy local, LGBT, culture, culinary, international, green, and group tourism. Itineraries would be leveraged with the other areas to create longer stays.
- **Website**—A major focus of Salem's marketing efforts focused on driving traffic to the website, www.Salem.org. Eighty-seven percent of Salem's visitors get their information from the site. The site was updated to reflect the new branding, as well as seasonal promotions and special events. One tactic included reaching out to niche markets and adding new web outlets for promotion, including blogs and social networking sites, ultimately driving more business to the website. Some suggested new website sections included: suggested itineraries, cruise ideas, a "media only" section, special values/packages, social events (weddings and reunions), group tours, and meetings and events.

Niche Markets

Salem would develop individual suggested itineraries and/or packages for targeted markets (see above). Included in the packages would be the development of campaigns that would identify and attract these niche market groups. Some of those identified by Destination Salem included:

- **LGBT**—The LGBT population, particularly from the Boston area, would be communicated to about events through LGBT publications.

- **Family travel**—One promotion idea was to develop three family-friendly school vacation week packages annually.
- **Culinary**—To attract culinary-focused tourists Salem would promote the existing Restaurant Weeks.
- **International**—A series of suggested itineraries for the international visitor from Japan, China, and South Korea were proposed to capitalize upon the new nonstop JAL flight from Tokyo to Boston.
- **Cruise**—Activities and programs designed specifically for the cruise passenger were proposed along with strengthening its partnership with the Historic Ports Initiative.
- **Green**—Promote the Cool Pass during August that includes cultural passes and trails to escape to the cool shore, as well as a cool night out in the city for tourists on the shore.
- **Meetings and Group Tours**—Another segment of the tourism market included the conference and meeting sector. Salem's marketing efforts would pursue the meeting and group tour markets to help mid-week and off-season business. Small, market-focused educational trips to Salem for both trade media, as well as meeting/conference planners, would be hosted as appropriate.

Evaluation

The success of Salem's tourism programs would be measured by:

- Tracking industry trends;
- Tracking the number of inquiries received;
- Measuring museum, attraction, and visitation statistics;
- Measuring hotel occupancy, ADR, and RevPAR statistics;
- Following up with key target markets to gauge level of success in campaigns;
- Collecting, maintaining, and analyzing statistical data on web visitors;
- Analyzing fulfillment statistics based around promotional campaigns; and
- Tracking the amount of media coverage received.

QUESTIONS FOR DISCUSSION

1. What is the historical significance of Salem, Massachusetts?
2. What types of events happen in October?
3. Why does Salem want to expand beyond its witch city image?

4. What groups might not appreciate the witch city heritage?
5. Why is Boston a focal area for Salem's tourism efforts?
6. What are the tourism niche groups that Salem focused on?
7. How could media relations play a pivotal role in changing Salem's image?
8. How could other public relations and marketing tactics change Salem's image?

Dig Deeper

Review Salem's 2011–2012 Marketing Plan available on the textbook's companion website. What are Salem's competitive destinations? What are some of the travel trends? What are Salem's initiatives and goals? Review Salem's operating budget overview ("Salem Budget—General Overview—FY2013 Operating Budget"), available on the textbook's companion website. What are some of the factors affecting Salem's economic health?

Read the research article "Marketing Destinations with Prolonged Negative Images: Towards a Theoretical Model" available on the textbook's companion website. Describe the two approaches of media strategies for changing negative images. What is the better approach? Why?

19

Getting Away from It All

Trade Association Sells Affordability and Convenience

Do you live to work or work to live?

It's a question commonly asked when "the job" demands seep into all areas of life. Home, once a safe harbor from the pressures of work, now serves as a secondary office for many workers, especially those connected to their primary office by smart phones and computers. Less time for home, friends, and relaxation creates stress, missed opportunities, or simply misplaced priorities.

One trade association is doing its best to make sure that Americans get back their life balance and focus on what it says is important—family and fun.

The Recreation Vehicle Industry Association (RVIA) is the national association that represents nearly 400 manufacturers and component suppliers of that uniquely American institution, the RV. While RV manufacturers and dealerships in this $9 billion industry compete with each other for consumer sales, promoting the concept of the RV and its overall ownership benefits are the purview of RVIA. By pooling their financial resources, manufacturers fund RVIA's well-crafted national consumer marketing and public relations campaigns, research, industry education and training, government affairs, RV standards, and national shows.

About nine million Americans are RV owners. While the vast majority of these owners use their RVs on a regular basis, there are "full timers," who have sold their homes and have become "modern-day nomads in a high-tech covered wagon," as the Smithsonian described them in a historical retrospective. With more than 16,000 RV parks and campgrounds located along scenic routes and interstates, in cities and small towns, the ability to use an RV anywhere is appealing to many.

There are RVs to fit all types of lifestyles and pocketbooks. The industry's two major groups are the "towables," ranging from economical pop-up tent campers to large trailers hauled by trucks, and "motorized vehicles," everything from van-sized to enormous 40-foot home-away-from-home vehicles with home conveniences and luxuries as well.

FIGURE 7.11 *Go RVing's television commercials stressed getting away from it all and finding "your away." In the commerical, "Within Your Means," nature's beauty and family togetherness are both available on a budget.*
http://www.gorving.com/
Courtesy of Go Rving, Inc.

Recreational vehicles beckon their owners to jump in, rev the motor and take off for an adventure or simply find a quiet part of nature to rediscover. Airline tickets, hotels, and restaurants aren't a factor. An RV can be transportation and food and lodging all in one.

Yet, even with all these advantages, some consumers remain skeptical. After all, gas prices can give RV operators a continuing shock at the pump. Larger motorhomes, for example, can get less than ten miles to a gallon. Other hurdles for potential buyers: the price of the RV itself, cramped accommodations, and the potentially intimidating reality of driving a large vehicle or pulling a towable down a highway.

Yesterday's image of RV owners as senior citizens is changing. Today's typical RV owner is 48 years old, married, with an annual household income of $62,000, and owns his or her own home, according to RVIA. The largest segment of RV owners is the 35–54 age category (11 percent of all U.S. households) with those 55 and older comprising 9.3 percent of U.S. households. As the large baby boomer population ages, RV sales are expected to rise steadily, despite the tough economy and high gas prices.

RESEARCH

Smart business people know not only the merits of their product but its weaknesses as well. Effective organizations conduct research on their strengths, weaknesses, opportunities, and threats, such as a SWOT (strengths, weaknesses, opportunities, threats) analysis or other research methods, to make product improvements and determine communication strategies. Such organizations are outward-looking, scanning the environment to take advantage of opportunities and to plan for potential threats.

While gas prices might be a psychological barrier for some potential RV buyers, RVIA has sought to put rising gas prices into perspective. Higher gas prices, it has argued, have affected all modes of transportation and are just one small factor to consider when purchasing an RV.

According to RVIA's research, people buy RVs mainly for:

- Flexibility and convenience
- Family togetherness
- Nature and outdoor activity
- Savings and affordability
- Escapism.

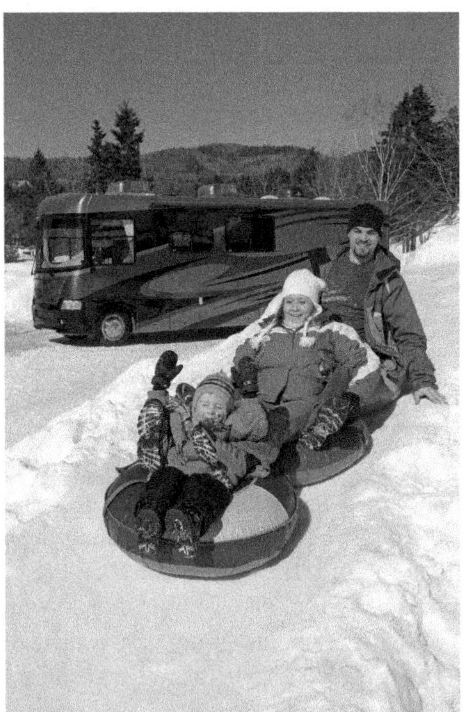

FIGURE 7.12 *Nearly all of Go Rving's print advertisements stressed three benefits: family time, nature, and fun.*
http://www.rvia.org/
Courtesy of Go Rving, Inc.

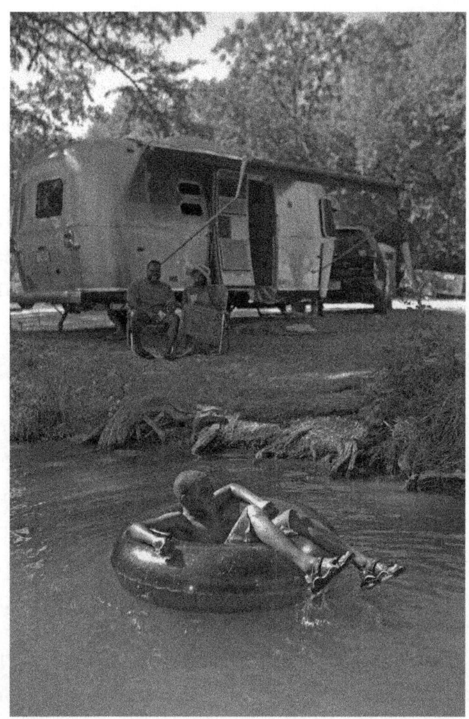

FIGURE 7.13 *Go RVings print advertisements stressed three benefits: family time, nature, and fun.*
http://www.rvia.org/
Courtesy of Go Rving, Inc.

Today's buyers find RVs the easier way to travel, without the hassle of airports and the restrictions of a schedule. RVs are fairly comfortable, with amenities such as flat-screen TVs and surround-sound stereos, fully equipped kitchens and baths. Keeping family pets with the family (54 percent) is another factor in RV ownership. Travel with an RV tends to bring families closer together. Even when factoring in the cost of RV ownership, a family of four can travel cheaper than other transportation modes. Nature and RVs have historic ties with many parks hosting RV camping and recreational areas. There are more than 16,000 public and privately owned campgrounds nationwide and a growing number of luxury RV resorts. And while camping is the most frequently thought of use of RVs, they can be used for any activity that involves travel—even tailgating at sporting events and festivals.

Although consumers may not think of RVs as good for the environment, their carbon footprint is getting attention by manufacturers who are constructing RVs with lightweight materials and aerodynamic design for improved fuel efficiency. The "greening" of RV design now includes solar panels for power. Another growing trend is the recognition by owners that RV travel makes them more active, providing a health benefit.

RVIA used research extensively to build credibility in its media relations strategy. These studies in particular are regularly commissioned by RVIA and referenced in its media efforts:

- **Vacation Cost Comparison Research**—PKF Consulting, an international consulting firm with expertise in travel and tourism, found that a family of four can spend 23 percent to 59 percent less on RV vacations compared to vacations using other modes of transportation, such as cars, planes, and cruises. For an "empty-nester" couple traveling by RV, savings were 11 percent to 46 percent. Even after accounting for factors such as RV ownership costs and fuel prices, the study confirms that RV vacations offer greater savings than those taken using a personal car or airline, and staying in a hotel or rental house or condominium. According to the study, for a family of four, fuel prices would have to more than quadruple for RV vacations to lose their economic advantage over other forms of travel. For an adult couple, fuel prices would have to more than double before RV vacations would become more costly.

- **RV Owners Travel Forecast Biannual Survey**—The annual Spring/Summer Campfire Canvass Survey of 424 RV owners conducted in 2012 by RVIA and Cvent found 64 percent of RV owners intended to use their RVs more during the spring/summer than they did the previous year; 24 percent said they'd use their RVs the same amount and 7 percent indicated they'd use their RV less. More than half (58 percent) said that fuel prices would affect their RV travel plans. Respondents indicated they would still travel by RV, but would adjust plans by traveling to destinations closer to home (74 percent) and driving fewer miles in their RVs (68 percent), according to RVIA. "The top reasons for using their RVs more include enjoying outdoor activity, taking mini-vacations, spending quality time with family and escaping from the stress and pressure of everyday life," according to RVIA. The survey found out what were the favorite types of activities that RV owners engaged in which included: Sightseeing, 77 percent; cooking, 75 percent; visiting friends and family, 58 percent; hiking, 57 percent; fishing, 50 percent; and visiting festivals or fairs, 49 percent.

- **RV Manufacturing Industry Survey**—The third study focused on manufacturing industry growth predictions and was conducted by Dr. Richard Curtin, an RV industry analyst and director of consumer surveys at the University of Michigan. Entitled "RV Roadsigns," this quarterly study in August 2012 predicted moderate growth with a gain of 8.4 percent over 2011 and the highest annual total (273,600 units) since 2007, the year before the Great Recession began. States buying the most RVs were Texas, California, Michigan, Florida, and New York.

- **RV Consumer Demographic Profile**—A consumer profile prepared every four years for RVIA by Richard Curtin of the University of Michigan Research Center, said 8.5 percent of U.S. households now have an RV parked in the driveway. In good news for RV dealers, 21 percent of all U.S. households plan to purchase an RV in the future. Of current RV owners, 70 percent said they expect to replace their existing rig with another RV and expressed a strong preference for purchasing a new, more energy-efficient RV. In addition, 14 percent of Americans who have never owned a recreational vehicle said they plan to purchase an RV in the future, with a third indicating they would prefer to buy a new RV. Twenty-seven percent of former RV owners also indicated their intent to purchase an RV in the future, with former owners under the age of 35 more likely to return to RVing than older former owners. Rapidly increasing consumer interest in RV ownership is being driven largely by consumers between the ages of 35 and 54, the RV nation's fastest-growing consumer demographic. However, empty-nesters from the Baby Boomer generation have also spurred a healthy increase in RV ownership. Among people over the age of 55, RV ownership increased to 9.3 percent in 2011.

PUTTING RESEARCH INTO ACTION

In addition to providing manufacturers with clues to American purchasing decisions and the type of features important to the prospective buyer, RVIA's research provided guidance in developing media campaign messages, both visually and audibly. Since

FIGURE 7.14 *Nature is just steps away when RVing. In this television commercial still "Closer," a family can see nature's wonder from their camper.*
http://www.gorving.com/
Courtesy of Go Rving, Inc.

national media buys are expensive it was helpful in determining key messages that resonated with current RV owners and prospective buyers for a single campaign.

Research revealed that messages, for the most part, could be used for current and prospective owners; one difference was that current RV owners were almost twice as likely to have a strong belief in environmental responsibility as non-owners.

Since many RV owners and prospective buyers said camping was a favorite activity and that family pets were a part of the adventure, advertising should include visual depictions of camping and pets. Other commonalities included the strong belief that RVs helped cultivate family togetherness and engagement with nature and outdoor activities. A Harris Interactive survey found that RV owners and prospective owners said RV travel encouraged more physical activity than a typical vacation. Interestingly, respondents said RV travel reduced exposure to illness and other health risks.

STRATEGY

Every year, RVIA applies its research to guide its national advertising efforts. For 2012, it had about $10.4 million for a marketing campaign that ran from February to November and included print, television, Internet, and social media components. Campaign funding came primarily from a mandatory assessment of all new units built by RVIA member manufacturers.

The Richards Group produced three new thirty-second commercials for its "Away" campaign. Each commercial, "Within Your Means," "Closer," and "Comforts," focused on families enjoying together time in nature—the experience made possible by affordable RVs.

The commercials were built around one simple word: "Away," Stan Richards, founder and creative principal of the Richards Group, said in a news release.

FIGURE 7.15 *Virtually every commercial and print advertisement for Go RVing's campaign stresses family time in nature.*
http://www.gorving.com/
Courtesy of Go Rving, Inc.

But in this campaign, "Away" becomes much more than just a word. It's a place. It's a state of mind. It's out there somewhere, and it's different for everyone, depending on who you are or what you like to do. And traveling in an RV is the best way to find it.

Each commercial ended with a call-to-action tagline "Find Your AWAY. Go RVing." The key message stressed the idea of escapism but also togetherness with loved ones. The television campaign was designed to drive consumer traffic to GoRVing.com, which provided information to guide the consumer through the purchase process and travel experience, according to RVIA. The site included interactive travel cost calculators and videos featuring real RVers who talked about their RV experiences.

The tug-at-the-heart-strings commercials, featuring the voice of actor Tom Selleck, subtly featured several types of RVs. RVIA budgeted $4.8 million to air spots on forty networks including Travel Channel, Outdoor Channel, Discovery, TBS, TLC, USA, and HGTV, which fit the RVIA buyer profile.

RVIA understood that consumer viewing patterns of commercials had changed over the years, with fewer people paying attention. RVIA extended its television advertising dollars by developing promotional partnerships with networks that allowed RVIA messages to be inserted into television brand content popular with its target audience, such as messages popping up during sporting events when there was a pause in the action.

Beyond traditional ad buys, RVIA invested heavily in integrated media buys with carefully selected partners who fit the prospective RV profile. For example, RVIA paid for the use of influencers such as popular network program hosts and celebrities, games and sweepstakes, and intermingled Go RVing commercial messages superimposed over the program content—as well as more traditional thirty-second commercials. Here are some of the partnerships RVIA developed for its 2012 campaign:

- Great American Country (GAC) network that included a national sweepstake, the Ultimate Country Music RV Giveaway, to win an RV and VIP access to CMA's Music Festival in Nashville. Country music was a good fit for RV users since research showed they liked country music. Go RVing messages and ads appeared on GAC's television programming and its website, GACTV.com. The GACTV website included Go RVing interactive banner ads that provided information about RVs and "roadworthy recipes." GoRVing.com cosponsored a six-page pull-and-save brochure in *People Country* magazine and an online GAC guide to 2012 summer concert tours, fairs, and festivals.
- Great American Country and GoRVing.com produced two sixty-second RV travel vignettes featuring country recording artist Chuck Wicks using a Lance travel trailer. In one, Wicks enjoys a weekend getaway with friends; in the other he takes a hunting trip with his father.
- A Major League Baseball (MLB) partnership included an eight-stadium RV motorhome tour that functioned as a broadcast studio featured on MLB programs covering baseball spring training. The motorhome was wrapped with visuals

from the new Go RVing "Away" national advertising campaign as well as logos for GoRVing.com, MLB Network, and the manufacturer. Go RVing graphics were displayed during on-air reports and interviews with players conducted both inside and outside the motorhome on the popular *On Deck Circle*, the network's signature show featuring Major League Baseball highlights and analysis.

- National Football League (NFL) *GameDay Morning* program featured Go RVing and editorial and advertising within the *NFL Magazine*. Football tailgating and RVs were also featured.
- Go RVing worked with CBS Sports Network to include RV-specific content as part of packages celebrating unique college football tailgating traditions.
- The SPEED Channel and National Geographic Channel aired custom RV travel content. SPEED host Rutledge Wood and his family publicized a family trip in a type A motorhome.
- The Outdoor Channel cosponsored a sweepstakes with an off-road folding camping trailer as the grand prize. Four Go RVing vignettes featuring the network's hunting and fishing hosts were created.
- *Fox and Friends* morning show provided Americans with new cooking ideas for tailgating with a fifth-wheel RV, provided by RVIA and an RV manufacturer. The live two-minute cooking demonstration featured the Feasty Boys.

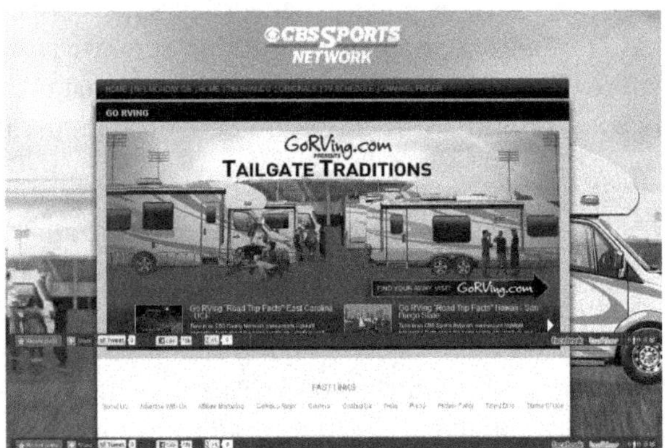

FIGURE 7.16 *Go RVing partnered with CBS to produce custom vignettes from footage filmed at SEC football games where RV tailgating is revered. The six sixty-second to ninety-second vignettes, titled "The College Football Tailgating Tradition Series," aired during* Inside College Football *or* SEC Studio Show *throughout the season. They celebrate the legions of faithful fans who follow their college teams, often turning stadium lots into impromptu RV towns for days preceding the game.*
RVIA
Courtesy of Recreation Vehicle Association of America

FIGURE 7.17 *RVIA described the concept of "away" in these terms: "AWAY is a place that's easy to find, and it's a feeling that's impossible to forget. It can be as far as the horizon or as close as the afternoon. AWAY is a place that's not on any map, but you know it when you find it. Whatever your idea of AWAY may be, an RV can help you find it."*
http://www.gorving.com/
Courtesy of Go Rving, Inc.

Corresponding print magazine ads were produced for a national ad buy of $2.7 million in twenty national and regional magazines. The ads had QR codes that when scanned by mobile devices, such as cell phones, took the reader to the Go RVing website to find nearby RV dealers, locate a campground, watch free videos, and more. James Ashurst, RVIA vice president, public relations and advertising, said, "Consumers now expect instant information and giving them access at their peak moment of interest is also the best time to invite them to supply us with personal data and become leads," according to an RVIA news release.

Magazines selected fit the buyer profile, had consistently produced strong consumer leads, and offered strong editorial content. They included: *Garden & Gun, Real Simple, Everyday with Rachael Ray, Reader's Digest, Guideposts, National Geographic Traveler, Better Homes & Gardens, Family Circle,* and *Good Housekeeping.*

RVIA's consumer website, GoRVing.com, was the most efficient lead generator of its media campaign components. RVIA redesigned its web content and created new content for its social media Facebook page, Twitter account, and YouTube presence to extend Go RVing messages. Creating a mobile-compatible version of its website was important because research predicted that nearly 50 percent of all web searches would be conducted by mobile by 2014. A $2.6 million Internet advertising buy included ads on Google, Yahoo, and Bing search engines, along with advertising on twenty other sites that fit the buyer profile including GACTV.com, Active.com, Eventful.com, and Zumobi.com.

RVIA used Apple iAd to allow Apple users to play a custom Go RVing game without ever leaving the ad. The Go RVing iAd features a large "Find a Dealer" option at the top of each game screen that takes users to GoRVing.com with one click.

Consumer research revealed that 39 percent of mothers handed off their smart phones to children during road trips to play games. RVIA's sponsorship of GSN.com's road trip games such as Funny Fill-Ins, Destination Alphabet, and Drive and Spy helped carry the RV message to a younger generation.

A special app was developed for one of the largest RV shows, the California RV show, that lasts ten days. The Apple/Android app provided a show map, helped consumers find exhibitors, provided information on show seminars, and provided a fun way to vie for prizes with a scavenger hunt photo game.

RV industry-related businesses such as dealers who wanted to tie into the national campaign could purchase tagable TV spots or stock (B-roll) footage for local commercials. A nine-minute B-roll video featured footage of all varieties of RVs driving along scenic roads.

RVIA also offered campaign posters and a new image library of high resolution photos and other graphics for advertisements and websites. The tie-in program provided access to Go RVing's Leads-Plus Program that assessed a consumer's likelihood of buying an RV with an assessment of the consumer's credit bureau data, according to an RVIA news release.

Reaching credible and influential bloggers about the benefits of RV ownership was another priority of RVIA's media team. RVIA sponsored the Digital Family Summit, a Philadelphia conference for family bloggers who wanted to increase their blogging skills and network. RVIA set up a mock campsite display that provided an opportunity to introduce the family merits of RVing to bloggers and establish connections with these potentially influential bloggers, including the influential "mommy bloggers" that could develop into future partnerships.

RVIA supports local RV consumer shows that are held across the U.S. by hosting information on its GoRVing.com website and providing media relations when requested.

RESULTS

The campaign's success was judged by a number of key indicators which included consumer awareness, attitudes, and behaviors related to activities that would lead to purchasing or renting an RV. Here are some of the campaign's results:

- Go RVing's "AWAY" campaign delivered a 15 percent increase in leads from the previous year and it was projected to increase another 4 percent in 2013. Increased awareness of the campaign was up across nearly every audience segment.
- Shipments of RVs saw significant growth in 2012 with wholesale shipments up 13.2 percent over 2011, despite a continued sluggish economy.

- Respondents who were aware of the "AWAY" campaign were twice as likely to indicate they would purchase an RV someday (43 percent vs 20 percent unaware) and were significantly more likely to rent an RV, both someday (45 percent vs 25 percent) and within the next twelve months (28 percent vs 10 percent).
- Respondents aware of the 2012 campaign (18 percent) were more than four times as likely as those unaware (4 percent) to have visited the website.
- Visits to GoRVing.com, held steady from the previous years; page views were up 11 percent, and leads from the website were up 147 percent from the previous year.
- Prominent digital advertising on partners' web pages linked to GoRVing.com helped generate new leads. RVIA also used Apple's iAd product to create a game-like version of the "AWAY" ads, plus ads at a digital game hub on GSN.com, helped Go RVing messaging reach consumers in an engaged way. Other analytics included a tap-through rate (TTR) from the banner ad to the game of 0.75 percent, which exceeded the 0.60 percent benchmark. Time spent on the ad unit/game was ninety-three seconds, thirty-three seconds more than the sixty-second benchmark.
- National sweepstakes with the GAC network and Outdoor Channel drew more than 811,000 entries and yielded 46,239 leads from entrants who willingly opted to receive information from Go RVing partners.
- Major League Baseball's (MLB) Home and AWAY Tour, National Geographic Channel and Nat Geo Wild's *Untamed Americas* series and the Cooking Channel Memorial Day Marathon raised awareness for Go RVing and helped drive traffic.
- *The Rachael Ray Show* featured a motorhome on her "Million Pound Makeover" program in which she interviewed guests in and out of the motorhome provided by RVIA and an RV manufacturer, on weight loss, wellness, and fitness issues.
- HGTV's *House Hunters* RV Special featured a couple looking to purchase an RV for a two-year full-time road trip. RVIA helped *House Hunters* find an appropriate couple for the show.

MEDIA RELATIONS RESULTS

The RVIA media relations team continuously promotes RV benefits to the news media. During the 2012 year, the RVIA media team arranged for a *New York Times* reporter to test drive a 2013 Winnebago Via motorhome for a family beach trip. It garnered a positive review in the newspaper's "Wheels" column on nytimes.com. A travel writer wrote a positive piece on the Winnebago Via motorhome after a

FIGURE 7.18 *Go RVing's print advertisements "Roasting Marshmallows" stressed three benefits: family time, nature, and fun.*
RVIA
Courtesy of Go Rving, Inc.

test drive from Colorado to Las Vegas in About.com. Other national media stories included:

- National Public Radio ran a story about a reporter's eight-day trek through Oregon and California in a rented RV.
- *ABC World News Tonight* broadcast a story about RVing's increasing popularity with American families.
- The Associated Press ran a story about how RVers adapted to fluctuating gas prices. The report included information from RVIA's vacation cost comparison study, as well as a mention of new fuel-efficient motorhomes now on the market. More than one hundred newspapers picked up an AP story on the state of the industry.
- The *Financial Times* reported on the RV industry's continued growth in shipments despite a sluggish economy and jittery consumer confidence.
- An MSNBC.com story from a *Today* show contributor described how Americans love RVs for the "much-needed, uninterrupted family time."
- RVIA president Richard Coon appeared in a live interview on Fox Business to discuss the resurgence of RV sales.
- *PBS Newshour* examined the RV industry's comeback despite the nation's economic uncertainty.

A successful part of RVIA's media relations program was its strategic spokesperson program, led by RVIA's president and travel expert Richard Coon. An authoritative and credible spokesperson for industry-wide trends concerning recreational vehicles, Coon was widely interviewed and quoted by the national media.

RV historian David Woodworth, owner of the largest-known collection of antique RVs including a 1916 Telescoping RV, was available to discuss the RV industry dating back more than a hundred years.

Representing Generation X, authors and RVIA media spokespersons Brad and Amy Herzog traveled from Chicago in a Winnebago Via and visited twenty-two media markets in eighteen states with stops in Minneapolis, Kansas City, Memphis, Albuquerque, and Des Moines. They focused on how RVs provide stress-free and affordable vacations that are eco and budget friendly. Their passion for RV travel generated local TV and newspaper stories wherever they went. Their travel blog, "You are Here," also promoted RV life.

BARRIERS TO RV OWNERSHIP

Beyond raising awareness about RVs, RVIA grappled with issues that affected potential buyers' decision-making process about RV ownership. Those included affordability including gas prices, the carbon footprint of RVs, and the health issue of formaldehyde from building materials used in RVs that was reported in the news media about Hurricane Katrina trailers.

RVS' AFFORDABILITY

During the Great Recession that began in 2008, Americans were pummeled by low returns on their retirement savings accounts, low to nonexistent salary increases or worse—loss of a job—and rising prices for food and energy. From seniors to young families, everyone was affected by the anemic economy. Still, many Americans wanted to enjoy their retirements or vacation time even on a budget. To convince Americans that RVs were still a good option when gas prices were high and family budgets were tight, Go RVing's consumer website created a "Vacation Comparison" value generator based on the research of PKF Consulting, an international consulting firm with expertise in travel and tourism. Its research found that typical RV family vacations were on average 28 to 59 percent less expensive than other types of vacations studied. For the "empty-nester" couple, the savings were 15 percent to 45 percent. The research firm found that gas prices would have to double or triple, depending whether the RV was a motorhome or a towable trailer, to erase the RV's financial advantage over other more costly vacation options. Since nearly 80 percent of RVs sold were towables, the gas price issue was greatly diminished.

GoRVing.com's interactive program allowed users to select the type of RV to be used for the trip and compare it to one of four other vacation transportation options, such as driving a personal car while staying in local hotels and eating at restaurants. Users could select a sample vacation trip such as Chicago to Branson, Missouri, for seven days and 1,455 miles, or just get the average calculated cost for a seven-day trip. In the case of a motorhome traveling from Chicago to

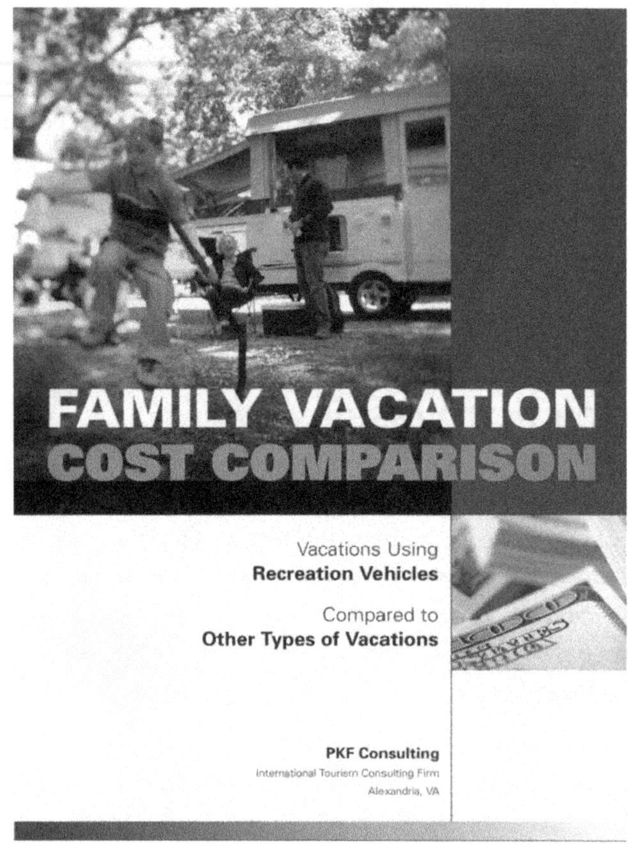

FIGURE 7.19 *RVIA sponsors research into the cost of various modes of transportation to show the affordability of RVing.*
RVIA
Courtesy of Recreation Vehicle Association of America

Branson, Missouri, for a seven-day trip, it would cost $2,173, opposed to $3,739 for flying, renting a car, and staying in a hotel and eating at restaurants. Here are the results:

Family Vacation from Chicago, Illinois, to Branson, Missouri

Seven days/1,455 miles

	RV	*Air/Car/Hotel*
Airfare (for a family of 4)	$—	$1,604
Rental car	$—	$310
Fuel	$482	$45
Cost of owning car	$—	$—
Cost of owning motorhome/trailer	$1,138	$—

Hotel	$—	$—
Campsite	$279	$700
Rental home/condo	$—	$—
Meals	$274	$1,080
Total	$2,173	$3,739

Fuel costs are uppermost in Americans' minds when money is tight. Go RVing's website offered ways to cut fuel costs:

Tips to Conserve Fuel

- Camp closer to home. With more than 16,000 campgrounds nationwide, RVers can enjoy the outdoor experience whether they travel five miles or 500 miles.
- Stay longer in one place. Many RV parks are vacation destinations in their own right, offering pools, playgrounds, hiking trails, entertainment centers, organized activities, convenience stores, and so much more.
- Cook your family favorites in the convenience of an RV, to avoid the high costs of eating out.
- Drive 55 instead of 65. Keeping speed constant and lower saves fuel, saving you money.
- Pack lighter by not topping off fresh water tanks until at the campground and by purchasing firewood and other camping materials on-site to keep the RV lightweight while traveling. Be sure holding tanks are dumped before heading out to further lighten the load.
- Tune up the engine of your motorhome or tow vehicle, inflate tires properly, and conduct regular maintenance to maximize fuel efficiency.
- Use the grade of fuel recommended by the engine manufacturer to increase miles per gallon.
- In the summer months, travel earlier in the day when the weather is cooler and the vehicle air conditioning is needed less.

Some other facts to keep in mind:

- Fuel is typically only the fourth largest expense on a road trip, behind lodging, food, vehicle payment, and maintenance.
- Airfares and hotel rates also rise when fuel costs increase and fuel surcharges are added. You can avoid those costs in an RV.
- Fuel prices would need to more than triple from their current level to make RVing more expensive for a family of four than other forms of travel.

RV'S CARBON FOOTPRINT—GOING GREEN

RV users are actually a green bunch. A survey funded by RVIA showed that most RVers minimize water use on trips; almost half recycle more on RV vacations than on other types; nearly half turn off home utilities while away, and a growing number (20 percent) use solar panels to power some of their electrical needs. In addition, 94 percent of all RVers travel with two to seven people, which further conserves fuel.

RVIA used PKF Consulting to analyze the CO_2 emissions of vacations varying in length from three to seven, ten, and fourteen days to destinations such as Orlando, Florida; New Orleans, Louisiana; and Napa, California. The RV vacations analyzed included car/folding camping trailer; SUV/travel trailer; Type C motorhome; and Type A motorhome (diesel).

RVIA and PFK Consulting reported the following in one of their news releases:

Using the carbon calculator methodology developed by Conservation International, an organization that promotes biodiversity conservation, PKF found that RV vacations, in

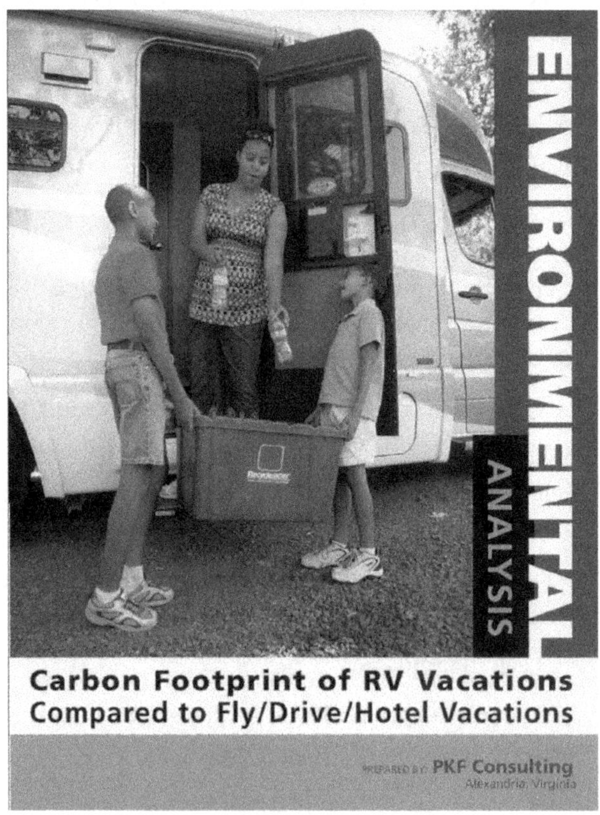

ENVIRONMENTAL
ANALYSIS
Carbon Footprint of RV Vacations
Compared to Fly/Drive/Hotel Vacations
PKF Consulting
Alexandria, Virginia

FIGURE 7.20 *RVIA conducted research to investigate the carbon footprint of RV vacations compared to other forms of transportation.*
RVIA
Courtesy of Recreation Vehicle Association of America

all cases, had a softer environmental impact than the typical airline/rental car/hotel vacations.

For example, comparing to a ten-day trip from Minneapolis, Minn., to Branson, Mo., the study showed that a fly/drive/hotel vacation creates 1.81 more tons of carbon emissions than vacation using a car/folding camping trailer; 1.35 more tons than an SUV/ travel trailer trip; 0.92 more tons than a Type C motorhome trip; and 1.26 more tons than a vacation by Type A motorhome (diesel).

In calculating the CO_2 emissions, RV miles per gallon estimated to be were 12.5 mpg for a Type A motorhome (diesel) and 10 mpg for a Type C motorhome, based on industry averages supplied by RV manufacturers. PKF used a conversion rate of 1.18 road miles to 1.00 airline mile in its calculations. To determine CO_2 impact of the folding camping trailer and lightweight travel trailer, PKF added one additional gallon of fuel per 100 miles traveled per 1,000 pounds. PKF used a weight of 2,000 pounds for the folding camping trailer and 4,000 pounds for the lightweight travel trailer.

RVS AND FORMALDEHYDE

Another issue associated with RVs was formaldehyde exposure and its associated health risks. Formaldehyde, a colorless gas, is a component of almost all glues used to make wood products commonly found in most American homes and offices. It is present in particle board and plywood used in making the cabinets and countertops common in RVs and mobile homes. The issue with formaldehyde and RVs emerged after Hurricane Katrina in 2005 displaced tens of thousands of people in Louisiana and Mississippi with no shelter. The Federal Emergency Management Administration (FEMA) purchased thousands of RVs to house victims of the devastating storm. Within a year, health complaints including headaches, nausea, and nosebleeds were reported by some RV users. FEMA stopped using the RV trailers after it was determined that formaldehyde emissions from wood products exceeded recommended safety levels. The news made national headlines and prompted calls for stronger federal regulation.

RVIA voluntarily raised its formaldehyde emissions standards for its members, which included most of the country's RV manufacturers that already met the Department of Housing and Urban Development standards. In 2008, RVIA adopted the most stringent standard in the nation—the California Air Resources Board's (CARB) new formaldehyde emissions level—as a mandatory condition of membership starting January 1, 2009. This put RVIA at the forefront of the industry and helped prepare its members for rapidly changing standards. On July 7, 2010, President Obama signed the Formaldehyde Standards for Composite Wood Products Act (Congressional Act S1660). This regulation mirrored CARB's standards which were implemented January 1, 2013.

RVIA developed educational materials on its website about formaldehyde and how RVIA and its members had responded to the issue.

THE INDUSTRY'S PERFORMANCE IN 2012

The year 2012 was good for RV business, thanks in part to its advertising and media relations program. From its 2012 Industry Profile the following highlights were noted:

- Wholesale RV shipments reached their highest annual level since 2007 at 285,700 units, a 13.2 percent increase over the previous year.
- The total retail value of those shipments neared $11 billion ($10.8 billion), a 20 percent increase over the $9.03 billion total in 2011.

QUESTIONS FOR DISCUSSION

1. What are the barriers to recreational vehicle ownership?
2. Why are fuel prices such a concern for the Recreation Vehicle Industry Association? What are the other factors involved in purchasing an RV?
3. Apply a SWOT (strengths, weaknesses, opportunities, and threats) analysis to RVs.
4. What key publics are the Recreation Vehicle Industry Association attempting to reach? Explain the rationale for each.
5. What are the elements of the Recreation Vehicle Industry Association's "Go Green" initiative? Why is it a focus of the industry?
6. How does the industry use research to inform its promotional campaign?
7. How does the Recreation Vehicle Industry Association use media relations to promote its industry?
8. If you were the media relations coordinator for the Recreation Vehicle Industry Association, how would you develop key messages that appeal to the youth generation, including Generation Y, Generation X, teens, and "tweens"? If you were pitching to a women's magazine, what would you emphasize? If you were pitching to a health magazine, what would you emphasize?

Dig Deeper

Review "Fuel Prices and the RV Industry—Research and Talking Points," available on the textbook's companion website. What talking points do you believe present the strongest case for the RV industry? Why? Read "Green RV Innovations," available on the textbook's companion website. What talking points do you feel make the strongest case for the RV industry? Why? Review "National Campaign Fact Sheet—2012 Media Campaign" fact sheet that is available on the textbook's companion website. What, in your opinion, are the best advertising elements for reaching a younger audience?

20

Making the Potato Top of Mind

Consumer Research Connects "Linda" to Potatoes

Each year, more than nineteen million tons of potatoes are grown in the United States, according to the U.S. Department of Agriculture. The marketing and public relations effort to sell those spuds is a highly sophisticated collective effort managed by the United States Potato Board.

USPB, established in 1971 by a group of potato growers, coordinates the promotion of potatoes nationally and internationally. As a collective, the USPB pools growers' financial resources to build demand for potatoes. It is the largest vegetable commodity board in the U.S.

A collective approach to promotion is common for food commodities: staple, in-demand products—potatoes, wheat, rice, bananas, etc.—that lack unique characteristics. After all, a potato is a potato is a potato, no matter who grows it or how it is grown (although there are more than a hundred varieties grown commercially throughout the United States). The USPB is managed by a professional staff of marketing and public relations professionals and is guided by elected representatives from all aspects of the potato industry, including growers and sellers.

The average American eats about 117 pounds of potatoes annually, according to USPB. The group's goal, described formally in its mission statement, is to attract wide attention and convince potential buyers that potatoes should be on their grocery list, instead of rice, bread or some other starchy alternative: "The mission of the United States Potato Board is to increase demand for potatoes and potato products through an integrated promotion program, thereby providing US producers with expanding markets for their production."

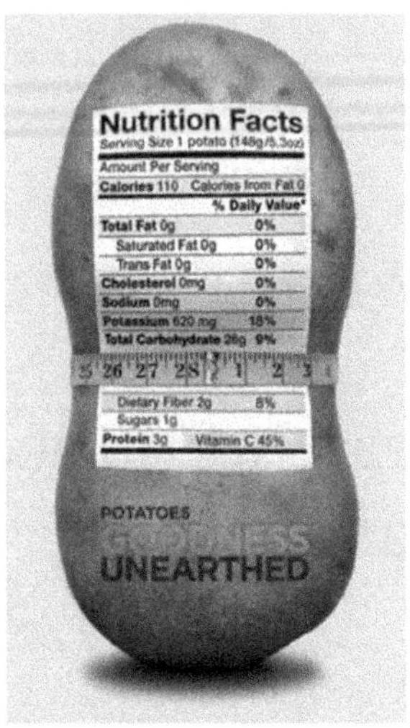

FIGURE 7.21 *The U.S. Potato Board's nutritional labeling guideline to promote potatoes' healthy features.*
http://www.uspotatoes.com/
Courtesy of U.S. Potato Board

THE STATE OF THE POTATO

While nearly 80 percent of all U.S. households eat potatoes 1.8 times per week at home, American consumption of potatoes has steadily declined over the past two decades, according to USPB. Part of the decline can be traced to the controversial—but perennially popular—Atkins Diet, a high-protein, high-fat, low-carbohydrate diet that first swept the country in the 1990s. For the first time, many people associated excess carbohydrates with getting fat. The potato's 26 grams of carbohydrates per 5.3-ounce serving were suddenly considered taboo and pushed away from the dinner plate. It wasn't just the Atkins Diet, however. Other reasons for the decline are cited by USPB research:

- Busy households that wanted quicker and easier meal preparation.
- The decline of traditional families, the core of fresh potato consumers, who are now a minority.
- The growth of one- and two-person households that eat out frequently and aren't buying five- and ten-pound bags of potatoes.
- Consumer demand for new and different eating experiences, especially for ethnic foods.

By the mid-2000s, another more complex concern emerged—the rise of diabetes, among children and adults. Foods high in carbohydrates and calories were once again an issue for those watching their weight. Potatoes, called a "starchy" vegetable, have more carbohydrates and calories than non-starchy veggies such as carrots and celery. When compared to less starchy vegetables, potatoes were less attractive.

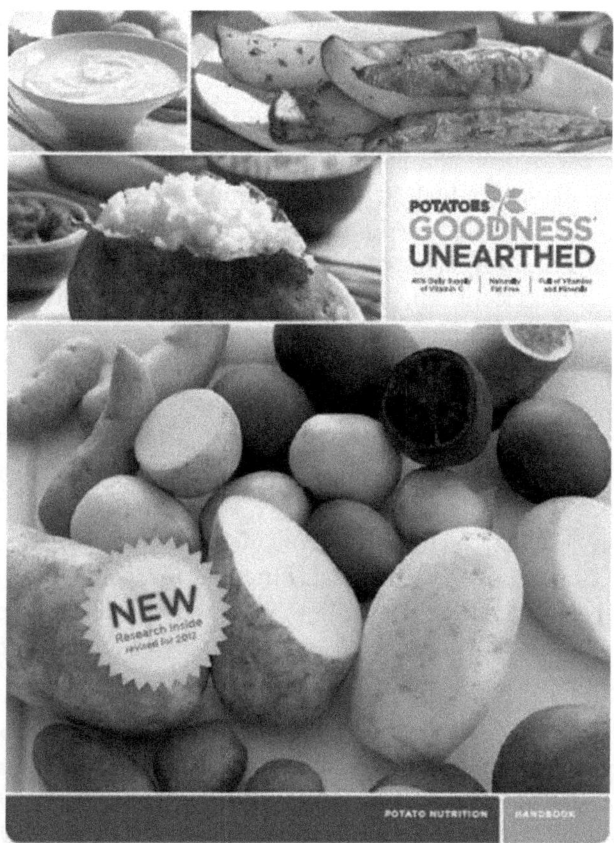

FIGURE 7.22 *This* Nutrition Handbook *publication by Potato Goodness Unearthed provides information about the healthy aspects of potatoes, including healthy recipes.*
http://www.uspotatoes.com/
Courtesy Potato Goodness Unearthed, Inc.

More recently, researchers developed a way to categorize different types of carbohydrates using the glycemic index. This index shows that starchy vegetables, such as potatoes, rapidly increase a body's insulin levels, causing strain on the pancreas, which makes insulin. More nutritionists began to recommend less consumption of so-called "high glycemic" foods. While there are many factors that affect a person's ability to make insulin, the glycemic index was considered another blow to the potato's healthy reputation.

THE POTATO'S NUTRITIONAL ATTRIBUTES

As Americans' attitudes toward this kitchen staple grew more ambivalent, the USPB sought to clarify the misperceptions about potatoes and reverse declining potato consumption. According to USPB's *The Fresh Grower/Shipper Update* newsletter, by 2004, "34 percent of consumers held negative attitudes about potatoes and their nutrition."

USPB developed multi-tiered nutrition campaigns to set the record straight about the potato's nutritional benefits. USPB started with its Healthy Potato campaign in 2004, which focused on the potato's nutritional benefits. The campaign's key nutrition facts: potatoes are high in vitamin C and potassium, low in calories and contain no fat. The campaign used a nutrition label on a potato to visually drive home its points with clever "Skinny Potato" advertising materials. A follow-up campaign featured Hasbro's iconic Mr. Potato Head to continue the nutritional messages: an average-sized potato has more potassium than a banana and about half of people's daily vitamin C needs, according to the FDA-approved nutrition label. *Healthy* MR. POTATO HEAD® was featured at the Macy's Thanksgiving Day Parade over the course of three years and was incorporated throughout its marketing and educational materials. Its cartoon persona was also attractive to children, who are an important public for USPB's nutritional messages.

In addition, USPB created a long-term messaging campaign. In 2008, the "Potatoes . . . Goodness Unearthed®" tagline and campaign (referred to as its "industry campaign signature") were introduced after two years of consumer research. Bart Connors, a Washington State fresh grower-shipper and 2008–2009 USPB chairman, explained the campaign in a USPB newsletter:

> *I think "Potatoes . . . Goodness Unearthed" gives our industry the tool to promote how potatoes are an important part of consumers' lives by providing some health benefits, but also on an emotional level that connects with consumers' feelings about potatoes. The combination of the health and emotional benefits creates a powerful message that rings in consumers' minds.*

Research was critical to the success of the USPB's marketing and public relations effort. In all, 3,827 consumers were interviewed as part of USPB's research over an eleven-month period, according to USPB's *Industry Update* newsletter. Two major consumer research projects were conducted by Sterling Brands of New York City to develop and test the proposed "Potatoes . . . Goodness Unearthed®" signature, which contained the position, image, and tagline. More research was conducted to test the advertising campaign "Peel Back the Truth," and a final research project established benchmarks on USPB's key demographic—female heads-of-household who served potatoes at home—regarding their attitudes towards potatoes, according to USPB.

The "Peel Back the Truth" advertising campaign's nutrition message featured a russet, yellow or red spud and a potato peeler at the ready. Superimposed on the potato was the question: "A fattening worthless starch with empty calories? It's time to peel back the truth." The partially peeled potato provided the answer: "Actually, a medium-size spud has only 110 calories. Is naturally fat free, high in vitamin C and packs more potassium than a banana. So a little respect please."

Another advertising campaign entitled "The Many Sides of Potatoes" was launched in 2011; it focused on quick and creative ways to add potatoes to family dinner plates. A departure from previous myth-busting educational advertising

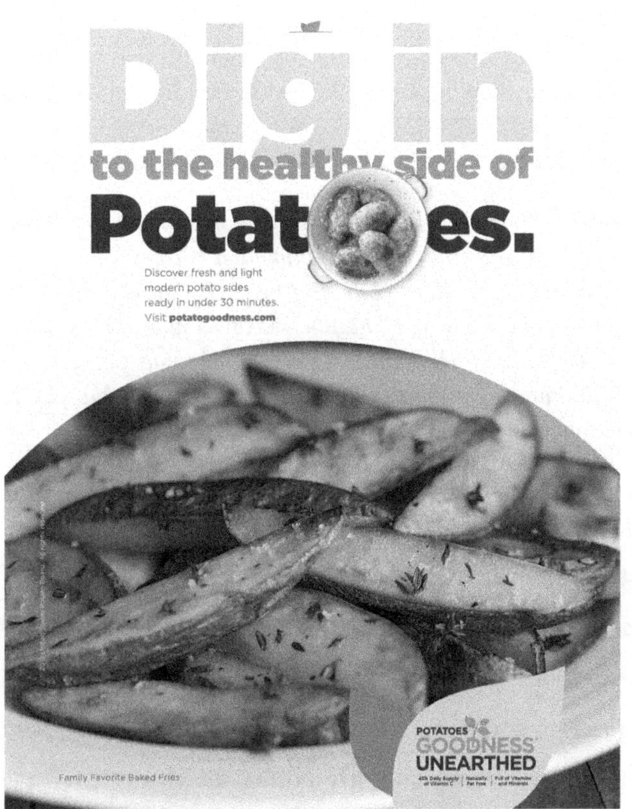

FIGURE 7.23 *An example of "The Many Sides of Potatoes" advertising campaign to increase potato consumption in the home.*
http://www.potatogoodness.com/
Courtesy Potato Goodness Unearthed, Inc.

campaigns, its message was more proactive, identifying opportunities for more fresh consumption of potatoes. The campaign urged readers to visit PotatoGoodness.com to find recipes that encouraged potato purchases. By April 2011, "only 18 percent of consumers held negative attitudes about potatoes," according to USPB's *The Fresh Grower/Shipper Update* newsletter, a dramatic decline from 34 percent in 2004.

LEARNING ABOUT LINDA

Key to building USPB's successful educational and marketing effort was its comprehensive and illuminating research about key consumer preferences, lifestyles, and attitudes. USPB worked with the Sterling Rice Group (SRG), a consulting company that specializes in strategy, innovation, consumer research, and communication to build brands. Their research helped USPB understand the consumer behavior that leads to potato purchases. To better visualize USPB's key demographic, SRG created a composite person, "Linda." According to USPB, she represents thirty million U.S. women (48 percent of women with kids and 12 percent of the adult population). Linda "influences nearly one-third of the U.S. population as the gatekeeper for her husband and children, making food choices for her and an additional 82 million people and 57 million kids."

Here's how Linda was described in USPB's *Industry Update* newsletter:

> *"Linda" is a mother with children under 18 years old at home. "Linda" is heedful of her family's taste when it comes to eating and is concerned for her and her family's health/wellness. She tries to buy healthy foods, but is aware of price. And even though she doesn't have a lot of extra time, making dinner at home is important to her. "Linda" is a person who will make a difference for potatoes. She is most open to our message, and ultimately is most likely to eat more potatoes and spread the good news to her friends and family.*

Some additional facts USPB learned about Linda were included in USPB's *2011 Potato Statistical Yearbook*. Linda:

- Likes to experiment and try new recipes;
- Cooks frequently throughout the week;
- Prefers to cook with fresh rather than frozen;
- Plans meals in advance;
- Buys a lot of the same brands her mother did when she was a child;
- Makes a lot of the same meals her mother did when she was a child;
- Is influenced by her family in the brands and products she buys;
- Spends slightly more time preparing dinner (thirty-nine minutes) than all consumers (thirty-four minutes);
- Is more likely to consider her children's preferences when choosing foods for dinner;
- Thinks meals should be "something everyone would enjoy" and "appealing to kids' tastes," which are relatively more important to Linda when choosing what to serve for dinner.

The USPB used this profile to better understand a major portion of its consumer market. Here are some additional facts that its consumer research discovered about Linda, according to its *2011 Potato Statistical Yearbook*:

1. Linda is a medium user of potatoes and buys them to have on-hand. She serves them one to three times per week, and dinners at home account for more than 60 percent of Linda's potato occasions. She believes potatoes are a food her whole family loves.

2. Linda cooks most often with fresh potatoes (russet, red, and/or yellow) making up 77 percent of Linda's potato occasions. Mashed, baked, and French fries are the top three ways Linda prepares potatoes.
3. Potatoes are almost exclusively used as a side dish. Linda would serve rice or pasta in place of potatoes, but she believes potatoes outperform rice or pasta as being fresh and natural. However, Linda believes rice or pasta outperform potatoes on being easy to prepare, good for weight management, and low in calories.
4. Linda knows how to prepare potatoes in many different ways and believes they are good value. Yet, despite their versatility Linda feels she is in a "potato rut" as she continues to prepare the same potato dishes for her family, unaware of new usage ideas.
5. Key areas that are important to Linda, but where potatoes currently fall short, are healthy, very flavorful, and quick and easy to prepare.

Research also found that Linda shifts her purchasing habits depending on the time of the year, according to USPB's *The Fresh Grower/Shipper Update* newsletter. There are five "seasons" in which Linda looks at potatoes differently. For example, the "Back-on-Track" period refers to the September and October timeframe when summer is

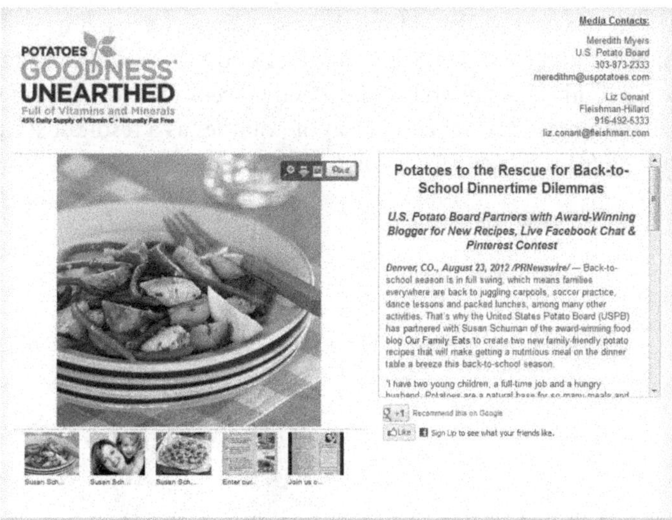

FIGURE 7.24 *This multimedia news release was developed for the back-to-school time to help moms get back on track with their home cooking routines. This news release offered information on a Pinterest contest, recipes, the nutrition handbook, and a live chat with a mommy blogger via the Potatoes, Taters and Spuds Facebook page.*
http://www.multivu.com/
Courtesy of U.S. Potato Board

done and children are back at school and schedules become more hectic. That's the time, according to USPB, to introduce time-saving recipes and messages that stress convenience as well as the nutritional messages. The other seasons: "Plus-Up Potatoes" for November and December; "Nurture Me," January and February; "Spring Ahead" for March through May; and "Lighten Up" for June through August.

MAGAZINE AND ONLINE ADVERTISING

USPB's exhaustive research made it much easier to determine what medium was best suited to reaching Linda. Her key attributes were matched to a variety of potential mass media's viewer or reader profiles. Surprisingly, it was not social media sites but that stalwart traditional medium—magazines. Research determined that certain women's magazines would reach Linda, and millions of target readers, cost effectively. The "Peel Back the Truth" advertising campaign appeared in *Southern Living BBQ, Cooking Light, Taste of Home, Family Circle, Weight Watchers, Redbook, Woman's Day*, and *Parents*.

Similarly, the "Many Sides of Potatoes" campaign featured carefully selected potato recipes, such as Family-Favorite Baked Fries and Mediterranean Sun-Kissed Savory Salad that could be made in thirty minutes; these ads were inserted into nine popular women's magazines. This time, the one-third page ads included QR codes allowing Linda to scan the recipes with a mobile device for later use.

The ad effectiveness testing showed that by June 2012, 29 percent of readers who recalled the ad said they would purchase potatoes as a result of seeing the ad and that 22 percent of readers who recalled the ad said they would consider purchasing potatoes as a result of seeing the ad. Fourteen percent of readers who recalled the ad said they have a more favorable opinion of potatoes as a result of seeing the ad, according to USPB's *Maximizing Return on Grower Investment*.

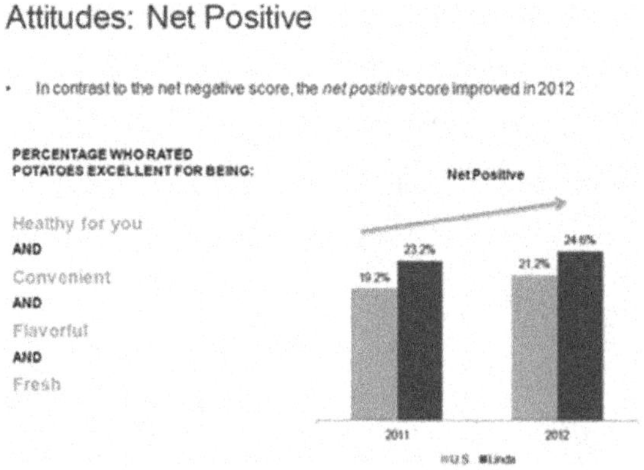

FIGURE 7.25 *A net positive attitudes metric was introduced in 2012 to reflect the value of the USPB's demand-building programs and strategies on the market for potatoes and potato products.*
http://www.uspotatoes.com/
Courtesy of U.S. Potato Board

In addition to traditional print ads, USPB had a robust on-line advertising program that complemented the "Many Sides of Potatoes" print ads with paid digital ads on popular recipe websites such as AllRecipes.com, MyRecipes.com, BHG.com (Meredith Networks), and FoodNetwork.com. Consumers who clicked on an ad's recipe were also directed to www.potatoegoodness.com/transformpotatoes. The key effectiveness test for USPB's online advertising was the click-through rate (CTR) which was 0.23 percent (0.13 percent higher than industry standards), according to USPB's *Maximizing Return on Grower Investment*. There were also 80,000 interactions with the "Quick and Healthy Potato" recipes.

The FY 2012 campaign was successful, building on momentum from the previous two years; total recipe interactions nearly quadrupled. That's 212,712 online recipe interactions, evidence that highly qualified users were engaged with potato recipes in contextually relevant spaces. Several high-impact placements on All Recipes.com significantly boosted overall site and campaign success. Through sponsorships in the site's "The Daily Dish eNewsletter" and the "Recipe of the Day", a combined CTR of 6.11 percent was attained. This resulted in 56,501 clicks to an All Recipes branded page and 8,827 clicks to the USPB's "Potato Goodness Transform Potatoes" landing page.

A small advertising purchase on Facebook for the Linda profile in 2012 attracted 3,000 new fans to USPB's "Potatoes, Taters and Spuds" Facebook page. This drove an increase in posts on the page's message wall, which increased "conversations" about potatoes on their own pages: a key metric of user engagement. This user-initiated activity is referred to as "People Talking about This" which is tracked during a seven-day period on a particular page and includes: likes, comments, and shares of page content or the page itself. When a USPB child's coloring cookbook was offered a similar spike in user engagement occurred.

In 2012, the advertising reached 75 percent of potential Lindas 5.5 times through about 110 million impressions, according to USPB's *Maximizing Return on Grower Investment*.

OTHER LINDA OUTREACH ACTIVITIES

Beyond paid advertisements, USPB had many other activities to connect with Linda. Those included media relations, social media, key influencer relations (third-party endorsers), special events, publications, and research.

Media Relations

USPB has a robust media relations effort. USPB's target news media editors are the food, nutrition, and lifestyle sections of newspapers, magazines, television programs, and other food-related news publications, and it has an integrative media relations package surrounding the five seasons of Linda for consumer media relations. For example, USPB released a multimedia news release that included all aspects of the

"Back-on-Track" seasonal campaign, including a press release, new recipes developed by "Our Family Eats" blogger spokesperson Susan Schuman and corresponding photographs, Pinterest contest information, Facebook "Real Moms" chat details, and more.

During the summer of 2011, USPB's public relations team focused on a perennial summer favorite—potato salad recipes. This included the "Grilled Pesto Potato Salad" recipe mat release (a pre-formatted article for placement in print publications) that generated twenty-four million impressions and syndicated placements of potato salad recipes: "Purple Potato Salad with Beets and Arugula" and "Quick & Healthy Potato Salad" that gained nearly four million impressions, according to USPB's *Industry Update*. Another coup involved *Eating Well* magazine. The magazine and USPB collaborated on an article for Yahoo's Shine!, one of the most popular women's lifestyle websites that produced "All-American Food Faceoff: Which is Healthier, Potato Salad or Pasta Salad?" According to the article, "potato salad has one advantage over pasta salad—it's almost all vegetable." The writer explained, "Potatoes actually have many redeeming health qualities: they're a good source of potassium and vitamin C and naturally deliver some fiber (especially when you keep the skin on) and protein."

Each year, USPB develops a significant new angle on potatoes to attract the news media's attention. A "Seven Days, Seven Ways" potato types press kit was developed containing new recipes, photography, and a video series. Featuring celebrity nutritionist and registered dietitian Katie Cavuto Boyle, the videos introduced a new potato type and recipe for each day of the week. This new way of looking at potatoes was fresh and intriguing to food editors (and readers/viewers) who may not have been as familiar with some potato varieties such as petites, fingerlings, and blue potatoes.

FIGURE 7.26 *The U.S. Potato Board has partnered with registered dietitian Katie Cavuto Boyle to develop a series of videos on how to use different potato varieties and healthy recipes.*
http://www.potatogoodness.com/
Courtesy of Potato Goodness Unearthed, Inc.

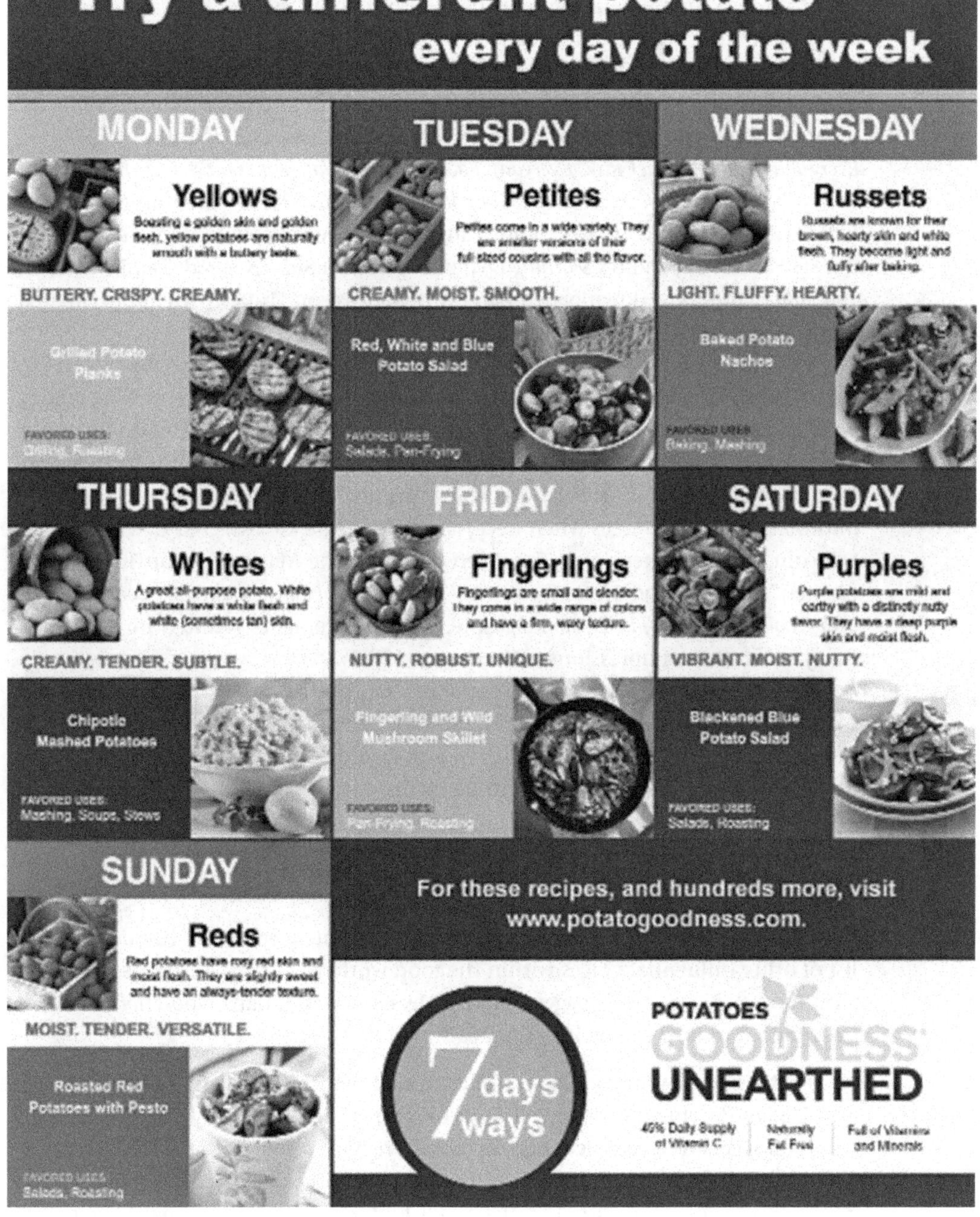

FIGURE 7.27 *"Seven Days and Seven Ways" to enjoy potatoes every day of the week with recipes provided by Potato Goodness Unearthed.*
www.potatogoodness.com/
Courtesy Potato Goodness Unearthed, Inc.

USPB public relations members traveled to New York City in 2011 where they had paid access to a small networking event with seventy-nine members of the New York City area food media through the "Editor's Showcase Cooking and Entertaining" event. The next night USPB hosted an invitation-only dinner at an upscale restaurant in the East Village for key media and influencers. Thirteen high-value media members attended and were treated to a seven potato types themed menu and program about the benefits of potatoes. Representatives attended from *USA Today, Every Day with Rachael Ray, Everyday Food, Weight Watchers, O, the Oprah Magazine, Self, Whole Living, Woman's Day, Glamour, Fitness*, and *FIRST*, according to USPB's *Industry Update*. While in NYC, Katie Cavuto Boyle conducted interviews with Martha Stewart Living Radio's *Morning Living* program on SiriusXM radio and with *Mom Talk Radio*, the most downloaded parenting podcast on iTunes with approximately 500,000 listeners on fifty stations in the U.S., according to USPB.

The "Seven Days, Seven Ways" press package was also distributed to USPB's database of 700-plus newspaper, magazine, and online contacts across the country. A ready-to-print feature release was also distributed to support the potato types program. The media kit was designed to help food editors easily adapt it to their own formats. The USPB public relations team was also available to provide additional information and resources when necessary. The media kit attracted USAToday.com, Self.com, "Health Bites" blog, FoodNetwork.com, the Martha Stewart Living "Test Kitchen" blog, Detroit News, *Every Day with Rachael Ray* magazine, *Cooking Light*, and *Cooking with Paula Dean* magazine. These placements resulted in more than thirty-two million impressions, according to USPB.

In addition to the public relations staff's targeted efforts with the news media, sometimes, the word about potatoes gets out naturally. The internationally syndicated column "Hints from Heloise" ran a potato nutrition feature that was picked up by more than sixty print and online media outlets across the country for about fifteen million impressions, according to USPB.

Third-Party Influencers

In addition to the third-party food editor news influencers, USPB has developed a list of other influential voices within the food world to develop relations, including with food and mommy bloggers, family physicians, dietitians, and chefs. Here are some activities undertaken in 2011–2012:

- **Bloggers**—During National Nutrition Month, USPB teamed up with Kitchen Play (kitchen-play.com), a food blogger group, to work with six top food bloggers to create new healthy potato recipes using two of the seven varieties of potatoes. These recipes were featured on their blogs, the Kitchen Play blog, and then posted to the USPB Pinterest page. Additional blogger and home cooks were encouraged to develop other recipes in a recipe contest. USPB participates in key food blogger conferences such as the International Food Bloggers Conference in Portland, Oregon, where their participation promoted the latest multimedia news releases and nutritional information, as well as introduced the USPB "Real Moms, Real Meals" program, which launched by featuring food blogger Susan Schuman of Our Family Eats.

- **Family physicians**—USPB sponsored a booth at the American Academy of Family Physicians (AAFP) Conference that reaches 5,000 family physicians. A public relations member and a USPB nutritionist consultant provided nutrition handouts about potatoes, including USPB's researched stance on health issues such as diabetes, weight control, and the glycemic index. Doctors could also sample potato bruschetta, providing a real example of the potato's flavorful, versatile, gluten-free and nutritional qualities.
- **Nutritionists**—Registered dietitians and nutritionists are another key group of influencers that USPB actively courts to explain the potato's nutritional benefits to a wider audience. In 2012, celebrity chef (Food Network's *Healthy Appetite* show) and nutritionist Ellie Krieger, M.S., R.D., featured potatoes in her popular "USA Weekend" column with "Recipe for Guilt-Free French Fries." The article reached twenty-two million readers, according to USPB.
- **Supermarket dietitians**—USPB has made a special effort to educate grocery store staff dietitians who help customers with food selections. In 2012, USPB created an e-newsletter called "Seasons" for "Supermarket RDs" filled with nutritional information and healthy potato-centric seasonal recipes for use in their shopper communications (such as in-store magazines, retail websites, newsletters, or blogs), social media platforms (Twitter, Facebook, and Pinterest), and in-store promotions. The newsletter drives readers to USPB's consumer website PotatoGoodness.com.
- **Chefs and food service professionals**—This group is vastly influential with the consuming public. Beyond restaurants, food service professionals also operate large food service operations such as corporate and hospital cafeterias, as well as school district cafeterias, where thousands of employees and the public dine daily. This group is constantly looking for new inspirations and information on nutrition and unique food varieties. In 2011, USPB launched an e-newsletter called "Get Creative" to provide recipes, nutrition information, and information on potato types. The newsletter drives readers to USPB's consumer website PotatoGoodness.com. USPB also sponsors a two-day annual culinary seminar at the Culinary Institute of America (CIA) in Greystone, California, the leading continuing education school for professional chefs. During the seminar, chefs receive updates from USPB staff on the nutritional benefits of potatoes and other industry information.
- **Health and nutrition reporters**—USPB is constantly monitoring academic and other peer-reviewed research that relates to the potato's health and nutrition benefits to share with top-tier health and nutrition reporters.

USPB's own research, titled "Potatoes are the Largest and Most Affordable Source of Potassium of Any Vegetable or Fruit," released in 2011, received generous attention from health and nutrition writers and resulted in twenty million impressions. USPB-sponsored researchers use important health conferences such as the American Dietetic Association's annual Food & Nutrition Conference & Expo to debut research findings. USPB's nutrition consultants also share information with top-tier health and nutrition journalists at invitation-only lunches that offer chef-prepared potato entrees.

Internet

- **Website—www.PotatoGoodness.com** is the USPB's consumer website designed to be the go-to resource for all-things-potatoes. Previously HealthyPotato.com, the site was renamed and redesigned in 2008 to conform to its new "Potatoes . . . Goodness Unearthed®" nutrition signature. Additionally, for three years USPB had a recipe blog called MomsDinnerHelper.PotatoGoodness.com, but it was integrated into the site to alleviate consumer confusion. PotatoGoodness.com underwent another major redesign in late 2012, so it could provide special portals for its main audiences to "find themselves" (home cooks, professional chefs, media, food developers, and nutrition educators). The goal was to provide consumers the inspiration to serve potatoes just once more a week, with new ideas, information, and preparation techniques found throughout the site. The site has an enhanced recipe section with more than 350 recipes and an expansive video collection, along with "Meet a Potato Grower," "Just for Kids," and "All About Potatoes" sections. The site is dynamic, with new content posted weekly to engage consumers and keep them coming back. Over the course of a year that involved a concentrated search engine optimization effort, traffic to PotatoGoodness.com increased 30 percent.
- **Website—www.USPotatoes.com** is USPB's industry website. Its focus is on providing information and tools for growers, shippers, and sellers to help promote potatoes at every level, including local farmers' markets to grocer displays. The site includes comprehensive information about national and international marketing efforts, including the latest consumer research.
- **Weekly recipe e-mails**—In 2012, USPB began providing a weekly e-mail service, offered on PotatoGoodness.com and on its Facebook page. Every Tuesday the professionally designed e-mail featured one healthy, easy-to-prepare potato recipe, its photo, and a potato "fun fact." The e-mail also linked to PotatoGoodness.com, the "Potatoes, Taters & Spuds" Facebook page and Potato Goodness YouTube channel. The e-mail consistently generates open rates of 25 percent and click-through rates of 10 percent which are results far beyond industry standards.

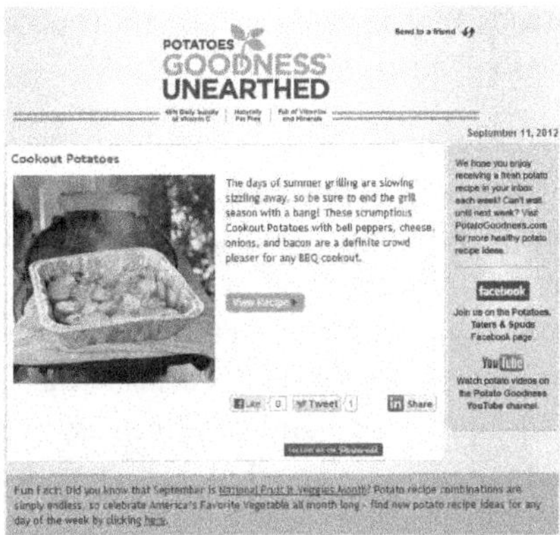

FIGURE 7.28 *Consumers, chefs, and nutritionists can sign up for a monthly e-mail newsletter that provides a potato-based recipe, a fun fact, and other useful links to keep stakeholders engaged.*
http://www.potatogoodness.com/
Courtesy of Potato Goodness Unearthed, Inc.

Social Media

- **Facebook**—USPB created its Facebook page "Potatoes, Taters and Spuds" in 2009 and has integrated it into many of its other marketing and public relations activities. It is a good place to repurpose many of its public relations information releases, including recipes, and it drives traffic to USPB's PotatoGoodness.com site and other links. By the end of 2012, there were more than 18,000 fans. To encourage fans to interact with potatoes and share their discoveries, USPB created the "Holly Jolly Potatoes Photo Contest" that invited consumers to upload a photo of a festive holiday potato recipe for the chance to win a cash prize or slow cooker. Another promotion aimed at Linda was the "Chef Solus Potato Party Coloring Book" giveaway, a children's cookbook available when a reader clicked on "like." A "Summer of Sides Sweepstakes" asked readers a question each week, such as: "What is your favorite outdoor mealtime memory?" Participants were eligible for prizes and many visited the USPB's "Summer of Sides" web page. As previously discussed, user-initiated activity is a key engagement metric gauged by "People Talking about This" which is tracked during a seven-day period and includes actions such as likes, comments, and shares of page content or the page itself.
- **Twitter**—Twitter is integrated into its Facebook and "Potato Goodness Unearthed" campaign. Some efforts have been made to help growers and grocers use Twitter to promote potatoes locally.
- **YouTube**—USPB developed its own YouTube channel in 2009 called "Potatoes, Taters and Spuds" that links to its Facebook page by the same

name. It offers videos that provide information about potatoes and recipe demonstrations.

- **Pinterest**—USPB developed its own Pinterest page in 2012 as a way to increase interaction with Linda through potato-centric recipes and other information about potatoes in a visual format. New boards have been developed to provide unique recipe ideas for holidays throughout the year, including Thanksgiving, Christmas, Easter, St. Patrick's Day, and others. USPB ran a "Real Meals: Pin to Win" contest that invited participants to create a "Real Meals" pin board and pin five easy weeknight meals, two of which must include potatoes. The winner received a slow cooker and a Spa Finder gift card. USPB's Pinterest activity is integrated with its Potato Goodness Unearthed consumer website as well as its Facebook page and weekly recipe e-mail blast.
- **QR codes**—The barcode readable by smart phones using free available apps is helping USPB growers and sellers to link consumers to more information about potatoes, such as links to recipes, videos, nutrition, e-mail letters, and to loyalty promotions, such as contests or free items.

RESEARCH PROMOTING POTATOES' GOODNESS

The USPB has used research to guide all of its activities. It sponsors research in the following areas: consumer/demographic, retail, food service, innovation, and international. These reports are available to anyone in the potato industry to guide local and state growers' and retailers' efforts. USPB is also focusing more efforts on developing international markets and has increased its research dramatically in recent years.

To combat negative views, translate new research, and develop its own research initiatives about potatoes, the potato industry formed the international Alliance for Potato Research and Education (APRE) in 2011. According to its mission statement on its website:

> *The Alliance for Potato Research and Education (APRE) is 100% dedicated to expanding and translating scientific research into evidence-based policy and education initiatives that recognize the role of all forms of the potato—a nutritious vegetable—in promoting health for all age groups.*

USPB's president and CEO is a member of APRE's board of directors. The organization hired Maureen Storey, a respected nutritionist with a Ph.D. who had been the chief scientist for the American Beverage Association. In that role, Storey helped defend sugary sodas that researchers had linked to an increased risk for obesity, diabetes, and high blood pressure. Storey's debunking strategies in the sugary soda debate and her ability to clearly communicate complicated scientific information to

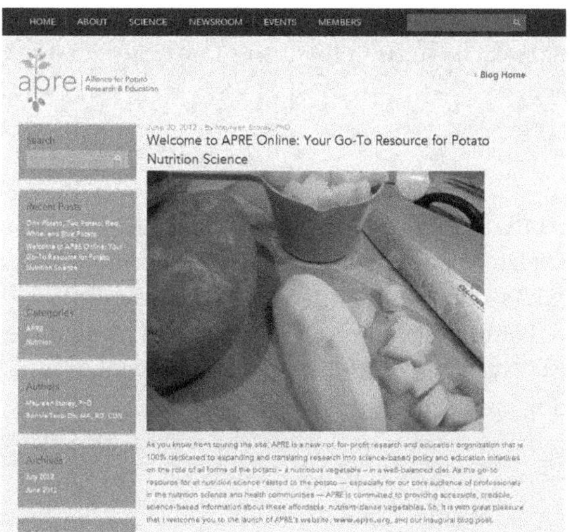

FIGURE 7.29 *The U.S. Potato Board sponsors the Alliance for Potato Research and Education (APRE) dedicated to expanding and translating scientific research into evidence-based policy and education initiatives that recognize the role of all forms of the potato—a nutritious vegetable—in promoting health for all age groups, according to its website. http://www.apre.org/*
Alliance for Potato Research and Education

the consuming public and news reporters made her a valuable resource for defending the potato's nutritional reputation. The APRE has a website that provides resources and other information for registered dietitians and medical doctors.

QUESTIONS FOR DISCUSSION

1. What is a food commodity?
2. What were the reasons for the decline in potato consumption?
3. What role did research play in the U.S. Potato Board's strategy for increasing market demand for potatoes?
4. Media relations is key to potato promotion. How does the United States Potato Board keep potatoes interesting to the news media?
5. What third-party influencers were the most effective for potato promotion in your opinion? Why?
6. What social media tactics were the most effective for potato promotion in your opinion? Why?

7. Through what new initiative has the United States Potato Board begun to strengthen its research efforts? Why is this important for potato promotions in the future?

Dig Deeper

Read the U.S. Potato Board's 2012 Annual Report available on the textbook's companion website. Explain the significance of the net positive attitudes metric. What are some of the USPB's strategies for international marketing?

Read the PowerPoint presentation entitled "U.S.P.B. Training Session: The Power of Public Relations," available on the textbook's companion website. Describe the tactics for leveraging public relations at the store level.

21

Sony PlayStation: It Only Does Everything!

(Except Protect Private Data and Communicate Effectively)

Each year, an estimated nine million Americans are victims of identity theft, according to the Federal Trade Commission. These thefts account for billions in losses to consumers and businesses.

Sony, a global technology company famous for decades of electronic innovations—the first personal stereo system, the Walkman, the compact disc—found itself involved in the "Great Brinks Robbery of cyber attacks."

Ironically, Sony's popular advertising campaign at the time featured character Kevin Butler who touted the amazing features of PlayStation 3. The funny commercials always ended with the slogan "It only does everything!" Owners of PlayStation, however, found Sony didn't do nearly enough when it came to protecting their private information from hackers and keeping them in the loop when their data was compromised.

PlayStation 3, a sleek video game console, was introduced in 2006 to global fanfare, competing with Microsoft's Xbox360 and Nintendo's Wii for digital gaming supremacy.

SONY'S RESPONSE TO THE ATTACK

On April 20, 2011, PlayStation 3 online gamers were enjoying *Battlefield, Call of Duty 2, Awesomenauts* and other games when everything suddenly stopped, and a very long and frustrating wait began. The PlayStation Network, which allows PlayStation 3 gamers to play multiplayer games online and purchase software, had shut down, along with Sony's other network service, Qriocity, which allows users to download music, videos, and television shows.

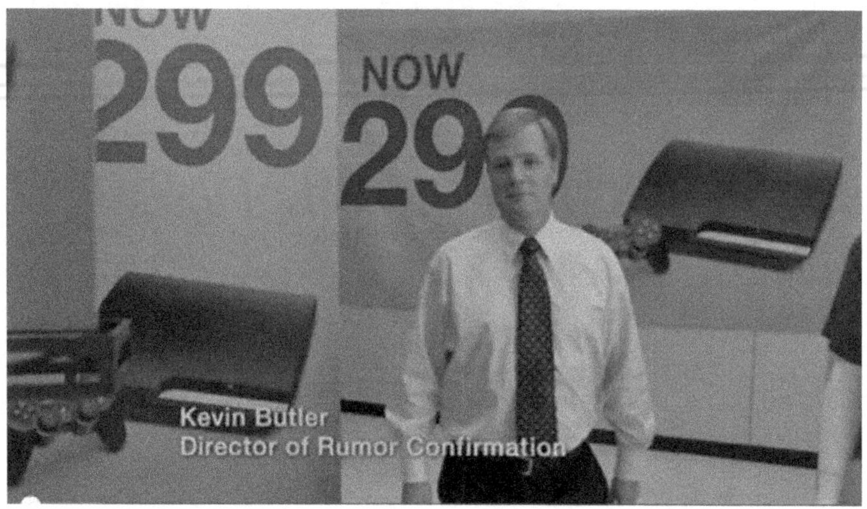

FIGURE 7.30 *Sony Playstation's "It Only Does Everything" commercial series featuring Kevin Butler was a big hit with consumers.*
http://www.youtube.com/
Sony Computer Entertainment America LLC

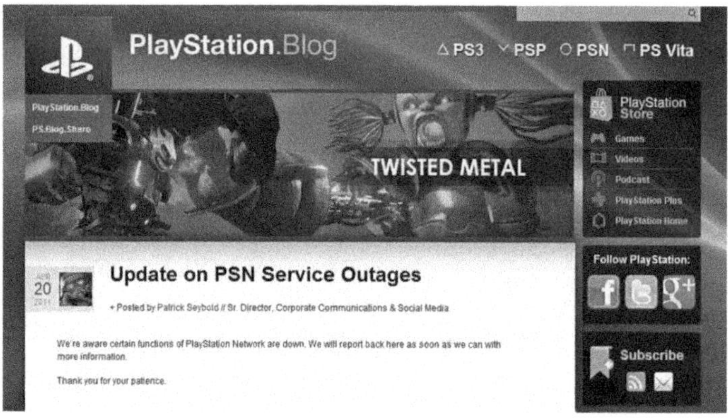

FIGURE 7.31 *The PlayStation blog was the chief communication channel during the crisis.*
http://blog.us.playstation.com/
Sony Computer Entertainment America LLC

Sony initially characterized the event as an "outage," posting short messages to its PlayStation blog on April 20 and 21, 2011, and promising more information soon.

The April 21, 2011, post said Sony was "investigating the cause," and that it might be a "full day or two" before service was fully restored. All of the blog posts were written by Sony's Senior Director of Corporate Communications and Social Media, Patrick Seybold.

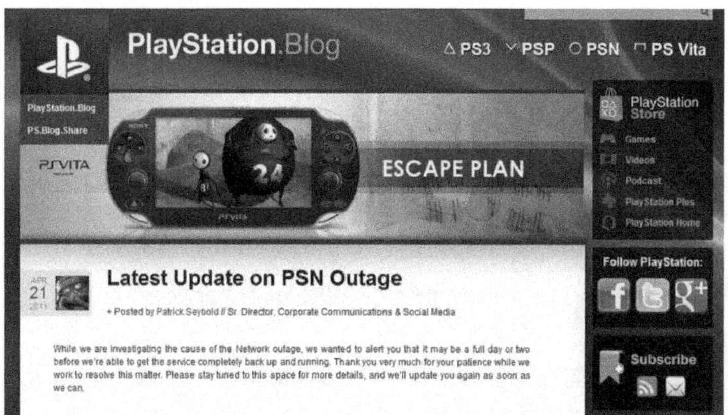

FIGURE 7.32 *PlayStation did not inform its customers of the customer security breach until April 26, 2011.*
http://blog.us.playstation.com/
Sony Computer Entertainment America LLC

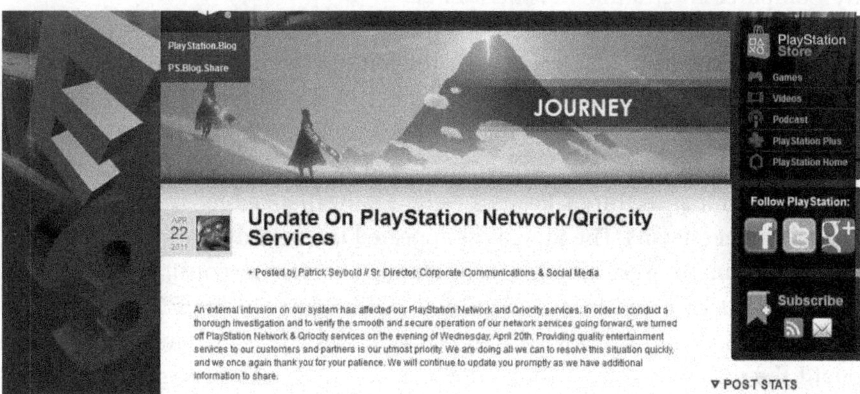

FIGURE 7.33 *The PlayStation blog admitted it was hacked ("external intrusion") but customers were not told their private information had been stolen.*
http://blog.us.playstation.com/
Sony Computer Entertainment America LLC

On April 22, 2011, Sony admitted what many had already surmised: the system had been hacked. "An external intrusion on our system has affected our PlayStation Network and Qriocity services." Sony explained that the shutdown was necessary to conduct a thorough investigation, and that it was doing everything possible "to resolve this situation quickly." Customers were thanked for their patience and asked to stay tuned for more updates.

FIGURE 7.34 *Four days later the system was still down and its systems needed to be rebuilt.*
http://blog.us.playstation.com/
Sony Computer Entertainment America LLC

The next day, April 23, 2011, with the shutdown ongoing, a new post took a more apologetic tone: "We sincerely regret" the shutdown, it began. Sony was "working around the clock," and the continued delay in restoring service was due to "re-building our system to further strengthen our network infrastructure" and provide "additional security." Readers were, again, thanked for their patience and promised further details. The same post appeared the next day, April 24, 2011.

Already rumors were running wild about who was responsible. At the time, Sony had been involved in a legal dispute with George Hotz, a 21-year-old who had posted PlayStation 3 security information on a blog in January, but many thought the secretive hacker group known as Anonymous was responsible because it had openly called for "denial-of-service attacks" against Sony. However, Anonymous issued a statement saying it was not responsible for the attack—"AnonOps was not related to this incident and does not take responsibility for whatever has happened"—and suggested that Sony's servers were to blame.

Still, shortly after the "denial-of-service" attacks, Tim Schaaff, president of Sony Network Entertainment, announced that one or more hackers had infiltrated the services of PlayStation Network.

In a brief PlayStation blog entry on April 25, 2011, Seybold recognized that readers were eager to get back to their gaming and other services. "Unfortunately, I don't have an update or timeframe to share at this point in time," his post read. The work being done was a "time intensive process" and service would resume as quickly as possible. It wasn't until six days after the network shutdown, on April 26, 2011, at about 4 p.m., that Sony posted a longer statement on its PlayStation blog; it also e-mailed the information in the blog post in the form of a "consumer alert" to all registered PlayStation users. The attacks on Sony's computer systems, the post read, actually began on April 17, 2011, and continued through April 19, 2011. PlayStation users' personal information was possibly "compromised" or, more to the point, stolen by an unknown hacker or hackers; no evidence had surfaced to confirm that credit card information had been stolen. Sony characterized the breach as an "illegal intrusion" of its Internet network. Sony's response included turning off the network, hiring an outside security firm to complete a full investigation, and quickly enhancing its security by rebuilding its network system.

The hackers, Sony said, could have taken a customer's name, address, country, e-mail address, birth date, PlayStation Network/Qriocity password and login, and handle/PSN online ID. Other information possibly stolen included profile data, purchase history, billing address, password security answers, and credit card numbers and their expiration dates. While the investigation was ongoing and nothing had been confirmed regarding the theft of credit card numbers and other sensitive information, the possibility was being released "out of an abundance of caution." Readers were advised to be on the alert for e-mail, telephone, and postal mail scams: "To protect against possible identity theft or other financial loss, we encourage you to remain vigilant, to review your account statements and to monitor your credit reports."

PlayStation/Qriocity users were told how to contact the three major U.S. credit bureaus to obtain a free credit report annually and how to place a "fraud alert" on their file.

Once again, readers were thanked for their patience and were told that Sony was still working "around the clock" to fix the problem. No timeframe was provided on when services would resume.

What consumers didn't know from these messages was how massive the breach was: nearly eighty million user accounts were affected worldwide. While many posted their thanks for the information update, others were upset that it took Sony so long to respond. Tacotaskforce commented on the PlayStation blog: "You waited a WEEK to tell us our personal information was compromised? That should have been said Thursday." PlayStation owners weren't the only ones upset.

Shortly after Sony's announcement, U.S. Senator Richard Blumenthal (D-Conn.) wrote the company, criticizing its slow response to the massive data breach and citing the need for customer service protections:

> *I am troubled by the failure of Sony to immediately notify affected customers of the breach and to extend adequate financial data security protections . . .*
>
> *When a data breach occurs, it is essential that customers be immediately notified about whether and to what extent their personal and financial information has been compromised. Additionally, PlayStation Network users should be provided with financial data security services, including free access to credit reporting services, for two*

> *years, the costs of which should be borne by Sony. Affected individuals should also be provided with sufficient insurance to protect them from the possible financial consequences of identity theft.*

Sony admitted that it did not know that customer information had been stolen until an external consultant figured it out. Such an admission by a technology giant was not comforting news for its millions of loyal customers.

Seybold clarified the reasons for the delay on April 26, 2011, after the initial blog post:

> *There's a difference in timing between when we identified there was an intrusion and when we learned of consumers' data being compromised. We learned there was an intrusion April 19th and subsequently shut the services down.*
>
> *We then brought in outside experts to help us learn how the intrusion occurred and to conduct an investigation to determine the nature and scope of the incident. It was necessary to conduct several days of forensic analysis, and it took our experts until yesterday to understand the scope of the breach. We then shared the information with our consumers and announced it publicly this afternoon.*

Sony's April 26, 2011, announcement was widely reported by the traditional news media and social media outlets, especially technology bloggers. Reports focused on the enormity of the breach and the type of personal information potentially stolen.

The PlayStation blog also carried two question-and-answer posts responding to the most frequently asked security questions related to the stolen data. The second Q&A focused on PlayStation Network player concerns.

SONY'S APOLOGY

At a news conference held in Tokyo May 1, 2011, Sony's executive deputy president Kazuo Hirai broke his silence, saying: "We apologize deeply for causing great unease and trouble to our users." During the news conference, Hirai and other senior managers bowed deeply, a significant display of remorse in Japanese culture. Hirai, the number two Sony executive widely believed to be in line to succeed CEO and president Howard Stringer, acted as chief spokesman at the event; Stringer was absent. Hirai said that portions of the network services would be restored by the end of the week.

- Hirai and two other executives agreed that Sony's network security needed to improve and pledged to make that happen.
- A customer appreciation program was being planned that would include free software downloads and thirty days of free network service.
- "I see my work as first making sure Sony can regain the trust from our users," Hirai said, according to The Associated Press.

FIGURE 7.35 *Sony Computer Entertainment President and CEO Kazuo Hirai, center, bowed along with two other executives at the start of a press conference at the Sony Corp. headquarters in Tokyo, May 1, 2011. The three executives bowed in apology for a security breach in the company's PlayStation Network that caused the loss of personal data of some seventy-seven million accounts on the online service. Next to Hirai are Sony Corp.'s senior vice presidents Shiro Kambe, left, and Shinji Hasejima, right.*
AP Photo/Shizuo Kambayashi

Seybold clarified information discussed at the news conference surrounding the type of security protocols for protecting passwords May 2, 2011, on the PlayStation blog. He said:

> *While the passwords that were stored were not "encrypted," they were transformed using a cryptographic hash function. There is a difference between these two types of security measures which is why we said the passwords had not been encrypted. But I want to make very clear that the passwords were not stored in our database in cleartext form.*

A link to further explain the security issue was provided, with another reminder for customers to change their network passwords and remain vigilant for phishing schemes and other scams. Once again, Seybold apologized for "causing users concern over this issue."

MORE SECURITY BREACHES

Ironically, on the day of its public apology, May 1, 2011, Sony discovered that another online multiplayer network (Sony Online Entertainment) had been hacked and personal data potentially stolen. The company shut down the network and notified users. This time 24.6 million accounts were affected; Sony said the new security breach stemmed from the original April 17–19, 2011, attacks. Investigators found a file on one of its servers named "Anonymous" with the words "We are Legion" attached to it, adding to the speculation that Anonymous was to blame for the malicious intrusions.

By the end of the month, another three smaller intrusions into Sony's services were announced to the public.

CONGRESSIONAL INVESTIGATION

The U.S. House Subcommittee on Commerce, Manufacturing and Trade sent Sony a letter April 29, 2011, asking questions about the security breach.

Lawmakers wanted to know, among other things, why Sony waited to notify customers of the breach. Sony explained the difficulty in detecting the intrusion:

> *Detection was difficult because of the sheer sophistication of the intrusion. Second the detection was difficult because the criminal hackers exploited system software vulnerability. Finally, our security teams were working very hard to defend against denial of service attacks and that may have made it more difficult to detect this intrusion quickly—all perhaps by design.*

At the beginning, Sony explained, the internal security team only had small indications that something was amiss. It hired a security forensic consulting firm on April 20, 2011, to conduct the investigation. As the investigation grew in scope another team was hired to assist. It took nearly three days to "mirror" or copy the information on its massive servers for forensic examination. On Easter Sunday a third forensic team was added to help with the forensic analysis. It wasn't until April 25, 2011, that Sony confirmed the scope of the personal data that it believed had been taken. Even so, Sony was still unable to confirm whether credit card information had been accessed and who had stolen the information.

Sony said it had taken steps to prevent future attacks, including: adding monitoring and configuration management software; more levels of data protection and encryption; more firewalls; moving its system to a new, more secure data-center site; and hiring a chief information security officer.

REGULATION PROPOSED

U.S. Representative Mary Bono Mack (R-Calif.) announced that she would introduce legislation requiring companies to quickly inform customers when their personal information had been compromised. During the House Subcommittee on Commerce, Manufacturing and Trade's May 4, 2011, hearing, Mack cited Americans' growing frustration with corporations who had compromised the data of their customers to hackers:

> *Yet for me, the single most important question is simply this: Why weren't Sony's customers notified sooner of the cyber attack? I fundamentally believe that all consumers have a right to know when their personal information has been compromised,*

> *and Sony—as well as all other companies—have an overriding responsibility to alert them . . . immediately.*
>
> *In Sony's case, company officials first revealed information about the data breach on their blog. That's right. A blog. I hate to pile on, but—in essence—Sony put the burden on consumers to "search" for information, instead of accepting the burden of notifying them. If I have anything to do with it, that kind of half-hearted, half-baked response is not going to fly in the future.*
>
> *This ongoing mess only reinforces my long-held belief that much more needs to be done to protect sensitive consumer information. Americans need additional safeguards to prevent identity theft, and I will soon introduce legislation designed to accomplish this goal. My legislation will be crafted around a guiding principle: Consumers should be promptly informed when their personal information has been jeopardized.*

Tim Schaaff, president of Sony Network Entertainment International, later responded to Mack's criticism of using its blog as a primary communication vehicle in Congressional testimony June 2, 2011:

> *On Friday, April 22nd, we notified PlayStation Network customers via a post on the PlayStation Blog that an intrusion had occurred. That blog, by the way, has been rated one of the top-twenty most influential on the Internet, right behind the White House's blog. It has a highly visible and deeply engaging relationship with our customers and is one of the best, fastest and most direct means of communicating with them.*

Schaaff defended the response time and amount of information its customers received during the crisis in Congressional testimony:

> *Let me address the specific issue you are considering today—notification of consumers when data breaches occur. Laws—and common sense—provide for companies to*

Let me address the specific issue you are considering today – notification of consumers when data breaches occur. Laws – and common sense – provide for companies to investigate breaches, gather the facts, and then report data losses publicly. If you reverse that order – issuing vague or speculative statements before you have specific and reliable information – you either confuse and panic people, without giving them useful facts, or you bombard them with so many announcements that they become background noise.

As recently noted by Director of National Intelligence James Clapper, "...almost two-thirds of US firms report that they have been the victim of cyber security incidents or information breaches." So we must strike the right balance between giving people the information they need, when they need it, without sounding false alarms or so many alarms that these warnings are ignored.

FIGURE 7.36 *Tim Schaaff, president of Playstation Networks, responded to Congressional questions about Sony's slow reponse to telling its customers about the security breach.*
http://republicans.energycommerce.house.gov
Tim Schaaff, president of Sony Netowrk Entertainment International

investigate breaches, gather the facts, and then report data losses publicly. If you reverse that order—issuing vague or speculative statements before you have specific and reliable information—you either confuse and panic people, without giving them useful facts, or you bombard them with so many announcements that they become background noise.

As recently noted by Director of National Intelligence James Clapper, "almost two thirds of US firms report that they have been the victim of cyber security incidents or information breaches." So we must strike the right balance between giving people the information they need, when they need it, without sounding false alarms or so many alarms that these warnings are ignored.

SONY'S RESPONSE

Sony's executive deputy president Kazuo Hirai responded by letter to a request from Senator Richard Blumenthal who had demanded answers to the company's then-failure to notify millions of customers of the data breach in a timely manner. Sony agreed to provide one year of free credit monitoring service to users, as well as a $1 million insurance policy to cover the possibility of them becoming victims of identity theft, at Blumenthal's request.

Dear Senator Blumenthal:

I am writing in response to your letters dated April 26, 2011 and May 3, 2011. I regret not responding to you sooner but I assure you that my attention and the attention of my colleagues literally around the world has been keenly focused on remedying the harm caused by the large scale criminal cyber-attack perpetrated upon Sony and its customers. I welcome your questions and hope that Sony can be helpful in crafting a public policy solution that reduces the chances that cyber-attacks such as this occur in the future.

With respect to your specific questions, please understand that the PlayStation Network is an extremely complex system that consists of approximately 130 servers, 50 software programs and 77 million registered accounts. To determine what meaningful information we could tell consumers about the attack on that network required a thorough investigation to understand what had occurred.

The basic sequence of events is as follows: On Tuesday, April 19, 2011, the Sony Network Entertainment America (SNEA) network team discovered that several PlayStation Network servers unexpectedly rebooted themselves and that unplanned and unusual activity was taking place on the network. This activity triggered an immediate response.

The network team took four servers off line and an internal assessment began. That process continued into the evening. On Wednesday, April 20, 2011, SNEA mobilized a larger internal team to assist the investigation of the four suspect servers. That team discovered the first credible indications that an intruder had been in the PlayStation Network system, and six more servers were identified as possibly being compromised. SNEA immediately decided to shut down all of the PlayStation Network services in order to prevent any additional damage.

On the afternoon of April 20, 2011, SNEA retained a recognized security and forensic consulting firm to mirror the servers to enable a forensic analysis. The type of mirroring required to provide meaningful information in this type of situation had to be meticulous and took many hours to complete.

The scope and complexity of the investigation grew substantially as additional evidence about the attack developed. On Thursday, April 21, SNEA retained a second recognized security and forensic consulting firm to assist in the investigation. That firm's role was to provide additional manpower to image the servers and to conduct a forensic analysis of all aspects of the suspected security breach.

The team took until Friday afternoon, April 22, to complete the mirroring of the first nine servers that were suspected of being compromised. By the evening of Saturday, April 23, the forensic teams were able to confirm that intruders had used very sophisticated and aggressive techniques to obtain unauthorized access to the servers and hide their presence from the system administrators.

Among other things, the intruders deleted log files in order to hide the extent of their work and activity within the network. At this point, SNEA knew it was dealing with a sophisticated hacker and on Sunday, April 24 (Easter Sunday) decided that it needed to retain a third forensic team with highly specialized skills to assist with the investigation. Specifically, this firm was retained to provide even more manpower for forensic analysis in all aspects of the suspected security breach and, in particular, to use their specialized skills to determine the scope of the data theft.

By Monday April 25, 2011, the forensic teams assembled by SNEA were finally able to confirm the scope of the personal data that they believed had been taken, but they could not rule out whether credit card information had been accessed.

SNEA was aware of its affirmative obligations under various state statutes to conduct a reasonable and prompt investigation to determine the nature and scope of the breach and to restore the integrity of its network system. SNEA also understood its obligation to report its findings to consumers if certain, specific kinds of personal information could have been compromised. As you are aware, there are a variety of state statutes that apply, and several that have conflicting or inconsistent requirements, but given the global nature of the network, SNEA needed to be mindful of them all—and has endeavored to comply with them all.

Throughout the process, SNEA was very concerned that announcing incomplete, tentative or potentially misleading information to consumers could cause confusion and lead them to take unnecessary actions. SNEA felt that it was important—and that it was in keeping with the mandate of state law—that any information SNEA provided to customers be corroborated by meaningful evidence.

Indeed, many state statutes (e.g., AZ, CT, CO, DE, FL, ID, ME, MD, MS, NE, VT, WI, WY) essentially require disclosure without unreasonable delay once an investigation has been done to identify the nature and scope of what happened and who was affected. That is precisely the course we followed.

While the forensic teams had not completed their investigation as of April 25 and could not determine if credit card information had been accessed, SNEA did not know when or if it would be able to rule out that possibility. And so, on Tuesday, April 26, SNEA and Sony Computer Entertainment America (SCEA) notified consumers of the situation.

SNEA and Sony Online Entertainment (SOE) continued to investigate the potential scope of this criminal attack even after consumers were notified of the breach. In the course of that investigation, on Sunday, May 1, using information uncovered by the forensic teams, engineers at SOE discovered that data had also been taken from their servers. They, too, shut down operations and on Monday, May 2, notified their consumers of the discovery.

Both SNEA and SOE notified consumers about the theft of data in a variety of ways. They issued global press releases that received widespread circulation across a range of media. Both companies have posted notices on the first page of their websites where most consumers are first likely to seek information. SNEA has posted a notice on the PlayStation website (www.PlayStation.com) that directs consumers to PlayStation Network Data Security Updates, and on the Qriocity website (www.Qriocity.com) that directs consumers to the customer support page with an "IMPORTANT Service Announcement". SOE has posted a "Security Notice" on its home page. Sony Computer Entertainment America, the company most associated with the PlayStation® brand, has communicated with its consumers via the PlayStation Blog and has placed a prominent notice on its home page. Finally both SNEA and SOE have been sending the e-mail notices to individual consumers that you mentioned in your letter.

In your letter you suggest that sending 500,000 e-mails an hour is not expeditious; however this limitation exists because these e-mails are not "batch" e-mails. The e-mails are individually tailored to our consumers' accounts. To comply with the various state laws that recognize personal notice (such as via e-mail) may be delayed or otherwise undeliverable we, in the forms noted above, provided what is known as "substitute notice" to our consumers. (I do not believe the e-mail pace relates to the decision to announce on April 26, as apparently suggested by someone to your staff; these issues are unrelated, and we apologize for any confusion.)

With respect to your question about credit cards potentially involved, SNEA had approximately 12.3 million active and expired credit cards, approximately 5.6 million of which were in the U.S. As of this writing, there remains no evidence that the credit card information was stolen and the major credit card companies are still reporting that they have not seen an increase in fraudulent transactions due to this event.

Unfortunately, our forensic teams still have not been able to rule out that credit card data was taken. That is why we have continued to be cautious in alerting our customers to the possibility it was stolen.

Since SNEA gave its first notice that the PlayStation Network and Qriocity services were compromised, SOE has subsequently announced the possible theft of personal information from approximately 24.6 million SOE accounts and also announced that approximately 12,700 credit cards (with expiration dates but not security codes) and approximately 10,700 direct debit records—all from non-US consumers—may have been taken.

You have questioned why SOE did not disclose this loss of data from its servers until May 2. The reason was because SOE did not discover that theft until May 1. The intruder carefully covered his or her tracks in the server systems. In fact, as noted above, the discovery was made only after SOE rechecked their machines—which earlier showed no evidence of theft—using information developed by our forensic experts working in collaboration with our technical teams.

Notices as required by various state statutes were prepared and the information was made available to consumers through a press release and e-mails to SOE customers beginning on May 2.

You have also asked how we will protect consumers going forward. We have already advised our consumers in the U.S. that we would offer a complimentary identity theft protection program, the details of which we will announce shortly. SNEA is finalizing details of this offer and SOE has agreed to participate in the offer and will make it available to its consumers as well.

In addition to offering this identity theft protection, SNEA has announced a series of steps that it will take—most of which were in progress before this theft occurred—to enhance security before the service is restored. SOE has taken or will take similar steps. Those steps are:

- *additional automated software monitoring and configuration management to help defend against new attacks;*
- *enhanced levels of data protection and encryption;*
- *enhanced capabilities to detect software intrusions within the network, unauthorized access and unusual activity patterns;*
- *implementation of additional firewalls;*
- *expediting a planned move of the system to a new data center in a different location with enhanced security; and*
- *appointment of a new Chief Information Security Officer.*

Please allow me to attach a letter delivered yesterday to the House Committee on Energy and Commerce, Subcommittee on Commerce, Manufacturing and Trade, which provides additional information that might be of interest.

We of course deeply regret that this incident has occurred and have apologized to our customers. We believe we are taking aggressive action to right what you correctly perceive is a grievous wrong against our consumers: a wrong that is the result of a malicious, sophisticated and well-orchestrated criminal attack on us and our consumers.

While those who perpetrated this crime no doubt relish putting us in the cross-hairs of controversy, I know you can appreciate how widespread the problem of cybercrime is in society today. What happened to us, though more vast in scope, has happened to many others before. And cybercriminals will continue to attack businesses, consumers, and governments, posing a real threat to our economy and security.

We believe a strong coalition among government, industry, and consumers is needed to identify ways that the public and private sectors can work more closely together to enact strong laws, promote stronger enforcement of those laws, educate people about the threats we face, share best practices and make the Internet a safe place for everyone to engage in commerce. In this we commend you for your leadership.

We do not want what happened to us and our consumers to happen to any other business, consumer or organization, and we look forward to bringing the lessons we have learned to all who are concerned about the threat of cybercrimes to our way of life.

Very truly yours,
Kazuo Hirai
President and Group Chief Executive Officer

CUSTOMER APPRECIATION PROGRAM

Sony knew it needed to compensate its customers for the twenty-three-day outage. A customer appreciation program was announced May 16, 2011, and included: a selection

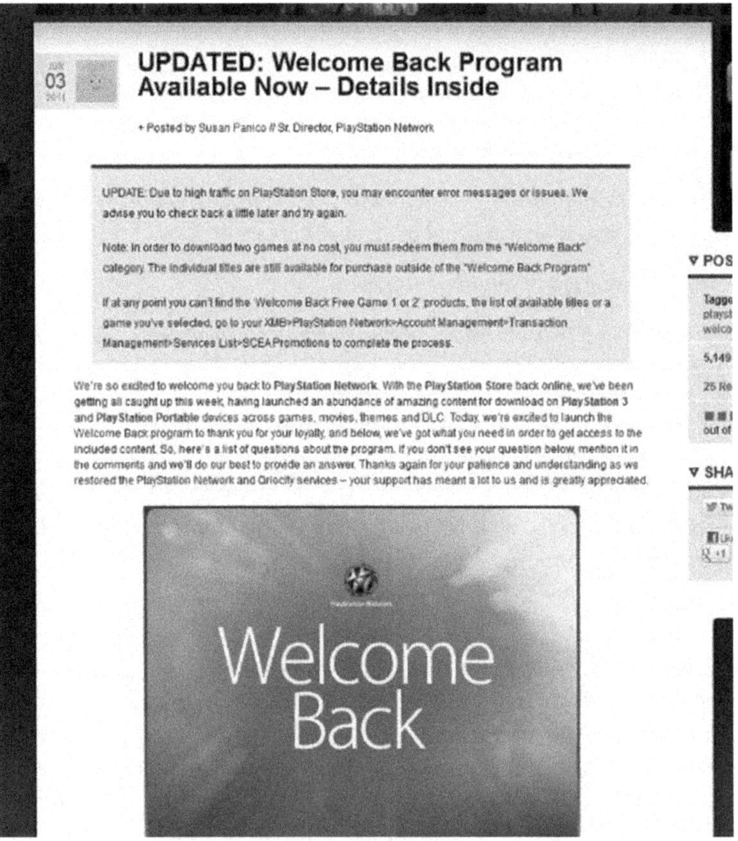

UPDATED: Welcome Back Program Available Now – Details Inside

+ Posted by Susan Panico // Sr. Director, PlayStation Network

UPDATE: Due to high traffic on PlayStation Store, you may encounter error messages or issues. We advise you to check back a little later and try again.

Note: In order to download two games at no cost, you must redeem them from the "Welcome Back" category. The individual titles are still available for purchase outside of the "Welcome Back Program"

If at any point you can't find the 'Welcome Back Free Game 1 or 2' products, the list of available titles or a game you've selected, go to your XMB>PlayStation Network>Account Management>Transaction Management>Services List>SCEA Promotions to complete the process.

We're so excited to welcome you back to PlayStation Network. With the PlayStation Store back online, we've been getting all caught up this week, having launched an abundance of amazing content for download on PlayStation 3 and PlayStation Portable devices across games, movies, themes and DLC. Today, we're excited to launch the Welcome Back program to thank you for your loyalty, and below, we've got what you need in order to get access to the included content. So, here's a list of questions about the program. If you don't see your question below, mention it in the comments and we'll do our best to provide an answer. Thanks again for your patience and understanding as we restored the PlayStation Network and Qriocity services – your support has meant a lot to us and is greatly appreciated.

Welcome Back

FIGURE 7.37 *Sony offered its Playstation customers two free game downloads for the month-long power outage.*
http://blog.us.playstation.com/
Sony Computer Entertainment America LLC

of free downloadable games; free access to PlayStation Plus for thirty days; a selection of "On Us" rental movie titles; free access to Music Unlimited Premium for thirty days; and free items for PlayStation Home. Most customers responded positively to the offers, especially the free games, which were considered high quality and sought after.

SONY CRITICISM AND HACKER REALITIES

The fallout of this massive security breach was expensive, both for Sony's bottom line and for its reputation. According to PC World, more than one hundred million users of PlayStation had personal information hacked, and it could not rule out that 12.3 million credit card numbers had been obtained by the hackers.

A month after the historic security breach, Sony estimated the financial damage at $171.2 million. This did not include the class action lawsuits related to the security breach for negligent protection of personal data and failure to users that their credit card information may have been stolen.

During this time, Sony characterized the criminal(s) behind the cyber intrusion as "malicious" and sophisticated and the investigation as complex and time consuming. Sony also repeated its assertion that the murky hacker group known as Anonymous was somehow responsible. After all, Anonymous admitted it was behind the "denial of service" attacks that preceded the massive intrusion. Sony characterized itself as a victim of "malicious actions" that affected innocent gamers.

As more details became known about the security breach, security experts were critical of Sony's lax security protections. According to an article by VentureBeat.com, a technology news site,

> *An experienced security analyst examining the PSN's logs on a regular basis should have been able to detect the earliest warning signs of the upcoming breach. We don't know exactly what measures Sony had in place before the breach, but it has clearly tried to bolster security measures since then.*

Sony, its cyber critics said, was great at making sleek and effective game consoles but not secure websites.

Sony undoubtedly suffered reputational damage as a result of the security breach and twenty-three-day service outage. Still, to this day, there was no evidence that anyone's personal information was ever published or that anyone's identity was stolen from the Sony security breach. Sony's senior vice president for strategic communication Jim Kennedy said its actions were effective:

> *Sony told people more and told them more quickly than most victims of sophisticated cyber attacks. And so, nearly two years later, the PlayStation Network has many millions more accounts than it did at the time of the criminal intrusion.*

Since the Sony security breach, many more high-profile breaches have been published, including the Federal Reserve, *The New York Times*, the *Wall Street Journal*, *The Washington Post*, Apple, and Facebook, to name a few. Some critics say that a large percentage of companies have been breached but (1) don't know that they have been breached or (2) know it but don't publicize it because it might affect their stock value and reputation.

One cyber-security expert was quoted in *The Washington Post* two years later in 2013: "'The dark secret is there is no such thing as a secure unclassified network,' said James A. Lewis, a cyber-security expert at the Center for Strategic and International Studies."

Another not-so-comforting reality expressed in another article was that companies often have no idea what information, if any, was stolen if the hacking is not discovered quickly. As Dmitri Alperovtich, formerly McAfee's vice president for threat research and chief technology officer for Crowdstrike, said in a *New York Times* article: "I divide the entire set of Fortune Global 2000 firms into two categories: those that know they've been compromised and those that don't yet know."

THE NEXT TIME

When another security breach was detected in October 2011, Sony responded quickly with a post on its PlayStation blog:

> *We want to let you know that we have detected attempts on Sony Entertainment Network, PlayStation Network and Sony Online Entertainment ("Networks") services to test a massive set of sign-in IDs and passwords against our network database. These attempts appear to include a large amount of data obtained from one or more compromised lists from other companies, sites or other sources. In this case, given that the data tested against our network consisted of sign-in ID–password pairs, and that the overwhelming majority of the pairs resulted in failed matching attempts, it is likely the data came from another source and not from our Networks. We have taken steps to mitigate the activity.*
>
> *Less than one tenth of one percent (0.1%) of our PSN, SEN and SOE audience may have been affected. There were approximately 93,000 accounts globally (PSN/SEN: approximately 60,000 accounts; SOE: approximately 33,000) where the attempts succeeded in verifying those accounts' valid sign-in IDs and passwords, and we have temporarily locked these accounts. Only a small fraction of these 93,000 accounts showed additional activity prior to being locked. We are currently reviewing those accounts for unauthorized access, and will provide more updates as we have them. Please note, if you have a credit card associated with your account, your credit card number is not at risk. We will work with any users whom we confirm have had unauthorized purchases made to restore amounts in the PSN/SEN or SOE wallet.*
>
> *As a preventative measure, we are requiring secure password resets for those PSN/SEN accounts that had both a sign-in ID and password match through this attempt. If you are in the small group of PSN/SEN users who may have been affected, you will receive an e-mail from us at the address associated with your account that will prompt you to reset your password.*

Similarly, the SOE accounts that were matched have been temporarily turned off. If you are among the small group of affected SOE customers, you will receive an e-mail from us at the address associated with your account that will advise you on next steps in order to validate your account credentials and have your account turned back on.

We want to take this opportunity to remind our consumers about the increasingly common threat of fraudulent activity online, as well as the importance of having a strong password and having a username/password combination that is not associated with other online services or sites. We encourage you to choose unique, hard-to-guess passwords and always look for unusual activity in your account.

QUESTIONS FOR DISCUSSION

1. Explain the core message of "PlayStation: It Only Does Everything!" What made those commercials so successful?
2. What caused the Sony crisis? Was it preventable?
3. Was three days too long for customers to get a better idea of what had happened to its PlayStation system?
4. Was the use of the PlayStation blog the appropriate way to communicate to all its stakeholders?
5. It wasn't until nine days after the first cyber attacks began that Sony explained what was really going on. Sony decided to blame the hackers instead of its lax security system. How did that further damage Sony's reputation and trust with its customers?
6. The actual size of the security breach took Sony several days to reveal. How did it justify its actions?
7. How effective was Sony's apology to its customers?
8. What did Sony do to help with its recovery efforts? Do you feel it was adequate? Why or why not?

Dig Deeper

A May 3, 2011, letter, available on the textbook's companion website, from Sony's chairman of the board of directors to the investigating Congressional subcommittee explained the facts of the case at that point in time. On June 2, 2011 Sony president Tim Schaaff explained why Sony delayed reporting the suspected security breach in his statement to a Congressional subcommittee. Did these statements make a persuasive case for delayed reporting? What did Sony support for federal data breach legislation?

22

Kryptonite: Radioactive Publicity

Crisis Response in an Instant Internet World

The pen is mightier than the sword—and it's a pretty good bike burglary tool too.

Leading bicycle lock manufacturer Kryptonite of Canton, Massachusetts, found itself at the center of an Internet storm when bike owners discovered some tubular cylinder U-locks could be easily opened with a plastic Bic pen.

While the security vulnerability applied to many tubular cylinder U-locks, such as locks for vending machines and laptops as well as other manufactured bicycle locks, national coverage of the security problem focused on industry leader Kryptonite, partly due to its revered brand status and because initial customer reports focused on Kryptonite locks.

It all started when bike enthusiast Chris Brennan told a friend about the recent theft of custom-made wheels from his 2004 Bianchi bicycle. His friend asked if Brennan knew that a Bic pen could open Kryptonite locks.

Brennan didn't believe it—at first. But when he tried it at home on his Kryptonite Evolution 2000 lock, it worked. In fact, he said it was as easy as using a key and took less than thirty seconds on his first try.

THE INTERNET POSTING

Brennan's disbelief soon turned to anger and then concern. If this security flaw affected him, it also affected thousands of other cyclists who relied on bike locks to protect their property. He sat down at his computer and typed out an urgent post late that night on an Internet bike site called Bike Forums (www.bikeforums.net) where hundreds of bike enthusiasts swap information about all things related to cycling.

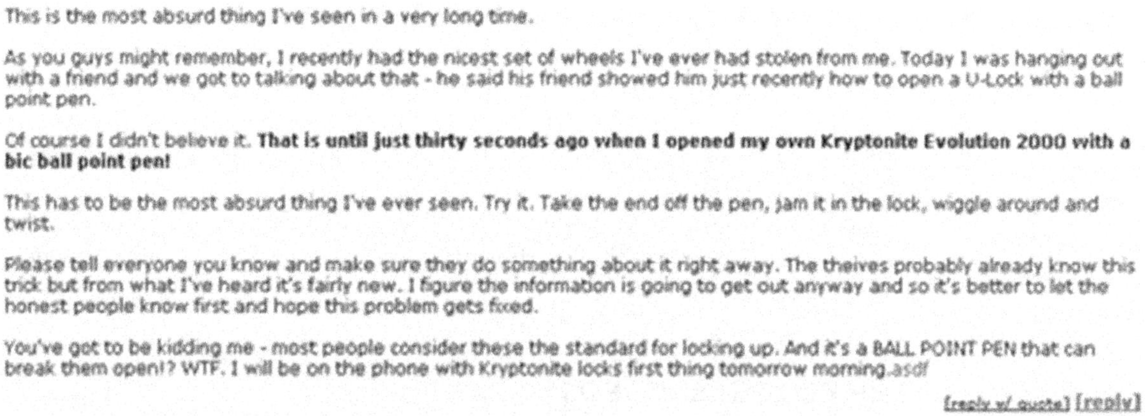

This is the most absurd thing I've seen in a very long time.

As you guys might remember, I recently had the nicest set of wheels I've ever had stolen from me. Today I was hanging out with a friend and we got to talking about that - he said his friend showed him just recently how to open a U-Lock with a ball point pen.

Of course I didn't believe it. **That is until just thirty seconds ago when I opened my own Kryptonite Evolution 2000 with a bic ball point pen!**

This has to be the most absurd thing I've ever seen. Try it. Take the end off the pen, jam it in the lock, wiggle around and twist.

Please tell everyone you know and make sure they do something about it right away. The theives probably already know this trick but from what I've heard it's fairly new. I figure the information is going to get out anyway and so it's better to let the honest people know first and hope this problem gets fixed.

You've got to be kidding me - most people consider these the standard for locking up. And it's a BALL POINT PEN that can break them open!? WTF. I will be on the phone with Kryptonite locks first thing tomorrow morning.asdf

[reply w/ quote] [reply]

FIGURE 7.38 *Chris Brennan was so concerned after he learned how to "Bic" his bike lock that he quickly started a discussion thread on the Bike Forum's website to warn others. BikeForums.net*
www.BikeForums.net

Brennan's headline to a new Bike Forum discussion thread warned: "Your brand new bicycle U-Lock is not safe!" The September 12, 2004, post, under Brennan's username Unaesthetic, stated:

> *This is the most absurd thing I've seen in a long time.*
>
> *As you guys might remember, I recently had the nicest set of wheels I've ever had stolen from me. Today, I was hanging out with a friend and we got to talking about that—he said his friend showed him just recently how to open a U-Lock with a ballpoint pen.*
>
> *Of course I didn't believe it. That is until just thirty seconds ago when I opened my own Kryptonite Evolution 2000 with a Bic ballpoint pen.*
>
> *This has to be the most absurd thing I've ever seen. Try it. Take the end off the pen, jam it in the lock, wiggle around and twist.*
>
> *Please tell everybody you know and make sure they do something about it right away. The thieves probably already know this trick but from what I've heard it's fairly new. I figure the information is going to get out anyway and so it's better to let the honest people know first and hope this problem gets fixed.*

Word spread quickly as the Internet post began to attract other postings; the forum's discussion thread circulated via e-mail and was easily pasted into other Internet bicycle sites. According to BikeBiz, a digital cycling magazine, an estimated 340,000 readers had read the Bike Forums postings during the first week.

Within the cycling community there was early debate and lingering doubt about Brennan's claim. Subsequent postings that followed in the first hours of Brennan's post claimed they also replicated Brennan's Bic trick, while others said they couldn't get it to work.

Soon a Bike Forums poster successfully "Bic-ed" his bike lock, recorded the feat with a digital camera, and e-mailed the video to Kryptonite's customer service department by 12:18 p.m., just about fourteen hours after the original post appeared. A copy of the video was sent to another Bike Forums member named Benjamin Running, who volunteered to host the video on his blog site. It was a big hit.

Brennan, who wrote the original thread post, aptly summarized the first twenty-three hours in his twenty-sixth posting about the bike lock flaw: "I think I opened a very big can of worms."

THE BLOGGER VIDEOS

Early the next morning, September 14, Running successfully opened his bike lock with a ballpoint pen—to his utter amazement. Running also decided to re-create the feat on camera. He digitally recorded the "Bic-ing" with his small digital camera, and posted it to his blog, Thirdrate.com, alongside the other digital video *Bic-ing*. Running made both videos available on Bike Forums with Internet links. His September 14 blog entry started this way:

9.14.04 take this quiz kryptonite bike locks are:

- *the best on the market*
- *the most secure*
- *the most indestructible*
- *open-able in a few seconds with a 10 cent Bic pen.*

and the correct answer is "open-able in a few seconds with a 10 cent Bic pen." details of how to pen any bike lock using a cylindrical key (including most kryptonite locks) has been blowing up a number of bike websites and discussion boards in the last few days and sure enough, it's easy as pie.

check out this quicktime video of me cracking my $90 kryptonite EV disc lock in about 20 seconds [link]. bike owners beware, that same bright yellow lock that once said 'don't screw with me' now screams 'steal me!' obviously, i post this information as a warning to lock owners—not as a how-to. stealing is bad. stealing bikes is worse.

The next day, his blog chronicled the growing interest in his QuickTime movie:

so. This kryptonite lock deal: is getting big. I called kryptonite on tuesday morning and was called back by a customer service rep who assured me that they are working on this and will come up with a solution of some sort within 48 hours (like. tomorrow?).

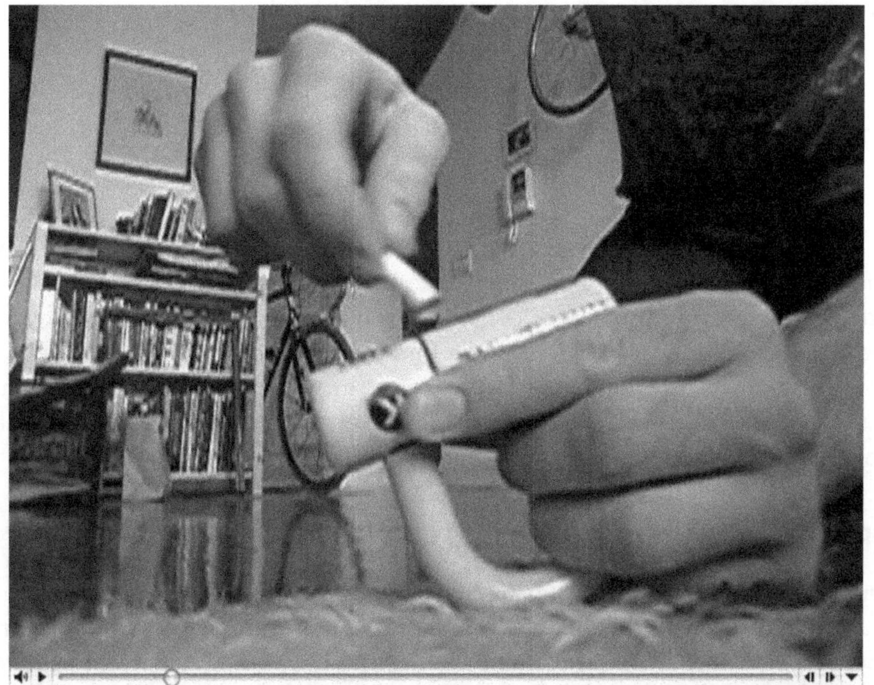

FIGURE 7.39 *The Kryptonite bike lock at the time was susceptible to "Bic-ing" with a plastic pen. Benjamin Running demonstrated the simple procedure with his home video camera.*
Benjamin Running
Courtesy of Benjamin Running

meanwhile, back at the web: the lock cracking videos that I and another guy recorded are linked from everywhere and have been downloaded over one hundred and twenty thousand times in 48 hours (um.damn?)

i'm going to have to unload these soon.

Actually, seeing Running's Bic pen easily unlock the Kryptonite lock within seconds made believers out of doubters at Bike Forums and other Internet sites. The video was posted on various websites, including Bike Forums. According to BikeBiz, the video was downloaded three million times within days of its posting as word about it was spread by numerous media reports including CNN.com, Wired.com, many broadcast cable and local network news affiliates, *The Boston Globe*, and the front page of *The New York Times*.

KRYPTONITE: TOUGH WORLD, TOUGH LOCKS

Kryptonite, a Massachusetts company owned by Ingersoll-Rand, is widely recognized by cyclists as the premiere bike lock business. Its slogan, "Tough World, Tough Locks," and its reputation for building theft-proof locks were legendary. Its website recounts how the legend was born in 1972.

The Second Avenue Bicycle Shop in New York City, under Kryptonite founder Michael Zane's direction, locked a three-speed bicycle to a signpost in New York City's Greenwich Village. Like a lamb awaiting slaughter, the bicycle remained for thirty days and thirty nights. All removable parts of the bike were immediately

FIGURE 7.40 *Kryptonite: Tough World, Tough Locks*
http://www.kryptonitelock.com/
Kryptonite

stripped by marauders, but a month later the lock and the bike frame were still in place, even though it had been mauled by repeated break-in attempts. Publicity from this event gave Kryptonite the boost it needed, forever changing the face of bicycle security.

The company's reputation continued to grow when Zane returned to New York in 1994 to once again pit his latest innovation, the New York Lock, against the city's toughest streets. Once again, an expensive, shiny new bike stayed put for forty-eight hours locked to a parking meter in the East Village. The bike frame and lock were secure. The experiment, witnessed by a *New York Post* employee, was also tried in other high-crime New York neighborhoods, with the same result

In addition to the street test, the *New York Post* ran its own battery of tests using common bike theft tools: "a 4-foot bolt cutter, a crowbar and a hammer. The non-Kryptonite locks cracked in seconds, but all methods failed on the New York Lock, even the monstrous bolt cutter, which ended up useless with large dents in its jaws."

INTERNET POSTINGS ATTRACT TRADITIONAL NEWS MEDIA

Since Brennan's first Bike Forums message, posted before midnight September 12, 2004, information about Kryptonite's tubular cylinder U-locks' vulnerabilities circulated quickly within blogs, e-mails, and Internet communities; it wasn't long before the mainstream news media became interested in the story. Kryptonite's Public Relations Manager Donna Tocci was designated to develop the media relations response.

Kryptonite began issuing public statements September 15, 2004.

Meanwhile media calls had been pouring into Tocci's office. She responded to all news media e-mails by creating a distribution e-mail list of those who had e-mailed or called with questions, "I felt it was important to respond as quickly as possible even if we didn't have specific details about our plan at that time," she said. "Our message was that we were aware of their concerns and that Kryptonite would be responding with a plan within 48 hours. Please bear with us."

When communicating with the people most affected—owners of its tubular cylinder locks—Kryptonite's customer service department handled the consumer questions, including telephone and e-mailed questions, on a daily basis.

Kryptonite's headquarters, which employs twenty-five people, did not have a formal crisis communication plan, especially one that dealt with an inconceivable product failure. Tocci said a response team was immediately assembled comprising about fifteen Kryptonite administrative staff people, including representatives from customer service, marketing, product management, and the general manager. The goal was to "provide constant and honest communication" and resolve the problem in a responsible way, she said.

KRYPTONITE'S MEDIA RELATIONS RESPONSE

Tocci, a one-person public relations office responsible for Kryptonite's public relations efforts worldwide, received more than a hundred calls from the media in the first days of the crisis. Because of the sheer volume of phone calls and her need to be away from her desk in executive crisis management meetings, Tocci changed her voice mail message, asking the media to leave a name, phone number, and e-mail address so that she could respond to requests by telephone or via e-mail. "I was taking my laptop home and responding to e-mails usually until midnight during the first week."

Information for the media was developed by the response team Kryptonite set in place.

"For me, it was a big deal to get back to [media and consumer information] requests," she said. "It's okay to say you don't know—just get back to them." Requests from top-tier media, such as *The New York Times* and *San Francisco Chronicle,* were answered in person. Tocci functioned as the company's main spokesperson, although other executives were also quoted in stories. Second-tier media were either answered in person or by an individual or group e-mail. "We actually got compliments from the media," Tocci said. "Major news organizations couldn't believe we got back to them," including one busy reporter who received three messages from Tocci.

According to the Internet cycling magazine *BikeBiz,* when it contacted Kryptonite September 14, 2004, for a comment, "the company said it was aware of the Bike Forums debate and wanted 24 hours to formulate a response." The next day another media call came from *The Boston Globe,* Kryptonite's local paper with a national reach. Tocci decided to call *Globe* reporter Ross Kerber, whom she had dealt with before and who, she knew, would "listen and tell the story the right way"—fairly, "PR is all about relationship building," Tocci said.

Kryptonite issued a written statement September 15, 2004, which was repeated by *BikeBiz* and other sources the following day:

> *We understand there are concerns regarding tubular cylinders used in some Kryptonite locks. The tubular cylinder, a standard industry-wide design, has been successfully used for more than 30 years in our products and other security applications without significant issues.*
>
> *The current Kryptonite locks based on a tubular cylinder design continue to present an effective deterrent to theft. As part of our continuing commitment to produce performance and improved security, Kryptonite has been developing a disc-style cylinder for some years. In 2000, Kryptonite introduced the disc-style cylinder in its premier line of products, the New York series. In 2002, Kryptonite began development of a new disc cylinder system for both its Evolution and KryptoLok product lines, which currently use the tubular cylinder design. These products are scheduled to be introduced in the next few weeks.*

We are accelerating the delivery of the new disc cylinder locks and we will communicate directly with our distributors, dealers and consumers within the coming days. The world just got tougher and so did our locks.

The Boston Globe story that ran September 16, 2004, quoted from the statement mentioning the company had accelerated plans to upgrade the KryptoLok and Evolution lines of U-locks which were prey to pens. The story included a quote from Tim Clifford, Kryptonite's director of sales, noting: "Unfortunately, this takes the thunder out of the launch at Interbike [trade show], but we'll do what's right by the bicycle community."

The Associated Press also issued several versions of its story September 16, 2004, including one with this headline: "Bike Lock Can Be Picked with a Pen." The Associated Press article was picked up by hundreds of newspapers and broadcast media around the country. *The New York Times* ran an article titled "The Pen Is Mightier than the Lock" with video still frames from Running's homemade *Bic-ing* video on September 17, 2004. Out of a lengthy 1,142-word article, Kryptonite only received sixty-eight words in the story based on an e-mailed statement from Kryptonite saying the company was aware of the problem and was working on a solution.

A slightly modified news release statement, developed the day after Kryptonite's initial statement, was distributed by Business Wire on September 16, 2004.

Kryptonite Issues Statement on Tubular Cylinder Lock Consumer Concerns

CANTON, Mass., Sept. 16, 2004

For more than 30 years, Kryptonite has focused on delivering innovative advances that establish the benchmark for lock technology, product performance and enhanced security.

In light of recent demonstrations on the Internet that explain how to criminally defeat tubular cylinder lock technology, which has performed successfully for more than three decades, Kryptonite intends to expedite the introduction of its upgraded Evolution and KryptoLok lines.

These products will have the disc-style cylinder that has the same technology as the company's famous New York Lock. Specifically, Kryptonite will provide the owners of Evolution and KryptoLok series products the ability to upgrade their cross bars to the new disc-style cylinder, where possible. This new cylinder provides greatly enhanced security and performance. Kryptonite is finalizing the details of this upgrade process and will publicly communicate these details as soon as possible.

The national news media and its websites were used to carry Kryptonite's messages during the crisis, with mixed results. For example, the focus on solving the problem quickly was not the message contained in company officials' quotes. A *New York Times* article mentioned that Tocci said the "locks made by other manufacturers shared the same vulnerabilities," and another Kryptonite spokesperson talked about how this problem would not affect earnings.

Kryptonite used Business Wire to disseminate two additional news releases September 17 and 22. The first formal announcement about Kryptonite's broad upgrade exchange program came September 17, five days after the initial problem was identified by Brennan, the cyclist. The statement said the company would begin providing "free product upgrades for certain locks purchased since September 2002."

Kryptonite Offering Free Upgrade Worldwide for Consumers' High End Tubular Cylinder Locks

CANTON, Mass., Sept. 17, 2004

Kryptonite today announced it will provide free product upgrades for certain locks purchased since September 2002, in response to consumer concerns about tubular cylinder lock technology. Consumers can visit the company's website (www.kryptonitelock.com) on Wednesday afternoon, September 22, 2004, to learn how they can participate in the security upgrade program.

Consumers who have purchased an Evolution lock, KryptoLok lock, New York Chain, New York Noose, Evolution Disc Lock, KryptoDisco or DFS Disc Lock in the last two years are eligible for a product upgrade free of charge from Kryptonite. Customers will need to have either registered their key number, registered for the Kryptonite anti-theft protection offer or have proof of purchase to qualify.

Specifically, Kryptonite will provide for free cross bars featuring the company's new discstyle cylinder lock technology to consumers who have purchased Evolution and KryptoLok series products. In addition the company will replace for free recently purchased Evolution Disc Locks on New York Chain and New York Noose with its "Molly Lock," a heavy duty solid steel padlock. Kryptonite also will upgrade recently purchased disc locks.

Consumers who have had one of the Kryptonite locks mentioned with a tubular cylinder for longer than two years will be eligible for a sizeable rebate on the upgraded products. This program will be administered through Kryptonite dealers and distributors.

A distributor and dealer swap program will be rolled out through direct communication from Kryptonite to all its partners.

Full details about this unprecedented program will be available on Kryptonite's website by afternoon Eastern Standard Time, Wednesday, September 22, 2004, at www.kryptonite.com.

Confusion about the exchange program and growing complaints from owners whose locks were not included in the exchange program led Kryptonite to expand the offer to anyone who owned a Kryptonite tubular cylinder lock. The full details of the exchange program came on September 22, 2004, when Kryptonite said in a news release and on its website that it would offer free product exchanges to "all customers who are concerned about the security of their tubular cylinder locks." The upgraded models used disc-style cylinders in which cuts in the key are angled, providing a more secure design.

Not everyone was happy with Kryptonite's response.

Frustrated lock owners accustomed to rapid communication and a "fast-food" lifestyle did not understand the seemingly slow response of Kryptonite, said Tocci. Many customers told Kryptonite, "We want our new lock today." Kryptonite's steel locks are made in Asia, and the unscheduled need meant a newly designed lock that took weeks, not hours, to manufacture, ship, and distribute, said Tocci. Even though people live in an age of instant communication, manufacturing is not instant—"steel locks can be made only so fast," said Tocci. Fortunately, production for an upgraded product line that had been scheduled to hit stores in January was accelerated to accommodate the rush orders.

Other problems also hindered Kryptonite's response. Kryptonite's phone system crashed during the initial days of the crisis due to the large volume of calls, the website crashed (and the webmaster was out of the country), and Tocci's personal laptop broke.

INTERNET RESPONSE

Kryptonite chose not to respond directly on Bike Forums, where Brennan's original post started the crisis, or other Internet sites. Tocci said the potential flood of questions and comments that a posting could generate would easily overwhelm Kryptonite's ability to respond responsibly. "We didn't want people to think Kryptonite was ignoring them [by not answering]."

This decision also meant rumors and inaccurate information that appeared in some Internet forums and blogs were not responded to, although they were monitored. Instead, Kryptonite relied on its website, the mainstream media, and its Business Wire statements to communicate with its customers and other key publics. Tocci noted that minutes after an official statement was released to the media, it would appear on Bike Forums, posted by a user with access to the information.

Bloggers presented a new problem for Kryptonite. Running's site, Thirdrate.com, basically came out of nowhere. Blogs were a relatively new communication phenomenon at the time. And Running's blog was not considered a credible source of information by Kryptonite; it wasn't even a cyclist's blog. It was just Running's thoughts about his everyday activities that sometimes included thoughts about cycling. Still, its video *Bic-ing* wreaked havoc for Kryptonite.

Unlike the mainstream media, which follow strict journalistic standards and ethical practices, bloggers are accountable to no one. There are no fact-checkers or senior editors to complain to if a blogger's work is inaccurate, incomplete, one-sided, or biased. "You are left with no recourse other than trying to build relationships with them," said Tocci.

Another problem was determining which blogs were legitimate with influential audiences. "We were asking ourselves, 'Who are these bloggers? Are they 15- or 16-year-olds, experts or people who just think they're experts?' "

At the time, Kryptonite decided not to formally communicate with Running and his blog, just as it had decided not to communicate directly with Bike Forums.

MONITORING THE ENVIRONMENT

Tocci was not familiar with Bike Forums prior to the crisis, but she routinely monitored many cycling Internet sites. Her Internet and traditional media monitoring usually took an hour or more each morning. Kryptonite executives kept an eye on other sites and passed along pertinent information. Tocci also routinely scanned dozens of magazines and newspapers. Keeping up is a challenge, she said, because Kryptonite also caters to motorcycles plus power sports such as ATVs, snowmobiles, scooters, skis, and snowboards. Another niche area for the company is in mobile security.

While Kryptonite had two media-tracking services in 2004, its staff did not monitor Internet and blog activity. Kryptonite was considering such a service in the future to help manage the ever-expanding Internet universe, said Tocci.

EPILOGUE

According to *PR News*, by February 2005, the lock upgrade program had cost Kryptonite about $10 million, with about 40,000 locks affected.

In an interview with *PR News*, Steve Down, Kryptonite's general manager, spoke about the lessons he learned from the experience with blogs:

> *This was a totally new experience for me and my team, and I don't think anything can fully prepare you for this. We tried to communicate as much as possible up front, but could we have communicated a little more? Yes, I'm sure we could have. But the difficulty was that [being tripped up by the blogosphere] wasn't only new to our company but to our industry and all industries. We wrestled with the idea of going out in a clandestine way to try and influence the blog but felt that wasn't the right thing to do because we could have damaged ourselves even more.*

When asked, "How do you think blogs have started to impact the ways in which companies communicate with their various stakeholders?" Down responded:

> *When you are dealing with traditional media, there are some balances. The difficulty with blogs is that anyone can put out information in an anonymous way. [But] for any business, blogs are a reality, and companies have to look at what they do and be able to respond adequately to concerns that are raised in such a forum.*

QUESTIONS FOR DISCUSSION

1. What is an Internet forum? What is an Internet community?
2. What problems does the Internet pose for organizations faced with a crisis? What are the benefits for an organization?

3. How did Bike Forums ignite Kryptonite's crisis?
4. What is a blog? How did the blog Thirdrate.com make the crisis even worse for Kryptonite?
5. Evaluate Kryptonite's mainstream media relations response to the crisis. In your opinion, did Kryptonite have key messages communicated? Would you do anything differently? Explain.
6. Evaluate Kryptonite's decision not to respond to Internet postings or blogs. Would you do anything differently? Explain.
7. How might the trend of participatory journalism, the decline of traditional media readers and viewers, and the demand for information customization affect organizational responses similar to the Kryptonite case?
8. How can public relations practitioners monitor the web effectively?
9. What key messages would you stress if you were the public relations manager for Kryptonite? Beyond customers and the media, would you target other key audiences? Why?

Dig Deeper

This case study deals with a crisis situation that involves communication with its customers for a product recall. Using the following documents, available on the textbook's companion website, from the Small Business Administration, assess how these documents could have been useful to Kryptonite communication staff:

- "Crisis Communication Plan"—SBA
- "Emergency Communications Plans"—SBA
- "Table Top Exercise"—SBA
- "How to Use Social Media to Do a Better Job of Customer Service"—SBA.

CHAPTER 8

Entertainment and Leisure

While leisure time and entertainment public relations have a strong connection to consumer relations, these industries deserve a separate look because of their size, their cultural impact on our society, and the attention they get from the mass media.

Simply put, sports, entertainment, travel and tourism are major players in determining how Americans spend their spare time and money. These industries span the performing arts (dance, drama, and music), sports, books, movies, art, video games, and travel to various destinations for leisure-time pursuits.

TRAVEL AND TOURISM INDUSTRY

The travel and tourism industry generated $1.2 trillion and supported 7.6 million jobs in the U.S. in 2011. Travel and tourism spending also grew 3.5 percent, according to the U.S. Department of Commerce. The U.S. leads the world in revenues from international travel and tourism and ranks second in the number of international visitors, according to the government's *National Travel and Tourism Strategy* report. In 2011, sixty-two million international visitors came to the U.S. and spent a record $153 billion on U.S. travel- and tourism-related goods and services, which are counted as U.S. exports. The U.S. hopes to increase international visits to one hundred million by 2021 and bring in an estimated $250 billion.

Worldwide, the industry is predicted to account for one out of every ten jobs by 2022, according to the World Travel and Tourism Council.

Since tourism is big money, competition for both domestic and international visitors is extremely intense. Individual destinations, regions, states, and entire nations are aggressively marketing their own natural, historic and cultural offerings. Marketing and public relations are needed to keep visitors interested in visiting and returning.

Two traditional travel and tourism categories include business travel for meetings, conventions and exhibitions, training and incentive programs, and the leisure category for personal trips to visit family and friends, and destination trips, such as the time-honored beach vacation or trip to Disney.

Niche tourism has grown over time and can include virtually any interest as long as enough people are interested to make the promotion worthwhile. Destinations are creating suggested travel itineraries to cater to the special interests of these groups but also can add on new related ideas that might have an appeal. Here are a few trends in targeted tourism:

- **Food tourism**—As the Food Network and other forms of food entertainment grew, so did food tourism, which WorldFoodTravel.org described as "the pursuit and enjoyment of unique and memorable food and drink experiences, both far and near." One of the oldest forms of food tourism is the wine tour which connects wine lovers with a number of wineries for tasting sessions.
- **Ecotourism**—This type of tourism has been described as "responsible travel to natural areas that conserves the environment and improves the well-being of local people" by the International Ecotourism Society. TravelGreen.org, an organization developed by the U.S. Travel Association, expects eco-friendly opportunities to grow significantly in the future.
- **Shopping tourism**—Good deals, unique or better quality goods, and/or better shopping experiences encourage some to travel abroad or within their own countries to satisfy their consuming needs.
- **Medical tourism**—Healthcare costs and quality have inspired people who live in one country to travel to another country to receive medical, dental or surgical care at a more affordable price or better quality. Some people also travel to other cities within their own country for access to better facilities and physicians.
- **Historical and literary tourism**—These are more often found in older cities with rich histories. They can include tours based around literary or historical people, places and events.

Some of the key performance indicators used to track and evaluate the tourism industry include:

- Economic indicators related to travel spending, such as overnight visits through the hotel occupancy, average daily rates (ADR) and receipts from attractions; foreign visitors can be tracked through visas and other travel trends;
- Attraction receipts, attendance numbers;
- Airport, train traffic to destination;
- Customer satisfaction measured through customer satisfaction surveys and other feedback.

One consulting group, KWE Group, which specializes in luxury travel, recommended the following key ideas for marketing content for high-end tourists looking for a unique experience:

- Insider insights can help grow audiences; interviews, behind-the-scenes photos, and "a day in the life" stories can provide that sense of insider privilege that clients are looking for.
- Create rewards for Facebook likes and followers, which allows fans to become part of an inner circle; some hotels reward fans with periodic passwords that earn guests a surprising reward, such as room upgrade at check-in.
- Hold online events with limited attendance. This can be anything from a sneak preview video to early access to new stuff.
- Be invitation-only to increase your following for that sense of being "part of the club" feeling.
- Seek feedback through comments, contests and quizzes. The more you seek their opinions, the more they'll come back.

SPORTS AND ENTERTAINMENT INDUSTRY

Our society loves its leisure time; there are many business opportunities to market these commodities to their fullest. High-profile opportunities need creative and sophisticated marketing communication campaigns to generate buzz and fight for attention from the news and entertainment media.

Sports are a growing part of what Americans do with their spare time. Plunkett Research estimated that the entire industry in 2012, including equipment and apparel sales, could range from $375 to $435 billion annually.

In addition to the organized sporting industry, the National Sporting Goods Association reports that exercise walking is the most popular sports activity in America, with 97.1 million people participating. Exercising with equipment follows as a distant second at 55.5 million, then swimming at 45.0 million, overnight camping at 42.8 million, aerobic exercising at 42.0 million, bicycle riding at 39.1 million, and hiking also at 39.1 million.

Another sector of the entertainment industry worth mentioning is the entertainment software industry (computer and video games). According to the Entertainment Software Association, sales for computer and video games were $25 billion in 2011. Like Hollywood, these often elaborate games provide a true multimedia experience and require promotional activities much like a Hollywood movie blockbuster.

Beyond the sheer size of these industries and their economic impact on the economy, the entertainment and leisure industries must engage in marketing and public relations activities to maintain the business's or entity's reputation. The entertainment world's exciting dimension of star power adds a certain amount of

volatility, however. People can be all too human, and their foibles and eccentricities get top billing in the media. After all, inquiring minds want to know what is happening with red-carpet icons and sports stars. Entertainment companies hire public relations professionals to polish their reputation; celebrities have publicists who can also function as spokespeople, publicity agents, and special events coordinators.

Entertainment-related organizations are eager to attract consumer attention to spur sales of event tickets or merchandise. A marketing communication approach (see Chapter 7, "Consumer Relations") is used to create awareness and interest in the product. In addition to advertising, media relations and special event planning are major components of this coordinated communication effort.

Celebrities are, in reality, products that project their own image, and this image changes depending on what the celebrity does or doesn't do. In the textbook *Public Relations Strategies and Tactics,* the authors suggest the following for conducting a personality campaign:

1. **Interview the client.** This first step helps the publicist find "interesting and possibly newsworthy facts about the person's life, activities, and beliefs" that often are unrecognized by the individual for their publicity value.

2. **Prepare a biography of the client.** Based on the interview and other sources, assemble a short biography, with the most interesting or newsworthy information mentioned prominently so editors and producers can locate the information easily. Photos of the client and other material can be included in a media kit.

3. **Plan a marketing strategy.** Similar to any strategic marketing communication plan, identify the public relations goals and what audiences to reach.

4. **Conduct the campaign.** Based on the public relations goals and defined publics, the next step is to determine which tactics will meet the campaign's objectives. This includes news releases with hooks about the client's activities, interesting photographs of the client, public appearances, awards, and nicknames or labels.

The last three tactics are unique to celebrity promotion. Celebrities are often asked and paid to attend organizational events (i.e., public appearances) to generate interest in an event. The client may be asked to talk at a meeting or sign autographs and chat and pose for photographs with fans.

Awards given to the client also generate publicity. It is acceptable to put forward the name of a client for awards or even suggest that an award be created for the client. Some additional tactics include fans' clubs and a celebrity website with a blog, or Twitter, with musings directly from the celebrity, and other informational items. Another growing tactic is book-writing, such as Rolling Stone Keith Richard's *Life,* Justin Bieber's *First Step 2 Forever: My Story*, Kim Kardashian's *Kardashian Konfidential* or Jon Stewart's *The Daily Show with Jon Stewart Presents Earth: A Visitor's Guide to the Human Race*.

DAMAGE CONTROL

Under the relentless glare of the media spotlight, mistakes, misstatements and other gaffes that could potentially hurt or even ruin a celebrity's reputation are increasingly common. Fortunately, history shows time and again that fans usually forgive their celebrity heroes. Most realize that celebrities are human too and make mistakes. The celebrity apology is a frequent media phenomenon: Lance Armstrong's apology for doping, actress Kristen Stewart's apology to Robert Pattinson for cheating, and Apple CEO's apology to iPhone users for a dysfunctional Apple maps app.

According to *Public Relations Tactics and Strategies*, for celebrities in trouble

> *Experts suggest immediate response so that the momentum of subsequent stories is minimized. A brief, honest statement of regret for bad behavior or denial of rumors works well . . . Then the celebrity needs to disappear from sight and take care of personal matters.*

Most celebrity communication in these situations occurs through publicists who provide oral statements to reporters individually. There is usually no written record available. However, sometimes the celebrity will do the communicating himself/herself through a social media platform, such as Twitter.

CRISIS COMMUNICATION

Organizations that are inexorably connected to celebrities can be embroiled in controversy that requires more than damage control's quick-fix tactics. Consider these examples: Rush Limbaugh's on-air remarks about college co-ed Sandra Fluke, Tiger Woods' infidelities, and Olympian swimmer Michael Phelps' pot-smoking photo had immediate implications for their advertisers and sponsors. The tourism industry, as well, can be severely damaged by man-made and natural disasters such as massive oil leaks or monster hurricanes.

These major problems can cause considerable apprehension and sometimes even direct anger toward the organization involved. Customers and investors may shy away from once desirable destinations. Such incidents require a well-thought-out plan of action based on crisis communication and image repair principles.

Special concerns of the travel and tourism industry, according to *Public Relations Strategies and Tactics*, include addressing terrorism fears, the growing use of the Internet and social media to provide information and travel arrangements, and the appeals to target audiences, such as families and seniors.

Despite the problems with celebrities and the fickle nature of consumers whose attention does not seem to last that long, organizations will continue to seek out opportunities to partner with the next big thing—celebrity, destination, or sport. It's up to public relations practitioners to manage the entity's communication and reputations proactively, ethically, and responsibly.

23

Penn State Fumbles

Child Abuser Operates Undetected in Happy Valley

The Pennsylvania State University, a statewide network of twenty campuses, comprises about 95,000 students, 41,000 full- and part-time faculty and staff, and more than half a million living alumni. It has more Fulbright scholars than any other college; it conducts about $800 million in research annually. *The Wall Street Journal* has ranked Penn State grads among the most sought-after by top corporate recruiters. Penn State's annual dance marathon ("Thon") by 2012 had raised more than $89 million since 1977 for the Four Diamonds Fund at Penn State Hershey Children's Hospital, making it the largest student-run philanthropy in the world.

Its largest campus, University Park, located in the center of Pennsylvania, has about 45,000 students. Known for its small town atmosphere, the campus and town are located at the base of Mount Nittany and in what locals call "Happy Valley." It is a relatively secluded, tight-knit community.

THE NITTANY LIONS PRIMER

The Nittany Lion, the official mascot of the PSU athletic teams, is a legendary Pennsylvania mountain lion that once roamed Mount Nittany and the valleys of central Pennsylvania that eventually became the birthplace of the Pennsylvania State University, according to Penn State's website. Shortly after the turn of the twentieth century, the Nittany Lion began to represent the athletic spirit of the university.

Each home game offers a full-day experience that is touted as one of the best in the country. It starts with the huge tailgating party which often includes a trip to the Berkey Creamery for ice cream. The blue buses carrying the team slowly roll through the tailgating cook-outs where fans honk their horns and cheer their team. The game's creative show begins with the Blue Band's pre-game show that includes the "Floating Lions," alma mater, drum major flip, and the drumline's cadence to lead the band onto the field. There's also the dance team and many other entertaining activities.

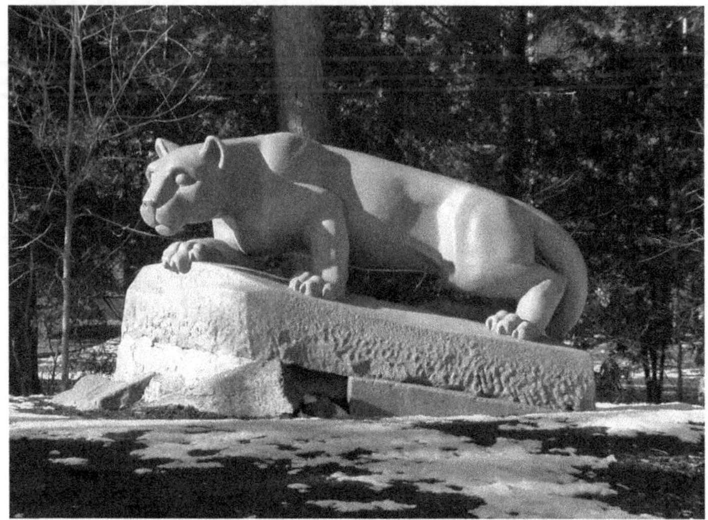

FIGURE 8.1 *The Nittany Lion.*
http://wikimedia.org/
Nathaniel C. Sheetz

FIGURE 8.2 *Penn State fans are among the most loyal and enthusiastic. One favorite tradition is the Penn State white-out where fans create a "white-out" for their team.*
© David Bergman/Corbis

Some of the game traditions include the home game "white-outs" when more than 107,000 screaming fans dressed in white (and some with white painted faces) cheer on the Nittany Lions. At big game moments, fans burst out singing "Zombie Nation" to deafening limits. Another favorite chant is the defiant "We Are Penn State." Another tradition is to protect the Lion Shrine, the massive limestone lion statue,

FIGURE 8.3 *In this September 4, 2004, file photo, Penn State coach Joe Paterno leads his team onto the field before an NCAA college football game against Akron in State College, Pa. Paterno, the longtime Penn State coach who won more games than anyone else in major college football but was fired amid a child sex abuse scandal that scarred his reputation for winning with integrity, died Sunday, January 22, 2012.* AP Photo/Carolyn Kaster

from any high jinks from visiting teams, such as painting it the color of the opposing team.

The team's uniforms are not flashy and there are no names on the backs because it's all about team effort on the field.

Finally, the top ritual for Penn State football fans was seeing its legendary coach Joe Paterno leading his team out onto the field, wearing his traditional khaki pants, sneakers, and iconic thick spectacles.

"JOEPA"

In 1950, Paterno began his Penn State career as a 23-year-old assistant football coach for the Nittany Lions. At the time, the University Park campus was known as a small agricultural college, a reputation that changed over time as the campus became a football powerhouse under Paterno's long reign as head football coach. Paterno led the Nittany Lions to two national championships and five undefeated seasons. He also held the title for most bowl victories—twenty-four—and was the "winningest" coach in the history of Division 1 college football with 409 victories in forty-six seasons, although the NCAA removed 111 of these wins after his death.

In Happy Valley, Paterno was truly beloved. His small frame, nerdy, Coke-bottle glasses, white socks, black sneakers, and high-tide trousers endeared him

FIGURE 8.4 *The seven-foot bronze statue in front of Beaver Stadium of Joe Paterno running onto the field with his players was an iconic site for football fans young and old.*
AP Photo/Gene J. Puskar

to generations of loyal players and fans. He lived in a modest four-bedroom home near campus, and he walked to work. His folksy ways, his generous nature (his family donated more than $4 million to the university), and his devotion to his players were evident. He also took academics seriously and called the dual emphasis on athletic and educational excellence his "Grand Experiment." The experiment worked; his players achieved an 89 percent graduation rate, remarkable for Division 1. Under "JoePa's" fatherly supervision, Penn State never had a serious NCAA sanction.

Penn State football was a major source of revenue, bringing in $53.2 million in profit in 2010, according to Forbes.com. Its stadium is the second largest in the western hemisphere with a capacity of 107,000 seats. Its separate football facilities added to its elite status on campus. A seven-foot bronze statue depicting Paterno running onto a field was erected in 2001 outside the stadium.

It is not surprising that football insiders noted that Paterno kept his job for sixty-one years by being tenacious and strong-willed. In fact, Penn State's president and athletic director were rebuffed in 2004 when they suggested that it might be time for Paterno to retire at age 77.

But all was not perfect. According to an ESPN report, forty-six players had been charged with 163 crimes from 2002 to 2008. An event in 2007, known as "the apartment incident" by many, involved up to two dozen football players who forced their way into an off-campus apartment party in which several students were severely beaten. The players who were arrested saw the charges dropped and just two players pleaded guilty to misdemeanor offenses.

The university's internal investigation into the apartment brawl did not result in any meaningful repercussions for players either. There had been a running power struggle between Paterno and Penn State's vice president of student affairs, Vicky Triponey, over disciplinary actions for football players, according to news media accounts. A *Wall Street Journal* article quoted a 2005 e-mail by Triponey, who summed up Paterno's views this way: he

> *believed she should have "no interest" (or business) holding our football players accountable to our community standards. The Coach is insistent he knows best how to discipline his players . . . and their status as a student when they commit violations of our standards should NOT be our concern . . . and I think he was saying we should treat football players different from our students in this regard.*

At one point, Paterno told administrators to fire Triponey or he would stop fundraising for the university, according to the *WSJ*. Paterno decided the punishment for the apartment brawl involving his players would be team members picking up trash at the stadium after each home game. Triponey resigned; some news reports said she was forced out. She later described the conduct of administrators (including the president) to the Daily Beast as "A blind sense of loyalty—not just at the top, but at all levels."

ESPN's *Outside the Lines* program ran a segment in 2008 that examined the large numbers of PSU football players charged with criminal offenses and Paterno's alleged interference with the internal investigations. Most media outlets did not challenge the deity status of Paterno.

JERRY SANDUSKY

Jerry Sandusky was the Nittany Lion's defensive coach for thirty-two years, including twenty-three years as coordinator. Often, Penn State was known as "Linebacker U" because of the number of Penn State National Football League linebackers it produced. Sandusky was thought to be Paterno's heir apparent until Paterno told him otherwise. Sandusky retired in 1999 at age 55 and said he would devote more time to his foundation. Called The Second Mile, it was a charity that worked with at-risk children. As part of his retirement package, Sandusky was given an office and full access to PSU's football facilities. Sandusky also began volunteering at Central Mountain High School, working with the football players in 2002. But his celebrity status with the Nittany Lions and his charitable and volunteer work masked a terrible secret. Sandusky was a serial sexual predator. As investigators later discovered, his victims were young vulnerable boys; Sandusky befriended them and gave them gifts, including access to Penn State football players and games. Over the years, he was frequently seen with young boys in public, behavior that was explained, at the time, by his charity work. Boys were also allowed to stay in Sandusky's home basement so he could spend more time helping the boys, who, people thought, were benefiting from a famous father figure.

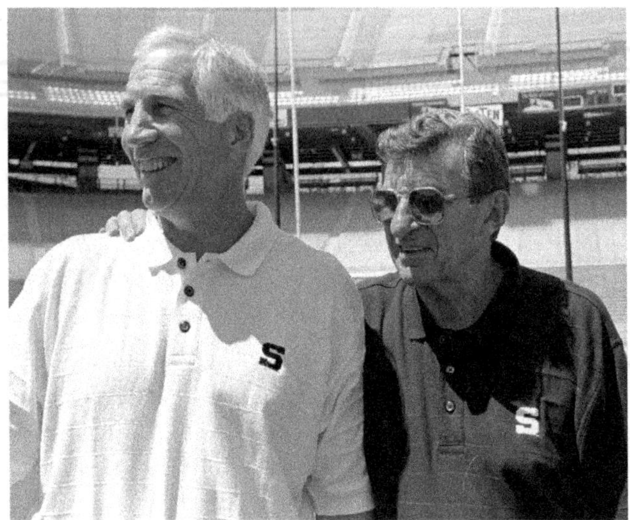

FIGURE 8.5 *In this August 6, 1999, file photo, Penn State head football coach Joe Paterno, right, poses with his defensive coordinator Jerry Sandusky during Penn State Media Day at State College, Pa.*
AUG. 6, 1999, FILE PHOTO Paul Vathis/Associated Press

THE GRAND JURY REPORT

On November 4, 2011, a Harrisburg, Pennsylvania, grand jury issued an explosive report based on a two-year investigation. It provided graphic detail of Sandusky's alleged criminal sexual behavior with eight boys over a fifteen-year period from 1994 to 2009. At least three incidents occurred at PSU football facilities; two of the PSU incidents were witnessed by employees. However, it was a boy's mother, not PSU, who ultimately started the investigation that stopped Sandusky. Sandusky was arrested on twenty-one felony counts for abusing eight boys.

The following information is derived from the grand jury report and focuses only on the initial victim and the PSU assaults.

A MOTHER'S CALL

The investigation began when a boy's mother called the high school in 2009 to report her son had been sexually assaulted by Sandusky. The school's football and wrestling coaches both attested to observing suspicious, but not abusive, behavior involving Sandusky and the boy. He had access to young boys at the school as a volunteer football coach and Second Mile mentor. Victim 1 was a participant in the Second Mile program. The report said that Sandusky had performed oral sex on the boy a number of times and had Victim 1 perform oral sex on Sandusky at least once.

In 1998 another mother, whose son was also in the Second Mile program, called the university police to report Sandusky had bear-hugged her 11-year-old boy in the PSU football shower. Investigators were allowed to eavesdrop on a conversation between the mother and Sandusky in which he admitted he had showered naked with her son: "I was wrong . . . I wish I were dead." The district attorney did not file charges and the investigation was closed.

Two other PSU Sandusky incidents, both witnessed by employees, were reported but no further investigation occurred. In 2000, a janitor saw Sandusky with "a young boy pinned up against the wall, performing oral sex on the boy." The janitor reported what he saw to his supervisor and other coworkers but no report was filed. They were afraid they would lose their jobs.

In 2002, Victim 2, a child of about 10 years whose identity is still unknown, was seen by Mike McQueary, a graduate assistant coach, "with his hands up against the wall, being subjected to anal intercourse by Sandusky" in the shower.

WHO KNEW WHAT AND WHEN

The grand jury's report explained in detail what Penn State officials said they knew and did with the information provided by McQueary.

McQueary immediately left the locker room and contacted his father. He was advised to visit Paterno, which McQueary did the next morning. After the meeting Paterno called Tim Curley, Penn State's athletic director and Paterno's immediate superior. They met the next day. Paterno told Curley that Sandusky had been seen "fondling or doing something of a sexual nature to a young boy." About ten days later, McQueary met with Curley and Gary Schultz, Penn State senior vice president, whose duties included overseeing the university police. McQueary told them he had "witnessed what he believed to be Sandusky having anal sex with a boy in the Lasch Building showers."

As a result of McQueary's report, Sandusky's keys to the locker room were confiscated, and he was prohibited from bringing children to campus. Curley also reported the incident to the director of the Second Mile program. Both Curley and Schultz confirmed that Penn State president Graham Spanier knew of the incident and approved of the steps taken. No one reported the incident to the university police or any other police agency or child protective service. There were no additional interviews with McQueary.

Both Curley and Schultz denied that McQueary told them that a child was raped. Instead they recalled that McQueary had seen "inappropriate conduct" or activity that made him "uncomfortable."

Schultz also testified that he was aware of the 1998 incident and the investigation conducted by a child protection agency.

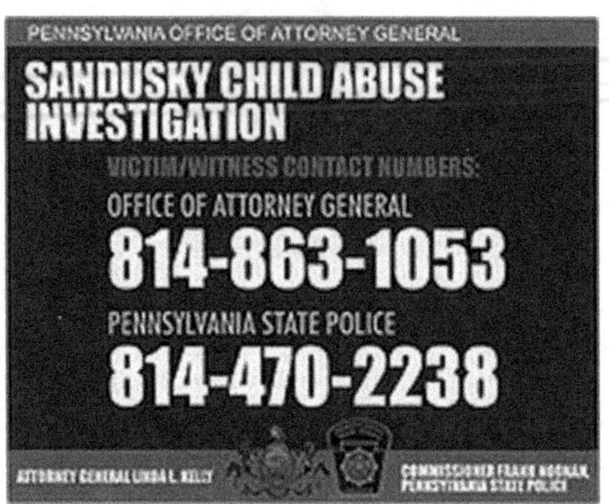

FIGURE 8.6 *On November 14, 2011, Pennsylvania Attorney General Linda Kelly made an appeal to the public for information related to the ongoing investigation into the case against former assistant football coach Jerry Sandusky.*
http://live.psu.edu/
PennState

Spanier testified he was told Sandusky was in the shower with a younger child and "they were horsing around." He denied that he was told the incident "was sexual in nature." He also denied knowing about the 1998 university police investigation.

Curley and Schultz were formally arraigned November 7, 2011, in Harrisburg on charges of perjury in testimony to the grand jury and failing to report the alleged abuse to the police or other authorities.

PSU'S RESPONSE

While the sports world was rocked by news of Penn State and Sandusky on November 5, 2011, the indictment and arrest came as no surprise to Penn State administrators. Paterno, Curley, Schultz, and Spanier had all testified, and even though grand jury proceedings are secret, people involved tend to talk. A reporter for Harrisburg's *Patriot-News* reported in detail the nature of the grand jury investigation as early as March 31, 2011, eight months before the grand jury's report was made public.

Still, Penn State's response was chaotic and insensitive to the victims as events quickly unfolded. President Spanier gave a statement that defended Curley and Schultz's actions:

> *The allegations about a former coach are troubling, and it is appropriate that they be investigated thoroughly. Protecting children requires the utmost vigilance.*
>
> *With regard to the other presentments, I wish to say that Tim Curley and Gary Schultz have my unconditional support. I have known and worked daily with Tim and Gary for more than 16 years. I have complete confidence in how they have handled the allegations about a former University employee.*

Tim Curley and Gary Schultz operate at the highest levels of honesty, integrity and compassion. I am confident the record will show that these charges are groundless and that they conducted themselves professionally and appropriately.

Steve Garban, chairman of the board of trustees, did not read the grand jury report until twenty-four hours after it was released, according to *The New York Times*.

On November 6, 2011, Paterno issued his own statement:

If true, the nature and amount of charges made are very shocking to me and all Penn Staters. While I did what I was supposed to with the one charge brought to my attention, like anyone else involved I can't help but be deeply saddened these matters are alleged to have occurred.

Sue and I have devoted our lives to helping young people reach their potential. The fact that someone we thought we knew might have harmed young people to this extent is deeply troubling. If this is true we were all fooled, along with scores of professionals trained in such things, and we grieve for the victims and their families. They are in our prayers.

As my grand jury testimony stated, I was informed in 2002 by an assistant coach that he had witnessed an incident in the shower of our locker room facility. It was obvious that the witness was distraught over what he saw, but he at no time related to me the very specific actions contained in the grand jury report. Regardless, it was clear that the witness saw something inappropriate involving Mr. Sandusky. As Coach Sandusky was retired from our coaching staff at that time, I referred the matter to university administrators.

I understand that people are upset and angry, but let's be fair and let the legal process unfold. In the meantime I would ask all Penn Staters to continue to trust in what that name represents, continue to pursue their lives every day with high ideals and not let these events shake their beliefs nor who they are.

On November 7, 2011, the board of trustees issued the following statement titled "Trustees Announce 2 Officials to Step Down While Case is Investigated:"

Following an executive session held Sunday night (Nov. 6), members of Penn State's Board of Trustees and President Graham Spanier received a request from athletic director Tim Curley to be placed on administrative leave so he can devote the time needed to defend himself against recent allegations by the Pennsylvania Attorney General. Gary Schultz, interim senior vice president for finance and business, will step down so that he also can defend himself and return to retirement.

Both men have been charged with failure to report and perjury. Both deny any wrongdoing.

"The board, along with the entire Penn State family, is shocked and saddened by the allegations involving former assistant coach Jerry Sandusky," said Steve Garban, chairman. "Under no circumstances does the University tolerate behavior that would put children at risk, and we are deeply troubled."

Sandusky retired from the University in 1999.

Schultz, who served as senior vice president of finance and business and University treasurer from 1993 until his retirement in 2009, recently returned to Penn State in an interim capacity to help the University transition as it fills the position. The University has been interviewing candidates for the post and expects to fill the position in the coming weeks.

Spanier said that Senior Associate Athletic Director Mark Sherburne will serve as interim athletic director until Curley's legal situation is resolved.

"The protection of children is of paramount importance," said Spanier. "The University will take a number of actions moving forward to increase the safety and security within our facilities and make everyone aware of the protocols in place for handling these issues."

Garban announced the following steps:

1. *The chair of the board will appoint a task force to engage external legal counsel to conduct an independent review of the University's policies and procedures related to the protection of children. This action is not intended to interfere with the ongoing judicial process;*
2. *Publicize the findings of the independent review;*
3. *Review with administrators police reporting protocols; and*
4. *Enhance educational programming around such topics.*

"Members of the Board of Trustees reinforced that Penn State is committed to honesty, integrity, and upholding the highest ideals," said Garban.

It wasn't until the third day of the crisis, November 9, 2011, that Penn State took action; Curley and Schultz were removed from their positions and the board issued its own statement:

The Board of Trustees of The Pennsylvania State University is outraged by the horrifying details contained in the Grand Jury Report. As parents, alumni and members of the Penn State Community, our hearts go out to all of those impacted by these terrible events, especially the tragedies involving children and their families. We cannot begin to express the combination of sorrow and anger that we feel about the allegations surrounding Jerry Sandusky. We hear those of you who feel betrayed and we want to assure all of you that the Board will take swift, decisive action.

At its regular meeting on Friday, November 11, 2011, the Board will appoint a Special Committee, members of which are currently being identified, to undertake a full and complete investigation of the circumstances that gave rise to the Grand Jury Report. This Special Committee will be commissioned to determine what failures occurred, who is responsible and what measures are necessary to insure that this never happens at our University again and that those responsible are held fully accountable. The Special Committee will have whatever resources are necessary to thoroughly fulfill its charge, including independent counsel and investigative teams, and there will be no restrictions placed on its scope or activities. Upon the completion of this investigation, a complete report will be presented at a future public session of the Board of Trustees.

Penn State has always strived for honesty, integrity and the highest moral standards in all of its programs. We will not tolerate any violation of these principles. We educate over 95,000 students every year and we take this responsibility very seriously. We are dedicated to protecting those who are placed in our care. We promise you that we are committed to restoring public trust in the University.

On Tuesday, November 8, 2011, the administration canceled Paterno's regular pre-game news conference one hour before its scheduled time. The action was seen by many as an indication that Paterno was on his way out.

The next day, Wednesday, November 9, 2011, Paterno announced his retirement without consulting the board:

I am absolutely devastated by the developments in this case. I grieve for the children and their families, and I pray for their comfort and relief.

I have come to work every day for the last 61 years with one clear goal in mind: To serve the best interests of this university and the young men who have been entrusted to my care. I have the same goal today.

That's why I have decided to announce my retirement effective at the end of this season. At this moment the Board of Trustees should not spend a single minute discussing my status. They have far more important matters to address. I want to make this as easy for them as I possibly can. This is a tragedy. It is one of the great sorrows of my life. With the benefit of hindsight, I wish I had done more.

My goals now are to keep my commitments to my players and staff and finish the season with dignity and determination. And then I will spend the rest of my life doing everything I can to help this University.

However, the board had decided on a different path. It fired Paterno and Penn State President Spanier for failing to do more for the victims when they had the opportunity. It had already decided to fire Spanier, and by 10 p.m. it had made the same decision about Paterno. According to *The New York Times*, the board thought delivering the news by phone was the best and safest option. *The Times* said that Paterno hung up after the news was delivered.

What followed was an outpouring of emotions from supporters of Paterno and Penn State who didn't understand the board's actions. Students filled the streets protesting that Paterno was not allowed to finish the season and some gathered at Paterno's home shouting their support.

Paterno came out on his porch with his wife and said a few words to students:

I wanted to say hello to all these great students . . . hey, look, get a good night's sleep. Study . . . alright? We still got things to do, alright? I'm out of it maybe now. The phone call put me ahead of it but we'll go from there, okay? Goodnight everybody. Good luck everybody. And thanks a lot.

Also that night, Spanier issued a statement:

It has been my great privilege and honor to serve Penn State for more than 25 years, including the past 16 as president. I have said before that the position I occupy is the dream job in American higher education, and I am proud of what we have all done together to advance our programs, support our students, and enhance pride in our institution.

Our great university has been rocked by serious charges against a former coach. The presentment by the Attorney General describes acts that should never be tolerated or ignored. I was stunned and outraged to learn that any predatory act might have occurred in a University facility or by someone associated with the University.

I am heartbroken to think that any child may have been hurt and have deep convictions about the need to protect children and youth. My heartfelt sympathies go out to all those who may have been victimized. I would never hesitate to report a crime if I had any suspicion that one had been committed.

The acts of no one person should define this university. Penn State is defined by the traditions, loyalty and integrity of hundreds of thousands of students, alumni and employees.

Penn State and its Board of Trustees are in the throes of dealing with and recovering from this crisis, and there is wisdom in a transition in leadership so that there are no distractions in allowing the University to move forward.

This University is a large and complex institution, and although I have always acted honorably and in the best interests of the University, the buck stops here. In this situation, I believe it is in the best interests of the University to give my successor a clear path for resolving the issues before us.

I will always value the wonderful relationships that I have developed with the many thousands of Penn Staters, community leaders and members of the higher education community throughout the country. I will continue to serve the University in every way possible and celebrate the greatness of Penn State.

THE PUSH FOR TRANSPARENCY

The new PSU board of trustees chairman, Karen Peetz, provided remarks at the January 20, 2012, board meeting that described the board's three new core values: justice for abuse victims, increased transparency, and balance between athletics and academics. Regarding transparency she said:

the board will increase our own transparency with the public as well as work with President Erickson to improve the entire University's openness. President Erickson has already begun this process through town hall meetings with alumni. I and other members of the board will begin holding similar town hall meetings with students, faculty, and alumni later in the year. The more we learn, the more we can communicate our thoughts, the better.

In addition, the board is going to form our own task force to examine our governance and determine whether we can make changes that would improve our oversight of the University as well as our accessibility to it. We will certainly take into account what we hear from the University community.

Three weeks later, on February 13, 2012, Penn State President Rodney Erickson and the university's board of trustees announced the creation of a new Openness

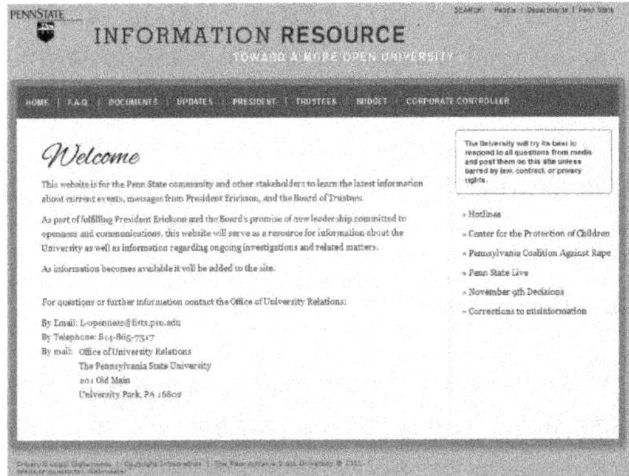

FIGURE 8.7 *This "openness" website was established during the crisis to provide information to stakeholders.*
http://openness.psu.edu/
PennState

website at http://openness.psu.edu. "This is a reminder of the commitment to open communication to the fullest extent possible," said Erickson.

The site provided its stakeholders answers to their questions regarding ongoing investigations and related matters. "This new website represents reform and change and our commitment to improve the University's openness with the public," said Karen Peetz, chairwoman of the board.

The website has information under various categories: Frequently Asked Questions, Documents, Updates, and Messages from the President of the University and Board of Trustees. The site also includes links to the university budget office, right-to-know information, hotlines, and several other sources.

Four months after the November 9, 2011, decision to fire Paterno and Spanier, the PSU board of trustees explained its decision regarding Paterno's and Spanier's firing in a report:

> **The removal of Graham Spanier as Penn State president and Joe Paterno as football coach**
>
> *The Pennsylvania State University Board of Trustees has been asked by members of the Penn State community, including students, faculty, staff and alumni, to state clearly its reasons for the difficult decisions that were made unanimously on the evening of Nov. 9, 2011—to remove Graham Spanier as president of the University and Joe Paterno as head football coach for the remaining three games of the 2011 season. Our decisions were guided by our obligation as Trustees, always, to put the interests of the University first.*
>
> *We share the grief of the entire Penn State family at the passing of Coach Paterno. We also continue to respect and appreciate Dr. Spanier's and Coach Paterno's lasting contributions to Penn State. We especially honor the great legacy of Coach Paterno in*

making his football program a model for his emphasis on academic as well as athletic performance and for his generous support of Penn State through the years.

We offer this report guided by one overriding commitment going forward—to remember the children who may have been victims of sexual abuse on or near the University Park campus over the last 10 or more years and to support their healing process as best we can.

President Graham Spanier

We determined on Nov. 9 that Dr. Spanier should be removed because he failed to meet his leadership responsibilities to the Board and took insufficient action after learning of a 2002 incident involving former assistant coach Jerry Sandusky and a young boy in a Penn State facility. This failure of leadership included insufficiently informing the Board about his knowledge of the 2002 incident. He also made or was involved in press announcements between Nov. 5–9 that were without authorization of the Board or contrary to its instructions.

On Nov. 9, Dr. Spanier asked the Board for a vote of confidence. Since for the reasons cited above we were unable to provide it, we voted that evening unanimously to remove him as president and informed him of that decision. Dr. Spanier remains a tenured professor at Penn State.

Coach Joe Paterno

Also on Nov. 9, the Board unanimously made the decision to remove Coach Paterno for the last three games of the season. He had announced earlier that day that he would be retiring at the end of the season. Our most important reason—by far—for this difficult decision flowed from what we learned on Nov. 5, for the first time, from a "presentment" (report) by a Pennsylvania Grand Jury about Coach Paterno's early 2011 sworn testimony.

The report stated that a Penn State graduate assistant had gone to Coach Paterno's home on Saturday morning, March 2, 2002. The report quoted Coach Paterno as testifying to the Grand Jury that the graduate assistant told him that he had seen Jerry Sandusky, the coach's former assistant coach up to 1999, "in the Lasch Building showers fondling or doing something of a sexual nature to a young boy."

While Coach Paterno did his legal duty by reporting that information the next day, Sunday, March 3, to his immediate superior, the then Penn State Athletic Director Tim Curley, the Board reasonably inferred that he did not call police. We determined that his decision to do his minimum legal duty and not to do more to follow up constituted a failure of leadership by Coach Paterno.

The Board spent hours on conference calls between Saturday, Nov. 5, and Tuesday, Nov. 8, discussing appropriate action and our fiduciary responsibility as the Trustees. On Wednesday evening, Nov. 9, we met in person in State College. At about 9 pm, we unanimously made the difficult decision that Coach Paterno's failure of leadership required his removal as football coach.

We are sorry for the unfortunate way we had to deliver the news on the telephone about an hour later to Coach Paterno. However, we saw no better alternative. Because Coach Paterno's home was surrounded by media representatives, photographers and others, we did not believe there was a dignified, private and secure way to send Board representatives to meet with him there. Nor did we believe it would be wise to wait until the next morning, since we believed it was probable that Coach Paterno would hear the news beforehand from other sources, which would be inappropriate.

Thus, we sent a representative of the Athletic Department to ask Coach Paterno to call us. When the coach called, the Board member who received the call planned to tell him that (1) the Board had decided unanimously to remove him as coach; (2) the Board regretted having to deliver the message over the telephone; and (3) his employment contract would continue, including all financial benefits and his continued status as a tenured faculty member. However, after this Board member communicated the first message, Coach Paterno ended the call, so the second and third messages could not be delivered.

Penn State announced April 25, 2012, that it had hired two firms, Edelman, the world's largest public relations firm, and La Torre Communications, a public relations and public affairs firm based in Harrisburg, Pennsylvania, to assist with its corporate communications, media relations, and stakeholder engagement. In a statement, PSU said:

The primary objective of this work is to ensure broader and more transparent communications with key Penn State stakeholders, including current and prospective students, alumni, faculty and staff, parents, local communities, and state and national media. The firms also will support the University throughout upcoming litigation, ensuring rapid and accurate dissemination of information to the extent possible given the ongoing investigations.

"Earlier this year, I announced five promises to guide Penn State in recovery from our recent crisis and rebuild trust with the Penn State community," said Penn State President Rodney Erickson. "Retaining these communications firms puts us more firmly on the path toward accountability, openness and preserving our reputation as one of the world's leading research universities."

This move ensures Penn State will have a comprehensive communications infrastructure with significant expertise within Pennsylvania and across the country.

The board of trustees announced May 16, 2012, that it had launched a new website. Karen Peetz, chair of the board of trustees, said in a statement: "This is, of course, a continuation of the board's pledge for openness and for providing more and better information to the Penn State community and beyond. It's an ongoing process."

On June 4, 2012, PSU President Erickson announced the relaunch of the Openness website, renamed "Progress" (http://progress.psu.edu). Here's what part of the statement said:

The new version of the website is the next step in the University's work to ensure broader communications with key Penn State stakeholders, including current and

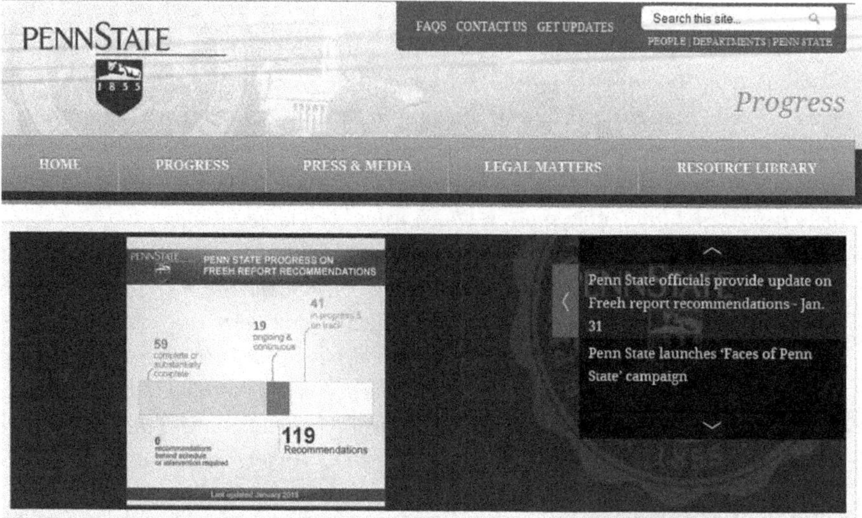

Feb 10, 2013

Freeh investigation findings used to improve Penn State operations

In November 2011, the Penn State Board of Trustees appointed former FBI director and federal Judge Louis Freeh to conduct an independent investigation of the University's response to the allegations of sexual abuse committed by former Penn State assistant coach Jerry Sandusky. The goal of this investigation was to uncover facts and identify where failures occurred in the University's governance and compliance structure and to make recommendations to help ensure that such failures never happen again. This was an internal investigation into Penn State's response to the allegations.

It was not within the scope of Judge Freeh's engagement to review the actions, motives or functions of entities outside of our University community. This was an internal investigation into Penn State's response to the allegations, and that is how the University has utilized the report.

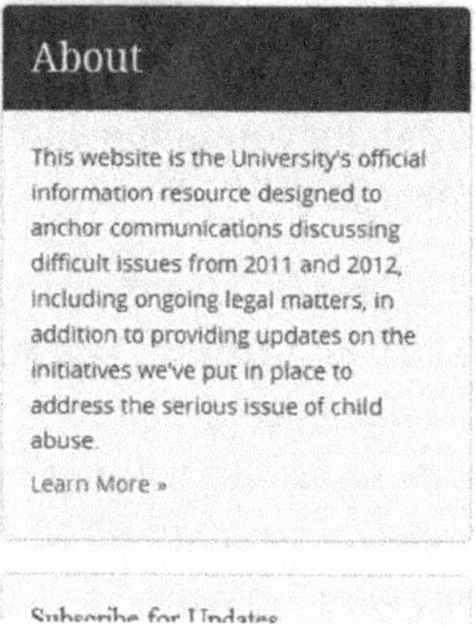

FIGURE 8.8 *A new website was launched June 4, 2012, called Progress, which shared information about the ongoing investigations and corrective actions.*
http://progress.psu.edu/
PennState

prospective students and their families, alumni, faculty and staff, local communities, and state and national media. The Progress website includes new functionality and features that make it easier to find, receive and share information.

"This is the next iteration of our information resource that is designed to anchor communications discussing difficult issues from the last year, including ongoing legal matters, in addition to providing updates on the initiatives we've put in place to address the serious issue of child abuse," said Penn State President Rodney Erickson. "This step is a natural progression of our original website and will help keep the Penn State community informed on the important work and progress taking place."

REORIENTING THE CULTURE

Debate continued regarding the role of Paterno in the crisis. Many could not believe that "JoePa" could have erred. After all, he had been head coach for nearly forty-six seasons without a single major scandal. And, he did report the alleged abuse to the proper administrators. Some thought that the victims had come forward to cash in from future litigation.

Abuse experts explained that abused children often don't report abuse because they are embarrassed, confused, and are afraid they won't be believed. Serial sexual child predators, experts said, are often well-liked individuals in positions of authority with access to children.

There were similar parallels to the Catholic Church abuse scandal. Many church supporters found it difficult to believe that priests who were in positions of respect, authority and responsibility did not protect those in their care.

At the height of the scandal, on November 11, 2011, the board of trustees and Penn State's new president, Erickson, provided some much-needed direction and action. In a statement to the Penn State community, Erickson said that he and others would "begin to rebuild the confidence and trust that has been shaken this past week" and offered five specific promises:

1. He would "reinforce to the entire Penn State community the moral imperative of doing the right thing—the first time, every time." This would include appointing an ethics officer, reporting directly to the president, who would

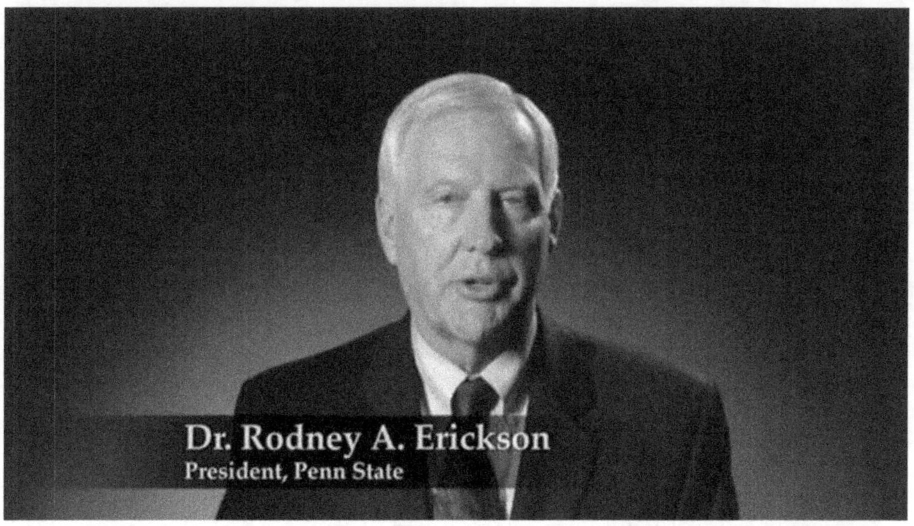

FIGURE 8.9 *Dr. Rodney Erickson, president of Penn State, developed three thirty-second videos during the crisis period that reassured viewers that Penn State would move forward to solve its problems.*
http://progress.psu.edu/
Penn State

review all standards, policies, and programs to meet "not only the law, but Penn State's standard." He also said he would "reorient" Penn State's culture to ensure no one would "feel scared to do the right thing. My door will always be open."

2. He would "lead by example" and would "expect no less of others."
3. There would be more transparency including updates about the investigations. He would provide frequent updates, dialogue with key stakeholders.
4. Everyone would be "respectful and sensitive to the victims and their families." Penn State would "seek appropriate ways to foster healing and raise broader awareness of the issue of sexual abuse."
5. The administration would completely support the Special Committee's investigation work and recommendations which would be led by trustees Ken Frazier, president, chief executive officer of Merck & Co. Inc., and Ronald Tomalis, state education secretary.

Erickson also provided a thirty-second video message that day:

> *This has been one of the saddest weeks in the history of Penn State and my heart goes out to those who have been victimized; I share your anger and sorrow. Although we cannot go back to business as usual our university must move forward. We are a community. Our work is as vital as ever. We remain committed to our core values and we will rebuild the trust, honor and pride that have endured for generations. Please join me in this effort. We are Penn State.*

AFTERMATH

Penn State lost its final 2011 season home game, against Nebraska, without Paterno in his usual spot. Fans wore blue to show support for victims of child abuse, and there was a pre-game moment of silence for the alleged victims of abuse, which *Sports Illustrated* noted was "at once poignant and sadly ironic, given the role silence played in aiding the unfathomable."

Later, Erickson met with students and held town hall meetings with alumni groups in Pittsburgh, New York, and Philadelphia to gather input on Penn State's future direction and explain what was happening.

After criticism from the Penn State Faculty Senate that PSU's own investigation needed to be independent, on November 21, 2011, Penn State announced that it had hired Judge Louis Freeh and his firm to conduct an independent, external investigation. Freeh, a former FBI director and federal judge, would report his findings to the board of trustees special committee led by Frazier. The findings would be made public and Freeh said no one would be "above scrutiny."

The Pennsylvania Attorney General announced new charges against Sandusky on December 7, 2011.

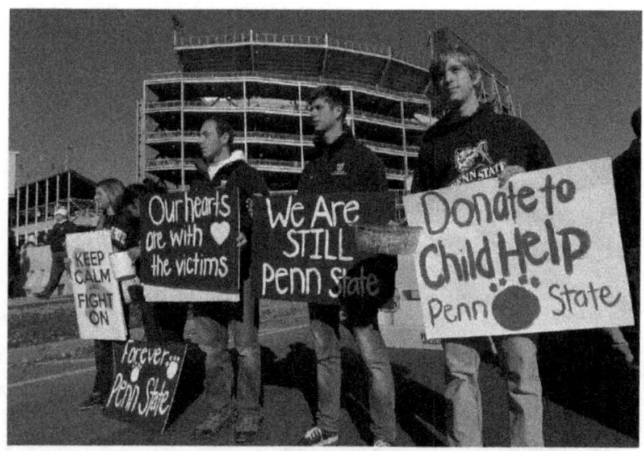

FIGURE 8.10 *A group of students at Penn State collect money for childhelpusa.org outside Beaver Stadium before an NCAA college football game against Nebraska Saturday, November 12, 2011, in State College, Pa. Penn State was playing for the first time in decades without former head coach Joe Paterno, after he was fired in the wake of a child sex abuse scandal involving a former assistant coach.*
AP Photo/Alex Brandon

FINDINGS

The most saddening finding by the Special Investigative Counsel is the total and consistent disregard by the most senior leaders at Penn State for the safety and welfare of Sandusky's child victims. As the Grand Jury similarly noted in its presentment,[1] there was no "attempt to investigate, to identify Victim 2, or to protect that child or any others from similar conduct except as related to preventing its re-occurrence on University property."

Four of the most powerful people at The Pennsylvania State University – President Graham B. Spanier, Senior Vice President-Finance and Business Gary C. Schultz, Athletic Director Timothy M. Curley and Head Football Coach Joseph V. Paterno – failed to protect against a child sexual predator harming children for over a decade. These men concealed Sandusky's activities from the Board of Trustees, the University community and authorities. They exhibited a striking lack of empathy for Sandusky's victims by failing to inquire as to their safety and well-being, especially by not attempting to determine the identity of the child who Sandusky assaulted in the Lasch Building in 2001. Further, they exposed this child to additional harm by alerting

FIGURE 8.11 *An excerpt from the independent investigative report by Louis Freeh and his law firm.*
http://progress.psu.edu/
PennState

FIGURE 8.12 *A web page was developed to provide information relating to the Freeh investigative report.*
http://progress.psu.edu/
PennState

The next day, Penn State said it would create the Center for the Protection of Children and partner with Pennsylvania Coalition Against Rape for education and outreach. Both efforts would be funded from football revenues.

A faculty-led, university institute for the study and treatment of child abuse was proposed, according to Erickson's January report to the board of trustees. He also reported that a Sexual Assault and Relationship Violence hotline was established "so abuse or suspected abuse can be reported anonymously."

There were dozens of activities and actions in the intervening months that showed the university's commitment to protecting its vulnerable populations and ensuring that the events that had led to the scandal would not be repeated. For example, by April 17, 2012, the university had revised significantly its policy overseeing the supervision and treatment of minors involved in university-sponsored programs or programs housed or held at any Penn State campus. The school's students launched a drive to fight child sexual abuse called "One Heart," and workshops to discuss kids' sexual health and safety were promoted. And alumni and students raised more than $528,000 for a national anti-sexual violence organization.

A few months after Paterno was fired, Bill O'Brien, offensive coordinator for the New England Patriots, was appointed the new head coach of the Nittany Lions. Paterno died January 22, 2012, of lung cancer, which was diagnosed soon after his firing.

On June 22, 2012, Sandusky was found guilty of forty-five out of forty-eight counts of child sexual abuse against ten boys. He received a thirty- to sixty-year sentence and was remanded to Greene State Prison. He maintained his innocence throughout the scandal.

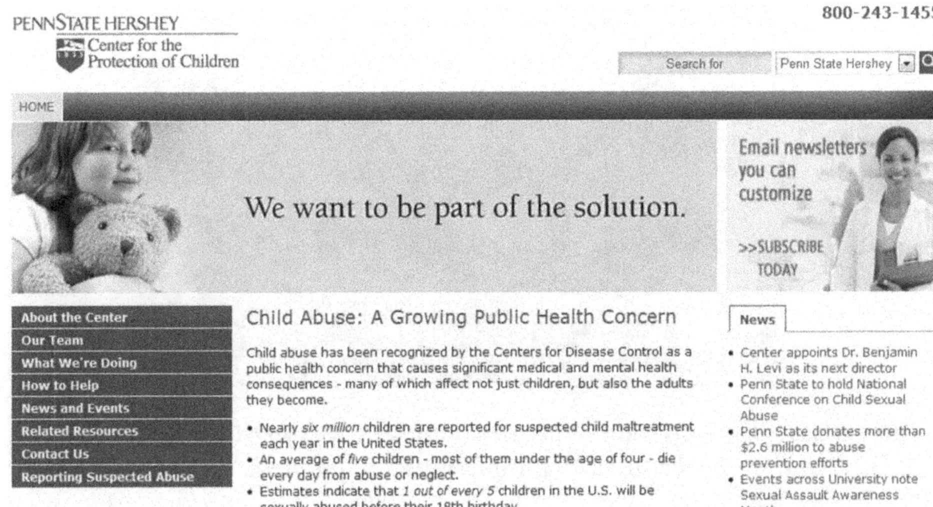

PENNSTATE HERSHEY
Center for the Protection of Children
800-243-1455
Search for
Penn State Hershey
HOME
We want to be part of the solution.
Email newsletters you can customize
>>SUBSCRIBE TODAY
About the Center
Our Team
What We're Doing
How to Help
News and Events
Related Resources
Contact Us
Reporting Suspected Abuse
Child Abuse: A Growing Public Health Concern
Child abuse has been recognized by the Centers for Disease Control as a public health concern that causes significant medical and mental health consequences - many of which affect not just children, but also the adults they become.
• Nearly six million children are reported for suspected child maltreatment each year in the United States.
• An average of five children - most of them under the age of four - die every day from abuse or neglect.
• Estimates indicate that 1 out of every 5 children in the U.S. will be sexually abused before their 18th birthday.
News
• Center appoints Dr. Benjamin H. Levi as its next director
• Penn State to hold National Conference on Child Sexual Abuse
• Penn State donates more than $2.6 million to abuse prevention efforts
• Events across University note Sexual Assault Awareness Month

FIGURE 8.13 *Launched in December 2011, a month after the scandal began, the Center for the Protection of Children brings together an interdisciplinary group of Penn State clinicians and researchers who are well respected for their achievements in the field of child abuse.*
http://www.pennstatehershey.org/
PennStateHershey.org

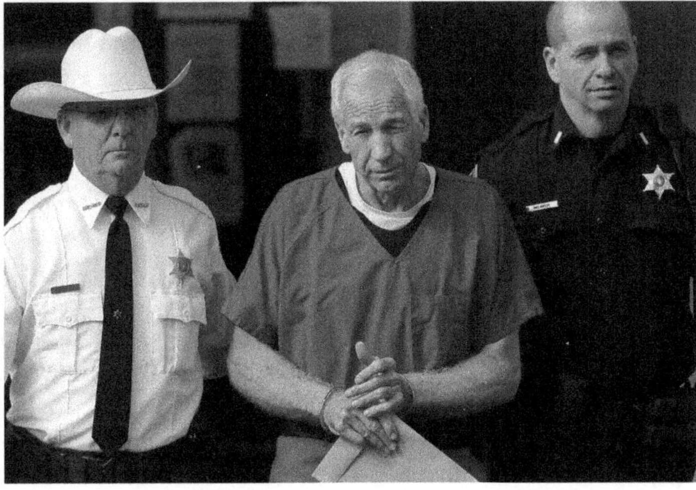

FIGURE 8.14 *Jerry Sandusky, former Penn State University assistant football coach, was sentenced to thirty to sixty years in prison for child sexual abuse October 9, 2012.*
AP Photo/Matt Rourke

FIGURE 8.15 *The Paterno statue was hauled away after the crisis had passed and a new Penn State president was appointed.*
AP Photo/Centre Daily Times, Christopher Weddle

Leaked e-mails, first reported by CNN, surfaced months after the grand jury report that indicated Curley and Schultz knew about the negative legal consequences if they did not report what McQueary had seen. The e-mails included Paterno and Spanier. Critics predicted future legal action against Spanier, Paterno's estate, The Second Mile program and Penn State. By November 1, 2011, Schultz and Curley were charged with perjury, obstruction of justice, endangering the welfare of children, criminal conspiracy, and failure to report suspected child abuse. Spanier was charged a year later on similar charges. The trail of these high-level officials would surely keep the scandal—and Penn State—in the news for months to come.

The most symbolic action was the unceremonious removal of the famed Joe Paterno seven-foot tall bronze statue in front of Beaver Stadium a few weeks after the release of Freeh's devastating independent investigative report July 12, 2012. PSU President Erickson provided the following statement explaining the removal of the statue, while keeping Paterno's name attached to the library, to the news media:

> *Since we learned of the Grand Jury presentment and the charges against Jerry Sandusky and University officials last November, members of the Penn State community and the public have been made much more acutely aware of the tragedy of child sexual abuse. Our thoughts and prayers continue to go out to those victims of Mr. Sandusky and all other victims of child abuse. I assure you that Penn State will take a national leadership role in the detection and prevention of child maltreatment in the months and years ahead.*
>
> *With the release of Judge Freeh's Report of the Special Investigative Counsel, we as a community have had to confront a failure of leadership at many levels. The statue of Joe Paterno outside Beaver Stadium has become a lightning rod of controversy and national debate, including the role of big time sports in university life. The Freeh Report has given us a great deal to reflect upon and to consider, including Coach Paterno's legacy.*

Throughout Penn State, the two most visible memorials to Coach Paterno are the statue at Beaver Stadium and the Paterno Library. The future of these two landmarks has been the topic of heated debate and many messages have been received in various University offices, including my own. We have heard from numerous segments of the Penn State community and others, many of whom have differing opinions. These are particularly important decisions when considering things that memorialize such a revered figure.

I now believe that, contrary to its original intention, Coach Paterno's statue has become a source of division and an obstacle to healing in our University and beyond. For that reason, I have decided that it is in the best interest of our university and public safety to remove the statue and store it in a secure location. I believe that, were it to remain, the statue will be a recurring wound to the multitude of individuals across the nation and beyond who have been the victims of child abuse.

On the other hand, the Paterno Library symbolizes the substantial and lasting contributions to the academic life and educational excellence that the Paterno family has made to Penn State University. The library remains a tribute to Joe and Sue Paterno's commitment to Penn State's student body and academic success, and it highlights the positive impacts Coach Paterno had on the University. Thus I feel strongly that the library's name should remain unchanged.

Coach Paterno's positive impact over the years and everything he did for this University predate his statue. At the same time it is true that our institution's excellence cannot be attributed to any one person or to athletics. Rather, Penn State is defined by our actions and accomplishments as a learning community. Penn State has long been an outstanding academic institution and we will continue to be.

The world will be watching how Penn State addresses its challenges in the days ahead. While some may take issue with the decisions I have made, I trust that everyone associated with our University will respond in a civil and respectful manner.

I fully realize that my decision will not be popular in some Penn State circles, but I am certain it is the right and principled decision. I believe we have chosen a course that both recognizes the many contributions that Joe Paterno made to the academic life of our University, while taking seriously the conclusions of the Freeh Report and the national issue of child sexual abuse. Today, as every day, our hearts go out to the victims.

An NCAA probe launched soon after the scandal went public released its investigative ruling implicating Penn State for "hero worship" and a warped athletic culture. On July 23, 2012, the NCAA imposed a four-year postseason ban from bowl games, massive scholarship reductions, a vacation of all Penn State's victories from 1998 through 2011, and a $60 million fine spread over five years. This amount was equal to the average annual gross revenue of the football program. Pennsylvania's Governor Tom Corbett filed suit to dismiss the penalties.

By December 2012, the university admitted that it had spent $41 million on costs associated with the scandal, including $8.1 million for the Freeh investigation. This did not include the settlements with the victims of Sandusky's sexual abuse which could rise to as many as thirty victims, from the original ten identified in the district attorney's investigation. Another lawsuit was filed against the university by McQueary, the former assistant football coach, who witnessed some of the abuse by Sandusky. He claimed that the university had defamed him during the controversy.

Mark Emmert, the president of NCAA, said:

> *We hope we would never, ever see anything of this magnitude or egregiousness again in our lives. But we do have to make sure that the cautionary tale of athletics overwhelming core values of the institution and losing sight of why we are really participating in these activities can occur. That's the balance that every university needs to strive for.*

Beyond the impact on the team, legal actions by victims would go on for years.

Clearly, Penn State would be haunted for years to come by the scandal. Some said Happy Valley had lost its innocence while others said it had fumbled badly when it came to protecting its own children.

QUESTIONS FOR DISCUSSION

1. What was the football culture like at Penn State?
2. What were some early signs that the football team and its head coach Joe Paterno were not in alignment with expectations that other programs followed at Penn State?
3. Head coach Joe Paterno was considered a power unto himself at Penn State. What was the responsibility of the board of trustees and the administration for maintaining control over the athletic program?
4. When did Penn State know about the grand jury proceedings?
5. In what way was Penn State's initial response to the grand jury report insensitive to the alleged victims?
6. Explain how the board of trustees' new chairwoman Karen Peetz provided leadership in PSU's recovery from the scandal. What were the key elements of her statement regarding transparency in the recovery process?
7. Why is transparency important during the recovery process?
8. What other actions did the board of trustees and the new president take to recover from the scandal? What were the most effective steps?

Dig Deeper

For more background on this case, read the grand jury report on Jerry Sandusky and the Sandusky criminal complaint available on the textbook's companion website.

When Graham Spanier, president of Penn State, was removed November 9, 2011, Executive Vice President and Provost Rodney Erickson was named the interim president. Review the following videos and documents, available on the textbook's companion website. Assess the efforts of President Erickson to start the rebuilding efforts for PSU:

11.10.11 *A Message from Rodney Erickson* (video)

11.10.11 A message from Rodney Erickson (statement)

11.16.11 A message to students (statement)

11.17.11 *A Message of Appreciation from Dr Erickson* (video)

11.21.11 A message from President Dr Rodney Erickson (statement)

11.23.11 *A Message from Dr Rodney Erickson* (video)

12.13.11 A message from President Rodney Erickson (statement)

- PSU actions fact sheet
- Grand jury report
- Sandusky criminal complaints 2011.

24

Rush to Judgment

Advertisers Flee Conservative Radio Show after Crude Remarks

Politics and its accompanying gamesmanship were on full display during a debate that contained a potpourri of hot-button issues: government power, religious freedom, women's rights—and sex. The cast of characters included elected officials—Democrats and Republicans—a law school student and Rush Limbaugh, the nation's most popular conservative radio commentator. When the dust settled, Limbaugh's program had lost advertising support and gained what it needs to thrive: publicity.

RUSH LIMBAUGH

Rush Limbaugh, the immensely popular conservative talk show host, has dominated AM radio since the mid-1980s. His daily three-hour program reaches millions via 600 radio stations. A leading figure in the national conservative movement, Limbaugh is credited with influencing Republican politics and policies; he has built a loyal following and an equally lengthy list of detractors by delivering the conservative message in an entertaining and dramatic way.

The program consists of Limbaugh holding forth on a variety of current political and cultural topics, supportive callers agreeing with his positions, and occasional interviews with well-known conservative figures. Among his favorite targets are Democrats, the "liberal mainstream" news media, Republicans he deems are not conservative enough, bloated government agencies, and "liberal" movie stars and activists. In one instance, Limbaugh took on actor Michael J. Fox, who has Parkinson's disease, for his appearance in an advocacy commercial supporting stem cell research; he said Fox's involuntary muscular movements were either an act or he had purposely not taken his medication. Limbaugh later apologized for the comment.

Limbaugh and the program have developed a sardonic vocabulary: outspoken feminists are described as "feminazis" and those who give in to the "liberal agenda" are "the new Castrati." Callers who say they agree with everything Limbaugh

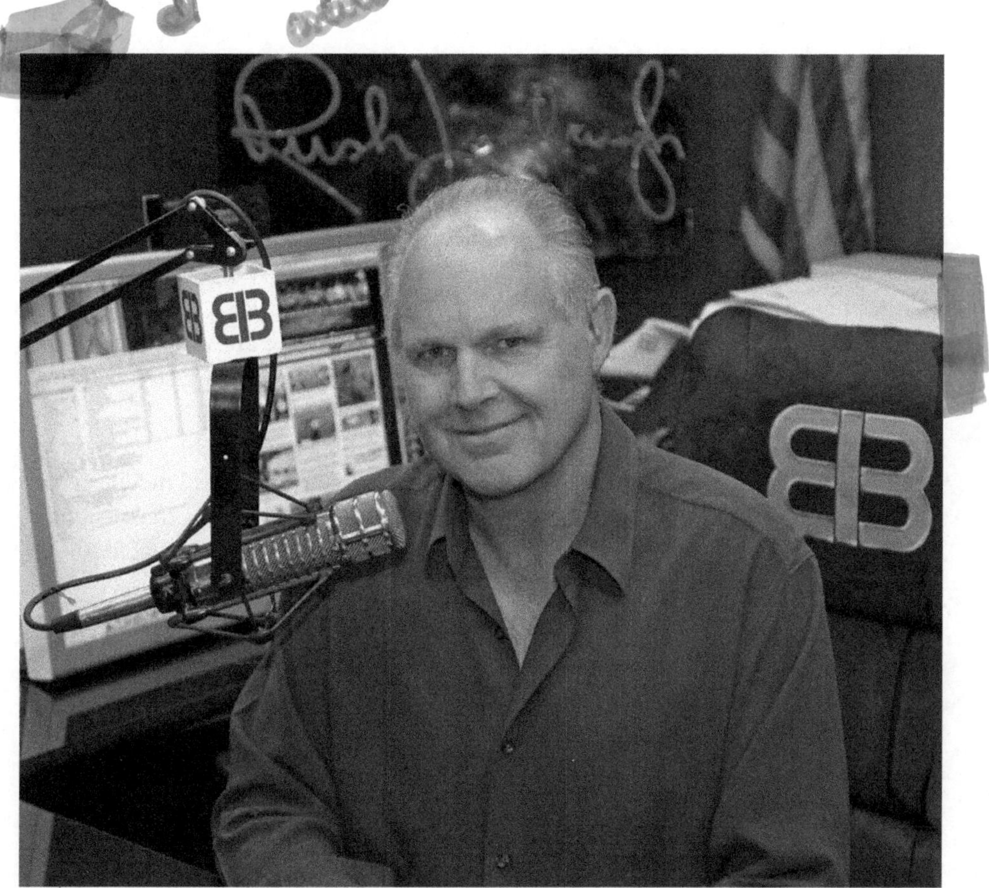

FIGURE 8.16 *This photo provided by Rush Limbaugh shows Limbaugh in his Palm Beach, Fla., radio studio, September 2009.*
See note on Copyright Holder
Photo Courtesy of Rush Limbaugh/AP

says, and everything he espouses, proclaim themselves "ditto-heads." In his on-air persona, Limbaugh alternates between thundering denunciations of his targets and self-mockery. He is, he says, a "harmless, loveable little fuzzball and all-around good guy" using "talent on loan from God," conducting his show "with half my brain tied behind my back just to make it fair."

While some view him as an entertainer, Limbaugh has built a commercial empire; he has authored best-selling books and at one time hosted a TV version of his program. Still, the centerpiece of his persona and his business success remains his weekday radio program. He reportedly signed a contract for $400 million in 2008 through 2016 with Clear Channel subsidiary Premiere Radio Networks, the company that syndicates *The Rush Limbaugh Show*. Limbaugh is a bright spot in the troubled radio industry, which overall has suffered from audience erosion and declining advertising revenue. Much of his success is due to a loyal conservative base of listeners, a base that is largely older and predominantly male.

Wealthy and influential though he may be, Limbaugh is not without his own problems including three failed marriages and an admitted addiction to pain medications. He was arrested in 2006 for "doctor shopping" for prescriptions, including OxyContin; the charge—which Limbaugh and his attorney denied—was dropped after he agreed to continue treatment and pay the $30,000 cost of the investigation. Critics pointed out the irony of Limbaugh's brush with the legal system, in light of his 1995 statement—on his TV program—that "if people are violating the law by doing drugs, they ought to be accused and they ought to be convicted and they ought to be sent up."

Limbaugh explained in a 2008 *New York Times* interview that his conservative politics are his bread and butter. Limbaugh said, "First and foremost I'm a businessman. My first goal is to attract the largest possible audience so I can charge confiscatory ad rates. I happen to have great entertainment skills, but that enables me to sell airtime."

His hardball tactics have made him a target of Democrats and liberal activists.

HOUSE COMMITTEE ON OVERSIGHT AND GOVERNMENT REFORM

In 2012, the U.S. Department of Health and Human Services (HHS) proposed that to comply with the Affordable Care Act's Women's Preventive Services Amendment, religiously affiliated institutions such as hospitals, universities, and social service agencies must provide birth control coverage without cost-sharing in their employee and/or student health plans; the policy excluded churches and "houses of worship." A modification to the proposal allowed the institutions to avoid providing the contraception coverage themselves by permitting insurance companies to handle it indirectly. Some Catholic and other religious groups protested that these institutions were being forced to breach their own religious teachings. Some religious leaders said that the Constitution's separation of church and state, and its protections of religious freedoms, should allow religious-based institutions to disallow insurance coverage of contraceptive and sterilization procedures for their employees and/or students.

This proposal affected institutions such as Georgetown Law School, a Jesuit school opposed to offering its students contraceptives or providing them indirectly in student insurance coverage paid for by the insurance companies.

Religious organizations that opposed this government proposal appealed to Congress to help resolve the issue. Congressman Darrell Issa (R-CA), chairman of the House Committee on Oversight and Government Reform (COGR), ordered a committee hearing to examine the HHS proposal. The COGR investigates how federal taxpayer money is spent and the efficiency of that spending, seeking to eliminate fraud and other abuses in governmental agencies.

At the time, the Republicans were the majority party in the U.S. House of Representatives. COGR chair Issa and his Republican colleagues on the committee entitled their hearing "Lines Crossed: Separation of Church and State; Has the Obama Administration Trampled on Freedom of Religion and Freedom of Conscience?" A variety of religious leaders, college presidents, ethicists, and medical doctors were invited by the committee's Republican majority to testify about the new mandate, which they unanimously opposed. The minority Democratic committee members wanted one person in particular to provide a counter viewpoint as part of the hearing, a woman named Sandra Fluke.

A LAW STUDENT'S TESTIMONY

Sandra Fluke was a third-year law student at Georgetown Law and a past president of Georgetown Law Students for Reproductive Justice. She agreed to offer testimony on behalf of her organization at the committee hearing. However, Chairman Issa, controlling the hearing, did not allow Fluke's testimony.

During opening statements at the COGR hearing, several minority members, including Rep. Elijah E. Cummings (D-MD) and Rep. Carolyn B. Maloney (D-NY), blasted the lack of viewpoints provided on the issue, particularly the exclusion of Fluke's prepared testimony in which she had planned to say she knew students who "suffered financial, emotional, and medical burdens because of this lack of contraceptive coverage." Cummings said it was politics as usual:

FIGURE 8.17 *Sandra Fluke gave her testimony on women's health issues at an unofficial hearing sponsored by Democrats.*
http://www.c-span.org/
C-Span

I think everyone understands what is going on here today. The Chairman is promoting a conspiracy theory that the federal government is conducting a "war" against religion. He has stacked the hearing with witnesses who agree with his position. He has not invited the Catholic Health Association, Catholic Charities, Catholics United, or a host of other Catholic groups that praised *the White House for making the accommodation they made last week.*

Maloney questioned the absence of female witnesses on the panel regarding an issue so closely tied to gender:

What I want to know is, where are the women? I look at this panel, and I don't see one single individual representing the tens of millions of women across the country who want and need insurance coverage for basic preventive health care services, including family planning. Where are the women?

House Democratic leader Rep. Nancy Pelosi (D-CA) jumped into the fray that same day during her weekly news conference, framing the issue as one of women and healthcare rather than religious freedom.

Right now, as we gather here, in another part of the Capitol, there is a hearing. Five men are testifying on women's health. My colleague Carolyn Maloney, who is on the committee, looked down at this panel from which a woman who was the Democratic witness was excluded, and said "Where are the women?" And that's a good question for the whole debate. Where are the women? Where are the women on that panel? Imagine having a panel on women's health and they don't have any women on the panel. Duh! What is it that men don't understand about women's health and how central the issue of family planning is to that? Not just if you're having a family but if you need those kind of prescription drugs for your general health, which was the testimony they would have heard this morning if they had allowed a woman on the panel.

Pelosi concluded her remarks on the lighter side:

the Republican leadership of this Congress thinks it's appropriate to have a hearing on the subject of women's health and purposely exclude women from the panel. What else do you need to know about the subject? If you need to know more, tune in. I may, I may at some point, be moved to explain biology to my colleagues.

The following week, the House Democratic Steering and Policy Committee held a hearing at which Fluke testified. After the hearing, the Democratic website for COGR posted videos of the minority members' comments during both hearings and it also posted Fluke's testimony. Fluke discussed students' experiences with affordable contraception:

Without insurance coverage, contraception can cost a woman over $3,000 during law school. For a lot of students who, like me, are on public interest scholarships, that's practically an entire summer's salary. Forty percent of female students at Georgetown Law report struggling financially as a result of this policy.

Fluke told of Georgetown students who needed contraceptive medicine for medical care. She recounted a friend's experience; she had polycystic ovarian syndrome that "needed a prescription birth control to stop cysts from growing on her ovaries." Eventually, Fluke's friend was unable to afford her out-of-pocket birth control and went without, resulting in the loss of an ovary.

> *You might respond that contraception is accessible in lots of other ways. Unfortunately, that's not true. Women's health clinics provide vital medical services, but as the Guttmacher Institute has documented, clinics are unable to meet the crushing demand for these services. . .*
>
> *In the media lately, conservative Catholic organizations have been asking; what did we expect when we enrolled at a Catholic school? . . . We refuse to pick between a quality education and our health, and we resent that, in the 21st century, anyone thinks it's acceptable to ask us to make this choice simply because we are women.*

RUSH FINDS A CONTROVERSY

Like any entertainer, Limbaugh knows the benefit of publicity—good or bad. Limbaugh's caustic remarks endear him to a loyal audience while sometimes sparking controversy that nets him national media coverage and, perhaps, more listeners. Less than a week after Fluke testified at the House Democratic Steering and Policy Committee, Limbaugh read from a conservative news service about Pelosi's hearing. His take on the issue: women at Georgetown Law were "having so much sex that they're going broke, so you and I should pay for their birth control . . . Apparently, four out of every ten co-eds are having so much sex that it's hard to make ends meet." And then he singled out Fluke:

> *What does it say about the college co-ed Sandra Fluke, who goes before a congressional committee and essentially says that she must be paid to have sex, what does that make her? It makes her a slut, right? It makes her a prostitute. She wants to be paid to have sex. She's having so much sex she can't afford the contraception. She wants you and me and the taxpayers to pay her to have sex. What does that make us? We're the pimps. The johns? No! We're the johns. Yeah, that's right. Pimp's not the right word. Okay, so she's not a slut. She's "round heeled." I take it back.*

Limbaugh continued his analysis of Fluke's testimony for three days. On the second day, March 1, 2012, Limbaugh said that Fluke purposely chose Georgetown Law because it did not offer contraceptives: "She wanted to go there to stir it up! She's a plant, an anti-Catholic plant from the get-go on this," Limbaugh said. He explained:

> The Washington Post *reports that Fluke "researched the Jesuit college's health plans for students before enrolling, and found that birth control was not included." And she enrolled anyway. Why? Quote, Fluke, "I decided I was absolutely not willing to compromise the quality of my education in exchange for my health care."*

Limbaugh also defended his use of "slut" and "prostitute" from the previous day and further inflamed the controversy:

> *So, Ms Fluke and the rest of you feminazis, here's the deal: If we are going to pay for your contraceptives and thus pay for you to have sex, we want something for it. And I'll tell you what it is. We want you to post the videos online so we can all watch.*

It wasn't long before politicians used the controversy to score some points, especially with their female constituents. Rep. Jackie Speier (D-CA) criticized Limbaugh's choice of words and called on consumers to boycott companies that advertised on his show:

> *I rise this morning to say to Rush Limbaugh, shame on you. Shame on you for being the hatemonger that you are. Shame on you for being misogynistic. Shame on you for calling the women of this country sluts and prostitutes, 'cause that's what he did. Ninety-eight percent of the women in this country at some time in their lives use birth control, and yet he went on the air recently and called Sandra Fluke a slut and a prostitute because she was trying to access birth control pills as a third-year law student at Georgetown. So I say to the women of this country, do something about this. I say to the women of this country ask Century 21, Quicken Loans, Legal Zoom and Sleep Number to stop supporting the hatemongering of Rush Limbaugh. And if they do not do that I ask them to boycott those companies.*

On March 1, 2012, Senator Frank Lautenberg (D-NJ) took Limbaugh to task for what Lautenberg described as anti-woman rhetoric:

> *What he said yesterday—and I had it checked because I wanted to be sure that I'm not misquoting anything. Said a woman who wants affordable birth control is, and I quote here, "a prostitute." Talking about your wife, your sister, your daughter, your child. Hateful! Ugly language! And we condemn it. Republicans like to talk about the Constitution and freedom. But once again when it comes to women they don't get rights, they get restrictions.*

Limbaugh fired back. After airing two Democratic Congresswomen's responses to his description of Fluke, he said he would buy Georgetown women "aspirin to put between their knees" in lieu of birth control pills.

THE CONTROVERSY GROWS

On March 2, 2012, the White House weighed in. President Barack Obama called Fluke, according to White House Press Secretary Jay Carney,

> *because he wanted to offer his support to her. He wanted to express his disappointment that she has been the subject of inappropriate, personal attacks, and to thank her for exercising her rights as a citizen to speak out on an issue of public policy. And it was a very good conversation.*

Georgetown University president John DeGioia, in a letter to the Georgetown community, said that while Fluke

> *was respectful, sincere, and spoke with conviction . . . provided a model of civil discourse . . . some of those who disagreed with her position—including Rush Limbaugh and commentators throughout the blogosphere and in various other media channels—responded with behavior that can only be described as misogynistic, vitriolic, and a misrepresentation of the position of our student.*

Many professors and administrators at Georgetown University Law Center and other law schools responded with their public support for Fluke's right to express her opinions and strongly condemned "the recent personal attacks on our student, Sandra Fluke."

On day three of the controversy, Limbaugh tried to explain his remarks with a counterattack. Republicans, he said, don't hate women; Democrats had tried to reframe the controversy about the Republican OCGR hearing and his remarks as a "War on Women." Instead, Limbaugh said the debate was really about the "unconstitutionality of Obama's mandate that churches and religious schools pass out abortion pills, contraception pills and so forth." And he continued to attack Fluke's testimony and willingness to speak publicly on the issue. Fluke's parents, who had expressed pride in their daughter's actions, should be embarrassed. "I'd disconnect the phone. I'd go into hiding and hope the media didn't find me."

Some Republicans and conservatives sought to distance themselves from Limbaugh's remarks. House Speaker John Boehner (R-Ohio), the highest-ranking House Republican, said through a spokesman that Limbaugh's choice of words was "inappropriate."

AN APOLOGY OF SORTS

On March 3, 2012, Limbaugh issued a statement:

> *For over 20 years, I have illustrated the absurd with absurdity, three hours a day, five days a week. In this instance, I chose the wrong words in my analogy of the situation. I did not mean a personal attack on Ms Fluke.*
>
> *I think it is absolutely absurd that during these very serious political times, we are discussing personal sexual recreational activities before members of Congress. I personally do not agree that American citizens should pay for these social activities. What happened to personal responsibility and accountability? Where do we draw the line? If this is accepted as the norm, what will follow? Will we be debating if taxpayers should pay for new sneakers for all students that are interested in running to keep fit? In my monologue, I posited that it is not our business whatsoever to know what is going on in anyone's bedroom nor do I think it is a topic that should reach a Presidential level.*
>
> *My choice of words was not the best, and in the attempt to be humorous, I created a national stir. I sincerely apologize to Ms. Fluke for the insulting word choices.*

EIB WEB PAGE DISGRONIFIER

Archive Search Go EMAIL HELP? Tweet

Home > Archives (Mar 3, 2012) > A Statement from Rush

A Statement from Rush

March 03, 2012

For over 20 years, I have illustrated the absurd with absurdity, three hours a day, five days a week. In this instance, I chose the wrong words in my analogy of the situation. I did not mean a personal attack on Ms. Fluke.

I think it is absolutely absurd that during these very serious political times, we are discussing personal sexual recreational activities before members of Congress. I personally do not agree that American citizens should pay for these social activities. What happened to personal responsibility and accountability? Where do we draw the line? If this is accepted as the norm, what will follow? Will we be debating if taxpayers should pay for new sneakers for all students that are interested in running to keep fit?In my monologue, I posited that it is not our business whatsoever to know what is going on in anyone's bedroom nor do I think it is a topic that should reach a Presidential level.

My choice of words was not the best, and in the attempt to be humorous, I created a national stir. I sincerely apologize to Ms. Fluke for the insulting word choices.

FIGURE 8.18 *Rush Limbaugh's apology to Sandra Fluke.*
http://www.rushlimbaugh.com/
RushLimbaugh.com - © 2013 Premiere Radio Networks

The following Monday, on March 5, Limbaugh explained his apology to his audience—saying his mistake had been in stooping to the level of his critics:

> *But this is the mistake I made. In fighting them on this issue last week, I became like them. Against my own instincts, against my own knowledge, against everything I know to be right and wrong, I descended to their level when I used those two words to describe Sandra Fluke. That was my error. I became like them, and I feel very badly about that. I've always tried to maintain a very high degree of integrity and independence on this program. Nevertheless, those two words were inappropriate, they were uncalled for, they distracted from the point that I was actually trying to make, and I again sincerely apologize to Ms. Fluke for using those two words to describe her.*

SOCIAL MEDIA BACKLASH

As expected, the news coverage of Limbaugh's remarks made headlines. Social media, including blogs and social networks such as Facebook, quickly spread the latest developments in the unfolding story.

A blog called "Think Progress," a project of the liberal organization the Center for American Progress, was a major engine behind a boycott campaign to eliminate Limbaugh's advertisers. Supporters tweeted and posted on corporations' social media sites demanding that they stop advertising on Limbaugh's show.

On March 9, a radio insider newsletter, "Taylor on Radio-Info," reported that Premiere Radio Networks had circulated an internal memo to radio station traffic managers nationwide with a list of ninety-eight advertisers who wanted to avoid "environments likely to stir negative sentiments." Those no-go radio zones included Limbaugh and other controversial radio talk shows. The internal memo was posted on the "Think Progress" blog, which reported daily on the status of the boycott and posted comments from organizations that had dropped Limbaugh show advertising. Eventually, a web page was created on Pinterest, a social media site that allows users to categorize and organize information visually; 141 organizations were depicted as no longer advertising on Limbaugh's show, according to "Think Progress."

One national advertiser, Carbonite, issued a statement:

> *No one with daughters the age of Sandra Fluke, and I have two, could possibly abide the insult and abuse heaped upon this courageous and well-intentioned young lady. Mr Limbaugh, with his highly personal attacks on Miss Fluke, overstepped any reasonable bounds of decency. Even though Mr. Limbaugh has now issued an apology, we have nonetheless decided to withdraw our advertising from his show.*

Netflix, which found its commercials had inadvertently aired during Limbaugh's show, explained what it had done as a result of consumer pressure:

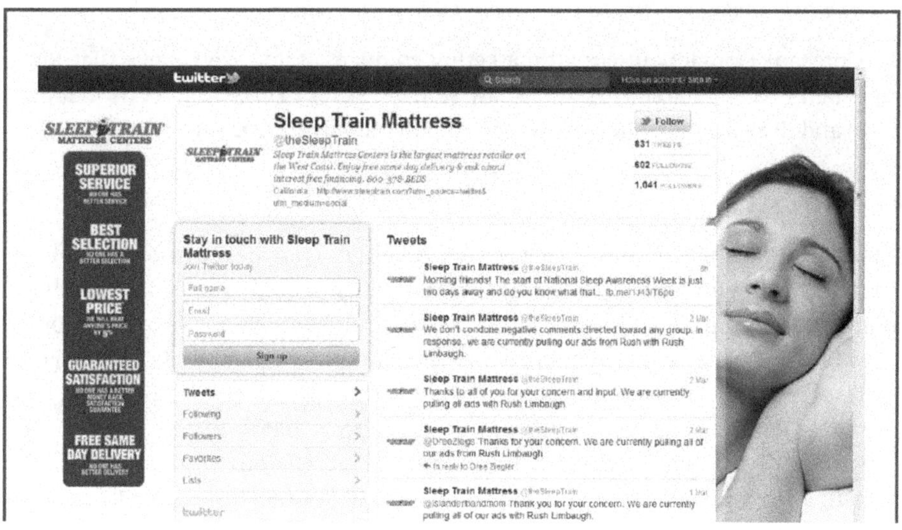

FIGURE 8.19 *Sleep Train Mattress's Twitter response.*
https://twitter.com/theSleepTrain
Sleep Train Mattress

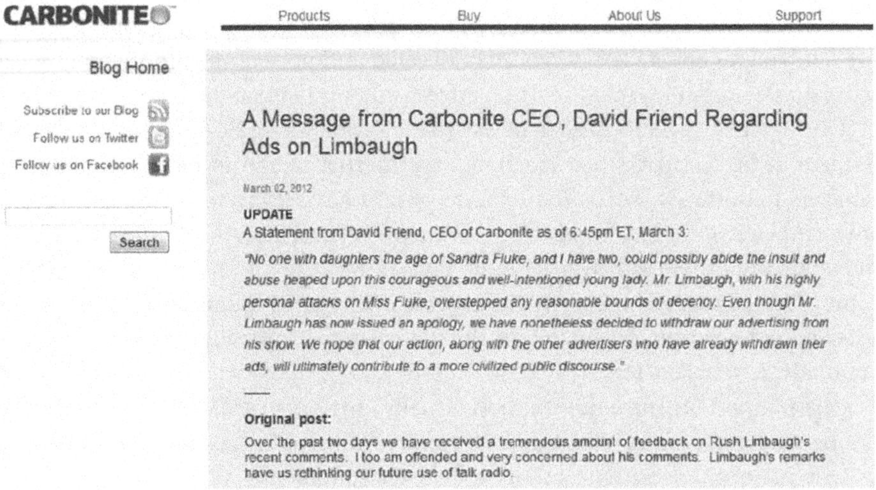

CARBONITE

Products Buy About Us Support

Blog Home

Subscribe to our Blog

Follow us on Twitter

Follow us on Facebook

Search

A Message from Carbonite CEO, David Friend Regarding Ads on Limbaugh

March 02, 2012

UPDATE

A Statement from David Friend, CEO of Carbonite as of 6:45pm ET, March 3:

"No one with daughters the age of Sandra Fluke, and I have two, could possibly abide the insult and abuse heaped upon this courageous and well-intentioned young lady. Mr. Limbaugh, with his highly personal attacks on Miss Fluke, overstepped any reasonable bounds of decency. Even though Mr. Limbaugh has now issued an apology, we have nonetheless decided to withdraw our advertising from his show. We hope that our action, along with the other advertisers who have already withdrawn their ads, will ultimately contribute to a more civilized public discourse."

—

Original post:

Over the past two days we have received a tremendous amount of feedback on Rush Limbaugh's recent comments. I too am offended and very concerned about his comments. Limbaugh's remarks have us rethinking our future use of talk radio.

FIGURE 8.20 *Carbonite CEO wrote his decision to discontinue adverting on Rush Limbaugh's show because of the offensive nature of his remarks. http://www.carbonite.com/*
Carbonite

> *Spotted your tweets and wanted to let you know that Netflix has not purchased and does not purchase advertising on the Rush Limbaugh show. We do buy network radio advertising and have confirmed that two Netflix spots were picked up in error as part of local news breaks during the Rush Limbaugh show. We have instructed our advertising agency to make sure that this error will not happen again.*

Constant Contact, an e-mail marketing company, said "We believe that Rush Limbaugh's recent statements about law student Sandra Fluke were both inappropriate and disrespectful, and we decided to pull our advertising on his program."

AFTERMATH

Entertainers generally must seek the media spotlight to keep the attention on them so that they are not forgotten by their advertisers, audiences, and others who feed their commercial enterprises. This case illustrates that unfavorable publicity can sometimes backfire even for entertainers who welcome controversy. While Limbaugh is no stranger to criticism and threatened boycotts, the social media's impact does give pause to commercial sponsors. The controversy also provided the Democrats with an opportunity to shift the debate—from an attack on religious freedom to a war on women. With a presidential election shifting into high gear with just eight months until Election Day, this was another win for the Democrats. They made sure people knew this message: Democrats respect women and Republicans don't.

The National Organization for Women (NOW) created the "Enough Rush" campaign aimed at targeting local radio stations that broadcast *The Rush Limbaugh Show* and local businesses that continue to advertise on it, according to NOW's website. On May 18, 2012, protests at various radio stations in Washington, D.C., New York City, West Palm Beach, Florida, and Phoenix, Arizona, were held.

In typical Limbaugh style, he responded to NAGS ("National Association of Gals"—Limbaugh's moniker for NOW) and developed "Rush Babes for America" on Facebook to provide a place for "the millions of conservative women who know what they believe in: family, American Values, and not being told by Faux Feminist Groups how to think," according to the Facebook site. The site gained more than 70,000 fans in a short period of time.

Outrage is hard to sustain. After all, there are always new outrageous behaviors and events on the horizon and the media spotlight can't linger long. According to *The Christian Science Monitor*, Media Matters, a nonprofit organization that monitors and analyses conservative "misinformation," spent over $100,000 to encourage local stations to drop the Limbaugh show. Media company Clear Channel Communications said that few had done so, according to WND U.S., an independent news network.

However, outrage can cause significant monetary impact—in the short and long term. Immediately after his remarks, Limbaugh's radio show lost more than a hundred advertisers. This also had a lasting impact, even several months after Rush verbally attacked Fluke. Cumulus Media—a major affiliate of Limbaugh's show—reported millions of dollars in losses attributable to the advertiser troubles caused by Limbaugh's remarks, according to Politico.com. During a call with investors, CEO Lew Dickey alluded to Limbaugh as a "drag" on business, explaining how "extraordinary issues" such as "the boycott that we saw from some remarks in a talk radio show impacted us," according to a *Huffington Post* story. That impact cost the company $5.5 million, according to Dickey. While he projected that revenue for the company would pick up again during the summer of 2012, he informed investors in August of that same year that the "drag" would continue for the next six or twelve months.

In 2013, Cumulus Media negotiated its new three-year contract for *The Rush Limbaugh Show*. While neither Rush Limbaugh, Premier Networks nor Cumulus were talking, industry watchers speculated that Premier Networks, which syndicates *The Rush Limbaugh Show* and is owned by Clear Channels, took a major hit on its licensing revenue. Limbaugh also lost its powerful 50kW home at WABC in New York City as a result of the new agreement.

QUESTIONS FOR DISCUSSION

1. How would you describe the influence of the Rush Limbaugh radio show within the political and entertainment spheres?
2. How did Rush Limbaugh's comments about Sandra Fluke spark publicity for his show?

3. Why did Democrats make an issue out of this incident?
4. What groups led the charge to discredit Rush Limbaugh's comments about Sandra Fluke?
5. What was the involvement of "Think Progress" in this controversy? What tactics did it use against Rush Limbaugh?
6. What was the reaction from Rush Limbaugh's advertisers to the controversy?
7. How did Rush Limbaugh respond to the criticism after advertisers from his show began to respond to pressure groups and customers?
8. How effective was Rush Limbaugh's apology?

Dig Deeper

For background, read the full committee hearing transcript "Lines Crossed: Separation of Church and State" and Sandra Fluke's testimony before House Democratic Steering and Policy Committee on women's health and contraception, available on the textbook's companion website. Review some of the Twitter, Facebook and Pinterest communications of companies who responded to requests to pull their advertising from *The Rush Limbaugh Show*, available on the textbook's companion website. How did companies convey their actions to consumers?

Read the research article "Excellence in Broadcasting? Rush Limbaugh and Image Repair in the Sandra Fluke Controversy" that is available on the textbook's companion website. According to the author, what image repair strategies did Limbaugh use to deal with the controversy?

25

Tabloid Tiger

Scandal Derails Storied Career

Celebrity endorsements are a common advertising and public relations tactic. They bring fan and media attention to products and causes. They also associate the celebrity's positive qualities with the product—the so-called halo effect.

When the halo drops off, however, it's not just a problem for the celebrity's personal brand but for the product he or she is endorsing.

A CHILD PRODIGY NAMED TIGER

Tiger Woods was born Eldrick Tont Woods in Cypress, California, a state with the second highest number of golf courses in the nation. He was given the nickname Tiger in honor of a friend of his father. Woods's ancestry is diverse: African American, Native American, Thai, Chinese and Dutch.

Woods was a golf prodigy trained by his father, an amateur but serious golfer; Woods made his national television debut at the age of 2 on *The Mike Douglas Show* putting against comedian Bob Hope. He was featured in *Golf Digest* by age 5 and amassed numerous youth amateur golf awards, including three consecutive U.S. amateur titles, a record.

Woods lasted just two years at Stanford University before turning pro at the age of 20. In one year he won his first major golf tournament, the Masters. He was the youngest player and the first African American or Asian to don the green jacket, the symbol of the ultra-exclusive Augusta National Golf Club; the club whose tournament's founder infamously said: "As long as I'm alive, golfers will be white, and caddies will be black."

Woods rocketed to number one in the Official World Golf Rankings for 1997. He was an instant sensation, drawing fans of all ages who liked his clean-cut image and his astonishing ability for powerful drives and clutch putts. He was also generous, starting a foundation in 1996 that provides scholarships and golfing activities for inner-city youth.

Woods leveraged his golf talents and positive personal qualities for lucrative product endorsements. After turning pro, he signed endorsement deals worth $60 million with Nike, the sportswear and athletic equipment giant, and Titleist, a leading golf products company. In 2000, Rick Burton, director of the Warsaw Sports Marketing Center at the University of Oregon, said: "Think of him as the offspring of Arnold Palmer and Michael Jordan," according to *ESPN The Magazine*.

By 2009, experts estimated Woods's earnings at $1 billion from golf prizes, appearance fees, endorsement deals, and earnings from his golf design business, according to *Forbes*. His appeal was so great that Gatorade created the Gatorade Tiger drink; Nike launched its first golf enterprise around Woods's endorsements; Wheaties, "the breakfast of champions," put his image on their cereal boxes and made him a permanent spokesperson, and Tag Heuer, the Swiss luxury watchmaker, worked with Woods to create a golf watch. Everyone, it seemed, wanted to associate their brands with a winner like Woods. He showed as much control over his

FIGURE 8.21 *Tiger Woods.*
© Duomo/CORBIS

golf game as he did in his private life and interactions with the news media. When Woods married the former model Elin Nordegren, they honeymooned on his yacht, called *Privacy*. Woods's circle of friends and employees were expected to keep details of Woods's private life private or risk being banished.

TIGER TANTRUMS

In 2008, Woods tore a knee ligament but continued to play golf for ten months, according to ESPN.com. His knee injury was exacerbated by a double stress fracture in the same leg, occurring two weeks before the U.S. Open, which he played and won. But it also ended his season. Eight months after surgery and rehabilitation, Woods was ready to return to golf. And the golfing world welcomed his return early in 2009. A recession and lower TV viewer ratings had pummeled the U.S. PGA Tour, which had grown accustomed to the fans and sponsors that Woods attracted wherever he went.

Woods made an uneven comeback in 2009 with six victories on the PGA Tour but no Majors wins. At the time, with fourteen Majors championship wins, Woods was chasing Jack Nicklaus's all-time eighteen career Majors record. Still, Woods ended the season with his tenth PGA Player of the Year Award (Jack Nicklaus Trophy), which is determined by player votes. With the lowest adjusted scoring average for the year, Woods won the PGA Tour's Byron Nelson Award, and he was the top money winner on the PGA Tour. To date, he had won eighty-two pro golfing events around the world.

During the 2009 season, sports commentators and writers were not only commenting on Woods's difficult golfing season but also on his poor manners. *ESPN The Magazine* writer Rick Reilly wrote a scathing column about "Tiger Tantrums" which included "slamming his club, throwing his club and cursing his club," all in front of a worldwide audience. At age 33, with a wife and two children, Woods needed to grow up, Reilly suggested, and be a better role model for his young fans. Reilly spoke for many when he wrote: "He's grown in every other way. He's committed, responsible, smart, funny and the most talented golfer in history. I just thought we'd be over the conniptions by now," according to *ESPN The Magazine*. Reilly noted that Woods was one of the very few golf pros who acted so disrespectfully to the game and fans.

THE 2:25 A.M. CAR ACCIDENT

The cascade of events that led to the Tiger Woods scandal began the day after Thanksgiving when Woods was home with his family. On November 27, 2009, Woods crashed his Cadillac Escalade into a fire hydrant and a neighbor's tree just outside his home at 2:25 a.m. Early news reports said Woods was leaving his home, an exclusive gated community near Orlando, Florida. Police officials said Woods was found lying on the ground and that his wife had used a golf club to break the rear passenger-side window to get Woods out. He was treated and released from a hospital for lacerations to his upper and lower lips. He also had blood in his mouth and was in and out of consciousness when police arrived, according to police reports.

Woods soon returned to his home and avoided the news media—and everyone else. Even the Florida Highway Patrol was turned away the following day, and the day after.

THE MEDIA CIRCUS BEGINS

On November 29, 2009, two days after the crash, *The New York Times* ran a story entitled "Speculation Fills the Gap Left by Woods's Silence." The story quoted experts who said that Woods's silence was "allowing an online rumor mill to produce conjecture and opinion" that could damage his carefully crafted image.

While most of the mainstream media did not publish material from unnamed or questionable sources, they were asking questions and not getting answers. Speculation was almost immediate with online tabloid and celebrity sources such as TMZ.com. By 1 p.m. on the day of the crash, TMZ.com reported details of the accident including quotes from the police report and an aerial photo of the accident scene from a local television station. By 10:35 p.m. that day, TMZ.com reported that an argument between Woods and his wife had happened before the accident. TMZ.com also reported that an unnamed Florida law enforcement official had said it was a "domestic issue." The next day, November 28, 2009, TMZ.com ran a story based on unnamed sources from the hospital where Woods was treated, saying that his wife had confronted Woods about an alleged affair with another woman. Other unnamed sources said that Elin scratched Tiger's face and struck his vehicle with a golf club.

The *National Enquirer*, a tabloid newspaper known for paying sources, was the first to break the story—and it did so two days before Woods's accident. The cover story "Tiger Woods Cheating Scandal" detailed allegations about Woods's affair with a New York City event planner, Rachel Uchitel. According to an interview months later with ESPN's *E:60*, an investigative journalism newsmagazine show, *National Enquirer* Executive Editor Barry Levine said the publication used "all its investigative reporting techniques—surveillance, telephone work, cultivating sources and staking out individuals—and spent months traveling from Las Vegas to Los Angeles to Melbourne, Australia, seeking information on Woods." The story was based on off-the-record interviews with unnamed sources and an on-the-record interview with one of Uchitel's friends. The *National Enquirer*'s story was quickly linked to Woods's car accident.

On November 29, the Florida Highway Patrol, still not allowed access to Woods to finish its investigation, released a 911 call made by a Woods's neighbor. The unidentified caller said that a person was on the ground outside his vehicle.

The speculation grew as traditional and tabloid news organizations increased their reporting. TMZ.com, for example, published a story November 29, 2009, titled "Tiger: I need a 'Kobe Special'" based on unnamed sources that claimed Woods had said his wife had "gone ghetto" and needed a "Kobe Special." The "Kobe Special" referred to basketball superstar Kobe Bryant's sex scandal and the "special" was a large expensive ring described as "A house on a finger."

Even mainstream media got into the act when the *Miami Herald* and the *Chicago Sun-Times* among others quoted British tabloid *News of the World* about one alleged mistress who said that Woods liked "rough" sex, according to the *American Journalism Review*.

TIGER TALKS, SORT OF

With rumors and speculation running wild online and in news and entertainment sources, Woods finally broke his silence on November 29, 2009, by posting a statement on his official website entitled "Statement by Tiger Woods," in which he said:

> *As you all know, I had a single-car accident earlier this week, and sustained some injuries. I have some cuts, bruising and right now I'm pretty sore.*
>
> *This situation is my fault, and it's obviously embarrassing to my family and me. I'm human and I'm not perfect. I will certainly make sure this doesn't happen again.*
>
> *This is a private matter and I want to keep it that way. Although I understand there is curiosity, the many false, unfounded and malicious rumors that are currently circulating about my family and me are irresponsible.*

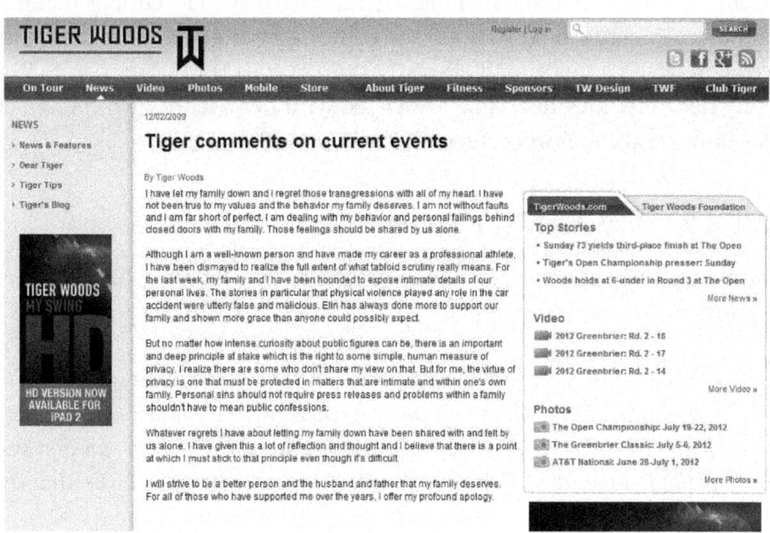

TIGER WOODS

On Tour | News | Video | Photos | Mobile | Store | About Tiger | Fitness | Sponsors | TW Design | TWF | Club Tiger

NEWS
- News & Features
- Dear Tiger
- Tiger Tips
- Tiger's Blog

12/02/2009

Tiger comments on current events

By Tiger Woods

I have let my family down and I regret those transgressions with all of my heart. I have not been true to my values and the behavior my family deserves. I am not without faults and I am far short of perfect. I am dealing with my behavior and personal failings behind closed doors with my family. Those feelings should be shared by us alone.

Although I am a well-known person and have made my career as a professional athlete, I have been dismayed to realize the full extent of what tabloid scrutiny really means. For the last week, my family and I have been hounded to expose intimate details of our personal lives. The stories in particular that physical violence played any role in the car accident were utterly false and malicious. Elin has always done more to support our family and shown more grace than anyone could possibly expect.

But no matter how intense curiosity about public figures can be, there is an important and deep principle at stake which is the right to some simple, human measure of privacy. I realize there are some who don't share my view on that. But for me, the virtue of privacy is one that must be protected in matters that are intimate and within one's own family. Personal sins should not require press releases and problems within a family shouldn't have to mean public confessions.

Whatever regrets I have about letting my family down have been shared with and felt by us alone. I have given this a lot of reflection and thought and I believe that there is a point at which I must stick to that principle even though it's difficult.

I will strive to be a better person and the husband and father that my family deserves. For all of those who have supported me over the years, I offer my profound apology.

TigerWoods.com | Tiger Woods Foundation

Top Stories
- Sunday 73 yields third-place finish at The Open
- Tiger's Open Championship presser: Sunday
- Woods holds at 6-under in Round 3 at The Open

More News »

Video
- 2012 Greenbrier: Rd. 2 - 18
- 2012 Greenbrier: Rd. 2 - 17
- 2012 Greenbrier: Rd. 2 - 14

More Video »

Photos
- The Open Championship: July 19-22, 2012
- The Greenbrier Classic: July 5-6, 2012
- AT&T National: June 28-July 1, 2012

More Photos »

TIGER WOODS MY SWING HD
HD VERSION NOW AVAILABLE FOR IPAD 2

FIGURE 8.22 *Tiger Woods' website provided just three statements on the scandal. The first one was posted November 29, 2009.*
http://web.tigerwoods.com/
TigerWoods.com

The only person responsible for the accident is me. My wife, Elin, acted courageously when she saw I was hurt and in trouble. She was the first person to help me. Any other assertion is absolutely false.

This incident has been stressful and very difficult for Elin, our family and me. I appreciate all the concern and well wishes that we have received. But, I would also ask for some understanding that my family and I deserve some privacy no matter how intrusive some people can be.

The next day, Woods withdrew from his upcoming tournament, the Chevron World Challenge, which supported his foundation and drew top players. On December 1, 2009, the Florida Highway Patrol closed its investigation, despite no post-accident interview with Woods. With no evidence to the contrary, Woods was issued a careless driving citation and fined $164. *The New York Times* reported the next day that Woods's neighbors, who made the 911 call at the accident scene, said they saw no evidence of domestic violence the night of the car crash. The lawyer, Bill Sharpe, said about Woods: "The scratches on the face were consistent with somebody in a minor car accident . . . None of his injuries looked like he was beat up by his wife."

The lack of information surrounding the world's number-one player increased the media's questions about the circumstances surrounding the accident. The mysterious incident grew into a full-fledged scandal on December 1, 2009, when a Los Angeles cocktail waitress named Jaimee Grubbs claimed to have had a thirty-one-month affair with Woods, according to the celebrity gossip magazine *US Weekly*. Unlike Uchitel, who denied she had had an affair with Woods, Grubbs had no such compunction; she claimed to have 300 text messages from Woods. On December 2, *US Weekly* released a voice mail allegedly from Woods three days before his accident asking her to remove her name associated with her telephone number because Woods's wife was calling numbers from his cell phone.

"I HAVE LET MY FAMILY DOWN"

On December 2, 2009, another statement was issued by Woods on his website, titled "Tiger Comments on Current Events."

I have let my family down and I regret those transgressions with all of my heart. I have not been true to my values and the behavior my family deserves. I am not without faults and I am far short of perfect. I am dealing with my behavior and personal failings behind closed doors with my family. Those feelings should be shared by us alone.

Although I am a well-known person and have made my career as a professional athlete, I have been dismayed to realize the full extent of what tabloid scrutiny really means. For the last week, my family and I have been hounded to expose intimate details of our personal lives. The stories in particular that physical violence played any role in the car accident were utterly false and malicious. Elin has always done more to support our family and shown more grace than anyone could possibly expect.

But no matter how intense curiosity about public figures can be, there is an important and deep principle at stake which is the right to some simple, human measure of privacy. I realize there are some who don't share my view on that. But for me, the virtue of privacy is one that must be protected in matters that are intimate and within one's own family. Personal sins should not require press releases and problems within a family shouldn't have to mean public confessions.

Whatever regrets I have about letting my family down have been shared with and felt by us alone. I have given this a lot of reflection and thought and I believe that there is a point at which I must stick to that principle even though it's difficult.

I will strive to be a better person and the husband and father that my family deserves. For all of those who have supported me over the years, I offer my profound apology.

MORE WOMEN . . .

More women emerged with stories about their relationships with Woods. By December 7, 2009, nine women including a porn star, pancake house waitress and models were providing details about their affairs with Woods. ABC News and other traditional sources were publishing the salacious details of Woods's purported sexual activities. More women would emerge over time to tell their stories to various tabloid sites that paid for such information. A slow jam musical remix of his voice message to Grubbs was also making the rounds online.

Beyond the tabloid news and gossip sites, comedians were having fun with Woods's situation. Hundreds of jokes were making their rounds including:

Jay Leno: "This Tiger Woods thing is having an effect on a lot of people. In fact, earlier today, Elizabeth Edwards went out and bought a new set of golf clubs. I didn't even know that she played."

David Letterman: "President Obama is sending troops to Afghanistan. Hell, he ought to be sending them to Tiger Woods's house."

Many unattributed jokes circulated, such as: "Have you heard that Tiger has a new nickname? It's cheetah." The *New York Post* ran a version of this on one of its covers: "Tiger Admits: I'm a Cheetah."

One comedic effort that some thought crossed the line was NBC's *Saturday Night Live*'s skit that depicted Woods as a victim of domestic violence. He was portrayed in a series of news conferences giving bungled apologies for his transgressions. Woods's wife (played by *Gossip Girl* Blake Lively) calmly stands behind Woods (played by actor Kenan Thompson), wielding a golf club as he reads his apologies; after each bungled apology he incurs more injuries that lead to his surreptitious pleas for help.

TIGER TAKES A BREAK

By December 11, 2009, after increasingly intense media attention, Woods announced on his website that he would take an indefinite leave of absence from golf:

> *I am deeply aware of the disappointment and hurt that my infidelity has caused to so many people, most of all my wife and children. I want to say again to everyone that I am profoundly sorry and that I ask forgiveness. It may not be possible to repair the damage I've done, but I want to do my best to try.*
>
> *I would like to ask everyone, including my fans, the good people at my foundation, business partners, the PGA Tour, and my fellow competitors, for their understanding. What's most important now is that my family has the time, privacy, and safe haven we will need for personal healing.*
>
> *After much soul searching, I have decided to take an indefinite break from professional golf. I need to focus my attention on being a better husband, father, and person.*
>
> *Again, I ask for privacy for my family and I am especially grateful for all those who have offered compassion and concern during this difficult period.*

SPONSORS REACT

Business analysts estimated that most of Woods's wealth came from his many sponsorship agreements. In 2008, for example, only 7 percent of his $100 million came from "on-course earnings," according to *Sports Illustrated*. For the first weeks of the scandal Woods's sponsors stood by him and offered support. But as the number of women claiming affairs with Woods grew to the double digits, companies began to reassess their commitments with Woods. An Internet "endorsement deathwatch" began in early December 2009 with onlookers and experts offering their take on the sponsorship situation.

At the time, Woods had many endorsement deals including Nike ($30 million), Accenture ($20 million), Gillette ($15 million), Electronic Arts ($8 million), and deals with PepsiCo./Gatorade, Golf Digest, NetJets, Tag Heuer, Upper Deck, and AT&T for unspecified amounts, according to CBSNews.com. Most issued short statements supporting Woods and his family at the beginning of the crisis. However, some sponsors took preemptive steps to isolate the brand damage. No television commercials featuring Woods ran after November 30, and Tag Heuer began taking down in-house ads by December 10. Citing low sales, Gatorade said it would cancel the Woods-themed drink.

After Woods announced a leave of absence, more companies began to reassess their sponsorships. Accenture, a business consulting firm with many Fortune 500 companies, was using the ad tagline, "Go on, be a Tiger." The company decided to cut its ties with Woods December 13, 2009, in a statement: "After careful consideration and analysis, the company has determined that he is no longer the right representative for its advertising." AT&T ended its relationship December 31.

Tag Heuer, the luxury watchmaker, whose advertising tagline was "What are You Made of?" dropped him December 18. On February 26, 2010, Gatorade (the company's Tiger's drink slogan was the unfortunate "It's in Tiger, is it in You?") parted ways with Woods. A spokeswoman for Gatorade said: "We no longer see a role for Tiger in our marketing efforts and have ended our relationship." Gillette decided not to renew its contract at the end of 2010.

Nike and other companies stood by him. A Nike spokesman said: "Tiger has been part of Nike for more than a decade," according to a Nike statement reported in USAToday.com. "He is the best golfer in the world and one of the greatest athletes of his era. We look forward to his return to golf. He and his family have Nike's full support."

Nike also created a controversial commercial titled "Earl and Tiger" that featured an audio clip from Tiger Woods's deceased father Earl that seemed to question his son's philandering actions. The commercial aired before Woods's highly anticipated return to professional golf.

Articles such as "The Temptation of Tiger Woods," published March 31, 2010, by *Vanity Fair*, did not help. It provided an in-depth accounting of Woods's womanizing, gambling, and other indiscretions.

TIGER'S RETURN TO GOLF

Woods retreated from the world and went into therapy at a clinic in Mississippi. On February 19, 2010, Woods spoke directly to the public in his first live address since his accident. While his wife did not attend, his mother did. Woods appeared nervous, but his apology was direct and detailed. He did not take any questions. According to CNN.com's transcript of the event, he began with an apology: "I want to say to each of you, simply, and directly, I am deeply sorry for my irresponsible and selfish behavior I engaged in." He noted the pain he caused his family and supporters.

> *I am also aware of the pain my behavior has caused to those of you in this room. I have let you down. I have let down my fans. For many of you, especially my friends, my behavior has been a personal disappointment. To those of you who work for me, I have let you down, personally and professionally. My behavior has caused considerable worry to my business partners.*

He said he intended to support and commit himself to his foundation's future success.

> *I know I have severely disappointed all of you. I have made you question who I am and how I have done the things I did. I am embarrassed that I have put you in this position. For all that I have done, I am so sorry. I have a lot to atone for.*

FIGURE 8.23 *In this February 19, 2010, file photo, Tiger Woods pauses during a news conference in Ponte Vedra Beach, Fla. Woods called a news conference to apologize for his infidelities saying, "I was unfaithful. I had affairs. I cheated."*
A FEB. 19, 2010 FILE PHOTO/Associated Press

Woods then refuted the allegations that there had been any incidents of domestic violence in his marriage "ever." He said his wife had "shown enormous grace and poise throughout this ordeal. Elin deserves praise, not blame." He then said that he was to blame for his "repeated irresponsible behavior." Woods said: "I was unfaithful. I had affairs. I cheated. What I did is not acceptable. And I am the only person to blame. I stopped living by the core values that I was taught to believe in."

Woods then explained his behavior:

> *I knew my actions were wrong. But I convinced myself that normal rules didn't apply. I never thought about who I was hurting. Instead, I thought only about myself. I ran straight through the boundaries that a married couple should live by. I thought I could get away with whatever I wanted to. I felt that I had worked hard my entire life and*

deserved to enjoy all the temptations around me. I felt I was entitled. Thanks to money and fame, I didn't have far—didn't have to go far to find them.

I was wrong. I was foolish. I don't get to play by different rules. The same boundaries that apply to everyone apply to me. I brought this shame on myself. I hurt my wife, my kids, my mother, my wife's family, my friends, my foundation, and kids all around the world who admired me.

Woods admitted that his golf achievements were secondary to personal integrity:

Character and decency are what really count. Parents used to point to me as a role model for their kids. I owe all of those families a special apology. I want to say to them that I am truly sorry.

Woods then briefly addressed that he had been in inpatient therapy for forty-five days "receiving guidance for the issues I'm facing." He asked for privacy for himself and his wife.

He denied that he had ever taken performance-enhancing drugs.

Woods then said that his family should be shielded from the scandal and the media. He pleaded for the media to stop hounding his wife and children: "Whatever my wrongdoings, for the sake of my family, please leave my wife and kids alone."

Woods said he was determined to "become a better man." He then discussed something that few knew: he had been raised as a Buddhist but had "drifted away from it." He said: "Buddhism teaches that a craving for things outside ourselves causes an unhappy and pointless search for security. It teaches me to stop following every impulse and to learn restraint. Obviously, I lost track of what I was taught."

Woods said that he would be returning for more therapy and that he would be working to apply what he had learned in therapy to regain a balance between his spiritual life and his professional life.

He finished his statement by partially answering the question on the minds of all his fans—his return to golf. He said he didn't know when that would happen but that it might be sometime in 2010. "When I do return, I need to make my behavior more respectful of the game," he said. He ended his statement this way:

Finally, there are many people in this room and there are many people at home who believed in me. Today, I want to ask for your help. I ask you to find room in your hearts to one day believe in me again. Thank you.

The next month, Woods announced that he would return to golf at the Masters tournament in Augusta, Georgia. At the time, it was reported that Woods had been advised on his transition back to public life by Ari Fleischer, a former White House spokesman who owned his own sports consulting business. This relationship ended by

March 22 amid complaints from critics that Woods was being managed by someone who himself had negative baggage from his days in the George W. Bush White House.

Woods offered media interviews for the first time since November 2009 with the restriction that they be limited to five minutes, with no limits on what questions were asked. ESPN and Golf Channel got the interviews. He also conducted a pre-Masters news conference at Augusta's golf course. He admitted his infidelities and offered this comment to Kelly Tilghman of the Golf Channel: "You strip away the denial, the rationalization and you come to the truth and the truth is very painful at times, and to stare at yourself and look at the person you've become, you become disgusted."

He also answered questions about his golf game and discussed his uncertain future golf plans. Legions of fans eagerly awaited Woods's much publicized 1:42 p.m. tee-off at the Masters April 8, 2010. While he did not win, but placed second behind Phil Mickelson, it marked a new beginning for Woods as he began to rehabilitate his badly tarnished image. Two years later, Woods was back with his winning swing—returning to the world number one spot with a victory at the Arnold Palmer Invitational in March 2013. His PGA Tour earnings by September 2013 were $8,231,839 from fourteen events, making him the top earner. And Forbes listed him at number fifteen on its Celebrity 100 list. He also was getting sponsorships again, beginning with the 2012 announcement of an endorsement deal with Fuse Science, Inc., a sports nutrition firm, and Woods signed a new deal with Nike in 2013; other endorsement deals included Rolex, NetJets' EA Sports, and Kowa.

QUESTIONS FOR DISCUSSION

1. What golfing accomplishments made Tiger Woods a superstar athlete?
2. What were Tiger Woods's estimated earnings from endorsements?
3. Why was Tiger Woods considered such a strong celebrity endorser?
4. How does an athlete like Tiger Woods help sell products?
5. How long did it take for Tiger Woods to break his silence after the car accident? Was his statement effective? Explain.
6. Tiger Woods's second statement was issued December 2, 2009. Why did his privacy concerns not end the controversy?
7. Why did Tiger Woods's apologies, offered in his December 2 and December 11, 2009, web statements, not end the controversy? Who had he hurt other than his family?
8. Most critics thought the February 19, 2010, apology was effective. What was different about this apology/statement?

Dig Deeper

Read the research article "Media Portrayals for Tiger Woods: A Qualitative Deconstructive Examination." How do the media portrayals "reinforce historical practices and common stereotypes of the golf community," according to the authors?

26

What Price the Regal Reputation?

Protecting the Royal Investment from Scandal

Rambunctious royals are nothing new.

Many Americans across the pond have been fascinated by the British royal family's ups and downs, a fascination fed by the innate frailties of human nature and an aggressive paparazzi. Playboy reputations have existed down through the ages including Queen Victoria's eldest son, Albert Edward, who waited and played 60 years before being crowned, and his heir, George, who later abdicated the throne to marry a woman deemed unsuitable for court. In the 1980s, the world watched as Prince Charles wed Princess Diana in what many called a charming fairy-tale wedding, memorable for its stunning display of royal pomp and circumstance. The young and stylish princess set fashion trends and ignited a hairstyle craze. The marriage ultimately did not go well; Prince Charles and Princess Diana's separation and affairs were tabloid fodder for years. It all ended tragically with Princess Diana's death in a high-speed car crash which some blamed in part on the paparazzi.

The slow and painful dissolution of the royal marriage wasn't the only drama occurring in the House of Windsor. Prince Charles's younger brother, Prince Andrew, also had a marriage that ended in divorce; Sarah Ferguson, Duchess of York, or "Fergie" as she was known, had embarrassed the royal family in a variety of ways. In one instance, she was photographed sunbathing topless while a male companion sucked her toes.

While these types of celebrity scandals play out daily in the media and on gossip sites for all sorts of celebrities, negative coverage presumably had its limits even for British royalty. A backlash of public dissatisfaction occurred in the 1990s as coverage of the failing royal marriages and other foibles were played out for all to see. A public debate on the necessity of maintaining a constitutional monarchy gathered momentum as taxpayers, who funded much of the bill, began to question the value of their investment.

"THE FIRM"

As a constitutional monarch, Queen Elizabeth II has only ceremonial duties which are supported by parliamentary grants derived from taxes. In addition to the Queen, the royal family covered by the state includes: the Queen's husband, Prince Philip; the Prince of Wales (Charles); Camilla, Duchess of Cornwall; the Duke and Duchess of Cambridge (William and Kate); and Prince Harry. Other royal family members' support is funded by the Queen. The state underwrites staff salaries, state visits, public engagements, ceremonial functions, and maintenance of the royal households. Security and transportation are also covered by government grants. According to Brand Finance, a financial consultancy group, the full estimate of annual royal expenditures is £461 million and travel at £195 million (£1 equals about $1.60 in U.S. currency).

Forbes estimated the monarchy's net worth at around $500 million in 2011. The British monarchy is sometimes referred to as "The Firm" because of its massive holdings, similar to those of a corporation, in real estate, fine art, antiques, and other treasures of the empire. The monarchy is actually big business and plays a vital role in the U.K.'s massive tourism economy. Here are a few financial facts about the House of Windsor from Brand Finance as reported in its *Jubilee Report 2012*:

- The total assessed value of the monarchy is £44.5 billion (tangible and intangible assets).
- The monarchy's royal palaces and crown jewels are worth £18.1 billion.

FIGURE 8.24 *The royal family. http://wikimedia.org/* Carfax2

- The monarchy generates £26.4 billion for the UK through tourism and other industries annually.
- The Crown Estate properties generate £8.3 billion annually.
- The monarchy generates more than £4 billion in free publicity overseas annually.

The primary role of the monarchy is ceremonial and requires the royal family to be available for a rather grueling schedule of events. Queen Elizabeth II, at age 85 in 2011, participated in 444 engagements, fifty-seven of them overseas. Her husband, the Duke of Edinburgh, at age 89, had 356 engagements; their son, Prince Charles, had 585. In addition to their military service, Prince William and Prince Harry had seventy-three and fifty-three engagements respectively in 2011. Some economists have estimated that the cost for funding the monarchy in that year was just 62 pence per British citizen.

To keep the family business on solid ground, the monarchy keeps tabs on its younger members to protect its brand image. Everyone has a role to play and even the younger generation must toe the line. Here are a few incidents that have caused some consternation in the royal household.

PRINCE HARRY'S NAZI COSTUME CHOICE

Prince Harry, grandson of Queen Elizabeth II and then third in line to the throne, got more than the usual tabloid treatment in 2004. He was photographed wearing a Nazi uniform at a costume party—two weeks before the sixtieth anniversary of the liberation of the notorious Nazi death camp, Auschwitz.

The photograph showed the young prince, who was 20 at the time, at a friend's party holding a drink in one hand and a cigarette in the other while sporting a red-and-black swastika armband and an army shirt with Nazi regalia.

As the embarrassing photo was reprinted around the world, it clashed with the somber Holocaust anniversary, seen as particularly poignant because it was considered the last major gathering of Holocaust survivors; world leaders, including Queen Elizabeth, planned to commemorate the event.

The Nazi gas chambers, like those at Auschwitz, were part of a camp system that exterminated more than six million Jews and "undesirables"; millions more were subjected to imprisonment and forced labor during World War II.

In a two-sentence statement released to the media the day after the photo was published, Prince Harry said: "I am very sorry if I have caused any offence. It was a poor choice of costume and I apologize."

Ned Temko, editor of the London-based *Jewish Chronicle*, was unimpressed with the apology:

> *It implied this was a wardrobe problem. Whatever further statement he makes, there has to be some reflection that a swastika armband isn't just a fashion item, that it*

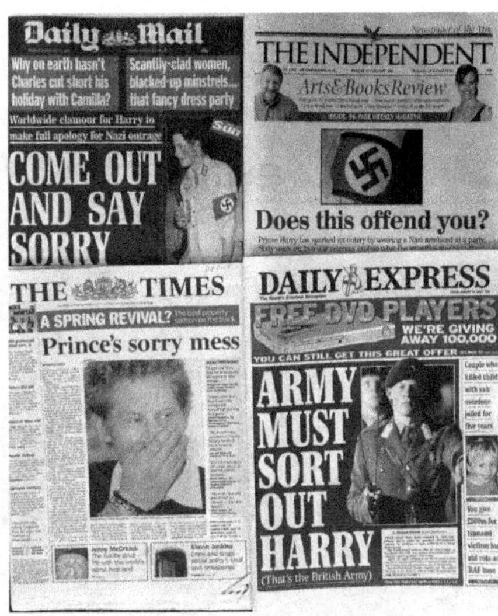

Daily Mail

Why on earth hasn't Charles cut short his holiday with Camilla?

Scantily-clad women, blacked-up minstrels... that fancy dress party

Worldwide clamour for Harry to make full apology for Nazi outrage

COME OUT AND SAY SORRY

THE INDEPENDENT

Arts & Books Review

Does this offend you?

THE TIMES

A SPRING REVIVAL?

Prince's sorry mess

DAILY EXPRESS

FREE DVD PLAYERS

WE'RE GIVING AWAY 100,000

YOU CAN STILL GET THIS GREAT OFFER

ARMY MUST SORT OUT HARRY

(That's the British Army)

FIGURE 8.25 *Prince Harry's headlines over the Nazi costume choice.*
Associated Press

> *symbolizes a lot more. One of the most dismaying aspects for Jews and non-Jews is that there seems to be an utter lack of awareness of the context of the Holocaust and the war.*

Prince Harry did not make an in-person apology. Amid calls for Prince Harry to do more than apologize, the royal family ruled out his attendance at Auschwitz ceremonies. An official said: "It would be a distraction and a detraction from the importance of the occasion because it would become a different story in media terms . . . He recognizes he made a very bad mistake and he apologizes for that."

PRINCE HARRY'S VEGAS PARTY PHOTOS

Years later, things were going very well for the royal family. The "wedding of the century" between Prince William and Kate Middleton was a smash hit with the British public and millions of fans around the world tuned in to see the televised event or traveled to London to see the spectacle in person. It was estimated that the $30 million wedding, paid for mostly by the Queen, generated £107 million tourism revenue in London alone, with an overall economic benefit of £620 million, according to Slate.com. While most economists said the event operated at a loss due to the "bank holiday," the wedding also was an incalculable morale boost for a country mired in a dreary worldwide recession and a long and costly war in Afghanistan.

The wedding was followed by the Diamond Jubilee, a year-long series of commemorative events to celebrate Queen Elizabeth's sixty-year reign. The celebration

FIGURE 8.26 *Prince Harry of Wales greeting people.*
commons.wikimedia.org/
John Pannell

included her participation in the 2012 London Olympics and subsequent Paralympic Games. By all accounts, the Jubilee and Olympics were flawless in their execution, full of pageantry and memorable moments.

All of this goodwill and national pride was tainted by what some called a youthful indiscretion weeks after the Olympics.

Just shy of Prince Harry's twenty-eighth birthday and before a second deployment to Afghanistan, he was again the subject of embarrassing photos, which appeared first on the celebrity gossip website TMZ.com. He was shown naked during a party in a Las Vegas hotel room after playing a game of strip billiards. One photo showed a nude Prince Harry, cupping his genitals, with a woman, apparently nude, behind him. Another showed a nude Prince Harry giving a woman, also apparently nude, a bear hug with his backside exposed. The photos, of course, "went viral" and were seen by millions online.

While some in the news media said that Prince Harry was letting off steam before potentially dangerous deployment as an Apache helicopter pilot, others said such playboy behavior was harmful to the royal brand. In Britain, the photos received just as much media attention as the chilling effect of the British Leveson

Inquiry on news reporting. The inquiry, which focused on news media actions following a phone hacking scandal, resulted in many newspapers not publishing the TMZ photos. A debate ensued: Did Prince Harry's nude photos taken in his room at a private hotel constitute an invasion of privacy under British law? Still, the British press fully described the scandalous photos and told readers where to find them.

What was more serious was the result of Prince Harry's publicized military deployment. Two U.S. Marines were killed and five British soldiers injured after powerful insurgent attacks on the airbase where Prince Harry was stationed. The insurgents had reportedly threatened to kidnap the prince, a high-value target. Some cynics said the unusual pre-deployment publicity was an effort to rehabilitate a tarnished image through military service. Other critics questioned whether or not deploying a royal to a war zone was acceptable since it put others in harm's way unnecessarily.

KATE'S TURN

Prince William's wife, Kate, was also embarrassed when photos of her sunbathing topless were published by a French magazine. Taken while she and William were vacationing at a private home in France, the pictures were captured by a high-powered camera lens capable of producing clear images from a half-mile away. While not considered responsible for this embarrassment, members of the royal family were nonetheless on the defensive again. The photos were published while the couple were on an official tour of Southeast Asia and the South Pacific as part of the British Commonwealth's Diamond Jubilee celebration.

QUESTIONS FOR DISCUSSION

1. How does the royal family respond to embarrassing incidents such as those described in this case study?
2. How is the royal spokesman used?
3. How is the official royal website used to promote the monarchy?
4. How does the monarchy use transparency to promote a positive reputation?

Dig Deeper

The British royal family is big business, especially for the tourism industry. Read the *Guardian*'s "Royal Wedding Gives £2bn Boost to UK Tourism," published April 29, 2011, and Brand Finance's "How We Valued the Monarchy as a Brand: UK Tourism Contribution" at brandfinance.com, which is also available on the textbook's companion website.

CHAPTER 9

Community Relations

"No man is an island," a famous poet once wrote—and likewise, no organization can succeed in isolation. Organizations constantly interact with and depend on all kinds of groups: employees, customers, members, government officials, other businesses, suppliers, educational institutions, and many others.

The traditional definition of community has included groups loosely or tightly associated through some unifying trait or issue such as ethnicity, politics, gender, work, and geographic location. Since technology and globalization have erased many geographic barriers in the last generation, the definition of *community* has changed dramatically. Just as people of like minds are now easily connected through online communities, multinational organizations, while headquartered in one place, may have plants and other operations scattered across the globe.

Even though the meaning of community has expanded, the traditional definition based on geographic location still counts today because organizations rely on attracting good employees and operating in business-friendly environments.

BUILDING POSITIVE RELATIONSHIPS AT HOME

In either case, public relations seeks to build positive relationships with community groups whose activities can have an impact on an organization's reputation and livelihood. Issues such as pollution, working conditions, hiring practices, compensation, the economic impact of the organization on other businesses—even traffic, noise, and other quality-of-life issues—all can grow into major controversies that may disrupt operations and damage the reputation of the organization.

An organization can develop a good-neighbor approach to community relations that balances the needs and concerns of community partners with its mission. This approach, called *corporate social responsibility,* recognizes an organization's obligation to contribute to society in some way because it's the right thing to do. Many organizations have found that giving back to the community is good business and often leads to stronger consumer loyalty. Such activity can foster company pride and provide opportunities for employees to be involved in their communities.

An effective community relations program should be conducted purposely with goals and objectives. This starts with an examination of the organization's strengths and weaknesses, from facilities to human resources. While many businesses have big

hearts and deep pockets, they want to see a benefit, even for charitable activities. An organization should inventory what it has to offer beyond money. For example, a professional baseball team could offer to run a baseball camp for underprivileged children, or executive leadership could be "loaned" to nonprofits for a year. Often organizations seek a natural fit that extends their brand recognition. Organizations should also consider employee interests. Employees are often willing volunteers for a good cause when their company provides the necessary resources.

Next, an organization needs to get acquainted with the community and its challenges. Organizational leadership should connect with elected community leaders and other organizations' executives by joining key civic or nonprofit organizations. Some of these could include the United Way, Rotary International, and cultural institutions.

Once an organization has examined its strengths and determined community needs, it must decide what it can do to help. Effective outreach may be as simple as a library that offers its meeting rooms to nonprofits, displays local artists' works in its lobby, or offers reading programs and craft activities for children.

Whatever an organization decides to do should be planned and executed with care. A poorly run program will reflect negatively on the organization. The same diligence that goes into planning a public relations campaign should apply to charitable events.

The good deeds of an organization should also be communicated to key publics through the contributing organization's own organizational media as well as community channels. Effective outlets can include the local news media, the organization's employee and community newsletters and website, the chamber of commerce newsletter, and the available communication channels of the organization receiving the help. A Girl Scout council that receives building materials for an office renovation project from a hardware store, for example, could be featured in the Girl Scouts' community publications or recognized at an annual volunteer dinner.

CORPORATE PHILANTHROPY

Similar to the good-neighbor concept of community relations is corporate philanthropy. By law, corporations are allowed to donate up to 10 percent of their earnings to charitable organizations. The authors of *Public Relations: The Profession and the Practice* suggest a strategic approach to philanthropy that considers the following factors:

- **Do no harm.** Contributions should not be made to any cause that may be contrary to the best interests of the donor or the recipient.
- **Communicate with the recipient.** Effective grant making requires a close partnership between donor and the recipient.
- **Target contributions toward specific areas.** Gifts should achieve maximum impact on the community and maximum benefits for the donor. In

this regard, donations should go to areas where individual corporations have unique expertise not available in the nonprofit sector.

- **Make contributions according to statements of corporate policy.** Fully developed policies of this nature should include the charitable aims and beliefs of the company, the criteria to be used in evaluating requests for funds, the kinds of organizations and causes that will and will not be supported, and the methods by which grants will be administered.
- **Plan within the budget.** Corporate giving should be tied to a set percentage of net earnings.
- **Inform all persons concerned.** Employees and the community at large should be fully aware of corporate activities.
- **Do a follow-up.** The corporation does a valuable service by demanding high levels of performance and proper financial accounting from recipients.
- **Remember that more than money may be needed.** An effective corporate contribution program requires more than checkbook charity. Volunteer workers, managerial expertise, and corporate leadership are essential elements of an effective program.

27

I'm Watching You . . .

School-Issued Laptop "Spycam" Invades Privacy Rights

For years, computers have been a reality in the K-12 educational environment. At its best, technology offers all kinds of possibilities for engaging young people in the learning process. But as anyone who has ever purchased a new gadget knows, technology can have its downside as well. So it was for students at Harriton High School, who discovered that their school-issued Apple laptops could monitor them at home—or anywhere else.

BACKGROUND

Harriton High School is one of two high schools in the Lower Merion School District (LMSD) that serves 62,000 residents of Lower Merion Township and the Borough of Narberth. The district, located west of Philadelphia, is one of the oldest public schools in Pennsylvania and is affluent, with a median household income of $112,300 in 2010 and a median home value of $583,900. A large renovation project modernized all nine district school buildings, and in 2010 a new $100 million Harriton High School was completed; a $108.5 million Lower Merion High School was under construction. The district's per student expenditure was one of the highest in the state.

According to the district's website, LMSD offers a quality educational program and students are high-achieving. Each school:

> *received recognition for excellence by the Commonwealth and seven have received the National Blue Ribbon Award for Excellence in Education. LMSD schools rank among the highest in Pennsylvania for SAT and PSAT scores, AP Participation rate, total number of National Merit Semifinalists, total number of International Baccalaureate diplomas granted and in numerous publications' "Top Schools" lists. Approximately 94 percent of high school graduates attend institutions of higher learning.*

Newsweek's "Best High Schools" ranked Harriton High School first in the state; its other high school was ranked third. Famous graduates included NBA basketball legend Kobe Bryant and Alexander Haig, former secretary of state.

A DISTURBING DISCOVERY

Thanks to state and federal funding secured by the district's technology department, each high school student was provided an Apple laptop to enhance his or her learning experience. Students were allowed to take home their assigned laptops to take full advantage of the technology.

On November 11, 2009, Harriton High School student Blake Robbins was confronted by an assistant principal who said that Robbins was engaged in "improper behavior" in his home. Cited as evidence, according to court documents: a photograph from the school-issued laptop webcam showed Robbins eating something that looked like pills on a bed. The photo was taken without his knowledge, permission, or authorization.

Students were unaware that the school district had loaded a software program onto each laptop that gave the district's technology department the ability to remotely activate the camera embedded in the laptop. When the laptop was operating, the technology department could view the environment in front of the laptop as well as "see" what was on the computer screen, such as documents and e-mails.

The district had installed LANrev, a computer management software system, on all of its district's 6,500 networked computers, including the laptops. This software allowed the district technology staff to efficiently disseminate software updates and patches and other maintenance work remotely from a central server, which eliminated the need to service each computer individually.

A feature of LANrev was Theft Track, which, when enabled, could assist district officials in locating stolen or lost computers by providing valuable data such as a computer's geographic environment, visuals of its users, and information from documents. The software could take still photos of anything in front of the laptop from the webcam and screenshots of what was on the computer screen.

At the time, students and their parents were required to sign an Acceptable Use Guidelines document to use the district-owned laptops; it included a reference to the district's policy for appropriate use of the district's network, but the signed agreement did not include information about the Theft Track feature specifically. No district policy was created to handle issues regarding Theft Track. In addition, there were no restrictions imposed on district technology staff use of LANrev's tracking features. The technology administrator hired after the purchase of LANrev later described the technology department as the "Wild West" because of the lack of protocols to guide staff about rapidly advancing technology issues.

In most instances, the Theft Track feature was activated on specific laptops when a school administrator or technology department member was informed that a student had reported his or her laptop stolen or lost. The intent was to use the tracking features to help locate the missing laptop. Within a year and a half, thirteen student laptops had been reported stolen and six of those were recovered by the local police with district-provided information.

AN EARLY WARNING FROM A STUDENT INTERN

Some students had noticed a green camera light flicker on their laptops from time to time, and a few decided to cover the lens. Fifteen months before Blake Robbins was confronted with a webcam photo of himself at home, a student intern in the district's technology department raised questions about privacy and the LANrev software. According to the district's own investigative report:

> *On August 11, 2008, shortly before the rollout of the One-to-One program at HHS, an HHS student who had been a student intern in the IS Department e-mailed Ms. DiMedio [the district's technology coordinator] with the subject line "1:1 concern (Important)." He wrote that he had recently learned of the District's purchase of LANrev and, describing his discovery of its ability to remotely manage computers while they are outside LMSD's network as "something startling," stated: "I would not find this a problem if students were informed that this was possible, for privacy's sake. However, what was appalling was that not only did the District not inform parents and students of this fact . . . "*
>
> *He further wrote: "[W]hile you may feel that you can say that this access will not be abused, I feel that this is not enough to ensure the integrity of students and that even if it was no one would have any way of knowing (especially end users).*
>
> *"I feel it would be best that students and parents are informed of this before they receive their computers.*
>
> *"And while this only slightly sways my opinion on 1:1, I could see not informing parents and students of this fact causing a huge uproar."*

Virginia DiMedio
Director of Technology and Information Services
Lower Merion School District
301 Montgomery Avenue
Ardmore, PA 19003
610-645-1925
dimedio@lmsd.org

From:
Sent: Monday, August 11, 2008 5:12 PM
To: DiMedio Virginia
Subject: 1:1 concern (Important)

Dear Ms. DiMedio,

As you are fully aware I have been constantly been supportive of the 1:1 initiative in Lower Merion School District. However, finally as 1:1 nears implementation I have come across 2 severe concerns (1 is much less important than the other so i wont talk about it in this email). I recently learned of the districts purchase of software known as "LANRev." Being a curious person I did a little reading/research/telephone calls (to the company) on the product and discovered something startling. This was the fact that the district can remotely manage computers that are outside of the network, should they so choose, as long as the computer is on the internet. Now, I would not find this a problem if students were informed that this was possible, for privacy's sake. However, what was appalling was that not only did the District not inform parents and students of this fact however they stated:

Internet Protection Act (CIPA) guidelines. At home students will not pass through this filter. Parents are asked to supervise their children when using Internet access. Checking the browser history is one way of knowing which sites users have visited."

While this does not cover remote monitoring it does implicate that at home you will not be able to be monitored and no where does it explicitly say otherwise. In addition, after coming through the AUP i don't see anything about monitoring 1:1 machines off property, only saying:

"the network administrator may review files and communications to maintain system integrity and ensure that students are using the system responsibly
" (and that is only pertaining to the networks integrity).

Also, now rereading it I only see clauses about firewall software and not about monitoring the computers whenever the technology department feels like it (although it s common knowledge when on school grounds). And while you may feel that you can say that this access will not be abused, I feel that this is not enough to ensure the integrity of students and that even if it was no one would have anyway of knowing (especially end users).

I feel it would be best that students and parents are informed of this before they receive their computers.

And while this only slightly sways my opinion on 1:1, i could see not informing parents and students of this fact causing a huge uproar.

FIGURE 9.1 *One Lower Merion School District student intern in the technology department raised a red flag regarding privacy concerns related to the tracking software months before the lawsuit was filed.*
http://www.lmsd.org/
Lower Merion School District

Respond to me ASAP

Virginia DiMedio
Director of Technology and Information Services
Lower Merion School District
301 Montgomery Avenue
Ardmore, PA 19003
610-645-1925
dimedio@lmsd.org

From: DiMedio Virginia
Sent: Monday, August 11, 2008 5:19 PM
To:
Subject: RE: 1:1 concern (Important)

I am not sure that what you've found is correct. What I do know for absolute certainty is that there is absolutely no way that the District Tech people are going to monitor students at home. There is no plan, no staff, no desire and I believe no technical way to do that. I will definitely confirm the technical piece. If we were going to monitor student use at home, we would have stated so. Think about it--why would we do that? There is no purpose. We are not a police state. Lower Merion is one of the few school districts that only filters what we are required by federal law. There is no way that I would approve or advocate for the monitoring of students at home.

I suggest you take a breath and relax.

FIGURE 9.3 *A school district administrater dismissed the student's concern, saying that it was unwarranted and that no one would monitor students at home.*
http://www.lmsd.org/
Lower Merion School District

Ms. DiMedio responded seven minutes later:

> *I am not sure what you've found is correct. What I do know for absolute certainty is that there is absolutely no way that the District Tech people are going to monitor students at home. There is no plan, no staff, no desire and I believe no technical way to do that. I will definitely confirm the technical piece. If we are going to monitor student use at home, we would have stated so. Think about it—why would we do that? There is no purpose. We are not a police state. Lower Merion is one of the few school districts that only filters what we are required by federal law. There is no way that I would approve or advocate for the monitoring of students at home.*
>
> *I suggest you take a breath and relax.*

According to the district's investigative report:

> *Ms. DiMedio then forwarded the e-mail chain to Mr. Perbix, who proposed a lengthy further response to the student intern that detailed LANrev's non-tracking features and described Theft Track. With Ms. DiMedio's approval, Mr. Perbix sent an e-mail to the student intern that included the following:*
>
> *"I will tell you that this feature is only used to track equipment that is reported as stolen or missing. The only information that this feature captures is IP and DNS info from the network it is connected to and occasional screen/camera shots of the computer being operated. This information is provided to police to hopefully assist in getting the*

> *laptop back to us. This feature has already been used to retrieve laptops that would have otherwise been lost and can only be activated by two people in the department. Once again, it is only used in the case where a laptop is reported as stolen or missing.*
>
> *"The tracking feature does NOT do things like record web browsing, chatting, email or any other type of 'spyware' features that you might be thinking of."*

That was not exactly true. In fact it was far from the truth, as the investigation later determined.

A lawsuit seeking class-action status was filed in U.S. District Court for the Eastern District of Pennsylvania against the Lower Merion School District by the Robbins family on February 17, 2010. The suit sought damages for invasion of privacy, theft of private information and unlawful interception and access to acquired and exported data and other stored electronic communications in violation of the Electronic Communications Privacy Act, the Computer Fraud Abuse Act, the Stored Communications Act, the Civil Rights Act, the Fourth Amendment of the United States Constitution, the Pennsylvania Wiretapping and Electronic Surveillance Act, and Pennsylvania common law, according to the lawsuit. Three days later, the news media reported that the FBI had opened an investigation to determine whether federal wiretap or computer intrusion laws were violated.

In particular, the invasion of privacy was noted in that the "images captured and intercepted may consist of images of minors and their parents or friends in compromising or embarrassing positions, including, but not limited to, in various stages of dress or undress." The students often used their laptops constantly. They were frequently left on twenty-four hours. One distressed female student interviewed on national television said that she brought her laptop into the bathroom to play music while she showered.

At the center of the controversy was 15-year-old Harriton sophomore Blake Robbins. With a sweep of hair over his forehead, he looked like a typical teen caught up in an unusual circumstance. His laptop was remotely monitored by the district because his family had not paid a $55 insurance fee required of every student who wanted to bring their laptop home. While about twenty other students had not paid the insurance fee, Robbins was the only one monitored by the district. At the time of the lawsuit, Blake's family did not know the extent of the monitoring since the assistant principal had provided only one printed image of him allegedly taking pills. Blake said in media interviews that the "pills" were Mike and Ike's candy.

NEWS COVERAGE ERUPTS

A website called BoingBoing.net published a story about the laptop lawsuit before midnight February 17, 2010. The next morning, district officials began to learn about the story and lawsuit. National and international news media and Internet blogger coverage quickly followed once the lawsuit was filed. At the time,

LMSD was one of the first districts in the country to provide all its high school students with a laptop computer that could be used at home. The clash of technology and privacy was of interest to many. Terms and phrases such as "spycam," "spycamgate," "spy kids," and "spy high" were frequently employed in media headlines. An Associated Press dispatch distributed on February 19, 2010, was widely republished throughout the country by bloggers and the news media. Newspapers such as *The New York Times* and *The Washington Post* also covered the story.

Two days after the suit had been filed *The CBS Early Show* interviewed a female student who attended Harriton High School. She said that when she heard about the lawsuit "I was shocked. Someone told me in my chem class. I e-mailed my mom right away. I was like 'Mom, I have this open all the time—when I'm changing, when I'm in the shower—this is disturbing.' "

That night, *CBS Evening News* interviewed Marc Rotenberg, director of the Electronic Privacy Information Center, who said: "This is one of the most egregious privacy violations I've ever heard."

The next morning on *The CBS Early Show*, Blake Robbins, his older sister, his parents, and his lawyer were interviewed. Blake said he was not taking or selling drugs, as had been alleged by the school administrator.

> *They called me to the office and they notified me that they had called my parents and she starts accusing me of selling drugs throughout Harriton and saying that I was taking pills. And I thought I've never done that before. That's not possible. It must have been Mike and Ike's, my favorite candy.*

FIGURE 9.4 *The Robbins family made themselves available for media interviews during the crisis.*
http://mainlinemedianews.com/
Main Line Media News

FIGURE 9.5 *CBS Evening News report February 19, 2010.*
http://www.cbsnews.com/
CBS Evening News

On the local ABC news affiliate in Philadelphia, Blake's mother said: "It's really scary . . . It was an invasion of privacy; it was as if we had a peeping tom in our house. I sent my son to school to learn, not to be spied on."

Another high-profile story appeared on ABC's *Good Morning America*, February 22, 2010, which included interviews with Blake and his mother. Blake again denied the drug allegations and his mother commented on the privacy issues. The local news media including *The Philadelphia Inquirer* covered the unfolding story on the front pages of its newspaper and website.

Blake Robbins provided an impromptu interview in front of his house to a gaggle of reporters eager for his story February 22, 2010. He said what the district had done was "real messed up" and "I just hope they're not watching me . . . It's terrible," according to *ABC News 10* in Philadelphia.

LOWER MERION SCHOOL DISTRICT'S RESPONSE

LMSD's District Superintendent Dr. Christopher W. McGinley became aware of the Robbins' lawsuit February 18, 2010, and developed an e-mail statement containing preliminary answers to questions which was posted at 4:45 p.m. Later that evening a letter from McGinley for parents was also posted on the district website at 9:26 p.m. and shared with the news media.

> *Dear LMSD Parents/Guardians,*
>
> *Our history has been to go to great lengths to protect the privacy of our students; whether it comes to student health, academic or other records. In fact, many of you may remember the heated debate over whether to have security cameras monitor some of our food vending machines. Privacy is a basic right in our society and a matter we take very seriously. We believe that a good job can always be done better.*

FIGURE 9.6 *NBC 10 Philadelphia interviewed a fidgetty teen at home about the controversy, saying, "It's terrible." http://www.nbcphiladelphia.com/*
NBC 10 Philadelphia

Recent publicity regarding the District's one-to-one high school laptop initiative, and questions about the security of student laptops prompted our administration to revisit security procedures.

Laptops are a frequent target for theft in schools and off school property. District laptops do contain a security feature intended to track lost, stolen and missing laptops. The security feature, which was disabled today, was installed to help locate a laptop in the event it was reported lost, missing or stolen so that the laptop could be returned to the student.

Upon a report of a suspected lost, stolen or missing laptop, the feature was activated by the District's security and technology departments. The security feature's capabilities were limited to taking a still image of the operator and the operator's screen. This feature was only used for the narrow purpose of locating a lost, stolen or missing laptop. The District never activated the security feature for any other purpose or in any other manner whatsoever.

As a result of our preliminary review of security procedures today, I directed the following actions:

- *Immediate disabling of the security-tracking program.*
- *A thorough review of the existing policies for student laptop use.*
- *A review of security procedures to help safeguard the protection of privacy; including a review of the instances in which the security software was activated. We want to ensure that any affected students and families are made aware of the outcome of laptop recovery investigations.*
- *A review of any other technology areas in which the intersection of privacy and security may come into play.*

FIGURE 9.7 *Attorney Henry Hockeimer of Ballard Spahr provided a summary of the investigation's preliminary findings during a school board meeting April 19, 2010.*
http://www.lmsd.org
Lower Merion School District

> *We are proud of the fact that we are a leader in providing laptops to every high school student as part of our instructional program. But we need to be equally as proud of the safeguards we have in place to protect the privacy of the users, as well as to safeguard district-owned property while being used by students.*
>
> *We regret if this situation has caused any concern or inconvenience among our students and families. If you have any questions or concerns, please email us at info@lmsd.org.*
>
> *Additional information has been posted on our website, www.lmsd.org.*
>
> *Thank you for your time and attention.*
>
> *Sincerely,*
>
> *Dr. Christopher W. McGinley*
> *Superintendent of Schools*
> *Lower Merion School District*

LMSD's School and Community Relations Director Doug Young also provided comments for news media stories.

The following day, February 19, 2010, McGinley posted another letter to parents and residents regarding the situation. It included a Q&A section that provided answers to many questions that residents were asking at the time:

> *Dear LMSD Parents/Guardians*
>
> *Yesterday I reported to you on the early phases of the school district's response to questions raised about the security-tracking software feature that was installed on student laptop computers. While we were able to address many of your initial questions and concerns, I regret we were not immediately in a position to answer all of your questions. Our goal is to be as open as possible, while preserving student privacy, and ensure that over time we have answered to your satisfaction every question about this situation and the broader issue of technology and privacy.*

We are a school district that embraces the use of leading-edge technology in our instructional program, encourages all forms of free expression, and must do everything possible to safeguard individual privacy. For these and other reasons, this matter is of the highest importance. In this regard, we have retained the services of Henry E. Hockeimer, Jr, Esq., a local attorney and former federal prosecutor, to assist in our comprehensive review of relevant policies and past practices, as well as assist us in implementing appropriate improvements.

Despite some reports to the contrary, be assured that the security-tracking software has been completely disabled. As I noted yesterday, this feature was limited to taking a still image of the computer user and an image of the desktop in order to help locate the reported missing, lost, or stolen computer (this includes tracking down a loaner computer that, against regulations, might be taken off campus). While we understand the concerns, in every one of the fewer than 50 instances in which the tracking software was used this school year, its sole purpose was to try to track down and locate a student's computer. Before answering additional questions below, it is important to clear up the matter of notice to students and parents of the existence of the security software. While certain rules for laptop use were spelled out—such as prohibitive uses on and off school property—there was no explicit notification that the laptop contained the security software. This notice should have been given and we regret that was not done.

Once again, we regret this situation has been a source of concern and disruption, and trust that we will soon have stronger privacy policies in place as a result of the lessons learned and our comprehensive review that is now underway. If you have any questions or concerns, please email us at info@lmsd.org. Additional information has been posted on our website, www.lmsd.org.

1. *Did an assistant principal at Harriton ever have the ability to remotely monitor a student at home? Did she utilize a photo taken by a school-issued laptop to discipline a student?*

   No. At no time did any high school administrator have the ability or actually access the security-tracking software. We believe that the administrator at Harriton has been unfairly portrayed and unjustly attacked in connection with her attempts to be supportive of a student and his family. The district never did and never would use such tactics as a basis for disciplinary action.

2. *How were the decisions made to develop the original security plan? Were there/are there safeguards in place to ensure student privacy with regard to use of the security application?*

   Concerned about the security of district-owned and -issued laptops, the security plan was developed by the technology department to give the District the ability to recover lost, stolen or missing student laptops. This included tracking loaner laptops that may, against regulations, have been taken off campus.

   Only two members of the technology department could access the security feature.

3. *Were students and families explicitly told about the laptop security system?*

   No. There was no formal notice given to students or their families. The functionality and intended use of the security feature should have been communicated clearly to students and families.

4. *How many thefts have there been? How many times was the system used? What have been the results in terms of recovery of computers?*

   During the 2009–10 school year, 42 laptops were reported lost, stolen or missing and the tracking software was activated by the technology department in each instance. A total of 18 laptops were found or recovered. This number (18) is an updated number given the information we have compiled today.

5. *What was the total cost of implementation of the laptop program?*

   The approximate cost of each laptop is $1,000 and during the two years of the program, there were 2,620 laptops purchased.

6. *How was funding obtained for the laptop program?*

   Laptops were purchased using a combination of district funds and Classrooms for the Future grants.

7. *When was the district notified of the allegations contained in the lawsuit?*

   The district learned of the allegations Thursday, February 18th. No complaints were received prior to this date. The district's initial response was posted on the district webpage and communicated to students and parents the same day. The district will not be commenting on the specifics of the plaintiff's complaint, however, outside the legal process.

8. *In the future, will students be required to use district-issued laptops?*

   The district believes students received significant benefit from the one-to-one laptop program and has no intention of discontinuing the program.

9. *Is remote access activity by the district logged?*

   Yes. There is a log entry for every instance of the security feature activation. The logs will be reviewed as part of the special review conducted under the direction of special outside counsel.

10. *Can parents return currently issued laptops to the district at this time?*

    They can, but we note that the laptops are an integral component of the educational program in the district. The security feature has been deactivated and there is no reason to be concerned about the use of the laptop on campus or at home.

11. *Did the district remotely access any laptops which were not lost, missing or stolen?*

    No.

12. *Are students allowed to cover the camera on their school-issued laptops with tape?*

    Yes. There is no requirement that a student use the camera's standard webcam feature.

FAQs Posted February 18 on the District Website

1. *Why are webcams installed on student laptops?*

   The Apple computers that the District provides to students come equipped with webcams and students are free to utilize this feature for educational purposes.

2. *Why was the remote tracking-security feature installed?*

   Laptops are a frequent target for theft in schools and off school property. The security feature was installed to help locate a laptop in the event it was reported lost, missing or stolen so that the laptop could be returned to the student.

3. *How did the security feature work?*

   Upon a report of a suspected lost, stolen or missing laptop, the feature was activated by the District's security and technology departments. The tracking-security feature was limited to taking a still image of the operator and the operator's screen. This feature has only been used for the limited purpose of locating a lost, stolen or missing laptop. The District has not used the tracking feature or webcam for any other purpose or in any other manner whatsoever.

4. *Do you anticipate reactivating the tracking-security feature?*

   Not without express written notification to all students and families.

Sincerely,

Dr. Christopher W. McGinley, Superintendent of Schools, Lower Merion School District

A few days later, on February 22, 2010, the judge in the case issued several orders including a gag order. The district was directed not to contact any student or a student's family that had been issued a computer by the district since they were potentially part of the class-action lawsuit request. The district was allowed to discuss educational and other matters with the students unrelated to the issues in the lawsuit. Another order required the district to preserve data on the computers issued to students.

While the gag order did not prevent people from talking about the case to the news media, it did curb the public conversation by district officials, employees, and board members. The board president, David Ebby, provided some updates at board meetings about the district's internal investigation but details were limited until April 13, 2010, when Ebby released preliminary data on the forensics investigation. A full presentation of the internal investigation was planned for May 3, 2010.

FIGURE 9.8 *Lower Merion School District Board President David Ebby, center, provided some updates on the investigation. School Superintendent Christopher McGinley, left, also provided information.*
http://www.lmsd.org
Lower Merion School District

According to the district, the following statement was issued April 13, 2010:

As we shared with you about a month ago, the District has retained Ballard Spahr and L3 Communications to conduct a review of the use of the tracking feature of the LANrev software application. This review has included the interviews of over 30 witnesses and the review of hundreds of thousands of documents, primarily emails and an analysis of the LANrev database. This analysis continues and we are hopeful that a report from the investigative team will be available to the public in the next few weeks.

We are able to share tonight the following information:

1. *The investigation has uncovered no evidence of intentional misuse of the LANrev tracking feature.*
2. *The investigation has confirmed that there were fewer than 50 activations during the current school year that would have resulted in photos, IP address identification and the capture of a desktop screenshot.*
3. *Once activated, there is no way to manipulate LANrev to capture images in "real time" or video.*
4. *All relevant evidence has been turned over by the District and will continue to be shared with the FBI.*

Again, the investigative team will be providing much more complete information in their report. We felt it was important to share these preliminary findings—as reported to us today—with you tonight.

DISTRICT PARENTS REACT

The gag order did not silence parents in the district. In fact, it mobilized them and helped the district communicate its story. A Facebook group called "Reasonable LMSD Parents Refusing to Rush to Judgment" and a second group called "lmsdparents.org" were organized. Doug Young, the district's community relations director, said these groups were a turning point for the district.

The Parents Refusing to Rush to Judgment described its purpose:

> *The sensational news reports following the filing of the recent federal lawsuit and its invasion of privacy allegations . . . have been almost exclusively driven by the plaintiffs and their lawyers. This is a discussion forum for parents of current and former LMSD students who believe it is important to know the facts before we or anyone else can claim the right to judge and condemn LMSD teachers, Administrators or our school board. Let's lead our children by fighting for the truth.*

In time, Parents Refusing to Rush to Judgment moved the Facebook discussion from talking about the spying issues to talking about the ramifications of a class-action lawsuit on the taxpayers and district services, said Young. More than 700 people joined the group.

The "lmsdparents" group was created soon after the gag order was implemented by lawyers pro bono who were district parents. In early March 2010, about 150 parents attended a town hall meeting to discuss the situation. They were in "opposition to the class action that was filed in connection with the laptop/Webcam issue," according to its FAQ page on its website. This group realized that a class-action lawsuit had the potential to cost the district (i.e., the taxpayers) millions of dollars and drag out for years in the courts. More than 1,000 people joined this group. In addition to sharing information about the lawsuit and the district's actions, it created a petition on ipetitions.com that stated:

> *As parents who consider the teachers and officials at our schools to be respected partners in educating our children as well as people to whom we entrust some of the work of molding their character, including their understanding of moral behavior, we wish to express our solidarity with Dr. Christopher W. McGinley, the Superintendent of Schools for the Lower Merion School District and the Board of Directors, as they handle the issue of privacy with regard to the free laptop program.*
>
> *We are aware that the addition of security-tracking software to laptops on loan should have been clearly communicated to students and parents alike, but we do not believe that there was any malice or duplicity underlying the omission. It was a misstep that could have been avoided, but we do not believe that it was done deliberately. We understand that the feature was activated only when a laptop was reported missing, or when it had been removed without authorization, and that over one third of those laptops were recovered through its use without any complaint.*

We understand that the use of the webcam feature on the laptops is optional and that students routinely appreciate its existence and use it frequently even though there is no requirement that they do so, and that they are free to disable the feature by placing tape over it. As such, we value the trust placed in the integrity and good sense of our children, and the expectation that the learning of discretion and honorable behavior is as important a part of their education in this school system, as the acquisition of graded skills.

We believe that our children are both willing and able to rise up to the standards of behavior expected of them as students who have been given access to personal laptops, a program that is not available to most students in this country, and that we have done our part, as their parents, to ensure that they understand the responsibilities that come with it.

We therefore stand together as parents who value the work of the remarkable human beings in whose care we place our children, both teachers and all staff, from the janitors who manage the facilities to the administrative officials who form policy, and call for a non-litigious end to this issue which has only served to detract from the far more important work of addressing their educational needs.

The petition garnered 799 signatures.

TENS OF THOUSANDS OF IMAGES

The attorney representing Blake Robbins said that in a court motion filed April 15, 2010, in addition to at least 400 images taken of Robbins "thousands of webcam pictures and screen shots have been taken of numerous other students in their homes."

In response, the next day LMSD board president Ebby said in a statement that was posted on LMSD's website and e-mailed to parents:

Dear LMSD Parents/Guardians:

As you know, our outside counsel and a computer forensic/computer security expert have been investigating the circumstances surrounding the use of the LANrev "tracking" feature. They will provide us their findings in the next few weeks and we will release them to you. We will do so regardless of whether or not we resolve the Robbins litigation . . .

. . . We do not feel it is appropriate for anyone other than the investigators to dictate the timing of the investigation and the release of complete findings. As we have made clear since day one, we are committed to providing all of the facts—good and bad—at the conclusion of the investigation. In light of what has been raised by plaintiffs' counsel, however, we feel it is critically important to provide immediate clarification regarding key items.

A substantial number of webcam photos have been recovered in the investigation. We have proposed a process to Judge DuBois whereby each family of a student whose image appears in any such photos will be notified and given the opportunity to view such photographs. Our counsel proposed that Chief Magistrate Judge Thomas Rueter handle that process. While our counsel has not yet met with Judge Rueter, Judge DuBois has agreed that such a process makes sense. We hope to start that process shortly. During that process the privacy of all students will be strongly protected.

Also, the plaintiffs' Motion suggests that the LANrev tracking feature may have been used for the purposes of "spying" on students. While we deeply regret the mistakes and misguided actions that have led us to this situation, at this late stage of the investigation we are not aware of any evidence that District employees used any LANrev webcam photographs or screenshots for such inappropriate purposes. Please also be reminded that we continue to fully cooperate and provide transparency to the United States Attorney's office in its investigation of the matter. To the extent there is any evidence of inappropriate conduct, it will be disclosed in the findings of the current investigations.

We are committed to disclosing fully what happened, correcting our mistakes, and making sure that they do not happen again.

Thank you for your continued patience during this process.

Sincerely,

David Ebby

President, LMSD Board of School Directors

The district's investigator provided the preliminary results of the investigation on April 29, 2010: at least 56,000 images had been captured by LMSD's monitoring software on students' computers. Most of the image captures happened after stolen or missing computers had been recovered and given back to students.

The number of images was vast and startling to parents, students, and residents who had been told repeatedly by the district that only forty-two security software activations had occurred on the laptops in 2010. While that was true, it misrepresented the situation since the software had been used for two years and captured images every fifteen minutes. About ten school officials had the right to request an activation of a student laptop and two employees were authorized to do the activation.

What would be reported May 3, 2010, by the district's investigative experts were the following key facts:

During a two-year period, Theft Track had been activated 177 times which included automated information-capturing every fifteen minutes when the computer was operating. Activations on 101 computers in question used an IP address (a numeric sequence identifying the network to which the computer is connected) tracking feature and did not include the capture of any visual data tracking. The seventy-five other activations included more than 30,564 webcam photographs and 27,428 screenshots stored in the district's technology department systems—nearly 58,000 images in all. According to the district's investigative report, "the vast majority

Ballard Spahr
LLP

Report of Independent Investigation

Regarding Remote Monitoring of Student Laptop Computers by the Lower Merion School District

May 3, 2010

FIGURE 9.9 *The Lower Merion School District investigative report. http://www.lmsd.org/*
Lower Merion School District

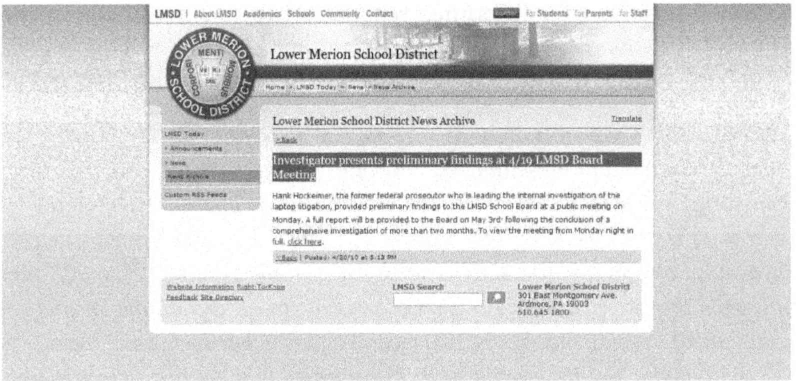

FIGURE 9.10 *Lower Merion School District established a special web page to provide updates for its stakeholders on the controversy. http://www.lmsd.org/*
Lower Merion School District

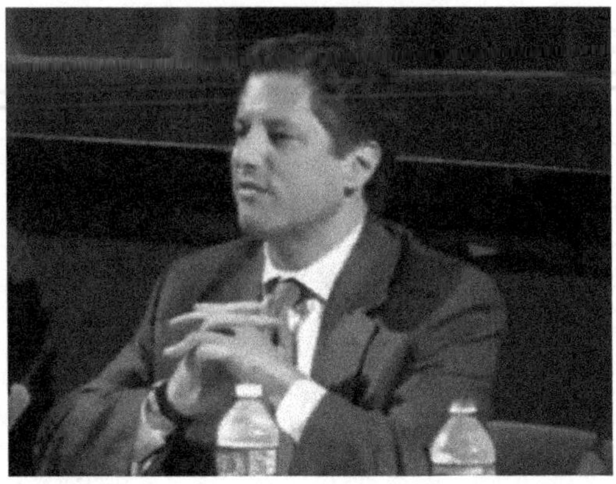

FIGURE 9.11 *Lower Merion School District Board President David Ebby answers questions at a board meeting.*
http://www.lmsd.org
Lower Merion School District

(87 percent) of the images recovered resulted from the failure to deactivate Theft Track on 12 laptops after they had been found or recovered."

AFTERMATH

Lower Merion School District sent out another letter for the LMSD community explaining the preliminary investigative data and provided another Q&A based on feedback from the community. As planned, on May 3, 2010, the district released the full report by Ballard Spahr including the L3 forensic investigation. LMSD provided a video of the meeting and all printed reports related to the investigation on its website. While the investigative report found a number of things to be corrected, it did not find the district had been intentionally spying on students. The report said:

> *Notwithstanding the large quantity of images collected by LANrev Theft Track, we found no evidence that the feature was used to "spy" on students. Although there is no forensic method to determine with certainty how often images stored on the LANrev server were viewed, we found no evidence that any District personnel surreptitiously downloaded images from the LANrev server. Rather, the collection of images from laptops while they were in the possession of students resulted from the District's failure to implement policies, procedures, and recordkeeping requirements and the overzealous and questionable use of technology by IS personnel without any apparent regard for privacy considerations or sufficient consultation with administrators.*

The judge in the case developed a plan that allowed nearly forty Lower Merion students surreptitiously photographed by their school-issued laptops to privately view their images with their parents. The photos were later destroyed.

Lower Merion paid more than $1.6 million in 2011 to litigate and settle claims that it surreptitiously spied on students through webcams on the laptops it gave to each of its nearly 2,300 high school students. Blake Robbins was awarded $175,000. The class-action lawsuit was later dismissed. On August 17, 2010, the U.S. Attorneys' office announced that there would be no criminal charges in the case.

An outside consultant was brought in to develop new technology and information systems and the district switched from LANrev to Casper Suite, which did not offer the theft-tracking features.

A technology advisory council comprising parents, students, and administrators was formed to offer feedback and guidance and a subcommittee for privacy and security was also formed. A technology report is provided at every board meeting.

Still, 2010 wasn't all bad for LMSD. The district completed $200 million in high school construction projects; endured high-profile lawsuits over a redistricting plan, and celebrated the renaming of the Lower Merion High gymnasium after its most generous and famous alumnus, Kobe Bryant, who donated $411,000 to the district.

QUESTIONS FOR DISCUSSION

1. How did student Blake Robbins find out he had been monitored in his home by his school-issued laptop?
2. How did the controversy over student laptops with visual tracking features become an instant news bombshell?
3. What were the main issues for parents and students regarding the Theft Track software installed on school district-owned laptops for students?
4. What was the early warning sign that predicted the issue with Theft Track?
5. Why did an insufficient technology policy covering student laptops become a focus of the investigation?
6. What were the first steps the school district took to respond to the controversy?
7. How well did the school district respond to the controversy?
8. Why did some parents come to the support of the school district? How did they support the school district specifically?
9. The school district released preliminary findings of the investigation. Why did they do this and was it effective?

Dig Deeper

For more background, read the *Class Action Complaint by Blake Robbins et al v. the Lower Merion School District* available on the textbook's companion website. The independent investigation by Ballard Spahr, including the forensic investigation report, is available on the textbook's companion website. Review the "Adoption of Board Policies Relating to District-Issued Laptop Computers" PowerPoint presentation and "LMCD—Policy P893 Remote Access, Monitoring and Tracking of District-Issued Laptops." Does this new policy resolve the laptop tracking issues? How?

28

"It's the Real Thing"

Protest at the Jewish Museum

Art exhibitions sometimes attract criticism and greater public attention when individuals or groups find fault with the subject matter. In the case of the Jewish Museum in New York City, the uproar came before the exhibition had even opened.

Mirroring Evil: Nazi Imagery/Recent Art featured nineteen works by thirteen contemporary artists from eight nations; many of the works used Nazi-era images and symbols in combination with pop culture symbols and consumer products to "raise questions about commercialization and iconic images of the Holocaust." Using the imagery of the Third Reich and the challenging language of conceptual art, the artists led viewers of their work to question how images shape perceptions of evil today. Some of the offending art included:

Giftgas Giftset, by New Yorker Tom Sachs, replicated three Zyklon B gas canisters using the colors and logos of Chanel, Hermès, and Tiffany. Zyklon B, a commercial preparation of hydrocyanic acid, was used in the Nazi death camps.

LEGO Concentration Camp Set, by Polish-born artist Zbigniew Libera, consisted of LEGO pieces used to construct small-scale models of concentration camps including barracks and crematoria. Libera created fake LEGO packaging that looked like boxes for commercial LEGO children's building blocks. The viewer saw a suite of these boxes, but not the actual models. The work was intended to remind the viewer of the Third Reich's propaganda aimed at children as well as the pervasiveness of violence in children's products today.

Self-Portrait at Buchenwald: It's the Real Thing was a web image of artist Alan Schechner holding a Diet Coke digitally inserted into Margaret Bourke White's famous photograph of emaciated Jews in their bunks shortly after the liberation of Buchenwald concentration camp.

Four of the artists, including Sachs and Schechner, were Jewish; some were descendants of Holocaust survivors. Most were born after World War II; many were in their thirties or forties. While the art did not approve of the Holocaust or suggest that it did not happen the way history records it, many survivors and descendants felt the works trivialized a horrific period in which six million people lost their lives.

FIGURE 9.12 Self Portrait at Buchenwald: It's the Real Thing.
http://dottycommies.com/holocaust01.html
Courtesy of Alan Schechner

However, the exhibition and its accompanying art were not about the Holocaust; instead it was current social commentary.

The Jewish Museum, established in 1904, is considered a cultural gem that explores the intersection of 4,000 years of art and Jewish culture. Its exhibitions and educational programs appeal to people of all cultural backgrounds; 35 percent of its visitors at the time of the *Mirroring Evil* exhibition had no Jewish background. The museum maintains a collection of 26,000 objects—paintings, sculpture, works on paper, photographs, archaeological artifacts, ceremonial objects, and broadcast media. According to its website, its collection is "the largest and most important of its kind in the world." On average about 170,000 people visit the museum annually and many thousands participate in the museum's educational offerings.

While the Holocaust theme had been explored by the museum in other exhibitions, including the Holocaust-era paintings and drawings of Charlotte Salomon in 2000, the March 17—June 30, 2002, *Mirroring Evil* exhibition was the first show featuring works by a younger generation using Nazi imagery in combination with current pop culture themes and consumer products. The resulting works of art made powerful (and, for many, disturbing) comments about modern cultural issues. The exhibition's wall text described the approach:

> *This art is cautionary rather than memorial. It warns us not to take for granted the symbols of oppression that pervade our outlets of news and entertainment. It conveys a sense of wariness about techniques of persuasion, including those we encounter in the marketplace.*

CONTROVERSY

Ultimately, the aims of artists, the exhibition's curator, and museum alike were obscured by controversy. The negative public reaction followed the catalog copublishers' decision to release the exhibition catalog, complete with color photographs of the featured art, three months before accompanying educational materials were completed and before the exhibition was open to the public. Museum Director of Communications Anne Scher said at the time the decision would leave the institution "vulnerable" to criticism. She shared her concerns with the exhibition's curator and deputy director but not with the museum's director.

In a city that boasts the largest concentration of Jews anywhere outside of Israel who had experienced the Holocaust firsthand, some found the works disrespectful and painful.

The 164-page catalog, edited by exhibit curator Norman Kleeblatt, featured essays by well-known academic scholars who wrestled with the exhibition's aesthetic, historical, and cultural issues; short essays about each piece in the exhibit were also included.

In the museum's news release, Kleeblatt said the exhibit's artists represented a new generation and viewpoint that weren't exactly in line with traditional ways:

> *A trend has emerged over the past decade in which younger artists have departed from the more traditional ways of addressing the Holocaust and have begun to find new ways to confront the evil of the Third Reich. Many of these artists base their works on material of popular culture, which is a potent source of information for their generation. Others wed Nazi imagery to coveted consumer products, warning us about the fragile boundaries between propaganda and promotion, desire and destruction. I believe all of these artists invite us to look at ourselves, to reflect on the role the Holocaust plays in our lives today—as memory, as point of reference, even as a subject for the entertainment industry—and to question the adequacy of our own response to evil.*

Soon after the catalog's publication, a small educational program was held at the museum to discuss the upcoming *Mirroring Evil* exhibition, including the curator and some of the contributing catalog essayists. A few participants objected to the art during a question-and-answer session, and a few attendees, one of whom may have been a Holocaust survivor, walked out of the event, said Scher, who heard about the reaction from those attending the program.

A *Wall Street Journal* reporter heard about the program and began researching the exhibition. Scher provided information and sources for the reporter's story. The resulting January 10, 2002, article entitled "Coming Museum Show with Nazi Theme Stirs New York's Art World" drew a connection with a controversial 1999 shock art exhibit by noting in its lead the exhibit could be the "next art-world *Sensation*." That exhibition included, among other highly charged works, a painting of the Virgin Mary splattered with elephant dung.

The *New York Daily News* ("Jewish Museum's Holocaust Storm: Show with a Lego Concentration Camp Hit for Trivializing Horror") picked up the story the next day, as did the *New York Post*. The Associated Press released a domestic wire story entitled "Jewish Museum Exhibit Criticized for Lego Concentration Camp, Designer Gas Canisters" and another story for its state and regional wires entitled "Jewish Museum Exhibit Criticized for Including Nazi Art." Both AP stories quoted Menachem Rosensaft, a founding chairman of the International Network of Children of Holocaust Survivors, who criticized the exhibition, and the exhibition's curator, Norman Kleeblatt. The AP propelled the story nationwide and beyond.

ORGANIZATIONAL RESPONSE

Calls from reporters came flooding into Scher's office, which included just one other staff member. "There was a call every minute and we did our best to respond." Scher worked many late nights responding to media requests. "It was overwhelming."

An extensive press kit included a six-page news release, biographies of the artists, a backgrounder that described the museum's art holdings that related to the Holocaust and its past Holocaust-related exhibitions, and a backgrounder on the museum.

To get its messages out, the Jewish Museum worked to place op-ed pieces or letters to the editors in such publications as the *Daily News*, *The Jewish Week*, *The Washington Post*, and *The New York Times*. It provided third-party advocates to speak on its behalf in interviews for newspapers, magazines, and television news segments.

A small public relations firm helped Scher draft materials for the media, and its senior management served as a "sounding board" for strategy sessions. The firm's crisis management experience was limited, and Scher said the firm had never before experienced such a controversy.

One month before the exhibition's opening, the American Gathering of Jewish Holocaust Survivors, a national organization with ties to about seventy Holocaust survivor groups, urged a boycott if the museum did not cancel the exhibition.

New York State Assemblyman Dov Hikind, whose mother survived Auschwitz, and a group of about ten Holocaust survivors and children of survivors met with Jewish Museum representatives on March 1, 2002, sixteen days before the exhibition's opening, to ask for the removal of the three most offending pieces. The meeting lasted two hours and ended with museum officials agreeing to give more consideration to the group's request.

Three days later the Jewish Museum announced that it would post signs at the point where visitors are about to encounter the most troubling artwork. The sign would read: "Some Holocaust survivors have been disturbed by the works of art shown beyond this point. Visitors may choose to avoid the works by exiting the exhibition through the door to the left." Carpenters would also build a special exit from the gallery allowing visitors to avoid those works. And the museum would mount Schechner's *Real Thing* Buchenwald image on a computer that displayed it only after the viewer had read a content warning. Still, critics were unhappy. Hikind was quoted in a New Jersey newspaper six days before the opening:

> *But I don't think they get it. When I saw that thing with the Coke can, hey, give me a break. I can't think of anything [the museum should do] to frame the art that would make it acceptable. I will be out in front of the museum with such a large group of protesters on March 17 when it opens.*

Robert J. Hurst, chairman of the Jewish Museum and the son of a Holocaust survivor, said in a statement prepared for the news media that his initial reaction to Sachs's and Schechner's pieces changed once he saw them at a member preview showing:

> *When I heard of artist Tom Sachs'* Giftgas Giftset*—three gas canisters packaged in Chanel, Hermès and Prada—my reflex was anger. Confronting it in person, seeing it in context, made me think about how in fact the Nazi party itself was "packaged" in a kind of inflated glamour that led otherwise rational individuals to buy into them in a way not dissimilar to how we buy into cult brands today. Another contentious piece, Alan Schechner's self-portrait at the Buchenwald concentration camp—where he inserts himself holding a Diet Coke can into an historic photograph of emaciated prisoners—also earned my ire—before I saw it. But giving up my indignation I gained much more by considering—and in fact relating to—the way in which this artist tried to find his place in an oppressive past that claimed many of his family members.*

The museum issued this news release March 3, 2002, about two weeks prior to the exhibition's opening:

> ***THE JEWISH MUSEUM TO PRESENT* MIRRORING EVIL: NAZI IMAGERY/ RECENT ART, *A NEW EXHIBITION ACCOMPANIED BY PROGRAMS AND CATALOGUE***
>
> *From March 17 through June 30, 2002, The Jewish Museum will present* Mirroring Evil: Nazi Imagery/Recent Art, *a contemporary art exhibition accompanied by extensive education programs, forums for discussion, and a major publication. At the core of this initiative is a selection of recent works by thirteen internationally recognized artists, all of whom make new and daring use of imagery taken from the Nazi era. Employing the challenging language of conceptual art, the artists bring the highly charged imagery of the Third Reich out of the past and into the present, leading us to question how images shape our perception of evil today.*

"As an art museum that presents all of Jewish culture, we are committed to showing works of contemporary artists who have used images of the Nazi era to make a powerful and timely investigation of the nature of evil," stated Joan Rosenbaum, Helen Goldsmith Director of The Jewish Museum. "These artists ask each viewer to consider his or her responsibility toward civil society, and to be vigilant about the bigotry and dehumanization that continue in the world more than fifty years after the Holocaust."

The exhibition Mirroring Evil: Nazi Imagery/Recent Art *has been conceived and organized by Norman L. Kleeblatt, the Susan and Elihu Rose Curator of Fine Arts at The Jewish Museum. "A trend has emerged over the past decade," Mr. Kleeblatt says, "in which younger artists have departed from the more traditional ways of addressing the Holocaust and have begun to find new ways to confront the evil of the Third Reich. Many of these artists base their works on the material of popular culture, which is a potent source of information for their generation. Others wed Nazi imagery to coveted consumer products, warning us about the fragile boundaries between propaganda and promotion, desire and destruction. I believe all of these artists invite us to look at ourselves, to reflect on the role the Holocaust plays in our lives today—as memory, as point of reference, even as a subject for the entertainment industry—and to question the adequacy of our own response to evil."*

The artists represented in Mirroring Evil *come from eight different countries. They are Boaz Arad (born 1956, Israel); Christine Borland (born 1965, Scotland); Mat Collishaw (born 1966, England); Rudolf Herz (born 1954, Germany); Elke Krystufek (born 1970, Austria); Mischa Kuball (born 1959, Germany); Zbigniew Libera (born 1959, Poland); Roee Rosen (born 1963, Israel); Tom Sachs (born 1966, U.S.); Alan Schechner (born in England 1962, lives in U.S.); Alain Séchas (born 1955, France); Maciej Toporowicz (born in Poland 1958; lives in U.S.); and Piotr Uklański (born in Poland 1968; lives in U.S.).*

Interpretive Videos

The exhibition includes two specially commissioned interpretive videos. The first, produced by the noted art historian Maurice Berger and shown in the entrance gallery, introduces major themes of the exhibition by exploring how popular films and television programs have used similar, potent images of the Nazi era. This video raises questions that are present throughout the exhibition—questions to which there are no simple answers. They are:

- Who can speak for the Holocaust? *Can only survivors speak? How can subsequent generations gain understanding and apply the lessons of the past?*
- How has art used Nazi imagery to present evil? *What happens to our understanding of history, as film, television, and other art forms convert the Nazis into symbols?*

- What are the limits of irreverence? *To what extent may artists overstep the bounds of taste, in confronting facts that are outrageous and terrifying? Do some art forms work against themselves?*
- Why must we confront evil? *What are the dangers of ignoring the past, or being complacent about the present?*
- How has art helped to break the silence? *When reality seems to be unspeakable, how may art open a dialogue and keep memory alive?*

The second video, produced and directed by Maxine Wishner, is shown at the end of the exhibition. It provides a range of commentaries and responses to the artworks, taken from interviews with the artists and with curators, educators, Jewish community leaders, and Holocaust survivors. The Executive Producer for this video was Carole Zawatsky, The Jewish Museum's Director of Education, who worked with Creative Content and Program Designer Karen Michel, and Cinematographer and Editor Ralph Toporoff.

Public Programs

The Jewish Museum has organized Mirroring Evil: Nazi Imagery/Recent Art *and its related programs as a means of prompting meaningful discussion about the questions raised by the artworks. Like all of the Museum's presentations of art related to the Holocaust and the Nazi era, this exhibition is part of an ongoing dialogue between the artists and the public.*

During the presentation of the exhibition, The Jewish Museum will offer programs for adults, school groups, and educators organized in partnership with other institutions throughout New York City. Programming partners include The Vera List Center for Art and Politics, New School University; The New York Public Library, Humanities and Social Sciences Library; CLAL—The National Jewish Center for Learning and Leadership; Columbia University; and Facing History and Ourselves.

The public programs associated with Mirroring Evil *have been selected by Americans for the Arts as a component of that organization's prestigious Animating Democracy Lab. Supported by the Ford Foundation, the Animating Democracy Lab fosters artistic and humanistic activity that stimulates civic dialogue on important contemporary issues. The Jewish Museum is one of only five New York City institutions, and one of only sixteen nationwide, to participate in this year's Animating Democracy Initiative.*

Exhibition Catalogue

In conjunction with the exhibition, The Jewish Museum and Rutgers University Press have published the catalogue Mirroring Evil: Nazi Imagery/Recent Art, *edited by Norman L. Kleeblatt. The 164-page book, featuring 79 illustrations (26 of them in color), includes a foreword by James E. Young and essays by Mr Kleeblatt, Sidra DeKoven Ezrahi, Reesa Greenberg, Lisa Saltzman, Ellen Handler Spitz, and Ernst van*

Alphen. The book is available for $65 hardcover and $30 paperbound in the Museum's Cooper Shop and at bookstores nationwide.

The Jewish Museum and Art Related to the Holocaust

Mirroring Evil: Nazi Imagery/Recent Art *is the most recent of many art exhibitions at The Jewish Museum that have addressed the period of the Holocaust. These exhibitions have notably included a 1985 retrospective of the work of Felix Nussbaum, a young Jewish artist who perished in the Holocaust; The Art of Memory, a groundbreaking 1994 exhibition that examined how and why public memory of the Holocaust is shaped by museums and monuments; and an exhibition in 2000 of the Holocaust-era paintings and drawings of Charlotte Salomon, titled* Charlotte Salomon: Life? Or Theatre?

The Jewish Museum also collects artworks and artifacts related to the Holocaust. Examples of them, such as George Segal's pivotal 1982 sculpture The Holocaust, *are included in the permanent exhibition* Culture and Continuity: The Jewish Journey.

From March 17 through June 30, 2002, while Mirroring Evil *is on view in its first-floor galleries, the Museum will also present* An Artist's Response to Evil: "We are Not the Last" *by Zoran Music. This exhibition, to be shown on the Museum's second floor, is comprised of a series of paintings and watercolors reinterpreting the drawings of the dead that Zoran Music made during his two-year internment at the Dachau concentration camp, where he was sent after his arrest by the Gestapo for anti-German activity in 1944.*

Exhibition Sponsorship

Mirroring Evil: Nazi Imagery/Recent Art *is supported, in part, by the Animating Democracy Initiative, a program of Americans for the Arts, funded by The Ford Foundation.*

Major gifts have also been provided by The Blanche and Irving Laurie Foundation, The Ellen Flamm Philanthropic Fund, Peter Norton and The Peter Norton Family Foundation, The Andy Warhol Foundation for the Visual Arts, The Schnurmacher Foundations, the Joseph Alexander Foundation, Inc., Goldie and David Blanksteen, The Dorsky Foundation, Agnes Gund and Daniel Shapiro, and other generous donors.

A week before the exhibition opening, a press preview event attracted about 150 people from the news media, including twelve television crews. Much of the news coverage focused on the controversial aspects reported earlier by *The Wall Street Journal*, The Associated Press, and others

As a result of the pre-publicity, nearly one hundred protesters were on hand for opening day. From behind police barricades across the street from the Manhattan museum, protesters chanted, "Don't go in" and "Shame on you"; some held signs with messages such as "Nazi Museum."

A written statement released by museum officials to the news media the opening day of the exhibition (March 17, 2002) said:

Mirroring Evil: Nazi Imagery/Recent Art *is not an exhibition about the Holocaust. It is about the way some younger artists are commenting on today's society, using images taken from the Nazi era.*

We feel that comments, both pro and con, should now come from the people who see the exhibition.

We hope that public debate will now move on to the issues the artists raise.

Beyond providing viewing options for individuals who might be disturbed by portions of the exhibition, the museum also developed a broad educational program, a major exhibition catalog publication, and another more traditional Holocaust exhibit during the time *Mirroring Evil* ran.

At the museum's entrance gallery, an interpretive video by noted art historian Maurice Berger introduced the major themes of the exhibit and discussed Nazi images in popular films and television programs.

Some of the questions raised by the video included: Who can speak for the Holocaust? How has art used Nazi imagery to present evil? What are the limits of irreverence? Why must we confront evil? How has art helped break the silence?

The second video, produced and directed by Maxine Wishner, was shown at the end of the exhibition. It contained commentaries and responses to the artworks, taken from interviews with the artists and with curators, educators, Jewish community leaders, and Holocaust survivors.

Throughout the exhibit's fourteen-week presentation, the Jewish Museum sponsored public programs for adults, school groups, and educators organized in partnership with other institutions throughout New York City. Programming partners included the New York Public Library, New School University, Columbia University, and the National Jewish Center for Learning and Leadership. Each program was designed to promote dialogue between the artists and the public on the ideas represented by the exhibition.

Hardly noticed in the media storm was a concurrent Jewish Museum exhibition entitled *An Artist's Response to Evil: "We are Not the Last"* by Zoran Music. The series of paintings and watercolors by Zoran Music reinterpreted the drawings of the dead that Music made during his two-year internment at Dachau concentration camp.

Once the *Mirroring Evil* exhibition opened to the public and was reviewed by art critics—after several weeks—the intense scrutiny died down and the *Mirroring Evil* exhibition finished without further incident. The Jewish Museum continued its robust cultural offerings to a now much larger audience eager for events that made them think more deeply.

QUESTIONS FOR DISCUSSION

1. What is the mission of the Jewish Museum? How does it relate to the controversial exhibition *Mirroring Evil*?

2. The release of the *Mirroring Evil*'s exhibition's catalog three months before the exhibition opening created unique problems for the Jewish Museum as the images were shown to the news media without the exhibition's context. Explain why the catalog's early release ignited the controversy.

3. The museum's director of communications had reservations about the early release of the exhibition's catalog. Analyze the director's actions in this situation, and suggest another course of action.

4. Analyze the museum's media relations response to the initial national media coverage after the initial *Wall Street Journal* article appeared January 10, 2002. What other course of action would you suggest?

5. What crisis communication tactics could be used in this situation?

6. Analyze the organization's accommodative response after meeting with Holocaust survivors and children of Holocaust survivors. Do you feel the accommodations were appropriate? Would you do anything differently?

7. What third-party advocates would you suggest the museum use to communicate its goals?

8. The *Mirroring Evil* exhibition was compared to another exhibit called *Sensation*. What was the controversy with *Sensation*? What were the similarities and differences between the two exhibitions?

9. Who can speak for the Holocaust? Can only survivors or descendants of survivors speak out?

Dig Deeper

There have been many controversial pieces of artwork over the years. A few examples are listed below. Explain why they were considered controversial by some people. What was the artist trying to express?

- *Holy Virgin Mary*, Chris Ofili
- *Piss Christ*, Andres Serrano
- *Madame X*, John Singer Sargent
- *Yo Mama's Last Supper*, Renee Cox
- *Mother and Child Divided*, Damien Hirst

Hallmark Writers on Tour

Connecting Employees with their Hometown Audience

For more than a century, Hallmark has been helping people express their feelings and touch the lives of others. As anyone who has received one knows, a greeting card can communicate love, humor, sympathy, and much more. And, not just any card will do. Hallmark's well-known slogan—"When you care enough to send the very best"—radiated quality above all.

With an array of product lines that includes not only greeting cards but also ornaments and television entertainment, Hallmark netted $4.1 billion in 2011. The company leads domestic greeting card sales with a 50 percent market share in the United States; it publishes products in more than thirty languages and distributes them in more than one hundred countries. Its 625 artists, designers, writers, editors, and photographers generate more than 10,000 new and redesigned greeting cards and related products each year. Hallmark offers more than 49,000 products in its model line at any one time.

Clearly, consumers understand the power and value of a greeting card; almost 90 percent of U.S. households use them. According to the Greeting Card Association, Americans purchased about 6.5 billion greeting cards annually adding up to an industry worth about $6–$7 billion. GCA said the most seasonal cards are Christmas cards, which sold 1.6 billion units, followed by Valentine's Day (145 million units) and Mother's Day (133 million units). It's estimated that 80 percent of all greeting cards are purchased by women. The GCA said seven out of ten card buyers surveyed consider greeting cards "absolutely" or "almost" essential to them.

However, greeting card sales have slowed in recent years, in part because busy lifestyles can lead to forgetfulness and missed purchasing opportunities. Increasing postal rates also have curtailed greeting card purchases as e-mail and cell phone usage substituted for personal greetings. To expand its reach electronically, Hallmark has developed a full line of e-mail cards and in 2012 it developed a partnership with Shutterfly to create customized Hallmark greeting cards. In 2013, Hallmark's website

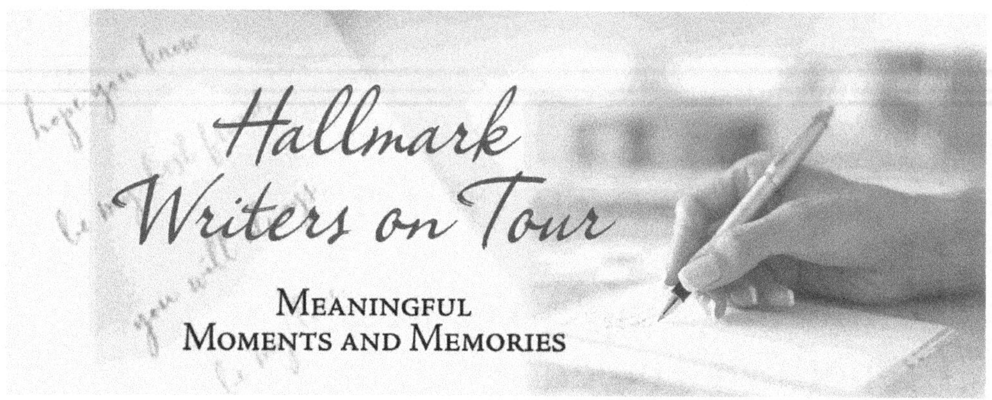

FIGURE 9.13 *Hallmark writers on Tour.*
Hallmark

offered a personalized trifold photo card for Valentine's Day that Hallmark called "visual love letters."

FINDING NEWS VALUE IN GREETING CARDS

Cards in and of themselves are not news. Typical card news opportunities are usually limited to holiday times, such as Valentine's Day and Mother's Day, or when new card themes illuminate social trends. At other times of year, few holidays support card giving: Summer's most celebrated holiday, the Fourth of July, is not especially known as an occasion to send a greeting card.

One unique solution to get Americans (and the news media) to reflect on the importance of greeting cards and their ability to send just the right message at the right time involved a community relations effort. The idea also served as a creative card-based publicity campaign to promote sales.

The public relations staff's creative solution to help grow the greeting card category was the Hallmark Writers Tour (later including Hallmark artists). It was an opportunity to express to consumers directly and through news stories the emotional benefit of greeting cards. The program would take writers on the road, allowing them to interact with consumers through small events and creating media relations opportunities to share their work and solicit consumer memories about special greeting cards. These consumer stories could then be leveraged for additional news coverage.

Hallmark wanted to remind consumers in person and through the news media of the emotional benefit of greeting cards. Other objectives included reinforcing and personalizing the Hallmark brand and using the freshly media-trained creative staff and consumer testimonials to feed other promotional efforts. Hallmark partnered with Fleishman-Hillard to develop the media tour.

Beyond the promotional benefits of sending its writers on tour, a secondary outcome happened: The customers and their stories inspired Hallmark employees. The tour became an effective employee relations program that helped renew employees' sense of purpose; by hearing directly from consumers how their daily work had affected others' lives, they gained new insight to feed future endeavors, said Lydia Steinberg, Hallmark's media relations manager at the time.

The program was designed to allow people to share their stories about how cards have helped them connect with others in a meaningful way. "Whether you send greeting cards or write them, we all have experiences that speak to our spirits, that touch us in important ways," said Pat Daneman, Hallmark writing director. "Greeting cards are often part of those memories. We hope to gain inspiration and insight from others' stories, as well as share some of our own."

CONNECTING WITH THE COMMUNITY

One of the stories shared by a couple in Texas was posted to Hallmark's Meaningful Moments website and was also re-created in a television commercial. A customer's web posting told about a Valentine *déjà vu* experience:

> *During the second year of our marriage, my husband, Mike, was serving in the Army in Viet Nam. Anxious to find the perfect valentine, I searched diligently to find a card that expressed exactly how I felt in my heart during our separation. Finally, I found that special valentine, a large Hallmark card, and mailed it with the hope that it would*

FIGURE 9.14 *A Hallmark writer shares his work inspirations.*
Hallmark

arrive on time. Imagine my shock and disappointment when I went to the mailbox and opened a large card only to think, "Oh, no! My valentine to Mike was returned to me. He never got it!" After looking carefully at it for a moment, I realized that the card was actually from my husband. He had bought the identical card at the PX in Da Nang that I had bought in Beaumont, Texas! I have kept those cards to remind myself of the miracle of love and God's goodness to me. Those special thoughts I searched so hard to send to my husband, he had also sent to me.

Beyond inspirational moments, Hallmark writers discovered new consumer needs for greeting cards. At the Minneapolis–St Paul tour stop, writers Scott Emmons and Molly Wigand, a city native, heard a need for more cards to help men, especially husbands and sons, express themselves. Customers told them that in times of polarized opinions, there was also the need to help people say, "Let's agree to disagree."

At a second stop in a cozy Twin Cities bookstore, the writers heard stories like this: Two women shared how they had often found a card so perfect for their friendship that they would send the same card back and forth for years. Later that day at a coffee house, another woman talked about her long-distance relationship with a man who is now her husband. The pair never lived in the same town until they were married, but they got to know each other through the cards they exchanged.

The Writers on Tour market locations were selected for media receptivity, heavy consumer card purchasing, "hometown" connection between the writers and the market, and their nearby location to a Fleishman-Hillard office or other in-market resource.

Audiences were generated by invitations to Hallmark Gold Crown members, advance media relations stories, fliers in Hallmark Gold Crown stores, fliers at event venues, and affinity group outreach, said Steinberg. Writers on Tour was tested in Lawrence, Leavenworth, Leawood, and Topeka, Kansas, and Kansas City, Missouri. Pilot events allowed the public relations team an opportunity to tweak the "run of show" and help the writer pairs and host gain comfort in their roles.

The pilots also helped the team identify which program elements were meaningful to guests, which were extraneous or disruptive, and which venues worked best before the investment in travel was made. Official tour stops included San Diego, Cincinnati, Philadelphia, St. Louis, Nashville, Minneapolis–St. Paul, Las Vegas, and many other cities.

Hallmark decided that the sessions would not be held in Hallmark stores to keep the events from seeming too commercial. "We sought smaller, casual venues with engaged proprietors so that audiences would feel comfortable enough to tell very touching, personal stories in public," Steinberg said. Typical venues were libraries, coffeehouses, tearooms, bookstores, community centers, and cafes. Writers were scheduled for three days and two nights in each market. This allowed time for media interviews, four to five event appearances, and retailer interaction and store visits.

An event format usually included a host and two writers, an introductory video, writer presentations including background and sources of inspiration, a question-and-answer session, story sharing, and informational packets containing card samples, story forms, bookmarks, and gift cards.

To give the initiative a year-round presence outside specific tour markets, the Hallmark Visitors Center, at the company's Kansas City headquarters, offered a display showcasing videos and card samples from the touring writers and seeking guests' greeting card memories. Hallmark launched a website for an additional source of consumer stories and to showcase the entire program.

RESULTS

Within nineteen months, Writers on Tour made seventy-seven appearances in fifteen markets. "We laughed, we cried, and sometimes we scratched our heads . . . but mostly we marveled at the way greeting cards touch people in strange and wonderful ways," Steinberg said.

Internally, the public relations staff used this project as a way to inspire employees about their company. Writer profiles and consumer stories were featured in employee newsletters. Hallmark employees, as well as CEO Donald J. Hall, Jr, were also solicited to share stories in the company newsletter and on the company's intranet site. Weekly e-mails highlighting consumer stories to Hallmark writing staff and other employees allowed tour members to share their experiences and maintain enthusiasm for the program. The company made presentations to writers and editors to celebrate the program's success, and an all-employee meeting recapped the program and recognized everyone's contributions.

In the first year, Hallmark writers talked face to face with more than 2,500 employees and members of the public, Steinberg said. The program netted about 600 written consumer stories from events, its visitors center, website, and mail. The program's website (Hallmark.com/meaningfulmoments) had more than 75,000 visitors.

The media helped tell the story: More than 131 million media impressions resulted from top-tier media coverage about the Writers on Tour project. Major print and online clips included *The New York Times*, *The Wall Street Journal*, *The New Yorker*, *The Philadelphia Inquirer*, the St. Paul *Pioneer Press*, the South Florida *Sun-Sentinel*, *The Kansas City Star*, and *The Cincinnati Enquirer*. Some of the in-market articles, most notably in the Nashville *Tennessean* and *The Salt Lake Tribune*, were syndicated to other newspapers around the country. Twenty-one radio interviews reached 5.5 million listeners, and seventeen television interviews reached eight million viewers. Overall, the team was successful in generating one to three television appearances, one or more radio interviews, and a daily newspaper feature in each market.

Additional Writers on Tour messages fed other Hallmark campaigns, yielding 143 million more impressions. Consumer stories were used in Valentine's Day publicity efforts, and media-trained writers were prepared to participate in a successful campaign supporting a relaunch of the popular Shoebox card line.

Ninety percent of the news coverage carried the program's key message: "This tour is not only about sharing how we work at Hallmark, but also about listening to real people talk about how cards have made a difference in their lives."

Those surveyed at Writers on Tour events enjoyed their time. When asked if the program helped them realize how important cards are to people, 83.5 percent strongly agreed. Participants said that their respect for what goes into the creation of a greeting card was increased (95 percent), and 50 percent said they had purchased or used greeting cards more than normal the week following the event.

The success of Hallmark's Writers on Tour rested in its authenticity. "It was a campaign built around our DNA," Steinberg said.

> *It did not portray us as something other than what we are. The writers were able to completely be themselves, sincerely delivering the message about the benefit of greeting cards—because it is with their words that the magic begins. As a result, audiences had no problem with embracing the concept. It basically reinforced our brand promise.*

The support of Hallmark employees was key, Steinberg said. When employees embrace a campaign, it becomes part of the corporate culture. As a result,

> *card planning teams began to ask for relevant consumer stories when assigning new projects to writers; the company's chairman referred to the program in his annual Thanksgiving letter to employees and many volunteered for the second and third years of the program . . . The stories were shared throughout Hallmark, reinforcing the importance of each job and improving morale.*

Consumer stories also have been used in communication to Hallmark's independent retailers to reinforce their role in enriching consumers' lives as well.

Stories such as a single mother who spoke of her elation at receiving a card "To Mom on Father's Day" from her daughter, and a woman who recalled the reassurance she felt on finding a card from her family tucked in her suitcase when she was headed away for a college semester abroad underscored the belief and values of Hallmark—to enrich people's lives through creativity, quality, and innovation.

QUESTIONS FOR DISCUSSION

1. What business problem did the Hallmark Writers and Artists on Tour program attempt to solve?
2. Why was it important that the Writers on Tour program be authentic—part of Hallmark's "DNA"?
3. How did the Hallmark Writers on Tour program create positive publicity for Hallmark?
4. How did Hallmark avoid overcommercializing Writers on Tour?

5. How did the Hallmark Writers on Tour program promote quality products?
6. What are some traditional ways that public relations practitioners build strong employee relations?
7. Analyze Hallmark's brand legacy information available under "Our Brand" on Hallmark's corporate website (corporate.hallmark.com). What is Hallmark's brand?
8. Analyze Hallmark's beliefs and values statement available under "Our Culture" on Hallmark's corporate website (corporate.hallmark.com). Why is it important for an organization to have such a statement?

Dig Deeper

For additional background to this case view the Hallmark communication's office presentation on the Writers on Tour available on the textbook's companion website. Also, learn more about the greeting card industry by viewing "Facts About the Greeting Cards Industry Fact Sheet" and "Industry Backgrounder and Timeline" provided by the Greeting Card Association, both available on the textbook's companion website.

CHAPTER 10

Cultural and Other Considerations

Racial, ethnic, cultural and religious differences can lead to misunderstanding or worse. Compounding factors—war, scarcity, climate change, economic and social inequalities—create complex problems that often require equally complex solutions.

Addressing the many challenges facing society today requires a broad understanding of the social sciences such as sociology, psychology, anthropology, language, history, economics, political science, and government. One of the best ways to understand differences is to examine a group's value system—what people value or place importance on. These values can form the basis for a group or nation's cultural identity. Culture is a system of shared meanings within a social group that can develop over generations. Culture reflects how people live their lives or how things are done; it includes shared experiences and activities, such as language, religion, dress, food, and the environment, as well as the common history and government that bind a group, region, or country together into a distinct social system.

Well-known American brands and popular culture, from McDonald's to *Desperate Housewives,* are present in many nations around the world. Concerned about the dominance of U.S. culture and its values, many nations are attempting to maintain their distinct, native cultures by preserving cultural sites, objects, and forms of traditional cultural expression. Many countries and the U.S. Bureau of Educational and Cultural Affairs have been involved in supporting these efforts, which include the restoration of ancient, historic buildings, conservation of rare manuscripts, and protection of important archeological sites and other projects.

Beyond protection of countries' heritage and history are the stark realities facing many countries just trying to provide basic necessities for their populations. *The Human Development Report 2012* noted "extreme inequalities" exist around the world. Some 1.7 billion people in 109 countries lived in "multidimensional" poverty in the decade ending in 2012. According to the report, half of the world's population lives on less than $2.50 a day. Obviously, what many take for granted—fresh water, access to clean energy, and nutritious food and basic shelter—are daily struggles for many others.

Sensitivity to and appreciation for cultural differences and socioeconomic factors are necessary to build trusting relationships with any group. The U.S. has a rich diversity of human resources and public relations expertise to actively participate in developing multinational public relations programs. This is often accomplished when public relations firms partner with other practitioners "born into the culture." Public relations practitioners responsible for developing a cooperative partnership in another country should make every effort to learn that country's history, language, and other cultural dimensions.

Communicating poorly in one language is bad enough, but doing so in a second language can send unintended and, at times, humorous messages. Fraser Seitel's book *The Practice of Public Relations* gives some examples:

A food company named its giant burrito a *Burrada,* which means "big mistake" in colloquial Spanish.

Estée Lauder's proposed "Country Mist" got a name change because *mist* is German slang for "manure."

When Chevrolet introduced its Nova model, it didn't take off among Spanish-speaking customers, since *nova* in Spanish means "does not go."

All translated messages, including brand names, should be reviewed by native speakers and tested within the target market before they are implemented.

Beyond language and meaning, practitioners should understand the demographics and technological infrastructure of the country. Some populations, for example, are highly educated with accompanying high literacy rates while others are not. Some countries are industrialized, with access to sophisticated communication technology. South Korea, for example, is considered one of the most "wired" populations on earth. All of these factors and population characteristics will affect communication strategies.

Scholar Maureen Taylor described eight societal factors that influence the practice of international public relations: the level of media development and professionalism; the level of economic development; political ideology; societal tolerance for activism; the strength of labor unions; the level of development of the legal system; state-to-state relations; and the relationship between government and business.

In the book *Toward the Common Good: Perspectives in International Public Relations,* several themes emerge in the study of public relations abroad: "the interplay of democratic movements and emerging free-market economies; press freedom; the empowerment of public opinion; and the conflict of an aroused, mediated citizenry with authoritarian regimes and entrenched special interests." The book also noted:

> *A convergence of three factors contributed to the emergence of public relations as a profession: a growth in the global acceptance of democratic principles, growing global social interdependence, and the emergence of direct instantaneous communication abilities. These factors have now empowered public opinion to a degree that public relations performance is no longer a choice on the part of the organization.*

Two freedoms U.S. citizens are used to—freedom of expression and freedom of assembly—are not enjoyed universally. According to Freedom House's Freedom of the Press 2012 report, of 197 countries and territories examined, sixty-six (34 percent) were rated free, while seventy-two (36 percent) were rated partly free and fifty-nine (30 percent) were rated not free. The report further stated: "only 14.5 percent of the world's inhabitants lived in countries with a free press, while 45 percent had a partly free press and 40.5 percent lived in not free environments."

Limitations on freedom of expression can adversely affect an organization's ability to communicate freely, particularly with the news media. Related to freedom of expression are the integrity and credibility of the country's news media. The "cash for editorial" practice is a growing concern. According to the International Public Relations Association's Campaign for Media Transparency survey of public relations professions, cash payment for story placement is common in eastern and southern Europe, and in Central and South America. Even websites, which Americans assume are unregulated and unstoppable on the Internet, can be shut down. China, for example, has frequently clamped down on or blocked websites not authorized by the government.

Limits on freedom of assembly can also present challenges. Since public relations is responsible for building relationships, simply gathering people together in some countries for meetings, events, or demonstrations could be monitored or stopped. This eliminates an effective face-to-face communication tool.

Other practical considerations include the effect of female practitioners in a paternalistic society, where men make virtually all important life decisions. Also, the experience and educational level of the partner practitioner as well as the way public relations is practiced in a particular country can make a difference. Authors of *This Is PR: The Realities of Public Relations* note that "in only a few countries is public relations practiced at the strategic level where the PR person has the power and authority to affect policy."

30

Quran Burning

Cultural Insensitivity Leads to Deaths and Multiple Apologies

Remote, rugged and deeply religious, Afghanistan is a mostly tribal and conservative nation whose fiercely independent citizens have shown themselves willing to fight for their freedom. The Soviet Union tried unsuccessfully to subdue the country during a ten-year war that ended in 1989. That was followed by a civil war and then the U.S.-led invasion in 2001.

The war in Afghanistan began in October 2001, one month after the terrorist attacks of 9/11 that killed nearly 3,000 persons. Operation Enduring Freedom, as it was named, was launched by the U.S., with the help of the United Kingdom, Australia, and the Afghan United Front. The operation's goals were to defeat and dismantle al-Qaeda, the terrorist organization responsible for the U.S. attacks, and remove from power the Taliban, the extremist Islamist militant group that ruled Afghanistan and gave safe haven to al-Qaeda. The U.S. and its allies also sought to bring to justice al-Qaeda's leader, Osama bin Laden. It took ten years, but the goal was achieved; he was killed in 2011 by the U.S. military in Pakistan.

By the end of 2012, the Afghan war—the longest war in U.S. history—had resulted in the deaths of more than 3,000 coalition troops, nearly 2,000 of them American military. More than 17,000 U.S. military had been wounded. There is no official casualty record for Afghan civilians, but it is estimated in the tens of thousands. In 2011 alone, 3,021 Afghan civilians died and 4,507 were wounded, according to the United Nations. The UN attributed most of the deaths to Taliban attacks aimed at NATO coalition forces.

CULTURAL TRAINING FOR SOLDIERS

Modern warfare is not decided by superiority of force alone; it often relies on the battle for the "hearts and minds" of the people. The U.S.-led NATO effort in Afghanistan needed the support of the country's tribal leaders, government, and people to

FIGURE 10.1A *U.S. Army 1st Lt. David J. Leydet, with 3rd Platoon, Bear Troop, 8th Squadron, 1st Cavalry Regiment, greets an elder during a population engagement in Taktehpol, Afghanistan, on March 2, 2010. http://www.defenseimagery.mil*
U.S. Department of Defense

FIGURE 10.1B *Army Staff Sgt. John Newland helps an Afghan boy try on new boots in Zanto Kalay, Afghanistan, on January 11, 2006. U.S. Army soldiers are bringing medical assistance, donated winter jackets, sweaters, blankets, and food to the people of Zanto Kalay during a medical outreach program. Newland is attached to the Army's 492nd Civil Affairs Battalion. http://www.defense.gov/*
U.S. Department of Defense

FIGURE 10.1C *A U.S. Army soldier with Charlie Company 2508, Task Force Furry, shakes the hand of a young Afghan child during a dismounted patrol, February 5, 2010, southern Afghanistan.*
http://www.defense.gov
U.S. Department of Defense

FIGURE 10.1D *A group of local Afghan children bump fists with U.S. Army soldiers assigned to the 1775th Military Police Company during a mission to Kuchi village, Afghanistan, May 27, 2011.*
http://www.defense.gov
U.S. Department of Defense

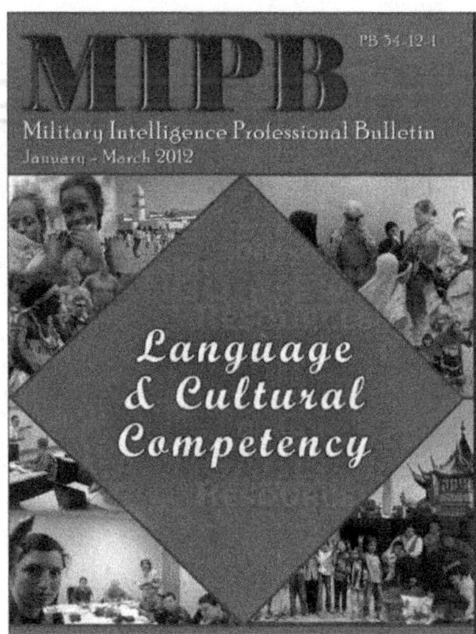

FIGURE 10.2 *The Army's cultural and foreign language advisors discussed cultural relativism, ethnography, and culture training as it applies to military warfare.*
http://www.fas.org/
U.S. Department of Defense

effectively battle al-Qaeda and the Taliban. Yet, many Afghans did not know about the 9/11 attacks, and many believed the Taliban's message that the foreign forces were invaders seeking the destruction of Islam.

The majority of U.S. Army cultural training for soldiers deploying to Afghanistan and other countries involved three groups: the U.S. Central Command (CENTCOM), the Army's Training and Doctrine Command's (TRADOC's) Center for Army Lessons Learned (CALL), and the U.S. Forces Command (FORSCOM).

Briefly, CENTCOM oversees all branches of the military in a theater-level operation. Among its activities, it identifies and requests training needs for active and deployed troops. TRADOC's culture center develops and provides educational resources for troop training. FORSCOM also provides more tailored troop training based on ever-evolving needs in conflict zones. Its readiness training includes specific training scenarios with complex cross-cultural challenges. One training center has an urban combat landscape with many role players acting as combatants and civilians.

TRADOC was created in 1973 and oversees troop training, the development of operational doctrine, and the attainment of new weapons systems. Regarding its role in troop training:

> *The U.S. Army Training and Doctrine Command (TRADOC) established the TRADOC Culture Center to provide the U.S. Army with mission-focused culture education and training. The TRADOC Culture Center is located at the U.S. Army Intelligence Center,*

Fort Huachuca, AZ. The TRADOC Culture Center's mission includes training all units and Soldiers preparing to deploy, and enabling all institutional organizations to effectively educate and train culture. The TRADOC Culture Center:

- *Develops culture education and training support packages.*
- *Conducts culture education and training as part of professional military education.*
- *Conducts culture training via transition teams and embedded training teams.*

The U.S. Army recognized that building trust with local Afghans was crucial to success. This required respect for its culture and some basic communication ability.

In January 2010, TRADOC issued the second edition of its *Afghan Smart Book.* The purpose of the smart book was to ensure U.S. Army personnel had a relevant, comprehensive guide to use in capacity building and counterinsurgency operations while deployed in Afghanistan that included how to handle religious items.

By fall 2010, the Army for the first time required all soldiers and reservists deploying to Afghanistan (and other regions) to complete a six-to-eight hour online language and culture training program. The training programs were developed specifically for soldiers' survival needs in a radically new environment. They provided military-focused vocabulary and scenarios, and cultural information. Computerized instruction, such as a computer software program called *Rapport,* offered digitally animated soldier avatars and interactive features to appeal to a new generation of learners. Each language and culture program, available online and on CD, could be accessed after deployment for further training.

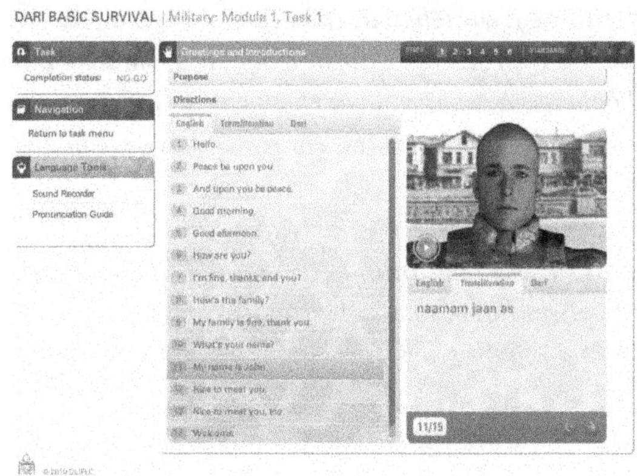

FIGURE 10.3 *The Army's Defense Language Institute developed an online six-hour interactive training program using Rapport software to teach basic language and cultural survival skills.*
http://rapport.lingnet.org/
Defense Language Institute/U.S. Department of Defense

In addition, each platoon was required to have a "language-enabled" soldier who had taken a more extensive language training program that included either a hundred-hour online HeadStart program or a sixteen-week course offered at many installations.

John Paul Boyce, deputy chief, U.S. Army Forces Command Public Affairs office, said unit training involved face-to-face cultural training of soldiers deployed to Afghanistan that included the following:

> *Because Muslims believe the Quran is the literal word of God, they treat all copies of book with extreme veneration. Every complete copy, or even partial passages, are considered holy. This includes verses that have been hand-written and that include the name of God. It is considered culturally insensitive for any non-Muslim to touch a copy of the Quran. Even Muslims are supposed to perform ablution (a ritualistic hand washing) before holding the Quran. Quran verses need not be in a book or even on paper to be sacred to Muslims. You will likely not be able to read the highly decorative script in Arabic. Use your interpreter to identify Qurans or Quranic verses.*
>
> *Verbal disrespect for Islam and/or the Quran is considered as inappropriate as physical desecration of the Quran. Insulting the Quran is an act of blasphemy. Expect to encounter a copy of the Quran or other Islamic Religious Materials when you search a person's belongings or home. Ask the person or homeowner to remove the sacred text or place it in a secure location before conducting a search.*
>
> *Insurgents will use even perceived disrespect to Islam and/or the Quran to their advantage to substantiate their claim that NATO ISAF forces are dishonoring Afghan religious and cultural values.*
>
> *Non-Muslims should NEVER handle an Arabic version of the Quran. While non-Muslims are permitted to handle a translation of the Quran, one should make it a general practice to treat all religious materials with extraordinary respect. If in the performance of your duty, you are required to handle a Quran or other Islamic Religious Material, you should use a clean cloth or clean gloves. It is important to recognize that even partial copies or hand-written verses of the Quran are equally sacred and must be handled in the same manner.*
>
> *As well as the Quran, service members may come in contact with other Islamic Religious Materials. These may include the Sunnah (Islamic guidance based on the behavior of the Prophet Muhammad), the Hadiths (sayings of the Prophet Muhammad on various major and minor issues), or various other printed or hand-written religious materials.*
>
> *Remember when securing items that you must still use proper procedures when handling Islamic Religious Materials, even if you are not certain of the exact nature of the materials you are have discovered. Proper handling ensures no offense will be given should these materials be deemed sacred in nature.*

Troops at training centers at Fort Irwin, California, or at Fort Polk, Louisiana, also received training with numerous scenarios including one about the handling of the Quran.

Another training supplement for troops led by FORSCOM was Rapid Afghanistan Experience Project (RAEP) in 2011. It consolidated the knowledge, skills, lessons learned, and the tactics, techniques, and procedures (TTPs) currently employed in Afghanistan. This resource included a classified website for tools, TTPs, links to other websites and portals, lessons learned and timely topics of interest.

Also in 2011, TRADOC began working with a university partner to develop a "serious game" that combined training for intelligence gathering and cultural immersion at the tactical level, according to the Army's website. "Its immersive gaming environment provided interactive engagement with indigenous community leaders under varied cultural contexts and conditions."

AFGHANS AND THE QURAN

Afghanistan is an Islamic republic, and more than 99 percent of its citizens are Muslims, followers of Islam. Muslims believe that there is only one true God, Allah, and that none other should be worshiped. Their beliefs are contained in the Quran, which is considered the verbatim word of God as revealed by the prophet Muhammad through the angel Gabriel over a period that spanned twenty-three years beginning in 610 CE. Muslims believe the Quran has survived to present times in its original form and is God's final revelation to humanity. The Quran is considered holy and its handling requires respect by all, including non-believers. The Quran says "Indeed, We have sent down the Quran, and surely We will guard it [from corruption]" (Quran, 15:9).

QURAN DESECRATION INCIDENTS

While many Americans revere religious objects, such as the Bible and the Torah, it is generally not illegal in the U.S. to destroy or mistreat them. Some artists, for example, have created and exhibited what religious conservatives consider blasphemous depictions of religious objects and themes, including *Piss Christ*, a plastic crucifix submerged in a glass of the artist's urine; and *The Holy Virgin Mary*, a painting that contained sexual images and elephant dung. These and other art objects have sparked protests in America.

Many states have laws that prohibit defiling or defacing the American flag in public, especially when it incites people to unrest. Still, most state laws handle flag mistreatment as a misdemeanor offense, and many believe that any attempt to suppress desecration of the flag would be an infringement of an individual's constitutionally protected right to free speech.

Americans learned how seriously Muslims regarded the Quran when riots broke out in Kabul, Afghanistan, after a church pastor in Florida threatened to burn a Quran on September 11, 2010. The pastor, Terry Jones, initially gave up his plans after religious leaders and government officials, including U.S. Secretary of Defense Robert Gates, asked him to stop. But months later, on March 20, 2011, he burned a

FIGURE 10.4 *Florida church pastor Terry Jones provoked a worldwide furore when he burned a Quran in his church in March 2011.*
http://www.youtube.com/
answeringchristian

Quran in his small church, and the event was streamed live online; later recorded versions with Arabic spread subtitles circulated around the world. The incident sparked deadly riots in Afghanistan; at least twenty-one people were killed, including seven United Nations employees, and more than 150 were injured, according to news reports. A $2.4 million bounty for Jones was ordered by religious leaders in Pakistan, according to *The Washington Post.*

The Florida incident was not the first. An earlier incident occurred in 2005 at a U.S. military base in Guantanamo Bay, Cuba, where suspected terrorists from the Afghan war were held. It was reported that U.S. military personnel desecrated the Quran. In one news account it was said that a copy of the Quran had been flushed down a toilet. This report sparked angry riots that led to seventeen Afghans killed. While the toilet flushing incident was later retracted, a military report did confirm other less serious abuses of the Quran.

QURAN BURNING IN AFGHANISTAN

The incident of Quran desecration that caused the most controversy occurred in Afghanistan on the night of February 20, 2012. A number of printed items were delivered to the coalition's Bagram Airbase incinerator from a nearby detention center. According to news reports, several hundred Islamic publications from the detention center's library, including copies of the Quran and other Islamic religious writings, had extremist messages written in them or had extremist content deemed inappropriate for the detainees. Afghan workers pulled remains of charred copies of

FIGURE 10.5 *Afghans burn an effigy representing U.S. President Barack Obama during anti-US protest over burning of Qurans at a military base in Afghanistan, in Ghani Khail, east of Kabul Friday, February 24, 2012. http://www.corbisimages.com*
© Rahmat Gul/AP/Corbis

the Quran out of the fire when they saw what was in the burn pit. Once the coalition troops realized what had happened, the operation was halted.

While none of the material was destroyed, the act of mixing holy books, especially the Quran, with garbage and then burning them was beyond comprehension for Muslims. According to some reports, Afghan workers took the charred copies of the Quran off base and showed other Afghans what had happened.

The results were immediate and severe. Within days, deadly protests broke out in Afghanistan resulting in thirty Afghans killed and the shooting deaths of four American soldiers that many believed were connected to the incident. A grenade explosion during one protest injured six other American service members.

As Davood Moradian, a former adviser to Afghan president Hamid Karzai, explained, "They have been here for more than ten years and they still fail to understand the sensitivities of Afghanistan . . . For Afghans, [burning the Quran] is an unacceptable, unforgiveable incompetence," according to *Stars and Stripes*.

Many criticized NATO soldiers for not taking the time to know Afghans and their values. If they had, they would understand that Afghans "are a mostly religious people whose interpretation of the world is a religious one," said Waliullah Rahmani, executive director of the Kabul Center for Strategic Studies, reported *Stars and Stripes*.

The importance of religion above everything else, even loss of human life, was a hard concept to understand for many Americans following the story.

As Mullah Qayoom explained, "Humans were sent here to worship and protect religion . . . That is what the purpose of a Muslim's life is," according to *The New York Times*.

THE NATO AND U.S. RESPONSE

The following documents are NATO International Security Assistance Force (ISAF) and U.S. military news releases, briefings and statements that were released after the February 20, 2012, nighttime incident during the early days of the crisis.

The first responses came within hours of the Quran burning incident. General John R. Allen, commander of ISAF, issued the following statement in a print and video release format February 21, 2012:

> **General Allen, Commander ISAF issued the following statement:**
>
> *To the noble people of Afghanistan—*
>
> *I have ordered an investigation into a report I received during the night that ISAF personnel at Bagram Airbase improperly disposed of a large number of Islamic religious materials which included Korans.*
>
> *When we learned of these actions, we immediately intervened and stopped them. The materials recovered will be properly handled by appropriate religious authorities.*
>
> *We are thoroughly investigating the incident and we are taking steps to ensure this does not ever happen again. I assure you . . . I promise you . . . this was NOT intentional in any way.*

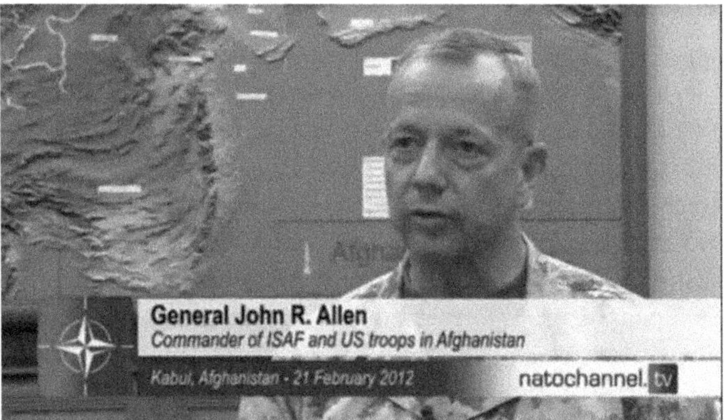

FIGURE 10.6 *General John Allen, Commander of ISAF, apologized to the Afghan people and said that an investigation had been launched and would include Afghanis, and that he had ordered that all military under his command would be required to receive training in how to handle Islamic religious materials to prevent the situation from happening again.*
http://www.youtube.com/
NATO Community

I offer my sincere apologies for any offense this may have caused, to the President of Afghanistan, the Government of the Islamic Republic of Afghanistan, and most importantly, to the noble people of Afghanistan.

I would like to thank the local Afghan people who helped us identify the error, and who worked with us to immediately take corrective action.

Manana, Tashakur.

This news release was issued by U.S. Secretary of Defense Leon Panetta on February 21, 2012:

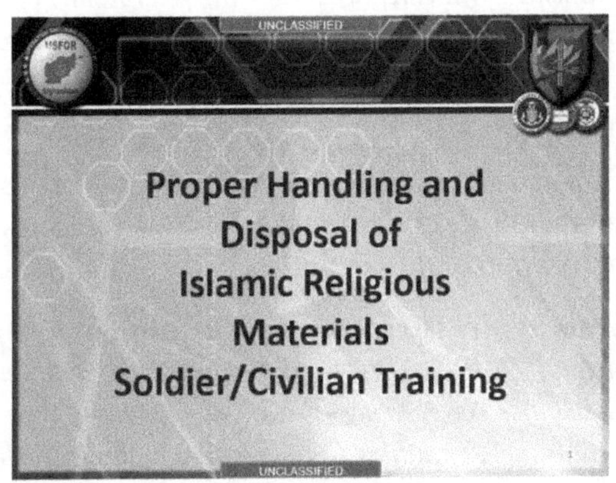

FIGURE 10.7 *The PowerPoint presentation developed by the U.S. Army on "Proper Handling and Disposal of Islamic Religious Materials".*
U.S. Army
U.S. Department of Defense

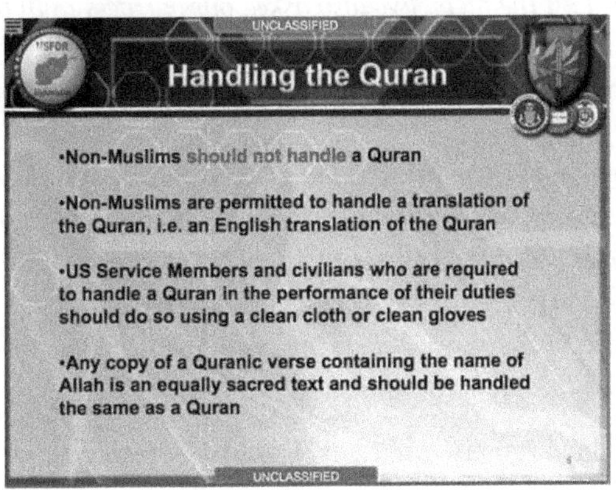

FIGURE 10.8 *An example slide from the U.S. Army's training PowerPoint.*
U.S. Army
U.S. Department of Defense

Statement by Secretary of Defense Leon E. Panetta on the Treatment of Religious Materials at Bagram Airbase

This morning ISAF Commander Gen. John Allen notified me of the deeply unfortunate incident involving the inappropriate treatment of religious materials, including the Koran, at Bagram Airbase. He and I apologize to the Afghan people and disapprove of such conduct in the strongest possible terms. These actions do not represent the views of the United States military. We honor and respect the religious practices of the Afghan people, without exception.

I support Gen. Allen's swift and decisive action to investigate this matter jointly with the Afghan government. I will carefully review the final results of the investigation to ensure that we take all steps necessary and appropriate so that this never happens again.

A news release issued by ISAF for the first of three investigations was issued February 21, 2012; it included the requirement for new training. Soldiers' mandatory pre-deployment language/culture training did not provide specifics on how to handle religious materials. Instead, the training provided a short overview of Islam that included a brief mention of the Quran.

ISAF Commander Issues Directive on Handling of Religious Materials
KABUL, Afghanistan (Feb. 21, 2012)—Gen. John R. Allen, commander of the International Security Assistance Force, today issued a new directive that all coalition forces in Afghanistan will complete training in the proper handling of religious materials no later than March 3. The new guidance comes in the wake of an incident that occurred last night at the Detention Facility in Parwan in which religious materials, to include Qurans identified for disposal, were inadvertently taken to an incineration facility at Bagram airfield. The incident is currently under investigation.

"On behalf of the entire International Security Assistance Force, I extend my sincerest apologies to the people of Afghanistan," said Gen. Allen. "To assist us in ensuring we have uncovered all the facts, I've also asked our partners from the Afghan Ministry of Interior to assist us with this investigation."

The training will include the identification of religious materials, their significance, correct handling and storage.

"Along with our apology to the Afghans is our certainty and assurance to them, that these kinds of incidents, when they do occur, will be corrected in the fastest and most appropriate manner possible," continued Allen. "We've been shoulder to shoulder with the Afghans for a long time. We've been dying alongside the Afghans for a long time because we believe in them; we believe in their country, and we want to have every opportunity to give them a bright future."

On the second day after the incident, Deputy Defense Secretary Ashton Carter arrived in Afghanistan and offered his apologies for the Quran burning. The U.S. Department of Defense American Forces Press Service issued the following news release:

Carter Offers Apologies to Afghan Leaders

KABUL, Afghanistan, Feb. 22, 2012—Deputy Defense Secretary Ashton B. Carter today joined other senior officials in condemning the improper disposal of religious materials, including Qurans, at Bagram Airfield.

Carter arrived here yesterday to meet with Afghan and International Security Assistance Force officials for the first time since he took the Pentagon's No. 2 post in October.

Defense Secretary Leon E. Panetta and Marine Corps Gen. John R. Allen, ISAF commander, offered apologies yesterday for the incident, and all ISAF personnel now will receive training on handling religious materials.

Carter said the mishandling was inadvertent, but shouldn't have happened.

"It's inexcusable—an act of ignorance—and it's very unfortunate because it has unfortunate consequences and gives people a chance to misunderstand what we're all doing here," he said.

In meetings today with Afghan President Hamid Karzai, Defense Minister Abdul Rahim Wardak and members of the Afghan parliament, Carter offered his personal apologies for the incident. In each meeting, the deputy defense secretary made it clear these were "ignorant" actions that were unacceptable.

He also pledged his full support for a joint Afghan–ISAF investigation into the incident, Pentagon spokesman Navy Capt. John Kirby said.

Two days after the incident, a joint ISAF and Afghan investigative team went to the detention facility to investigate what led to the Quran burning incident. The following news release was issued by the ISAF public affairs office February 22, 2012:

Joint ISAF/Afghan Investigative Team Visits Parwan Detention Facility

KABUL, Afghanistan (Feb. 22, 2012)—A joint investigation team comprised of members of the ISAF staff and representatives of the Afghan government visited the Detention Facility in Parwan today to examine the circumstances surrounding the disposal of religious materials there Sunday night.

"This visit is an extremely important first step in resolving this issue, and I am grateful to President Karzai for his support in sending this group of representatives to assist us," said Gen. John R. Allen, commander, International Security Assistance Force. "The only way we can demonstrate our sincerity to the people and government of Afghanistan is through our actions, and we are already taking measures to ensure this never happens again."

Afghan representatives included members of a ulema that will report directly to the President of Afghanistan. The ISAF team included a representative of the ISAF Commander and staff from the detention facility.

"The purpose of the investigation is to discover the truth surrounding the events which resulted in this incident," said Gen. Allen. "We are determined to ascertain the facts, and take all actions necessary to ensure this never happens again."

The U.S. Department of Defense conducted a press briefing with ISAF spokesman Brigadier General Carsten Jacobson via teleconference from Afghanistan on February 22, 2012. Below is his opening statement and portions of his comments on the Quran incident:

Well, good morning from Kabul. As you already know, we had an unfortunate incident early yesterday at Bagram Airbase, where ISAF personnel improperly disposed of some religious materials, which we believe included Qurans. As soon as we learned of this mistake, we stopped this action, and General Allen quickly initiated an investigation to discover how and why this happened.

This incident was completely unintentional. Material was inadvertently given to troops for burning. The decision to burn this material had nothing to do with it being religious in nature or related to Islam. It was a mistake. It was an error.

Today an Afghan delegation joined the investigation at Bagram, as we want to be as transparent as possible in determining how this incident occurred. We have deeply—we're deeply concerned about the possibility that Qurans or religious materials were damaged in this incident, and we will get to the bottom of what actually happened.

ISAF has complete respect for Islam and the reverence in which the Quran is held. We are very serious about making certain that it—that if someone failed to follow our rules, they will be held accountable.

Last night General Allen issued a new directive that all coalition forces in Afghanistan will complete training in the proper handling of religious material no later than the 3rd of March. The training will include the identification of religious materials, their significance, correct handling and storage.

General Allen and ISAF, again, give sincere apologies for any offense that this may have caused to the president of Afghanistan, the government of the Islamic Republic of Afghanistan and, most importantly, to the noble people of Afghanistan.

Answers to two questions posed by a CBS reporter addressed the nature of the joint investigation and the cultural training that NATO troops receive before deploying to Afghanistan:

Q: *David Martin with CBS. I'm not sure I understand what part of this was inadvertent. Was it inadvertent that these religious materials were taking—taken out of the prison or was that a deliberate decision? Was it—or was it just inadvertent that they were given to the troops for disposal or was it inadvertent that the troops then took them—took them to the burn pit?*

Gen. Jacobson: *Well, the mistake that I'm talking about—and it is a great mistake, and we're obviously all aware about the grave implications that this mistake has, in particular, when it comes to mishandling Qurans—was made somewhere down the line, and that is what has to be found out in the investigation: who basically failed to discover the quality of this material, who basically told soldiers to take it and to dispose of it in an improper way. It is part of the orders that left the headquarters yesterday, signed by General Allen, in how to handle and how to store Islamic material, to increase the awareness, to know what is inside a library, what is inside a facility, what* *is the type of the material, to lead to the correct decision and to not take this—these decisions unanimously but to always ask for cultural advice when it comes to questions like this.*

Somewhere down this line lies the mistake. The mistake was made. The mistake led to General Allen immediately coming forward yesterday morning and apologizing in the way that I said in my initial statement. And we basically have to wait for the results of the investigation on where, what went wrong.

Q: *Thank you. General, I wonder if you could elaborate just a little bit more on the nature of the cultural and religious sensitivity training that the troops receive both before deployment and after deployment. And how will that differ from what General Allen has ordered?*

Gen. Jacobson: *Well, General Allen's order of yesterday deals specifically with the consequences that have to be drawn out of this incident. And that is that somewhere in the chain of command, or right down to the personnel who have given the order to dispose of this material, somebody did not recognize the importance and the nature of the material which right from the beginning should have led to the involvement of cultural advisers.*

And as I say, we have cultural advisers and translators—Afghans—on every level, and we have Afghan workers with us on every level.

The training of forces before their deployment and their training on deployment are regulated by the troop contributing nations, but they all involve standards of cultural awareness. And as I said, we have a considerable number of Muslim members in the coalition, and we are working together on a daily basis with Afghans—130,000 soldiers of the coalition with 300,000 Afghan national security forces—who are going out sometimes in the most extreme situations and conditions.

In general, we are quite confident that the measures that we are taking pre-deployment and on deployment are sufficient. In this case, we have seen a mistake; in this case, we have seen misjudgment; in this case, we have seen what should have happened, what should have been guided, where guidance should have been asked for, not happening, and that led to this tragic mistake. By touching the Quran—obviously, a mistake that has considerable consequences; in particular, here in Afghanistan. And we've seen that in the demonstration over the last—in the demonstrations over the last 48 hours.

A question was asked by *The Washington Post* about the long-term consequences of the incident:

Q: *General, Craig Whitlock with* The Washington Post. *If I could ask more broadly what kind of strategic setback do you think this incident poses for ISAF's campaign? You know, whether it's intentional or not, or unintentional, you know, it seems to confirm a lot of the Taliban propaganda about the motives of foreign forces, non-Islamic forces in Afghanistan. Do you see this resonating for a long time to come?*

Gen. Jacobson: *Without going into speculation on long-term effects, we are obviously aware about the graveness of what has happened, about the graveness of this incident.*

Desecrating the Quran, mistreating the Quran, is a grave incident in the Muslim world. And as we are not only here to protect human rights, but also religious freedom, and obviously here to protect the people of Afghanistan and the way that they live and in—what they believe in, this is a grave incident.

We have seen the implications, the understandable anger of people of Afghanistan about what they have seen and what they have heard. The important thing is now that we are all together—together with Afghan authorities and together with the people of Afghanistan, treat this with the necessary care; explain to the people as much as possible that mistakes were made. And as I said in my initial statement, if we do find that there are responsibilities down the line, yes, there will be legal consequences to this, and we have to look into this in detail.

It is important that we deal with this rightly in the coming hours. What is important for ISAF, and what is important for Afghanistan—government and people of Afghanistan—is that violence does not flare; that this is not used to inflame the people of Afghanistan; that this is not used to drive a wedge between the people that we are working closely with on a very daily basis—the Afghan national security forces side by side with us on operation, in very dangerous missions on a day-to-day basis, trainers who are training Afghan personnel in every aspect, not only in the security sector.

We are very close to each other, and therefore it is of the utmost importance that we explain very, very clearly what happened; explain how sorry we are about what happened; explain that this was a mistake; explain what led to it and talk about the consequences.

The Department of Defense American Forces Press Service issued a news release February 22, 2012, that repeated apologies from officials, mentioned the protests, and explained the joint investigation and required cultural training for military personnel:

Quran Incident Inquiry Under Way, ISAF Official Says

WASHINGTON, Feb. 22, 2012—Coalition members are working with Afghan leaders to quickly and fully investigate the "grave mistake" that yesterday ended in partially burned Qurans at the Parwan detention facility near Bagram, Afghanistan, an International Security Assistance Force spokesman said today.

Speaking from the Afghan capital of Kabul in a teleconference with Pentagon reporters, Brig. Gen. Carsten Jacobson of the German army said it's of the utmost importance that officials "explain very, very clearly what happened, explain how sorry we are about what happened, explain that this was a mistake, explain what led to it, and talk about the consequences."

Afghan government and religious leaders are investigating the circumstances behind the incident along with ISAF representatives, Jacobson said, and the results of that inquiry could be available within hours.

The inadvertent desecration of the Islamic holy book kindled protest demonstrations that began with a 2,000-person disturbance outside the detention facility yesterday, and continued today with at least four more protests, featuring 200 to 500 demonstrators each, around Kabul, Jacobson said. News reports count the death toll from the protests at seven, though Jacobson said no violence has been specifically directed against ISAF troops.

Jacobson said the Qurans were mistakenly included in a mass of material delivered to the detention facility's burn pit for routine disposal. Local workers at the facility noticed the books and pulled them from the fire, he added.

"Material was inadvertently given to troops for burning," Jacobson said. "The decision to burn this material had nothing to do with it being religious in nature or related to Islam. It was a mistake. It was an error."

Marine Corps Gen. John R. Allen, ISAF commander, quickly ordered an investigation to discover how and why the mistake happened, the spokesman said.

"ISAF has complete respect for Islam and the reverence in which the Quran is held," Jacobson said. "We are very serious about making certain . . . that if someone failed to follow our rules, they will be held accountable."

All 50 coalition member nations require their troops to take part in cultural training before and after deploying to Afghanistan, he noted. While such training has been effective overall, the spokesman said, Allen ordered yesterday that all coalition forces in Afghanistan will complete training in the proper handling of religious material no later than March 3.

"The training will include the identification of religious materials, their significance, correct handling and storage," Jacobson said.

Defense Secretary Leon E. Panetta and Allen each issued statements yesterday apologizing for the event.

Jacobson repeated those sentiments today.

"General Allen and ISAF, again, give sincere apologies for any offense that this may have caused to the president of Afghanistan, the government of the Islamic Republic of Afghanistan and, most importantly, to the noble people of Afghanistan," he said.

Jacobson said he can't confirm news reports that the Qurans may have contained writing by detainees using the books as a means of communication with each other. "We haven't got any proof of that yet, and that is a vital part of the investigation that is ongoing," he said.

All material recovered at the burn pit was turned over to Islamic authorities, he noted, reiterating that Afghan officials are taking part in the investigation. Findings from that inquiry should determine exactly what material was involved, who gave the orders to dispose of it, how it got to the burn pit, and what actually happened when it got there, Jacobson said.

"We have to be very careful in what we do, what we say, what we look at," he added. "This is a very sensitive subject, and we have to be exactly clear on what was found, what was the reason for decisions that were taken, and it has to be done together with the Afghans."

Keenly aware of the Afghan public's interest in the investigation, the ISAF issued a follow-up news release the next day, asking for patience as the investigation continued:

Joint Investigation Continues into Parwan Incident

KABUL, Afghanistan (Feb. 23, 2012)—*A joint ISAF and Afghan investigation into events surrounding the mishandling of religious materials at Bagram Airbase continues. Witnesses to the incident are being interviewed, with a date for completion to be determined.*

"Working together with the Afghan leadership is the only way for us to correct this major error and ensure that it never happens again," said Gen. John R. Allen, Commander International Security Assistance Force.

"I call on everyone throughout the country—ISAF members and Afghans—to exercise patience and restraint as we continue to gather the facts surrounding Monday night's incident."

The joint investigation team is comprised of members of the ISAF staff and representatives of the Afghan government.

President Barack Obama issued an apology in a hand-delivered letter by U.S. Ambassador Ryan Crocker to Afghan President Hamid Karzai on February 23, 2012. The letter's complete contents were not made public because it included other information. Karzai issued a statement which also appeared on his office's website sharing the president's apology:

I wish to express my deep regret for the reported incident. I extend to you and the Afghan people my sincere apologies. The error was inadvertent; I assure you that we

FIGURE 10.9 *Concern for the safety of all U.S. military personnel in Afghanistan was so high following the Quran burning that President Barack Obama sent a letter to President Hamid Karzai to apologize for the incident. This received prominent placement in the news media and Karzai's website.*
http://president.gov.af/en
e-Government of Afghanistan

will take the appropriate steps to avoid any recurrence, to include holding accountable those responsible.

Karzai told members of the Afghan parliament that a U.S. officer was responsible for the burning, which was done "out of ignorance," his office said.

White House Press Secretary Jay Carney spoke to reporters aboard *Air Force One* en route to Miami on February 23, 2012, providing some context to President Obama's apology to President Karzai:

Q: *Jay, the President apologized to Karzai over the burning of the Koran. Is the President worried, or is he frustrated that he has to do this and that it feeds a kind of a political narrative that the Republicans have created that he's—*

Mr. Carney: *That's a fully false, fallacious and ridiculous narrative that is not borne out by any facts. The President, following up on a telephone conversation, the likes of which he has routinely with President Karzai, wrote a long letter on a variety of issues related to our bilateral engagement, including reconciliation, including the trilateral talks between—with Pakistan last week in Islamabad, in which he also expressed his condolences and—or rather, his apology for the inadvertent burning of religious materials by American personnel in Afghanistan.*

It is wholly appropriate, given the sensitivities to this issue, the understandable sensitivities. His primary concern as Commander-in-Chief is the safety of American men and women in Afghanistan, of our military and civilian personnel there. And it was absolutely the right thing to do.

And I would simply note that Secretary Panetta, Joint Chiefs Chairman Dempsey and I have all conveyed apologies on behalf of the United States for this incident.

Q: *Did President Karzai ask him for that letter after their phone call?*

Mr. Carney: *The letter, which I can't show you because it's not appropriate to show, but it's a lengthy three-page letter on a host of issues, several sentences of which relate to this matter.*

Q: *What's the reception been to the letter, Jay?*

Mr. Carney: *I don't have an update for you. I understand that President Karzai released some quotations from the letter. But I don't have any readout for you on the reception. I think that the message that we're trying to convey here is that this was inadvertent. We take this very seriously. There is an ISAF investigation. And even prior to any completion of that investigation, General Allen is taking steps to ensure that this kind of thing can't happen again by instituting training on the handling of religious materials.*

Q: *President Karzai's office said today that they'd like a trial of those involved in this incident. Do you have any reaction to that?*

Mr. Carney: *As I said, there's an investigation going on to find out exactly what happened. The inappropriate handling of these materials was inadvertent, but sensitivities here are ones that we understand and we have great respect—the actions here, while inadvertent, do not reflect the great respect that our military personnel have for the religious traditions of the Afghan people.*

Q: *What's the precedent for apologizing when the military has already apologized?*

Mr. Carney: *Well, in this case, again, the President was—had been—had a conversation with President Karzai the day before he was—in a follow-up to that conversation, wrote an extensive letter on a number of topics, including the Afghan-led reconciliation process and our bilateral relationship with Afghanistan, in which he included an expression of his regret and apologies for the inappropriate and inadvertent mishandling of religious materials.*

I would note that one of my predecessors, Dana Perino, the Press Secretary for President George W. Bush, following an incident in which an American serviceman apparently shot or did damage to a Koran in 2008, she expressed apologies on behalf of the President. And that's appropriate for the same reason, because our concern—this President's concern, as was surely the case with President Bush—is the safety and security of our men and women in uniform, as well as our civilians in Afghanistan.

And one of the reasons that it's appropriate to express our sincere apologies for this incident is that the kind of reaction that it can cause risks putting our men and women in harm's way, or in further risk than they already are. So I think that precedent is a useful one to look at.

A White House press briefing by Principal Deputy Press Secretary Josh Earnest was held February 24, 2012 on the Quran burning incident. Here are some of his answers to questions posed by reporters:

Q: *Two topics. On Afghanistan, the President's apology of the burning of the Korans has not seemed to quell the violence, the protests at all. I believe that now twenty people have been killed. I'm wondering if the White House is worried that there's no clear end in sight to this.*

Mr. Earnest: *Well, as you pointed out, Ben, General Allen, Secretary Panetta, and President Obama have all, in different forms, expressed their apology on behalf of the American people and the American military to the Afghan people to articulate that the United States military and, indeed, the American people have enduring respect for the religious views and religious practices of the Afghan people.*

We were pleased today to see that President Karzai himself has also called—or appealed for calm in Afghanistan. And while this is a difficult circumstance that we're working through, we're confident that our goals in Afghanistan—which I'll remind you is to defeat, disrupt and dismantle al Qaeda and to ensure that al Qaeda [Afghanistan] cannot be used as a safe haven for al Qaeda or other religious extremists—violent extremists—so it is our view that we will work through these difficult circumstances and remain on track to making progress on our goals there.

Q: *Also I'd like to follow up on a question from Ben about the apology that President Obama—the apology letter to President Karzai. That's also emerged as an issue that Republicans have criticized the President on. Without getting into their charges, can you walk us through the process and decision-making when it comes to issuing an apology? What concerns are taken into account? When is it thought that something rises to the level of needing an apology? When is something not? When is there a concern* *that that's probably too much, or the United States doesn't need to be too apologetic about such-and-such? I mean, how is a decision made to do such a thing? Is it only the lives of people protesting in the street, or the U.S. service members that are taken into account?*

Mr. Earnest: *This is a difficult thing to discuss in a hypothetical context, but I can talk about this specific context.*

Q: *Okay.*

Mr. Earnest: *And it was the President's view that an apology was appropriate because he's putting the best interest and safety and welfare of our service members and our civilians who are currently serving in Afghanistan right now—that we have seen a spike in violence around this mistake. And the President believed that it was in the best interests of their safety to make it clear that an apology was appropriate, and that the American people and the American military in particular does have respect for the religious views and the religious practices of the Afghan people.*

So in this case, the President believed it was in the best interests and in—of safety for American servicemen and women in Afghanistan, and for the civilians that are serving in Afghanistan.

Q: *Yes. My understanding is that there is now some training of the service members in terms of how to deal with this kind of situation—disposal of the Koran, respect for holy books, things like that—for service members serving in Afghanistan. Why has this not been done before? We've been there for ten years now, and we've had this sort of situation previously with burning of Korans.*

Mr. Earnest: *It's my understanding that there are some new training methods that are being put in place. I don't have any details about what those training methods are, though, so I'd refer you to ISAF for that.*

Q: *But why has it not been in place before? And are you also confident that the kind of cultural training that is in place for service members is sufficient?*

Mr. Earnest: *Well, again, I can't speak to the training standards that were in place before and in place now. For those kinds of details you're just going to have to check with my colleagues over at ISAF.*

Q: *The classified report that came out from NATO about a month or two months ago that talked about the uptick in attacks by Afghan soldiers on NATO soldiers talked about how most of those attacks were as a result of personal issues, feeling that the NATO soldiers—in particular the U.S. soldiers—were disrespecting their culture. Do we have a cultural disconnect here?*

Mr. Earnest: *Well, I haven't seen the report that you're referencing, Victoria. But the issue that you're raising is precisely the reason that the President himself—and General Allen, and Secretary Panetta—have made clear to President Karzai and to the Afghan people that the actions that took place at Bagram Air Force Base do not* *reflect the official United States policy and flagged that they were a mistake. And it was important in the view of General Allen, Secretary Panetta and President Obama to make sure that that was clear to the Afghan people.*

Q: *To follow up on Jake's—the substance on the Koran burning. Since you laid out the criteria where the President decides when he thinks the U.S. government should apologize, is the President seeking an apology from President Karzai for the fact that U.S. service personnel were killed because of this?*

Mr. Earnest: *The President is certainly gratified that President Karzai has appealed for calm in Afghanistan, as we work through what is a very challenging situation. At the end of the day, what the President and his national security team and our generals in Afghanistan are focused on is making sure that we accomplish our goals in Afghanistan. There is no doubt that we're working through a difficult situation there. But we are going to stay on track of accomplishing our goal and continuing to make the significant progress that we have made in ensuring that Afghanistan cannot be a safe haven for al Qaeda or other violent extremists.*

Five days after the incident, with Afghan national forces bearing the brunt of most of the protest violence, General Allen issued a news release thanking Afghan National Security Force members:

ISAF Commander Praises ANSF Efforts to Quell Violence
KABUL, Afghanistan (Feb. 25, 2012)—"I want to thank those brave Afghan National Security Force members for the sacrifices they have made this week to minimize violence throughout the country," said ISAF Commander Gen. John R. Allen. "For many years, these brave ANSF soldiers and policemen have stood together alongside us, shoulder to shoulder, shohna ba shohna, *in dutifully seeking to protect the Afghan population from a merciless insurgency."*

"In the wake of this week's ongoing violence, we honor the sacrifices of our Afghan brothers in arms," added Allen. "Their courage and steadfast resolve in maintaining their integrity, their professionalism and their commitment to providing the Afghan population a bright future is an example to all Afghan citizens."

AFTERMATH—WHAT THE INVESTIGATIONS FOUND

In March 2012 a NATO investigation found six U.S. soldiers responsible for the Quran burning incident but found that their actions were not deliberate with "malicious intent" to "defame the faith of Islam," said Army Brigadier General Bryan Watson, as reported in *The Christian Science Monitor.*

In August 2012, the Pentagon released its report on the investigation. It found that while soldiers generally knew the Quran was a holy text, "they were ignorant of the extreme cultural offense their mishandling of it could cause," according to *The Washington Post* in its report on the investigation. Investigators concluded that:

- The soldiers' cultural and language training was not sufficient.
- U.S. troops ignored Afghan soldiers and prison guards at the detention center who objected to the plans to destroy the library material.
- Most of the library material, which included 474 Qurans and 1,100 religious tracts, was not extremist in nature, according to *The Washington Post.* It was Afghan workers at the Bagram Airbase who immediately stopped the incinerator once they realized what type of material was being burned and called other Afghan workers to help rescue the material.

USA Today reported that the investigation "found that the service members relied too heavily on one linguist's conclusion that the Qurans, which also had militant messages in them, were rewritten versions that were extremist and would not be considered real Qurans." The investigative report also said that soldiers misunderstood a "commander's order to get rid of the books as permission to take them to the burn pit."

The soldiers received unspecified administrative punishment but did not face criminal charges.

A subsequent tragic incident happened a few weeks after the Quran burning in which a U.S. Army staff sergeant left his base and shot and killed seventeen Afghan civilians, including nine children and three women in their homes. High-level apologies were issued, including a statement from President Barack Obama; the gunman was taken into custody, and financial restitution was made to the families. There were no deadly protests in the wake of this tragedy.

FORSCOM pre-deployment training for soldiers now includes the following reminder regarding the "Disposal of Islamic Religious Materials:"

The proper disposal of Islamic Religious Materials SHOULD NOT be performed by US personnel.

- *Only unusable/damaged/worn-out Qurans should be disposed of—with proper procedures.*
- *Only Muslims should dispose of Qurans and/or other Islamic Religious Materials.*
- *Methods include: wrapping the Quran in a pure cloth and burying it in a grave or fastening the Quran with a heavy object like a stone and placing it respectfully in flowing water.*

QUESTIONS FOR DISCUSSION

1. What is culture?
2. Why was cultural sensitivity important for the U.S. military forces in Afghanistan?

3. How did the Army prepare soldiers culturally who were deploying to Afghanistan?
4. What are some of the cultural difference between Afghanistan and the United States?
5. What are the issues surrounding the handling of Islamic materials such as the Quran?
6. How did the U.S. forces respond to the Quran burning incident initially? Was it effective?
7. What rhetorical tactics were used within the apologies to express sincerity?
8. Beyond rhetorical tactics, what actions were taken during the crisis?
9. Why did Barack Obama issue an apology?
10. What are some of the more innovative training initiatives underway to improve the cultural sensitivity of soldiers in combat zones?

Dig Deeper

The U.S. military has published many documents discussing the need for language and cultural understanding for its missions in other countries. Below are some that address the military's activities to build cultural capacity within its ranks, which are all available on the textbook's companion website. Of particular interest is the document "Proper Handling–Disposal of Islamic Religious Materials—Training Material–CDR–526" that Army personnel stationed in Islamic countries now receive as a result of the Quran burning controversy.

- "Building Cultural Capability for Full-Spectrum Operations"
- "Improving Cultural Awareness in the US Military"
- *Afghanistan Smart Book*
- "Arab Cultural Awareness": fifty-eight fact sheets
- *Rapport*—"Pashto Cultural Orientation"
- "Proper Handling–Disposal of Islamic Religious Materials—Training Material–CDR–526"
- "Military Intelligence Professional Bulletin—Cultural Awareness."

31

Fukushima Nuclear Meltdown

A Disaster "Made In Japan"

The island nation of Japan is part of the Pacific Ring of Fire, an area known for seismic and volcanic activity where tectonic plates meet. By itself, Japan is home to 10 percent of the world's active volcanoes. As a result of the tectonic activity, earthquakes are common. According to the Japan Meteorological Agency, Japan can have as many as 1,500 earthquakes annually; earthquakes registering between magnitudes 4 and 6 are not uncommon.

On March 11, 2011, the Great East Japan Earthquake hit about forty-three miles off the east coast of Japan at 2:46 p.m. Although it lasted only 170 seconds, the magnitude 9.0 earthquake was so powerful it moved the main island of Japan, Honshu, eight feet east and shifted the earth on its axis by an estimated four inches, according to the National Institute of Geophysics and Volcanology in Italy. It was the largest earthquake on record in Japan and the fifth largest in the world's recorded history.

Tsunami waves breached many of the sea walls that cover 40 percent of Japan's coastline. In Miyako, in northern Japan, tsunami waves reached an estimated record height of 133 feet; in the Sendai area a thirty-nine-foot wave traveled six miles inland. According to Japan's National Police Agency the earthquake and tsunami killed nearly 16,000 people; 6,100 people were injured and more than 3,000 people were listed as missing. The agency also noted that nearly 46,000 buildings were destroyed and 144,000 buildings damaged. An estimated 340,000 people were displaced by the event.

While Japan enjoys the third largest economy in the world, it is among the poorest nations in terms of natural resources. For example, it must import 84 percent of its energy. According to the U.S. Energy Information Administration Japan is the largest importer of liquefied natural gas, the second largest importer of coal and the third largest importer of oil. Prior to the earthquake, 13 percent of Japan's total energy needs were met by fifty-four nuclear power plants. Japan was the third largest generator of nuclear power in the world, behind the United States and France.

In 2008, an *Asahi Shimbun* poll found public support for nuclear-generated electricity was about 40 percent.

FIGURE 10.10 *A large ferry boat, rests inland amidst destroyed houses after a 9.0 earthquake and subsequent tsunami struck Japan.*
U.S. Navy

FUKUSHIMA DAI-ICHI

The Fukushima nuclear power station, built in 1971, was one of the twenty-five largest nuclear power stations in the world. Its six reactors generated 4.7 gigawatts of electricity when fully functioning. Fukushima Dai-ichi was situated on the east coast of Japan about 140 miles from Tokyo and 140 miles from the epicenter of the quake.

According to meteorological experts, the earthquake generated seven major waves that caused massive damage to Japan's coastal cities. The first wave hit twenty-six minutes after the quake. The tsunami that hit Fukushima Dai-ichi power plant was estimated at forty-nine feet high. The plant's protective sea wall was designed to withstand a nineteen-foot wave. While the plant's base was about thirty-three feet above sea level, it was swamped by the forty-nine-foot wave.

According to Japanese government officials, the wave destroyed emergency backup generators that provided water to cool the plant's nuclear reactors. With no other power source to pump in cooling water to the reactor core, its rods began to melt. The first of three hydrogen explosions began the next day at Unit 1 and caused further damage. The loss of the cooling systems and the explosions triggered partial nuclear meltdowns at three of the Fukushima reactors. Significant amounts of radiation were detected over a 700-mile region, forcing the evacuation of 100,000 people. The affected area included a mandatory twelve-mile radius evacuation zone.

WARNINGS UNHEEDED

As early as 1990, the risks associated with emergency electricity generators were known, according to a report by the U.S. Nuclear Regulatory Commission. The report said that nuclear plants located in seismically active regions were at highest risk of cooling system failures because of potential problems with backup generators. According to the *Guardian*, an internal report by Tokyo Electric Power Co (TEPCO) in 2008 also suggested that a tsunami 10.2 meters high could damage the Fukushima plant. It was ignored.

TEPCO had predicted Fukushima's reactors could withstand a tsunami height of 3.1 meters (10.2 feet) when the nuclear power station was built in 1971. This was later upgraded to a new maximum height of 5.7 meters (18.7 feet) in 2002. TEPCO ignored other simulations showing waves between 13.6 and 15.7 meters (44.6–51.5 feet) based on previous Japanese tsunamis because there had been no recorded tsunamis in the Fukushima location. In 2009, the Nuclear and Industrial Safety Agency (NISA) asked TEPCO to consider the Jogan earthquake of 869 AD, but because it had not occurred in the Fukushima area it was ignored. The tsunami that hit Fukushima was 14 meters high (46 feet).

JAPANESE NEWS MEDIA

The Japanese are enthusiastic consumers of news. The five largest Japanese newspapers are among the top ten highest circulation newspapers in the world; the Japanese *Yomiuri Shimbun* and *Asahi Shimbun* papers have circulations of more than fourteen million and twelve million respectively. According to *Japan's Media: Inside and Outside Powerbrokers*, many of the nation's 120 newspapers have morning and evening editions. Japan's public service broadcasting company, NHK, employs 12,000, ranking it second in staffing after the British Broadcasting Corporation (BBC).

Reporters without Borders' Press Freedom Index for 2011–2012 ranked Japan twenty-second compared to the United States' forty-seventh ranking. And the Japanese trust their news media, too. According to *Japan's Media: Inside and Outside Powerbrokers* by Jochen Legewie,

> *more than 70 percent of Japanese believe in the overall reporting of newspapers and NHK . . . Trust in dailies and NHK also clearly exceeds that in all other social institutions such as the government (28 percent), the Diet (30 percent) and even the courts (61 percent).*

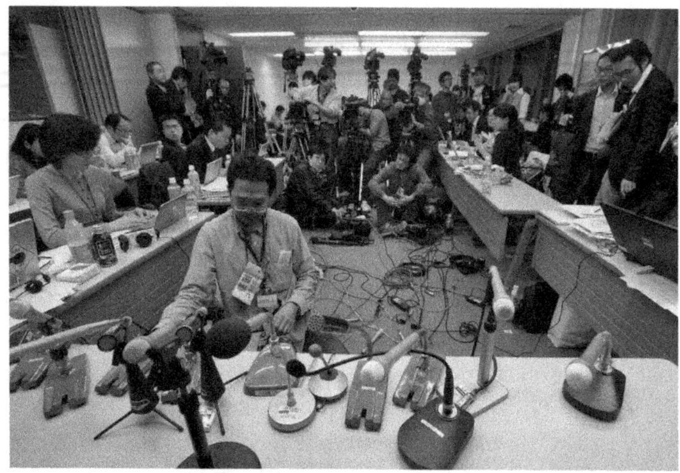

FIGURE 10.11 *Media members wait for Tokyo Electric Power to deliver a press conference at the company headquarters, Tokyo, March 15, 2011. Japan's Prime Minister Naoto Kan reportedly entered a Tokyo Electric Power executive meeting early March 15 demanding replies to questions regarding the current procedures and scope of damage at TEPCO's nuclear plants in Japan's tsunami-ravaged coastal area.*
http://www.corbisimages.com
© STRINGER/epa/Corbis

However, there are critics of Japan's journalism culture. Specifically, reporting access is determined by membership in press (*kisha*) clubs; historically, the foreign press has been excluded. Press clubs are associated with various organizations such as the parliament, ministry offices, and the prime minister's office. This system provides reporters with "highly privileged access to news and to news sources," according to *Japan's Media: Inside and Outside Powerbrokers*. While credentialed foreign media are sometimes allowed into press clubs, most foreign news agencies are not able to keep reporters there full time to develop the relationships with Japanese officials necessary to gain valuable insider information.

Freelance journalist Takashi Uesugi, author of *The Collapse of Journalism*, said:

> *[Japanese] Reporters see the press clubs as protecting their interests. Being a member is like being part of a cartel. You can just be an information receiver and don't need to be a chaser. The system is also convenient for politicians and bureaucrats, because they can release only what they want the media to report.*

Uesugi said that officials screen reporters' inquiries and can refuse to answer questions. He also described the collusive nature of the relationship between

Japanese reporters and their sources: "It is a relationship in which the media and the authorities strongly rely on each other, or even cooperate. At the same time, they both work to manipulate each other."

Another unique Japanese journalism practice that leads to the impression that all the country's newspaper coverage is oddly similar in tone and content is *memo-awase,* which translates as "share what's in your memos." According to Uesugi, after a press conference, Japanese reporters will gather together to share their notes so that no one misses anything.

The close relationship between government officials and the news media, however, reduces the incentive for probing, independent journalism that might embarrass the government. After all, critics point out that journalists are unlikely to risk losing high-level access provided by the press club system by not conforming to tacit government expectations. *Japan's Media: Inside and Outside Powerbrokers* points out that no press club journalists broke any government scandals in the past three decades; that news was relegated to the outside press or handed over to the paper's "social affairs" bureau.

Another factor: Uesugi said that reporters are reluctant to ask hard questions because TEPCO has a twenty billion yen advertising budget that benefits newspapers financially. In an interview with *The Asia-Pacific Journal*, he said that no Japanese reporters asked TEPCO officials if plutonium had leaked after Unit 3 reactor exploded. It wasn't until two weeks after the explosion that Uesugi asked the first question about plutonium leakage. According to *The Asia-Pacific Journal*: "TEPCO stated 'We do not measure the level of plutonium and do not even have a detector to scale it.' Ironically, the next day, Chief Cabinet Secretary Edano announced that 'plutonium was detected.'" When TEPCO released plutonium radiation readings two days later without any explanation regarding their toxicity, the Japanese press reported the plutonium readings without additional analysis and followed the TEPCO line that it "posed no human risk."

Two Japanese professors wrote "TEPCO's Criminal Error and the Media's Responsibility," an analysis that faulted not only TEPCO's negligence regarding safety issues surrounding the Fukushima disaster but also the Japanese news media's lack of initiative to get answers to difficult questions. In a presentation to the Foreign Correspondents' Club of Japan, Morinosuke Kawaguchi, a committee member of the Fukushima Project, said that Japanese journalists are more likely to accept information at face value from government officials rather than digging deeper to check the facts. Japanese journalists, he said, value harmony over debate, and belief over skepticism. During the Fukushima disaster, Japanese journalists were slow to respond to rumors and erroneous information published by outsider journalists. Those reports severely damaged Japan's reputation among foreign readers and resulted in losses of tourism, business opportunities, and foreign students. For example, Britain's *Daily Mail* published side-by-side photographs of the devastation of the tsunami and Hiroshima's atomic bombing, which looked eerily similar.

JAPANESE VALUES

Much has been said about business etiquette practices in Japan, including gift giving and business card exchanges. Less is said about Japanese values, which include consensus (harmony) and loyalty and obedience to authority. Regarding harmony, the concept of "saving face" is often mentioned. It refers to Japanese respect and one's dignity and reputation. Basically, one does not embarrass another or confront others in a way that would catch people off guard. The Japanese are an interdependent society with strong ties to family, community, and company. Hierarchy is observed in family and business interactions. As a result, the Japanese are not eager to question people in authority because of their loyalty and obedience to those in higher social and business settings.

The Japanese value their interdependence as a society. They value personal responsibility and a cooperative attitude in which people work together for the good of society. This is different from the value Americans place on individualism and personal accomplishments.

More than a year after the Fukushima disaster an independent government report said that "its fundamental causes are to be found in . . . Japanese culture: our reflexive obedience; our reluctance to question authority; our groupism; and our insularity."

TOKYO ELECTRIC POWER COMPANY

The Tokyo Electric Power Co. (TEPCO) was formed in 1951 and is the largest electric utility in Japan, according to its website. One of several power companies in Japan, TEPCO operates 162 hydroelectric plants, twenty-five thermal power plants and three nuclear power plants, including Fukushima Dai-ichi. The company employs about 38,500 throughout its facilities.

In 2003, all seventeen of TEPCO's boiling-water reactors were shut down for a time when the Japanese government reported that the company had falsified technical data supplied for routine governmental inspections and had concealed safety incidents over two decades. This resulted in the resignations of TEPCO's president, vice president and chairman. "TEPCO had failed for years to report—or fix—cracks in many of its reactors," according to *The Economist*. "Some fissures had first been spotted in the 1980s."

A 6.8 magnitude earthquake in northern Japan damaged one of TEPCO's nuclear reactors in 2007. Leaks of radioactive material caused a reactor in Kashiwazaki to be shut down. Japan's Nuclear Safety Commission said TEPCO had a "bungled response to a quake-triggered fire at an electrical transformer," according to The Associated Press:

> *Plant officials said they had no chemical fire vehicle at the plant, and local fire officials took 90 minutes to respond to their call. Despite Japan's propensity for earthquakes,*

TEPCO said the force of the quake had exceeded its resistance guidelines at all seven reactors, sometimes by more than double.

TEPCO, critics say, took advantage of the cozy relationship between Japanese government regulatory agencies and the nuclear industry.

One investigation "revealed a long history of nuclear power companies conspiring with governments to manipulate public opinion in favor of nuclear energy."

GOVERNMENT'S RESPONSE

The following is a day-by-day analysis of the Japanese government's communication regarding the conditions at the Fukushima nuclear power station. This analysis includes news coverage by the *Asahi Shimbun*, Japan's second largest daily newspaper. This paper had access through the press club system to top government officials and TEPCO officials. While the government was responding to a number of major concerns, including rescue operations, blackouts, and emergency operations for those displaced by the earthquake and tsunami, this analysis focuses only on the Fukushima nuclear plant situation during the first week of the disaster.

Foreign journalists were not allowed into the Japanese press club news conference briefings. Instead, they were provided their own press conferences with lower government officials. Journalists were not allowed to visit Fukushima nuclear power plant until eight months after the earthquake.

In fairness, it should be noted that the Fukushima nuclear disaster created the most complex set of problems ever encountered in the history of nuclear energy. Fukushima's nuclear problems will take decades to resolve. The accident was also exacerbated by the enormous challenges created by the massive earthquake and tsunami damage throughout northern Japan. Still, follow-up investigations called Japan's preparedness and response woefully lacking. This basic analysis provides some lessons in emergency communication. Press conference materials quoted below are available in the textbook's teaching materials and online.

THE GOVERNMENT'S COMMUNICATION AND RESULTING MEDIA COVERAGE

The following information provides a summary of the key messages communicated by the Japanese government and TEPCO officals about the tsunami and resulting nuclear disaster during the first eight days of the crisis. This section also explores the reporting of these events by one national Japanese newspaper, *Asahi Shimbun*. It is interesting to observe the type of information provided by Japan's leaders and the resulting newspaper coverage during this massive crisis. Critics of Japan's news media have noted its reluctance to challenge the government's claims.

DAY ONE—FRIDAY, MARCH 11, 2011

There were no *Asahi Shimbun* articles on the Fukushima nuclear reactor plant on the first day of earthquake coverage.

The Prime Minister of Japan, Naoto Kan, issued a statement about two hours after the earthquake. He described the earthquake but did not mention the tsunami. He said this about the nuclear facilities in the region affected: "As for our nuclear power facilities, a portion of them stopped their operations automatically. At present we have no reports of any radioactive materials or otherwise affecting the surrounding areas." He also said he had set up his emergency headquarters and he asked people to remain calm.

DAY TWO—SATURDAY, MARCH 12, 2011

Japan's national press began reporting on Fukushima's situation the day after the earthquake and tsunami.

A story "Crucial Safety Feature Fails at Fukushima Nuclear Plants" said the emergency generators failed at Fukushima. Unnamed experts explained the purpose of the generators in cooling the reactors. Another story, "Nuclear Fuel Rods Melt," said NISA reported a partially melted fuel rod. Residents within 10 km (6.2 miles) were told to evacuate.

FIGURE 10.12 *A worker wearing a protective suit and mask works atop destroyed No. 4 reactor building of Tokyo Electric Power Co. (TEPCO)'s tsunami-crippled Fukushima Dai-ichi nuclear power plant in Fukushima prefecture, February 20, 2012.*
http://www.corbisimages.com/
© Issei Kato/Pool/Corbis

FIGURE 10.13 *In this handout picture taken on September 29, 2011, released by TEPCO, the owner of the nuclear power plant, overview of reactor building of Unit 3 is seen at the Fukushima Dai-ichi Nuclear Power Plant in Fukushima, Japan.*
http://www.corbisimages.com/

An article titled "Explosion Hits Fukushima Nuclear Plan, Fuel Begins to Melt," said NISA officials thought a meltdown was occurring at Fukushima's Unit 1 following a hydrogen explosion. Japan's Chief Cabinet Secretary, Yukio Edano, said the explosion did not compromise the inner containment vessel. "The reactor core's containment vessel was not affected at all." He explained that radioactive substances measured in the air had actually gone down following the explosion, which indicated the containment vessel was intact. TEPCO was not quoted in the article, but its news releases on radioactivity in the area were mentioned. Edano said during a news conference that radioactivity levels were being monitored. A state of emergency had been declared the previous day and that residents within 20km should evacuate.

No additional sources beyond NISA, the cabinet, or TEPCO were referenced. No officials, except Edano, were identified by name.

Prime Minister Kan issued a statement that he had had a telephone conversation with President Barack Obama, who expressed his sympathy and offered U.S. assistance. A second brief statement was issued that the mobilization of Japan's Self-Defense Force in the emergency response was underway.

DAY THREE—SUNDAY, MARCH 13, 2011

At Chief Cabinet Secretary Edano's 11:30 a.m. press conference, he explained the actions taken at Fukushima, followed by the recent radiation readings at Fukushima. He tried to reassure residents and explain the next steps for evacuees:

We are continuing to monitor the situation on an ongoing basis. At present the situation is that as a result of the venting, gas is being released that includes small, controlled amounts of radioactive material within the expected levels. These steps are being carried out in accordance with the procedures for dealing with a situation of this kind. Please be assured that the level of radiation being released is not sufficient to have any effect on human health.

However, I understand that concern is high about the risk of exposure among evacuees. We are considering taking the following measures, while confirming the desires of Fukushima Prefecture.

We are compiling a list of all evacuees in Fukushima Prefecture. As a matter of national responsibility, the government is liaising with Fukushima Prefecture in establishing first aid stations staffed by specialists in each emergency evacuation area. Multiple specialist teams will be assigned to monitor all evacuees and other concerned persons for radiation exposure, as well as providing follow-up evaluations and liaisons with medical response services where necessary.

In a follow-up press conference at 3:30 p.m., Edano provided another update on the Fukushima situation including radiation readings.

This is the situation as it stands. The possibility cannot be ruled out that hydrogen is being produced and is collecting at the top of the reactor structure. But even in the event that another explosion like yesterday's does occur, then just as was the case yesterday this will not result in any problem within the reactor itself or the containment vessel. Even if an explosion does occur, it will be limited to the area outside the reactor itself, and the structure of the reactor and the containment vessel are designed to withstand an impact on that level.

Furthermore, even if an explosion or similar event does occur, because the levels of radiation in the nearby area are as I have indicated, we do not believe that this would cause a situation that would put the health of evacuees in the vicinity at risk. I am releasing this information immediately because of the concerns we have raised about a possible explosion or similar event, and because it has become clear that this possibility cannot be ruled out.

A fourth news conference was held at 8 p.m. in which Edano gave another update on Fukushima:

The third point concerns the situation in Unit 3 at the Fukushima Daiichi Nuclear Power Station. I mentioned earlier that water levels had begun to rise since injection of sea water into the pressure vessel began. Levels continued to increase steadily for a certain time, but since then the figures indicating the water levels inside the pressure vessel are no longer showing an increase. We are continuing to supply water to the reactor. It is not clear how we should assess this situation. There was a similar situation for a time following the explosion in Unit 1 yesterday.

This time, there is a high possibility that the valves in Unit 3 have failed. At the present time people on the scene are doing their utmost to resolve the malfunction of the

> *valves in order to lower the air pressure inside the reactor. Meanwhile, there has been no notable change in the radiation levels observed in the vicinity of the power station.*

Prime Minister Kan updated the country on the emergency response in a statement that night (7:50 p.m.) that included his first direct reference to the Fukushima nuclear situation:

> *Against this backdrop, the alarming situation remains ongoing regarding the nuclear power plants in Fukushima that are the cause of such concern among the public. Chief Cabinet Secretary Yukio Edano will be providing a detailed report on this point later.*

Kan went on to explain the country's electrical shortages and the need for rolling blackouts to conserve enough power to meet the crisis. He also asked citizens to conserve energy and noted the significance of the crisis:

> *I consider this earthquake and tsunami along with the current situation regarding the nuclear power plants to be in some regards the most severe crisis in the 65 years since the end of the Second World War. I believe that whether or not we Japanese are able to overcome this crisis is something now being asked of all Japanese individually. We Japanese have overcome many very trying situations in the past to create our modern society of peace and prosperity. I firmly believe that through our citizens working together to respond to this great earthquake and tsunami, we will certainly be able to overcome this crisis.*

The news media were more forthright in their assessment of the situation at Fukushima. An article entitled "Cooling System Fails at Another Fukushima Nuclear Reactor" focused on Unit 3 when its emergency cooling system also quit working, exposing fuel rods and causing a buildup of hydrogen. "We are dealing with the situation as though a core meltdown has occurred," Chief Cabinet Secretary Yukio Edano said at a Sunday morning news conference. "While TEPCO officials were unsure if core meltdown had occurred," the company was injecting water into the core, and by 11:30 a.m. the fuel rods were under water. Edano said that if another hydrogen explosion similar to the one at Unit 1 occurred it would not damage the core containment vessel nor would it release large levels of radioactive materials. Edano said that there was no need for additional actions for evacuees.

A NISA official said, "The situation is not one that should cause concerns among the public."

No new evacuation orders were ordered. Residents were asked to remain calm.

DAY FOUR—MONDAY, MARCH 14, 2011

Chief Cabinet Secretary Edano held five press conferences. In the first one, he added more detail to Kan's announcement of planned rolling blackouts to conserve energy during the crisis. In the second press conference, Edano discussed the recent explosions at the No. 3 reactor. Edano said he had confirmed with the director of the power station that "The condition of the containment vessel remains sound and risk of a large-scale release of radioactive materials is low at the present time." He also noted that pressure within the reactor vessel was stable. He said that workers were evacuated and six workers were injured. Later in the day, at another press conference, Edano said:

> *First, an update on developments following the hydrogen explosion in the Unit 3 reactor at the TEPCO Fukushima Daiichi Nuclear Power Station. As you know, we have been announcing the monitored radiation levels in the area around the power station. At present, no unusual readings have been detected. The work of supplying water to the reactor was interrupted for a time as a result of the explosion, and a team of people on the scene are working at present to restart this process. As of now, the latest data is stable for all reactors, and we are working on a long-term recommencement of water supply operations.*
>
> *Following the explosion in Unit 1 and Unit 3, the cooling system stopped in another reactor, Unit 2, and water levels are falling. Therefore adding to Unit 1 and Unit 3, where water supply operations were already underway, and preparations for injecting sea water into Unit 3 are underway.*

Edano also said that people within the 20 km (12.4 mile) area around the power plant should evacuate and he provided details about eleven workers who had been injured by the blast.

In the final press conference of the day, Edano explained that water injection had begun again at Units 1 and 3. At Unit 2, the cooling system had stopped; a fuel shortage for a pump had been part of the problem. Next, he said:

> *The water levels dropped, it is considered that there was a short period of time when the fuel rods were exposed above the water surface.*
>
> *However, after 20:00 these problems were resolved, and we were able to start injecting water. Rises in the water levels are now being observed. In all cases we have been able to restart reactor-cooling operations by injecting water. If cooling operations by injecting water develop, it is expected that the conditions will be stabilized. The personnel on site are working their hardest to continue these steps and further stabilize the situation. We are also making every possible effort to ensure safety on site.*

An article entitled "Explosion Hits Another Reactor; Cooling Functions Fail" explained that an explosion at No. 3 reactor had occurred and the cooling system at No. 2 reactor had reportedly failed. Edano said there was a "strong likelihood" of core meltdowns at reactors 1–3. He was quoted as saying:

> *While the earthquake itself may have lasted but an instant, the response thereafter was conducted under a certain level of control and, at the present time, the situation is moving in a direction of stability. We believe that even foreseeing the worst-case outcome it will not turn out like Chernobyl.*

NISA confirmed the No. 3 explosion. TEPCO reported eleven people had been injured but the containment vessel was intact. Edano also said, "The possibility is low that large quantities of radioactive substances have been released." TEPCO also reported two instances of exposed fuel rods at No. 2 reactor.

An article, "Crucial Vents Were Not Installed Until 1990s," by a senior staff writer about the containment vessel vents installed in the 1990s, explained how twenty years after Fukushima was built, belated action probably averted a "major nuclear catastrophe." The reporter said other countries installed vents after the Three Mile Island and Chernobyl nuclear power plant meltdowns. He noted Japanese officials "believed a core meltdown could never occur in Japan" but eventually gave in once Japan's Nuclear Safety Commission recommended the installation of vents. He ended the article with a whiff of criticism:

> *Whatever the outcome of the current crisis at the No. 1 Fukushima plant, the facts are that a core meltdown has occurred, that a large number of people have been evacuated and that radioactive materials have been released into the atmosphere. That reality will decisively change how the Japanese people think about nuclear energy.*
>
> *The issue cannot be explained by repeating the excuse, "It was beyond what we could foresee."*

There was no official statement from Prime Minister Kan.

People within the 20 km radius were told to remain indoors.

DAY FIVE—TUESDAY, MARCH 15, 2011

In a short early morning press conference, Edano said that the prime minister had visited TEPCO to "figure out the current situation again." He also said Unit 2's suppression pool, connected to the containment vessel, had been damaged. "However, the readings of radiation levels in the surrounding area have shown no sudden rise, and are not at values that would represent a threat to the people's health."

The Prime Minister's statement at 11 a.m. began with a request to "listen calmly to this information." He continued:

> *As I explained previously, the reactor at the Fukushima Daiichi Nuclear Power Station was shut off following the earthquake and tsunami, but none of the diesel engines that would normally power the emergency cooling system are in a functioning state. We have been using every means at our disposal to cool the nuclear reactors. However, the concentration of radioactivity being leaked into the vicinity of the station has risen considerably following hydrogen explosions caused by hydrogen produced at the Unit 1 and Unit 3 reactors, and a fire in the Unit 4 reactor. There is a heightened risk of even further leakage of radioactive material.*

Prime Minister Kan explained in the statement the current evacuation orders for those living near the Fukushima power plant. He ended by saying:

> *At present we are doing everything possible to prevent further explosions or leakage of radioactive material. At this moment, Tokyo Electric Power Company (TEPCO) workers in particular are taking great personal risks in their tireless efforts to supply water*

> *to the reactor. I realize that people in Japan are greatly concerned about the situation but I sincerely urge everyone to act in a calm manner, bearing in mind the tremendous efforts underway to prevent further radiation leaks.*

There were no further government briefings as the situation was worsening.

An article "Nuclear Crisis Worsens; Dangerous Radiation Levels Detected" started this way: "The crisis at the No. 1 Fukushima nuclear power plant was quickly running out of control Tuesday, after two explosions, a fire and dangerous levels of radiation compounded the problems at four of its six reactors."

The article described a fire in reactor No. 4 and an explosion thought to be caused by accumulated hydrogen from overheated fuel rods. Edano said the radiation released "clearly would affect people's health." An area south of Fukushima had radiation readings 400 times normal. It was reported that Prime Minister Naoto Kan had addressed the nation and said those living between 20 and 30 km from the nuclear power station should remain indoors. TEPCO and NISA officials explained the emergency operations at Fukushima, along with Edano.

Another article, "No. 4 Reactor Poses More Danger than Other Reactors," featured, for the first time, three named outside experts explaining the serious conditions occurring at No. 4 reactor. They were professors from different Japanese universities with expertise in nuclear power.

Another article, "Radiation Detected which 'Clearly Would Affect People's Health,'" featured excerpts of Chief Cabinet Secretary Yukio Edano's statement on March 15, 2011, and parts of his question-and-answer session. He reminded those within the 20–30 km zone to

> *remain indoors and to not go outside.*
>
> *At this time, I want everyone to shut the windows and make their houses as airtight as possible. Please do not use ventilation. We want people to hang their laundry indoors. The farther away one is, the lower is the concentration of the radioactive materials.*

While there was still much confusion on what actually had occurred at Fukushima, Edano confirmed that radioactive materials had leaked at reactors No. 1, No. 2, and No. 3, and that sea water was being pumped into the reactors. Edano downplayed the radiation emitted as "at a level that would have little effect on human health." The fire at No. 4 caused an evacuation of all workers except fifty employees who would be referred to as the "Fukushima 50."

A commentary by a senior staff writer, Keiji Takeuchi, titled "Unprecedented Disaster Tests Resilience of Society," provided only mild criticism of those responsible: "Japan should have developed nuclear energy not only with pride in its advanced technology, but also with cautiousness as a nation hit by atomic bombs."

DAY SIX—WEDNESDAY, MARCH 16, 2011

At an 11 a.m. press conference, Edano first addressed the fuel shortages and asked people not to hoard. He then discussed the conditions at Fukushima. He said "white smoke" was visible from Unit 3, but no cause was known at the time. He also reported radiation levels changing frequently and that "they remain within a range that could impact the human body." He provided some of the radiation readings from the area. At 10 a.m., the radiation "jumped rapidly" and workers were "temporarily evacuated." Before the press conference, he said that the radiation levels had begun to fall. He ended the brief press conference by saying:

> *Experts are hard at work analyzing the situation, but at present, we have not confirmed anything. The most probable case is that vapor is being released from part of the containment vessel, as took place in the Unit 2 reactor, and this is appearing as smoke. As this is vapor that has been absorbing the contained radiation, this may be the reason for the temporary rise in measured radiation levels. I repeat, this is not confirmed. This is the situation judged to be most likely according to the analysis at this time.*
>
> *Right now we have people monitoring the radiation levels, in particular, and confirming conditions such as whether water is actually continuing to flow, with the end goal of swiftly analyzing this situation and deciding measures to take in response.*

At a second news conference, Edano announced the appointment of a university professor and expert in radiation safety as a special advisor to the cabinet and said many nuclear specialists were being consulted during the crisis. Edano then gave summary details about the radiation monitoring being conducted outside the 20 km zone. He stressed that people living outside the 20 km zone should stay indoors but also said that there was no "immediate risk" to doing outside activities. He repeated:

> *According to the preliminary summary issued by specialists based on data obtained from radiation monitoring carried out today by the Ministry of Education, Culture, Sports, Science and Technology, the levels detected do not pose an immediate risk to human health.*

However, Edano then said the radiation levels might cause "problems" for those exposed on a daily basis for a year. He said that some people were not delivering emergency goods and supplies to the areas outside the 20 km zone due to fears of radiation. Edano said again:

> *I want you to understand that even inside the area where we have called for people to remain indoors, the levels are not sufficient to have any immediate effect on the health of someone carrying out activities outdoors, even inside this area. This is even more the case in areas beyond 30 km from the power station.*

In the news media, more explosions and fires were reported at Fukushima in an article headlined "High Levels of Radiation at Stricken Reactor," which used the typical official sources.

An interesting article was an opinion piece by the former vice chairman of the Nuclear Safety Commission of Japan entitled "Responses from TEPCO, NISA Came

Too Late." The author criticized TEPCO and NISA for going it alone instead of reaching out to others in the nuclear industry and related sources, as was done following a 1999 nuclear-criticality accident. He said NISA was not "fully functioning" and said its actions were ineffective since it operated under the Ministry of Economy, Trade, and Industry, "which promotes nuclear power generation."

DAY SEVEN—THURSDAY, MARCH 17, 2011

Prime Minister Kan issued a statement on the second phone call from a concerned President Obama. The statement said that "Japan intended to confer closely with the United States . . . nuclear power experts dispatched by the United States and Japanese specialists would continue to collaborate closely."

In Edano's morning news conference he also discussed Obama's conversation with Kan and repeated that the government would "collaborate closely with nuclear power experts dispatched from the United States." He said that the Self-Defense Forces were now transporting supplies to the affected regions and were also supplying water to the Fukushima reactors by air, and that the police were providing water at the ground level with high-pressure pumps to cool the affected reactors. He said people in the immediate vicinity should evacuate and that those within the 20–30 km zone should remain indoors. Edano said that evacuees and those asked to stay indoors were receiving "the necessary attention."

A second press conference announced new appointments to deal with the emergency as well as disaster victims. Edano also asked people to conserve energy to avoid power failures.

DAY EIGHT—FRIDAY, MARCH 18, 2011

In a news conference one week after the earthquake, Prime Minister Kan had this to say in an opening statement about Fukushima:

> *Meanwhile, the situation regarding the nuclear power accident in Fukushima remains precarious. At the moment, all the people involved from TEPCO, the Self-Defense Forces, the police, and fire departments, are literally risking their lives to work on overcoming this crisis. I too am resolved to do absolutely whatever it takes to resolve this incident. Together with the people of Japan and the people working to resolve the situation, particularly those on the scene, I am determined to overcome this crisis and restore peace of mind to the people. With this determination in my heart, I will work even harder from now on until the situation is resolved.*

He took three questions after his statement. The first question was from a reporter with Nippon TV:

> *With regard to the Fukushima Daiichi Nuclear Power Station, I believe this is an accident that is now causing considerable worry among all the people of Japan, not just*

the people in the surrounding area. Furthermore, distrust in the information released by the government is spreading in certain quarters. As prime minister of Japan, how dangerous would you say the current situation is? Alternatively, to what extent should we be setting our minds at ease? Finally, what outlooks are there for the future? Please tell us these things, including as many concrete examples as you can.

Prime Minister Kan responded:

Both I and the chief cabinet secretary have released all of the facts we have learned about the ongoing accident at the nuclear power station. Let me take this opportunity to make this clear once more to the people of Japan and to the global community as a whole.

Having said that, the present conditions at the Fukushima nuclear power station are such that we cannot say for certain how things will turn out. I will tell you this frankly. Right now, Tokyo Electric Power Co. and the Self-Defense Forces, firefighters, the police, and other personnel are prepared to make the ultimate sacrifice as they take measures to deal with the situation.

Today we carried out operations to spray water onto the Unit 3 reactor. While it is still far too early to say for sure, in the not-too-distant future we should be able to bring the situation firmly under control and extract ourselves from the present situation. I want the people of Japan to know that we are doing our utmost to move things in this direction.

Another reporter asked Prime Minister Kan if "the present government response is truly sufficient. Do you feel that the government's current posture is sufficient?" Kan replied: "The government moved swiftly to take action immediately after the earthquake struck, and since then has been doing everything in its power to resolve these problems and overcome the crisis."

Edano's press conference provided a similar update. Regarding the water spraying operation at Unit 3, he said: "Water vapor has been rising from the reactor, which we believe indicates that water has definitely reached the reactor. At this point, however, we have no conclusive data on how much water is actually inside."

A team from the Tokyo Fire Department had arrived and was going to attempt to inject water into Unit 1, as long as it didn't interfere with the Unit 3 water injection efforts. Edano said this:

The situation at the Unit 1 reactor is not as urgent as that at the Unit 3 and 4 reactors, but I have been informed that such operations are being considered since it is important to do everything possible to cool the reactor.

Edano concluded his press conference by downplaying radiation levels near the power station:

[L]evels that could pose a risk to human health have not been indicated, although high figures have been detected from time to time. Even slightly high figures detected at some monitoring points are not an immediate threat to human health. Terrain, climate, and other factors can influence these figures, though, so we are now advancing efforts to

boost monitoring activities in the surrounding areas to enable a more detailed analysis of the situation

In Edano's opening statement for his final press conference of the day he expressed his "deepest condolences for the many people who lost their lives in the disaster, as well as my sympathy for the victims still suffering from its aftereffects." He also said "It is with deep shame that the Government of Japan recognizes that many people continue to bear shortages of food, means of staying warm, and many other things as they live in a state of evacuation."

AFTERMATH

Several independent investigations were launched after the disaster. One prepared for Japan's parliament said that beyond the technical problems, there was the issue of the nuclear industry's political power to operate as it pleased. "Its regulation was entrusted to the same government bureaucracy responsible for its promotion," the report noted. The Japanese regulatory body, the Nuclear and Industrial Safety Agency from the Ministry of Economy, was often ignored by powerful energy companies like TEPCO amid the country's overarching energy needs. One investigation said accident management measures were "basically regarded as voluntary efforts by operators, not legal requirements, and so the development of these measures lacked strictness."

FIGURE 10.14 *Peaceful anti-nuclear protest in Tokyo, Japan, escorted by policemen.*
http://commons.wikimedia.org/
VOA

FIGURE 10.15 *Tunehisa Katsumata, chairman of TEPCO, announced at its headquarters in Tokyo, Japan, April 17, 2011, the utility's schedule for the moment for bringing the complex in Fukushima prefecture under control, while offering an apology for the ongoing nuclear crisis. http://www.corbisimages.com*
© Noboru Hashimoto/Corbis

The question of whether the earthquake or the tsunami was to blame for Fukushima's disaster was still being debated a year after the disaster. TEPCO officials said it could not have predicted such a powerful earthquake and resulting tsunami. It maintained that the tsunami was to blame for the loss of backup generators that could run the cooling systems. Reports from some employees at the power plant said that the earthquake damaged elements of the reactor, but it was uncertain whether they were critical to the reactors' operations. If further investigations prove that the Fukushima reactors were damaged by the earthquake, then that would bring into question the safety of all Japan's nuclear power plants to provide safe energy in such a seismically active country.

TEPCO had maintained that an earthquake and tsunami of the size that hit March 11, 2011, were out of the realm of possibility. According to one investigation, "The operator, regulators and the government 'failed to correctly develop the most basic safety requirements—such as assessing the probability of damage, preparing for containing collateral damage from such a disaster, and developing evacuation plans.'" However, on December 15, 2012, *Japan Today* reported that the operator of Fukushima Dai-ichi nuclear power plant's "lack of safety and bad habits were behind the nuclear accident."

As the Fukushima plant operator told the investigative commission: "We weren't prepared for a nuclear accident."

During the summer of 2012, a growing antinuclear movement gathered strength in Japan. Large rallies and marches became weekly occurrences in Tokyo and in communities with nuclear reactors. More than 100,000 marched peacefully in Tokyo and other spots when Prime Minister Yoshihiko Noda gave approval to restart the Oi reactor. Protests of this magnitude had not been seen since the tumultuous protests of the late 1960s and early 1970s.

Political elections in early 2013 brought back the conservative Liberal Democratic party (LDP), under Shinzo Abe, which wanted to review the previous government's pledge to phase out nuclear power in Japan. A skeptical and traumatized population, however, would probably need significant evidence of changes to the industry's safety performance and record of transparency to bring back nuclear power to the pre-tsunami era.

QUESTIONS FOR DISCUSSION

1. How dependent is Japan on nuclear power for electricity?
2. What were some of the early warnings that Japan's nuclear power plants may not be as safe as some thought?
3. What is the role of press (*kisha*) clubs in Japan? How does it prevent investigative reporting on sensitive subjects?
4. How does the phrase *memo-awase*, which translates as "share what's in your memos," impact Japanese journalism?
5. How did some traditional Japanese values contribute to the communication problems during the crisis?
6. What did critics say was the real reason TEPCO was not prepared and did not respond appropriately to the crisis?
7. During the eight days following the tsunami, did the Japanese government provide enough information on radiation levels for its citizens?
8. The Japanese government led the response on the nuclear disaster. Prime Minister Kan and Chief Cabinet Secretary Edano were the official government spokespersons. Did their comments build trust with the Japanese population?
9. What role did Japanese journalism play in the response to this crisis?
10. Governments, including that of the United States, were concerned about the way Japan was handling the crisis. What did they want the Japanese government to do?
11. The main communication activity of TEPCO, the owner and operator of the nuclear plant, was issuing news releases. It was not until November 2011 that TEPCO began offering more communication tactics such as videotaped news conferences. After examining TEPCO's news releases during the early days of the crisis, how would you assess their value?

Dig Deeper

Review the International Atomic Energy Agency's Communicator's Toolbox (located at www.iaea.org/nuccomtoolbox/index.html#). What are some of the recommendations of this site for effective communications? Peter Sandman's website (www.psandman.com/#index) also has many articles about risk communication and especially about how to deal with "risk familiarity." Review the following publications, all available on the textbook's companion website, from the IAEA. What are some of the communication lessons learned about Fukushima?

- "Communicating Fukushima the IAEA Experience"
- *Nuclear Communications: A Handbook for Guiding Good Communication Practices at Nuclear Fuel Cycle Facilities* (the most recent edition is located on the IAEA website)
- "IAEA International Fact Finding Expert Mission of the Fukushima Dai-ichi NPP Accident Following the Great East Japan Earthquake and Tsunami"
- "Public Communication Program Before and After Fukushima Accident"
- "Communicating in a Crisis: Risk Communication Guidelines for Public Officials."

32

Containing the Deadly Marburg Virus

Taking a Culturally Based Communication Approach

Burial customs are an important social tradition for many indigenous Angolans. The body often is laid out for a full day and buried the following day. The funeral rites include spending significant time with the body and often performing a ceremonial body washing and kissing it goodbye. The deceased are handled with loving care and respect because, according to traditional beliefs, a neglected spirit might "turn vengeful." A large crowd accompanies the coffin to the cemetery, often with a female family member sitting on the coffin to the gravesite.

In outbreaks of viral hemorrhagic fevers, including Marburg, unprotected exposure to dead bodies is a significant cause of further spread. Safe burial is essential to controlling the outbreak. Foreign health workers from various organizations have worked with local villages to help establish effective containment strategies.

The established protocol included having a technical team talk to the family and the community leader prior to the burial to give information about the Marburg virus and what was needed to occur to safely handle the body. Traditional burial practices ultimately had to be modified in ways that allowed families to mourn in accordance with their beliefs yet minimize the risk of exposure to the body and disease. If families were not allowed to maintain some semblance of their burial tradition, the fear was that they would secretly bury their loved ones without protections and spread the deadly infection.

These cultural considerations were ignored initially in the rush to contain a deadly outbreak of Marburg identified in Uige, Angola, in March 2005.

FIGURE 10.16 *In outbreaks of viral hemorrhagic fevers, including Marburg, unprotected exposure to dead bodies is a significant cause of further spread. Safe burial is essential to controlling the outbreak. Prior to the burial, the team talk to the family and the community leader to give information on Marburg. Traditional burial practices must be modified in ways that allow families to mourn in accordance with their beliefs yet minimize the risk of exposure to the body and disease.*
http://www.who.int/
WHO/CNRS/Alain Epelboin

MARBURG HEMORRHAGIC FEVER

Marburg hemorrhagic fever is a frequently fatal disease caused by a virus from the same family as Ebola. The disease has worked its way from the Congo to Angola and was present in Uganda in 2012. Fatality rates range between a low of 24 percent and a high of 88 percent, which was the case in 2005 in Angola where 429 died. There is no vaccine or curative treatment available. While incidents are rare, outbreaks of the disease in Africa received widespread media attention due to its horrific hemorrhagic symptoms and fears of global spread.

The Marburg virus is transmitted to people from fruit bats and spreads among humans by human-to-human transmission through direct contact with a victim, involving exposure to blood, saliva, or other bodily fluids, according to the World Health Organization (WHO). The virus has been known to survive for several days on contaminated surfaces. The incubation period can be from two to twenty-one days. Symptoms include fever, chills, and headache and become increasingly severe. Of the initial 124 cases reported between October 1, 2004, and March 29, 2005, 117 were fatal. International agencies working with Angola's ministry of health included the WHO, the Centers for Disease Control and Prevention (CDC), and the medical charity Médecins Sans Frontières (MSF). Outbreak control efforts included providing technical assistance for the medical care of victims, improving infection control in hospitals, improving surveillance and contact tracing, and educating local residents about the disease and its modes of transmission.

The source of the outbreak was a hospital in Uige, where thirteen nurses in addition to patients died from the Marburg fever. Panic ensued and hospital workers abandoned their posts. The country's medical system lacked basic necessities, including equipment and trained staff. This caused residents also to panic. Families arrived and took their sick and dead family members and hid them in their homes or in the bush, which placed more people at risk. Many Uige residents were afraid to take their loved ones to the hospital because initial lack of protective clothing for healthcare workers had helped spread the disease.

Many rumors were circulating, including:

- The hospital director bought the virus to intentionally kill patients, which would endow his brother with magical powers.
- MSF developed the virus to kill the population.
- The spirits of two dead female nurses were seen roaming the streets because they had not been buried properly according to their burial rites.

With the people not trusting foreigners or hospital personnel, traditional healers were sought for remedies; these did not provide any protection.

When foreign health workers showed up in Uige's outlying villages, they did not offer a friendly handshake or condolences to distraught families, nor did they

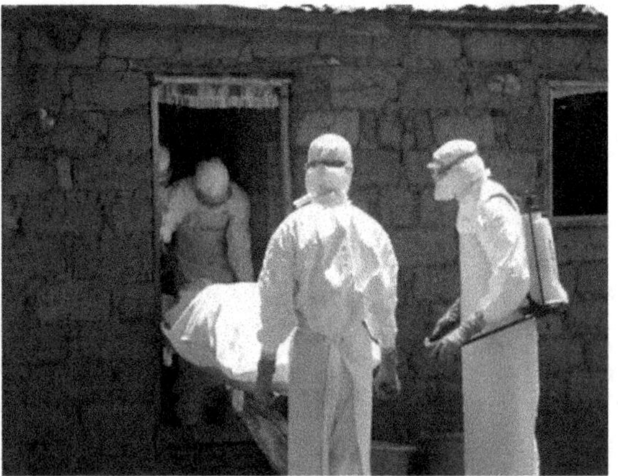

FIGURE 10.17 *In outbreaks of viral haemorrhagic fevers, including those caused by Marburg virus, unprotected exposure to dead bodies is a significant cause of further spread. Here, mobile teams in Uige, Angola, prepare for the safe transport and burial of fatal cases of Marburg haemorrhagic fever. WHO/Dr. Pierre Formenty*
http://www.who.int/csr/imagesangola/en
WHO/Dr. Pierre Formenty

FIGURE 10.18 *Marburg hemorrhagic fever is transmitted through close contact with blood or other bodily fluids of an infected person. Illness begins abruptly with symptoms of headache, muscle ache, and fever, followed by rapid debilitation and watery diarrhea, nausea, and vomiting. It is almost always fatal eight to nine days after the symptoms begin.*
http://www.who.int/
WHO/CNRS/Alain Epelboin

allow families to perform traditional burial customs. Bodies were placed in body bags and transported to a cemetery. Dressed from head to toe in white protective clothing—a color associated with ghosts—the alien-looking health workers were focused only on containing the disease quickly. Patients who died in the hospital were buried without any rites or family members present. Families did not receive notification, a death certificate or cause of death.

While well-meaning, the health workers did not take the time to understand villagers' concerns, frustrations, and traditions. They did not tap into the existing social structure of traditional healers and village leaders. Residents did not feel that the outsiders were listening to their concerns and felt they were not included in the management of the epidemic. Fear, distrust, and grief soon turned to anger. In one location, villagers threw rocks at mobile contact unit vehicles sent in search of suspected Marburg cases or hidden bodies.

To build trust with villagers, better communication efforts were implemented and procedures were altered. The provincial political and administrative authorities with the WHO began to listen to the residents; they also expressed empathy for their losses. Two medical anthropologists were added to the social mobilization teams to develop positive relationships. A WHO communications specialist joined the team. Other groups were also involved: a UNICEF team, Angola Red Cross volunteers, and others.

Then the social mobilization and communication teams worked with community leaders, healers, and midwives to convince Angolans of the importance of providing information on suspected Marburg cases and deaths. Educational pamphlets were printed in Portuguese, the official Angolan language, as well as in French, Lingalla, and Kikongo. Five television spots were produced in Portuguese, and five radio

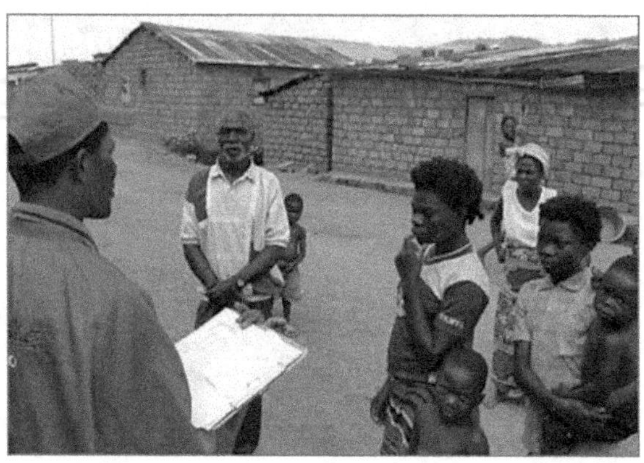

FIGURE 10.19 *Monitoring those who have been in contact with people who are ill or who have died of suspected Marburg hemorrhagic fever is vital in stopping the outbreak.*
http://www.who.int/
WHO/Pierre Formenty

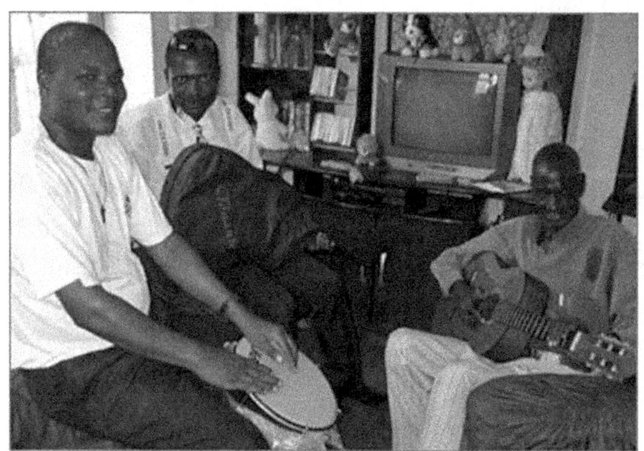

FIGURE 10.20 *"O trio contra o Marburg"—three singers against Marburg-prepare to record a Marburg song. The song, aimed at raising awareness of the disease, has been distributed on CD and cassette tape to the people of Uige, who also hear it every time the WHO social mobilization van drives through their neighborhood. The song is sung in four languages: Portuguese, French, Lingalla, and Kikongo.*
http://www.who.int/
WHO/CNRS/Alain Epelboin

spots were translated into eight of the country's most widely spoken indigenous languages. Daily messages were developed to combat rumors and misinformation.

To reduce fears, health workers arrived at homes in street clothes and then, in view of the family, put on personal protection garments. They took the time to talk

FIGURE 10.21 *People and communities have been extremely anxious about Marburg—it sets in quickly, there is no vaccine or treatment, and most infected people die. Community involvement and understanding is key to interrupting the chain of transmission, and training sessions for teachers and young public health students have been an important component.*
http://www.who.int/
WHO/CNRS/Alain Epelboin

to families and formally recognized their loss or expressed concern for a sick family member.

Burial customs were modified to allow families to carry out burial rites safely. For example, bodies were placed in open body bags for viewing, and ceremonial washings were replaced with sprinkling the body with a mixture of water and bleach. The family members were present when the body was removed from the home, and could accompany the body to the burial site.

The New York Times quoted Dr. Pierre Formenty, a virologist assisting in the Angolan disease containment efforts: "We are fighting the battle of the disease. But first we have to win the battle of the heart, and the battle of the funeral."

When Marburg claimed the life of a well-known Uige musician, the singer's band renamed itself the Trio against Marburg and wrote "Song against Marburg." The song advised listeners what to do when they suspected a Marburg case.

Most deaths in Uige, the outbreak's epicenter, occurred in children under the age of 5; as the outbreak grew, more adults were affected. When a local teacher died from Marburg, this provided an opportunity to step up educational efforts within the schools.

Complicating the response efforts to the Marburg outbreak was minimal infrastructure, a result of a devastating twenty-seven-year civil war that ensued after Angola's independence from Portugal in 1976. At the time of the outbreak, life expectancy was thirty-six years, and half the population was illiterate. Seventy percent lived below the poverty line, with 80 percent of the population involved in subsistence farming.

According to the CDC guidelines for infection control of hemorrhagic fevers such as Marburg, the following steps are recommended to mobilize community resources and conduct community education:

- Create a mobilization committee.
- Identify key community resources.
- Meet with community leaders and assess the current situation.
- Describe the target population.
- Describe problems contributing to transmission risk.
- Identify barriers to carrying out recommended changes or actions.
- Develop specific messages.
- Select activities for communicating messages.

	Audience		
	Households (caregivers, decision-makers)	Community health workers, traditional healers, religious leaders, volunteers, extension and animal health workers, village leaders	Media (local, national, international) Journalists, producers, editors, owners
Sources of information that are trustworthy and credible	Health workers Traditional healers Religious leaders Village leaders Volunteers	Peers Hierarchy (administration) Other agencies	First-hand accounts of experience Expert knowledge and opinion Institutions and agencies
Channels of information dissemination	Word of mouth Local radio Group meetings Face-to-face meetings Information leaflets and posters Mobile phones	Memos and circulars Standard operating procedures Telephone, mobile phone Information leaflets Group meetings Face-to-face meetings	Telephone, mobile phones E-mail Face-to-face meetings Group meetings Press releases and briefings
Feedback to ensure that the strategy is effective	Interviews (key informants) Self-reporting Observation	Reporting Observation	Media surveillance Journalists' reports to health officials Accuracy, consistency and correlation of health advice in media with public health advice
Settings (locations)	Houses Neighbourhoods Villages	Health clinics Training venues Meetings	Press briefings Interviews and interview opportunities (e.g. events such as drug distribution and locations like local hospitals) Informal

FIGURE 10.22 *A template example for developing the appropriate channels and settings for message delivery.*
http://www.who.int/
WHO

- Assign tasks and carry out activities.
- Evaluate activities.
- Obtain community feedback.
- Meet regularly with the mobilization committee.

According to the CDC guidelines, healthcare workers should initially assess the community's resources, such as local governments, religious groups, businesses, schools, and service organizations. Workers would then gather and record information about each group's expertise, leaders, and available resources.

The next step was the identification of community leaders and educating them on the disease. In Angola, this included building relationships with traditional healers. The social mobilization committee would communicate the outbreak status to community leaders, and they would be educated in the symptoms of the disease, how it is spread, personal precautions to prevent its spread, the importance of notifying healthcare workers of suspected cases, proper decontamination methods, and so forth.

COMMUNICATION AND CULTURAL CONCEPTS MODIFIED FOR OUTBREAK PREVENTION AND CONTROL

In 2012 the WHO developed "Communication for Behavioral Impact (COMBI): A Toolkit for Behavioral and Social Communication in Outbreak Response" to help health workers in the field effectively build trusting relationships with the community they are serving. Here's what the publication says about the use of anthropological techniques:

> *In an anthropological approach to outbreak prevention and control, a collaborative model of dialogue and engagement is created rather than a "top-down" model of broadcast communication. Anthropological research during an outbreak involves determining how to:*
>
> - *ensure maximum involvement of affected communities,*
> - *identify local resources and obstacles for effective social mobilization,*
> - *obtain sometimes sensitive and critical information, and*
> - *avoid misunderstandings and prevent and resolve conflicts.*
>
> *Such research takes into account the social organization of the community and emphasizes the importance of kinships and gender roles in households and the community, as well as local knowledge and beliefs about illness and outbreaks. Using many of the tools in this toolkit, anthropologists can identify and analyze local behavior, community beliefs and everyday practices that could affect disease transmission. This*

can help to identify behavior that is a priority for reform and also cultural resources or practices that could improve the effectiveness of an outbreak response. Outbreak response planners can use anthropological research to design more culturally sensitive and humane measures, which will not only improve the effectiveness of behavioral and social interventions but can also minimize the risk for community alienation or inflicting additional trauma on the population. Maintaining good community ties is not just cultural sensitivity; as many of the case studies in this toolkit show, community engagement and trust combined with culturally sensitive interventions can be crucial for preventing behavior such as hiding cases that would otherwise exacerbate the risk for transmission and spread of infection (see the case study of Marburg virus).

By involving communities as fully as possible, anthropologists can give them a sense of ownership in managing and controlling an outbreak of infectious disease. Affected communities will respond positively if they feel that the intervention teams are listening to their questions, understand their concerns and give straightforward answers that make sense from a local point of view. Such participatory community engagement not only minimizes the risk for alienating populations but also creates opportunities for the collection of data and feedback that can help planners to adjust and maximize the effectiveness of social mobilization strategies for outbreak prevention and containment.

For developing effective messages, COMBI had this to say about the type of message to develop for emergency situations:

In a study on emergency readiness and health behavior in the USA, Paek et al. found that campaigns to increase people's perceptions of self-efficacy and response efficacy were more effective than those that emphasized such issues as the likelihood or potential severity of emergencies and disasters. They also found that emotional appeals based on subjective norms, i.e. those that appealed to what the family and loved ones might think or want, might be effective. In addition, to increase self-efficacy, you should identify the barriers, e.g. knowledge, skills, cost, belief and emotions, that inhibit a person's perceived ability to perform an action, and you should address these directly in the strategy.

Regarding the appropriate sources for message delivery, COMBI had this to say:

Who are the currently credible, trustworthy sources of information in the community? What makes them so? Are there particular individuals (sports personalities, actors, politicians) who would be seen as credible, trustworthy sources of information? Do credible, trustworthy sources have particular characteristics that the community holds dear? For the particular behavior being promoted, who might be credible, trustworthy sources of information about the behavior in the community? To what extent is the health staff a credible and trustworthy source of information? To what extent do their training and appearance (e.g. a uniform) enhance perceptions of credibility and expertise? To what extent are teachers and schoolchildren sources of information?

COMBI planning steps 6 and 7: Monitoring and evaluating interventions

Tool 16: Develop a monitoring table

The tool below lists examples of questions asked in each form of monitoring, with some examples of indicators and methods of collecting the information.

Key questions	Indicator	Data collection method
Are activities being implemented as planned? Are outputs being delivered as planned? Are activities within the budget?	On the basis of the implementation schedule, plan of action and budget, for example: ▪ number of participants in meetings ▪ number of posters produced and distributed ▪ number of radio spots aired ▪ number of volunteers trained and engaged in social mobilization ▪ number of households visited ▪ costs within budget	Activity reports Attendance sheets Financial reports
Process	**Indicator**	**Data collection method**
Is the message or activity reaching the people for whom it was designed? Is participation good? To what extent are outbreak interventions being adapted to local needs? Is there a recent change or trend that should be considered? Are there any changes in the social, political or policy context that might affect the control measures and the COMBI strategy?	Examples of quantitative indicators: ▪ % of target population who have heard or seen messages and activities ▪ % of target audience who understand, like or agree with messages ▪ % of target audience who know the symptoms of the disease ▪ numbers of women and men who have been actively involved in social mobilization and other outbreak control interventions Examples of qualitative indicators: ▪ Existence of circulating rumours or messages that promote non-participation ▪ Participants feel that their concerns and ideas are taken into account by the local outbreak management committee ▪ Interventions are perceived as relevant and responding to the expressed needs of the target population ▪ Examples of quantitative indicators ▪ % accurate media reporting and coverage ▪ Examples of qualitative indicators: ▪ Evidence of communication hoaxes that undermine response strategies	Rapid surveys, interviews and observation through: ▪ central location intercept interview ▪ focus group discussions ▪ observation at service and delivery points ▪ interviews with field personnel involved in outbreak response ▪ observation of field staff carrying out interventions in local communities ▪ review and analysis of media coverage Informal conversations and meetings with key, grass roots organizations, journalists etc

FIGURE 10.23 *An example of a monitoring table for monitoring and evaluating interventions.*
http://www.who.int/
WHO

The credibility of the person who delivers the message influences the degree to which it is accepted. For instance, people may pay more attention to a message if a well-known doctor rather than a local shopkeeper delivers it, and a young person might be more likely to persuade other young people to take action rather than an older person, who may be seen as authoritarian. Remember that appearance makes a difference in how a source is perceived; therefore, care and sensitivity should be shown in dressing and presenting oneself. Credibility, expertise, trustworthiness and empathy are important.

By July 2005, after 329 deaths, the outbreak had been mostly contained. While the WHO relied on traditional methods, such as case finding, contact tracing and isolation, and high-quality care for infected people, it also learned that effective communication and cultural awareness were required to truly accomplish its mission.

QUESTIONS FOR DISCUSSION

1. What were the cultural or geographic problems posed by the Marburg outbreak in Angola?
2. What steps were taken to regain the trust of Angolans during this crisis?
3. What were the complicating factors from a political and historical perspective?
4. Rapid response to this crisis after confirmation of the Marburg outbreak led to deployment of sophisticated diagnostic field teams in the affected towns and villages. Why did this response backfire?
5. How would you reduce fear and rumors within the population?
6. What would be your key messages and communication channels based on the demographic, economic, and other social conditions of Angola?
7. How would you use the Trio against Marburg to further communication goals?

Dig Deeper

Read the WHO's "Communication for Behavioral Impact: A Toolkit for Behavioral and Social Communication in Outbreak Response," available on the textbook's companion website. What are the main components of an outbreak response strategy?

33

Shark Fin Soup

Hong Kong Disneyland Loses Magic for Some

Despite careful planning, the grand opening of the first magic kingdom in China—Hong Kong Disneyland—was overshadowed by weeks of unfavorable international news coverage involving complaints over its cost, its noisy and polluting fireworks, the mistreatment of laborers and stray dogs, and its shark fin cuisine.

The 310-acre amusement park was a joint venture between the Hong Kong government and Disney. Hong Kong owns 57 percent of the project after a $2.9 billion investment. The government expected the Western-styled resort to become a family vacation destination to complement the city's already vibrant financial hub. The project also created jobs—18,000 for the local economy, including 4,000 construction workers and 5,000 Disney employees, which would eventually grow to 36,000 new jobs with an economic value of $19 billion over a forty-year period. A whopping 5.6 million visitors were expected its first year of operation.

Located thirty minutes from downtown Hong Kong on the island of Lan Tau, the resort took seven years to build from its initial announcement. Hong Kong, a British colony until 1997, is a modern commercial city of seven million people. Because Hong Kong is a special administrative region of China, its successful ventures are often considered preludes to future expansion to the much larger market on mainland China.

Hong Kong Disneyland, with the Lan Tau mountains behind it and Hong Kong's dramatic skyline in front of it, was faithfully adapted from the original American Disneyland but on a smaller scale. Visitors can experience Tomorrowland, Adventureland, and Fantasyland, just like the fifty-year-old versions half a world away.

Several Chinese touches were included to ensure its Asian guests felt comfortable while still getting an authentic Disney experience.

FIGURE 10.24 *On stage in front of the Sleeping Beauty Castle: (Left to right) Donald Tsang, Chief Executive of the Government of the Hong Kong Special Administrative Region; Zeng Qinghong, Vice-President of the People's Republic of China; Michael D. Eisner, Walt Disney Company Chief Executive Officer; and Robert A. Iger, Walt Disney Company President, Chief Operating Officer, and CEO-elect, at the grand opening of Hong Kong Disneyland Park.*
http://www.corbisimages.com/
© Disney/epa/Corbis

HONG KONG DISNEYLAND

Feng Shui Design

Disney made changes to the new resort's design after consulting a feng shui master who recommended rotating the orientation of the entire park by several degrees and placing three large boulders in certain locations to ensure harmony with spiritual forces.

Two new features designed especially for Hong Kong were Fantasy Gardens and a musical extravaganza called *The Golden Mickeys at Disney's Storybook Theater.* Fantasy Gardens' lush and fanciful surroundings provided visitors "picture perfect" opportunities for autographs and photos with their favorite Disney characters.

The Golden Mickeys at Disney's Storybook Theater honored many Disney films with plenty of glitz and glamour reminiscent of a red-carpet Hollywood awards show.

Opening Ceremonies

Hong Kong Disney opened September 12, 2005, with children singing in English, Cantonese, and Putonghua (standard Mandarin); Chinese acrobats; and a performance

FIGURE 10.25 *Disney character Minnie Mouse stands in front of the Sleeping Beauty Castle inside Hong Kong's Disneyland Park. The Hong Kong Disneyland Resort, consisting of a theme park, two hotels, and a lakeside recreation area, opened on September 12, 2005.*
http://www.corbisimages.com

of the traditional Chinese lion dance in front of the pink Sleeping Beauty's Castle. The ribbon-cutting ceremony included the chief executive officer and president of Walt Disney; Zeng Quinghong, vice president of the People's Republic of China; and the chief executive of Hong Kong. The day before the grand opening, the resort invited special guests and the media to a preview event that featured numerous well-known singers and entertainers from Hong Kong.

Asian-Friendly Language and Food

In another nod to cultural sensitivity, rides and shows were trilingual, using Cantonese, Mandarin, and English. Employees' prescribed banter, delivered to customers during rides, was carefully checked by linguists to ensure accurate translation.

A food and beverage team carefully tested Western, Chinese, and Asian items to provide a diverse menu to satisfy all taste buds. Popular dishes from the Jiangnan region in northwest Asia and Guangdong province in mainland China were included on menus. Different styles of cooking, such as steamed dishes (dim sum), stir fries, noodles, curry dishes, and barbecue dishes such as Hong Kong char siew pork were featured.

Community Relations

Hong Kong Disneyland follows the long Disney tradition of taking an active role in the local community. Eight days before the grand opening, its first Charity Day was held to benefit the city's largest charity organization, the Community Chest. Hong Kong Disneyland and its volunteers hosted storytelling sessions at public libraries during the summer and participated in charity walks and hospital visits. It sponsored the annual Jiminy Cricket's "Environmentality-Challenge," which encourages young students to "think green," and Disney's Imagination Day, which challenges students to apply their creative energies.

ACTIVISTS GRAB HEADLINES

Despite careful planning, Hong Kong Disneyland attracted negative publicity before and after its grand opening on September 12, 2005.

Shark Fin Soup

Months before its opening, Hong Kong Disneyland encountered the wrath of environmentalists worldwide when Disney unveiled its Fairy Tale Wedding packages. Couples could choose from a Western-style celebration or an elegant Chinese-banquet style reception. The menu included shark fin soup, a cultural mainstay of most Chinese banquets and upscale restaurants. According to *The New York Times*, "Without shark fin, a Chinese banquet does not look like one at all," said Chiu Ching-cheung, chairman of the Shark Fin Trade Merchants' Association.

Shark fin, a delicacy in middle- and upper-class Asian diets, has been under scrutiny by environmentalists around the world who claim overfishing has led to sharp declines in the world's largest shark species. Environmentalists also oppose the practice of shark "finning," in which fins are chopped off and the rest of the shark is thrown back into the ocean and dies. Environmentalists said fishermen were not interested in shark meat because of its "rough texture and poor taste." Shark fin merchants in Hong Kong said the "finning" practice seldom occurs and that shark meat is eaten in poor countries. Shark fin fans believe the delicacy offers medicinal or aphrodisiac qualities; a bowl of shark fin soup can cost up to $200, making sharks a highly lucrative business.

Protests came from groups such as the Sea Shepherd Conservation Society and the World Wildlife Fund, and Hong Kong environmentalists.

At first, the park responded to the controversy by offering to give guests leaflets describing the ecological harm of shark finning in hopes of dissuading shark fin soup orders. It also said it would buy from only "reliable and responsible suppliers," and it would offer non shark fin soup options for banquets. After a month of protests, Disney President Robert Iger announced the park was removing shark fin soup from its wedding menu.

Air and Noise Pollution

Another controversy emerged when environmentalists protested the traditional nightly fireworks show because of increased air and noise pollution, although the fireworks display is smaller than the U.S. display. Hong Kong already suffers from smog pollution created by factories elsewhere in China and the use of coal in Hong Kong. Environmentalists requested Disney use new pyrotechnics technology that uses compressed air to lift fireworks, significantly reducing noise and ground-level smoke from black powder. Since the fireworks' pollution levels were within regulatory limitations, Hong Kong Disneyland did not implement the new technology.

Labor Issues

News media reports carried charges by labor activists that Disney forced its park staff to work eleven- and thirteen-hour days, provided inadequate breaks, and rewrote daily work schedules without notice. Student groups, who investigated factories on China's mainland that produced products for the park, found labor abuses. They accused Disney of underpaying its workers for a ten- to twelve-hour day and a six-day week.

Wild Dogs

Animal rights activists protested the killing of about forty-five dogs that were part of a wild dog pack roaming the hills surrounding the park. According to news accounts, the wild dogs, which are common on the island, threatened workers and visitors. While government workers tried to find homes for the dogs, sick ones were killed to protect the safety of workers and visitors.

FIGURE 10.26 *Protesters with Mickey Mouse dolls around their shoulders and covering their eyes hold placards during a demonstration at the entrance of the Hong Kong Disneyland to Protest what they claim to be Disney contractors' labor exploitation in China, August 30, 2005. The placards in Chinese read "Exploiting Chinese workers, Community Caring Just Talk."*
http://www.corbisimages.com/

Overcrowding

Some visitors complained that the park was too small, with only twenty-one attractions, and was overcrowded. This was especially true when the park encountered an unexpected snafu for the Lunar New Year holiday, the biggest holiday of the year. The park was swamped with visitors trying to use a dual system of "flexible" tickets, which allowed one visit within a six-month period, and "date-specific" tickets, which are issued for special events or holidays. Many mainland tourists with eager children were turned away at the gate.

Bill Ernest, executive vice president and managing director of the park, apologized:

> *We regret that anyone may have been inconvenienced . . . No one is more disappointed than we are. As a father, I understand how frustrating it is to disappoint your children . . . But our first priority is to protect our children.*

The *South China Morning Post* noted in its story that the theme park giant needed a better understanding of Chinese culture.

POST HONG KONG—SHANGHAI DISNEYLAND!

Without a doubt, all of the problems encountered by Hong Kong Disney were examined when Disney and China embarked on a cooperative venture to build the sixth Disney theme park in the world—Shanghai Disneyland, scheduled to open in 2016. It will be three times the size of Hong Kong Disney and cost quite a bit more. Before building even began, some critics charged that Disneyland's focus on American culture was a form of "cultural aggression" and that its relatively high prices would allow only the wealthy to enjoy its magic.

No doubt this mammoth project will attract its own controversies and provide challenges for its public relations team.

As its website noted in 2013, it was working to develop beneficial community relationships and develop a socially responsible mindset:

> *As we build this new world full of fantasy, imagination and adventure, the Shanghai Disney Resort is also building relationships in the growing Shanghai community. Through the Disney VoluntEARS program, Shanghai Disney Resort Cast Members have already started to volunteer locally. The resort is also working with local non-profit organizations to address key community needs which align with Disney's corporate social responsibility and philanthropy goals, focusing on compassion, creativity and conservation.*

QUESTIONS FOR DISCUSSION

1. What is culture?
2. Why is an understanding of culture important in public relations and communication?

3. What actions did Disney take to ensure that Hong Kong Disney would cater to Asian culture?
4. What were the specific cultural problems presented in this case study?
5. Why did environmental activists target Hong Kong Disney for proposing to serve shark fin soup when other restaurants and banquet halls offered the same dish?
6. Disney did not issue any corporate news releases in response to problems outlined in this case study. Hong Kong Disney managers did respond to media requests and were quoted in news media stories. What do you think about this strategy?

Dig Deeper

Another conservation group, WildAid, has developed a shark conservation program which includes public service announcements (PSAs), using Chinese celebrities such as former NBA superstar Yao Ming, to advocate against shark fin soup; it is available on the textbook's companion website. Other WildAid shark conservation PSAs are available on WildAid's YouTube channel. Are these types of celebrity PSAs effective? Why or why not? Read "China's State Council Makes Historic Decision to Protect Sharks" news article on WildAid's website, which credits Ming and others for bringing awareness to Chinese officials about shark conservation.

CHAPTER 11

Financial Communications and Investor Relations

Public relations professionals are known for their ability as communicators—not always for their business acumen. Often, professionals bemoan the lack of basic business knowledge exhibited by public relations graduates.

If public relations' goal is to ensure the survivability of an organization, shouldn't the practitioner understand how the organization's bottom line works? After all, if the practitioner doesn't know how the organization makes money, he or she will be unable to effectively communicate it to the public. It only takes one blank look in a room full of senior management to sideline the public relations practitioner who can't explain the basics of a company balance sheet.

Public relations students should take business classes, including economics and accounting, as part of their educational program. Students can also pick up business knowledge on their own by paying attention to business-related news publications and shows. The business section of a local newspaper is a good place to begin. Start monitoring your favorite shopping destinations or entertainment outlets. Check out their annual reports online. Little by little, the world of business will begin to make sense.

Not only does a general knowledge of an organization's business model and strategy help a practitioner do his or her job better with credibility among management, but it can eventually lead to opportunities to specialize in investor relations.

This specialized area of public relations deals with publicly held companies. According to the National Investor Relations Institute:

> *Investor relations is defined as a strategic management responsibility that integrates finance, communication, marketing and securities law compliance to enable the most effective two-way communication between a company and the financial community and other constituencies, which ultimately contributes to a company's securities achieving fair valuation.*

Publics that investor relations managers communicate with include financial analysts and current and prospective investors: institutional, individual, and employee investors. Another important public that investor relations professionals focus on is the financial news industry. This includes financial writers and their publications such as *The Wall Street Journal*, *Forbes*, *Barron's*, *Business Week*, *Fortune*, and *The Kiplinger Letter*, along with financial columnists, and cable and broadcast television and radio shows with a financial emphasis. The financial blogging community is a growing constituency that investor relations professionals need to be aware of as more members of the investment community are seeking information and insight from these often times independent sources. SeekingAlpha, a popular website, is one of the oldest and largest aggregators of financial blogs, offering essentially a "one-stop shop" for financial blog posts. In addition, the investor relations officer provides feedback and competitive intelligence to senior management.

A QUICK BASIC BUSINESS PRIMER

This section provides a very basic overview of some business terms and concepts to start, but further reading and discussion are helpful.

The first lesson of business is that businesses exist to make money. The goal of financial relations is to build positive relationships with all key stakeholders who affect the business's ability to survive and make money.

Every business needs capital (i.e., money) to operate. Businesses can be either privately or publicly owned. Private companies are often run by the company's founders, management, or a group of private investors. Private businesses use profits, bonds, or bank loans to provide the necessary money to expand or undertake new activities.

A publicly held company has sold a portion of itself to the public by selling stock (a piece of the company) or by issuing debt (usually in the form of corporate bonds), which means that its shareholders (owners of stock) and/or debt holders (owners of the bonds) have a claim on the company's assets and profits. The money raised from public offerings allows companies to expand, modernize, conduct research, or engage in other activities to expand the business. Publicly held companies have thousands, if not millions, of owners, thanks to the popularity of average Americans' investing in stocks and bonds for retirement savings.

As long as investors are confident that the company is on the right track and either provides a share of its profit earnings (a dividend) or has good indications of future profits, investors are likely to keep their money in the company. Management must share its business strategy plan with its investors so that they can determine whether the strategy is likely to move the company in the right direction. Financial analysts examine these business strategies and other company indicators (earnings, debt, and competitors, etc.) to comment positively or negatively about a company's performance and future prospects. With positive future prospects and accompanying high investor confidence, the company's stock value rises. This is because there are a limited number of shares available, and if demand outstrips supply, the price for a share of stock rises. In this situation, future stock purchases by investors in the company will cost more, but it's usually worth more too, because of positive future profit predictions. If an investor eventually sells his or her stake in the company, the profit should be higher than the initial investment.

All kinds of factors and events, anticipated or not, can combine to create either positive or negative business conditions. Some of these factors include earnings or sales growth, new product releases, leadership changes, and legislation. Rising gas prices that increase the cost of transporting goods or powerful hurricanes that destroy a company's facilities can have negative impacts on a business's ability to make a profit. Either could lead shareholders to pull their money out of the company and invest it somewhere else or prevent potential investors from buying shares. This loss of monetary investment reduces the overall value of the company, reduces its access to money, and often leads companies to find ways to reduce its costs, such as closing plants and laying off workers.

INVESTOR RELATIONS' ROLE

Investor confidence in a company is key to a publicly held business's success. It should be inspired by the company's financial performance, leadership, and future prospects truthfully communicated through various information tactics directed to investors and the financial media. Along with senior management, investor relations professionals are responsible for getting the message out about the company's well-being. The key to investor relations is disclosure of material information needed for informed decision making and dissemination of that information to those who need it.

To protect investors from companies involved in misconduct, the federal government's U.S. Securities and Exchange Commission (SEC) "seeks to detect problems in the securities markets, prevent and deter violations of federal securities laws, and alert investors to possible wrongdoing." The agency fosters informed investment decision making by "reviewing disclosures of companies and mutual funds to ensure that clear, complete, and accurate information is available to investors." For example, *regulation fair disclosure* (commonly called Reg FD) is a Securities and Exchange Commission rule that attempts to prevent selective disclosure of information; in the past, individual investors may not have been privy to the same information provided to bigger institutional investors. Today, conference calls and informational meetings conducted by the company are open to the general public. The right to equal access to this nonpublic "market-moving information" was required by the SEC's Regulation Fair Disclosure in 2000.

Another regulation, the Sarbanes–Oxley Act (SOX) of 2002, was created to protect investors from fraudulent accounting activities. Today, publicly traded companies must follow stricter auditor regulations and disclosure in their financial statements. The Public Company Accounting Oversight Board (PCAOB) oversees the enforcement of this regulation.

If investors cannot get timely, reliable, and truthful information about a company's operations or other factors that may affect its operations, then they will not risk their money. The most well-known type of disclosure problem is called *insider trading*. This involves a person having important knowledge, known as *material information*—such as advance information about a company sale, merger, product innovation, or launch—that other investors don't have and then using that information to make money by buying or selling stock. Material information is defined as any event or information considered important enough to influence a decision to buy or sell a publicly listed security and/or to influence a company's stock price.

According to the National Investor Relations Institute (NIRI):

> *Anyone in the spokesperson role must be completely familiar with the company's record of disclosure in order to guard against unauthorized disclosures of material, nonpublic information . . . under Reg FD, to detect inadvertent disclosure of material, nonpublic information or to avoid potentially intentional disclosure of such information, the IRO [investment relations officer] should accompany senior officials in meetings with analysts or investors. If there should be an inadvertent disclosure of such information, the company must issue a news release within twenty-four hours of when the official became aware of such disclosure or before the next trading day, whichever is later.*
>
> *Credibility comes not only from knowledge of the company and provision of accurate, complete and timely information, but also from a demonstrated willingness to correct or update changes in information on a timely basis. Failure to do so may cause long-term or irreparable damage to the company's management and the spokesperson's credibility.*

NIRI suggests that IROs tread a narrow path that requires them to "balance public interests with those of their company and place those interests above their own." An IRO should possess the following qualities: personal integrity, professionalism, competence, and objectivity. He or she must also understand conditions for conflicts of interest and how to appropriately represent the company, especially when addressing matters related to future company performance.

IROs develop materials or directly interact with analysts and investors to accurately portray a business's value. The IRO constantly monitors investor communication and the competitive environment to respond to questions about trends, or other important developments in and outside the company that might have an effect on the business's value. This information is communicated back to management to develop effective communication strategies as part of the overall business strategy.

An investor relations counseling firm can provide any of the following strategic counseling and tactical activities to help organizations achieve their objectives:

- Analyst and investor meetings
- Investor days
- Communication counsel for program and policy development and implementation
- Crisis communication
- Disclosure issues relating to financial reporting and policy development
- Financial communication tactics

- IR spokesperson training
- Media relations
- Message development
- Perception audits
- Positioning strategies
- Research
- Overall strategy development.

To ensure that companies are telling all investors what is going on in a timely manner, the SEC requires publicly held companies to adhere to numerous reporting rules. It requires publicly held companies with assets of $10 million or more and 500 shareholders to file three types of reports throughout the calendar or fiscal year: Form 10K, Form 10Q, and Form 8K. Any SEC-required company filings can be accessed from SEC's website (www.sec.gov) using the EDGAR database. The following descriptions are from the SEC website:

REQUIRED FORMS

- **Form 10K (Annual Filings)**—The annual report on Form 10K provides a comprehensive overview of the company's business and financial condition and includes audited financial statements. Although similarly named, the annual report on Form 10K is distinct from the "annual report to shareholders," which a company must send to its shareholders when it holds an annual meeting to elect directors.
- **Form 10Q (Quarterly Filings)**—Form 10Q includes unaudited financial statements and provides a continuing view of the company's financial position during the year. The report must be filed for each of the first three quarters of the company's fiscal year.
- **Form 8K (Current Filings)**—Public companies must report material corporate events on a more current basis. Form 8K is the "current report" companies must file with the SEC to announce major events that shareholders should know about.

OTHER DOCUMENTS

Beyond these important reports, the investor relations officer should be familiar with other documents including:

- Registration statements for newly offered securities
- Proxy materials sent to shareholders before an annual meeting
- Annual reports sent to shareholders

- Documents concerning tender offers (an offer to buy a large number of shares of a corporation, usually at a premium above the current market price).

Filings Related to Mergers and Acquisitions

The New York Stock Exchange (NYSE) and NASDAQ also have requirements for companies listed on their exchanges.

The successful investor relations officer should develop and work to improve several skill areas, including a thorough knowledge of business concepts, communication, and relationship building and ability to research and analyze financial information. Also the investor relations officer should share information with management and help incorporate it into the organization's business strategy.

NIRI recommends the following information dissemination guidelines:

- **Technology**—Companies are encouraged to use multiple technologies to reach the widest audience possible, including the individual investor. These technologies include: major wire services, conference calls, broadcast fax and fax-on-demand services, e-mail, video conferences, websites, and electronic EDGAR filings. The broadly disseminated news release is considered essential to the communication program.

- **Internet**—While the Internet is widely used, companies must use more traditional sources of dissemination for those who request it. Companies should monitor Internet sites that discuss a company's performance but are not allowed to participate or respond in chat rooms as this could be considered a form of selective disclosure. Monitoring the Internet does help companies create communication strategies.

- **Conference Calls**—Following news releases to the wire services, fully accessible webcast conference calls are the most widely used means for disseminating corporate information to the investment community. Conference calls are often used as a forum in which the company disseminates detailed information, expanding on information contained in the news release that has been issued prior to the call.

Regulation FD considers a fully accessible, non-exclusionary webcast or telephonic conference call as a means for real-time, full and fair disclosure.

- **One-on-One Meetings**—Face-to-face meetings, such as one-on-one meetings with analysts and investors, help build goodwill and make a company more approachable in the eyes of the investment community. Companies should note that, as in all other types of meetings, there is the possibility that information may be selectively disclosed. Companies should conscientiously avoid discussing material or nonpublic information in one-on-one meetings. If there is an unintentional disclosure of such information, the IRO can issue a news release containing that information within twenty-four hours.

CHALLENGES IN INVESTOR RELATIONS

Investor relations is a demanding and important job. It requires high ethical standards, particularly in providing truthful information to all who require it even when pressured by others in the organization. The job also requires the ability to react quickly and appropriately in times of crisis; this includes reacting to rumors, actual poor performance reports, tender offers, or proxy fights.

A tender offer is an offer to buy a large number of shares of a corporation, usually at a premium above the current market price. Investor relations officers can help management strategize how best to communicate with shareholders, investors, and analysts to encourage confidence in the current leadership and company's direction.

A proxy fight happens when shareholders ask other shareholders, unable to attend an annual meeting, to cast their "absentee vote" for the issue advocated by the requesting shareholders. This often happens when shareholders are unhappy with management and want to vote down certain management proposals or change the organization's leadership by voting in new board directors. As with tender offers, a proxy fight requires the investor relations officer to help management communicate effectively with shareholders, investors, and analysts so that the current leadership maintains control of the company.

34

Paychex, Inc., Sees Big Payoff in First Investor Day

Donna N. Stein, APR, Fellow PRSA

Managing Partner of Donna Stein & Partners

Paychex, Inc., (NASDAQ: PAYX) is a leading provider of payroll, human resource and benefits outsourcing solutions for small to medium-sized businesses. Founded in 1971 by B. Thomas Golisano and headquartered in Rochester, New York, the company has more than one hundred offices and serves approximately 567,000 payroll clients as of May 31, 2012. Revenues for the company's 2012 Fiscal Year were $2.2 billion.

Paychex, Inc., went public on the NASDAQ Exchange in 1983 to the delight of not only Wall Street's institutional investors, but also the company's own employees, most of whom had received company shares as part of their compensation when Paychex was privately held. Most of senior management's attention was focused on growing the company's business, and Paychex embarked on opening a significant number of branches to extend its reach across the U.S. Soon the company expanded its product offerings to provide a one-source administration solution for payroll, human resource, benefits, and insurance services for the small business owners the company served. During the 1980s, 1990s, and early 2000s, the company experienced double-digit growth, which Wall Street admired and institutional investors favored.

The company's investor relations activities have always been the joint responsibility of the CEO and CFO and predominantly could be characterized as "reactive" rather than "proactive." The company has always practiced transparent communications and readily responded to phone calls from sell-side and buy-side research analysts, institutional investors and individual investors, as well as accepted invitations to attend brokerage-sponsored conferences and road shows. But the primary focus for both of these management positions was to run the company and run it well, leaving little time for proactively targeting new institutional investors or hosting company-sponsored meetings with analysts and members of the investment community.

Fast forward to 2011: Martin Mucci had been the CEO of Paychex for one year and Efrain Rivera had just joined the company as the new CFO. Both men had solid track records with the Wall Street community. In a prior position with another corporation, Rivera had engaged in what would be considered "proactive" investor relations activities which involved marketing his organization to new research analysts and institutional investors. Paychex's investor relations effort was facing new challenges; due to a poor U.S. economy and tight borrowing restrictions levied by the nation's banking institutions, new business formations had slowed considerably and the company was no longer achieving the growth trajectory it once enjoyed. The price of the company's shares had fallen in value, and Paychex, once considered a growth company, was now faced with re-positioning itself as a value investment, which some investors questioned. The company was paying a solid dividend, but was it enough to appease existing investors as well as attract new, long-term investors?

Clearly, the Paychex investment story had evolved; it was very different from what it had been under prior senior management administrations and needed to be communicated effectively and persuasively by the new CEO and CFO.

Both Mucci and Rivera agreed: they wanted to step up the company's investor relations efforts and be more proactive in communicating a new Paychex investment story with the company's existing research analysts and institutional investors, while hoping to attract new analysts and investor support as well.

PHASE ONE PLANNING

In January 2012, with the assistance of an investor relations consultant, Paychex embarked on the first phase of a new, proactive investor relations program. With board approval, Mucci and Rivera decided to host the company's first-ever Investor Day in Rochester, New York, in mid-July. Investor days are common practice in proactive investor relations programs, serving a number of purposes. For Paychex, Investor Day was an opportunity to achieve several investor relations objectives, including introducing several new members of Mucci's senior management team to the investment community, communicating a new investment story for Paychex, showcasing the technology investments and product innovations made in the company's new generation of mobile product offerings, and providing a "cultural" view of a company headquartered in the upstate New York city of Rochester.

Pre-Investor Day Audit

A pre-Investor Day perception audit of Wall Street sentiment toward Paychex was conducted in February 2012 via phone interviews with a number of the company's sell-side research analysts and institutional investors. All participants were offered anonymity to ensure the honesty and candor of their responses. The purpose of the audit was to determine if there was interest in attending the company's first-ever

Investor Day in Rochester during July 2012; identifying the Paychex senior executives the Wall Street community was most interested in meeting and hearing presentations from; soliciting topics for discussion at Investor Day; and providing audit participants with the opportunity to comment on the company's business strategies, financial performance, competitive position, and valuation. All of the information gathered was presented to Paychex senior management in a written report with specific recommendations that served as the foundation for the planning, message development and execution of Paychex's Investor Day.

PHASE TWO PLANNING

Under the theme "Charting the Future," work began in earnest in March 2012 for the July event. Paychex Director of Corporate Communications Laura Saxby Lynch was appointed project manager; she assembled a team of professionals from departments within the company including marketing, public relations, travel and transportation, IT, finance, and advertising. Saxby Lynch also solicited bids from outside vendors to assist with the design and delivery of management's PowerPoint presentations, banners, signage, and overall event planning. Due to the Rochester venue and limited flights in and out of the regional airport, Investor Day quickly expanded to include a dinner with management the evening before, breakfast in the morning and lunch following the conclusion of Investor Day presentations. A fluid, extensive timeline and flow chart of responsibilities were developed and followed by everyone on Saxby Lynch's team to keep Investor Day moving forward.

In addition to Mucci and Rivera, presenters at Investor Day included Michael Gioja, senior vice president, information technology, product management and development; Mark Bottini, senior vice president, sales; and Andrew Childs, vice president, marketing. More than fifty members of the investment community attended the event, and more than 200 others participated via a webcast on the company's investor relations website. Midway through the management presentations on July 18, the share price of Paychex stock reached a new fifty-two-week trading high. Analyst reports issued late that afternoon and early the next day praised the company's management team and innovative product offering demonstrated at Investor Day.

EVALUATION—PERCEPTION AUDIT

In the two weeks following Investor Day, a perception audit was conducted to solicit feedback from attendees regarding their overall impressions of the event, presentation content, and logistics. For many, Investor Day represented "a new era" for the company, including a charismatic and invigorated senior management team, a broad technology-inspired product offering and transparent, forward-thinking investor communications. The planning, message development, technology demonstrations, and overall attention to detail paid off handsomely for Paychex: Investor

Day was successful on all fronts and ushered in a more proactive investor relations effort for Mucci and Rivera.

QUESTIONS FOR DISCUSSION

1. Why did the CEO and CFO of Paychex want to host Investor Day?
2. What was the reason for the pre-Investor Day perception audit?
3. What was the reason for the post-Investor Day perception audit?
4. What should management include in the company's future investor relations efforts to maintain the positive momentum?
5. What types of logistics are needed to plan and execute an event like Investor Day?
6. What are the advantages of a webcast for investor presentations?

Dig Deeper

Read the Paychex, Inc., 2011 Annual Report, available on the textbook's companion website. What are its risk factors? What are Paychex's strategic relationships? What strategies are used to connect with these partners?

35

Best Buy Fights for Survival

Company Strives for Relevancy in an e-Commerce World

Best Buy, once the darling of big-box electronic stores, was fighting financial pundits' gloomy predictions that unless it radically changed its business strategy it would face the fate of other electronic stores such as Circuit City: bankruptcy and liquidation.

Founded in 1983, Best Buy was a $50 billion Fortune 100 company that at one time was the place to go for anything electronic. With 125,000 employees in the U.S. and 170,000 worldwide, it was the biggest consumer electronics chain in the country, with 1,055 stores in early 2013. In the company's own words:

> *Best Buy Co., Inc. (NYSE: BBY) is the global leader in consumer electronics. We offer a unique promise to our large and loyal customer base including the latest devices and services; competitive prices; and the ability to shop when and where you want. Additionally, our "Blue Shirt" sales associates and Geek Squad agents are the authority on consumer electronics, delivering unbiased, knowledgeable advice hundreds of millions of times a year and offering unmatched support for the lifetime of the products we sell.*

Even as one of the best-known electronic stores in the nation, Best Buy was not faring well in the digital commerce world. For the third quarter of 2012, the company reported a loss of $10 million, compared to a profit of $156 million in the same quarter a year earlier.

Its CEO, Brian Dunn, resigned in 2012 amid allegations that he had an improper relationship with an employee. Best Buy's founder, Richard Schultze, also left after forty-six years with the company when his protégé Dunn was forced out. During the summer Schulze offered a buyout valued as high as $8.8 billion, which was rejected,

There were several top administrative changes at the company in quick order including a new CEO, a new chief financial officer, a new digital, marketing and e-commerce administrator, a new vice president for U.S. retail, and a new communications and public affairs officer to help lead the changes.

Best Buy held an Analyst and Investor Day on November 1, 2012, in New York to discuss its new leadership team and preview its expected third quarter earnings. The event was hosted by Hubert Joly, Best Buy's new president and CEO. Joly shared his assessment of the business, its new structural organization, and renewed areas of focus. The event also included presentations by other members of the executive team. The presentations were streamed live via Best Buy's investor relations website (www.investors.bestbuy.com).

Joly said in a news release at the time:

One thing I have learned in helping turn companies around is that a business needs to have a nimble organization. Our new organization will help build a closer connection to our customers and front line employees, as well as accelerate our transformation.

Beginning in 2013, business analysts said that Best Buy needed to change its policy of matching competitors' prices and the massive size of its stores. A major problem, analysts said, was the phenomenon known as "showrooming," in which shoppers visit brick-and-mortar businesses, such as Best Buy, to test drive a product, and then purchase the same product from a lower-priced retailer, such as Amazon.

"There's not really any space in the marketplace for 150,000 square-foot stores that sell a bunch of TVs," said Jeff Macke, a business analyst, on Yahoo's "The Daily Ticker" on February 14, 2013. That was a dire statement to make for a company that had seen much better days. Best Buy was having difficulty competing with online competitors such as Amazon that did not have the extra financial burden of maintaining large stores, when consumers—buffeted by years of recession—were looking for the best deals.

It decided on a significant new business strategy: make permanent its holiday shopping offer of matching competitors' prices, and instituting significant price cuts.

On February 15, 2013, Best Buy issued this news release entitled "Best Buy Ends 'Showrooming' with Low Price Guarantee":

Best Buy's Low Price Guarantee hits online and in stores on March 3, signaling the end of "showrooming." Best Buy will price match all local retail competitors and 19 major online competitors in all product categories and on nearly all in-stock products, whenever asked by a customer.

Best Buy is the only retailer to offer a Low Price Guarantee in addition to having a full range of the latest and greatest devices and services, a sales force dedicated to providing impartial and knowledgeable advice and full support for the life of the product.

With a Low Price Guarantee, our customers will have the best of both worlds when they shop BestBuy.com or come to a Best Buy store. They will get unbiased service from our Blue Shirts and support for the life of their product while also knowing they have a Low Price Guarantee on nearly every item. This guarantee is available on BestBuy.com, at more than 1,000 Best Buy big box stores, more than 400 Best Buy Mobile standalone stores in the United States, as well as on the telephone.

The full Low Price Guarantee policy—including exclusions and the list of online retailers we will match prices from—can be found on BestBuy.com.

Best Buy spokesperson Matt Furman told Minnesota Public Radio after the announcement:

As part of our turnaround and transformation efforts, we've recommitted to improving the customer experience. And we know one of the key elements to the customer experience, of course, is being price-competitive. With that in mind, we decided to end showrooming for our customers and ensure them that they come in to our store and see a product they want, they'll get it at the lowest price.

At the same time, *The Wall Street Journal* reported that Best Buy founder and former chairman Richard Schultze had supposedly given up plans for a buyout and instead was working with a group of investors to purchase a minority stake in the company. Schulze already owned 20 percent of the company, and an even bigger stake in the company (with the group of investors) would increase his ability to pressure the board to adopt changes. However, it would take at least 51 percent ownership to control the company and board. Schultze was not considered a white knight by everyone, but plenty of people wanted to see him regain control of the company and put it on the road to profitability.

Some analysts, such as Blake Bos of the financial services firm The Motley Fool, said that a buyout would allow the company to return to a privately owned company and give it the room to make the changes needed to regain its stability outside the glare of the news media. He noted that big strategy changes are difficult to do when the news media are focused on a company's every move and investors are generally focused more on short-term gains than long-term strategy.

While a 2012 Schulze buyout offer was rejected, a new minority stake offer, which had not been officially reported by the company, was the subject of widespread speculation in the financial news media. Best Buy had given Schulze and his private equity partners until February 28, 2013, to make an offer. Best Buy's board would have the option of accepting the offer or turning it down, as it had done earlier in 2012. There was also the possibility that no bid would be tendered.

When uncertainty becomes common, investors tend to look for safer investments. Financial analysts gave the company lukewarm assessments during this troubled time, such as: "underperform," "neutral," and "hold." However, the uncertainty also brought in speculators who tried to guess what would happen so they could benefit accordingly. Consequently, Best Buy's stock price fluctuated. The day that Best Buy announced its price guarantee policy, its stock price climbed 7.4 percent to $16.87 per share. That represented a total of 42 percent increase since the start of 2013, but it was still 35 percent lower than a year earlier.

The strategy, embedded in Best Buy's February 15, 2012, news release, said that the price matching policy, along with a "full range of the latest and greatest devices and services, a sales force dedicated to providing impartial and knowledgeable advice and full support for the life of the product," would help Best Buy win back customers.

Under the "About Best Buy" section of its website, the company said that it wanted to be the:

> *preferred authority and destination for all your technology products and services. Under the leadership of President and CEO Hubert Joly, we are rejuvenating and refining our customer experience, driving value and innovation and continuing our leadership in making a positive impact on our world.*
>
> *Early results of Renew Blue have been positive: increased online revenue and an improved 2012 holiday season, investments in employee training and the introduction of a guaranteed low price policy have all made an impact.*

Official communication during this period of uncertainty was scrutinized by investors, analysts, and the news media. Also of interest were the company's marketing efforts. During the summer of 2012, Best Buy rolled out a new tag line: "Making Technology Work for You." One bright note was Best Buy's 2013 Super Bowl commercial, featuring actress and comedian Amy Poehler. The commercial used humor to tell the Best Buy story to millions of football fans and showed off the expertise of the company's famous "Blue Shirt" techies. Jokes aside, the message was clear: Best Buy's top-notch service was what differentiated it from online competitors.

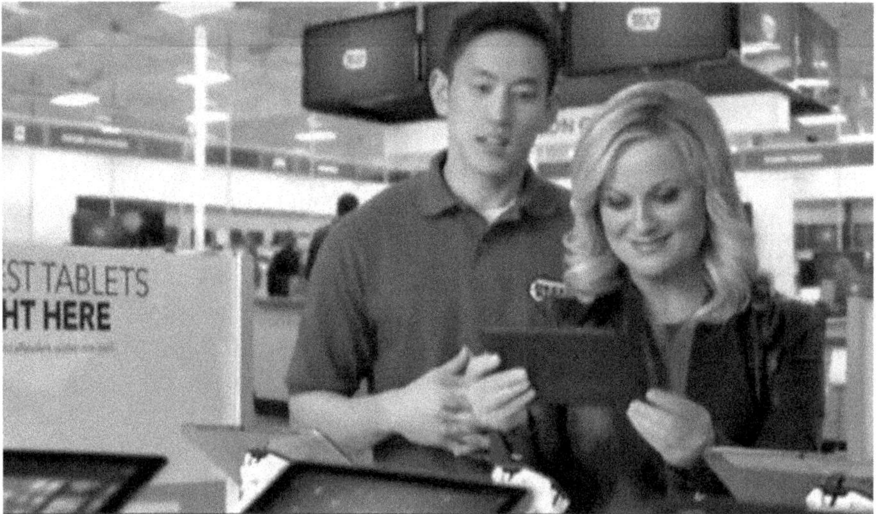

FIGURE 11.1 *Comedic star Amy Poehler was featured in a Best Buy Super Bowl commercial in 2013 that focused on its "Blue Shirt" experts in customer service.*
BestBuy.com
BestBuy

Scaled-down Best Buy "Connect Stores" were being developed in 2012; they offered high-end customer service in a streamlined setting. The middle of each Connect Store featured the Geek Squad Solution Center offering free tech support consultations and classes. A home theater design center allowed customers to try the latest video and audio technologies, and staff members were on hand to help configure home theater setups.

Ultimately, the market will decide whether Best Buy's administrative team makes the changes necessary to ensure survival in an increasingly competitive environment.

BEST BUY'S STRATEGY FOR GROWTH

In April 2012, Best Buy announced "Samsung Experience Shops" within Best Buy's larger stores, which was seen as innovative and as another positive step to its turnaround strategy.

Best Buy released its second quarter results August 20, 2013. In this report, Best Buy addressed its ongoing financial problems and its strategy to address them going forward:

> *Hubert Joly, Best Buy president and CEO, commented, "In November at our investor meeting, we talked about the two problems we had to solve: declining comparable store sales and declining operating margins. Since that time, the resolution of these two problems has become our Renew Blue rallying cry and the organization's goals and objectives have been prioritized accordingly. While we are clear there is much more work ahead, we have made measurable progress since we unveiled Renew Blue last year, including near flat comparable store sales, substantive cost take outs, and better-than-expected earnings in the past three consecutive quarters."*
>
> *Joly continued, "As expected, Domestic comparable store sales were down 0.4 percent. But this was driven by short-term disruptions caused by the retail deployment of the Samsung Experience Shops, Windows Stores, and floor space optimization, as well as our continuing rationalization of non-core businesses. Excluding these impacts, Domestic comparable store sales were flat to slightly positive for the quarter. In addition, we delivered a better-than-expected non-GAAP diluted EPS of $0.32."*
>
> *Joly concluded, "During the second quarter, we continued to make substantial progress on our Renew Blue priorities. This progress included (1) driving a more than 10 percent increase in Domestic comparable online sales; (2) improving our Net Promoter Score; (3) enriching our retail customer experience through the rollout of our Samsung Experience Shops and Windows Stores; (4) piloting our 'buy online—ship from store' initiative in 50 stores; and (5) eliminating an additional $65 million in annualized costs—bringing our 'nine-month' total of annualized cost reductions to $390 million toward our target of $725 million."*

While it was clear that Best Buy had many challenges ahead of it, investors were bullish on its future. Its stock was trading at $37.98 a share in September 2013, a fifty-two-week high, and a great comeback from its November 2012 low of $11.40. While not the $48 a share it had been in 2010, its September 2013 stock value showed Best Buy's management was aggressively moving forward to put the company on a sound financial footing and effectively communicating its strategy with its investors and financial analysts.

QUESTIONS FOR DISCUSSION

1. What is the advantage of being a privately owned company?
2. What is the advantage of being a publicly traded company?
3. In 2013, what differentiated Best Buy from its competitors?
4. How did "showrooming" become a problem for Best Buy?
5. What other issues affected Best Buy's financial performance in early 2013?
6. What was Best Buy doing to enhance its financial position?
7. What was Best Buy's marketing strategy?
8. What is the role of financial analysts for investors?
9. How effective is Best Buy's investor relations website? Provide examples.

Dig Deeper

Read Best Buy's FY12 Annual Report on Form 10-K that is available on the textbook's companion website. What are Best Buy's business strategy and core philosophies? How does its annual report describe its risk factors?

36

"A Plate of Black Beauty"?

Burger King Worldwide Deals with Horsemeat Reports

Burger King Worldwide began as a single restaurant in Miami, Florida, in 1954. In the nearly sixty years since it started, Burger King has grown into a worldwide brand with 12,667 restaurants in more than eighty countries, more than 40 percent of them outside of the U.S. and Canada. Approximately 95 percent of the company's restaurants are owned by independent franchisees, many of which are family-owned businesses that have operated for decades, and 595 restaurants are owned by Burger King Worldwide. In addition to the popular Whopper® sandwich, BKW's menu includes chicken sandwiches, salads, and breakfast items.

For years the second-largest burger chain, BKW fell to third place in 2012, surpassed only by Wendy's and top-selling restaurant chain McDonald's in U.S. system-wide sales.

HIGHLIGHTS OF BURGER KING HOLDINGS' HISTORY

- 1954: James McLamore and David Edgerton open their first Burger King restaurant in Miami, Florida.
- 1957: The company debuts its famous Whopper® sandwich.
- 1963: The company opens its first international franchise in Puerto Rico.
- 1967: The two founders sell the chain to food maker Pillsbury.
- 1988: Grand Metropolitan PLC, a British spirits and food maker, buys Pillsbury.
- 1997: Grand Metropolitan buys Guinness PLC and forms food and drink maker Diageo PLC.
- 2002: Private equity firms Texas Pacific Group, Bain Capital, and Goldman Sachs Group's Goldman Sachs Capital Partners buy Burger King for $1.5 billion from Diageo PLC.

- 2006: Burger King Holdings complete a successful initial public offering, and list its stock on the New York Stock Exchange.
- 2010: 3G Capital acquires Burger King Holdings. As a result of the acquisition by 3G, BK becomes a privately held company once again.
- 2012, Burger King Worldwide Holdings, Inc., and Justice Holdings Limited ("Justice") (LSE:JUSH), a publicly listed UK investment company, entered into a definitive business combination agreement to list Burger King on the New York Stock Exchange upon completion of the transaction. Shares were listed and began trading on June 20, 2012 under the ticker NYSE:BKW. Roughly 70 percent ownership of the company is retained by 3G Capital.

(Source: BK.com)

According to Burger King Worldwide's strategy and vision statement, it relies on four strategic strengths to drive future sales and traffic:

- **Menu Strength**—Its signature flame-grilled cooking process and its world-famous Whopper® sandwich set it aside from its competitors. In addition BKW has focused on developing new products for changing consumer palates. In 2012, it introduced twenty-one new or improved menu items. The varied menu options were an attempt to attract more women and seniors to BKW.
- **Marketing and Communication**—BKW has developed a metric-driven marketing strategy that is "food-centric" since it has a unique cooking process and menu.
- **Image**—BK's new contemporary "20/20 design" has been described "industrial" and features a "grill-centric" design with corrugated metal, exposed brick, hardwood-like floors, modern hanging lamps, a large flat-screen television, and earthy colors, such as deep red and beige. The exterior carries over the brick theme. The goal is to have 40 percent of its stores remodeled by 2015.
- **Operations**—Field employees use the "business coach" approach to help restaurants achieve their performance metrics. Focus areas include food quality, guest service, speed of service, and restaurant cleanliness.

In addition to these four strength areas, BKW has sought to accelerate its international development in high-growth emerging markets such as Brazil, Russia, and China. BKW also has been working toward a 100 percent franchised system to enhance profits and margins. To keep costs low, BKW has used a zero-based budget that required departments to justify costs and expenditures.

BKW's 2012 third quarter earnings (net profit) dropped 83 percent, mainly due to restructuring costs and unfavorable changes in the foreign-exchange rates. Its same-store sales rose 1.4 percent, better than analysts' expectations.

HORSEMEAT FOUND IN PATTIES

On January 15, 2013, news media reports said that traces of horsemeat had been discovered in British and Irish beef products. From tests on beef products sold in Tesco, the largest supermarket in Britain, the contaminated meat was traced back to Silvercrest Foods, a supplier for U.K. and Ireland-based BKW restaurants. Silvercrest shut down its production line and recalled ten million burgers from grocery stores January 21, 2013. While there was no evidence that BKW burgers had been tainted with horsemeat at that time, the company dropped Silvercrest Foods (owned by ABP Food Group) as its supplier as a "voluntary and precautionary measure," according to *The Times* of London. BKW said it uses only 100 percent beef in its burgers.

According to *The Times*, Irish food officials said the likely horsemeat contamination came from an imported filler ingredient used for inexpensive burgers.

While horsemeat is a culturally acceptable menu item in some countries, including China and the island of Sardinia, most Europeans and Americans are squeamish about eating it. As *National Geographic* put it, "horses are widely viewed as gentle companions or noble competitors . . . most Americans are uncomfortable with the thought to sitting down to a plate of Black Beauty or Seabiscuit."

Another concern raised was the possibility that a common anti-inflammatory painkiller used for sporting horses, but banned for human consumption for health reasons, could have entered the food chain.

The scandal began when a British frozen foods company found concentrations of horsemeat ranging from 60 to 100 percent in samples of its beef lasagna. Tesco, Britain's biggest retailer, found horse DNA exceeding 60 percent in some of its frozen spaghetti bolognese meals, and one tested hamburger contained 29 percent horsemeat, according to the Associated Press.

BKW'S RESPONSE

BKW issued a statement via PR Newswire January 31, 2013:

Burger King Worldwide Concludes Investigation of Silvercrest Foods

We know there has been concern regarding one of our former suppliers, Silvercrest Foods, and we want to thank our guests for their patience and understanding while we completed our investigation.

You wanted answers and so did we.

Earlier this month, we were notified that Silvercrest was under investigation for potential contamination of some retail products. At that time, they were approved to supply 100 percent Irish and British beef patties for BURGER KING® restaurants in the UK, Ireland and Denmark.

Despite assurances from them that our products were not implicated, we immediately launched our own internal investigation, which included scientific testing, inspection of the Silvercrest facility and scrutiny of traceability records.

As we confirmed on 23rd of January, we transitioned all of our restaurants in the UK, Ireland and Denmark to other BURGER KING® approved suppliers from Germany and Italy as a precaution. These suppliers have provided DNA evidence to confirm their products are free of equine DNA. These are the product being sold in our restaurants today.

Following the conclusion of our investigation:

Our independent DNA tests results on product taken from BURGER KING® restaurants were negative for any equine DNA. However, four samples recently taken from the Silvercrest plant have shown the presence of very small trace levels of equine DNA. This product was never sold to our restaurants.

Within the last 36 hours, we have established that Silvercrest used a small percentage of beef imported from a non-approved supplier in Poland. They promised to deliver 100 percent British & Irish beef patties and have not done so. This is a clear violation of our specifications, and we have terminated our relationship with them. Through our investigation, we have confirmed that this non-approved Polish supplier is the same company identified by the Irish Department of Agriculture as the source of Silvercrest's contamination issue.

Diego Beamonte, vice president, Global Quality, Burger King Corporation, said, *"While the Food Safety Authority of Ireland has stated that this is not a food safety issue, we are deeply troubled by the findings of our investigation and apologize to our guests, who trust us to source only the highest quality 100 percent beef burgers. Our supplier has failed us and in turn we have failed you. We are committed to ensuring that this does not happen again.*

"We will dedicate ourselves to determining what lessons can be learned and what additional measures, including DNA testing and enhanced traceability controls, can be taken to ensure that we continue to provide you with the quality products you expect from us."

We remain committed to identifying suppliers that can produce 100 percent pure Irish and British beef products for us that meet our high quality standards.

QUESTIONS FOR DISCUSSION

1. What are the risks to a franchise-dominated business model?
2. What is the benefit to a zero-based budgeting system?
3. Why did Burger King Worldwide want to sell off its company-owned restaurants and become a 100 percent franchise operation?
4. Did Burger King Worldwide handle the horsemeat scandal fast enough?
5. Did Burger King Worldwide's press release provide the right amount of information and concern for stakeholders? Explain.
6. What were the key messages in its news release?

7. What determines how Burger King Worldwide wants to be positioned in the investment community? What are the company's key messages? How will the company distinguish itself from other publicly traded restaurant stocks?
8. What communications vehicles will be used to communicate and conduct a proactive outreach to existing shareholders and members of the investment community?

Dig Deeper

Read Burger King's FY12 Annual Report on Form 10-K available on the textbook's companion website. How does it describe its risk factors to investors? In particular, what are some of the risks associated with franchisees?

APPENDIX A

Guidelines for Case Study in the Classroom

READ AND REREAD THE CASE

Case-based instruction is not the typical lecture-style class in which students sit and quietly take notes. In fact, the teacher does not usually have a central role in the classroom. Instead, the spotlight is on you, the student. Learning happens through student-led discussion of cases and group activities. The teacher guides the learning process by assisting discussion to ensure that key concepts and principles are discussed and to create alternative scenarios.

To make this an exciting learning environment, you must come prepared and have a thorough knowledge of the assigned cases. Know the characters' names, what happened, and in what order. It generally takes two readings, with note taking as you go along, to prepare each case for discussion.

There are opportunities to do your own research in a topic area or trace the case from its origins to its conclusion. Databases, such as the newspaper database LexisNexis, and organizational websites are great resources for background material. Websites often include mission statements, archived news releases, annual reports, historical information, and more. Activist sites can offer different views and their own evidence about certain issues and events.

Some of the best resources are your textbooks from prior public relations, communication, and business management classes. If you do not own these, your library will most likely have copies. Other public relations resources include research journals and industry publications such as the *Journal of Public Relations Research, Public Relations Review, PR Week* and public relations-focused websites such as Public Relations Society of America or the Institute for Public Relations.

Don't be afraid to go beyond the obvious public relations issues. Each case has unique attributes. Be curious and ask questions. Case analysis worksheets are provided to help you prepare for each case.

MAKE CONNECTIONS

Next, begin to tie in the public relations issues. You can start with a SWOT (strengths, weaknesses, opportunities, and threats) analysis. When possible, analyze the organization's strategy, response, communication techniques, and other tactics. What were the organization's options? What would you have done differently?

You may be surprised to learn that your assessment of a case strategy can be different from those of others in the classroom. What seems obvious to you may escape the notice of a classmate—and vice versa. Particularly in the choice of public relations tactics, there are many options. While many good communication theories and core principles have emerged from a growing body of knowledge, there is still plenty of room for debate about which strategies and tactics are "right"—and often, there may be more than one right answer!

Examine each case for elements of the public relations process (research, planning, communication, and evaluation). What's missing and how would you, as a practitioner, have added or changed these elements?

PARTICIPATE IN THE DISCUSSION

Participating in the discussion is the most important element of the class. Your active involvement will deepen your understanding of the public relations practice. Beyond the public relations principles, theories, and strategies, this class can also help you develop counseling, strategic thinking, and rhetorical skills.

The counselor role in public relations is an important function in organizations that can be learned in case-based instruction through role playing exercises. Advising management to see the big picture, carefully examining the potential consequences of its actions, and suggesting sound alternatives can be a tricky proposition even for experienced practitioners. While big egos, traditional ways of doing things, and management isolation sometimes prevent practitioners from providing this valuable service, you'll find that class discussions and role playing can help you develop counseling skills and build your credibility with managers.

That's because in public relations today, knowledge, experience, and strategy expertise aren't enough. Successful practitioners know how to present ideas to their peers and leaders in a convincing manner. While the business memo and proposal are alive and well, more often the ability to present your ideas orally when the golden opportunity arises is essential. Speaking up at the appropriate time and constructing logical and persuasive arguments are vastly underrated skills for new practitioners.

When you have to respond to direct questions from your classmates or teacher, you'll get valuable practice articulating your ideas—and you'll learn how to think on your feet, under pressure. When the boss asks for your opinion in a meeting or he/she gives you a minute in the hallway to present your case, can you do it logically, concisely, and persuasively? This is just one more good reason to be prepared: Have the facts and a strategy at your fingertips. If you tell the boss you're not prepared to offer your ideas—or, worse, you don't remember all the facts—you will have missed an opportunity. And the boss won't be impressed.

Beyond dealing with the boss, being articulate is helpful in other instances: How would you deal with persistent reporters during a crisis? How do you establish authority within your department without crushing teamwork and creativity? By creating a scenario based on a scene from a case, students can begin practicing their strategic thinking and speaking skills.

You may also be asked to lead class discussion on a case. This will give you practice at organizing your thoughts, participating in active listening, and encouraging others to speak up.

A student can start the case by presenting the key points concerning the case. Everyone should be prepared because it may be "your turn" to answer the next question or present your views or solutions to a problem posed. Anyone can be called on at any time to offer his or her reasoning and timing of certain actions. Students may also be subject to query, argument, and discussion from anyone in the classroom. Adding to the challenge, your professor may change an element in the case that will have to be factored into your problem solution.

Some case scenarios can expand into role playing activities. Students in your class may be asked to dramatize a particular scene within the case. Not only do students practice their rhetorical skills, but dramatizing gives students a chance to observe how everything has the potential to send messages: body language, tone of voice, eye contact, active listening, and nervous habits. New twists can be added to the dramatization to see how good you are at thinking on your feet. You may be a little self-conscious at first, but most students find role playing enjoyable and an effective way to learn.

Remember, whenever you speak in a role playing scenario, you may be quoted. Especially in times of crisis, when events are moving quickly, the chance for error is great. Could your words be taken out of context? Did you talk beyond the known facts and speculate? This class will help you learn how to choose your words carefully, stay focused, and communicate effectively.

Teamwork and other kinds of collaborative efforts are common practice in public relations today. Most cases can incorporate in-class group activities, such as group discussions, debates, research, and analysis assignments—all good ways to practice working in a group or as part of a team. Your professor may select teams prior to a class or during a class.

The idea is to provide a variety of ways for you to practice and sharpen your rhetorical, counseling, and leadership skills in different situations.

SHARE YOUR EXPERIENCES

Some of the best class discussions and learning occur when students share personal experiences related to the case topic. If you have completed an internship, for example, you might share your observations on how public relations is practiced in a corporate, agency, or nonprofit setting.

You may want to relate experiences a family member has encountered as an employee or customer. Even a job at the local mall can provide fodder for discussion, especially in employee relations, management practices, and interpersonal relationships.There's no substitute for real-life experience; you'll often find that incidents, which you, family members, and other students have encountered in the workplace or elsewhere, can illustrate some of the concepts in this textbook.

RESPECT OTHERS

Respect for all opinions is key to a successful discussion-based class. Everyone should have the chance to participate, and some students need more encouragement than others.

No one likes negative criticism or public embarrassment. While polite disagreement is encouraged, verbal attacks and dominating the discussion are not. Make your point and let others make theirs; be careful not to dominate the class discussion. Active listening should be as much a part of the class as forceful speaking.

APPENDIX B

Case Preparation

Not all the elements below will be present in all the cases. You may seek additional information about an organization, communication/public relations theories, and public relations concepts and tactics from suggested websites, including the website of the organization featured in the case study. Beyond examining the organization's website, look at activist sites or blogs that discuss the organization and/or issues relevant to the case study.

ORGANIZATION OVERVIEW

Based on the information provided, describe what you know about the organization.

- Basic facts of the organization/entity
- History of the organization
- Type of business/service (size, profit or nonprofit, new or old, etc.)
- Organizational culture: formal, informal?
- Organizational system: opened, closed? (transparency, interaction with outsiders)
- Environment: internal (managers, staff employees) and external (competitors and stakeholders such as customers and activists)
- Mission statement (if available)
- Annual reports (if available)
- Archival news releases or other communication (if available)
- Other ______________.

ORGANIZATIONAL HISTORY

Public relations practitioners should be familiar with their organization's history. Often, that history can explain something about an organization's current situation.

- How did the organization begin?
- Who founded it?
- How has the company changed since its inception?
- Has it grown or diversified?
- Does the executive officer have family ties to the organization's founder?
- Is the company publicly or privately owned?
- If it is publicly traded, look at its investor relations materials.

FINANCIALS

Key financial information listed below is available through the organization's investor website or at the Securities and Exchange Commission's database of regulatory filings (www.sec.gov) for publicly traded companies. Business publications such as Bloomberg's *Business Week* are also good sources for information about companies.

- Annual reports (10-k)
- Quarterly reports (10-Q)
- Dividend information
- Stock market value
- Earnings press releases
- Profit and loss statements
- Transcripts of conference calls and investor presentations
- Proxy statements
- Analysts' reports (usually for a fee).

SWOT ANALYSIS

Conduct a SWOT analysis: strengths, weaknesses, opportunities, and threats. SWOT analyses have been used by business professionals for many years to analyze products, services, and future markets. It is a good planning exercise for public relations professionals who need to assess where an organization stands.

PROBLEM OR OPPORTUNITY

What's the public relations issue that causes the concern?

- Explain the problem.
- Explain the opportunity.

TABLE B.1 This table illustrates the factors of a SWOT (strengths, weaknesses, opportunities, and threats) analysis.

STRENGTHS	WEAKNESSES/LIMITATIONS
Strong financial resources	Conservative culture
Superior market position	Outdated products
Industry leading products/services	High staff turnover
Respected leadership	Reactive communications
OPPORTUNITIES	**THREATS**
Emerging markets	Economic instability
Social changes	Cultural trends
Access to finance	Strong competitors
New legislation	Technological developments

Source: Courtesy *The Public Relations Strategic Toolkit*

TIMELINE

Often it is helpful to develop a timeline of events. Knowing when and in what order events occur can provide important insights.

STAKEHOLDERS

Who are the characters in this case?

- What did they do?
- Who's directly affected by the actions of the organization?
- Internal (employees, management)
- External (competitors, investors, community, government officials, activists, etc.)
- Other ______________.

TABLE B.2 Calculating the interest and power of stakeholder publics helps public relations practitioners prioritize their efforts.

	LOW INTEREST	HIGH INTEREST
Low power	Minimal effort	Keep informed
High power	Keep satisfied	Key players: Keep informed and satisfied

Source: Courtesy *The Public Relations Strategic Toolkit*

HUMAN FACTORS

Interactions with others in and outside the organization are important factors to consider.

- In particular, what did the public relations practitioner(s) do?
- Interpersonal relationships
- Organizational role, access to management
- Seniority
- Working with outside public relations firm employees
- Other ______________.

PRACTITIONER FACTORS

Experience, expertise of practitioner:

- What special skills or knowledge are necessary for success in this public relations setting?
- Media relations
- Investor relations
- Crisis communication management
- Public relations counseling
- Other ______________.

ETHICAL AND LEGAL CONSIDERATIONS

Following are some basic ethical questions:

- Is the action right or wrong? According to what—your own principles, your professional code, the law?
- Can someone be harmed by your decision (including your inaction)?
- Can you personally live with your decision?
- Can you justify your decision publicly for good reasons?

APPENDIX C

Theories of Public Relations, Communication and Related Theories

Here is a sampling of theories that can be used to analyze the case studies in this book:

- **Excellence theory**—Considered by many as the dominant public relations theory, it calls for symmetrical two-way communication between organizations and publics, compromise and shared power. Information, rather than persuasion, is considered the most ethical approach to achieving mutual understanding between the organization and its publics
- **Contingency theory**—Organizations behave in a variety of ways depending on the particular situation that an organization is involved in. Glen T. Cameron said that there is an axis of advocacy and accommodation. His matrix contained eighty-six variables that influenced the action of public relations professionals in deciding whether more advocacy or more accommodation was needed.
- **Situational theory of publics**—Building strategic relationships for an organization involves understanding publics. Situational theory describes the factors that contribute to creating active publics based on their situation. First comes awareness (problem recognition), followed by how the issue affects people's lives (constraint recognition), and, finally, the ability to do something about the problem (level of involvement).
- **Relationship management theory**—Scholars John Ledingham and Steven Bruning said that relationships are essential to public relations practice and that those relationships must be mutually beneficial if they are to continue. This theory helps explain the management of successful relationships.
- **Situational crisis communication theory**—This theory offers crisis response strategies depending on the threat/crisis type and an assessment of the organization's crisis history, to protect an organization's reputation.

- **Systems theory**—Organizations cannot survive alone. They are interdependent with others and must interact to some degree with various constituencies in the political, economic, and social realms to survive and thrive. Every organization has stakeholders, such as employees, customers, and government regulators, who must be dealt with. Public relations helps to identify, build, and monitor these crucial relationships.
- **Diffusion theory**—This theory by Everett Rogers claims people make decisions or accept ideas following ordered steps: awareness, interest, trial, evaluation, and adoption.
- **Indirect effects theory**—The media can have an effect on people, but that effect is usually indirect because it is often "filtered" through other people, such as friends and social groups.
- **Limited-effects theory**—The media have little effect on people because many factors intervene or mitigate the message.
- **Agenda building theory**—This is the process by which active publics and organizations focused on a cause can catch the attention of the news media and public officials to put a cause on the agenda for potential change.
- **Agenda setting theory**—While the media can't tell people what to think, the media can be effective in establishing what topics are talked about, according to Bernard Cohen's theory. An organization or issue can suddenly gain a national stage if the media decide it's worth a look.
- **Framing theory**—Journalists and editors make many critical decisions in their work, ranging from whom to interview to what questions to ask and what specific words to use when writing a story. These decisions can be affected by public relations "frame strategists."
- **Media uses and gratification theory**—People actively select and use the media to fulfill their own needs, such as finding information to make purchasing decisions or to be entertained.
- **Hierarchy of needs theory**—People pay attention to messages based on their personal needs. These needs have been arranged in a pyramid form according to the most basic physiological needs for survival to the most complex ones dealing with self-fulfillment.
- **Two-step and multi-step flow theories**—Some individuals actively take the time to seek and understand information on certain topics, making them, in effect, subject experts. These individuals are called *opinion leaders* and can have an effect on their followers. Later research has indicated that the most effective opinion leaders are those who share the same social status as their adherents. More research has indicated that two-step flow oversimplifies the complexity of communication and influence and has offered the multi-step

flow theory, positing that there are many individuals who can serve to influence other opinion leaders.

- **Social learning theory**—This theory says people use information processing to explain and predict behavior.
- **Cognitive dissonance**—Leon Festinger found people usually seek out and pay attention to media messages that do not threaten their established values and beliefs. Messages challenging a person's deeply held values and beliefs make a person uncomfortable (dissonance) and are often avoided.
- **Selective processes**—Leon Festinger found that because people are uncomfortable with information that challenges their values and beliefs, they generally seek information that is more attuned to their own values and beliefs.
- **Elaborated likelihood model**—Petty and Cacioppo's theory looks at how people make decisions based on their level of involvement in processing the persuasive message. In this model, persuasive messages fall into two main categories: those that contain a great deal of information and cogent reasons for some product or issue, and messages with simple associations of negative and positive attributes to some object, action, or situation. Those self-motivated to think about the more complex persuasive message will be influenced by good arguments, repetition, rewards, and credible spokespersons. Attitudes formed under high elaboration tend to stay stable.

MODELS OF PUBLIC RELATIONS

The following models describe how the role of public relations manifests itself within organizations. The four basic practice models include:

- **Press agentry**—Public information flows one way from the organization to its publics and stakeholders. It uses persuasion to achieve its organizational goals.
- **Public information**—This model also has information flowing one way from the organization to its stakeholders. It is not characterized by persuasive tactics of promotion or publicity.
- **Two-way asymmetrical**—While information flows both ways between the organization and its stakeholders and publics, this model uses scientific persuasion based on research and feedback from stakeholders; its goal is to convince others to accept the organization's way of thinking.
- **Two-way symmetrical model**—This is characterized by the two-way flow of information between the organization and its stakeholders and seeks to build mutual understanding through research, but does not focus on one-way persuasive tactics.

APPENDIX D

Ways Organizations Communicate

Here are the four categories suggested by the book *Strategic Planning for Public Relations* that provide an excellent guide to how organizations communicate. It's not exhaustive, but it gives some basic ideas to compare to case studies.

FACE-TO-FACE COMMUNICATION TACTICS

Public relations professionals generally agree the most effective way to communicate is face to face. However, it is often the most expensive way to reach audiences. The expense is usually justified when the publics targeted by the communication event are crucial to the organization's function. For colleges, that would be prospective students and their parents (open houses); for publicly held corporations, that would include stockholders (annual meetings); and for the local chapter of the American Red Cross, its volunteers.

Types of Face-to-Face Communication Tactics

- Special events: Annual meetings, groundbreakings, open houses, grand openings, anniversary celebrations, awards/recognition events, sporting events, fundraisers
- Group meetings: Question-and-answer sessions, civic club presentations
- Virtual town hall meetings
- Exhibits for products/services (and virtual exhibits)
- Demonstrations
- Executive round tables
- Road shows/city tours
- Speakers' bureau (subject matter experts' credentials on LinkedIn, etc.)
- Meetups (via meetup.com or Facebook, etc.)
- Other ______________.

ORGANIZATIONAL MEDIA TACTICS

Organizations often create their own communication for employees and the outside world. The design and content of these communication products are controlled by the organization, which ensures that every element of message is presented the way the organization intended.

Types of Organizational-Created Media Tactics

- Annual reports
- Blogs (including multimedia blogs such as Tumblr, etc.)
- Books (including e-books)
- Brochures
- Bulletin boards (including e-bulletin boards)
- Buttons
- Case studies
- Comic (graphic) books
- Customer-focused community websites
- Curation websites (Pinterest, etc.)
- Discussion forums.
- E-learning series
- E-mails
- Electronic chat rooms
- Gamification
- Ideation programs (collect ideas to solve solutions)
- Infographics
- Letters
- Logos (other graphic identifications)
- Magazines (digital and print)
- Micro blogging (Twitter, etc.)
- Mobile applications
- Newsletters (digital and print)

- Payroll stuffers
- Photographs
- Podcasts
- Posters
- Presentation sharing (slide shows on the web)
- Slide shows (PowerPoint)
- Social networking websites (Facebook, Pinterest, etc.)
- Testimonials
- Text messages
- T-shirts
- Videos (including video channels available at YouTube, etc.)
- Video shows (organizationally produced TV shows, etc.)
- Webinar
- Webcasts
- Website—Intranet
- Websites—Public
- White papers
- Wikis
- Other _______________.

NEWS MEDIA TACTICS

The news media are a powerful vehicle for getting organizational messages to large audiences at no cost—except in the production and dissemination of the information provided to the news media. The trade-off is the loss of control that comes with providing information to the media. There are no guarantees the information will be used or how it will be used.

Types of Organizational Tactics for Mass Media

In addition to the items listed below, many of the tactics here can be incorporated into an online newsroom concept which provides a one-stop site for reporters developing stories related to the organization.

- News releases (plain to multimedia)
- News release archives, by date and topic
- Statements
- Photo and graphics gallery, including the high resolution formats of the company's logo
- Media alerts
- News conferences
- Organizational media tours
- Media briefings (group and individual)
- Fact sheets (biographies, organizational histories, frequently asked questions, product specifications)
- Rapid response crisis websites
- Rumor refutation statements
- Third-party statements of endorsement
- Feature stories
- Press kits, print or electronic (can include many of the elements listed here but generally are focused on specific new promotional activities such as a new product or service)
- Satellite media tours: radio and television
- Online news rooms (can provide many of the elements listed individually here)
- Op-ed guest columns, letters to the editor
- Conference calls and transcripts
- Other ________________.

ADVERTISING/PROMOTIONAL MEDIA TACTICS

Mass media channels provide opportunities for placing messages within news, entertainment, or any setting where you think key audiences are likely to view messages. The message content, look, and placement are controlled by the organization, but for a price. Unlike news media tactics, which only incur production and dissemination costs, advertising and promotional media tactics also entail the cost of placement, which in mass media channels such as television and newspapers or magazines can become expensive.

Types of Advertising/Promotional Media Tactics

- Display print ads (newspaper, magazines, programs)
- Television commercials
- Radio commercials
- Internet ads
- Billboards
- Promotional gift items (key chains, etc.)
- Clothing items (T-shirts, hats, etc.)
- Software items (interactive games, virtual tours, etc.)
- Other ______________.

APPENDIX E

Effective Communication Considerations

Public relations practitioners are responsible for the organization's communication programs. Many cases in this textbook provide examples of the communication efforts in statements, news releases, advertising, and other collateral material. An analysis of key messages is helpful in reviewing many cases.

ANALYZING THE COMMUNICATION TIMING

- Create a chronology or timeline of events in the case.
- How much time elapsed between the pivotal information discovery, public communication of the information, and the organization's response to the information?
- If silence was used as a response to public information, was it effective?

ANALYZING USE OF LANGUAGE IN KEY MESSAGES

- Factual? Use of facts, statistics, examples, documents, other forms of evidence?
- Persuasive? There are many types of emotional appeal strategies including fear appeals, guilt appeals, and patriotic appeals. What type of persuasive appeal was made?

WRITTEN ELEMENTS

- Are certain word choices more powerful than others?
- Are words chosen to appeal directly to a certain key audience?
- Are the messages easy to understand?
- Are the words humorous, shocking, or offensive? In what way?

SPOKEN ELEMENTS

- Who was the organizational spokesperson? Do you feel he or she was an appropriate spokesperson? Why?
- What kind of credibility does the spokesperson possess?
- Analyze the quotes by organizational spokespersons in news media accounts. Are they effective? Why?

VISUAL ELEMENTS

- What are the visual elements present in the message? Photographic, illustrative, iconic?
- In what way are the images used to attract attention? Communicate a message?
- Does the image provoke a feeling? Does it have a connection to a cultural past?
- Is the type of font communicating a message as well?

APPENDIX F

Organizational Responses

A TYPOLOGY OF PROACTIVE ORGANIZATIONAL RESPONSES

There are many ways for organizations to act proactively so that activities are strategic and support the mission of an organization. Ronald D. Smith's *Strategic Planning for Public Relations* textbook describes the following action strategies: organizational performance, audience participation, special events, alliances and coalitions, sponsorships, strategic philanthropy, and activism. Communication strategies, he notes, include publicity, newsworthy information, and transparent communication. For case study, consider the following areas:

ENVIRONMENTAL SCANNING

- Mass media monitoring (Internet, newspapers, television, radio, etc.)
- Industry trend-watching through professional conferences and trade publications
- Internal monitoring (employee suggestion box, casual conversations or checking with departments, customer service trends)
- Issue identification and prioritization.

RESEARCH

- Informal research (discussions with key communicators, department heads, etc.)
- Secondary research (database research or Internet searches to help identify new trends or issues)
- Formal research (questionnaires, focus groups, content analysis, observations, and in-depth interviewing).

OUTREACH

- Management opportunities to interact informally with employees
- Management involvement with key community and industry organizations, including the formation of alliances and coalitions
- Organizational opportunities to interact face to face with the public through annual meetings, open houses, facility tours, key communicator group meetings, general meetings, speakers' bureau
- Formal media relations program to develop good working relationships between the organization and journalists
- Organizational communication programs, such as newsletters, brochures, websites, informational videos, news releases
- Community relations (sponsorships, philanthropy, and volunteerism).

A TYPOLOGY OF REACTIVE PUBLIC RELATIONS RESPONSES

There are many response options, especially when a problem or crisis emerges. They can range from the all-out attack, especially in instances of known hoaxes, to strategic silence, when an organization purposely chooses no comment or other responsive action in a situation. Here are the behavioral and verbal responses available to organizations when they are faced with accusations or other criticisms.

Preemptive Action Strategy

- Preemptive action.

Offensive Response Strategies

- Attack
- Embarrassment
- Threat.

Defensive Response Strategies

- Denial
- Excuse
- Justification.

Diversionary Response Strategies

- Concession
- Ingratiation
- Disassociation
- Relabeling.

Vocal Commiseration Strategies

- Concern
- Condolence
- Regret
- Apology.

Rectifying Behavior Strategies

- Investigation
- Corrective action
- Restitution
- Repentance.

Strategic Inaction

- Silence.

APPENDIX G

PRSA Member Code of Ethics

PRSA MEMBER STATEMENT OF PROFESSIONAL VALUES

This statement presents the core values of PRSA members and, more broadly, of the public relations profession. These values provide the foundation for the Member Code of Ethics and set the industry standard for the professional practice of public relations. These values are the fundamental beliefs that guide our behaviors and decision-making process. We believe our professional values are vital to the integrity of the profession as a whole.

VALUES

Advocacy

- We serve the public interest by acting as responsible advocates for those we represent.
- We provide a voice in the marketplace of ideas, facts, and viewpoints to aid informed public debate.

Honesty

- We adhere to the highest standards of accuracy and truth in advancing the interests of those we represent and in communicating with the public.

Expertise

- We acquire and responsibly use specialized knowledge and experience.
- We advance the profession through continued professional development, research, and education.
- We build mutual understanding, credibility, and relationships among a wide array of institutions and audiences.

Independence

- We provide objective counsel for those we represent.
- We are accountable for our actions.

Loyalty

- We are faithful to those we represent, while honoring our obligation to serve the public interest.

Fairness

- We deal fairly with clients, employers, competitors, peers, vendors, the media, and the general public.
- We respect all opinions and support the right of free expression.

RSA CODE PROVISIONS

Core Principle: Free Flow of Information

Protecting and advancing the free flow of accurate and truthful information is essential to serving the public interest and contributing to informed decision making in a democratic society.

Intent

- To maintain the integrity of relationships with the media, government officials, and the public.
- To aid informed decision making.

Guidelines

A member shall:

- Preserve the integrity of the process of communication.
- Be honest and accurate in all communications.
- Act promptly to correct erroneous communications for which the practitioner is responsible.
- Preserve the free flow of unprejudiced information when giving or receiving gifts by ensuring that gifts are nominal, legal, and infrequent.

Examples of Improper Conduct under this Provision

- A member representing a ski manufacturer gives a pair of expensive racing skis to a sports magazine columnist, to influence the columnist to write favorable articles about the product.
- A member entertains a government official beyond legal limits and/or in violation of government reporting requirements.

Core Principle: Competition

Promoting healthy and fair competition among professionals preserves an ethical climate while fostering a robust business environment.

Intent

- To promote respect and fair competition among public relations professionals.
- To serve the public interest by providing the widest choice of practitioner options.

Guidelines
A member shall:

- Follow ethical hiring practices designed to respect free and open competition without deliberately undermining a competitor.
- Preserve intellectual property rights in the marketplace.

Examples of Improper Conduct under this Provision:

- A member employed by a "client organization" shares helpful information with a counseling firm that is competing with others for the organization's business.
- A member spreads malicious and unfounded rumors about a competitor in order to alienate the competitor's clients and employees in a ploy to recruit people and business.

Core Principle: Disclosure of Information

- Open communication fosters informed decision making in a democratic society.

Intent

- To build trust with the public by revealing all information needed for responsible decision making.

Guidelines

A member shall:

- Be honest and accurate in all communications.
- Act promptly to correct erroneous communications for which the member is responsible.
- Investigate the truthfulness and accuracy of information released on behalf of those represented.
- Reveal the sponsors for causes and interests represented.
- Disclose financial interest (such as stock ownership) in a client's organization.
- Avoid deceptive practices.

Examples of Improper Conduct under this Provision:

- Front groups: A member implements "grassroots" campaigns or letter-writing campaigns to legislators on behalf of undisclosed interest groups.
- Lying by omission: A practitioner for a corporation knowingly fails to release financial information, giving a misleading impression of the corporation's performance.
- A member discovers inaccurate information disseminated via a Web site or media kit and does not correct the information.
- A member deceives the public by employing people to pose as volunteers to speak at public hearings and participate in "grassroots" campaigns.

Core Principle: Safeguarding Confidences

- Client trust requires appropriate protection of confidential and private information.

Intent

- To protect the privacy rights of clients, organizations, and individuals by safeguarding confidential information.

Guidelines
A member shall:

- Safeguard the confidences and privacy rights of present, former, and prospective clients and employees.
- Protect privileged, confidential, or insider information gained from a client or organization.
- Immediately advise an appropriate authority if a member discovers that confidential information is being divulged by an employee of a client company or organization.

Examples of Improper Conduct under this Provision:

- A member changes jobs, takes confidential information, and uses that information in the new position to the detriment of the former employer.
- A member intentionally leaks proprietary information to the detriment of some other party.

Core Principle: Conflicts of Interest

- Avoiding real, potential, or perceived conflicts of interest builds the trust of clients, employers, and the publics.

Intent

- To earn trust and mutual respect with clients or employers.
- To build trust with the public by avoiding or ending situations that put one's personal or professional interests in conflict with society's interests.

Guidelines
A member shall:

- Act in the best interests of the client or employer, even subordinating the member's personal interests.
- Avoid actions and circumstances that may appear to compromise good business judgment or create a conflict between personal and professional interests.
- Disclose promptly any existing or potential conflict of interest to affected clients or organizations.
- Encourage clients and customers to determine if a conflict exists after notifying all affected parties.

Examples of Improper Conduct under this Provision

- The member fails to disclose that he or she has a strong financial interest in a client's chief competitor.
- The member represents a "competitor company" or a "conflicting interest" without informing a prospective client.

Core Principle: Enhancing the Profession

- Public relations professionals work constantly to strengthen the public's trust in the profession.

Intent

- To build respect and credibility with the public for the profession of public relations. To improve, adapt, and expand professional practices.

Guidelines

A member shall:

- Acknowledge that there is an obligation to protect and enhance the profession.
- Keep informed and educated about practices in the profession to ensure ethical conduct.
- Actively pursue personal professional development.
- Decline representation of clients or organizations that urge or require actions contrary to this Code.
- Accurately define what public relations activities can accomplish.
- Counsel subordinates in proper ethical decision making.
- Require that subordinates adhere to the ethical requirements of the Code.
- Report ethical violations, whether committed by PRSA members or not, to the appropriate authority.

Examples of Improper Conduct under this Provision

- A PRSA member declares publicly that a product the client sells is safe, without disclosing evidence to the contrary.
- A member initially assigns some questionable client work to a non-member practitioner to avoid the ethical obligation of PRSA membership.

INDEX

Cases in Public Relations Management

Developed for advanced students in public relations, *Cases in Public Relations Management* uses recent cases in public relations that had outcomes varying from expected to unsuccessful. The text challenges students to think analytically, strategically, and practically. Each case is based on real events, and is designed to encourage discussion, debate, and exploration of the options available to today's strategic public relations manager.

Key features of this text include coverage of the latest controversies in current events, discussion of the ethical issues that have made headlines in recent years, and strategies used by public relations practitioners. Each case has extensive supplemental materials taken directly from the case for further student investigation and discussion. The case study approach encourages readers to assess what they know about communication theory, the public relations process, and management practices, and prepares them for their future careers as PR practitioners.

New to the Second Edition are:

- 27 new case studies, including coverage of social media and social responsibility elements
- Glossary
- End-of-chapter exercises
- Embedded hyperlinks in eBook
- Fully enhanced companion website that's seamlessly connected with the text
- Instructor resources: PowerPoint presentations, Syllabus, Test Bank, Video Clips, Case Supplements, Instructor Guides, Author Blog
- Student resources: Quizzes, Glossary, Case Supplements
- New chapters on corporate social responsibility and activism

Patricia Swann, former dean of the School of Business and Justice Studies, is an associate professor of public relations and journalism at Utica College. She is the assistant director of the Raymond Simon Institute for Public Relations and Journalism and the past head for the Public Relations Division of the Association for Education in Journalism and Mass Communication. She has 20 years of experience in the public relations and journalism industries and has garnered numerous awards for her work.